CATEGORIES IN SOCIAL INTERACTION

This book investigates the situated (re)production of categories, from the most mundane and unremarkable to those most strongly associated with power and privilege. By examining the reciprocal relationships between categorial phenomena and the basic structures and practices of social interaction, the book provides a new framework for integrating conversation analysis and membership categorization analysis.

Across its ten chapters, the book describes a conversation analytic approach to studying categories and categorization, charts the development and history of membership categorization analysis, and addresses core methodological challenges and practices associated with using this approach. After mapping out the new framework developed in the book, each chapter describes intersections between categorial phenomena and the domains that comprise the infrastructure of social interaction. The book concludes by exploring applications, interventions, and impacts of understanding categories in ways examined across the preceding chapters, and by considering future avenues for excavating categorial practices in the ordinary, institutional, and technological settings of human social life.

Categories in Social Interaction is essential reading for social scientists with an interest in categories of people and categorizing practices, and especially for practitioners and students of conversation analysis, membership categorization, ethnomethodology, and discursive psychology.

Kevin A. Whitehead is Associate Professor of Sociology at the University of California, Santa Barbara, USA, and Visiting Associate Professor in the School of Human and Community Development at the University of the Witwatersrand, Johannesburg, South Africa. His research uses ethnomethodological and conversation analytic approaches to study recorded talk-in-interaction, focusing in particular on practices through which social categories are used, reproduced, and resisted, and on their intersections with social problems including racism and violence.

Elizabeth Stokoe is Professor in the Department of Psychological and Behavioural Science at The London School of Economics and Political Science (LSE), UK. Her research uses conversation analysis and membership categorization to understand social interaction in diverse settings. She is also passionate about science communication and translating research findings for and with public, commercial, and third-sector partners.

Geoffrey Raymond is Professor of Sociology at the University of California, Santa Barbara, USA. His research interests include conversation analysis, the role of talk-in-interaction in the organization of institutions, and qualitative research methods.

CATEGORIES IN SOCIAL INTERACTION

Kevin A. Whitehead, Elizabeth Stokoe, and
Geoffrey Raymond

 Routledge
Taylor & Francis Group

LONDON AND NEW YORK

Designed cover image: Paul Blow

First published 2025

by Routledge
4 Park Square, Milton Park, Abingdon, Oxon OX14 4RN

and by Routledge
605 Third Avenue, New York, NY 10158

Routledge is an imprint of the Taylor & Francis Group, an informa business

British Library Cataloguing-in-Publication Data
A catalogue record for this book is available from the British Library

ISBN: 9780367637668 (hbk)
ISBN: 9780367637651 (pbk)
ISBN: 9781003120599 (ebk)

DOI: 10.4324/9781003120599

Typeset in Galliard
by Apex CoVantage, LLC

CONTENTS

ACKNOWLEDGEMENTS

This is a book about categories and categorizations of persons in social interaction. We would like to acknowledge the support of several categories of persons in writing it: editor, funder, research participant, illustrator, student, reviewer, friend, family member, partner, PhD supervisor, mentor, and member of the community.

We are grateful to Eleanor Taylor and Emilie Coin, our Editors at Routledge, for supporting our project and for several constructive suggestions about its organization.

The Institute for Advanced Studies at Loughborough University, UK, funded a generative week of intensive work together at Loughborough in September 2022 as we consolidated the book's key contributions and planned the final stages of writing.

We are indebted to the people who gave consent for their interactions to be recorded, over numerous projects, some of whom feature anonymously in the data extracts. Our work, and conversation analysis as a field of study, would not be possible without them.

We are delighted that Paul Blow accepted our invitation to design the book's cover and to A Dozen Eggs for the illustration that features on page 126 (Figure 4.1).

Several cohorts of the University of California, Santa Barbara students in the SOC 136A, 136C, 236, and 236C courses, served as attentive and constructive test audiences for analyses of many of the data extracts included in the book, and for earlier versions of its overall argument.

Tomone Komiya offered incisive comments and suggestions on some key conceptual and analytic matters over the course of several discussions during his visit to UCSB in 2022–2023.

Geoffrey Bowker, Natasha Shrikant, Sandra Thompson, and Hansun Zhang Waring provided generous and supportive readings of draft chapters.

Numerous colleagues, friends, family members, and especially our partners offered invaluable support, encouragement, and (during difficult periods and turbulent times) sympathy.

In addition to learning an enormous amount from each other during the course of writing this book, and from our collaborations prior to this project, each of us has benefitted profoundly from the mentorship we have received respectively from Manny Schegloff (for Geoff), Derek Edwards (for Liz), and Gene Lerner (for Kevin). What we have learned from them has undoubtedly shaped the work we have done separately and together for the book in more ways than we can adequately articulate, but no responsibility for its shortcomings should be attributed to them.

It is especially poignant that we completed the book during the week of Manny's passing. The project we have pursued is neatly captured by his reminder that "[b]ecause the relevance of categories of person can be intimately connected to characterizations of actions . . . we should not let our pursuit of one of them wander too far from our pursuit of the other" (Schegloff, 2005a, p. 474). We are sure he would have had many suggestions for how we could have improved this project, but we hope he would still have liked what we have done.

Loughborough, UK, and Santa Barbara, USA, June 2024

PROLOGUE

Why categories matter

0.1   What is this book about?

To categorize is human.[1] This book focuses on how, throughout our daily interactions, we categorize ourselves and other people, individuals and groups, unavoidably, in myriad ways. Although categories are implicated in places, spaces, and settings, and events, objects, and actions, the book pays most attention to categories of people. We ubiquitously invoke, describe, and construct such categories; we ascribe and resist them; we imply, infer, and deny them, in the course of doing the actions that comprise our day-to-day lives. Categories and categorizing can be mundane and ordinary; they can be profound and spectacular. Categorization is as ubiquitous as social action because it is a form of social action.

We begin this book by making a simple observation: categories matter to people. In particular, categories matter regardless of what any academic researcher might have to say about them, theoretically, methodologically, or empirically. Categories tell us – as ordinary people or researchers – the kinds of people there are in the world, and their continual emergence reveals new ways of being or struggling in the world. Categories are so pervasive that we could pick almost any case of spoken, embodied, visual, or written social text or interaction, on any day, in any place, to find examples like the ones we come to shortly, in which people show just how passionately they concern themselves with categories.

---

1 With acknowledgements to Bowker and Star (1999).

DOI: 10.4324/9781003120599-1

We started conceiving of this book in 2019 and finished writing in 2024. During this time, the world shifted in unprecedented ways: the Covid-19 pandemic arrived, impacting the global population (not equally, to be sure) and bringing with it a wealth of new categories (e.g., 'minimizer,' 'covidiot,' '[anti-]masker'). Longstanding political struggles took on new forms and gave us new ways to categorize the people who participated in them. Attempts to overthrow the 2020 presidential election in America gave us 'election deniers'; Britain's exit from the EU gave rise to 'Brexiters' and 'remainers.' The climate crisis escalated, wars continued and started, large language models suddenly made AI routinely accessible and dramatically more advanced, and misinformation on social media created "reality disjunctures" (Pollner, 1975) more than ever before. And a great deal of the public discourse about local, national, and global events centred around categories.

Thus, it is not difficult to find examples that show why categories matter, and that people care a great deal about them – the world is generating data at a dizzying rate. But we must start somewhere. We focus on the initial case shown in Extract 0.1 because it shows, clearly and without a conventional academic analysis, that people routinely conduct analyses of categories. And, importantly, they "do not have to consult a textbook before analysing the world. *They just do it*" (Silverman, 1998, p. 86; emphasis added). This extract is the headline from a British broadsheet newspaper, *The Daily Telegraph*. Beneath the headline, "Migrants side by side in hotels with public," was a story about then UK Home Secretary Suella Braverman's plans to reduce "overcrowding at [an] asylum processing centre" by temporarily housing "migrants" at hotels. The day after this story was published, a well-known British soccer pundit, Gary Lineker, posted on the social media platform Twitter (now 'X') a screenshot of *The Telegraph* front page with his own replacement headline, as shown in Extract 0.2.

Extract 0.1: *The Daily Telegraph*, 30.10.22
01 Migrants side by side in hotels with public

Extract 0.2: @GaryLineker[2], 31.10.22
01 Human beings side by side in hotels with fellow human beings.

In these opening extracts, embedded in alternate descriptions of the situation at hand, are categories of persons ("migrants," "public") and an alternative to them ("human beings"), as well as a category of place ("hotels"). The respective versions of the headline also imply something about the relationship between groups of persons and their rights and entitlements to be "side by

2 https://twitter.com/GaryLineker/status/1587010428005220353

side" with each other as equals ("human beings," "fellow human beings") or not ("migrants" and "public"). The alternate categories construct competing versions of the events being discussed and even different realities. There are no neutral categories: all engage in an action, and thus reveal a stance, a version, a view, a 'take' on the 'facts' at hand. But the extracts also illustrate that and how categories matter – not just to academics, researchers, and scholars, but to everybody, virtually inescapably.

Lineker's tweet went viral, occasioning a wealth of responses that unfolded in sequences of social interaction. The responses, either affiliating with or challenging his tweet, were suffused with further categories. As well as using categories in their posts, people included them in their short Twitter profiles (e.g., 'remainer,' 'mother,' 'immigrant,' 'Welsh'), showing the practical utility of categories for short-cutting a host of meanings about 'who they are.' For example, a "Germany-based Scot" replied in support of Lineker:

```
Extract 0.3: @isslater³, 31.10.22
01  I live in constant fear of being in the same hotel as a
02  Telegraph reader.
```

Here, the author leverages the name of the newspaper in which the original headline and article appeared, *The Daily Telegraph*, to produce the category, "a Telegraph reader." What it means to be "a Telegraph reader" – indeed, an "average Telegraph reader" (see Honeyman, 2023, p. 54) – is unspecified yet clear, at least for those familiar with in British politics and media. In this sense, since the paper is British and regarded as "right-wing, pro-Conservative" (Honeyman, 2023, p. 54), being "a Telegraph reader" invites inferences of membership in those national and political categories. More generally, newspapers are one of myriad entities that can be used in combination with other categories to produce new ones (e.g., a '*Daily Mail* woman,' a 'Florida man,' a 'tech bro'). Furthermore, we see that instances of categorizing are a form of social action. Calling a person "a Telegraph reader" is not a neutral description of them. For this author, it entails a moral judgment about the kind of person they are, which is clear from the rest of the sentence this category appears in.

Despite being a much-invoked category in public and academic discourse, at least in the UK, "a Telegraph reader" is not one of the categories that academic researchers regularly and typically interrogate, quantify, associate, correlate, or manipulate in their research (e.g., gender, race, class, sexuality, ability – which we discuss more fully in Chapter 1: An Introduction to Categories in Social Interaction). Nevertheless, the category "a Telegraph reader," in

---

3 https://twitter.com/isslater/status/1587094411447619584

its truncated form without 'The Daily,' shows that the author, at least, treats it as familiar enough to whoever is reading their post not to need its full title. Furthermore, this reduction is one way that the formulation constitutes this as a person *category* rather than a person *description* (e.g., 'a person who reads *The Daily Telegraph*').

Yet, as well as using already-familiar category-laden words and phrases, people often put together new combinations in ad hoc ways that, despite not being commonplace, are fully comprehensible for the rhetorical purpose of the message. Being "a Telegraph reader" makes for a contrast with being a member of the "Guardian-reading, tofu-eating wokerati," a description that the Home Secretary had used ten days previously to refer to people otherwise categorizable as oil protestors and members of British opposition political parties. The component categories ('Guardian-reader,' 'tofu-eater,' 'woke[rati]'), combined in an ad hoc way to produce a new compound category, serve to package a host of unspecified but treated as known-in-common attributes and stances that those thus categorized are claimed to share. As an ad hoc category, "Guardian-reading, tofu-eating wokerati" has been put together, on an occasion, to do something in particular – in this case, to stigmatize an otherwise mainstream political perspective. It shows how virtually anything can become a category or be used in categorizing ways. And it shows that, while originating in live, unfolding social interaction, members' categories can richly expand upon the familiar sets studied in research as well as cross over from public to academic discourse (e.g., Blitvich, 2022; Oliver et al., 2024). Indeed, being a member of the category 'Guardian-reading, tofu-eating wokerati' was immediately embraced by some social media users, and a clothing company turned it into a T-shirt and hoodie design.[4]

Extract 0.4 is another reply to Lineker's post, from an account with a biography including numerous direct and implied self-categorizations: "Animal lover especially cats and Huskies. Female. Mostly in Scotland, travelling to rUK or bella Italia. Centre right politics Pro-UK."

Extract 0.4: @Maxie_UK[5], 31.10.22

01 Illegal immigrants on freebies with fellow UK citizens paying

When comparing Extract 0.4 with the original *Daily Telegraph* headline, we see how "migrants," replaced by Lineker with "human beings," is replaced again by Maxie UK with "illegal immigrants." Furthermore, "side by side in hotels" is replaced with "on freebies," and "public" or "human beings" with "UK citizens." The latter categorization specifies national identity membership

4 https://twitter.com/balconyshirts/status/1582635340971798529
5 https://twitter.com/Maxie_UK/status/1587122355934994438

and associated rights in a way that "public" does not, at least not explicitly (cf. Billig, 1995 on banal nationalism), in the service of complaining about the arrangement reported in the headline and thereby aligning with the headline and opposing Lineker and those who have aligned with him.

Discussing her planned use of hotels, Home Secretary Suella Braverman made the following widely broadcast comments at the Westminster parliament, transcribed verbatim in Extract 0.5.

```
Extract 0.5: Suella Braverman, 31.10.22
01  SB:  The British people deserve to know which
02       party is serious about stopping the invasion on
03       our southern coast and which party is not.
         ---13.6 seconds cut---
04  SB:  So let's stop pretending that they are
05       all refugees in distress.
         ---37 seconds cut---
06  SB:  I Madame Deputy Speaker am utterly serious
07  SB:  about ending the scourge of illegal migration.
```

Braverman's speech makes heavy use of categories ("The British People," "party," "refugees") and category-implicative pronouns ("our," "us"), as well as descriptions that imply the categorization of others (e.g., "the invasion," "in distress," "scourge of illegal migration"). Video footage of her speech was shared widely online (e.g., on *Sky News*[6,7]). The footage included the concurrent responses of those co-present in Parliament, including one in which an observer cups and partially hides his face in a way that conventionally conveys something like disbelief and/or dismay as Braverman says "scourge" (line 07).

Following the broadcast, many responses on social media focused on Braverman's use of the word "invasion." For example, in Extract 0.6, a broadcaster and political correspondent at Yahoo News UK denounced its use as "dehumanising and grotesque," and countered with an alternative description of the people in question:

```
Extract 0.6: @nadinebh[8], 31.10.22
01  Make no mistake, describing asylum seekers as invaders is
02  straightforward far-right language, and should be reported as
03  such.
```

6 https://twitter.com/SkyNews/status/1587139142043201536

7 Accessed via Learning On Screen: News Hour with Mark Austin, 17:00 31/10/2022, Sky News, 60 mins. https://learningonscreen.ac.uk/ondemand/index.php/prog/3BFFD0E7?bcast=137740320

8 https://twitter.com/nadinebh_/status/1587135562888237056

```
04  It is a dehumanising and grotesque way to describe innocent
05  human beings trying to claim asylum
```

In Extract 0.6, as well as criticizing Braverman's uses of categories, the author attends to the practice of description itself. Braverman's use of the term "invasion" is generalized to "straightforward far-right language." At a sometimes-startling pace, categories are reified and take on a life of their own.

As we continued to complete this book, the unfolding story about Braverman's language erupted again. This time, Joan Slater, an "83-year-old" went "viral on the internet" in a video of her "confronting the UK home secretary, Suella Braverman" about her language (Salter, 2023). The UK Home Office controversially sought the removal of the video, which had been posted by an organization called Freedom From Torture.[9] However, the video remains publicly available. Extract 0.7 is a verbatim transcript of the key charge from Salter, along with Braverman's response.

```
Extract 0.7: @FreedomFromTorture[10] January 2023
01  JS: I am a child survivor of the Holocaust.
        ---16 seconds omitted---
02      Now, when I hear you using words against
03      refugees like "swarms," and an "invasion," (I am
04      reminded of the language used to dehumanise and
05      justify the murder of my family and millions of others.
07      Why do you find the need to use that kind of
08      language.
        ---tape cut; unknown length of time omitted---
09  SB: I won't apologise for the kind of language that I've used
10      to demonstrate the scale of the problem.
```

Salter's first-hand account following the incident, published in *The Guardian* (Salter, 2023), contains her analysis of her interaction with Braverman and her reasons for saying what she did.

```
Extract 0.8: Joan Salter, The Guardian, January 2023
01  So when I hear the kind of rhetoric being used by our
02  politicians against desperate refugees trying to make
03  their way to safety here because they see the UK as a
04  welcoming place for them to settle and bring up their
05  children, I am concerned by how quickly we have forgotten
06  the lessons of the past.
07  . . .
```

9 www.freedomfromtorture.org/holocaust-survivor-confronted-suella-braverman-to-say-your-hateful-language-has-consequences
10 https://twitter.com/FreefromTorture/status/1614172335921303554

08   So, Ms Braverman, stop your dangerous rhetoric and find
07   other solutions, or history will not forgive you – and
08   the ordinary people who have swallowed your words will
09   eventually regret it.

Taken together, across the extracts we have presented thus far, several important features of categories are readily evident. First, categories, words, and language matter to people and yet, as we noted at the start of this prologue, people "do not have to consult a textbook before analysing the world. *They just do it*" (Silverman, 1998, p. 86; emphasis added). Second, categories are formulated and situated inextricably *in and through social interaction*, where, as Drew (2005, p. 74) points out, much of "our sense of who we are to one another" is managed, and where "[m]uch of the work of the core institutions of a society" is done (also see Schegloff, 1996a, 2006a). Third, categories are morally organized and often morally fraught, serving as fundamental sites for dispute and contestation, power struggles, political upheaval, and the management of relationships, affiliation, and argumentation. Through words, descriptions, depictions, and visible conduct, we deploy categories and, in so doing, construct ourselves, others, actions, events, and the world.

In light of these considerations, this book aims to advance a way of investigating how categories get used and produced by participants in everyday interactions. One might consider some of the categories we have encountered thus far (e.g., "invader," "migrant") as being at the 'profound and spectacular' end of a spectrum, nested in contexts of nationalism, racism, politics, and the like – and therefore plainly connected to some of the 'big topics' of social science. Yet they are also ordinary, or have become so, at least in the sense that they are recognizable, commonplace, and not technical or obscure for the people who use them. Each category can be put to different uses, depending on who utters or writes it, to whom, in response to what, in what setting, doing what action, in the service of what agenda(s), and so on. And words and categories can be combined to produce entirely new, but rapidly proliferating, ways to describe and categorize people.

Categories provide social scientists with a way into topics that are crucial to understanding social problems as they occur, evolving across different time horizons, generalized as "rhetoric" (Extract 0.8, line 01) and creating evidence for the very kinds of "history of sedimentation of usage" (Baker, 2000, p. 112), that perhaps is more familiar to social theorists and those working with discourses at a so-called 'macro' level: Categories "lock discourses into place" and are "quiet centres of power and persuasion" that "arrange relations of power, privilege and advantage. . . . Rearranging categories and associated activities is difficult excavation work because one encounters a history of sedimentation of usage and, therefore, of commonsense and 'logic'" (Baker, 2000, pp. 99, 106, 112, 113).

0.2   Why are we writing this book?

The book's origins are in a conversation at the International Institute of Ethnomethodology and Conversation Analysis (IIEMCA) conference in Mannheim, Germany, during summer 2019. One of us (Stokoe) had given a presentation on categories in interaction, and this prompted discussion of our mutual interests in, on the one hand, conversation analysis as the approach we all use in our research and, on the other, using this approach to study categories as sociological and psychological concerns. Although we knew each other previously, and different combinations of us had previously collaborated (see, e.g., Whitehead et al., 2018; Whitehead & Stokoe, 2015), our conversation at the conference propelled us to the first stage of this more thoroughgoing project. We made plans to meet in the summer of 2020 to begin working on a book proposal but then came the Covid-19 pandemic. We did meet regularly online though and managed to submit our proposal and then begin writing the book later in 2020. And we eventually met in person at Loughborough University, UK, in autumn 2022, to plan the book's completion.

Our reasons for writing the book are threefold. First, and foremost, we have recognized a need for a book that presents a specifically conversation analytic framework for the analysis of categorial phenomena. We hope that the book will thereby provide those who are interested primarily in the basic 'machinery' of social interaction (i.e., in conversation analysis) with ways of approaching the more traditional concerns of social science. It will also bring to researchers who are interested primarily in categorial topics – including the categories that underpin so much of social science – a way of investigating them that draws primarily on conversation analysis as an empirically based theory of human sociality and as a methodological approach. We hope to demonstrate the power of conversation analysis for conducting systematic and empirically rigorous analyses that take seriously the concerns and perspectives of participants in everyday interactions rather than seeking to replace them with those of analysts. Throughout the book's chapters, we present analyses of empirical cases that offer new insights into the workings of a wide range of categories that have been longstanding topics of conventional social scientific research, while also considering their relationships to categories conventionally deemed unworthy of scholarly attention.

Second, we write this book in part as a project to bring together the sometimes-contested trajectories of research that built on Harvey Sacks's (e.g., 1966, 1972a, 1972b, 1992) pioneering work in both conversation analysis and membership categorization. In so doing, we adopt what Watson (2021, p. 17) describes as an "inclusive approach" that "might work towards a convergence and, indeed, unification of areas of Sacks's work that are currently often treated separately." That said, we think it is fair to note that, while there are several book-length treatments that build on Sacks's work in theorizing and empirically analysing categorial phenomena using ethnomethodological, conversation analytic, and/or discursive psychological approaches, there are many more that focus on and/or use conversation analysis, but none that directly integrate CA's current and core concerns with attention to systematic features of categories and categorization. In terms of existing works that do focus on categories and that have shaped our thinking, we include books by Eglin and Hester (2003), Hester et al. (2016), Jayyusi (1984), Järviluoma et al. (2003), Lepper (2000), Silverman (1998), and Williams (2000); as well as a number of edited collections (e.g., Antaki & Widdicombe, 1998a; Fitzgerald & Housley, 2015; Hester & Eglin, 1997; Nguyen & Kasper, 2009; Smith et al., 2021); special journal issues (e.g., Fitzgerald et al., 2017); and journal articles that are too numerous to list, but are cited throughout the book.

Third – and we develop this point now in some detail – we seek to address claims about conversation analysis and membership categorization, as ethnomethodological approaches (among which we include discursive psychology), that we regard as erroneous or disingenuous – or both. Right from their inception, these approaches attracted criticism, particularly within sociology and psychology. For instance, Coser (1975, p. 696) infamously characterized ethnomethodology as "aggressively and programmatically devoid of theoretical content of sociological relevance," and a method "in search of a substance," foreshadowing a recent critique of conversation analysis as "a method in search of a problem" (see Stokoe & Albert, 2024). Other complaints about these approaches include claims about their 'pointless empiricism,' focusing on 'nothing but the text'; failing to address notions of subjectivity; being atheoretical and ahistorical; and thus failing to address the 'big and important questions' (see, e.g., Billig, 1999a, 1999b; Parker, 2005, 2012, 2013; Sarangi, 2017; Thorne, 1995; Wetherell, 1998). (Also see our related discussion of critiques of conversation analysis in Chapter 3: Methodological Principles, Practices, and Challenges.) Of course (!), we reject these criticisms. In our view, they are often based on 'straw person' versions of conversation analysis and its ethnomethodological family relations. Some commentators seem unaware of the strong traditions of research at the intersections of ethnomethodology, conversation analysis, discursive psychology, and membership categorization that address an expansive range of so-called 'big questions.' The examples we can list here do not do justice to the vast literature in this regard but to illustrate the strong and expanding tradition of research on categorial matters, including various combinations and domains of stereotyping, prejudice, discrimination, marginalization, and power in relation to them, we point readers towards work on:

- Gender (e.g., Edmonds & Pino, 2023; Fukuda, 2024; Henderson, 2022; Joyce et al., 2021; Kiguwa, 2018; Kitzinger, 2007a, 2007b; Kitzinger & Wilkinson, 2017; Miltersen, 2020; Nielsen, 2024; Pino & Edmonds, 2024;

Raymond, 2019a; de Rijk et al., 2024; Speer, 2002b; Speer & Parsons, 2006; Speer & Stokoe, 2011b; Stokoe, 2003, 2010a, 2015; Stokoe & Smithson, 2001; Stokoe & Weatherall, 2002; Tadic, 2024; Wowk, 1984; Yu, 2024);

- Race (e.g., Blain & Diskin-Holdaway, 2023; Byun, 2024; Cheeks & Whitehead, 2024; Creider, 2024; Fox et al., 2023; Garcia, 2022; Goodman & Burke, 2010; Hoey & Raymond, 2024; Joyce & Sterphone, 2022; McKenzie, 2016; Rafaely, 2021; Rawls & Duck, 2020; Rawls et al., 2018, 2020; Robles, 2015; Robles & Xie, 2024; Sambaraju, 2024; Shrikant, 2018, 2022; Shrikant & Sambaraju, 2021; Sterphone, 2022; Stokoe, 2015; Stokoe & Edwards, 2007; Tadic, 2024; Tadic et al., 2024; van den Berg et al., 2003; Whitehead, 2009, 2012b, 2015, 2018, 2020; Whitehead & Lerner, 2009; Williamson, 2024; Xie, 2024; Xie & Durrheim, 2024; Xie et al., 2021; Zhang, 2022, 2023);
- Ethnicity (e.g., Hansen, 2005; Moerman, 1974, 1988; Saft, 2024; Shrikant, 2021; Svensson, 2024; van de Weerd, 2019, 2020; Wieder & Pratt, 1990; Wilkinson, 2011a);
- Class and related matters of socio-economic inequality (e.g., Dominguez-Whitehead & Whitehead, 2014; Holmes, 2019; Lee, 2018; Robles & Joyce, 2024; Tam et al., 2024);
- Sexualities (e.g., Kitzinger, 2000, 2005a, 2005b; Land & Kitzinger, 2005; Raymond, 2019a; Speer, 2017; Speer & Potter, 2000);
- (Im)migration (e.g., Fox et al., 2023; Goodman & Burke, 2010; Goodman & Speer, 2007; Yu, 2024);
- Age, stage of life, and generational cohort (e.g., Baker Rosa & Hastings, 2016; Butler & Fitzgerald, 2010; Flinkfeldt et al., 2022; Liu, 2024; Nikander, 2000; Paoletti, 2002, 2024; Previtali et al., 2023; Rafaely, 2024; Rafaely & Whitehead, 2020; Willemsen et al., 2023);
- Family, friendship, and kinship (e.g., Benwell & Stokoe, 2006; Bilmes, 2009; Butler & Fitzgerald, 2010; Liu, 2023, 2024; Moody, 2023; Raymond & Heritage, 2006; Wilkes & Speer, 2021);
- (Dis)abilities (e.g., Chinn & Antaki, 2021; Due, 2024; Frankena et al., 2019; Yu & Sterponi, 2023);
- Mental health-related categories (e.g., Maynard, 2019; Maynard & Turowetz, 2022; Roca-Cuberes, 2008; Turowetz & Maynard, 2016); and
- Intersectionality (e.g., Bakshi, 2024; Figgou et al., 2023; Hummelstedt et al., 2021; Paravina, 2024; Whitehead, 2013b).

Also relevant in this regard is applied – that is, intervention- and/or policy-oriented – conversation analytic research across a diverse range of settings, including education, law, healthcare, defence, policing, medicine, politics, media, and artificial intelligence (e.g., Antaki, 2011; Haddington & Stokoe, 2023; Housley & Dahl, 2024; Jones et al., 2023; Lester & O'Reilly, 2018;

Raymond et al., 2022; Richards & Seedhouse, 2005). (Also see our discussion of applications in Chapter 10: What Now and What Next? Domain-Specific Applications of Categorization Practices.)

Thus, as Silverman (1998, p. 68) notes, although it might "be argued that there are more *important* social events than 'mere' talk – revolutions, murders, new laws and so on . . . it is difficult to resist the argument that conversation is a major medium of social interaction" and, indeed, it may be difficult to do any of the supposedly more important activities mentioned here without conversation. Moreover, as Schegloff (2006a, p. 70) points out, it is largely through social interaction that the abstract institutions of society – such as "the economy . . . , the law, religion, and so forth" are constituted and realized. In our view, critics of conversation analysis mistakenly equate attention to the details of talk-in-interaction at the level of granularity at which participants produce and attend to them (e.g., short silences, emphasis on words or sounds, pitch changes) with a focus on trivial matters, and lack awareness of research on categories in social interaction and of membership categorization analysis more generally. However, as decades of conversation analytic research have demonstrated – and as much of the research on categorial matters cited in the preceding paragraph affirms – details of this nature are crucial features of how categorial phenomena are interactionally constituted. In other words, our attention to them as analysts is warranted – and even required – by the demonstrable fact that participants in interactions are attending to them, using them, managing them, etc., in doing whatever they are doing (also see Schegloff & Sacks, 1973). This book is therefore designed to offer ways of understanding and studying both the apparently mundane details of the everyday (re)production of categories and social problems more widely recognized as important that we are currently facing and have faced historically – and to appreciate how the former constitute a crucial set of foundations for realizations of the latter. Our view is that conversation analysis provides the tools for the systematic empirical investigation of core social science topics via a focus on categories in interaction.

0.3   Chapter overviews

Following this prologue, the next two chapters set out the development, approach, framework, and methods for understanding and analysing categories in social interaction that inform the remainder of the book. In Chapter 1: An Introduction to Categories in Social Interaction, we describe the approach we develop in this book. We locate it both in its broader social science context, where categories have been theorized and studied, and in its origins in both Harvey Sacks's lectures on conversation and Harold Garfinkel's challenge to mainstream sociology: ethnomethodology. We explain a basic distinction between the way categories are deployed, on the one hand, by academics in the course of their research (*analysts' categories*) and, on the other, by (lay) people (*members' categories*) – the latter as exemplified in the extracts presented earlier. We chart the origins and trajectory of this fundamental distinction from Sacks's and Garfinkel's early work through to the development of membership categorization analysis and discursive psychology, where most of the research on categories (and category-adjacent topics, like identity) has been conducted. We draw on empirical examples throughout the chapter, before setting out the book's key themes and contributions, which centre on examining the reciprocal relationships between categorial phenomena and the 'generic' organizations of practice for talk-in-interaction described by Schegloff (2006a, 2007b).

Chapter 2: Approaching Membership Categorization introduces the apparatus of membership categorization devices (MCDs) first described in Sacks's early work, and subsequently developed by other researchers who adopted the label, 'membership categorization analysis' (MCA). Throughout the chapter, we illustrate and demonstrate the concepts of membership categorization using examples from various domains, from newspaper texts to messaging apps to ordinary conversational and institutional interactional encounters. We also consider the (ontological and epistemological) world-building and moral-ordering "force of categorization practices in social and institutional life" (Baker, 2000, p. 112).

Chapter 3: Methodological Principles, Practices, and Challenges addresses the practical concerns that arise in conducting research on categories in naturally occurring – and especially audio- or video-recorded – social interaction, using a conversation analytic approach. In particular, we discuss challenges associated with 'capturability' (also see Stokoe, 2012b), empirically grounding analyses in participants' orientations, and dealing with tacit and/or ambiguous cases, while addressing criticisms that have been levelled at conversation analysis in relation to these challenges. We also offer some practical advice for undertaking the characteristically conversation analytic approach of building and analysing collections of cases, particularly in relation to studying categorial phenomena.

The following six chapters then implement the primary contribution of the book, as described earlier, in sketching out a framework[11] for examining features of the reciprocal relationship between categories and other fundamental structures and practices of talk-in-interaction. These chapters largely

---

11 In characterizing his "partial sketch of a systematics" for person reference, Schegloff (1996b, p. 471) notes, "What I offer is really only a sketch, and I plead constraints of time and space; but even if I had much more time and space, I think our understanding (or at least mine) is at present at best a sketch; so I am offering a sketch of a sketch." It is in a similar spirit that we offer a sketch (or a sketch of a sketch) of a framework – with a lively sense that our current understandings are limited, and with the hope that future work will flesh out any number of details of this sketch that are missing, incomplete, or even incorrect.

correspond to the generic organizations of practice for interaction described by Schegloff (2006a, 2007b),[12] with two main exceptions. The first of these is that we do not include a separate chapter focusing on overall structural organization – although we do consider some features thereof in relation to categorial phenomena in various places throughout the other chapters (also see the illustrative analysis of categorial phenomena in relation to the openings of telephone calls in Whitehead et al., 2024). The second is that our examination of word selection focuses more specifically – in Chapter 5: Referring to and Addressing People – on person reference, as a sub-domain of word selection in which categorial phenomena are especially plentiful (Schegloff, 1996b). (Again, we touch on various other features of word selection in relation to categories throughout our analyses across the other chapters.)

In Chapter 4: Forming and Making Sense of Actions, we focus on how actions are formed by speakers and recognized by their recipients, using resources grounded in talk, other embodied conduct, and their position in unfolding interactions – and how, in the process, participants' observably take into account their respective memberships in particular categories. We begin by examining how categories can, both explicitly and tacitly, serve as bases for solving organizational problems encountered during the course of interactions. We then develop further accounts of how participants use explicit categorial practices to form and make sense of actions, and how they tacitly treat categories as bases for designing and evaluating actions.

In Chapter 5: Referring to and Addressing People, we examine how speakers' selection of particular words in forming up references to persons – including 'third person' references to a person other than the speaker or immediate recipients, 'second person' references to an immediate recipient, and 'first person' or self-references – can be done in ways designed to either do 'nothing more than referring' or to contribute to the action of the turn in which the reference is produced. In considering how these possibilities can be analytically distinguished, we examine some ways in which categories can be reproduced 'incidentally,' through their use as core resources for referring to persons, or can be deployed more directly or concertedly in the service of particular interactional work to which a person reference contributes.

Chapter 6: Taking Turns at Talking and Selecting next Speakers considers the categorial features of turn-taking, focusing on the system underpinning the construction and allocation of turns at talk – that is, the question of who should speak, when they should begin speaking, and for how long. We start by introducing the basic machinery of the turn-taking system, before focusing on how the system provides the basis for understanding turn allocation, and

---

12 We discuss these in more detail in Chapter 1: An Introduction to Categories in Social Interaction, Section 1.4.

overlapping talk or 'interruption,' as categorially tied practices. We show how conversation analysis may both challenge and specify stereotypical notions of 'interruption' as practices in and of themselves, and as associated with categories in ways that reveal the workings of power, participation, and exclusion.

Chapter 7: Organizing Sequences of Action sketches out the features of "adjacency pair" sequences, which serve as fundamental "building blocks" (Schegloff, 2007b, p. 12) for producing and maintaining mutually intelligible courses of action in interaction, while also demonstrating how they serve as basic structures and resources for producing and recognizing categorial phenomena. It then considers how categories may become relevant in and through the range of ways adjacency pair sequences can be expanded – namely 'pre-expansion,' 'insert expansion,' and 'post-expansion,' as well as in 'parenthetical sequences.' In doing so, it demonstrates both how the structures and expectations of sequences of action provide places for the use and/or management of categories and how categories serve as extra-sequential sources of the organization of interactional occasions.

In Chapter 8: Managing Troubles in Speaking, Hearing and Understanding, we examine how participants manage troubles that can occur when producing, partially producing, correcting or altering, hearing, and understanding categorial phenomena in social interaction. This includes exploring the practices of 'repair' – that is, how people attend to the moment-by-moment production of their actions, and how they may halt, go back, reformulate, start again, add something, and prompt their interlocutors to do the same, in order to maintain intersubjectivity and progressivity in and through their interactions. Specifically, we focus on how these practices can be rich sites for the examination of participants' orientations to and management of categorial matters, which are recurrently exposed through repair practices that implicate categorial considerations and troubles. We do this by explaining and illustrating the range of different structural positions at which (category-related) repair can be performed, including same-turn self-initiated repair, transition space repair, next-turn other-initiated repair, and repair after next turn.

In Chapter 9: Managing Knowledge, Experience, and Entitlement, we return to an original and important component of work on membership categorization, concerning 'category-bound rights and obligations' and subsequently developed as part of the conversation analytic subfield of 'epistemics.' We examine the practices participants use for composing and positioning utterances that reveal their orientation to managing their relative rights to knowledge, and how these are recurrently associated with categorial phenomena. We thereby specify ways of observing how participants' conduct reflects their pervasive monitoring, patrolling, and defence of rights to knowledge, experience, and entitlements associated with membership in particular categories.

Finally, in Chapter 10: What Now and What Next?' Domain-Specific Applications of Categorization Practices, we examine a number of different settings, including medicine, healthcare, crisis negotiation, sales encounters, and the proliferation of conversational technologies using artificial intelligence – and the relevance of categories to understanding those settings in ways that can be identified, described, and shared with practitioners in order to generate applications and impact. Such applications of category-based work include developing research-based materials and resources for helping multiple kinds of stakeholders to understand contemporary workplace concerns like allyship, speaking out, and discrimination. At the end of the chapter, we consider the categorial future and describe potential future directions for the field.

Reader, we hope you enjoy the book.

1

AN INTRODUCTION TO CATEGORIES IN SOCIAL INTERACTION

1.0 Introduction

Even before contemporary academia began to study categories, the word 'category' (from the Greek, *katēgoria*) was much discussed by philosophers as a concept of understanding, judgement, and language (see Alejandro, 2021) and as "an attribute, property, quality, or characteristic that can be predicated of a thing."[1] From very early on, the concept of a category emerged as an explanatory account for observable regularities and patterns.

In contemporary academia, social science understandings of 'categories' rapidly coalesced around particular groups of people. For example, writing about the neuroscience of social vision, Stolier and Freeman (2016, p. 141) refer to "the Big Three" of "sex, race, and age" through which people "group individuals based upon social information." In addition, they list "social status, occupation, and even perceptually ambiguous categories such as sexual orientation" (p. 141) as other significant sets of categories. From sociology, Drew (2021) lists age, ability, ethnicity, race, gender, sexual orientation, socioeconomic status, and religion. Alcoff and Mendieta (2003) also include nationality as a key category.

Towards the end of the twentieth century, the analytic and conceptual framework of "intersectionality" emerged as an explicit rejection both of "the tendency to treat race and gender as mutually exclusive categories" and of conceptualizing "subordination as disadvantage occurring along a single categorical axis" (Crenshaw, 1989, pp. 139–140). After advocating for analytic

---

1 Letter from Beck to Kant, June 20, 1797.

DOI: 10.4324/9781003120599-2

attention to be paid to the simultaneous and intersecting experiences of discrimination and marginalization on the basis of both race and sex/gender categories, Crenshaw and other theorists of intersectionality incorporated additional categories into this framework – including class, sexuality, ethnicity, nation, religion, ability, and age – while also noting the potential further expandability of this list (see Cho et al., 2013; Collins & Bilge, 2020). We return to the notion of 'expandability' in Chapter 2: Approaching Membership Categorization and Chapter 3: Methodological Principles, Practices, and Challenges.

Both individually and as intersections, these sets of categories serve as significant bases for the structuring of human societies and experiences in a wide range of explicit and tacit ways. They are also the categories of academia, since they appear, top-down, in research that pre-selects them, by dividing groups of participants to interview, survey, experiment, and theorize upon, and otherwise subject to research and scholarship. In so doing, such research both anticipates and reproduces, by design, the categorial basis of social science explanation. A key distinction we draw in this book is between the way categories are deployed, on the one hand, by academics in the course of their research (*analysts'* categories) and, on the other, by (lay) people (*members'* categories). This kind of contrast is frequently articulated as the difference between insider versus outsider perspectives when conducting research, 'emic' versus 'etic' (Pike, 1954), endogenous versus exogenous, micro versus macro, bottom-up versus top-down, even subjective versus objective. The approach we take in this book can be understood as insider, emic, endogenous, and so on, although these binaries are often reductive, and both construct and reify hierarchically organized categories themselves.

The collections of categories that comprise 'The Big Three' – plus the further additions listed previously – are those of conventional and widespread interest for social science researchers. Of course, this is because of their central importance both historically and ongoingly in organizing and structuring societies and, thereby, people's everyday lives. Thus, in seeking to differentiate between the categories that scholars most commonly deploy to frame research questions or identify participant groups and those which people themselves use in everyday life, we are not minimizing their importance or proposing that scholars give such categories undue weight. Often, as many examples in this book will show, analysts' and people's categories are the same. However, as we discuss throughout the book, using ordinary people's activities and orientations rather than those of researchers as a starting point opens up possibilities for investigating a wider range of categories than those that are conventionally regarded as worthy of social scientific attention.

Thus, our approach focuses explicitly on *members'* categories and categorial descriptions, objects, and actions – and how they are used – while, in so doing, "preserving in situ forms of social organization through which actual participants collaboratively produce social actions and social life in the first place" (Maynard, 2014, pp. 216–217). For example, in Chapter 2: Approaching Membership Categorization, we will explore how, during a dispute between neighbours, a participant mentions that she has been categorized by another as "a Barbra Streisand." What kind of category is "a Barbra Streisand"? What has occasioned its use? What is accomplished via this way of categorizing her? Is it a one-off category, while nevertheless completely understandable in the sequential context it appears (also see Hauser, 2011; Schegloff, 2007b)? What does it imply? Does she resist it, or embrace incumbency as a member? As a category, "Barbra Streisand" is highly unlikely to start life as an analyst's way of grouping research participants or constructing a theory. Yet it is formulated on a particular occasion, for a particular reason and is meaningful to those present as characterizing an aspect of their conversation and relationships.

Our principled starting point, then, is that we are interested in any and all things that people do with categories, including the ones conventionally used in academic research; the familiar ones ("a Telegraph reader," see the Prologue: Why Categories Matter); and the "ad hoc categories" (Hauser, 2011, p. 186) that are put together for an occasion of use (e.g., "Guardian-reading, tofu-eating, wokerati," again, see the Prologue: Why Categories Matter). Moreover, we do not make a distinction between 'social' and, say, 'natural' categories, since appealing to the 'naturalness' of a category is itself an action-oriented and rhetorical practice (see, e.g., Henderson, 2022). This means that the categorial scope of our research is potentially much wider ranging than traditional social science and raises the importance of people and their categorial concerns above those of researchers and analysts (Stokoe & Albert, 2024). Yet, as we will see, this does not mean that 'anything goes' or that gaining empirical purchase on a potentially infinite list of categories is impossible. Rather, it means that we need an empirical warrant for claiming the relevance of categories to whatever interactional conduct is occurring (also see our discussion of participants' orientations to categories in Chapter 3: Methodological Principles, Practices, and Challenges). While categories like "a Barbra Streisand" are often used as a way of invoking one or more other categories, the approach we advance can also include attention to many other categories typically not recognized as significant (also see our discussion of this issue in Section 1.4.2).

The examples we provided in the Prologue: Why Categories Matter introduce some important features of the approach and intention of the book. In the remainder of this chapter, we explore how categories have been researched and theorized across the social sciences, and how the approach we take differs from more conventional ones (Section 1.1). We then introduce the approach to categories and social interaction taken in this book, based on the work of Harvey Sacks (Section 1.2). Mapping the terrain, we next situate our approach in the foundational literatures of conversation analysis, membership categorization, discursive psychology, and, more broadly, ethnomethodology, on which we build (Section 1.3), before articulating and explaining the main themes and contributions of the book (Section 1.4). Before we leave this chapter, we explain our thinking behind the types of data we use in the book and their transcription, and the potential limitations of working with varieties of spoken and written English (Section 1.5). We end with some brief concluding remarks (Section 1.6).

1.1   Categories in the social sciences

As we saw in the Prologue: Why Categories Matter, one of the most common things that people do with categories is to refer to and/or describe themselves and others, individuals and groups of persons. The notions of self- and other-categorization may be thought of, superficially at least, as synonymous with notions of identity, role, self, and so on (cf. Hadden & Lester, 1978; Halkowski, 1990; McHoul & Rapley, 2005). Of course, there are already thousands of research papers and books that theorize and study these topics empirically (for overviews, see Benwell & Stokoe, 2006; Elliott, 2019; Leary & Tangney, 2012; Preece, 2016; Tieu, 2023; Williams, 2000). No one academic discipline 'owns' the study of self, identity, categories, or related concepts, and different entry points and traditions can be found across the social sciences and humanities, including in psychology, sociology, social policy, public administration, linguistics, anthropology, philosophy, communication, behavioural science, history, politics, and geography. Yet, some ways of thinking and writing about categories appear to be shared or are described in similar ways across these fields. For example, Schaller and Neuberg (2012, p. 43) observe that "[h]uman beings are implicit organizers; we like to lump people into categories." They write as experimental social psychologists but neatly capture something that may be the starting point for many different kinds of research (as well as what we see people doing in everyday talk and texts). However, although some of the academic language may sound similar, the details of the ways categories are theorized and studied empirically are starkly divergent. For example, categories may be conceived in many, and often antithetical, ways, as biological, cognitive, computational, linguistic, or social, and studied via associated conceptual frameworks, theories, models, and processes.

It is not our intention to review these different traditions in detail, but it is noteworthy that, across many approaches, categories are conventionally deployed by researchers as methodological and explanatory resources rather than interrogated in and of themselves. The uses to which they are put in this regard include for (1) selecting settings and/or people to study, and describing features of settings and people being studied; (2) studying identities or experiences shared by members of a group; (3) dividing populations to compare groups; and thus as predictors of and/or explanations for differential actions or outcomes between groups; (4) describing and accounting for relationships, conflicts, etc., between individuals or groups; and (5) theorizing social structures and politics. In this range of uses, categories are systematically treated as *analysts' resources* (also see, e.g., Alejandro, 2021; Heritage, 1984b; Järviluoma et al., 2003; Zimmerman & Pollner, 1970).

In the coming sections, building on the distinction between *analysts' categories* and *members' categories* introduced earlier, we position our approach in contradistinction to this mainstream social science approach. That is, our goal is to study how people use categories, rather than to use categories to study people (also see Zimmerman & Pollner, 1970). As Jefferson (2004b, p. 118) puts it, our business is to "analyze the workings of categories, not to merely use them as they are used in the world." In their book on classification, which they themselves say "straddles sociology, anthropology, history and information systems, and design" (p. xii), as well as "sociology of knowledge and technology" and" information science" (p. 6), Bowker and Star (1999, p. 286, emphasis added) summarize one kind of contrast between these two positions:

> Many scholars have seen categories as coming from an abstract sense of "mind," little anchored in the exigencies of work or politics. The *work* of attaching things to categories, and the ways in which those categories are ordered into systems, is often overlooked (*except by theorists of language such as Harvey Sacks*).

Our book is anchored in the work of Harvey Sacks, which we begin to explore in the following section. We aim to enliven this exploration with illustrative cases from various kinds of data.

1.2   Harvey Sacks, categories, and social interaction

The approach taken in this book sits squarely within the traditions of ethnomethodology, conversation analysis, membership categorization, and discursive psychology. It especially has roots in the writing of sociologist Harvey Sacks and his collaborators (e.g., Garfinkel & Sacks, 1970; Sacks, 1972a, 1972b, 1992; Sacks et al., 1974; Schegloff et al., 1977; Schegloff & Sacks, 1973). Since categories have been a founding concern for social scientists across a range of disciplines, it is not surprising that they were also a primary focus of Sacks's early work in pioneering what would become conversation analysis (CA) and membership categorization [analysis] (MCA). Sacks's approach to categories, however, was distinct from those that prevailed in the social sciences at the time – and that, as we noted earlier, continue to dominate to this day – and our focus on ordinary people's uses of categories in our examination of the illustrative materials in the previous section is in keeping with the spirit of this approach. We further illustrate the distinctiveness of Sacks's approach through an analysis of Extract 1.1, which shows the opening moments of a call to a holiday company (also see Flinkfeldt et al., 2022). The recording is transcribed using Jefferson's (2004b) conventions for conversation analysis (also see our discussion of data and transcription in Section 1.5). "S" is the salesperson and the person called; "C" is the customer/client and the caller.

```
Extract 1.1: Holiday sales
01  S:  G'd evenin' Rindley Leisure Hotels, you're speaking to
02      Diane.=↓How c'n I help.
03  C:  Uh- good evenin' Diane. .hh I'm trying to- um. (0.3) I'm
04      a lady of a certain age and going online's giving me a
05      headache.
06  S:  Mhm he heh, heh,
```

Conventional social scientific approaches might use what we see in this interaction as a catalyst for research on such matters as age differences in uptake and uses of such technologies, old(er) people's experiences of using relatively new web-based technologies, and/or possible ways of (re) designing online platforms to make these technologies more user-friendly for old(er) people. That is, such approaches might, as we have noted previously, deploy categories as *analysts'* resources. For example, they might use categories in selecting people and topics to study, explaining differences between groups, and designing evidence-based interventions to improve outcomes for specific categories of people.

In contrast, the approach developed by Sacks and other scholars who have built on his work focuses on how ordinary *members* of society use, manage, self-administer, or otherwise contend with categories in everyday naturally occurring interactions. In line with this approach, we can observe how the caller describes herself in a category-relevant way, as "a lady of a certain age" (lines 03–05), claiming membership of this occasioned category – implying, perhaps, but not saying 'old.' That is, the caller refers to herself using a euphemistic rather than a more direct form of self-categorization, such as 'I'm an old woman.' As we discuss in further detail in our analysis of this case in Chapter 4: Forming and Making Sense of Actions, this formulation serves as a resource for managing alternative ways in which the caller's in-progress action may be understood – that is, as doing self-justification rather than self-deprecation. More generally, such a description seems designed to take into account the normative constraints that make the use of particular category terms sensitive, delicate, or even prohibited.

In addition to using her age category in this way, the caller categorizes herself as a "lady" in describing herself as "a lady of a certain age." There are many ways such a description could be understood. For example, it is the title of a song, a prepositional phrase, a euphemism, a catchphrase, or an idiom. It is defined in the Urban Dictionary (2009) as an "[i]ronically polite term for a woman who does not want her actual age known, e.g. one who is close to or just over the menopause." Bishop (2018) refers to it as "over 60 at least." While one can discover numerous instances of the phrase in literature and other forms of discourse, and analyses thereof in research on language, gender and age(ism) (e.g., Caldas-Coulthard, 2010), it would require speculation on our part as to what precisely was meant by the caller's use of it in Extract 1.1.

However, rather than engage in speculations about which, if any, of these understandings is the 'correct' (but unspoken) one in this case, we focus on what Edwards (2006) refers to as the "rich surface" of the interaction that is visible, or treated as such, by the participants themselves (also see our discussions in Chapter 3: Methodological Principles, Practices, and Challenges of grounding claims in participants' orientations and analysing ambiguous cases). The rich surface is sequential, systematic, and organized. For instance, "a lady of a certain age" does not appear in the caller's first turn, but after a return greeting ("good evenin' Diane"). This return greeting itself appears after she has called the company, constituting a 'summons' (Schegloff, 1986), and after her summons has been responded to by the salesperson in her turn that opens the conversation (lines 01–02). Moreover, as we discuss in further detail in our analysis of this case in Chapter 7: Organizing Sequences of Action, "I'm a lady of a certain age" is positioned after the caller begins to articulate her reason for calling ("I'm trying to–"), and after she cuts off, hesitates, and pauses (line 04). In this way she positions the self-categorization as an element of her unfolding request rather than elevating it to the basis for her call.

Whatever we might make of "I'm a lady of a certain age," as analysts or readers, we can see that and how it is put to use in a particular setting, as an occasioned, ad hoc category. Language is "an inference-making machine" (Sacks, 1992), and here, as in so much of social interaction, the precise inferences that may be available are not spelled out; the turn is simply produced and (evidently) understood for the action it is doing in the moment at hand. Our evidence for this is, in part, that the salesperson does not, for example, display trouble understanding this categorization – for example, by saying "Huh?" (see Raymond, 2019a). Nor does the salesperson produce a reciprocal self-description (e.g., "I'm also one of those ladies!"), thereby showing her understanding that the caller's use of these categories here is designed in relation to her project of seeking assistance, rather than being done in pursuit of a similar self-disclosure from the salesperson. What the salesperson *does* do, at line 06, is produce a token of understanding, "Mhm" and some laughter particles. She thereby shows she understands the caller's self-description and the account it provides for the caller's actions, as well as affiliating with this account.

The gender and age categories used by the caller in Extract 1.1 are, of course, among the categories widely used by social scientists as analytic resources. However, as this extract demonstrates, such categories are typically available to ordinary people for a wide range of everyday non-specialist uses. And their use may involve participants orienting to normative expectations regarding the use of such categories – even as members – that are mostly overlooked when such categories are introduced 'from above' by analysts. Analysts' categories may therefore map onto members' categories, although perhaps not in the kinds of ways analysts could easily imagine or anticipate (also see our discussion of the use of 'naturally occurring' interactional data in Chapter 3: Methodological Principles, Practices, and Challenges).

In many cases, when categories of conventional social science interest do become relevant, it is through links with, or as alternatives to, other categories that have already been treated as relevant more locally or immediately. For example, in 2016, a medical emergency on a Delta Airlines flight from Detroit to Minneapolis became the subject of a widely followed media story (see, e.g., Levin, 2016; Wible, 2016). The story centred around accusations of "blatant discrimination" on the part of the airline and its cabin crew, after they reportedly refused the offer of help for a sick passenger from another passenger who was a doctor. The doctor, Tamika Cross, posted her account of the incident on Facebook, from which we reproduce selections in Extract 1.2.

Extract 1.2: TK Cross, Facebook, October 2016[2]

```
01   I'm sure many of my fellow young, corporate America working
02   women of color can all understand my frustration when I say I'm
03   sick of being disrespected.
04   Was on Delta flight DL945 and someone 2 rows in front of me was
05   screaming for help. Her husband was unresponsive. I naturally
06   jumped into Doctor mode as no one else was getting up.
07   . . .
08   A couple mins later he is unresponsive again and the flight
09   attendant yells "call overhead for a physician on board". I
10   raised my hand to grab her attention. She said to me "oh no
```

2 www.facebook.com/tamika.cross.52/posts/658443077654049

```
11  sweetie put ur hand down, we are looking for actual physicians
12  or nurses or some type of medical personnel, we don't have time
13  to talk to you" I tried to inform her that I was a physician
14  but I was continually cut off by condescending remarks.
15  . . .
16  Another "seasoned" white male approaches the row and says he is
17  a physician·as well. She says to me "thanks for your help but
18  he can help us, and he has his credentials". (Mind you he
19  hasn't shown anything to her. Just showed up and fit the
20  "description of a doctor") I stay seated. Mind blown.
21  . . .
22  She came and apologized to me several times and offering me
23  skymiles. I kindly refused. This is going higher than her. I
24  don't want skymiles in exchange for blatant discrimination.
25  Whether this was race, age, gender discrimination, it's not
26  right.
```

Despite reporting that she "naturally jumped into Doctor mode" (lines 05–06), and thus conveying that she could legitimately provide medical assistance by virtue of category membership, Cross was evidently not, for the flight attendant, categorizable as any of the categories subsequently listed: "physicians or nurses or some type of medical personnel" (lines 07–08). In her account, Cross formulates some category-bound features of members of the category "doctor," by referring to the " 'seasoned' white male" (line 16) who Cross proposes "fit the 'description of a doctor'" (line 20) by virtue of these visible characteristics. Cross thereby formulates the categorial inferences that she drew from conduct that would otherwise constitute a puzzle (Whitehead, 2009). That is, she treats the flight attendant's dismissal of her offers of assistance despite her self-categorization as a "doctor" as occasioning a search for an account, with the account she arrived at – of "blatant discrimination" (line 24) – making inferences relating to age, race, and gender (also see lines 01–02 and 25). Also note that Cross herself orients to the tacit and sometimes provisional workings of category ascriptions, since at the end of her account she says, "*Whether* this was race, age, gender . . ." (line 25; emphasis added), while at the same time listing categories that may serve to invoke a legally protected set of collections of categories known variously, depending on jurisdiction, as "protected group," "protected characteristics," "protected class," "sans distinction aucune," or "prohibited ground."

Extract 1.3 shows a further case with strikingly similar features to Extract 1.2 (also see our discussion of building and analysing collections of cases in Chapter 3: Methodological Principles, Practices, and Challenges). Here, another "young Black woman" (lines 03–04) doctor (line 03), Yasmin Walters, recounts her experience of offering medical assistance, in this case at the scene of an emergency on the London Underground (the "tube"):

Extract 1.3: Dr Yasmin Walters, X, March 2024[3,4]

```
01   [I] was supporting a medical emergency on a tube platform last
02   night. The attitude of one of your workers was disgusting. She
03   did not believe I was a doctor, presumably as I'm a young Black
04   woman, and insisted I show ID.
05
06   Also- a white male OT was present and all staff (and
07   paramedics!!!) continued to defer to him for
08   information/decisions, despite me being the ALS trained medical
09   doctor. He didn't correct them. He wasn't asked for ID. Being a
10   Black woman is exhausting.
```

As in Cross's account, Walters juxtaposes her treatment by an institutional employee in the scene (lines 02–04) with that of a "white male" (line 06). Both Cross and Walters thus used race, gender, and age categories as resources for seeing and describing the bases for the dismissive and/or suspicious responses to their respective offers of help, in contrast to the expectations provided for by their legitimate incumbency of the category "doctor" (we return to further consideration of the significance of these insights in Section 1.4.3).

1.3   Routes to analysing social categories in interaction

Having begun to explore Sacks's approach to categories in the previous section, we move on now to introduce the core fields of inquiry that originated in his writing and that particularly shape our approach. These are membership categorization, discursive psychology, and conversation analysis. Our aim in this chapter is to give a brief overview to enable readers to understand our basic stance and approach. We refer readers elsewhere for fuller histories, explanations, and critiques (including Chapter 2: Approaching Membership Categorization and Chapter 3: Methodological Principles, Practices, and Challenges in this book).

Each of the fields of membership categorization, discursive psychology, and conversation analysis are underpinned by or have a family relationship to ethnomethodology. Ethnomethodology, 'the study of people's methods,' is a programme developed by sociologist Harold Garfinkel (1967) which was, in turn, developed in response to the sociology of Talcott Parsons (e.g., 1937, 1951), and drawing on the phenomenological philosophy of Alfred Schütz (1962, 1964), and Goffman's (e.g., 1959, 1963) work on the interaction order (for detailed introductions and overviews, see, e.g., Button et al., 2022; Francis &

---

3 https://twitter.com/yasminleighw/status/1771460103532638649
4 https://twitter.com/yasminleighw/status/1771458720704160155

Hester, 2004; Heritage, 1984b; Maynard & Heritage, 2022; Psathas, 1979; Turner, 1974; Vom Lehn, 2014). Garfinkel's basic idea was that people in society, or *members*, continuously engage in making sense of and acting in the world, and in so doing methodically display their understandings of it, making their activities "visibly-rational-and-reportable-for-all-practical-purposes" (Garfinkel, 1967, p. vii).

As Zimmerman (1978, p. 11) further explains, ethnomethodology "proposes that the properties of social life which seem objective, factual and transituational, are actually managed accomplishments or achievements of local processes." That is, members endogenously produce the "objective reality of social facts" in ways that are "naturally organised, reflexively accountable, ongoing," achieved "everywhere, always, only, exactly and entirely" through "members' work, *with no time out*, and with no possibility of evasion, hiding out, passing, postponement, or buy-outs" (Garfinkel, 1991, p. 11; emphasis added). Although "Sacks did not set out to study conversation or language in particular" but rather "how ordinary activities get done methodically and reproducibly" (Schegloff, 1992b, p. xvii), social interaction became central to the ethnomethodological project of explicating members' methods for producing – with no time out – orderly and accountable social activities. This includes, as Thorne (1995, p. 498) writes, the "basic categories of difference and inequality," which points further towards topics like identity, categories, and categorization (Benwell & Stokoe, 2006). And this brings us back to ethnomethodology and some of its most influential proponents. Given its relevance to the study of categories, we turn next to a discussion of Garfinkel's work on a transgender woman named Agnes.

1.3.1 Ethnomethodology and the case of Agnes: from 'doing' to 'using' categories

One of the best-known pieces of writing in ethnomethodology is directly relevant to categories and social interaction. In 1967, Garfinkel published his research on the way gender is "rigorously dichotomized into the 'natural,' *i.e.*, *moral* entities of male and female" (p. 116, emphasis in original), through a case study of Agnes, "a nineteen-year-old girl raised as a boy" (p. 117). As "the first sociological analysis of a transitioning person," Garfinkel's work now sits within "the rapidly expanding area of the sociology of transgender studies" (Schilt & Lagos, 2017, p. 426). Garfinkel described the forms of common-sense reasoning and practices that people use to produce themselves as gendered beings, as well as the often-tacit norms implicated in the "seen but unnoticed" (Garfinkel, 1967, p. 36) production of what is now referred to as *cis*gender but was then termed "gender normal" (Schilt & Westbrook, 2009, p. 421). In the decades since its publication, Garfinkel's work "continues to be considered as a landmark for (trans)gender studies, being frequently reinterpreted and cited by academics in the humanities and social sciences" (Marques, 2020, p. 19; also see Crawley, 2022), with Garfinkel being read "as a queer theorist" (Crawley et al., 2021, p. 133).

Garfinkel set out "to understand how membership in a sex category is sustained across a variety of practical circumstances and contingencies, at the same time preserving the sense that such membership is a natural, normal, moral fact of life" (Zimmerman, 1992, p. 195). From his conversations with Agnes, Garfinkel (1967, p. 122) produced a list of the properties of "natural, normally sexed persons" as cultural objects. The crux of this work lay in his descriptions of Agnes's social achievement of gender, revealing her achievements as a "practical methodologist" (p. 180) to accomplish

> the tasks of securing and guaranteeing for herself the ascribed rights and obligations of an adult female by the acquisition and use of skills and capacities, the efficacious display of female appearances and performances, and the mobilising of appropriate feelings and purposes (p. 134).

Garfinkel's work was taken up by feminist commentators Stanley and Wise (1993, p. 147), who argued that traditionally feminist concerns are usefully examined from an ethnomethodological perspective, since oppression "isn't a once and for all phenomenon . . . [and ethnomethodology] looks to the processes involved in our construction of an objectively defined social reality as the scene in which oppression daily occurs." Postulating gender as a social production gives rise to notions of subversion and resistance, different social orders, and "multiplicity beyond the gender binary" (Marques, 2019, p. 206; also see Crawley, 2022; Crawley et al., 2021; Lorber, 2000). Although Garfinkel's work in this area has been criticized (e.g., Bologh, 1992; Collins, 1995; Maldonado, 1995; Marques, 2019; Rogers, 1992a, 1992b; Schilt, 2016; Schilt & Lagos, 2017; Takagi, 1995; Thorne, 1995; Weber, 1995; West & Fenstermaker, 1995b; Winant, 1995; Zimmerman, 1992), it provided a crucial step towards understanding "gender as an interactional (rather than biological) achievement for all people" (Schilt & Lagos, 2017, p. 429).

A core concept that emerged from Garfinkel's work was the notion of 'doing gender' (cf. Goffman's [1976] notion of 'gender display'; also cf. Cahill [1983]). This notion was developed by psychologists Suzanne Kessler and Wendy McKenna (1978) and sociologists Candace West and Don Zimmerman (1987). The concept also resonates with the influential philosophy of Judith Butler (1990) whose theorizing of "gender trouble" foregrounded the performative nature "not only of gender but also of sex, thereby undermining the last essentialist buttress of the distinction between male and female" (Poggio, 2006, p. 226; also see Crawley, 2022). As Crawley (2022, p. 367; emphasis in original) points out, the concept of 'doing' has much potential for queer and anti-racist social science, keeping it "*future-facing and in motion*" (also see Crawley et al., 2021). In later collaborations with Sarah Fenstermaker (Fenstermaker & West, 2002; West & Fenstermaker, 1995a), West extended 'doing gender' into a broader theory of "doing difference," adding parallel accounts of race and class to their theory of gender, and considering the relationships between all three (also see, e.g., Crawley, 2022; Whitehead et al., forthcoming).

The 'doing' of gender is conceived as "a situated accomplishment: the local management of conduct in relation to normative conceptions of appropriate attitudes and activities for particular sex categories" (West & Fenstermaker, 1993, p. 358). Of course, it was not just that Agnes produced conduct consistent with normative expectations associated with the gender category but that in justifying her claim to be a member of one category and not the other, she and the other participants reproduced the gender binary as a 'natural moral fact' and thus as an inescapable feature of social life. From this perspective, 'doing gender' "consists of managing such occasions so that, whatever the particulars, the outcome is seen and seeable in context as gender appropriate or, as the case may be, gender *in*appropriate – that is, *accountable*" (West & Zimmerman, 1987, p. 135; emphasis in original). For example, in her analysis of a murder confession, in which the victim is repeatedly categorized as a "girl" (rather than, say, a 'woman') and, moreover, a particularly kind of "girl," Wowk (1984, p. 75) examines the categorial practices through which the "objective reality" of sexual politics is a concerted achievement and interactional production rather than something existing "over and above their production by members."

One problem with the concept of '*doing* gender' is that it has sometimes been empirically translated in ways that leave a 'realist residue' (Velody & Williams, 1998). In other words, analysts start out "'knowing' the identities whose very constitution ought to be precisely the issue under investigation" (Kulick, 1999; cited in Stokoe, 2005, p. 125). Ironically, it was in an emerging tradition of conversation analytic research that a series of studies sought to establish empirical associations between gender and interactional phenomena, such as interruption (men interrupt women) or verbosity (men dominate interaction) (e.g., Ainsworth-Vaughn, 1992; Davis, 1988; DeFrancisco, 1991; Fisher, 1984; Fishman, 1978; West & Garcia, 1988). Although much of this research was inconclusive (see reviews by James & Clarke, 1993; James & Drakich, 1993) or criticized for committing what Cameron (1997, pp. 59–60) the "correlational fallacy," West and Zimmerman (1987) were cited by Schegloff (1997c) as an example of an endogenous, 'participants' category' approach to gender in contrast to critical discourse analytic work on the same topic (but see Stokoe & Smithson, 2001 for a critique; also see, e.g., Eglin & Wideman, 1986; Hepburn & Potter, 2011; Kitzinger, 1998; Speer & Stokoe, 2011a). As Kitzinger (2009, p. 97) argues, "the value of *Doing Gender* was its theoretical articulation of the ethnomethodological principles that underwrite an understanding of oppression and resistance in everyday life. What it left out was the key empirical method for advancing that understanding" – and CA is "uniquely fitted" (Kitzinger, 2009, p. 97) to this task. A more detailed discussion of the way in which gender, as a membership categorization device, offers a completely distinctive (and non-essentializing) alternative to treating categories as variables that 'cause conduct' and/or 'difference' can be found in Schegloff (2001), and in Chapter 6: Taking Turns at Talking and Selecting next Speakers.

For us, there is an important distinction between the 'doing' and the 'using' of categories. While the 'doing' approach has been associated with ethnomethodology, and therefore conversation analysis, it leads to problematic off-ramps into the kinds of research that reproduce essentialized or generalized category-based claims, and which we therefore seek to avoid. Instead, we argue that a thoroughly ethnomethodological approach focuses on the 'using' of categories. This removes the circularity with which categories are deployed, reproduced, and reified in much social science research.

1.3.2 *From ethnomethodology to the empirical study of categories in social interaction*

As collaborators writing this book, we bring different backgrounds and experiences to our work. While our degrees are in psychology (Stokoe, Whitehead) and sociology (Raymond, Whitehead), we share the broad ethnomethodological goal of understanding how society is produced by and for its members. This includes the "respecification" (Button, 1991, p. 1) of the conventional objects of social science as members' concerns and practices. In sociology, for example, conversation analysts have specified how everyday and institutional realities commonly conceptualized as social structures are produced and reproduced through situated interactional practices and participant-administered forms of social organization. In psychology, discursive psychologists have respecified "the dominant psychological notion of cognition" (Speer, 2005, p. 16), including psychological concepts like attitudes, emotion, memory, prejudice, and identity – and categories. In his deep dive into the Harvey Sacks Archive at the Charles E. Young Research Library, University of California, Los Angeles, Fitzgerald (2021, p. 98) reports that Sacks, in a seminar with Garfinkel, stated that "his interest was not so much in the study of the discipline of sociology, but the study of people doing sociology in their everyday actions." Similarly, discursive psychologists' interest is in "people doing psychology," or "how psychological matters are managed . . . via language but also through embodied actions" (Edwards & Potter, 2020, p. 277).

We do not aim to write an in-depth history of these fields as they pertain to the analysis of categorial phenomena because others have done this (e.g., Hester & Eglin, 1997; Hester et al., 2016; Schegloff, 1992b; Silverman, 1998;

Smith et al., 2021). Furthermore, since we more fully explore the concepts, terminology, implications, and empirical examples of Sacks's work on categories in Chapter 2: Approaching Membership Categorization, and we describe some of the foundations of conversation analysis throughout the remaining chapters, we do not do this here either. Instead, we summarize what we take to be some of the basic premises shared by the related approaches that have advanced the project of respecification in relation to categories, without necessarily endorsing or promoting any particular perspective or version.

As Mondada (2021, p. 101) puts it, "two indissociable facets, categorization analysis and sequential analysis" were initiated in Sacks's work (also see, e.g, Schegloff, 1992b; Stokoe, 2012b; Watson, 1997). Since then, conversation analysis (or "sequential analysis"[5]) has been more "developed" and "prolific" than work on membership categorization, yet the latter has been "quietly persistent" (Eglin & Hester, 1992, p. 247). It was in 1992, in a landmark article, that Peter Eglin and Stephen Hester formulated the term '"membership categorization analysis" or "categorization analysis" for short' to name an approach that they suggested had been "nameless to this point" (Eglin & Hester, 1992, p. 247). In their editorial introduction to Hester's posthumous book on membership categorization analysis (MCA), Eglin and Francis (2016, p. 7), further explain that the term came about

> as a replacement for 'MCD analysis' (the term under whose rubric the distinctive categorial dimension of social life had been analysed during the 1970s and 1980s). The reasons for this proposal were not merely aesthetic, nor were they name-changing for its own sake; they were that 'MCD analysis' privileged the analysis of membership categorization devices, and whilst this privileging acknowledged the originality of Sacks's notion of category collections, it obscured the fact that whilst membership categories always belong to some collection and whilst their intelligibility depends crucially on their membership in a collection, it is also equally the case that category collections are dependent for their intelligibility upon which categories they collect together.

In this article, Eglin and Hester (1992) discuss the work of several other researchers whose work they saw as underpinning the development of MCA as a field, locating the main momentum in Manchester, UK, which "became the engine-room of developments in categorization and activity analysis, and ethnographic CA more generally" (p. 247). In addition to Wes Sharrock,

---

5 We have reservations about using the term "sequential analysis" to describe conversation analysis, since it elides attention to a much wider range of generic structures and practices of interaction than just the analysis of sequences (also see our discussion of these generic organizations of practice in Section 1.4.1).

they list "Atkinson (J.M.), Atkinson (M.A.), Benson, Button, Coulter, Cuff, Francis, Hustler, Jayyusi, Lee, Payne and Watson . . . and related British colleagues such as Drew" as members of the "Manchester School" (p. 247). We would add Baker (e.g., 1984) and Wowk (e.g., 1984) to this list of key players in the early development of MCA.

Collectively, these authors extended the foundations laid by Sacks. Eglin and Hester (1992, p. 250) especially praise "the singular achievement" of Jayyusi (1984) "to bring this body of work together, elaborate its conceptualization and develop its problems through detailed attention to cases." In mapping the early terrain, Eglin and Hester (1992) also pay particular attention to Watson's (1987) work on police-suspect interviews, which we note includes analysis of both sequential action and categorial concerns, the latter through the introduction of the term "predicate" to refer to features that are tied to categories (also see Wowk, 1984). They also describe Drew's work on courtroom trial interactions (also analysed by Jayyusi, 1984), which investigates "how a practical interactional task – an accusation – may be achieved through the production of descriptions" (Drew, 1978, p. 1). Thus, we can see that, in those early years, the connections between the categorial and the sequential were closer and less contentious,[6] with proponents whose names latterly became synonymous with conventional CA (e.g., Drew, Schegloff) or MCA (e.g., Watson).

Eglin and Hester's own theoretical, methodological, and empirical work, with David Francis and Sally Hester, comprises a substantial contribution to the development of MCA. In their 1997 book, Hester and Eglin (1997, p. 3) set out its purpose and scope:

> The use of membership categories, membership categorization devices and category predicates by members, conceptualized as lay and professional social analysts, in accomplishing (the sociology of) 'naturally occurring ordinary activities.' MCA directs attention to the locally used, invoked and organized 'presumed common-sense knowledge of social structures' which members are oriented to in the conduct of their everyday affairs, including professional sociological inquiry itself.

Their work, focused on categories, is wide-ranging: from respecifying social science interviews as interactional encounters (Hester & Francis, 1994) to studies of different aspects of education, classroom interaction, children's disputes, and categorizing "deviance" in educational psychology referral meetings (e.g., Hester, 1998; Hester & Francis, 2000; Hester & Hester, 2012); from crime, disputes, and negotiation (e.g., Eglin & Hester, 2003;

---

6 Also see Drew's (1978) and Schegloff's (1972) work on place and location categories.

Francis, 1986; Hester & Eglin, 1992; Hester et al., 2016) to the visual organization of walking (Hester & Francis, 2003), and to critiques of conversation analytic research on institutional talk for a purported theory-driven and un-ethnomethodological "scientism" (Hester & Francis, 2000, p. 411). They are also critical of Sacks's "tendency towards cultural decontextualisation" and "tendency to reify membership categorisation devices and membership categories" in the way he wrote about "natural categories" (Francis & Hester, 2017, p. 57). In contrast, in formulating their approach to talk as 'culture in action' (Hester & Eglin, 1997; Hester & Hester, 2012), they foregrounded the interdependence of categories and sequential order and the notion that all categories are "indexical," in that they only make sense through their situated, embedded, and contextualized use (Hester & Eglin, 1997, p. 11).

Hester also collaborated with William Housley (e.g., Hester & Housley, 2002), who, in turn, generated with Richard Fitzgerald a further body of work on MCA. Together, they aimed to "reclaim lost ground" for membership categorization, in the context of well-rehearsed discussions of the dominance of conversation analysis and the "sidelining" of "other dimensions of members' work within talk" in the years since Sacks (Housley & Fitzgerald, 2002, p. 59). In their "reconsidered model of membership categorization analysis," following Hester and others, they argue for "an analytical mentality which is sensitive to context, the relationship between sequentiality and category work and the local production of social order" (Housley & Fitzgerald, 2002, p. 65). They also foreground the importance of Jayyusi's (1984) development of Sacks's work in focusing on "the moral organization of talk-in-interaction" (Housley & Fitzgerald, 2002, p. 65).

In their own collaborations and with other researchers, Housley and Fitzgerald have further broadened the scope of MCA, towards the study of big data and social media texts (e.g., Housley et al., 2017a, 2018; Wu & Fitzgerald, 2021) and television news (e.g., Burger & Fitzgerald, 2019; Fitzgerald & Evans, 2019), as well as publishing fresh insights about the early development of Sacks's work on MCA and CA (Fitzgerald, 2019). In a recent book "devoted to the reintroduction of the remarkably original approach to sociological inquiry developed by Harvey Sacks," Smith et al. (2021, p. 1) curated a collection of chapters that represent the wide-ranging scope of work carried out or inspired by Sacks, with a diverse set of chapters dedicated to the analysis of categories in social interaction.

Notably, Housley and Fitzgerald (2015) describe their understanding of MCA as

> not so much a fully worked out methodology but rather a collection of observed practices employed by members. Thus MCA has not tended to

establish a fully worked out set of methodological tools to be applied to data, but rather to develop a concern with the empirical examination of just what people seem to be orienting to in order to achieve whatever it is they are doing. That is to say MCA is interested in observing, uncovering and detailing the methods, techniques and orientations employed by members as they go about their routine tasks (p. 6).

They thereby tacitly acknowledge the potential for the development of a more "fully worked out set of methodological tools to be applied to data," as a basis for continuing to move research in this area forward (cf. Stokoe, 2012a, 2012b) – a matter we take up in this book, as we describe in more detail in Sections 1.4 and 1.5.

In addition to the important advances offered under the auspices of MCA, significant contributions to research on categories in social interaction have also been made within the field of discursive psychology (DP). The name of this field was first coined by Edwards and Potter (1992) in their book of the same title. In the decades since then, discursive psychologists have studied how language, in the form of social interaction and texts, builds action and constructs the world (Edwards, 1997; Potter, 1996; Tileagă & Stokoe, 2016). In a direct challenge to much of what might be regarded as 'mainstream' psychology, and across the social sciences more broadly, Edwards and Potter (1992) pushed researchers to understand how, and that, language *does* things, rather than treating it as providing access to the mind. With its antecedents in the discourse and rhetorical approaches of the Loughborough Discourse and Rhetoric Group, or DARG (see Stokoe et al., 2012), discursive psychologists promoted their blend of ordinary language philosophy, social studies of science, social constructionism, ethnomethodology, and conversation analysis. Rather than treat language as a tool or pathway to cornerstone psychological phenomena like attitudes, attributions, identities, personalities, emotion, or memory – via questionnaires, survey instruments, focus groups, and interviews – they examined how language builds worlds and minds alike. In DP, with its methodological partner conversation analysis, the core purpose of language – in the broadest sense across all its modalities – is the production and maintenance of human sociality and intersubjectivity (Stokoe, 2020; Stokoe et al., 2025).

While Sacks (as noted previously) did not set out to study language in particular, DP concertedly studied language from the outset, since a key focus was on the discursive representation of "'versions' and their actions . . . , and on how both text and talk (discourse) deal with, invoke, construct, make relevant, and so on the nature of cognition and reality" (Edwards & Potter, 2020, p. 276; also see Cuff, 1994; Smith, 1978). One clear point of connection, however, is between Sacks's (1992, p. 119; emphasis added) notion that "activities are *observables*" and that people "*see* activities . . . , *see* persons doing intimacy . . . , *see* persons lying, etc." and Edwards's (2006, p. 41) notion of "the rich surface of language and social interaction," through which discourse is analysed "not as the product or expression of thoughts or mental states lying behind or beneath it, but as a domain of public accountability in which psychological states are made relevant." Edwards (2006, p. 42) goes on to argue that, while

> language, or discourse, is not all that there is in the world, not all that psychology and society are made of, and not the same thing as experience, or reality, or feelings, or knowledge . . . , it is the primary work of language to make all those 'other' phenomena accountable.

When one considers the extent of attention paid to theorizing identity and the self (and related concepts like personality and role) in psychology, from Freud to Tajfel (see Benwell & Stokoe, 2006), the fact that categories and categorization feature prominently in discursive psychology as part of its respecification project is unsurprising. However, discursive psychology rejects both individualistic notions of self and personal identity and the process-based account of the way individuals' identity is established via identification with groups and membership thereof – as in "Social Identity Theory" (Tajfel & Turner, 1986) and "Self-Categorization Theory" (Turner et al., 1987) – in favour of the ethnomethodological approach described earlier. Indeed, in his essay on the relevance of Sacks's work for psychology, Edwards (1995, p. 593) writes that his "legacy might be construed as anti-psychological, in that he focuses on talk as social action rather than a product of mind."

In setting out a discursive psychology of categorization, Edwards (1991, p. 515) argued that "categories are for talking." Edwards (1991, pp. 517–518; emphasis in original) goes on to argue, in contrast to the cognitive approach that was (and remains) dominant in (social) psychology at the time:

> Categorization is *something we do*, in talk, in order to accomplish social actions (persuasion, blamings, denials, refutations, accusations, etc.). From this perspective, we would expect language's 'resources' not to come ready-made from a process in which people are trying their best to understand the world (whether as individuals or together), but rather, or at least additionally, to be shaped for their functions in talk, for the business of doing situated social actions. Rather than starting with the abstracted content of categories and then theorizing about how they are used, discursive psychology recommends starting with situated usage, and

the aim of analysis is to explicate 'what is being done'. This has a series of implications:

1. We are always dealing empirically with indexicality, with a specific thing, event, property, or group of things being referenced, not the entire possible set.
2. Categorization will always be encountered as part of an utterance, text, argument, description, account, etc.
3. It is therefore encountered as part of the accomplishment of some social action: a reporting, blaming, defence, justification, excuse, etc.
4. Situated categorizations therefore perform moral work on the world described, and indexically, on the current interaction and participants who are producing and receiving the description.
5. It seems reasonable to assume that this is what linguistic categories are for, to do these kinds of things in talk.
6. Category terms (their semantic content, etc.) might fruitfully be examined, therefore, in terms of the kinds of discursive work they are functionally designed for, rather than how well they correspond to cognitively natural or perceptually derived organizations of experience.

Discursive psychology, like MCA and CA, developed along somewhat divergent trajectories following the publication of Edwards and Potter (1992). First, in following Edwards's formulation discussed earlier, numerous psychology-based researchers examined the way social (identity) categories are claimed, resisted, and otherwise put to use in interaction (e.g., Antaki & Horowitz, 2000; Dickerson, 2000; Edwards, 1998; Kerby & Rae, 1998; Rapley, 1998; Widdicombe & Wooffitt, 1995). A second strand is more closely aligned to the post-structuralist and sociology of science approach articulated in Potter and Wetherell's (1987) discourse analysis, developed subsequently as "critical discursive psychology" by Wetherell and colleagues (e.g., Wetherell & Edley, 1999). Researchers in this tradition employ the language of postmodernism in their descriptions of identity as multiple and conflictual, rather than unitary and coherent, and use a more theory-heavy, explicitly political approach akin to critical discourse analysis (CDA). Writing from the original DP tradition, Edwards and Stokoe (2004) reject postmodern notions of identity as multiple and conflictual since, for one thing, consistency is demonstrably important to people (cf. Francis, 1994). This is not an empirical generalization about how consistent or variable people actually are, but a recognition that both are participants' concerted accomplishments: "consistency is a strongly sanctioned normative requirement for being a sensible, accountable, rational, reliable human being. . . . Fixity versus multiplicity are not best used as rival ontologies of the self" (Edwards & Stokoe, 2004, pp. 501–502). Perhaps most famously, Wetherell (1998) and Billig (1999a, 1999b) responded on the side of CDA in the published debate that started with Schegloff's (1997c) challenge to CDA (also see Schegloff, 1998c, 1999a, 1999b). Somewhat confusingly for outsiders, this debate apparently pitched DP against CA while, in fact, the 'split' was internal to DP. As Edwards and Potter (2020, p. 275) recently observed, "DP has incorporated CA more or less wholesale, becoming in some instances a branch of CA, and this extends into studies of embodied actions, gestural communication, and multimodality" (also see Wiggins & Osvaldsson Cromdal, 2020).

In an influential and wide-ranging edited collection, which is "theoretically and analytically motivated by Harvey Sacks's pioneering ethnomethodological and conversation-analytic studies of people's uses of categories" (Robinson, 2000, p. 494), Antaki and Widdicombe (1998a) bring together researchers in discursive psychology, conversation analysis, and membership categorization analysis. In their opening chapter, Antaki and Widdicombe (1998b, p. 3, emphasis in original), building on Sacks, set out five general principles for understanding identity as an achievement and a tool:

- For a person to 'have an identity' – whether he or she is the person speaking, being spoken to, or being spoken about – is to be cast into a *category with associated characteristics or features;*
- such casting is *indexical and occasioned;*
- it *makes relevant* the identity to the interactional business going on;
- the force of 'having an identity' is in its *consequentiality* in the interaction; and
- all this is visible in people's exploitation of the *structures of conversation.*

Having summarized the terrain through which emerged the distinctive theoretical and empirical approach to understanding and studying categories in social interaction we have articulated, we now arrive at a place where we can lay out the purpose of this book. In Section 1.4, we explain our approach to integrating research on categories with the foundational work in conversation analysis – and in doing so we describe the main contributions that our book aims to make in beginning to flesh out the resulting framework in the chapters that follow.

1.4   Key themes and contributions of this book

In this section, we articulate a set of themes that recur in the empirical analyses we provide throughout the subsequent chapters, and that together specify the main contributions the book offers. These include attending throughout to the ways that categories and actions are co-constituted by examining (1) categorial phenomena in relation to foundational conversation analytic findings on the basic structures and practices that constitute conversational and institutional occasions of talk-in-interaction; (2) the full range of different types, or categories, of categories by reference to which participants may design their interactional conduct and/or interpret the conduct of others; and (3) explicit and tacit practices participants use for introducing, invoking, mobilizing, maintaining, or altering the relevance of categories, on a moment-by-moment basis during the course of unfolding interactions. Each of these themes has origins in Sacks's work, and all have in various ways animated our own previous work on categorial phenomena and guided our plans as we embarked on the process of writing this book. However, each has also evolved in ways we had not anticipated at the outset of this process, as the empirical analyses we were developing during the iterative process of drafting and discussing each of the chapters shaped our understandings of their nature and import. They thereby represent both guiding considerations for the content of the chapters that follow – and, we hope, for future research this book may help to promote – and theoretical reflections derived inductively from the process of drafting the book, before we gathered them together in this introductory chapter as the final step in the process.

1.4.1 Categorial phenomena and generic organizations of practice for interaction

In using and building on Sacks's approach to categories in our work, we have – separately and in our collaborations – sought to conduct analyses that attend to both categorial features of talk-in-interaction and to the set of "generic orders of organization in talk-in-interaction" (Schegloff, 2007a, p. xiii) on which many of the foundational advances in conversation analytic research over the past six decades have focused (also see Schegloff, 2006a). Schegloff (2007a, p. xiv) describes these as

the various organizations of practice that deal with the various generic organizational contingencies of talk-in-interaction without which it cannot proceed in an orderly way:

(1) the "turn-taking" problem: who should talk next and when should they do so? How does this affect the construction and understanding of the turns themselves?

(2) the "action-formation" problem: how are the resources of the language, the body, the environment of the interaction, and position *in* the interaction fashioned into conformations designed to be, and to be recognizable by recipients as, particular

actions – actions like requesting, inviting, granting, complaining, agreeing, telling, noticing, rejecting, and so on – in a class of unknown size?

(3) the "sequence-organizational" problem: how are successive turns formed up to be "coherent" with the prior turn (or *some* prior turn), and what is the nature of that coherence?

(4) the "trouble" problem: how to deal with trouble in speaking, hearing and/or understanding the talk so that the interaction does not freeze in place when trouble arises, that intersubjectivity is maintained or restored, and that the turn and sequence and activity can progress to possible completion?

(5) the word-selection problem: how do the components that get selected as the elements of a turn get selected, and how does that selection inform and shape the understanding achieved by the turn's recipients?

(6) the overall structural organization problem: how does the overall composition of an occasion of interaction get structured, what are those structures, and how does placement in the overall structure inform the construction and understanding of the talk as turns, as sequences, etc.?

In addition, the period during which Schegloff (2006a, 2007a) was writing saw the identification (see Heritage & Raymond, 2005; Raymond & Heritage, 2006)[7] of what we can now list as a further "generic problem" of interaction, namely,

(7) the epistemics problem: how are relative rights to knowledge displayed and managed in sequentially organized activities?

As Schegloff (2007a, p. xiv) goes on to note, these generic problems give rise to a corresponding set of generic "organizations of practice" that are constitutive of conversation and other forms of talk-in-interaction: turn-taking, action formation, sequence organization, repair, word selection, and overall structural organization – and, we would add, as noted here, epistemics. Schegloff (2007a, pp. 263–264) also provides the following concluding reflections on how these organizations of practice "fit together," proposing that they

operate together all the time to inform the participants' co-construction of the observable, actual conduct in interaction that is the prima facie,

---

7 Also cf. prior work on the social constitution of knowledge (e.g., Garfinkel, 1967; Heritage, 1984b; Moerman, 1974; Raymond, 2000; Sacks, 1984b; Schütz, 1953; Sharrock, 1974).

bottom-line stuff of social life. Only by observing them all together will we understand how the stuff of social life comes to be as it is. Only by understanding them one by one will we get into a position to observe them all together.

A crucial feature of these organizations of practice is that, together and separately, they are what Sacks et al. (1974, p. 699) describe as both "context-free" forms of organization that are nevertheless "capable of extraordinary context-sensitivity" in any specific occasion of their use.[8] That is, on the one hand, their basic features can be recognized as such independently of "one or another aspect of situatedness, identities, particularities of content or context"; and on the other hand, their realization in particular cases and moments is sensitive to

> a wide range of situations, interactions in which persons in varieties (or varieties of groups) of identities are operating; it can be sensitive to the various combinations; and it can be capable of dealing with a change of situation within a situation (Sacks et al., 1974, p. 699; also see Lerner, 2003).

Thus, as Schegloff (2007a, p. 260) puts it, "the general always in real life . . . presents itself infused with its particulars, and it is not thoroughly understood without them."

One major and well-established basis for context specificity in relation to generic organizations of practice for interaction is participants' orientations to institutional matters. A large body of conversation analytic research on interactions in institutional settings has examined "the interactional practices through which [institutions] are talked into being" (Heritage & Clayman, 2010, p. 3), which involve modifications of the organizations of practice that constitute ordinary conversational interactions. As Drew and Heritage (1992a, p. 26; emphasis in original) note, these modifications

> commonly involve specific *reductions* of the range of options and opportunities for action that are characteristic in conversation and they often involve *specializations* and *respecifications* of the interactional functions of the activities that remain. The ensemble of these variations from conversational practice may contribute to a unique "fingerprint" for each institutional form of interaction – the "fingerprint" being comprised of a set of interactional

---

8 Sacks et al. (1974) made this characterization specifically with reference to turn-taking, but it has since been shown to be similarly applicable to the other organizations of practice we have described here.

practices differentiating each form both from other institutional forms and from the baseline of mundane conversational interaction itself.

This research has shown that, and how, "the institutionality of an interaction is not determined by its setting" (Drew & Heritage, 1992a, p. 3): participants situated in institutional settings may engage in mundane conversational interactions, and participants in non-institutional settings may undertake institution-related interactions. Moreover, when departures from institutional practices occur, interactions become more like mundane conversations in character (Clayman & Whalen, 1988; Greatbatch, 1992; Schegloff, 1988b). Thus, "interaction is institutional insofar as participants' institutional or professional identities are somehow made relevant to the work activities in which they are engaged" (Drew & Heritage, 1992a, pp. 3–4). The research is therefore focused on examining the practices through which various institutional roles are talked into being (cf. Halkowski, 1990).

In addition, however, participants conducting themselves within institutional settings, or elsewhere, may use or contend with categories associated with these roles – for example, 'doctor,' 'lawyer,' and 'teacher.' One can therefore appreciate the related but distinct character of roles, which are constituted in and as (institutional) activities, and categories of persons, which may involve common-sense knowledge of typical characteristics of the people seen as occupying them (we take up these and other features of categories in detail in Chapter 2: Approaching Membership Categorization). It is in this way that (as we saw in relation to Extracts 1.2 and 1.3) someone who is legitimately a doctor, and can therefore fulfil the role and associated activities of one, can nonetheless be seen by others in a scene as being disqualified from membership in the *category* 'doctor' by virtue of visible characteristics, including apparent membership in other categories such as 'Black'[9] and 'woman' (a form of discrimination that may also occur in hospitals or other medical settings). Moreover, as the data we examine throughout the book illustrate, the range of available categories extends far beyond the subset that is associated with institutions and roles therein. In addition, in institutional settings, persons occupying institutional roles may orient to both institutional and non-institutional categories of persons as relevant to the fulfilment of their institutional roles, or difficulties in doing so. Thus, while there is a permeable boundary between mundane conversational and institutional conduct,

---

9 Throughout the book we follow the current (at the time of writing) convention of capitalizing the racial category 'Black,' while not doing so for 'white.' We recognize, however, that this convention remains contested and that views on its merits (including our own) may change as time passes (also see further discussion of these matters by, e.g., AP, 2020; Appiah, 2020; Colman, 2020).

the interactional organization of categories cuts across both and may provide for their context-specific realizations (also see Psathas, 1999).

In light of these considerations, while we can recognize that analyses of talk in institutional settings provide a systematic basis for establishing features of context specificity in relation to generic organizations of practice for interaction, how people may categorize each other is another – and perhaps *the* other – systematic way that context specificity is realized in talk-in-interaction. This is by virtue of the ways participants composing and making sense of actions must contend with common-sense knowledge about the "types of persons in a culture's inventory, by reference to which are composed a society's understanding(s) of 'the sorts of people' there are, what they are like, how the society and the world work – in short, its culture" (Schegloff, 1996, p. 465). This association between categories and common-sense knowledge enables interactional participants to mobilize common-sense knowledge by mobilizing categories, and vice versa – whether doing so explicitly or tacitly – and thereby makes categories a rich resource for action and interpretation. Categories and associated common-sense knowledge are continually maintained as such because they are available for mobilization as resources across a virtually unlimited range of professional and everyday activities in which they can be used prospectively and retrospectively to achieve accountability; solve dilemmas or problems in relation to the distribution of social resources; allocate and manage entitlements and responsibilities; anticipate and make sense of conduct, including in relation to goals, motives, projects, etc., and in terms of the valence of actions (e.g., as positively or negatively oriented). In using categories in these ways, participants can be seen to take into account both 'proximate' and 'distal' contexts. That is, uses of categories are unavoidably deployed in particular interactional moments, and these moments are organized by reference to participants' uses of the generic organizations of practice for interaction (as described earlier) to conduct courses of action with one another. And yet, in just the ways categories are used in these courses of action, participants observably contend with features of context beyond the immediate interaction in which they are engaged, associated with what they treat as known-in-common about the categories at hand, and thereby invoke and reproduce these ostensibly 'distal' contexts in these interactional moments (cf. Schegloff's [1991, 1992a] discussions of the "paradox of proximateness").

It is in relation to these considerations that we offer a framework for integrating analyses of categorial phenomena with the generic organizations of practice for interaction. We observe that *all actions can be inspected for how they are designed by reference to particular categories of actor and/or recipients, and/ or how features of their design can be taken up as such by recipients.* (We return in more detail to consideration of the relationship between categories and actions in Chapter 4: Forming and Making Sense of Actions.) In this way, categories constitute a pervasive and wide-ranging basis for context-sensitivity in the uses and realizations of the generic orders of organization in talk-in-interaction, and an integral part of "how the stuff of social life comes to be as it is."

We have already begun to offer some non-technical observations on these features of categories and interaction in relation to our examples in the preceding sections. In the chapters that follow, we develop this approach more technically and systematically, thereby advancing a framework for empirically examining features of the reciprocal or "mutually constitutive" (Watson, 1997, p. 54; cf. Schegloff, 2001) relationship between categories and both basic and institutional organizations of practice for talk-in-interaction. That is, we attend to a range of ways in which organizations of practice for interaction constitute systematic bases for the emergent (re)production of categories; while at the same time showing how categories serve as systematic resources for participants' uses of these organizations of practice, and for managing prevailing contingencies in relation to them, in particular cases. This leaves intact the foundational conversation analytic findings of both mundane conversation and institutional interactions. It also provides opportunities to specify some features of "categorial systematics" (Stokoe, 2012a) that are produced in and through participants' interactional conduct, and by reference to which interaction is organized. To put it more simply, we consider both how interaction 'shapes' categories, and how categories 'shape' interaction.

1.4.2   Categories of categories

In keeping with our discussions of the empirical illustrations presented in the preceding sections, in the chapters that follow we attend to the full range of possible (types, or categories, of) categories to which participants may be oriented in relation to their own and/or others' conduct, and that may be observably consequential in and for the details of an interaction. These include the following, partially overlapping, category types, many of which we have already encountered in the preceding sections:

- The categories of conventional social scientific interest described earlier (e.g., gender, race, class, sexuality, age, ability).
- Categories associated with particular settings or types of interaction, often (but not always) institutionally identified (e.g., 'hotel guest,' 'cyclist,' 'salesperson,' 'customer,' 'passenger,' 'flight attendant,' 'friend').
- Pairs of categories arising from setting-based and/or other institutional arrangements and linking their incumbents relationally (e.g., 'friend/friend,' 'parent'/'child,' 'host'/'guest,' 'help-seeker'/'help-provider,' 'driver-pedestrian').
- Ad hoc and/or novel categories deployed in relation to particular prevailing circumstances or contingencies, often developed as combinations or modifications of other widely used categories – since language evolves constantly and neologisms are added to the public lexicon on a daily basis (see,

e.g., Ivanov et al., 2023) – but that may also become widely used in their own right, and/or be modified in further ways (e.g., 'Telegraph reader,' 'Guardian-reading, tofu-eating wokerati,' 'lady of a certain age').

Moreover, this range of categories may intersect with a range of recurrent social positions arising from the immediate details of an interaction and renewed or altered on an ongoing basis in and through its unfolding (e.g., 'caller,' 'called,' 'current speaker,' 'prior speaker,' 'storyteller'). Watson (1997, p. 66), drawing on Sacks (1992, pp. 360–366), refers to these as "turn-generated categories"[10] on the basis that they are associated with specific rights and obligations – for example, in telephone calls, 'called' is expected to speak first and 'caller' is expected to initiate the call's closing.[11] In contrast, we consider these social positions to be *alternatives to categories* in the sense that they provide locally organized solutions to contingencies associated with the production of talk-in-interaction (e.g., as a basis for who gets to speak, and what they are expected to do) that cannot be solved by reference to statuses or categories that are extrinsic to the forms of social organization used to manage them (e.g., turn-taking, sequence organization). And yet, participants' practices for managing such social positions can be inspected for the ways in which they are oriented to particular statuses or categories.

In Chapter 2: Approaching Membership Categorization, we introduce a more formal, technical vocabulary for working with some of these category types, but for now we note that many of them have commonly been treated as too mundane, trivial, or idiosyncratic to warrant sustained analytic attention. In contrast, we propose that the routine uses of apparently mundane categories are part of the infrastructure that enables the use of other, more familiar ones, and are therefore constitutive of the workings of the categories typically seen as more consequential and/or as central to how people manage issues of power, conflict, and so on. Thus, by looking at the places where categories are used, and by carefully attending to how the full range of them are used and

---

10 Sacks (1992) does not refer to 'caller' and 'called' as categories but instead as "*identities for conversation*," "*identities that the conversation makes relevant*" (p. 361; emphasis in original), and "conversational identities" (p. 362). Moreover, Sacks (1992, p. 360) contrasts these with "other identities, e.g., the names, sexes, social statuses, etc., of the parties," thereby treating them as distinct from rather than continuous with categorial bases for the organization of interaction. Similarly, Zimmerman (1998) uses the term "discourse identities" (rather than "categories") to refer to recurrently occupied social positions (including 'current speaker,' 'listener,' 'questioner,' 'answerer,' etc.) that are integral to the moment-by-moment organization unfolding of interaction.

11 Some forms of video-mediated interaction are organized in similar ways to conventional telephone calls, on the basis of 'caller' and 'called' identities (see, e.g., Ilomäki & Ruusuvuori, 2020), while others are designed to resemble physical meetings rooms with pre-scheduled meeting times, and are organized by reference to 'host' and 'attendee' or other setting-based categories (see, e.g., Seuren et al., 2020).

with what consequences, we can come to see crucial aspects of how they are recurrently produced and organized and yet may systematically be overlooked or forgotten. We therefore contend that dismissing the significance of seemingly trivial categories in favour of a focus on those more widely recognized as significant may result in analyses that miss important features of what is happening for participants and may even promote incomplete or inadequate understandings of the workings of the conventional categories of social science.

In attending to this range of categories, we consider ways in which they can on some occasions be treated as alternative or competing, and on other occasions as intersecting or combining, bases for action and interpretation. This provides for a set of empirical specifications of Sacks's crucial observation (which we also discuss in more detail in Chapter 2: Approaching Membership Categorization) that any person can be 'accurately' categorized in (potentially indefinitely) extendible ways (e.g., 'young,' 'Deaf,' 'student,' 'musician,' 'working-class,' 'Black'). Thus, the relevance of the category selected out of the potentially wide range of available options – whether it is used explicitly or in category-implicative ways – is inspectable for what it is doing interactionally on each and every particular occasion. We can thereby offer case-by-case, moment-by-moment analyses of how participants orient to, manage, and/or use (what they treat as) relevant intersections between categories – what we could call *members' intersectionality* or *practical intersectionality* – in contrast to the cumulative or distributional notions of intersectionality advanced and used as analysts' resources by the theorists who (as discussed in Section 1.0) first developed this concept and for whom the constituent categories are already somewhat solidified (cf. Hummelstedt et al., 2021; Whitehead, 2013b; Whitehead et al., forthcoming).

Attending to both well-established and novel or situation-specific categories also provides an empirically grounded basis for examining both the durability of categories that are central to the social organization of societies, and the processes of change that arise from and/or are reflected in participants' everyday uses of categories. As Sacks (1979, p. 14) notes,

> the important problems of social change, I would take it, anyway, would involve laying out such things as the sets of categories, how they're used, what's known about any member, etc., and beginning to play with shifts in the rules for application of a category and with shifts in the properties of any category.

Social change can thus be appreciated by reference to which categories participants use, create, resist, reject, etc., as well as to what participants on any given occasion appear to know, expect, dispute, etc., in relation to specific categories (also see, e.g., Baker, 2000, 2004; Plunkett, 2009; Rawls et al., 2020; Wowk, 1984). This also relates to the crucial matter of continuity versus change in relation to the categories to which participants are evidently oriented within the same interaction – as opposed to across different interactions over some period in time – and it is to this that we turn next.

1.4.3 *Category maintenance, category change, and category trouble*

In many cases, the category/ies by reference to which a stretch of interaction is unfolding remain entirely tacit and unspoken. Their use by participants as bases for inference and action in such cases can remain completely taken-for-granted – a " 'seen but unnoticed' background of common understandings" (Garfinkel, 1967, p. 44) that people rely on in going about their everyday interactional business without this ever explicitly rising to the surface of the interaction. This is particularly so when participants' orientations to some operative category/ies are unproblematically (and often tacitly) *maintained* across successive turns and actions in an interaction (also see our discussion of Sacks's "consistency rule" in Chapter 2: Approaching Membership Categorization). In contrast, *changes* in categorial orientations recurrently result in these orientations rising more explicitly to the surface, with participants using more explicit and/or readily observable practices in either *adding* new operative categories that intersect with prevailing ones or *shifting* from one set to another (with the prior set being replaced by a different one). Notably, this can occur prospectively or retrospectively in relation to, or during the in-progress course of, unfolding event(s) or action(s) (Stokoe & Attenborough, 2015; Watson, 2009a). That is, a participant may anticipate the relevance of additional or alternative categories for a projected upcoming action or course of action and may orient to and/or manage it accordingly in advance of producing it. Alternatively, participants may recognize the relevance of such categories only during or after the production of the conduct in question, and may observably contend with it 'in the moment' or through post hoc practices (also see Chapter 2: Approaching Membership Categorization).

While the particular (types of) categories implicated in these unfolding processes of maintenance and/or change are always a matter to be examined on a case-by-case empirical basis, our observations on Extracts 1.2 and 1.3 and our analyses of the cases we present throughout the book are suggestive of some patterned asymmetries between different category types. Specifically, we find that setting-based categories are recurrently routinely maintained as unspoken 'default' bases for action and inference, while additions of or shifts to the use of other categories are recurrently more exposed – including through their production using practices that treat them as departures from setting-based categories and the activities with which they are associated. That is, these other categories are recurrently treated as 'second alternatives' whose use may be characterized by various forms of category-related *interactional trouble*.

In this sense, categories of conventional social scientific interest may be seen to 'lie in wait' for use as "quiet centres of power and persuasion" (Baker, 2000, p. 112): They are ever-available to be drawn on as a set of interpretive resources through which anybody in a scene can be categorized, while nonetheless in many cases being mobilized only when the setting-based categories that have been presumptively organizing the scene are no longer adequate for meaningfully acting in relation to, or making sense of, events. That is, such categories can be used when what is happening is recognized as 'special' or remarkable, and/or when something 'goes wrong' or 'seems off'; in short, when something *accountable* is happening or has happened (also see Garfinkel, 1967; Heritage, 1984b; Schegloff, 2001). Because the knowledge associated with these categories is so wide-ranging and so significant for the structuring of societies, they can be used virtually any time as a basis for inference and action, even in situations in which they have previously been entirely backgrounded (West & Fenstermaker, 1995a; West & Zimmerman, 1987; Whitehead et al., forthcoming). This knowledge may, however, also be a basis for disputes over the relevance of particular categories, due to the systematic possibility of one party mobilizing additional categories as interpretive resources while another rejects or resists their applicability to the events at hand. Indeed, this is reflected in how conventional social science research commonly uses methodological workarounds in order to establish that particular categories of interest (for analysts) are relevant, and in doing so may elide the substantial work that was needed in order to establish their relevance.

This flexible, episodic use of these categories is one of the sources of the longer-term durability noted in the previous section. It also reveals how the enduring nature of these categories and the common-sense knowledge associated with them may in large part be (re)produced as "by-products of ambient organizations which are quite unconcerned with these outcomes, rather than as products which were the design target of some organization" (Schegloff, 1992b, p. xxiv). That is, these categories are "kept in good repair" (Heritage, 1984b, p. 210) every time they are used as resources for designing actions and making inferences about others' actions, even when reproducing them is not the 'main interactional business' at hand for the participants who do this (also see, e.g., Kitzinger, 2009; Raymond, 2019a; Sacks, 1986; Whitehead, 2012b, 2021) – and the conversation analytic approach to categories we present in the chapters that follow is especially well-equipped to elucidate the precise interactional mechanisms through which this reproduction of categories is done.

1.5 A note on data and transcription

The book draws on a diverse range of sources of social interactional data.[12] The research traditions that have built on Sacks's work have drawn in particular on transcribed audio- and video-recorded 'naturally occurring' interactional materials, from wide-ranging ordinary conversational and institutional domains, and we similarly make extensive use of such materials. In addition, however, we analyse newspapers, social media texts, fieldnotes, and fictional/television scripts, and in doing so we follow the example of pluralism in terms of data sources set by Sacks: As Fitzgerald (2021, p. 99) reports based on his examination of the Sacks Archive, "Sacks collected data from a range of different contexts including newsprint, overheard conversations, stories, children's street games, children's drawings, his own recollections, comic books, classic and contemporary research reports and, of course, transcripts of various forms of interaction" (for further discussion and examples of different data sources in conversation analysis, membership categorization, and discursive psychology, see Anderson, 1978; Drury & Stokoe, 2022; Kitzinger, 2008; McHoul, 1987). We hope that a wide range of sources will convey both the pervasive set of sites at which categorial phenomena can be observed and the wide range of possible trajectories for research on categories in social interaction (also see our further discussion of data sources in Chapter 3: Methodological Principles, Practices, and Challenges).

Starting with Chapter 4: Referring to and Addressing People, we begin each chapter with a high-profile or widely reported-on 'hook' case that includes a range of the features of categories and social interaction to be examined in the chapter and thereby provides for readily recognizing the implications of the chapter for matters of widespread public interest. We also (re)use a number of key cases in and across multiple chapters. This is designed to demonstrate how the categorial matters evident in the same stretch of interaction can intersect with features of multiple generic organizations of practice for interaction. Thus, by progressively introducing additional 'layers' of analytic resources, we can move towards more comprehensive analyses of the context-specific cases while also situating their features by reference to the context-free forms of organization around which these chapters are structured.

---

12 Our data are drawn from a diverse series of projects and shared data repositories. All data were collected, stored, transcribed, and used in this book in line with institutional ethics protocols. We have replaced all identifying information with pseudonyms in many of our extracts in accordance with these protocols. However, in cases of recordings that are in the public domain, we have used participants' real names. Moreover, in data drawn from shared repositories, we have used naming practices in accordance with the original source which, in some cases, involves participants' real names.

Audio- and video-recorded materials are transcribed using Jefferson's (2004a) system, which has become a standard set of conventions for conversation analysis. The system seeks to represent details of how turns at talk are designed, where they are placed sequentially in an unfolding interaction, timed gaps and pauses, the onset and end of overlapping talk, and features such as pitch, emphasis, laughter, and crying (Hepburn & Bolden, 2017). It has also been adapted for transcribing written social interaction – for example, on social media messaging services (see Meredith & Stokoe, 2014). Some have criticized CA's use of Jeffersonian transcription for contradictory attachments to incompatible views of reality (e.g., Ashmore & Reed, 2005); as a means of empiricist standardization (Anderson & Sharrock, 2017); as giving research that uses it a "structuralist or behaviourist flavor" (Atkinson, 1988, p. 447); as encoding "conventional sociological preconceptions" (Hester & Francis, 2000, p. 398); and as providing "excessive" and "surplus" levels of detail (Bogen, 1999). For others, however, the Jefferson system is not detailed enough, in terms of the phonetic details needed for auditory or acoustic analysis (Walker, 2012), and it has been augmented to incorporate embodied conduct such as gesture, body torque, gaze, and head nods (e.g., Goodwin, 1979; Laurier, 2014; Mondada, 2016; Whitehead, 2011).

Stokoe and Albert (2024, p. 198) argue that the Jefferson transcription system reveals the power of conversation analytic methods to expose far more of what happens in social interaction than is often included in other forms of qualitative research – including research that aims "to enfranchise research participants by eliciting what is important to them in their own voices and words." It is common to find that data extracts, such as quotes from interviews, are stripped both of their interactional context (including the interviewer's questions) and of the precise ways in which they were produced, often being 'tidied up' with pace, pauses, hesitations, emphasis, etc., removed (Potter & Hepburn, 2005). While, of course, Jeffersonian transcripts cannot include 'everything,' they preserve the voices and actions of participants to a much stronger degree than most other approaches. Conversation analysts have also shown systematically the serious problems of relying on standard orthographic records of spoken interaction in high-stakes contexts such as legally regulated evidence- and testimony-gathering interactions (e.g., Richardson et al., 2022). The transcripts also facilitate a particular kind of openness and transparency of the research and analysis, as Moerman (1988, p. 12) explains:

> . . . transcripts represent, or render, events that occurred in the world; they provide an inexhaustible resource for your own, and future, interests. My descriptions, analyses, and claims are based upon the transcriptional evidence they cite. You can therefore evaluate them.

The original language of our data sources is English, mostly British, American, and South African, simply by virtue of these being the sources and language to which we have access – and this might be seen as a limitation of the book's scope. That said, in much the same way that cross-linguistic conversation analytic research has shown in recent years, while the language used to build sequences of actions in interaction may vary, we expect the basic categorial structures and practices on which we focus throughout the book to be universally available to participants as a machinery, in much the same way that the generic organizations of practice for interaction (word selection, turn-taking, sequence organization, repair, etc.) have been shown to be largely universal across languages and cultures (see, e.g., Dingemanse et al., 2015; Enfield & Levinson, 2006; Kendrick et al., 2020; Schegloff, 2006a; Sidnell, 2009; Stivers & Enfield, 2009; Stivers et al., 2009). That is, although the 'content' of categories and category-based knowledge may vary linguistically and culturally, that there are categories in the first place, and that they are associated with knowledge and used to build actions, is evidently universal (cf. Levinson, 2005). Nonetheless, these are, of course, empirical matters, and we welcome research based on a wider range of languages and cultures that could affirm or challenge our expectations about the universality of the categorial phenomena we present here.

1.6   Summary and conclusions

> If you want to understand the big issues, you need to understand the everyday practices that constitute them (Suchman et al., 2019).

This chapter has aimed to introduce the landscape of categories in social interaction in and through texts and interactions of various kinds, with the further aim of showing their centrality to many of the themes and issues that social scientists have emphasized as central to the structuring of social life. We aimed to do this with limited use of the extensive technical language of membership categorization. However, having introduced the way that we will explore categories in social interaction in this book, and traced the origins of the approach through its emergence in several related fields of study, we move on now to unpack the conceptual and methodological apparatus in detail as we turn to Chapter 2: Approaching Membership Categorization.

2

APPROACHING MEMBERSHIP CATEGORIZATION

2.0   Introduction

This chapter will introduce the origins and purpose of the academic approach to analysing social categories in interaction explored and extended in this book: membership categorization. The possibility of analysing membership categorization was first articulated in Harvey Sacks's doctoral dissertation (Sacks, 1966), and subsequently in his lectures (Sacks, 1992), which were edited and published posthumously in two large volumes. Following on from our introduction to Sacks's approach in Chapter 1: An Introduction to Categories in Social Interaction, in this chapter we describe the core analytic concepts of Sacks's framework for understanding social categories, their features, their import, and how people use them, as these matters have been taken up across the social sciences – in particular, in ethnomethodology, conversation analysis, sociology, and (discursive) psychology. As well as building the foundation for understanding and deploying the practical steps for conducting analysis that we set out in Chapter 3: Methodological Principles, Practices, and Challenges, we consider some of the challenges associated with analysing categories, and their importance for studying the construction of society, social change, and social justice.

In an early lecture, Sacks (1972b, 1992) began to develop an account of an apparatus that came to be a core concept in his work: 'membership categorization devices' (MCDs). MCDs consist of a collection of categories along with a set of 'rules of application.' To empirically illustrate this concept, he provided a now-classic extract from a published collection of children's written stories: "The baby cried. The mommy picked it up" (Sacks, 1972b, p. 330). Sacks (1972b, pp. 330–331) observed that

DOI: 10.4324/9781003120599-3

one thing I hear is that the 'mommy' who picks the 'baby' up is the mommy of the baby . . . . (You will, of course, notice that the second sentence does not contain a genitive. It does not read 'It's mommy picked it up,' or variants thereof.) Now it is not only that I hear that the mommy is the mommy of that baby, but I feel rather confident that at least many of the natives among you hear that also . . . [w]e hear that it is the mommy of the baby who picks the baby up because she's the one who ought to pick it up, and (you might eventually add) if she's the one who ought to pick it up, and it was picked up by somebody who could be her, then it was her, or was probably her.

We might add that this hearing is also provided for in part because of the use of the indexical pronoun "it" in the second sentence, which refers indexically to "the baby" in the first and thus grammatically connects the two sentences and their subjects/objects together. This pronoun, is an example of a "locally subsequent" reference form (Schegloff, 1996, p. 450), which is typically used only after "locally initial" reference forms (in this case, "baby" and "mommy") are already in play (also see Chapter 5: Referring to and Addressing People) Interestingly, "it" is a way of not gendering the baby (as opposed to "the mommy picked her/him up"), thereby foregrounding the referent's membership *only* in the category 'baby' as a basis for hearing the events being described (also see our discussion later of Sacks's "economy rule"). Moreover, as the previous quote shows, Sacks himself repeatedly uses this pronoun in his discussion of this case without remarking on this feature. In the light of contemporary discussions about pronouns (including "it"; see, e.g., Greenfield, 2021), this raises questions about other things that are, in Garfinkel's (1967, p. 36) terms, "seen but unnoticed."

Sacks further suggests that observers will infer that "mommy picked up" the "baby" *because* the baby was crying. That is, there is a 'categorial obligation' for 'mommies' to attend to their babies, particularly when they are distressed, and it is a characteristic of 'babies' that they cry. It is not "simply a matter of one action following the other but that the actions as categories are morally ordered, such that if her baby cries then she *should* then pick it up" (Housley & Fitzgerald, 2009, p. 348, emphasis in original; also see Drew & Penn, 2016). The two sentences are thus rendered comprehensible by tacitly invoking this common-sense knowledge. Sacks argued that it is through an MCD that the categories are hearably linked together and comprehensible to all parties, including us as readers. More specifically, it is the 'family' MCD that allows the categories "mommy" and "baby" to be collected together. Of course, the category "baby" may also be part of the collection of 'stage of life' categories ('baby,' 'toddler,' 'child,' 'teenager,' etc.), or even the collection of 'forms of address' ('darling,' 'sweetheart,' 'baby,' etc.). However, these categories do not 'go together' in a decontextualized way, independent of any given stretch of interaction. Rather, their 'going together' is occasioned; it "is achieved and is to be found in the local specifics of categorization as an activity" (Hester & Eglin, 1997, p. 46). For this reason, we can also begin to see that 'culture' and 'common-sense knowledge,' as well as power and societal structures, reside in categories, categorization practices, and their occasioned use, in the ways we observed by reference to Baker (2000) in Chapter 1: An Introduction to Categories in Social Interaction.

If Sacks's "baby cried" example and our accompanying description of MCDs thus far seems old-fashioned and already rather technical, consider this series of much more recent newspaper headlines, all of which deploy similar categories.

Extract 2.1: *CE Noticias Financieras English*, 15.5.22
01   "Mommy come, please," cried two-year-old baby who was home
02   alone.

Extract 2.2: *Concord Times/AllAfrica Global Media*, 8.8.22
01   As a Month-Old Baby Suffers, Mother Cries for Help

Extract 2.3: *The Daily Star*, 24.8.22
01   Bloke fumes as airline makes him give up seat on 10-hour flight
02   for mum and crying baby

Extract 2.4: *Khaleej Times*, 7.8.20
01   Male flight attendant helps mother comfort crying baby

Extract 2.5: *London Evening Standard,* 2.10.18
01   Police officer hailed for consoling crying baby while mother
02   went for exam

Like the child's story from which Sacks's example was extracted, newspaper headlines are in written form and regularly contain explicit uses of categories, making them useful resources for introducing membership categorization (Eglin & Hester, 1992). In the examples provided, as in Sacks's example, we somehow 'know' that, say, the "baby" referred to in each case is the baby of the "mommy" (Extract 2.1), "mother" (Extracts 2.2, 2.4, 2.5), and "mum" (Extract 2.3). Also like Sacks's case, the adults are categorized by gender while the babies are not. There is a host of other things we 'know,' including that in Extract 2.2 the 'cries' of the baby are not the same as the 'cries' of the mother; the same verb is used but the activity it formulates is different. In

Extract 2.4, part of the newsworthiness is that the "flight attendant" who helped the "mother comfort crying baby" was "male"; replace this with 'female'[1] and we immediately see how the action of comforting a crying baby is treated as not routinely associated with the category "male." Similarly, in Extract 2.5, the "police officer" is "hailed" for doing an action ("consoling crying baby") that is not routinely tied to their occupational category membership (in this case, an accompanying photograph also shows that the police officer was male-presenting).

The aim of this chapter is to explore, in detail, the conceptual apparatus and terminology of membership categorization that Sacks used to account for the types of observations we have introduced thus far. We start with 'membership categorization devices' and 'categories' themselves, including the way their associated features and 'rules of application' have been described. Since categorization is fundamental to the practice of description and the construction of social and moral worlds, we examine the constitutive work done by categorization and the theoretical connections between categorization and social constructionism. We begin by introducing the terminology of membership categorization (Section 2.1) and then unpack the membership categorization device apparatus in more detail (Section 2.2), including how Sacks, and other researchers subsequently, have described and expanded upon category-bound qualities and features (Section 2.2.1) and the rules of application for membership categorization devices (Section 2.2.2). Towards the end of the chapter, we explore the connections between Sacks's early work on categories and the way social scientists have subsequently developed it to augment theoretical and empirical work on the morality, the practices of description, and the (dis)connections between social constructionism and ethnomethodology (Section 2.3), before offering some reflections (Section 2.4) that link our discussion in this chapter to the mutually constitutive relationship between categories and interaction introduced in Chapter 1: An Introduction to Categories in Social Interaction, and thus to the chapters that follow.

1 People's use of (often tacitly cis and binary) gender and sex category terms (e.g., 'woman'/'man.' 'women'/'men,' 'girl'/'boy,' 'female'/'male') is, as is clear from the numerous instances in our book, varied and empirically interesting. We use and refer to these categories in the ways participants do in cases where they are explicit in the data presented. However, in cases where these categories were evidently relevant but not explicitly mentioned by participants, we needed to decide which terms to deploy in our analyses. In the case of Extract 2.4, while 'female' does not appear in the data, we use it (rather than 'woman') since it is fitted to the mentioned category "male." Elsewhere, we have made case-by-case decisions that are informed by grammar and practice while avoiding, where possible, using 'female' and 'male' as nouns.

2.1 Introducing the terminology of membership categorization

To introduce and explain the core concepts of the membership categorization apparatus, we begin with a more extended empirical example. Extract 2.6 is from a telephone call with a new customer (C) who has called a double-glazing sales company to request a quotation for some new doors. Up until the portion of the call shown in the following transcript, the interaction has proceeded in accordance with the typical overall structural organization for encounters of this type, as described by Humă and Stokoe (2020). In contrast, our focus is on what happens as the customer begins to expand a sequence initiated by the salesperson (S) in order to elicit the customer's address. Specifically, the unfolding of this part of the interaction demonstrates how categories may be invoked and mobilized by participants in ways that, although completely ordinary and routine, nevertheless "assemble a social world in which their categories have a central place" (Baker, 2000, p. 112).

```
Extract 2.6: Sales call
01  S:  .hhh and your ↓surname please,
02  C:  Missus ↓Bowler,=bravo oscar whiskey lima echo ↓romeo,
03          (3.3)/((S: audible writing))
04  S:  #That's great#,=↑is it just yourself?=or is it mister
05      and missu:s? or[:.]
06  C:                 [Mi]ster and
07      m[issu:]s,
08  S:  [uhm- ] (0.2) °↑↑mis°[ter ↓a:n:]
09  C:                      [ and a ba]by,
10          (.)
11  S:  [↑(AW: ]::/OH:::) hh HEH HE[H HEH .hhh]=
12  C:  [thh HEH]                  [ heh heh ]=
13  S:  =[↑mist]er >and missus and a< little one ↓too:.=
14  C:  =[yeah, ]
15  S:  =hh HEH [heh      ]
16  C:         [yeah:(p),] (.) an' a ↓dog:
17      a[s well, y(h)eah,]
18  S:   [OH:   AND   A D ]OG.=OH HH HEH H[EH=
19  C:                                   [yeah:
20  S:  =heh
21  C:  Well.=mhnhhh heh heh it's a busy family,
```

Much is happening in this stretch of interaction, but let us start with the basic actions and their sequential organization: Lines 01–04 include the salesperson asking for the customer's surname and her supplying it; at lines 04–07, the salesperson asks a question about the customer's domestic status and the presence of a "mister" (also see Stokoe et al., 2017), and then, between lines

08 and 21 the sequence is humorously expanded by customer-initiated mentions of the occupants of, and relationships within, her domestic space ("and a baby,"; "an' a ↓dog:") with the upshot that the "missus," "mister," "baby," and "dog" are treated as 'going together' to comprise a collection that the customer characterizes as "a busy family."

In response to the salesperson's initial question (line 01), the customer supplies not only her surname (and its spelling) but also a title, "missus" (line 02). Note that this is not requested, implicitly or explicitly; the customer could just state her surname, or could add her first name, rather than a title. Each component of her response is, in Schegloff's (2006a, 2007b) terms, oriented to 'the problem of word selection.' While generally hearable as referring to 'married heterosexual woman,' "missus" is also used in practice by widowed and divorced women, which means that the automatic presence of a "mister" in cases where this title is used cannot be assumed (Stokoe et al., 2017) – an orientation reflected in the design of the salesperson's successive queries in lines 04 and 05. By referring to herself as "missus," the customer may also tacitly convey several possible (though implicit) further self-categorizations: she is a woman; she is heterosexual, she is (or was) married; she is an adult.

That the customer is categorizable as a woman is also an example of what Jayyusi (1984, p. 73) refers to as "perceptually available category features," though in this case the categorization is not via visual cues but via voice quality and pitch. As Martikainen (2022, p. 704) points out, although much work on membership categorization focuses on analysing verbal accounts, Sacks "recognized and acknowledged the role of visual perception in membership categorization from the very beginning" since "people categorize each other based on visual cues." For example, in discussing how a child might be categorized as the oldest in her class "by far," Sacks (1992, p. 539, emphasis in original) observes that " 'by far' is *glance-determinable*" – that is, "[i]t's visible, like anything else in the room, that she is older by far."[2] This does not mean, however, that categorizations produced on visual bases in this way are any more guaranteed to be accurate or uncontested by participants than those produced on any other basis. For example, as Jayyusi (1984, pp. 58–59) argues, "[a]lthough gender is oriented to as a perceptually available matter . . . it is still an accomplishment on the part of members that it is sustained and given as just such a perceptually available matter" (also see Flinkfeldt et al., 2022; Stokoe, 2015 for analyses of perceptually based miscategorization).

---

2 Relatedly, others have described the perceptual and embodied nature of categorization practices, such as the "visibility arrangements of urban public space" (Watson, 2005; also see Ablitt, 2020; Carlin, 2003; Crabtree, 2000; Mondada, 2021; Willemsen et al., 2023). For example, queues, and the activity of queuing, are "constituted by membership categories" with the predicates "head of the queue," "next in line," and so on, such that "the sequential and the categorial aspects of queues mutually inform each other" (Carlin et al., 2021, p. 4).

In the long gap at line 03, the salesperson can be heard to be writing and then, at line 04, she produces a sequence-closing third turn (see Schegloff, 2007b, p. 118), "#That's great#," which both confirms and appreciates that she has received the information (also see our discussion of actions in different sequential positions in Chapter 7: Organizing Sequences of Action). Immediately, S produces further turn constructional units (TCUs; see Sacks et al., 1974, p. 701) within the same turn (also see Chapter 6: Taking Turns at Talking and Selecting Next Speakers), initiating a new sequence "↑is it just your<u>s</u>elf?=or is it mister and <u>m</u>issu:s? or:" This action is thereby built from two complete yes/no interrogatives (Raymond, 2003), followed by a trail-off "or," which are designed to ascertain whether there is a second incumbent of the 'parties to a sale' MCD in addition to the customer and the salesperson (Stokoe et al., 2017). The two interrogatives manage competing relevancies relating to the project of the call and evident presumptions about relationships. The first query – "↑is it just your<u>s</u>elf?" – avoids any assumption or implication that there may be another party to the sale in addition to the customer – although the salesperson's use of "just" implies the absence of a partner as a less than optimal social arrangement. The second query – "or is it mister and missu:s?" – probes what the salesperson treats as a 'best case scenario' for her, even if it potentially complicates the prospective sale (also see Raymond & Heritage, 2013, 2021; Raymond, 2003). These redesigned questions handle the epistemic asymmetry between the customer and the salesperson (cf. Heritage & Raymond, 2005; Raymond & Heritage, 2006); that is, while the salesperson displays common-sense categorial knowledge about how households are organized in terms of heterosexual married couples living together and buying doors, the customer knows about her actual living arrangements and, furthermore, is entitled to do so (also see our discussion of epistemics in Chapter 9: Managing Knowledge, Experience, and Entitlement). The salesperson thereby uses these multiple queries as a method for avoiding a 'best guess' regarding the customer's likely relationship status, given the offence a wrong assumption may give rise to in the context of a sales call. In addition, the salesperson produces a trail-off "or:" that further manages the delicacy involved in asking about the customer's marital status (Stokoe, 2010b).

At lines 06–07, the customer opts for the second possibility introduced by the saleperson's questions, confirming that she is an incumbent of a "<u>M</u>ister and <u>m</u>issu:s," pair or couple. Sacks (1972a, p. 37) referred to such pairs of categories as "'standardized' relational pairs" (SRPs), observing that members treat them as being positioned in a normative relationship with one another that "constitutes a locus for a set of rights and obligations." Other SRPs include husband-wife, parent-child, friend-friend, neighbour-neighbour, doctor-patient, and so on (Sacks, 1972a). Standardized relational pairs, and collections of categories more generally, may be "duplicatively organized"

(Sacks, 1972b, p. 334), meaning that they are partitioned in a unit or 'team-like' way. For example, the categories that comprise the 'family' MCD can also be heard as referring to specific family units, and categories such as 'centre-forward,' 'goalkeeper,' 'midfielder,' and 'defender' may be part of not just a general 'football' MCD but also as categories of player within a specific football team (e.g., Liverpool F.C.).

Collections of categories may also be *positioned* (Sacks, 1972b), meaning they stand in a hierarchical relationship (e.g., 'baby,' 'teenager,' 'adult'). This provides for the use of such categories as resources for complaints or accusations like 'stop acting like a child!' when uttered to an adult (Sacks, 1972b, p. 336). In this regard it is noteworthy that when the customer confirms she is part of a "mister and missus" pair (lines 06–07) she retains the ordering used by the salesperson (lines 04–05), rather than rearranging it to "missus and mister," which would be hearably done on a "for cause" basis, for example relating to the business of the call. As Bowker and Star (1999, p. 319) have written, regarding the power of categorization as a fundamental human practice, "what is often the most invisible is right under our noses. Everyday categories are precisely those that have disappeared into infrastructure, into habit, into the taken for granted."

At line 08, the salesperson begins a turn ("uhm-") in overlap with the end of the customer's confirmation of her membership in the "mister and missus" pair, before pausing and beginning her turn again to receipt the customer's confirmation ("°↑↑mis°ter ↓a:n:") and thereby close the sequence (Schegloff, 2007b). However, and now in overlap with the salesperson and perhaps addressing the salesperson's "just yourself," the customer reopens and expands the sequence to add "and a baby" (line 09). Note the use of the indefinite article "a" to produce a specifically *categorial* formulation – as opposed to referring to a specific baby with, for instance, "and we have our baby." The customer delivers her turn with 'deadpan' intonation, but, as lines 11–12 show, this sequence expansion is not in the service of providing task-relevant information for buying windows but rather serves as an occasion for affiliation through sharing a joke.

The salesperson's response at line 11 begins with a particle, "AW:/OH:::," that conveys a "change of state," thereby treating it as news (Heritage, 1984a), as well as appreciatively assessing it, followed by laughter particles with which the customer joins in (line 12). The salesperson displays her understanding of "mister," "missus," and "baby" as a collection of categories that belong together in her immediate repetition at line 13, although she reformulates "a baby" as "a< little one." The marked downward intonation on "↓too:." produces this set of categories as a completed list which is, notably, a three-part one (see Jefferson, 1990). The participants collaborate in treating the collection of categories at hand as 'possibly complete' through the brief silence at line 16, before the customer proposes one further member (a ↓dog:), marking it as a hearably last element of the set through her use of "as well" (line 17), while using this species shift to produce a joke, which is registered as such and appreciated by the salesperson's laughter at line 18. In the final turn of the sequence, the customer formulates an upshot, "it's a busy family," (line 21), that links these departures from the salesperson's initial query (in line 01) to the larger project it may have been initiated to pursue, namely getting to know the customer.

By the end of Extract 2.6, three distinct MCDs have come into play. The first is 'parties to a marriage' – a married and (in this case, tacitly, normatively) heterosexual couple – comprised of the categories "mister" and "missus." That these categories 'go together' is not asserted outside their context of use; rather, the customer and the salesperson show a shared orientation to *this kind* of 'mister and missus.' There is no resistance and no repair initiation, for instance (cf. Land & Kitzinger, 2005). The second MCD is 'parties to a sale,' comprising 'buyer' and 'seller,' or 'customer' and 'salesperson.' By adding the further categories "baby" and "dog," the caller extends the MCD 'parties to a sale,' but in a non-serious way that simultaneously makes relevant the third MCD: 'family.' Unlike the two prior MCDs, which are activated but unspoken, this collection is explicitly named as "a busy family" (line 21) by the customer. And the property of duplicative organization provides for the participants (and us, as analysts and readers) – even without the explicit categorization at line 21 – to take the customer to be 'mum' and 'owner' for the 'baby' and the 'dog,' and thus to hear the incumbents of all of these mentioned categories as comprising a single family rather than as members of separate families who happen to occupy the same residence (Sacks, 1972b).

2.2 Membership categorization devices, categories, and rules of application

In continuing our discussion of membership categorization, we reflect on its origins in Sacks's doctoral research. Sacks conducted his PhD while working as "a fellow of the Centre for the Scientific Study of Suicide, Suicide Prevention Center, Los Angeles" (Sacks, 1966, p. ii). His analysis of telephone calls to the centre revealed that callers often accounted for their call by stating, "I have no one to turn to." This led Sacks to observe that the search for help is a "category-organized search" (Francis & Hester, 2004, p. 101). That is, if a person is in trouble of any kind, including being suicidal, there are categories of persons (e.g., friend, partner, sister) to whom one is entitled to turn for help and who are, by dint of the mutual category-based rights and obligations associated with standardized relational pairs (as described earlier in Section 2.1), obliged to give help. Sacks (1966, p. 36) termed one type of pair "Collection R": "a collection of paired relational categories." Within Collection R, "Rp" ('Relationship proper') refers to relational pairs where providing help is a mutual 'category-bound right and obligation' (e.g., friend-friend, partner-partner, sister-brother, parent-child, etc.) while "Ri" ('Relationship improper') refers to relational pairs where such help is not 'category-bound' (also see Sacks, 1972a, p. 40).

Sacks developed his analysis of calls to the Los Angeles Suicide Prevention Center to describe an entire research methodology for analysing categories and categorization practices and, specifically and importantly, ordinary people's, or members' categories, reflecting how Sacks's work was influenced by his connection to Garfinkel and ethnomethodology. In contrast to much mainstream social science, ethnomethodology pays "close attention to the knowledge that members possess and how they use it in producing their activities" (Francis & Hester, 2004, p. 18). (Also see our discussion of these matters in Chapter 1: An Introduction to Categories in Social Interaction.) Sacks's (1966, pp. 13–14; emphasis added) stated intentions for his research methodology were to

- "[S]ystematically develop a rigorous, methodical set of procedures for understanding how the actor interprets (reports upon, views, hears others' reports, etc.) the environment of person he [sic] confronts and discusses"
- "[P]rovide a theoretical statement of the necessary conditions for generating and verifying a theory of certain aspects of interaction"
- Provide "the basis for a generative grammar, the use of which enables members of the society to properly engage in their activities of describing, conversing, reporting, questioning, etc. *The elements of that grammar . . . consist chiefly of the categories which members of the society use in classifying one another.*"

The methods Sacks outlined underpin, or are compatible with, the vast majority of empirical and theoretical work on identity that takes a discursive, constructionist, interactionist, etc., approach (Benwell & Stokoe, 2006). Indeed, referring to the work of Ward H. Goodenough's work on role theory, Sacks (1966, p. 10) wrote, "[t]he fact that everyone has many more identities than they assume in a given interaction poses for the researcher the problem of how it is that for any given interaction, identities are selected." He also asserted that, since role theory does not deal with this core notion, this made his dissertation work distinctive. Sacks also cites Linton's (1936, p. 115) observation that "some identities are 'ascribed' and some 'achieved'" in his early work to contend that most categories that sociologists treat as ascribed are, in fact, achieved. Jayyusi (1984, p. 57; emphasis in original) developed an alternative to this distinction by introducing the concepts of *discoverable* and *disclosable* categories:

If we look at some examples of different categories, we will see that while, for instance, the category 'victim' is ascribable, the category 'woman' or 'child' is *perceptually applicable* (or discoverable in the absence of the so-categorizable person); the category 'policeman' is discoverable and expectably *disclosable* by the incumbent or perceptually applicable (in the case of uniformed persons); the categorization 'friend' is achievable/ ascribable.

In taking up Linton's (1936) observation, Sacks (1966, p. 13; emphasis added) makes crucial arguments about category ascriptions and achievements as 'members' practices':

> [M]embers of a society face several significant problems when categorizing each other . . . , have systematic methods for handling those problems . . . , and the nature of their problems of categorization are such as to require a *fundamental methodological stance* on the part of sociologists investigating their activities (Sacks, 1966, p. 13, emphasis added).

This "fundamental methodological stance" is cashed out in Sack's subsequent publications (e.g., Sacks, 1972a, 1972b, 1975, 1979), many of which were based on his lectures (Sacks, 1992). The "core of the machinery" for understanding categories and the "procedures are that Members have for selecting categories" (1992, p. 42) is, as noted earlier in Section 2.1, the 'membership categorization device' or MCD. This is probably the most commonly used term in studies drawing on Sacks's work on membership categorization but Sacks (1992, pp. 40–41) also refers to the "MIR device" – standing for "Membership – Inference-rich – Representative," or the "MIR Membership Categorization Device." It is worth remembering this formulation alongside MCD since the 'inference rich' properties of categories are among the most interesting, sometimes controversial, and possibly misunderstood aspects of the apparatus – which we return to in Section 2.3.

As discussed earlier, a membership categorization device explains how categories may be hearably linked together. Regarding his observations about "The baby cried. The mommy picked it up," Sacks emphasizes that "they are *not* proposed as sociological findings, but rather do they pose some of the problems which social science shall have to resolve" (Sacks, 1972b, p. 330; emphasis in original). He goes on to map out one of the purposes of what became the MCD framework:

> I want the apparatus to show how we come to hear those facts. If I asked you to explain the group of observations which I have made . . . you might say something like the following: we hear that it is the mommy of the baby, who picks the baby up because she's the one who ought to pick it up, and (you might eventually add) if she's the one who ought to pick it up, and it was picked up by somebody who could be her, then it was her, or was probably her. . . . *That "possible descriptions" are recognizable as such is quite an important fact, for members, and for social scientists"* (Sacks, 1972b, pp. 330–331; emphasis added).

Decades later, Schegloff (2007c) produced a "tutorial on membership categorization," with the aim of explicating Sacks's work in this area, given that "[t]hose who have tried to familiarize themselves with it, or make it part of their working competence, have often found the central texts difficult, even inaccessible" (Schegloff, 2007c, p. 462). In the next two sections, we continue to unpack, first, how the term 'category' has been defined and exemplified and, second, the 'rules of application.' As we proceed, we build in discussions of expanded parts of the MCD apparatus that have emerged in the years following Sacks's foundational writings. Taken together, and as is probably clear even at this point in the chapter, the amassed terminology of MCA may indeed be bewildering for newcomers or even for those who have been in the field for some time. While our overview aims to be as inclusive and comprehensive as possible, we also remain agnostic as to the practical utility of many of the terminological developments we introduce here. In the following chapters, we use some of these terms more heavily than others, and some not at all, and we similarly invite readers to select and use those they find useful for their own research.

2.2.1 Categories and their associated qualities

As we noted in Chapter 1: An Introduction to Categories in Social Interaction, categories include those commonly used by social scientists (e.g., gender, race, class, sexuality, age), but any list of them is indefinitely extendible, and might also include "Protestants, minors (or miners), professors, goalies, adults, cellists, conservatives, vegetarians, merchants, murderers, 20-year olds, cat-people, technicians, stamp collectors, Danes, 'looky-loos' (people who slow down on the highway to stare at an accident), lefties (both politically and handedly), surfers, Alzheimers, etc." (Schegloff, 2007c, p. 467). Others use the term 'category labels' (Moerman, 1988) and, following Sacks, "membership categories," which Jayyusi (1984, p. 20, emphasis added) defines as "the already culturally available *category-concepts* that members may, and routinely do, use in categorizational work and the accomplishment of various practical tasks." Jayyusi's (1984, p. 20) examples of "category-concepts" are similar to Schegloff's, and include "doctor; mother; poet; vandal; saint; murderer; child."

Jayyusi (1984, p. 20; emphasis in original) makes an important distinction between "membership *categories*" and "membership *categorizations*," the latter being "the *work* of members in categorizing other members or using 'characterizations' of them." The examples Jayyusi (1984, p. 20) provides of categorizations include "a nice man; a nervous person; a pretty girl; an intelligent woman; a dangerous driver; hippy type, etc." She points out that the component features of such categorizations are an adjective plus a category:

Often the sense of the categorization depends criterially (as in 'dangerous driver') on both parts of the categorization. The former are organized in such a way that they can be seen (and treated) as relating to other concepts as devices or as categories within a device (in Sacks's sense) for various practical purposes. The latter kind work, at best, as *umbrella categorizations*, subsuming various sorts of particulars and descriptions. The distinction between the two, important as it is, is not however meant to be taken as a rigid one (Jayyusi, 1984, p. 20).

Jayyusi (1984, pp. 106–107) provides an extended example of the work speakers can do with categorizations, thereby transforming categories and constructing the social world. In this case, drawn from a discussion of a violent incident at a tribunal, the Chair of the tribunal transforms the categories "young people" and "old people" used by a prior speaker (a possible perpetrator of violence), instead using the alternative categorizations, "young men" and "old men." Another way of seeing this as a practice is as "embedded repair" (also see Jefferson, 1987). In this case, the "category transformation" implicitly deletes "women" and "children" from the prior speaker's utterance in the service of building a case regarding the relative culpability of the perpetrators, since 'violence' may be more associated with the category 'young men' than with 'young people' in general. (Also see our discussion of repair in Chapter 8: Managing Trouble in Speaking, Hearing, and Understanding.)

While this example may be taken as implicating ways that such uses of categories may be treated (accusedly or otherwise) as invoking stereotypes, there are important conceptual distinctions between common-sense knowledge underpinning categorization practices versus conventional understandings (both social scientific and common-sense) of stereotypes and stereotyping. These include a view of common-sense knowledge as socially shared but not necessarily personally believed or 'bought into,' in contrast to stereotypes conventionally being treated as believed by individuals; the assumption (made by participants) that the common-sense knowledge they are using is accurate for the purpose at hand, until shown to be otherwise, in contrast to conventional understandings of stereotypes as necessarily inaccurate or at least of questionable accuracy; and that although common-sense knowledge may be morally problematized, in many cases it is treated by participants as mundane and completely unproblematic, with its competent use being morally expected or required, in contrast to the conventional treatment of stereotypes as morally proscribed or complainable (see, e.g., Jones et al., 2023; McHoul, 2007; Schegloff, 2007c; Whitehead, 2018; also see Edwards [1991] on the distinction between cognitive and discursive approaches to categories).

It is clear from Sacks's work, and that of scholars who have subsequently interpreted and/or further developed it, that there is no once-and-for-all set of categories that pre-exist their situated interactional uses, or whose absolute meaning can be found in the dictionary. For example, Sacks (1966, p. 16) writes that "[w]hich particular categories constitute the 'membership categories' of any given collection will, of course, vary according to the particular collections at issue, the society in question, and the concrete purposes of categorizing at hand." Hester and Hester (2012, p. 565) expand upon this, writing,

> the 'machinery' of MCA – category collections, membership categories, category predicates, etc. – can be thought of as one aspect of a society's culture but in the sense of 'culture-in-action' or as improvisational cultural practices rather than as a body of decontextualized knowledge, practice and convention.

Sacks (1966, p. 15, emphasis in original) states that his "attention shall be exclusively limited to those categories in the language in terms of which *persons* may be classified." When describing the collections of categories that comprise a 'category set,' or membership categorization device (e.g., 'occupation'), Sacks (1992, p. 40), also articulates "[a] first thing we can say" about such sets – that they are "which-type sets because questions about any one of these can be formulated as, 'Which, for some set, are you?'" Members can also use other resources, such as formulating places, occasions, or events, as entailing membership categories and categorization. For example, in his analysis of place formulations, Schegloff (1972) gives examples of the categorial work they do (e.g., a reference to 'a driving school' can formulate 'occupation'; also see Drew, 1978). As Jayyusi (1984, p. 36) observes, a "place or institution (object-category)" can "generate a relevant membership categorization," such as 'hospital' generating 'doctor' or 'dog kennel' generating 'kennel owner' (also see Schegloff, 1972). Whitehead and Lerner (2009) show how place references can be racialized, examining a case in which a speaker, in describing a town that his family frequents while on holiday, refers to two places where alcohol can be purchased – "one is at a *hotel* and one is (down) like in *the black section*" (p. 615, emphasis added). As Whitehead and Lerner (2009) note, this racialized place formulation both tacitly produces the hotel as 'not Black' and tacitly accounts for the white speaker's family having spent a lot of time and money there. Edwards (1997, p. 256; emphasis in original) describes how, in a newspaper article about a forthcoming USA-sponsored Palestine-Israel peace conference in Madrid, the place formulation "the Middle East" becomes a category:

> Senator James Baker was reported to be tentative about the conference's possible success: 'He said: "I prefer not to put odds on this or give percentages at this stage . . . *We are dealing with the Middle East.*"'

Edwards describes how this place formulation works like tautologies, idioms, and proverbs do. Nobody needed *informing* that they were dealing with the Middle East. It serves to invoke ready-made categorial knowledge about the

Middle East, and its rhetorical force is to claim for one's own particular, current argument, the status of common knowledge, and thus render it hard to deny. Such kinds of generalized devices make it difficult to refute the more specific positions they are used to protect.

Extract 2.7 demonstrates how categories can emerge in unexpected ways. It comes from a neighbour mediation group meeting between three parties or clients (C1, also pseudonymized as Gary at line 05, C2, and C3 – who does not appear in this extract) and two mediators, M1 (also pseudonymized as Joe at line 05) and M2. The parties are neighbours in a housing development for senior citizens, and they have a longstanding dispute over their shared garden. The mediators are attempting to help the clients to resolve the dispute. The focus of much of their 90-minute discussion is some plants that one neighbour, C1, has planted that the others have objected to. At line 03, C2 is referring to one of the plants as "DANgerous," in overlap with a new sequence initiated by C1 about what she takes to be the heart of the matter.

```
Extract 2.7: Neighbour mediation multi-party meeting
01  C1:  But uh: can I say this[:: uh: when we  [::     moved- first]=
02  M1:                                         [Yeh?
03  C2:                                         [Um: it's DANgerous]=
04  C1:  =[move]d i:n, and uh: (1.2) I:: remember (0.3) ~uh:~=
05  C2:  =[Joe.]
06  C1:  =having a word with Gary about something he accu:sed
07       me of being uh- (0.5) like a Barbra <Strei:sand.>
```

At line 01, C1 uses a preface in the form of a pre-request to "say this" to introduce a possibly delicate matter (see Lerner, 2013) – we note that M1's go-ahead in line 02 is produced in overlap following her continuation of the projected turn. In her continuation she establishes that the time frame of the events she is recounting occurred "when we:: moved- first moved i:n," (lines 01–04). A common practice in neighbour disputes is for parties to establish a narrative timeline of the dispute that shows one party to be predisposed to particular behaviours, prejudices, and so on, that are not occasioned by anything that the other party has done. In this case, C1 suggests that C2 had a problem with C1 before she had done anything to the garden, and thus that his issues with her arise out of his prejudice rather than her actions. She reports, "he accu:sed me of being uh- (0.5) like a Barbra <Strei:sand.>" (lines 06–07). As observed earlier, note again the use of the indefinite article 'a' to produce, in this case, a well-known person's name as a category – 'a Barbra Streisand' – apparently as a method for accomplishing off-the record what it would be plainly offensive, and specifically antisemitic, for him to do on the record.

At this point, C1 has not explicated what she assumes C2 to have meant by 'accusing' her of being "*like*" 'a Barbra Streisand' but we know that she regards C2's use of it as designedly offensive or problematic since he "<u>accu</u>:sed" her of this ascribed incumbency. However, C1 then goes on, within the same sequence, to unpack what she takes to be the features of the category "a Barbra <Str<u>ei</u>:sand.>" being ascribed to her by Gary:

```
08   C1:   which meant I must be agg<u>ress</u>ive: (0.5) Jewish, (0.3)
09          which I am neither,
10                (0.4)
11   C1:   Um::
12                (0.4)
13   M2:   I- I think- [I'm not- I'm not sure that this is helpful
14   M1:              [Is this helpful?
```

At lines 08–09, C1 expands upon and unpacks the meaning of "a Barbra <Str<u>ei</u>:sand.>" and its sense as an 'accusation,' thereby using it in formulating her own complaint against C2. For C2, C1 is "aggressive" and "Jewish"; for C1, C2 is hearably antisemitic. This is the work that the reported categorization, and its disavowal, is doing in and for this occasion. And in its unpacking, C1 also displays a concern that the category may not be seen as an antisemitic insult in the absence of further specification of its meaning. By C1's account, C2's complaint is not really about the garden; it is about C1's supposed incumbency in categories about which C2 holds prejudices (also see Stokoe, 2015). Moreover, in repeating C2's use of "a Barbra <Str<u>ei</u>:sand.>" in her retelling, C1 retains C2's effort to avoid a more straightforward expression of antisemitism, and thus his understanding that his conduct is objectionable.

Sacks (1972b, p. 335) introduced the notion of "category-bound activities," describing them as "activities taken by members to be done by some particular or several particular categories of members." This notion, as with many others in the MCA lexicon, has been developed and extended. For instance, Jayyusi (1984, p. 35) explains that categories and categorizations work on the basis that they carry with them, or convey and imply, "category-bound and category-constitutive features" (Jayyusi, 1984, p. 35). Extending this observation further, from activities to other category-bound associations, Jayyusi (1984, p. 35) includes "[t]he ties between categories and conventionally expected properties, habits, beliefs, etc." in a list of related concepts. She also develops related terms such as "category-tied and category-embedded attributes and actions" (p. 33) and, citing Watson (1978) and Sharrock (1974), "category-bound tasks," "category-bounds obligations and rights," and "category-bound knowledge" (p. 35). To bring this collection of terminology together, Jayyusi (1984, p. 35) proposed the use of the general term "category-bound features," suggesting that it provides "a more abstract analytic framework which comprises all of the above variants."

In another expansion, Järviluoma et al. (2003, p. 74) use the term "category-generated features" to describe "features . . . presented in discourse as having been situatedly produced through their tie to some category." Jayyusi (1984), however, credits Turner (1970) for first using the term "category-generated activities," which she describes as activities "provided for (or providable) in discourse as having been situatedly *produced through* their tie to some category" (p. 37; emphasis in original)." Jayyusi (1984, p. 36) also notes how categorizations may be "locally generated by the specifics of the situation under discussion," including formulations of the activities engaged in and other contextual particulars. She gives an example from the Scarman Tribunal, a report into violence and civil disturbances in Northern Ireland in 1968, in which formulating a place, or an 'object-category,' generates categories. In this case, the place was "the first-aid post" which generated "the categorization 'first-aider' from the specifics of the talk" (Jayyusi, 1984, p. 36). People can also be ascribed category memberships or 'incumbencies' (e.g., "he is a Hell's Angel") or can be "type categorized"; that is, characterized as a category 'type' such as "these are Hell's Angels types" (Jayyusi, 1984, p. 22). The 'category-predicate' is another term used to refer to features of categories; for example, the predicates of the category 'nun' may include praying, helping the needy and sick, abstaining, and so on (McHoul, 2007).

More recently, Rossi and Stivers (2020, pp. 55–56) introduced the term "category-sensitive action" (see also Stokoe, 2009a on "category-based actions") to

> focus on distinct moves within a sequence . . . [with] a strict relation with a specific social category . . . [and] to better account for instances where individuals perform actions that transgress the boundaries of social membership, including cases of borrowing incumbency of a given social category (Watson, 1978, p. 107) or otherwise claiming rights or responsibilities associated with that category by virtue of one's membership in a related category.

An example of such category-based or category-sensitive actions is provided in Extract 2.8, in which a complaint turns on what Schegloff (2007c, p. 480) refers to as "categorical resonances": "attributes [that] resonate category-relevance." The extract comes from an initial telephone inquiry between a mediator (M) working at a community mediation centre and a council worker (C) who is calling on behalf of a local resident whose house backs onto cricket club grounds. The resident has complained to the council that balls from the club are damaging her roof and making it unsafe to sit in her garden. The council worker wants the mediation centre to mediate between the local resident and the club and this is, therefore, a potential 'new client' and intake call.

Extract 2.8: Neighbour mediation initial inquiry

```
01  C:  She can't go in 'er ga:rden an' it's dam- she's paid
02      for: (.) tiles bein' fixed on 'er roof:. Without even
03      contactin' them,=she's says- she knows they're re- (0.2)
04      they kno:w they're responsible [hh       ] but she
05  M:                                 [.pt Yeh.]
06  C:  doesn't want to confront them: she's [eighty three].
07  M:                                       [.hhh ↑↑No: I]'d be
08  M:  uh ↑ye:[ah. ]=it's not *i-* uh y'know: *i-* b- *i-*
09  C:         [(Um)]
10           (0.5)
11  M:  Obviously age: (.) c- *i- i-* (.) could [be an i:ssue]
12  C:                                          [Ye:ah:      ]
13  M:  with'er but- .hh [↑y'know] it's ↑not something that-=
14  C:                   [(Yeah) ]
15  M:  =(0.3) a lo:t of people: um: do: easily.
```

The council worker provides an account for why the local resident has
not "confront[ed]" the club herself: "she's eighty three" (line 06). The
account formulates an attribute of the resident but does not explicitly categorize her as, say, 'old.' However, "eighty three" invokes a host of possible (but implied, not articulated) category resonances relevant to why this
person does not want to complain directly to the cricket club (e.g., 'too
old,' 'frail,' 'intimidated,' 'vulnerable'). The emphatic "↑↑No:" which begins the mediator's response (line 07) is responsive to, and affiliative with,
the council worker's account that the local resident does not want to "confront" the cricket club. The mediator continues to formulate an agreement
with the council worker's account "I'd be uh ↑ye:ah." (lines 07–08). Having now apparently heard the council worker's category-resonant description of the resident as "eighty-three," the mediator continues, cutting off
numerous times (line 09; also see our discussion of same-turn self-initiated
repair in Chapter 8: Managing Trouble in Speaking, Hearing, and Understanding) and pausing (line 10) before saying "Obviously age: (.) c- *i- i-*
(.) could be an i:ssue' (line 11). This displays her interpretation of "she's
eighty-three" as invoking the 'age' MCD, and "converts [an] individual attribute to [a] membership category" (Schegloff, 2007a, p. 445) – and the
parties thereby collaboratively transform description into categorization
(Stokoe, 2012b).

As a membership categorization device, 'parties to a dispute' may in some
ways implicate equivalent members (e.g., party A, party B), with the dispute
accordingly characterized (especially by disinterested third parties) as 'six of
one, half a dozen of the other.' However, parties can, alternatively, become
asymmetrical 'victim' or 'wronged party' and 'perpetrator'; indeed, the core
rhetorical goal for both parties in such disputes is incumbency in the category
'victim' (Stokoe, 2009a). As the case in Extract 2.8 demonstrates, membership

in these categories can be accomplished via the invoking and overlaying of other categories – here, Party A comprises one person, an elderly woman; Party B is multiple persons, likely to be (though not spelled out) many men of various ages. The action relevancies associated with the parties are elided by other categories – that is, being elderly is not to be remedied; being 'wronged' is, although being elderly may make one more readily categorizable as 'wronged,' and can also be used to warrant the intervention of a third party (also see our further analysis of this extract in Chapter 7: Organizing Sequences of Action).

As noted previously in relation to Extracts 2.1–2.5, one perspicuous setting for categories and their analysis is newspaper headlines, and there are several classic examples in the MCA literature that together make visible the ethnomethods through which journalists convey newsworthiness and readers make sense of the likely story to follow. For instance, in Lee's (1984) analysis of "GIRL GUIDE AGED 14 RAPED AT HELL'S ANGELS CONVENTION," he works through how we come to hear that the "girl guide" was raped *by* a "Hell's Angel," not some other convention attendee, despite this not being explicitly stated. He starts by noting that the co-presence of "girl guide" and "Hell's Angels" together in the headline is a 'category puzzle' or "category-and-predicate-puzzle" (Watson & Weinberg, 1982, p. 67), since they are not obviously linked by belonging to the same MCD. Another headline, "Killer Nuns!," creates a similar puzzle (McHoul, 2007). That 'killing' is not an activity bound to the category 'nuns' provides for an anomalous and unexpected combination being used to create an enticing headline and construct something as newsworthy – and this is a product of a members' orientation (in this case, the journalist). The inclusion of an exclamation mark also encourages the reader to understand this category-activity tie as non-serious in some way (i.e., this is not a story about serial killing). As McHoul (2007, p. 460) writes, the

> nuns in question were learning karate: hence they were (potential) killers . . . 'killer' and 'nuns' are rarely co-located. And this is how headlines routinely announce news: by deliberately mismatching membership categories (designations of types of persons) with their expectable actions (predicates).

A further illustration of how membership categorization is used in newspaper headlines comes from Hester and Eglin's (1997) analysis of the headline: "Engagement was broken – Temperamental young man gassed himself." Hester and Eglin (1997, p. 38) carefully explicate how it is that

> [w]e read this newspaper headline to mean that a young man's engagement to be married was broken by his fiancée and that this made him so unhappy (at losing her) that, (perhaps) somewhat impulsively, he committed suicide. (He probably did this by inhaling poisonous gas from his kitchen stove or from the exhaust of his car.)

We might add that there is also a presupposition in Hester and Eglin's account that the young man was in a heterosexual relationship and that his partner was a woman. They go on to describe how it is on the basis of "syntax and semantics" and the membership categorization apparatus that we know

> (a) that the engagement was for marriage (not for dinner), (b) that the young man was engaged (not someone else), (c) that the engaged parties were engaged to each other (and not to others), (d) that the broken engagement was the young man's (not another's), (e) that the gassing was a suicide (not an accident, and not less than terminal), (f) that first the engagement was broken and then the young man gassed himself (not the reverse), (g) that the second happened because of the first (not independently of it), and (h) that it happened because of desperation arising from the 'loss', assisted by the 'temperamental' aspect of the young man's character (rather than from religious ecstasy or moral outrage . . . .)? (Furthermore, how is it that we think that he probably did this in one of the manners described above (and not, say, by some more exotic method)?) (Hester & Eglin, 1997, pp. 37–38).

We do want to add one note of caution, or of something additional, to Hester and Eglin's analysis of headlines, which is that they provide for a special way of reading; specifically, a maximalist reading. The news headlines are about categories of persons, and not necessarily persons known to readers. Therefore, they pose different problems of interpretation in action than actions in conversation do. In fact, the only names of persons who typically appear in headlines are persons that can be assumed to be known to others; that is, famous people. Thus, we need to exercise caution in generalizing from analyses of headlines to analyses of social interaction more broadly, since the former are more properly considered in association with newspapers and the practice of journalism.

Returning to the newspaper headline examined by Lee (1984), the co-presence of "Girl Guide" and "Hell's Angels" is explained via the activity type, 'rape,' which co-selects 'victim' and 'perpetrator' within the MCD 'parties to a rape.' The category-bound features of the victim include the named category "girl" and attribute ("aged 14"), which tacitly categorizes her as a 'child.' Incumbents of the category "Hell's Angels" are commonsensically also members of the 'adult' and 'male' categories, with other possible resonances such as aggressive, leather, bikers, occult, drinking, etc., though none of these are explicitly formulated. It is revealed in the story that the victim was abducted, and this accounts for her presence at the convention, since members of these two categories are not normatively found in each other's company.

In both the neighbour dispute and the rape, the parties are explicitly and implicitly categorized by both 'age' and 'sex.' Sacks (1972a, p. 33) observes that these are collections whose categories could be used to categorize any member of a population, and uses the term "Pn-adequate" to refer to membership categorization devices with this property – where "P" stands for 'population' and "n" a number "equal to or larger than 1" (Sacks, 1972a, p. 32). In observing that members of all populations have at least two such MCDs, Sacks (1972a) notes that this provides for every member of any population being potentially categorizable by multiple different categories from different MCDs (also see Schegloff, 2007c, pp. 467–468). While Sacks (1972a) identifies the 'age' and 'sex' collections in particular as collections used in every known society, we can add that most also use a number of further MCDs of this sort, and that the resulting widely used set of Pn-adequate collections is similar to those of conventional interest for social science researchers, as discussed in Chapter 1: An Introduction to Categories in Social Interaction.

A consequence of the availability of at least two Pn-adequate MCDs in every society is that "correctness" alone does not provide an adequate warrant for the selection of a particular category to categorize any given member of a population (Sacks, 1972a, p. 33), since any categorization involves a choice between two or more "correct" options. Instead, the choice of a categorization is observably grounded in its *relevance* in relation to some feature(s) of the prevailing interactional context(s), the action being produced by the speaker doing the categorizing, the conduct and/or attributes of the categorized person, etc. (Sacks, 1972a; Schegloff, 2007c). While recognizing this as a "research problem," Sacks (1966, p. 13) is clear that its status as such is grounded in the "problems" of categorization faced by members of a society – and thus that the task for researchers in examining them is to describe the empirical features of these members' methods and the resources they use in deploying them.

While Sacks (1966, p. 16) writes of "natural groupings of categories" that "members of the society feel 'go together,'" he is clear that "whether or not a particular category is a member of a collection is, *in each and every case*, a matter to be decided empirically" (emphasis added). Sacks (1966, p. 13) is equally clear that different category terms may be used by different people and/or in different contexts:

[I]t is the case that the particular terms and devices employed by members of the society to classify each other are not invariantly the same. What constitutes the 'family' in some societies differs from the categories of persons thought to comprise that collection in our own [sic], both as regards the extensiveness of the collection, i.e., the number of categories it contains, as well as the particular member categories.

The provision and relevance of any and all of the features, predicates, entitlements, and so on that are 'bound' or 'tied' to categories, is, therefore, "situatedly provided for or invoked as being category-bound" and "an occasioned matter and a methodic achievement on the part of members" (Jayyusi, 1984, p. 35) and "cannot simply be asserted on the analyst's authority" (Schegloff, 1992b, p. xlii), separate from sequentially grounded warrants for such claims (also see our further discussion of these matters in Chapter 3: Methodological Principles, Practices, and Challenges). This is why categorization is *work*, and an *accomplishment*. What counts as a *category incumbency* or *ascription* and how it is made relevant to a setting and action – that is, "displayed, accomplished, ascribed, perceived, avowed and/or recognized . . . is different for different settinged categorizations and is in part contingent on the conventional category-incumbent relationship known in common by members" (Jayyusi, 1984, p. 63).

In her expansion of Sacks's work, Jayyusi paid much attention to the way that the practices of describing are intrinsically constitutive of the 'moral order.' One of her examples takes up the situation of an accident. If one is present, a doctor at the scene may avow membership of the category, which "requires a certain set of abilities," and this gives a person "eligibility" or entitlement, and "practically enables" them, to perform as a category member (Jayyusi, 1984, p. 63; also see our discussion of Extracts 1.2 and 1.3 in Chapter 1: An Introduction to Categories in Social Interaction). However, as Jayyusi (1984, p. 63) points out, if it later turns out that a doctor attended the scene but did not offer help, they may be complained about based on not fulfilling their category-bound duties, obligations, and entitlements. If the doctor offered help but "badly bungled" their intervention, their category membership may be challenged or subverted (Jayyusi provides this example: "You're not a surgeon – you're a butcher!," p. 44) via what Jayyusi (1984, p. 44) calls a "competence categorization." Furthermore, 'doctor' may be used as a "moral performance categorization" – "You're not a doctor, you're just into money making" – where the category-bound obligations of the category 'doctor' are overridden by category predicates that should not be so tied (Jayyusi, 1984, p. 44; also see Strong & Dingwall, 2018).

Schegloff's (2005a) analysis of "complainability" develops a similar set of observations by reference to analyses of the details of recorded encounters, focusing on how participants can anticipate and attempt to subvert complaints before they are actually produced, and on how complaints produced by reference to explicitly mentioned membership categories – for example, "he's just a student" (Schegloff, 2005a, p. 453) – as well as ones that are tacitly oriented to by participants, are managed when and where they arise. As Schegloff (2005a, p. 452) observes in discussing these matters, "[t]he complainability of some form of conduct can be contingent on the identity of the agents and the recipients of the conduct – identities often grounded in category memberships."

We noted earlier that while the term 'membership categorization device' is very commonly used, Sacks (1992, pp. 40–41) also referred to the "MIR device" – standing for "Membership – Inference-rich – Representative" or the "MIR Membership Categorization Device." A key facet of categories is that they are "inference-rich," referring to "the knowledge that members of a society have about the society" which is "stored in terms of these categories" (Sacks, 1992, p. 41). As Schegloff puts it, categories are "the store house and the filing system for the common-sense knowledge that ordinary people – that means ALL people in their capacity as ordinary people – have about what people are like, how they behave, etc." (Schegloff, 2007c, p. 469). Category 'inferences' made by a speaker may be picked up, developed, or countered in subsequent turns in an interaction (also see Raymond, 2019a). Sacks gives the example of how categories can be implied, along with their inferential upshots, by mentioning some category-incumbent features. Sacks uses an example of how this can contribute to antisemitism without the category 'Jew' ever being explicitly mentioned: merely by listing the (identifiably Jewish) names of those on trial for "economic crimes" in the Soviet Union in the early 1960s, those names could be "seeable as belonging to Jews. And you could leave the rest to everybody's routine procedures: 'See? Jews are economic criminals, as everyone knew'" (Sacks, 1992, p. 42). This brings us back to Extract 2.7, in which the category 'a Barbra Streisand' is used as a proxy for a complaint implied to be based upon antisemitism.

Since category membership can be implied like this, speakers can tacitly "propose membership in some category, where that category stands as the adequate basis for inferring these certain other things" (Sacks, 1992, p. 46). Sacks gives the example of a conversation between a psychiatric social worker and a suicidal man. The man had previously been married and the social worker asks about his previous interests. The man replies, "I was a hair stylist at one time, I did some fashions now and then, things like that." Later, the social worker asks about sexual problems, and the man replies that "naturally" he has such problems: "You probably suspect, as far as the hair stylist and, uh, either one way or the other, they're straight or homosexual, something like that" (Sacks, 1992, p. 46). As Sacks (1992, p. 47) observed, the categorization machinery, and the inference-rich properties of categories, means that "there are ways of introducing a piece of information and testing out whether it will be acceptable, which don't involve saying it" (also see Whitehead, 2009).

People can therefore imply possible or provisional categorizations, of oneself or others, and inoculate themselves from the interactional consequences of overt categorization: attributions of category membership in such cases are deniable. As Edwards (1997) observes, the semantic nature of categories, with labels and a set of incumbent, typical or associated features, lends them to being invoked implicationally, in the management of accountability. Again, this provides a functional basis for categories to have those semantic properties, rather than the fixed and definitive properties they are often assumed by social scientists to have.

Just as someone can be incumbent in a category, and taken as a presumptive member thereof, they can also attempt to subvert, block, or modify what is taken to be 'known' about such category members. This is illustrated by Extract 2.9, which comes from a call from a council worker (C) to an 'antisocial behaviour officer' in another department of the same local council (A) about a council tenant, pseudonymized as "Mrs Tindall." Mrs Tindall is an alleged victim of harassment from her neighbours. This sequence appears near the start of the call, where the council worker is attempting to explain what he has called a "complicated situation" – a formulation that subsequently becomes apparent to be preparing for a description of Mrs Tindall's limited or compromised competence as a member of society.

```
Extract 2.9: Antisocial behaviour council office
01  C:  Missu- (Oh-) sorry missus Tindall h. herself,
02              (.)
03  A:  Mhm:,
04              (0.2)
05  C:  Is:: agoraphobic.
06              (0.3)
07  A:  Mhm:,
08              (0.4)
09  C:  .pt .hhHHH um:: a:nd she's (0.9) uh:: hh uh heh she's
10      fifty three::.=b't, (.) I mean she's a- (0.2) she's what
11      you'd call an o:ld fifty three.=[I suppose.]
12  A:                                  [.pt .hh  ] ye:ah,
```

The council worker's first description of Mrs Tindall, "Is:: agoraphobic" (line 05), formulates agoraphobia as an attribute of Mrs Tindall while avoiding categorizing her as a mentally unwell person (e.g., 'she's *an* agoraphobic'). But of particular interest is the council worker's subsequent description, in which, like in Extract 2.8, he specifies her age "she's fifty three::." (lines 09–10). However, the turn design and action are different to those in Extract 2.8. First, the age attribution occurs in a turn that is not (at least not yet) designed to account for something Mrs Tindall may or may not have done (e.g., confronted the other party). Second, the turn is a continuation of prior description ("um:: a:nd . . ."), and the council worker treats it as delicate by pausing, hesitating, and inserting laughter particles before producing the age attribution (also see Lerner, 2013). Third, unlike "she's eighty-three," it is not immediately clear what being "fifty three" might mean in the context of discussing a victim of harassment. The laughter particles anticipate and project a stance towards the age attribution, which will establish the relevance of this information in the moments following it.

After completing this formulation of the age attribution, the council worker goes on to explicate the relevance of naming such an attribute of Mrs Tindall. He starts with 'b't,' indicating a contrast or problem with the previous description, before saying, "I mean she's a-," in which "I mean" projects a forthcoming explanation of what has so far only been projected, and "she's a-" begins the explanation (also see Maynard, 2013). However, the council worker then halts and restarts this formulation, "she's what you'd call an o:ld fifty three" (also see our discussion of same-turn self-initiated repair in Chapter 8: Managing Trouble in Speaking, Hearing, and Understanding). Through this self-repair, the council worker provides a characterization of Mrs Tindall that marks her as worse off than her possible category membership as 'middle aged' might suggest. In describing her in this way, the council worker can be heard to denigrate Mrs Tindall – even if in the service of helping her. Thus, the council worker's turn is filled with the sorts of hesitation and restarts that cast his doing of this as reluctant and delicate.

Furthermore, the council worker's reformulation is a 'modifier,' providing "that what is that may be said about any member is not to be said about the member in hand" (Sacks, 1992, p. 44). That is, modifiers block the operation of presuming that the inferences stored in the category apply to this particular member of it, neutralizing "the applicability of the presumptive knowledge" (Schegloff, 2007c, p. 469). The insertion of "what you'd call" generalizes the council worker's description – this is not just something he has observed about Mrs Tindall but is what anybody would see about her – and he places her into a category "an o:ld fifty three." In contrast, being "fifty three" in other contexts (e.g., talk about being a Premier League footballer) may immediately be understood as meaning (too) 'old.'

Stokoe (2012b) shows how Sacks's notions about the 'inference-rich' nature of categories – which is often misunderstood – can be observed through the ways categorial formulations themselves are designed and built. It is not just that categories are, in theory and before empirical observation, 'inference rich,' but that we can see that, and how, people treat categories *as* carrying inferential resources, in the design of their turns in which categorial formulations appear. In other words, the inference-rich nature of categories is observable from the endogenous orientations of participants. As we will see in Chapter 8: Managing Trouble in Speaking, Hearing, and Understanding, for instance, as part of self-initiated self-repair operations, when speakers replace one category with another, they display an understanding *that* there are different ways of referring to women and *that* different categories carry different resonances and inferences. Consistent with our discussion in Chapter 1: An Introduction to Categories in Social Interaction, participants show us all the time that "the word selection problem" (Schegloff, 2006a, 2007b) implicates – for members themselves – that choices of category terms carry common-sense associations, resonances, predicates, features, etc. Category selection matters, even when a first term is referentially adequate, and second chosen to replace it is its near synonym (Stokoe, 2011a). It matters not only for ensuring that the 'right' category resonances and inferences are made relevant for the object of description and the action underway but also for the 'subject-side' inferences (Edwards, 2005) that can be made about the speaker as the kind of person to use one category rather than another. Moreover, how a speaker categorizes others may reflexively give rise to inferences about how the speaker can be categorized – a phenomenon Whitehead (2009) calls "categorizing the categorizer." As Edwards (1995, pp. 581–582) observes, categories:

> are not just sense-making devices that get triggered by events; that kind of perceptual-cognitive theory, common in cognitive and social psychology, grossly underspecifies situated talk. People have a lot of flexibility in their choice and deployment of words, which permits particular choices of words to perform, on actual occasions of use, important interactional and conceptual work.

In contrast to the explicit uses of categories in the preceding extracts, in Extract 2.10 a participant treats a prior speaker's description as resonant of a particular category without the prior speaker having explicitly mentioned it. This extract comes from a police interview in which the suspect (S) has admitted criminal damage to her neighbour's door. Here, she has asked the police officer (P) if she can explain some mitigating circumstances and has listed several things, including tiredness.

```
Extract 2.10: Police interview
01  S:  I'm um:: (0.5) menstruatin'?
02            (0.5)
03  P:  A'right.
04            (0.3)
05  S:  (Which/it) doesn't add to one's um:: (1.0) normal frame
06      of mi:nd, [y'know y'kind'f] get a bit irrational an'=
07  P:            [Mhm, yeh     ]
08  S:  =things:
09  P:  £I've got a girlfriend yeah,£
```

Since the suspect's description at line 01 contains the category-bound activity "menstruatin'?," the category to which this is tied, 'female' is implicitly oriented to as a feature of what Jayyusi (1984, p. 135) refers to as a "relevant category environment" – although it may be left implicit to avoid, in this case, affiliating with the suspect (also see Schegloff, 2005a). The police officer's acknowledgement (line 03) neither aligns with nor blocks the suspect's excuse, producing a sequential context that allows for the suspect's elaboration of her claim, and the possibility of soliciting the police officer's understanding and alignment with her view of the events. While police officers usually resist suspects' appeals to display shared category knowledge (e.g., "you know what women are like?"), or to occupy shared category memberships when these are produced in the course of denials (Stokoe, 2009b), here the suspect's invocation of such matters is produced in the service of an admission. What happens at lines 07 and 09 is, therefore, interesting. Following the suspect's euphemized or elaboration (via the use of a litote, "doesn't add to" – line 05), the police officer produces a compound continuer that asserts agreement ("Mhm, yeh" – line 07) in overlap with the suspect's subsequent "y'know" prefaced continuation of the claim that "menstruatin'" makes one "a bit irrational" (line 06). As foreshadowed by the police officer's minimal agreement in line 07, he then explicitly aligns with the suspect's claim by offering an independent basis for knowing, as a member of a different category, what she has asserted, "I've got a girlfriend yeah" (line 09). The police officer's selection of the category "girlfriend" to convey this understanding reflects the basis on which he could have knowledge or experience of such matters as a non-member of the category,[3] and thus treats the suspect's descriptions as resonant with or implicative of 'female.'

Consistent with this, note that the police officer says, "I've got *a* girlfriend," rather than something like 'my girlfriend's like that,' using the indefinite article "a" to construct "girlfriend" *as* categorial and therefore general to members of the gender category who occupy that role. Thus, although the police officer's alignment comes to be expressed in terms of 'girlfriends' who do irrational things when menstruating, his contribution is hearable as claiming 'women' do so, in part because his use of the category term invokes a heterosexual relationship, and thus his status as 'man.' We might add that such a hearing is the only basis on which the police officer's contribution could convey the form of

---

3   In using this practice, he can be understood to be managing the distance-involvement dilemma implicated in managing agreement that is described in Raymond and Heritage (2006), and further discussed in Chapter 9: Managing Knowledge, Experience, and Entitlement). That is, P must establish a basis for claiming agreement with S despite *not* being a member of the category about which the claim is being made. Invoking his intimate, ongoing experience with a member of the category who does have such experiences provides a method for claiming access to a phenomenon he cannot experience first-hand, and thereby avoids being overly distant. At the same time, the claim also avoids any possible assertion of access to the state of affairs that might suggest he is over-involved in, or usurping of, knowledge that belongs to members of that category (e.g., as might be entailed by a non-member's claim to know what challenges experiences by members are like). This points to ways in which knowledge about members of a category may be general and shared, while nevertheless distributed unevenly. Members and non-members will always retain different access to events and experiences associated with membership.

alignment it has been produced to display. The suspect also treats this as a matter of common-sense knowledge through her generalized formulation of the effects of menstruation on "one" (line 05) and her use of "y'know" (line 06). In addition to being a rare example of self-disclosure, the police officer's affiliative categorization at line 09 ratifies the common-sense knowledge the suspect has proposed, and introduces P*n*-adequate alternatives to the setting-based 'police officer' and 'suspect' categories, in the form of 'heterosexual man' and 'woman.'

The common knowledge aspects of the practice seen in the previous extract proffers a speaker's description-turned-categorization (also see Schegloff, 2007a) into an invitation to see what is claimed *as recognizable* common-sense knowledge. Such claims and invitations are relevant precisely in those environments where such recognition of what is known-in-common is at stake – that is, where the recognition of what is claimed about members of the category matters for the course of action in progress. As McHoul (2007, p. 462) points out, categorizing someone as a 'postman' is sufficient for "competent members to hear (infer) just what it is he expectably does . . . unless when perhaps writing a reading primer for kids: 'Bill's the postman, he comes to our house each day and leaves mail in the mailbox.'" Categorial phrases therefore take on an idiomatic quality and work as summarizing devices: they are among Sacks's (1992, p. 8) "idiom-like things." Phrases like "you know what women are like" package and assert as common knowledge what people understand about particular category members. If a category-feature formulation 'works'; that is, it does not become the object of trouble in understanding, then it works on the basis that speakers share category knowledge and unspecified inferences, whether they agree with them or not, enough to enable forms of alignment that allow for progress in the sequence underway. The common knowledge component also makes relevant the co-participants' category memberships, such that as, for example, 'men,' 'women,' or 'heterosexuals,' they share mutual knowledge of what those being categorized are like. Common knowledge components can therefore have an affiliative function.

In Extract 2.10, we saw how, across a sequence, participants show that and how they are understanding and leveraging categorial phenomena to build actions – and that one would not exist without the other. That is, descriptions (e.g., "I'm um:: (0.5) menstruatin'?") may be treated by the speaker or a recipient as category-relevant (also see Deppermann, 2011; Hauser, 2011; Schegloff, 2007a). In turn, a party may then 'proffer' a category (e.g., "£I've got a girlfriend"), which can accomplish a variety of actions (e.g., affiliation). Across the sequence, these practices of categorization manage both "prospective" (Watson, 2009b) and "retrospective" (also see Hester & Francis, 1994) elements of the organization of action, thereby underscoring that practices of categorization exemplify how contributions to unfolding occasions of talk-in-interaction are both context-sensitive and context-renewing (also see Heritage, 1984b). The practices through which participants collaboratively build collections of categories, display understanding of a category's resonances, entitlements, activities, inferences, and so on, and use such features as members' resources both prospectively and retrospectively, are further illustrated in Extract 2.11. It comes from an online 'chat' between two friends, pseudonymized as Callum and Isla, using an instant messaging application (the spelling/typing errors at lines 05 and 11 are in the original).

```
Extract 2.11: Online chat (data from Meredith, 2014)
01   Callum:   you can teach me
02                   (2.0)
03   Isla:     I charge by the hour
04                   (35.0)
05   Callum:   you sound liek a prostitute there haha
06             but i wont take it like that
07                   (69.0)
08   Isla:     haha while that wasn't exactly the intention
09             it was the connotations lol - joke with -
10             my friend here - she just said the same
11             thing to another guy - agian in a different
12             context but with that sort of banter lol
```

Callum and Isla have been talking about sports coaching. A gloss on the work of naming and labelling that takes place here might be something like "what is this relationship that we are proposing to enter into?" Consider, for instance, Callum's initial "you can teach me" (line 01). While the text formulates, and summarizes, the conversation that precedes it, it is also composed as an offer (e.g., rather than a request, "can you teach me?"), positioning Isla as beneficiary and Callum as benefactor (also see Clayman & Heritage, 2014; Raymond & Zimmerman, 2016). To "teach," in and of itself, involves a social activity, rather than a category, but it is also bound to categories such as 'teacher' and 'coach,' and thus proposes that Isla could be, or become, an incumbent of such a category. Moreover, "*you* can teach *me*" specifies the relational pairing 'teacher' and/or 'coach'/'student' as one that each party to the interaction is collaboratively engaged in developing. Thus, whilst members can make inferences from a category to the kinds of activity that incumbents of that category might do, they can also invite others to make inferences in the other directions – from an activity (or predicted activity) to a certain kind of category, and category incumbency (also see Sacks, 1992; Schegloff, 2007c; Watson, 2009b).

This line of analysis is also consistent with Isla's response, "I charge by the hour" (line 03): it is what she, herself, proposes as the type of relational pairing that Callum has suggested. Her response orients to Callum's initial proposal and, in doing so, offers up the kind of action that incumbents of the 'teacher' or 'coach' categories might carry out: they not only "teach" but might also be reasonably expected to "charge" for those services. As such, while Isla partially aligns with Callum's proposal, she also attaches a condition to her prospective incumbency of the 'teacher'-'coach'/'student' pair of categories it invokes, thereby treating his offer as having been a request. In this way, she resists any possible implication in his proposal that she would be the beneficiary (and thus 'owe' him in some way), while also resisting the implication that she would share her time and expertise free of charge, and resisting the status as benefactor the offer of free services would convey. In his next response, Callum exploits a further set of links between categories, actions and predicates in the service of producing a sexualized joke. Specifically, Callum treats Isla's "I charge by the hour" as an activity relevant to incumbency in a rather different category, being "liek [sic] a prostitute," thereby invoking a different categorial pairing, 'prostitute'/'customer,' in which one party charges for something that in other contexts – among romantic partners – is given freely. In this way, across this exchange, his 'offer' of prospective membership in the 'student' category becomes recognizable as having actually been a 'request' pursued in seeking a different category relationship, involving sex rather than sports (also see our discussion of categorial bases of the formation and interpretation of actions in Chapter 4: Forming and Making Sense of Actions).

In doing so, Callum possibly also registers a tacit objection to Isla's indication that the acceptability of his initial proposal is contingent on his willingness to pay – which is possibly grounded in a tacit claim that, given their co-membership in the category pair 'friend'/'friend,' she should teach him for free. That is, rather than, for example, agreeing to pay her, or at least indicating his willingness to do so by asking what her hourly rate is, he counters by (jokingly) suggesting that her mention of an hourly rate places her in a stigmatized category. His treatment of the "prostitute" category as stigmatized is shown by numerous features that mark this turn as carefully designed: consistent with the stance taken in earlier turns in the sequence, Callum ends the first part of his turn with a written laughter particle, "haha" (line 05); he downgrades the definitive nature of the categorization by noting that she only "*sounds like* a prostitute *there*" (line 05; emphasis added), in a temporally specific and limited way; and he concludes by claiming that he "wont [sic] take it like that" (line 06). In these ways, he displays awareness that even designedly non-serious attributions of the category pairing 'prostitute/customer' are potentially risky.

Isla begins her next response by reciprocating Callum's non-serious stance towards this category work ("haha," line 08). This is reinforced by her inclusion of other 'laughter' indicators ("lol," lines 09 and 12), and her characterization of the exchange as "banter" (line 12). However, she both resists and goes along with the categorization "prostitute" in several ways: as something that her turn in line 03 was not making relevant ("that wasn't exactly the intention," line 08); as something that may be prospectively referred to ("it was the connotations lol," line 09), and via the reporting of a concurrent chat with another friend who was involved in a similar prospective-retrospective categorization activity ("she just said the same thing to another guy," lines 10–11).

This section has set out the core components of Sacks's membership categorization apparatus and its subsequent extension by other scholars – membership categorization devices and collections of categories and the use of these in making inferences. The extracts we have analysed demonstrate the connections between categories and actions/activities in their sequential and other interactional contexts. In the following section, we turn to the maxims or "rules of application" Sacks observed participants systematically using or orienting to in relation to categories and their collections.

2.2.2 The rules of application for membership categorization devices

Earlier in the chapter, we introduced Sacks's core term, 'membership categorization device' (MCD), and his related use of the MIR acronym, the 'Membership Inference-Rich Representative' device. As Sacks (1992, p. 40) began to set out what he called the "very central machinery of social organization," he came to use the term MCD to refer to "a class of category sets," meaning "[a] set which is made up of a group of categories." He emphasized that the categories within such a set are not "made up" but are "Members' categories" (Sacks, 1992, p. 40). However, the fact that, as noted previously, multiple categories could be applied to any given person presents a challenge for analysts to establish "whose categories" are being used and how members "go about choosing among the available sets of categories for *grasping some event*" (Sacks, 1992, p. 41; emphasis added). (The notion that people select categories for "grasping some event" points forwards to Section 2.3 in the current chapter, where we consider the constructive and constitutive work done by categorization to "assemble" the social world [Baker, 2000]).

This 'problem of categorization' is resolved in part via a set of 'rules of application' that Sacks (1972b) observes members systematically using in this way. A first rule of application is "the economy rule," which Sacks (1972b, p. 333) describes as a "reference satisfactoriness rule" that "holds: A single category from any membership categorization device can be referentially adequate." That is, any person can be referred to or described using only one category, such that in cases where more than one category is used in referring to a person, their use can be inspected for what they accomplish interactionally, beyond merely providing referential adequacy (Sacks, 1972a, 1972b). Sacks (1972a, p. 32) also connects the economy rule to understanding childhood socialization through further examples of children's stories (e.g., "Once there was a baby pig. He played with his Mommy. He went to Mommy. Mommy went to Daddy."). He describes how children learn "what in principle adequate reference consists of," including "what categories must be added to 'Mommy,' 'Daddy,' and 'baby' to complete the collection of which they are members," and then learning more collections, and "occasions and rules of use of each of the devices" (Sacks, 1972a, pp. 34–35).

The economy rule is connected to "the consistency rule," which Sacks (1972a, p. 33) notes "can only hold for the use of Pn-adequate devices." The consistency rule states that

> [i]f some population of persons is being categorized and if some category from a device's collection has been used to categorize a first Member of the population, then that category or other categories of the same collection may be used to categorize further members of the population (Sacks, 1972a, p. 33).

As McHoul (2007, p. 461) explains, the consistency rule provides for the expectation that if reference is made to 'a postman,' a subsequent reference to another person would also use a category from the MCD 'occupation' (e.g., 'plumber'), rather than using a category from a different MCD (e.g., 'blonde'). Similarly, as Schegloff (2007c, p. 471) observes, in a series of introductions that focus on academic discipline (e.g., 'sociologist,' 'physicist,' 'psychologist'), the relevance for each subsequent categorization is provided for by the prior, and for a "next person to be identified or to self-identify as 'Canadian' is then registerable as a 'departure.'" Thus, just as departures from the economy rule can be inspected for what they accomplish interactionally, so can departures from the consistency rule.

As a corollary of the consistency rule, Sacks (1972b, p. 333) describes a "hearer's maxim," which holds that "if two or more categories are used to categorize two or more members of some population, and those categories can be heard as categories from the same collection, then: hear them that way." Watson and Weinberg (1982, p. 61) refer to the hearer's maxim as "a 'strong' form of the consistency rule" (p. 61). Sacks (1972b, p. 338) also describes a "viewer's maxim" for category-bound activities: "if a Member sees a category-bound activity being done, then, if one sees it being done by a member of a category to which the activity is bound, see it that way." The hearer's and viewer's maxims therefore serve respectively as instructions for hearing and seeing performed actions and activities as tied to a member's incumbency in a category.

The hearer's maxim applies to cases in which an action or activity (e.g., crying) is attributed to a member of a category (e.g., 'baby') that could be part of two (or more) distinct MCDs (e.g., 'stage of life' and 'family'). Sacks (1972b, p. 337) proposes that this ambiguity with respect to which collection of categories is being invoked will be resolved by hearing the category as being (at least) the one to which the activity is category-bound – in this case hearing the category 'baby' as being from the 'stage of life' collection (to which the action of crying is bound) rather than from the 'family' collection.

In contrast, the viewer's maxim provides instructions for using a visually available activity as a basis for seeing the category membership of the person who produced it. That is, seeing a person engaged in an activity (e.g., crying) that is bound to a particular category (e.g., 'baby') provides a warranted basis for seeing the person as a member of that category – that is, for seeing the crying person as a member of the category 'baby' rather than, for example, as a 'boy' (since, as *The Cure*[4] famously reminded us, "boys don't cry"). As Schegloff (2007c, pp. 472–473) notes, this involves treating the characterization of an activity as unproblematic to provide leverage for arriving at a characterization of the category of the actor producing it, but participants may also conversely treat the category of the actor as unproblematic in order to provide for a characterization of the activity (also see Chapter 6: Forming and Making Sense of Actions).

As an example of the consistency and economy rules, and their corollaries – as well as the perceptual availability of categorization – Rose (1994, cited in Carlin, 2003) provides the example of the following scene: A person he saw as a member of the category "adult" walking with another, who he saw as a "child" towards a place, "a school." As Carlin (2003, pp. 2–3) writes,

> When seeing an adult and child walking towards a school, on a school-day, first thing in the morning, it is inferred 1) that a parent is walking a child to school; 2) that a parent walks their child to school, rather than somebody else's child; and 3) that a child walks to school with their parent, rather than another child's parent. In this visual scene, Rose recognized the adult as a parent of the child who skipped around them, and that the child attended the elementary school that they were approaching. Thus, Rose 'saw' a parent escorting their child to school.

In observing this scene, Rose saw and described the people as each being members of just one category (the economy rule); with the activity he sees them as being engaged in, walking to school, providing for seeing them as members of these particular categories (the viewer's maxim); and with both categories coming from the same collection, 'family' (the consistency rule and

---

4 With direct relevance to the themes of our book, *The Cure's* lead vocalist and songwriter, Robert Smith, stated regarding their music genre categorization: "It's so pitiful when 'goth' is still tagged onto the name The Cure . . . *We're not categorizable.* I suppose we were post-punk when we came out, but in total it's impossible . . . I just play Cure music, whatever that is" (Reuters, 2006, emphasis added; see also Widdicombe & Wooffitt, 1995).

hearer's maxim), and the same family unit within that collection (duplicative organization – see Section 2.1).

In a similar vein, Hester and Francis (2003, p. 36) articulate the "categorial organization of observable scenes" through an extended set of fieldnote-based descriptions of the categories of persons observed during a walk to the supermarket. They draw on the observer's fieldnotes to show how much shortcutting and assuming is done via descriptions such as, "Just walking along, another car goes by, had a family in it": while "the car might have contained abductees," "it was utterly unproblematic that the passengers in the car were a family" (Hester & Francis, 2003, pp. 40–41). A possibly more grounded version of the relevance of categories for observations is exemplified by Garfinkel's (1967) "Boarders Experiment," in which he asked students to observe events in their homes as if they were strangers. One student's description begins, "A short stout man entered the house, kissed me on the cheek, and asked, 'How was school?'" (Garfinkel, 1967, p. 45). Produced as a stand-alone account of events, the description is troubling: what kind of man enters a house and assaults the first person he sees? However, once one knows that the "short stout man" is the student's father, the events described are routine, and even endearing. These examples invite us to appreciate how categorization in and of space and place is fundamental to inequities and privilege. For example, Vera-Gray's (2018, p. 13) account of how "women trade freedom for safety" presents multiple narratives collected from women describing the way they "walk kind of fast" to be categorizable as "not the type of woman they can joke around with"; or "give off this vibe that you're just completely not interested in anyone or you're busy." Similarly, during the Covid-19 pandemic, multiple studies showed that people who were perceptually categorizable as a "visible minority" felt less safe in public space and were more likely to be harassed or attacked on the basis of "race, ethnicity, or skin colour" (Heidinger & Cotter, 2020, p. 4; also see Anderson, 2022). Social categories, as ways of classifying people, can even disappear entirely, and as such are "powerful technologies. Embedded in working infrastructures, they become relatively invisible without losing any of that power" (Bowker & Star, 1999, p. 319). As Ásta (2018, p. 1) explains, in *The Categories We Live By*,

> While it is often only when we travel out of our comfort zones that we become aware of the many social categories we belong to, they are also there when we are comfortably not aware of them, framing our interactions with other people and our own self-understanding.

A further resource, in addition to the rules of application, that participants in some settings may use in resolving the problem of categorization, or characterizing an action performed by the actor, or both, is what Sacks (1992, p. 313) calls "omni-relevant" MCDs. This refers to collections of categories that – similarly to what we have described in Chapter 1: An Introduction to Categories in Social Interaction as setting-based categories, and what Zimmerman (1998, p. 90) calls "situational identities" – are tied to the types of activities that typically get done in a setting, such that the MCD serves "as background . . . as a kind of 'default' orientation that organises the participation context" (Fitzgerald et al., 2009, p. 45), with the participants' membership in a category from the collection being systematically *potentially* relevant at any point for the production and interpretation of actions by participants in the setting (also see Fitzgerald, 2021; Fitzgerald et al., 2009; Whitehead & Baldry, 2018). For example, Sacks (1992, pp. 313–314) describes how the omni-relevance of the MCD including the categories 'therapist' and 'patient' in group therapy sessions provides for an otherwise "cryptic" utterance by the therapist being heard by other participants as moving towards closing the session, by reference to the therapist's entitlement to decide when the session will end. While Sacks notes that other MCDs may also be (omni-) relevant at particular moments in such settings – and the identification of a setting-based omni-relevant device thus does not excuse the analyst from demonstrating precisely when and how a particular device or category is relevant (a challenge to which we return in Section 2.3 and in Chapter 3: Methodological Principles, Practices, and Challenges) – cases such as this provide ways of seeing the "reflexive co-determination" (Schegloff, 2007c, p. 473) of categories and actions that Sacks observed (also see Hester & Eglin, 1997; Schegloff, 2001).

The terminology around categories, membership categorization devices, and rules of application is not, as emphasized already, meant to be reified as a conceptual apparatus for analysts but rather a necessary use of language to describe what participants do as they themselves construct, reify, assemble, disassemble, and 'grasp at' the world. Categories are words in language, and people use these ready-made typifications in language to construct reality. In the next section, we briefly explore the constitutive and moral work done in and through membership categorization.

2.3 Description, construction, and moral worlds

In developing his account of membership categorization, Sacks (1992, p. 41) criticizes mainstream social science for its "unanalytic" starting point, "in the sense that they simply put some category in." In other words, social scientists deploy their own already-known categories to divide the population (and their research participants) and account for any findings in those pre-defined terms. In doing so, they treat the doing of categorization in an entirely arbitrary manner and overlook the centrality of 'membership' in membership categorization as the starting point of analysing members' categories. Furthermore, since Schegloff (2007c, p. 475; emphasis added) writes about the way "participants' *production of the world* is informed by . . . particular categorization devices," and that categories "are big-time players in how *common-sense culture* operates" (p. 471, emphasis added), any social scientist reading this book is likely to already see the similarity in the language used to write about categorization and social constructionist theory and methods. That is, such language practices are how members and analysts go about constructing, creating, and producing the world, rather than simply being proffered as " 'mirroring' an independent reality" (Hammersley, 2022, p. 134; also see Pollner, 1974). As Baker (2000, p. 112; emphasis added) explains, when members " 'do describing,' they assemble a social world in which their categories have a central place . . . these are powerful statements about what could be the case, how the social order might be arranged, *whether or not it really is.*"

Ethnomethodology and conversation analysis (EMCA) – and thus membership categorization, as a core component of both – are often aligned with social constructionism as an ontological position and epistemological approach, such as in Buttny's (1993) 'conversation analytic constructionism.' The same holds for discursive psychology (Edwards, 1997; Potter, 1996). Lynch (1993, pp. xiv–xv) argues that both EMCA and constructionism share a focus on the investigation of knowledge production: both take an anti-foundationalist stance by "seeking to describe the 'achievement' of social order and the 'construction' of social and scientific 'facts,'" and both "explicitly renounce the use of transcendental standards of truth, rationality, and natural realism when seeking to describe and/or explain historical developments and contemporary practices." Additionally, ethnomethodology's efforts to "point to some of the ways in which the world is rendered objectively available and is maintained as such" (Heritage, 1984b, p. 220) is aligned with the concept of methodological relativism as described in the field of "sociology of scientific knowledge" (Collins, 1983, p. 265) or, more recently "science and technology studies" (Hammersley, 2022, p. 133). Both EMCA and science and technology studies methodologically 'bracket off' reality, adopting the position of "ethnomethodological indifference" (Garfinkel & Sacks, 1970, p. 63) in order to study how people maintain a sense of a commonly shared, objectively existing world.

However, despite these similarities, the relationship between EMCA and constructionism is not straightforward, and it is not clear that EMCA (and the camps within them) practitioners regard themselves as 'constructionist' in the conventionally used senses of the term (Button & Sharrock, 1993; Hammersley, 2022). For instance, in a recent article, Lynch (2022, p. 258) argues that "ethnomethodology is distinct from both constructionist and post-constructionist research." Some, including Wowk (2007, p. 141), propose that ethnomethodology "takes no position on the continuum between realism and social constructionism (or any other dualisms either) and is, if anything, a-constructionist." In particular, it does not take up an ontological position with regard to the nature of 'reality.' Instead, it "respecifies" (Button,

1991, p. 6) issues of what is real and authentic, including what is 'true' about identity, as matters for members themselves to deal with. Since discursive psychology is to psychology what ethnomethodology is to sociology, the same holds regarding the respecification of psychological concepts (e.g., cognition, attitude, memory) as discursive practices displayed in and through "the rich surface" of social interaction (Edwards, 2006).

For some in ethnomethodology, then, it is a "basic mistake" to assume that we need to "adopt a theoretical stance on 'reality' at all" (Francis, 1994, p. 105), partly because preoccupations about ontology inhibit close analysis of members' practices (Button & Sharrock, 1993). Indeed, ethnomethodology is critical of some constructionist work for what it sees as subverting and ironizing participants' sense of the integrity of their world (Watson, 1994). That is, people use categories as 'practical realities' they can know about themselves and other people, and are not generally sent into a 'metaphysical spin' about ontological statuses (Francis, 1994; Schegloff, 2007c) – though, of course, people ascribe, resist, transform, and otherwise deploy categories and do categorization work throughout their interactional activities. The issue for constructionists and ethnomethodologists is not whether any given category is actually 'real' or 'true'; rather, it is the business of analysis to "analyze the workings of those categories, not to merely use them as they are used in the world" (Jefferson, 2004b, p. 118). As Bowker and Star (1999, p. 319) suggest, categories are ways of classifying, and "[c]lassifications are powerful" and important sites "of political and ethical work." Once embedded in language and society and systems, they can become invisible to the point that people "hardly know what we have built."

A strong theme in membership categorization research is a focus on "members' activities of describing, inferring and judging" (Jayyusi, 1984, p. 1), since "the description of persons turns out to be intimately embedded in the description and ascription of actions, in the work of practical judgment in everyday and in practical inferential activities" (Jayyusi, 1984, p. 2; also see Cuff, 1994). Most basically, practices of categorization and description are forms of social action, and thus entail claims about the moral justifiability of the type of person or conduct they describe (Garfinkel, 1967; also see Schegloff, 2005a). Jayyusi's focus on categories and description explicates this perspective in her argument that categorization is fundamentally moral:

> Further, in examining the ways in which persons are described and the ways in which such descriptions are used to accomplish various practical tasks – e.g. to deliver judgments, warrant further inferences, ascribe actions, project possible events, explain prior events, account for behaviour, etc. – it becomes clear that categorization work is embedded in a moral order, how that occurs and how that moral order operates practically and pervasively within social life (Jayyusi, 1984, p. 2).

This notion is further elaborated by Widdicombe (1998, p. 53):

> The fact that categories are conventionally associated with activities, at-tributes, motives and so on makes them a powerful cultural resource in warranting, explaining and justifying behaviour. That is, whatever is known about the category can be invoked as being relevant to the person to whom the label is applied and provides a set of inferential resources by which to interpret and account for past or present conduct, or to inform predictions about likely future behaviour.

A compelling example of the constitutive, constructed, and moral work done by description and categorization can be found in Drew's (1992) ex-amination of contested versions of events in rape trial courtroom interaction. The questions and answers of attorneys, witnesses, and the alleged victim and perpetrator, are all designed to manage the different stakes and interests of the parties in the pursuit of a 'true' version of events on which the outcome rests. A key stretch of interaction examined by Drew (1992, p. 489) is presented as Extract 2.12.

```
Extract 2.12: Courtroom
01   A:   An' you went to a:uh (0.9) ah you went to
02        a ba:r? in ((city)) (0.6) is that correct?
03             (1.0)
04   W:   It's a clu:b.
.  .  .
05   A:   It's where uh (.) uh gi:rls and fella:s
06        meet isn't it?
07             (0.9)
08   W:   People go: there.
```

Drew (1992, p. 490) points out that, while the attorney's (A) questions are "designed to elicit an answer which is either *yes* or *no*; that is, which will either confirm or disconfirm the version proposed in the question," in each case, the witness – the alleged victim – does not provide either of these pro-jected answers (also see Raymond, 2003). Instead, her responses "are quali-fied, guarded versions of what the attorney suggests" and "they manage to be defensive as well as to rebut his versions" (Drew, 1992, p. 490). In so do-ing, they also unmask the moral characterizing the attorney's descriptions and queries prepared the grounds for; she exposes the degree to which what the attorney offers as "mere" or benign descriptions position her can be revealed to have been on their way to impeaching her.

What we can also observe is the centrality of categories, category-bound activities, and categorial features to the way the attorney and witness con-struct and resist alternative versions of events and thereby potentially produce and maintain 'reality disjunctures' (also see Eglin, 1979; Pollner, 1975). For instance, the attorney's formulation "a bar" (line 02) as a place category is reformulated as "a club" (line 04) by the witness. The activities tied to the place are formulated by the attorney as "where (.) uh gi:rls and fe<u>ll</u>a:s <u>meet</u>" (lines 05–06), themselves invoking categories arranged in a standardized relational pair ("girls and fellas") with numerous inferences available: "girls and fellas meet" hearably categorizes the "place" as one known for meeting people for a flirtation, a date, to find a partner, romance, etc. These inferences are not explicitly unpacked, but the fact that that such inferences are available is evidenced in the witness's description of the place as somewhere "People go" (line 08), thereby reformulating the paired categories into a non-gendered, non-relational one, and thereby resists any implication that she entered the location with such a motive.

Examples of the constitutive and moral work done by description, including categorization, can be found in any discursive context, alongside the grammar, agency, and other language features that work in aggregate to construct the world of facts and reality. For instance, swapping the categories 'freedom fighters,' 'terrorists,' and 'murderers' within the same newspaper headline or account pushes towards or away from legitimacy, justification, condemnation, and so on (Jayyusi, 1984). A case in point is the emergent account, and its subsequent solidification, of 'what happened' during the bombings and mass shootings in Norway in July 2011, for which Anders Behring Breivik (described on Wikipedia as a "Norwegian far-right domestic terrorist") was arrested and convicted. Initial descriptions started in the media with the process of allocating, and distributing, relevant category incumbencies (for a fuller analysis, see Stokoe & Attenborough, 2015). While there was no doubt that there were 'victims,' whether events were an unintended accident, or deliberate, and caused by an offender were initially unclear. Rolling 24-hour news, both on television and online, variously categorized (and described) the event as (cf. Raymond, 2000):

- "A gas explosion"
- "Probably a bomb"
- "Terrorism"
- "A bomb"
- "An attack"
- "Europe's first Mumbai-style attack"
- "Carnage"
- "Massacre"
- "Terrorism"
- "Slaughter"
- "Assault"
- "Murder and mayhem"
- "Indiscriminate violence"

Categorizing events as "an explosion" avoids ascribing agency or cause to persons. Indeed, commentators were oriented to the ambiguity of the event categorization, as well as the moral need for caution in the rush for definition (e.g., "we have to be really careful"). In expressing such caution in the course of formulating descriptions of the events, commentators revealed a need for audience members – and themselves – to actively resist the default inferences or categorizations invited by the sort of events they are witnessing. In this way, commentators' warnings were also assertions of agency with respect to the machinery of culture: on the one hand, their warnings reveal how reporters, anchors, and audience members may experience the pull of the 'gravitational power' of the machinery of categorization and inference (which invites seeing the explosion in specific ways), while also emphasizing that they retain the capacity to resist taken-for-granted usage.

Accounts were formulated via retrospective and prospective categorizations, moving from what was known – "an explosion" – to what could be known in the future. Once the event was recategorized as "a bomb" – as deliberate rather than an agency-free accidental "gas explosion" – category-implicative accounts proliferated. As a 'bombing,' the unfolding event became accountable via a standardized relational pair of 'victim-perpetrator,' though with what kinds of perpetrators yet unknown and thus prospectively categorized. Across the news reports, 'what happened' gradually consolidated around a clear, but still prospectively categorized, standardized relational pair such that the victim was 'the West,' and the perpetrator was 'Islamism,' and references to (for example) "Al-Qaeda" were invoked in categorial ways:

- "The presence of Norwegian troops in Afghanistan . . . hunting down Al-Qaeda."
- "The military presence in Muslim countries such as Afghanistan or Libya, a move bound to anger fanatics"
- "Scandinavian countries have faced radical Islamic attacks"
- "Islamic suicide bomber"
- "Osama bin Laden"
- "No group had admitted responsibility last night for the bombing or the attack on. But the multiple nature of the assault, . . . bear the hallmarks of al-Qaeda."
- "The gun maniac was blond with blue eyes and spoke Norwegian – raising fears that he was a homegrown al-Qaeda convert."
- "The maniac"
- "The gunman – described as over 6ft, with blond hair and blue eyes – arrived on the island by boat posing as a policeman. He spoke fluent Norwegian – raising fears he was a homegrown Islamic convert."
- "One blond-haired, blue-eyed man"

Who the 'victims' were was less opaque, but different categorizations focused on 'youth,' on the one hand, and 'the Norwegian State' on the other, as events unfolded:

- "Young people camping on an island"
- "The Norwegian State"
- "Citizens at a youth camp"
- "A youth camp on the tiny Norwegian island of Utøya"
- "Island youth rally"
- "Friendly and civilised streets of one of Europe's most peaceful nations"

Retrospectively, as constructions solidified, the categories within the standardized relational pair 'victim-perpetrator' were adjusted and revised (also see Drew, 2003). 'Norway' became duplicatively organized with a family of crimes of the type committed by Timothy McVeigh in the USA rather than the same family as 9/11 and 7/7. The prospective categorization of the perpetrator as "Islamic," part of a networked Al-Qaeda and targeting 'the West' as a whole, became a "loner" with "personal grievances against the state." In order to make sense of the category puzzle of paired categories that do not conventionally go together ("Islam" and "Al-Qaeda" were paired with "blond with blue eyes" and "blue-eyed"), the "terrorist" category was replaced by "gun maniac" and "assassin." The solution to the puzzle was given by the further categories "home-grown" and "convert," which enabled the "blond and blue eyed" perpetrator to remain tied to the category "Al-Qaeda."

As the story rolled on, information that was potentially incongruous with the dominant version was initially worked into the accounts unproblematically, again via categories. The iteration of the story that became 'the facts of the matter'; what 'really happened,' severed the connection between the perpetrator and Islam:

Extract 2.13: *Newcastle Evening Chronicle* 23.7.11

NRK and other Norwegian media posted pictures of the blond, blue-eyed Norwegian. Police said later that the suspect had right-wing and anti-Muslim views, but the motive for the attacks was unclear.

Extract 2.14: *Daily Mail* 24.7.11

Media reports in Norway described Breivik as a 'loner', who lived with his mother in a wealthy suburb of west Oslo, was well-educated and enjoyed hunting.

Here, the retrospective categorization work established a new victim-perpetrator pairing, with the perpetrator being named as "Breivik"

(Extract 2.14), which, of course, rapidly spread across all news sources. "Home-grown Islamic convert" was replaced by "right-wing" and "anti-Muslim" (Extract 2.13); and a different narrative began to emerge, one of the "loner" killer, with various category-tied predicates including "lived with his mother" and "enjoyed hunting" (Extract 2.14). As Watson (2009a, p. 86) notes, "particulars may subsequently appear which may occasion a re-definition (again maybe involving nuance and 'fine-tuning' rather than neces-sarily involving a radical re-casting)." In this case, a "radical recasting" *was* involved in reconstruction of the case, accounts of which consolidated around a sole, white, Norwegian perpetrator who was operating from an anti-Islamic, 'right-wing extremist' ideology. Extract 2.15 shows headlines from subse-quent days' newspaper headlines:

Extract 2.15: Newspaper headlines

Sunday Mirror (24.7.11) THE LONE WOLF KILLER
Daily Mail (26.7.11) SMIRK OF THE MANIAC
Daily Mail (26.7.11) MIGRANT HATING MONSTER
The Sun (26.7.11) MADMAN RANTS
Daily Star (27.7.11) PSYCHO NAZI'S LUXURY JAIL

A week after the initial event, the categories in play were refined further, away from the "loner" committing a 'Timothy McVeigh' type of crime. Rather, Breivik was now simultaneously categorized in psychopathic terms ("lone wolf killer," "maniac," "monster," "madman," "psycho"), with a political flavour ("migrant-hating," "Nazi") and with particular category-tied predicates and activities ("smirk," "rant").

The 'category transformations' of the perpetrator, as laid out in the con-struction of 'what happened' in Norway in 2011, show "how the sense of an event can be transformed if the membership category of the person involved is changed" (Hester & Hester, 2012, p. 569; also see Jayyusi, 1984). Once an account has been constructed, it solidifies into taken-for-granted facts, and this includes what categories and category members are taken to mean and, equally, why modifiers such as 'not a typical X' both subvert and reify a cat-egory. As Baker (2000, p. 112) concludes:

> Rearranging categories and associated activities is difficult excavation work because one encounters a history of sedimentation of usage and, therefore, of commonsense and logic. This has been encountered in feminist work which has attempted to dislodge persistent and pervasive connections be-tween gender categories and associated activities such as forms of work and rights . . . a first step in challenging discourses and practices is to recognise the force of categorization practices in social and institutional life.

2.4   Summary and conclusions

The aim of this chapter has been to navigate the territory of membership categorization in terms of the conceptual and methodological apparatus built by Sacks and others, with explanations of terminology and approach provided through multiple data extracts. In reflecting on this apparatus, we might now suggest that it is in some ways *over*-built when it comes to examining participants' categorial work and orientations in many cases. It is surely the case that some 'core' features of categories and categorization we have described in this chapter – including most especially a range of MCDs and the common-sense knowledge associated with particular categories – are pervasively 'at play' across and throughout interactional occasions. However, participants seem seldom, if ever, to be oriented to anywhere near the full range of such features we have specified here – an observation borne out by our own experiences of conducting research on categories in social interaction, including in the analyses we present in the following chapters, in which a number of the concepts we have discussed in this chapter never feature.[5]

In contrast, one would be hard-pressed to find even a short stretch of interaction in which participants are not pervasively using or contending with most or all of the generic organizations of interactional practice we introduced in Chapter 1: An Introduction to Categories in Social Interaction – namely, turn-taking, action formation, sequence organization, repair, word selection, overall structural organization, and epistemics. This returns us to the pointed reminders by Sacks and others who have built on his work – as we have noted in various places throughout this chapter and the previous one – that categorial phenomena are always occasioned, produced, and managed by participants in and through their social conduct, and to be examined empirically on a case-by-case basis. This means that fully appreciating the import of the *categorial* systematics we have reviewed in this chapter requires appreciating precisely how and when they relate to *interactional* systematics – and most centrally to the aforementioned generic organizations of practice. We turn to these matters as we move to address methods for analysing categories in social interaction next, in Chapter 3: Methodological Principles, Practices, and Challenges, as well addressing as the practical concerns that arise in conducting research on categories in naturally occurring, and especially audio- or video-recorded, social interaction.

---

5   It might be suggested that, rather saying anything about the utility of the MCD apparatus, this is indicative of gaps in our analyses. While of course we open to constructive suggestions for how these analyses could be improved, we contend that many of the categorial phenomena described by these concepts are simply not pervasively relevant for the participants across the occasions we examine.

3

METHODOLOGICAL PRINCIPLES, PRACTICES, AND CHALLENGES

3.0   Introduction

In this chapter, we build on the foundations laid in the preceding chapters to establish a set of methodological principles and procedures on which the chapters that follow rest. That is, having mapped the development and terrain of research and theory on categories in social interaction, we now move on to introduce a set of practices that will facilitate the integration of analyses of categorial phenomena with attention to the generic organizations of practice for interaction, as described in Chapter 1: An Introduction to Categories in Social Interaction. We also address some of the challenges associated with using conversation analysis to conduct research on 'big' social science research topics that are often deeply embedded in categorial matters, as discussed in the Prologue: Why Categories Matter and in Chapter 1: An Introduction to Categories in Social Interaction, as well as relating to common critiques of the principles that guide a conversation analytic approach and its ostensible limitations.

While these principles, practices, challenges, critiques, and debates are interlinked in practice, in the interest of clarity we have separated them into sections that largely correspond with the main stages of conversation analytic research, beginning with matters relating to selection and/or collection of data sources (Section 3.1), before addressing the issue of 'capturability' of categorial phenomena in 'naturally occurring' data (Section 3.2). We then consider questions of whether and how, in the materials collected, evidence of 'participants' orientations' to categories can be established, rather than asserting their relevance by analysts' fiat (Section 3.3), as well as how to approach tacit categorization and ambiguous cases (Section 3.4). Before concluding

DOI: 10.4324/9781003120599-4

the chapter, we offer some practical advice on how to go about building and analysing collections of cases of categorial phenomena in social interaction (Section 3.5).

3.1 Using 'naturally occurring' recorded interactional data

A founding principle of conversation analytic research is the use of what has come to be called 'naturally occurring' – and especially audio- and/or video-recorded – interactional data as a primary basis for claims about the workings of social interaction. As Schegloff (1996, p. 169) observes, proceeding in this way "can yield empirically grounded results at variance with our commonsense intuitions about how some action is accomplished or what action some utterance is to be understood to have accomplished." Since the 1960s, conversation analysts have collected and analysed recorded data across a tremendous range of domains, from institutional and domestic telephone calls (themselves including a vast diversity of settings and participants) to broadcast media, courtrooms, classrooms, medical settings, police-civilian encounters, family mealtimes, human-robot interaction, dancing classes, and many more.

The term 'naturally occurring' was adopted as a way of distinguishing CA's target phenomena, and thus data sources, from those most widely employed in the social sciences at the time – and that indeed still dominate the contemporary social scientific landscape. These include the types of invented or idealized talk commonly invoked by (among others) philosophers of language and linguists to illustrate claims about interaction, as well as a range of approaches to generating empirical data that rely on self-reports (e.g., surveys, interviews, focus groups), experimental manipulation of participants' conduct, or real-time observations that rely on fieldnotes or coding schedules without the use of recording devices (see, e.g., Heritage, 1984b; Potter & Hepburn, 2005; Sacks, 1984a; Sacks et al., 1974; Schegloff, 1996, 2007a). By 'naturally occurring,' then, we mean data – whether recordings of interactions or collections of text-based materials – that pass what Potter (2002, p. 541) calls the "dead social scientist test," referring to the question of whether the data would "be the same, or be there at all, if the researcher got run over on the way to work." This can include recordings and materials produced or gathered by researchers themselves, but "where the researcher's active role is minimized" (Potter, 2002, p. 539), as well as what Jones and Raymond (2012, p. 112) call "opportunistic third party" data – referring to materials produced for non-research purposes, with no involvement on the part of researchers in the process, before subsequently becoming available for use by researchers. And 'interactional' may include all these types, since one can make the case that all forms of language use are "recipient designed" (Sacks et al., 1974, p. 727), from newspaper headlines to a social media post to a novel or film script.

Naturally occurring recorded interactional data thus contrast with these other data sources in being designed to capture participants' actual interactional conduct at its point of production, and at a level of detail that real-time observers would not be able to accurately record – but that, as decades of CA research has demonstrated, participants may be finely attuned to. This contrasts with the use of data that are invented, idealized, (experimentally) manipulated, or produced in the first instance for the purpose of research, and/ or rely on post hoc reports, thereby losing the emergent and/or contingent character of the conduct at hand. Indeed, as Dingemanse et al. (2023, p. 1) point out, "[t]hat social interaction matters is recognized by any experimentalist who seeks to exclude its influence by studying individuals in isolation."

Since occasions of interaction are the primary ecological niche for social actions, cultures, and institutions produced through human conduct (Schegloff, 2006a), analysts can rely on the forms of organization participants use to conduct occasions, including what has been called, following Sacks et al. (1974, pp. 728–729) a "next turn proof procedure." That is, any next action will display a participant's analysis of what has been done by the prior actor, and will thereby provide professional analysts with a powerful source of evidence for claims about the meaning or import of that prior action, grounded in the perspectives of the participants themselves (Sacks et al., 1974). It thereby provides for the use of participants' own interactionally displayed orientations as evidence for claims about the interactional workings of categories, rather than relying on analysts' assessments of which category/ies are in play at any given moment – a matter to which we return in Section 3.3 (also see our discussion of categories as *participants'* versus *analysts'* resources in Chapter 1: An Introduction to Categories in Social Interaction and Chapter 2: Approaching Membership Categorization).

The use of naturally occurring data offers the further benefit, in relation to category-focused research in particular, of providing for the examination of fine-grained details of how categories are used, managed, resisted, etc., by participants 'in the wild,' rather than (as is virtually unavoidably the case for other data sources) having participants 'primed' as to the relevance of the particular categories the researcher has used as a basis for recruiting them to participate in the research (Potter & Hepburn, 2005; Whitehead & Baldry, 2018). A striking illustration of the types of insights that might be gleaned from this – insights that may never be recognized as 'missing' in the absence of analysis based on naturally occurring data – can be found in the findings of two studies (Reynolds & Wetherell, 2003; Stokoe, 2003) published in successive issues of *Feminism & Psychology*. Stokoe's (2003) analysis, based on recordings of naturally occurring talk between disputing neighbours, showed how participants used the category 'single woman' as a basis for complaints about the conduct of those with whom they were in dispute, and as defences against complaints about their own conduct. In contrast, Reynolds and Wetherell's (2003) analysis of interview talk in which participants recruited on the basis of their membership in this category were questioned directly about its meanings for them made no mention of the types of phenomena described by Stokoe (2003). The everyday situated uses of this category were thus readily observable in Stokoe's (2003) naturally occurring data but evidently elided or overlooked as 'seen but unnoticed' aspects of experience in the reports elicited from the same category of persons in Reynolds and Wetherell's (2003) interview data.

Interview materials can also be studied as interactions in their own right – as *topic* rather than *resource* (e.g., Rapley, 2001; Roulston, 2019; Seale, 1998; Speer, 2002a), and as sites for "displaying the cultural knowledge that can be used to account for oneself" as a category member (Baker, 1997, p. 167). Furthermore, interactions in laboratory or experimental contexts can be examined for how the constraints introduced by experimental protocols are consequential for the interactional conduct of researchers/experimenters and research participants (Gashaj et al., forthcoming; Gibson, 2019; Hollander & Turowetz, 2023; Schegloff, 1991; Wooffitt, 2007); recordings of standardized survey interviews can be analysed to document how participants interactionally produce standardization in asking and answering questions, and/or manage troubles associated with the demands of standardization (e.g., Maynard & Schaeffer, 2006; Suchman & Jordan, 1990) – including categorization (e.g., Wilkinson, 2011a); research interviews and focus groups can be treated as naturally occurring sources of how participants collaboratively accomplish and interact in such settings (e.g., Puchta & Potter, 2004; Roulston, 2019) – and any or all of these can be examined for how participants use, manage, resist, etc., social categories apart from those associated with the research setting (e.g., Baker, 2004; Whitehead & Baldry, 2018; Widdicombe, 2015). However, as Potter (2002, p. 539) notes, "treating method as topic is not the same as using it to find something out." There is, for example, "a world of difference between the material gathered in a questionnaire from the record of an everyday phone conversation; what is gained by studying a video of a family therapy session is very different from the retrospective accounts of participants" (Potter, 2002, p. 541). This is because the "motive force" (Schegloff, 1997a, p. 99) that people have when providing accounts as interview participants is empirically different from the occasioned use of categories in building actions in settings where their stake is quite different (also see, e.g., Potter & Hepburn, 2005; Stokoe, 2010a).[1] Similarly, Jerolmack and Khan (2014, p. 179) describe "the error of inferring situated behavior from verbal accounts" generated in interviews and surveys,

---

1 For an interview-based study of participants' orientations to participating in interviews, see Bredal et al. (2024).

which they call "the attitudinal fallacy." Moreover, while Maynard (2014, pp. 216–217) appreciates Jerolmack and Khan's call for greater attention to interaction in concrete situations, he also emphasizes that approaches to addressing this fallacy should be grounded in analyses that attend to the details of "in situ forms of social organization through which actual participants collaboratively produce social actions and social life." Indeed, if our aim is to understand the range of situated ways in which people use and contend with categories during the course of their everyday lives, we should work to get as direct and detailed access as possible to the full range of settings and situations in which they do so.

While the chapters that follow are replete with further demonstrations of the advantages of working with naturally occurring recorded interactional data from a wide range of settings, Extract 3.1[2] provides an initial illustration.[3] This extract shows part of a segment of a US National Public Radio comedy quiz show, *Wait Wait . . . Don't Tell Me*, from March 2022. The stretch shown here features the show's regular host, Peter Sagal (PS) and co-host Bill Kurtis (BK), along with three featured guest participants, Alzo Slade (AS), Negin Farsad (NF), and Paula Poundstone (PP) – all of whom are, as is typical for guest participants on the show, professional comedians and/or comedy writers. This specific segment of the show is typically built around a celebrity guest participant, who is first interviewed and then participates in a quiz game with a theme selected as a comedic spin on some characteristic or topic for which the celebrity guest is well known. The celebrity guest in this case is Elana Meyers Taylor (EMT), who Sagal has earlier introduced as "the most decorated American Olympic bobsledder ever," thereby treating this set of categories as bases for her membership in the 'celebrity guest' category (cf. Roth, 1998).

The transcribed portion of the segment shown next begins as Sagal initiates a transition from the interview portion of the segment, which has taken place over the preceding six minutes or so, to the game portion, which he introduces in collaboration with Kurtis (lines 01–09 and 11–16).

Extract 3.1: NPR, *Wait Wait. . . Don't Tell Me*, 12.3.22

```
01  PS:   Well, Ela:na, we are de↑lighted to talk to you, we
02        have more questions but we have business to do, we
03        have a competition of our own, (.) Bill, (0.2) what
```

---

2 In addition to returning to this extract in illustrating our discussions in the sections that follow in the current chapter, we further develop our analysis of it in Chapter 9: Managing Knowledge, Experience, and Entitlement.

3 Further empirical illustrations of these considerations, and others throughout this chapter, are also available in Whitehead et al. (2024), which provides a set of methodological discussions that partially overlap with those in this chapter.

```
04              is the na:me of the ga:me?
05      BK:     pt=.hh "You've Medalled all Right in:: (0.2) Death
06              Metal:."
07      PS:     So, (.) we were ↑think↓ing, (.) Olympic medals, as
08              you well know, are famously quite heavy, so we
09              thought we'd ask you about (0.5) heavy metal.
10      EMT:    O(h)h(h) boy! heh [heh!
11      PS:                       [>Answer two out of three questions
12              about< heavy metal bands and you'll win >our prize
13              for one of our listeners, the voice of anyone they
14              might choose for their voicemail.< .hh Bill who:: is
15              Elana Meyers playing for?
16      BK:     Jason Ha:ll of Austin Texas.
17      PS:     All::: righty then.
18      AS:     I feel like this ain't right, Peter.
19      PS:     Why- why is it not ri[ght?
20      AS:                          [This ain't right. ih- ((chuckle))
21              d'y- I mean, .hh £it's enough that the: Black woman is
22              already in[: bobsledding, now you gonna ask her£
23      EMT:              [°hhh huh huh huh°
24      AS:     t[uh- tuh b(h)e- £tuh be knowledgeable about death=
25      EMT:     [huh huh huh .hh
26      AS:     =metal?£ [°hih   hih°  hih    hih    hih    hih
27      PP:              ['Ts- I- I think it's- she's a shill.
28      AS:     [ hih hih hih hih .hhh
29      PP:     [I think it's gonna turn out=
30              =[she knows a:ll:: abo[ut death metal.
31      NF:      [Yea:h:              [(she doe[s) ↑that is her thing ( ).
32      EMT:     [      uh  [ huh huh huh .hhh
33      PS:                            [A(h)l(h)l r(h)ig(h)ht.
34      PS:     [.hh All right. We- we're gonna find out.
35      EMT:    [I don't know ab- bout that. (But) let's go.
36              (0.2)
37      PS:     He:re (.) is your first question.
```

Notably, following the first part of Sagal's description of the game, Meyers Taylor registers this news using an exclamation that conveys a lack of confidence in her prospects of success (line 10). Slade may be oriented to this as he intervenes (cf. Lerner, 2019) at just the point where the game was projected to start by directing a negative moral assessment of the game at Sagal (line 18) and then repeating it (line 20) after Sagal's questioning response (line 19). Slade then jokingly remarks on the unfairness of expecting a "Black woman" to know about "heavy metal" (line 09) and/or "death metal" (line 24) – thereby invoking what he treats as common-sense knowledge that being a bobsledder is an unusual vocation for someone of these race, gender, and stage of life[4] categories (lines 21–22), and that

---

4 Note how the category "woman," although primarily and explicitly categorizing Meyers Taylor in terms of gender, also tacitly places her in the stage of life category, 'adult.'

being knowledgeable about heavy and/or death metal music would be even more unexpected for a member of these categories (lines 22, 24, and 26). He thus draws these two contrasts to mobilize what he treats as recognizable incongruities between category memberships (race, gender, and stage of life) and activities (bobsledding) and knowledge (of heavy/death metal music) respectively as resources for producing humour – while evidently also orienting to his co-membership with Meyers Taylor in the racial category "Black" as a basis for his entitlement to raise this joking objection (also see, e.g., Cheeks & Whitehead, 2024; Okazawa, 2021; Scarpetta & Spagnolli, 2009; Whitehead, 2013b, 2018).

This case thus shows how categories may be mobilized in the service of a participant's setting-specific agenda; that is, as a 'special' intervention into an activity in which Slade would not ordinarily be expected to participate, in the service of producing humour, in a setting in which doing so is the primary activity expected of participants – as opposed to being researcher-prompted or introduced in pursuit of a particular research agenda. Moreover, it demonstrates how the next turn proof procedure can be used to ground claims about the common-sense categorial knowledge mobilized in producing the action at hand – in this case, joking. For example, Meyers Taylor's laughter (lines 22 and 24), beginning just after Slade's mention of her race and gender categories, and well before Slade has completed the joke, displays her recognition of the common-sense knowledge he is invoking and her appreciation for the joke-in-progress. Also note how the onset of Slade's use of 'smile voice'– shown by the pound sign on line 20 – at just the point at which he launches the joke facilitates Meyers Taylor's recognition of his utterance *as* a joke-in-progress. Similarly, Poundstone and Farsad's follow-up jokes (lines 25, 27, and 29) display their recognition of the categorial incongruities Slade has invoked even as they jokingly propose its inaccuracy in this particular case – actions that may also reflect their own (non-Black) race category memberships and associated lack of entitlement to align with the racial stereotypes Slade is jokingly deploying (also see Whitehead, 2018). In addition, the level of detail in transcription and observations on the exchange permitted by repeated listening to the recording enables analyses of features such as the aforementioned precise timing of Meyers Taylor's laughter and use of smile voice by Slade, among others (also see Chapter 8: Managing Troubles in Speaking, Hearing and Understanding for discussion of the potential significance of disfluencies such as those evident in Slade's and Poundstone's launching of their jokes in lines 20 and 25, respectively).

There are nonetheless good reasons for avoiding a dogmatic interpretation of, and insistence on, naturally occurring recorded interactional data sources. As we noted in Chapter 2: Approaching Membership Categorization, Sacks developed his foundational work on membership categorization in part on the basis of the start of a story ("The baby cried; the mommy picked it up") published in a book entitled *Children Tell Stories* – that is, by reference to a textual, non-interactional data source – though 'naturally occurring' in the sense of it being 'found data,' rather than generated or 'got up' for the purposes of research (also see, e.g., Mair & Sharrock, 2021; Schegloff, 2007b). As discussed in Chapter 1: An Introduction to Categories in Social Interaction, conversation analytic and membership categorization researchers have regularly worked with written documents and other text-based interactions, including news media, and this has become commonplace with the proliferation of online forums and social media providing access to naturally occurring discussions of a virtually limitless range of topics and associated categorial phenomena (see reviews by, e.g., Giles, 2016; Housley et al., 2017b; Meredith, 2020; Paulus et al., 2016). Even scripted fictional recorded interactions "can be taken seriously as objects of conversation analysis" (McHoul, 1987, p. 83), by virtue of offering windows into the tacit interactional (including categorial) knowledge of the writers and actors who produced them (also see, e.g., Cheeks & Whitehead, 2024; Chepinchikj, 2022; Okazawa, 2021, 2022; Stokoe, 2008b).

One issue that has been raised in relation to the use of recording devices is what Labov (1972, p. 97) calls the "observer's paradox," referring to the possibility that the presence of a recording device prevents researchers from capturing "how people speak when they are not being observed." As van Dijk (1987, p. 119; emphasis added) argues, "researchers (with recorders!) usually have no *unobtrusive* access to natural communicative events, such as family conversations, talk during parties, or to other dialogues in a large variety of interpersonal situations." The impact of a recording device on behaviour is probably one of the questions most commonly asked of conversation analysts, and the presence of a recording device is seen by some as presenting a particular issue for researchers interested in categories, since participants may especially avoid saying and doing category-related things to avoid the associated troubles of '-isms' (Whitehead & Stokoe, 2015). However, the issue is not clear-cut, since some material collected and analysed by conversation analysts is recorded as part of the endogenous organization of the setting rather than for research purposes, such as police interviews, institutional telephone encounters, CCTV, media broadcasts, YouTube uploads, and so on (see, e.g., Jones & Raymond, 2012; Whitehead et al., 2018). Moreover, for better or worse, recording has become a ubiquitous and expected part of public life (Speer & Stokoe, 2014). Whether research participants who have consented to being recorded alter what they do, consistently throughout an encounter, is an empirical question. Numerous studies (e.g., Gordon, 2013; Jones & Raymond, 2012; Speer & Hutchby, 2003; Speer & Stokoe, 2014; Stokoe, 2009b; Tietbohl & White, 2022; Tuncer, 2016) have shown that the moments at which participants orient to a recording device (in occasions recorded for research and those recorded by third-parties) are circumscribed and re-currently observable; that rather than curtailing efforts to examine when and how participants may be contending with categorial matters, orientations to recording devices can instead offer rich evidence of such phenomena; that the great majority of participants' references to recording devices are retrospective reflections rather than prospective warnings about projected conduct or other apparent alterations made by reference to the presence of a recording device; and that participants appear to take no notice of the device much of the time, and instead simply get on with their interactional 'business' as if it were not present.

More complex questions may be raised with respect to the relationship between recordings of naturally occurring encounters and ethnographic fieldnotes about such encounters – that is, materials *produced* rather than collected by a researcher – along with questions concerning the relationship between ethnography and ethnomethodology. In a recent discussion of this relationship, Rawls and Lynch (2024, p. 2; emphasis in original) explain that, despite the same 'ethno' prefix, 'ethnography' and 'ethnomethodology' refer to quite different things: conventional ethnography comprises a set of research methods (e.g., immersive field studies with informants, fieldnotes, interviews, participant observation), while ethnomethodology "is a name for the *phenomenon* the research investigates, rather than the method of investigation" (also see, e.g., Jimerson & Oware, 2006; Meier zu Verl & Meyer, 2024; Pollner & Emerson, 2007; Shapiro, 1994; Wieder, 1999). While Rawls and Lynch (2024, pp. 117–118) observe that conversation analysts have "expressed ambivalence about ethnography," it is noteworthy that it is not unusual for prominent conversation analysts to use fieldnotes or vignettes as illustrations and/or additional cases of interactional phenomena that they systematically examine using recorded interactional data (e.g., Jefferson, 2004b; Pomerantz, 1980; Sacks, 1992; Schegloff, 2001, 2003, 2005c) – as we do, for example, in Chapter 4: Forming and Making Sense of Actions. Moreover, conversation analytic and membership categorization principles have been employed in both studies examining categorial phenomena by combining fieldnotes and/or other ethnographic materials with recordings (e.g., Duneier & Molotch, 1999; Jones et al., 2023), and in thoroughly fieldnote-based studies (e.g., Carlin, 2003; Drury & Stokoe, 2022). Beyond our brief treatment of these matters, numerous further discussions of the relationship between conversation analytic and ethnographic methods and data are available (see, e.g., DeLand, 2021; Kitzinger, 2008; Maynard, 2003, 2014; Moerman, 1988; Schegloff, 1988c; Weinberg et al., 2006), and surely much more remains to be written about these issues. However, it is fair to say that, for conversation analysts, recorded data are the gold standard, and thus are privileged over fieldnotes and other real-time observations in cases where there appear to be discrepancies between what they indicate.

3.2 Addressing the 'capturability issue'

The foundational focus in conversation analytic research on naturally occurring data sources has given rise to suggestions that researcher-generated sources such as surveys, interviews, and focus groups are more reliable ways of generating data on particular category systems in which the researcher might be interested, since we cannot be sure that specific focal categories will 'come up' in any given naturally occurring interaction (Stokoe & Edwards, 2007). This concern has been raised in particular by researchers committed to studying the collections of categories most commonly (as we noted in Chapter 1: An Introduction to Categories in Social Interaction) used as bases for the structuring of societies, and thereby associated with phenomena relating to power, oppression, exclusion, prejudice, and the like – which, as we noted in Chapter 2: Approaching Membership Categorization, are typically what Sacks (1972a, p. 33) called "Pn-adequate" collections. For example, in his influential study of communicative features of racism, van Dijk (1987, p. 119), argues that researchers cannot

> simply go into the field and observe how, when, where, and with whom people talk with others about ethnic groups. We would need hundreds of researchers and thousands of situations to record enough relevant data, simply because people talk about so many other topics as well. . . . Finding data, in such a case, would amount to a search for the proverbial needle in the haystack.

One striking feature of van Dijk's formulation of this argument is its treatment of talk *about* ethnic categories (and, by extension, other collections of categories) as the taken-for-granted proper focus of research on categories in talk-in-interaction – and the attendant implication that direct discussion of categories serves as the predominant mechanism for their interactional reproduction.[5] In contrast, CA research reveals the range of ways in which categories come to be used and reproduced during the course of the everyday actions and activities in which participants are engaged – including (as we discussed in Chapter 1: An Introduction to Categories in Social Interaction) in many cases as a 'by-product' of some other 'main business' at hand. That is, rather than the reproduction of categories being a primary goal pursued by participants and/or a direct *topic* of their talk, in many cases categories are reproduced by virtue of the common-sense knowledge and other features associated with them serving as a systematically available set of *resources* participants can

---

5 And that the categories under investigation will be ones that the researcher already knows, rather than (for example) setting-based categories or one of the ad hoc or novel categories, as discussed in the Prologue: Why Categories Matter and in Chapter 1: An Introduction to Categories in Social Interaction.

use in the service of the interactional projects they are pursuing at particular moments (also see, e.g., Raymond, 2019b; Schegloff, 1992b; Stokoe, 2009a; Whitehead & Lerner, 2009; Wilkinson & Kitzinger, 2003). As such, we do not necessarily need to find sustained periods of ideologically loaded discussion of categories of interest in order to discover aspects of their interactional reproduction, with even the briefest orientations to them by participants being potentially valuable additions to our analytic collections (also see Section 3.5).

Nonetheless, some conversation analytic researchers note similar concerns about reliably capturing instances of participants' orientations to particular categories of interest in naturally occurring interactional data. For example, in describing a CA approach to studying uses of relationship categories in interactions, Pomerantz and Mandelbaum (2005, p. 154) argue, "Because we cannot know in advance when a person will explicitly invoke a relationship category, there is no way to plan data collection of them," and that collections generated in this way "would not be instances of the same interactional phenomenon." In addressing this challenge, Stokoe (e.g., 2009a, 2010a) showed, over a range of studies and settings, that, in fact, it is entirely possible to identify the same occasioned use of similar categories in similar sequential environments doing similar actions. Other scholars wishing to examine collections of categories of conventional social science interest have made use of institutional interactional data sources in which such MCDs are omni-relevant in the setting at hand, thereby virtually ensuring the prevalence in the interactions of participants' management of matters relating to the focal MCD of interest. For example, Speer and Parsons (2006) studied psychiatric assessments of transgender patients in a gender identity clinic, where gender is reliably at stake for participants; Whitehead (2009) examined 'race training' workshops, occasions for which race is central; and Shrikant (2018, 2021) analysed meetings of an Asian American Chamber of Commerce, a setting constituted in part by participants' membership in ethnic and racial categories.

Indeed, there is ample and growing evidence that this type of approach to selection of data sources is far from being the only sure way to capture naturally occurring interactions involving categories of historical and contemporary interest to social scientists. As we noted in Chapter 1: An Introduction to Categories in Social Interaction, a substantial and growing body of conversation analytic research has examined how categories from these MCDs *do* get deployed in interactionally systematic ways in naturally occurring interactions, and thus how conversation analytic research can and does address 'big questions' in relation to them. This research has thus built on Sacks's (1984b, 1986, 1992; cf. Sacks, 1979) early observations[6] on the interactional

---

6 Also see Rawls et al. (2020) and Whitehead (2021) for further discussions of Sacks's early contributions in this regard.

organization of race and racism, demonstrating the power of conversation analytic methods and resources for rigorously examining the interactional mechanisms underpinning the everyday reproduction of a range of category systems associated with exclusion, inequality, and oppression. Contrary to the "needle in the haystack" argument advanced by van Dijk (1987) and others, the undoubted importance of these category systems in structuring everyday life in many societies should lead us to expect nothing less than their recurrent relevance in everyday conversational interactions. That is, we can expect them to regularly arise as observable features of interactions – and thereby become available for examination by *researchers* committed to studying them – precisely because they are potentially pervasive concerns for *participants* in interactions (a matter to which we return in the following section).

The foregoing considerations can be appreciated by reference to Extract 3.1 where, as we have noted, race and gender categories are used to interject, in the service of producing humour, into an activity for which other, setting-based categories (e.g., Olympic bobsledder and medallist) have been established as relevant. In producing humour that trades on common-sense knowledge associated in particular with her race category in relation to her profession and the activity she is now being prompted to engage in, Slade is evidently setting out in the first place to make a joke, but he does this in a way that reproduces race as a by-product of his action. Thus, rather than being an end in itself, the reproduction of this type of common-sense knowledge is a systematic possibility by virtue of it being a resource for pursuing other interactional ends, including in moments where it is not otherwise topicalized or treated as relevant immediately prior to being mobilized in this way.

An alternative approach to addressing the capturability issue is to examine category-related processes and practices that appear to be common across a wider range of MCDs than those typically examined by social scientists. As such, and consistent with Sacks's (1984a, p. 22) suggestion that we can examine interactions involving "whomsoever, wheresoever, and we get much the same things," and with our introduction to these matters in Chapter 1: An Introduction to Categories in Social Interaction, there is potentially much to be learned about the interactional organization of categories in relation to the generic organizations of practice for interaction, independently of the additional 'layers' that may constitute unique features of particular MCDs or categories, on particular occasions, in particular moments in history.

Moreover, as our previous discussions and examples in Chapter 1: An Introduction to Categories in Social Interaction and Chapter 2: Approaching Membership Categorization suggest, and as the chapters that follow further demonstrate, adequately addressing matters relating to the categories on which social scientists have conventionally focused may require also attending to intersections between these categories and other (e.g., setting-based) categories to which participants may be oriented. As such, focusing exclusively on particular categories that the researcher is committed to studying, to the exclusion of others to which the participants may be oriented, may result in analyses that primarily reflect the concerns and agendas of the analyst rather than those of the participants – a possibility we address in more detail in the following section. This can also be seen in relation to Extract 3.1, where Slade's use of a race category in making a joke is also tied to his membership in the setting-based 'comedian/comedy show guest participant' category. That is, although joking is something that participants may potentially do at virtually any time in any interactional setting, Slade's membership in this setting-based category provides him with a particularly systematic warrant or even obligation for engaging in this kind of action – and it is thus in part by reference to this category that his action is heard by recipients as a joking complaint rather than simply a complaint (also see Chapter 4: Forming and Making Sense of Actions). That it is a race category in particular that he uses as a resource for doing so is surely noteworthy – illustrating, for example, how Slade can take for granted the intelligibility of the common-sense knowledge he invokes by virtue of the significance of race in the society at large – but his use of it cannot be fully appreciated without also recognizing how it arises from his membership in an ostensibly more mundane setting-based category.

3.3   Empirically grounding participants' orientations to categories

As we discussed in Chapter 1: An Introduction to Categories in Social Interaction, a foundational principle of conversation analysis – and perhaps the most misunderstood and caricatured – is that of empirically grounding analytic claims about what is happening in interactions in evidence of the participants' interactionally displayed orientations. This is reflected in Schegloff and Sacks's (1973, p. 299) observation that "a pervasively relevant issue (for participants) about utterances in conversation is 'why that now'" – with this question thus being recognized as a centrally important one for conversation analysts precisely by virtue of being one that interactional participants pervasively (although largely tacitly) attend to (Schegloff, 1998c). The basis for this analytic privileging of participants' orientations is, as Schegloff (1997c, p. 166) puts it,

> because it is the orientations, meanings, interpretations, understandings, etc. of the *participants* in some sociocultural event on which the course of the event is predicated . . . it is *those* characterizations which are privileged in the *constitution of socio-interactional reality*, and therefore have a prima facie claim to being privileged in efforts to *understand* it (emphasis in original).

And, as noted previously, the next turn proof procedure provides a powerful evidentiary resource for checking potential analytic claims against participants' own displayed analyses of the import of a prior action.

While this principle is a crucial feature of the distinctiveness of conversation analytic research as a general matter, it has a particular import in relation to research on categorial phenomena, given the widespread use of categories as analysts' resources. In observing sociology's unexamined use of participant categories – thereby raising a critique that could easily be extended to much social science research – Sacks (1966, pp. 22–23) notes that

> Sociologists frequently treat some categorization which members have done . . . as providing them with materials which are descriptive, that is that may then be used, as they stand, for further sociological investigation. Alternatively, sociologists themselves frequently use members' categorization devices to categorize members as one step in doing sociological inquiries, for example, they decide to compare 'males' and 'females' for some purpose, or contrast 'young people' and 'old people' with respect to some dependent variable. In both cases – whether they use an already categorized population or engage in some categorization themselves – the presumptive warrant for this use is, or would seem to be, that demonstrable correctness of the categorization may be properly established by some such procedure as looking to see whether the person(s) so categorized was properly so categorized.

What makes such uses of members' categories by social scientists potentially problematic is that, as Sacks (1972a) crucially observed (and as noted in Chapter 2: Approaching Membership Categorization), any person can be 'accurately' characterized in terms of their membership in categories from multiple MCDs. As Schegloff (1997c, p. 166; emphasis in original) notes, "At a time when there appears to be deep scepticism about the possibility of establishing *anything* as true, we have here an embarrassment of truths." The problem, then, is how to establish which of the multiple possible ways any given participant could be categorized are not just *true*, but *relevantly* so, such that they can be warrantably deployed in analysing of some piece of interactional conduct of interest (Schegloff, 1997c). The recognition of this problem is also evident beyond conversation analytic discussions of it. For example, in discussing issues for the evolution of theory and methods for a field of intersectionality studies, Cho et al. (2013, p. 787) include "the eponymous 'et cetera' problem – that is, the number of categories and kinds of subjects (e.g., privileged or subordinate?) stipulated or implied by an intersectional approach."

The approach to addressing this conundrum taken by and large across various conventional social scientific approaches has been to adopt a standard of what Schegloff (1997c, p. 166) calls "explanatory adequacy," referring to the assertion that "that way is best which most reliably yields 'findings' – repeatable, reliable, objective, significant (for some statistically significant) observations about the world." This standard thereby privileges the theoretical methodological, etc., agendas or concerns identified by the analyst over those of the participants who produced the conduct being analysed, hence running the risk of producing or reinforcing stereotypic accounts that render members' doings in ways that obscure the situated orientations and contingencies that may feature in their conduct (or in the patterns it exemplifies), or that overlook and thus obscure some other category that may be relevant for an outcome, but which has not been considered by the analyst (cf. Galanter, 1974; Jefferson, 2004b). It thus concerns the danger of what Hauser (2016, p. 40) calls "culturalism," which

> involves the presumption that there exists a machinery that specifies once and for all what a category means, what its predicates are, as well as what collection it belongs to. It also entails analytic assertions of category understandings that are not adequately grounded in data. Critics argue that too often in MCA studies category understandings and inferences are posited arbitrarily by the analyst, based on nothing more than his/her own presumptions rather than the displayed orientations of participants.[7]

In short, adopting the standard of explanatory adequacy is more likely to stand in the way of possibly novel discoveries than to facilitate them.

In advocating for the privileging of participants' orientations rather than adopting the standard of explanatory adequacy, however, Schegloff (e.g., 1987a, 1991, 1992a, 1992c) identifies two analytic challenges, relating to the types of empirical evidence required in order to adequately ground claims by reference to participants' orientations. The first of these is what Schegloff (1992c, p. 108) calls "the problem of relevance," referring to the need for empirical evidence that a category was *relevant to the participants* at any given moment in an interaction as a way of warranting any claim in relation to that category. The second challenge concerns the establishment of the "procedural consequentiality" (Schegloff, 1992c, p. 110) of a category for *specific features of conduct* during the course of the moment(s) of the interaction on which the analysis is focusing. That is, even if a category can be shown to be relevant

---

7 These pitfalls have been further described in a range of related ways, including in terms of analysts' use of common-sense categorial knowledge as a *resource for analysis* rather than a *topic of analysis* (Zimmerman & Pollner, 1970, p. 81; cf. Järviluoma et al., 2003), or as a *presupposition* of analysis rather than an *outcome* thereof (Schegloff, 1997c, p. 170); or as reproducing categorial 'facts' under the guise of studying them (Hammersley, 2001; Jefferson, 2004b); or as implementing "theoretical imperialism" (Schegloff, 1997c, p. 167).

to the participants during some stretch of interaction, this does not imply that it is necessarily consequential for, or observably shaping, every possible detail of the participants' talk, and thus there remains a need to empirically demonstrate whether or how it matters for any particular detail of interest. Importantly, while this can include bringing ethnographic knowledge to bear on the analysis of the interaction, its use should also be grounded in the participants' conduct and orientations, rather than being "independently invoked by the analyst on extrinsic ethnographic grounds" (Schegloff, 1992a, p. 197; cf. DeLand, 2021; Maynard, 2003; Rawls & Lynch, 2024; Whitehead, 2020).

The issues of relevance and procedural consequentiality place a stringent evidentiary burden on analysts, calling for the development not just of apparently compelling (or 'adequate') explanations in terms of some category or categories but of analyses that point to the fine-grained details of participants' own orientations on the particular occasions under examination. As such, rather than us as analysts relying on our own categorizations of the participants as analytic resources, our analysis of Extract 3.1 has focused on how Slade uses race and gender as interactional resources, how his co-participants recognize and appreciate how he has done so, and how the participants systematically orient to their incumbency in setting-based categories throughout the exchange. Moreover, throughout these analyses, we have made claims with specific reference to the empirical details that serve as evidence for them – including by pointing to line numbers in a transcript, using brief quotes, or identifying the features of participants' conduct that serve as evidence for the claims – as well as specifying precisely how the pointed-to features serve as evidence for the claims being made. This principle is captured in the Schegloff's (2007a, p. 252) illuminating discussion of the distinction between identifying and/or naming features of an interaction versus analysing them:

> The single most troublesome misunderstanding harbored by those just exposed to conversation analysis, or still coming to terms with it, is that the work of analysis is done when a bit of data is recognized as belonging to some category, and the category term is applied to the data fragment. But that is a taxonomic act, not an analytic one. It locates one possible feature of the event being examined, but not how that event was achieved in its particularity – in those words or physical actions, by that participant, at that point in the interaction, understood in that way by co-participants, produced by some specifiable practices of conduct. The formal features do not add up to an analysis until they are filled out by the particulars that constituted that achieved event and relate it to what has come before and what interpretive shadow is cast on what is to follow.

For example, rather than simply asserting that Slade was using race to make a joke while leaving readers to see for themselves that and how he did so, we spelled out the details and timing of how he composed and delivered the joke, Meyers Taylor's appreciation of it as such through her precisely timed laughter, and Poundstone and Farsad's treatment and continuation of the activity of joking through their responsive and follow-up jokes. In sum, while analysts' intuitions or impressions as to the relevance of a category in some stretch of interaction may thus be a productive starting point, developing them into a robust analysis calls for case-by-case explications of precisely how analysing participants' selections of actions, their design features, and their placement serve as evidence for their orientations to and uses of particular categories, rather than merely identifying them and/or asserting their import by fiat (also see our discussions of these matters in later chapters, especially Chapter 4: Forming and Making Sense of Actions).

Not surprisingly, given that it unsettles the largely taken-for-granted use of categories as analysts' resources across a range of other social scientific approaches, Schegloff's advocacy for privileging participants' orientations over explanatory adequacy has been a source of some contention. Critics have suggested, for example, that the principles Schegloff describes constitute an "unacceptably narrow" sense of participant orientation (Wetherell, 1998, p. 402) and render " 'translocal' phenomena" difficult to incorporate analytically (Blommaert, 2001, p. 13). Relatedly, these principles have also been interpreted as an injunction to turn analytic attention away from categories of conventional social scientific interest (race, gender, etc.), and the matters of power, oppression, etc., associated with them, and instead focus exclusively on "overly myopic technicalities" (Korobov, 2001, p. 10).[8]

Contrary to such suggestions, the data we examine in this chapter and throughout the book, along with a wealth of conversation analytic studies that have taken these principles seriously, show that people talk *on the basis that* there is a world outside the interaction in which they are engaged (cf. Stokoe, 2012b) – one populated by categories of people with assumed known-in-common characteristics and ways of acting that provide for the kinds of inferences being made by (or at least made available to) other participants. However, in making such inferences – while making it evident to their recipients, and thus to overhearing analysts, that and how they are doing so – participants bring elements of this outside world into the interaction, making them part and parcel of how the interaction is constituted by and for each other, rather than being elements of an 'external' context that analysts must introduce to make sense of the interaction (cf.

---

8 For further specifications of these and other critiques, see, for example, Billig (1999a, 1999b); Blommaert (2005); Bucholtz (2003); Cameron (2008); Ehrlich (2002); Enfield (2007); Parker (2013); Whelan (2012); and Wowk (2007). For direct responses to some of these critiques, see Schegloff (1998c, 1999a, 1999b, 2009); Kitzinger (2000, 2008); and Speer (1999, 2012).

Schegloff, 1992a; Whitehead, 2020). Moreover, as noted in the previous section, the range of categories to which participants *may* be oriented, and with which they *may* be contending in observable ways, includes the full range of categories recognized by social scientists as central loci of social order and power. As such, the concerns of participants *may* converge in particular cases with the longstanding commitments of social scientists, enabling analysts to pursue their preferred agendas in this regard precisely by engaging with those of the participants – and, in so doing, potentially learning something new about how people use categories in everyday life.

Once again, these points are readily illustrated by Extract 3.1: as we have noted, it is a participant, Slade, who explicitly introduces gender and race[9] analyses of the unfolding interaction, and other participants who take this up in various ways, making this a case in which analysts' engagement with these categories is entirely commensurate with the displayed orientations of the participants. Furthermore, the incongruities between Meyers Taylor's race and gender categories, activities, and knowledge that Slade mobilizes in his joke are built on presumed shared knowledge of a 'world out there' in which Black women (or Black people more generally) do not typically pursue careers as bobsledders, and are not presumed to be knowledgeable about heavy metal music – and the other participants' uptake of the joke ratify these as features of a world beyond the interaction. The participants thus rely on these features of the ostensibly external world as resources for composing this action at just this moment in the interaction, and in doing so ratify and (re)produce them as known-in-common features of the world.

3.4   Analysing tacit and/or ambiguous cases

A further set of critiques of the principle of grounding analyses of categorial phenomena in participants' orientations entails claims that such an approach may not adequately account for phenomena such as the invisible workings of power, the unsaid or what is not oriented to (e.g., Billig, 1999b; Frith, 1998; Parker, 2005; Rawls & Duck, 2020; Wetherell, 1998); the pervasive relevance of MCDs of conventional interest to social scientists (e.g., Blommaert, 2001; Ehrlich, 2002; Sciubba et al., 2020; Weatherall, 2000); or the fact that very few features of (English) language explicitly index gender (e.g., Ochs, 1992). In other words, the principles Schegloff advances are claimed to be unable to deal with things that the

---

9 Although we can note that Sagal and/or his writing team may have tacitly done so by selecting a white-associated genre of music as the basis for the game Meyers Taylor is to play. Also see our discussion of tacit and/or ambiguous cases in Section 3.4.

analyst 'knows' – or assumes – are relevant but that participants do not helpfully make explicit at the 'interactional surface' (cf. Edwards, 2006). What, then, can we say about the workings of unarticulated, implied, or possible meanings in talk, or cases where the meaning is treated as shared but not unpacked, resisted, queried, or otherwise made explicit?

In many cases these critiques misconstrue the challenges of relevance and procedural consequentiality as amounting to a requirement that analysts be barred from addressing particular categories or MCDs unless the participants have explicitly mentioned them. In direct contrast to this mis-construal, Schegloff (2007d, p. 474; emphasis in original) contends that the analytic aim should be to describe "practice[s] of talking that arguably" make "some categorization device *possibly* relevant in the scene *whether it is actually articulated or not.*" For example, a number of CA studies (e.g., Baker et al., 2005; Flinkfeldt et al., 2022; Kitzinger & Mandelbaum, 2013; Nguyen, 2011; Rafaely & Whitehead, 2020; Stommel et al., 2022; Wilkinson, 2011a, 2011b) have shown how features of "recipient design" – that is, "the multitude of respects in which the talk by a party in a conversation is constructed or designed in ways which display an orientation and sensitivity to the particular other(s) who are the co-participants" (Sacks et al., 1974, p. 727) – may serve to tacitly categorize the recipient (also see Schegloff, 2001).

Analysts have also examined cases in which categorization is initially tacit or ambiguous before being explicitly exposed in a subsequent turn, thereby enabling empirical grounding of ostensibly 'invisible' categorization processes that may be occurring in many other cases without ever explicitly 'surfacing' (see, e.g., Whitehead, 2009, 2020; Whitehead & Lerner, 2009) – and pointing again to the powerful resource offered by the next-turn-proof procedure. Explicit categorial practices may also make relevant participants' membership in particular categories, even if they are never explicitly mentioned. For example, in Extract 3.1, Slade's explicit categorization of Meyers Taylor provides for the possible tacit relevance of Slade's and other participants' membership in categories from the MCDs he invokes in doing so, and especially for his joking defence of her having been done as a co-member of the category "Black" (also see our discussions of Sacks's consistency rule and Whitehead's [2009] observations on "categorizing the categorizer" in Chapter 2: Approaching Membership Categorization).

There are also myriad ways in which participants may display categorial orientations entirely tacitly, but nonetheless plainly observably. In line with this observation, we note the tendency to conflate *tacit* orientations with *ambiguous* ones, and the importance of recognizing that participants' tacit orientations to categories may well be readily evident. This can be seen in Extract 3.1, in which Slade, Poundstone, and Farsad orient to the 'comedian/comedy show guest participant' category by making jokes (as described earlier); Meyers Taylor orients to the 'celebrity guest' category by conveying her preparedness to play the game she is there to play (especially by saying "let's go" in line 32); and Sagal orients to the 'host' category by explaining the game and, following the series of jokes, prompting a return to the game (see lines 33–34). None of these setting-based categories is explicitly mentioned, but the participants' pervasive orientations to them are clearly evident in their conduct. Indeed, such categories may be at their most tacit precisely when they are the most pervasive, with their taken-for-grantedness enabling entirely unspoken understandings of their relevance, and participants' competence in the setting resting on their continued tacit use of these categories. Conversely, explicit mentions of them may be evidence of trouble arising from failures to maintain their taken-for-granted tacit relevance, and/or from the potential intersecting or competing relevance of alternative categories (also see our discussions of related matters in Chapter 1: An Introduction to Categories in Social Interaction and Chapter 4: Forming and Making Sense of Actions).

In contrast to the tacit-but-plainly-observable orientations to setting-based categories seen in Extract 3.1, Extract 3.2 offers an illustration of an at least partially ambiguous categorial orientation – one in which it is evident that *something* category-related is at play for a speaker, and where the range of categories he is likely contending with is evident, but where it is not unequivocally clear precisely which of them is or are operative. This extract shows the opening moments of a police encounter in an American city occasioned by a Black civilian calling 911. When the police arrive, they encounter the 911 caller in the parking lot of a convenience store, and he reports that a white couple inside the store were causing a disturbance and using racial epithets against him. The caller agrees to remain outside while the police officers enter the store to seek out the couple reportedly responsible for the trouble, and the extract begins at the point at which they first enter the store.

Having been called, attending police officers routinely claim rights to talk first as a basis for beginning to pursue a policeable project (Meehan, 1989; Raymond et al., 2022, 2023). In this case, however, as soon as the police officers enter the store to find three civilians, a Black man (C1) and a white couple (C2 and C3), the former seeks to establish his membership in the 'witness,' and later 'peace-keeper,' categories before the police officers ever say a word. The pre-emptive project he thereby launches evidently reflects his understanding that he will need to overcome the police officers' likely presumption that he is one of the antagonists, and thus a suspect (also see our further analysis of this case in Chapter 6: Taking Turns and Selecting Next Speakers). This raises a question as to the basis upon which he has arrived at such an understanding, with his membership in categories from at least three perceptually available MCDs, namely race, gender, and age offering a set of potential solutions to this 'puzzle' (also see Whitehead, 2009). That is, he appears to depart from a routine opening of the encounter in an attempt to counter the categorial biases that he thereby treats as being associated with the 'police officer' category – which he evidently fears may wrongly implicate him.[10]

```
Extract 3.2: Police encounter
((As two police officers walk in))
01  C1:  >Hey.=Honestly sir.< (.) I have no issues=
02  P1:  =Let's go out[side.
03  C2:             [These guys are cool.
04  C1:  This guy- I- hon[estly- honestly=
05  C3:                  [He's cool. He's,
06  C1:  =I'm the- I'm [the one that's keeping th[uh peace sir.
07  C2:               [those dudes out there, [
08  C3:                                        [He's- he's
09  C1:  I'm fine.
10  P1:  First of all you're coming outside too
11  C1:  Okay. [No(      ). fine sir
12  C3:        [Hey he's cool though. Please believe me man.
```

Similarly to our foregoing discussion of Extract 3.1, the participants' orientations to the setting-based 'police officer,' 'witness,' 'suspect,' and 'peacekeeper' categories are made evident through a combination of tacit and explicit practices, despite none of them being directly mentioned. Specifically, C1's pre-emptively interjected (as reflected in the rapid pace of talk) announcement disclaims any involvement in the dispute (line 01) and thus orients to his recipients' membership in the 'police officer' category and works to pre-empt their potential categorization of him as a 'suspect' by claiming membership in the 'witness' category. When one of the officers tells him to "go outside" (line 02) instead of taking up his claims, he further characterizes his role in trying to resolve the dispute, as a means of establishing how he should be treated. That is, in asserting that he is "the one that's keeping thuh peace" (line 06), and thereby explicitly claiming membership in a setting-based 'peacekeeper' category, C1 specifies a legitimate basis for his presence at a scene of trouble that the police have been called to – one that two other participants, C2 and C3, align with (see lines 02, 05, 07, 08, and 12). The work C1 does in this regard is consistent with his membership in the categories 'Black,' 'man,' and 'young,'

---

10 C1's use of the formal address term "sir" in this opening turn (line 01), as well as in his further pursuit of this action in line 06, underscores his orientation to his recipient's membership in this category. This contrasts with the later use of the informal "man" (line 12) by C3 in producing a pursued claim designed to appeal to the officer to abandon the institutional business he is pursuing in relation to C1. In addition, we can note C2's references to "These guys" (line 03), referring to the people currently in the store, and "those dudes" (line 07), referring to those with whom she has been in conflict: The shift in these reference forms may serve to index C2's treatment of the referents as members of contrasting 'peacemaker' versus 'troublemaker' categories, and thus as supportive of the project C1 is pursuing. Also see our discussion of person references and address terms in Chapter 5: Referring to and Addressing People.

which offer tacit accounts for his evident expectation of being treated by police officers as a suspect rather than a witness or peacekeeper (cf. Sacks, 1984b). While it is likely the case that he is thereby oriented to the "deficit of credibility" associated with his "provisional status" as, first and foremost, a Black person in a "white space" (see Anderson, 2015, pp. 13–14), he may also be treating his gender and/or age as secondarily contributing to these potential inferences. As such, while there is arguably strong evidence for his orientation to at least one of this set of categories, there remains a degree of ambiguity as to whether he is also treating one or both of the other two as contributing to, or even a primary basis for, his vulnerability in the scene.

In cases like this one, where evidence for the relevance of one or more categories or MCDs is plausible but nonetheless to varying degrees inconclusive and/or ambiguous, producing the types of carefully grounded analyses that conversation analysts call for can be a challenging undertaking (also see, e.g., Stokoe, 2012a, 2012b; Whitehead, 2012a, 2020). As our foregoing analysis demonstrates, one approach to such cases is to mobilize whatever evidence is available in support of claims, while nonetheless registering their equivocal nature, thereby allowing readers to make their own assessments of their plausibility. This also recognizes the potential value of putting such claims 'on record,' since doing so may be a catalyst for future efforts, based on different data, to more conclusively document the features of the practices involved (also see our discussion of building and working with collections in the following section).

A further (but not mutually exclusive) way of dealing with ambiguity is to recognize that language and embodied conduct may be resources for composing actions designed to imply, insinuate, hint, and otherwise do things in ways that are tentative and provisional (Stokoe, 2012a). As such, analysts can treat ambiguity as a participants' resource that provides for the "defeasibility" (Hart, 1948; also see Benson & Drew, 1978; Eglin, 1979) and provisionality, and thus, in some cases, deniability of the possible categorial basis of some piece of conduct (Benwell & Stokoe, 2006; Sacks, 1992; Stokoe, 2012a; Whitehead, 2020).[11] As such, it is not the job of analysts to be more definitive about participants' conduct than they are themselves (Edwards, p.c.), including in cases where the possible relevance of a category and/or the level of precision used in a description (see Drew, 2003) may be exactly what is at stake for the participants, or where ambiguity is part and parcel of the competent deployment of a practice (Edwards, 2006; Speer, 2017) – or, indeed, where the possible categorial basis of the conduct may be opaque for analysts but is evidently completely clear for the participants. In line with this

---

11 As Schegloff (2006b) notes, this is a generic feature of action rather than one particular to (possible) category-related actions.

approach, we might note that C1's claim of membership in the 'peacekeeper' category in Extract 3.2 may be specifically designed to contend with his possible alternative categorization as a suspect while leaving unspoken – and thus deniable – the presumed additional (race, and/or gender, and/or age) categorial bases for being categorized as such. That is, invoking and/or disclaiming the relevance of his membership in these categories more directly (e.g., "Don't assume I'm involved in this just because I'm Black!")[12] could be taken as a pre-emptive accusation of race/gender/age bias against the officers, which could occasion further trouble for C1.

It is also important to note that even if a category is explicitly mentioned, this does not necessarily mean that it is the category that the speaker is actually contending with. In this regard, Schegloff (2007b, p. 477) identifies as a "key issue" the following question:

> [H]ow can analysts show parties' orientation to the categories they want to claim are in play, without the parties saying things like, "as a woman, I . . ." (in fact, saying that does not make it so, and should be tracked for what its speaker is doing with it, and what other category is more compellingly in play).

Thus, for Schegloff, not only are explicit mentions of categories *not* a requirement for analytic claims regarding their relevance; they should also be carefully inspected for whether they are actually evidence for a speaker's orientation to some *other* unmentioned category or MCD. That is, explicit mentions of categories are neither necessary nor sufficient evidence for their relevance (also see Flinkfeldt et al., 2022; Sacks, 1992; Stommel et al., 2022; Whitehead, 2020; Whitehead & Lerner, 2022). Moreover, consistent with our earlier observation that explicit mention of a category may indicate trouble, a participant's disavowal of the relevance of a category may serve as evidence of an orientation to its (possible) relevance, since such disavowal would not be needed if the category was self-evidently not relevant (also see, e.g., Whitehead, 2009, 2020). Extract 3.2 also offers an illustration of this, with C1's explicit claim of membership in the setting-based 'peacekeeper' category apparently being designed to discount the relevance of the 'suspect' and/ or race and/or gender and/or age categories, while in the process serving as evidence for his tacit orientation to the potential relevance of these other categories for his recipients.

---

12 Also see Whitehead et al.'s (2025) analysis of a police encounter in which the participants invoke and dispute the relevance of race in the aftermath of an officer's use of violence against a Black civilian.

Finally, we note that Schegloff (1991, p. 66) explicitly considers potential instances in which

> an adequate account for some specifiable features of the interaction cannot be fashioned from the details of the talk and other conduct of the participants as the vehicle by which they display the relevance of social-structural context for the character of the talk, but rather that this must be otherwise invoked by the analyst, who furthermore has developed defensible arguments for doing so.[13]

Schegloff thus acknowledges the possibility that an analyst could provide a defensible argument for invoking a category (or other elements of social structure) in analysing an interaction even when evidence for participants' orientations to its relevance does not appear to be available, but emphasizes that this should be done only if an examination of the details of the interaction has failed to produce such evidence. What such arguments might look like is another matter – and Schegloff, perhaps deliberately, does not offer specific examples – but how they might be constructed, along with assessments of their merits would surely have to proceed on a case-by-case basis. In any event, a move towards mobilizing an argument in favour of introducing a category in the absence of evidence of participants' orientations to its relevance should be a 'last resort' rather than a routine practice.

At this point we can register that our discussion in this section has been addressed primarily to the question of how to deal analytically with particular cases of tacit or ambiguous orientations to categories. While the proposals we have set forth in this regard thus offer ways of tackling these challenges in relation to *singular* cases, in the following section we expand the resources for doing so by considering *collections* of cases.

3.5   Building and analysing collections of cases

The use of multi-case collections of interactional phenomena, including a focal practice, action, or feature of participants' talk or other conduct, is another distinctive hallmark of conversation analytic research (Clift & Raymond, 2018; Robinson et al., 2024; Schegloff, 1996, 1997b, 2006b). Using this approach to develop analyses of categorial phenomena thus involves identifying and building collections of category-related practices, actions, or features of talk and/or other conduct through which participants manage and thereby display their orientations to some interactional contingency or contingencies (also see Whitehead, 2020; Whitehead et al., 2024). This can be understood as a

---

13 We thank Gene Lerner for drawing our attention to this passage and its implications.

way of examining features of what Garfinkel (1967, p. 9; emphasis in original) described as " 'reflexive' practices":

> that by [their] accounting practices the member makes familiar, commonplace activities of everyday life recognizable *as* familiar, commonplace activities; that on each occasion that an account of common activities is used, that they be recognized for 'another first time.'

The collections-based approach used by conversation analysts thus enables empirical investigations that follow from these observations by Garfinkel. That is, as Maynard and Clayman (2018, p. 134) note, "each occasion combines features of 'anotherness' together with 'first time-ness'" – "features of social life can embody both distinctiveness and recurrence, which are equally fair game for analytic explication." Examining collections of cases of categorial phenomena provides for analyses that can contend with the potentially distinctive features of particular cases, while also documenting patterned features that occur recurrently across multiple cases, and are thereby produced, one case at a time, as 'durable' features of the categories or MCDs at hand. This also makes collections a powerful resource for dealing analytically with single cases that may on their own be ambiguous, but that become more readily recognizable in light of features that they share with other cases – and, in particular unequivocally clear ones – such that clearer cases may provide evidence that can be used to strengthen the more speculative claims that might (in line with our discussion in the previous section) be made about ambiguous cases (also see Speer, 2015, 2017; Whitehead, 2012a, 2020).

In light of these considerations, we offer later some practical suggestions for how to approach building and analysing collections of categorial phenomena (also see Whitehead et al., 2024). While we have formulated these as roughly the steps that one would follow in applying this approach, we nonetheless caution against treating them as an invariant 'recipe' and/or as being followed in a linear fashion. Instead, whether and precisely how any of the procedures we have formulated can or should be implemented will depend on the details of the data and the analytic claims they permit in relation to the project at hand. With these caveats in mind, we suggest the following in relation to *building collections* of cases of categorial phenomena in interaction:

1. Collect cases, both explicit and tacit, of interactional phenomena in which some MCD(s)/category(ies) become possibly relevant and procedurally consequential while intersecting with/implicating one or more of the generic orders of the organization of interaction introduced in Chapter 1: An Introduction to Categories in Social Interaction – word selection, action formation, turn-taking, sequence organization, repair, overall structural organization, and epistemics.

2. Build collections over-inclusively at least initially, including not just cases that appear to clearly exemplify the target phenomenon, but also those that seem to be only marginal candidate cases or "boundary cases" (Schegloff, 1997b) as well as "deviant cases" (Schegloff, 1996), but that may nonetheless ultimately enable more precise specifications of the target phenomenon.
3. Include cases from a range of differently constructed interactional settings, including ordinary conversational and institutional settings, if appropriate (i.e., if the target phenomenon is not especially tied to a particular setting or type of interaction).

As an illustration of how categorial 'collectables' may be generated from empirical cases, the following serves as a (likely partial) list of candidate instances for possible collections or sub-collections of categorial phenomena derived from our observations about Extract 3.1:

1. Mentions of a person's membership in a category or categories – as in Slade's reference to Meyers Taylor as "the Black woman" in line 21 (also see Chapter 5: Referring to and Addressing People).

   • More specifically, mentions of category memberships that depart from Sacks's economy rule (see Chapter 2: Approaching Membership Categorization) by using more than one category ("Black" and "woman" rather than, for example, simply "woman" or "[Black] person").

2. Departures from expectations of ordinary turn-taking and sequence organization as places where orientations to/uses of categories other than omni-relevant setting-based categories systematically arise – as in Slade speaking to produce a joke at a place where Meyers Taylor has been selected to speak next, and in doing so introducing race as an alternative to the prevailing setting-based categories for interpreting what has just happened (also see Chapter 6: Taking Turns at Talking and Selecting Next Speakers and Chapter 7: Organizing Sequences of Action).

   • More specifically, use of a category, and of co-category membership (in the race category "Black") – in particular, of a speaker (Slade) and a co-present but non-addressed recipient (Meyers Taylor) – as a basis for an "intervening action" (Lerner, 2019) by a participant who speaks when a different participant has been selected to speak next.

3. Uses of common-sense knowledge about categories as resources for producing actions – as in Slade's use of common-sense racial knowledge to produce the joke (also see Chapter 4: Forming and Making Sense of Actions).

   • More specifically, uses as resources for actions of incongruities between memberships in categories (Meyers Taylor, as a "Black woman") and what their incumbents are normatively expected to do (bobsledding), know (about particular types of music), etc.

4. Troubles in speaking, hearing, or understanding in relation to mentions of or orientations to categories – as in the disfluencies and restarts in Slade's talk as he produces the joke in lines 20–23, and in Sagal's display in line 19 of difficulty understanding the negative moral assessment Slade has produced in line 18 (also see Chapter 8: Managing Troubles in Speaking, Hearing and Understanding).
5. Participants' orientations to and/or uses of what members of particular categories are expected, obligated, entitled, etc., to know – as in Slade's mobilization of the aforementioned categories incongruities, and in Poundstone's subsequent use of the knowledge-based category "shill" (also see Chapter 9: Managing Knowledge, Experience, and Entitlement).

Collection-building may be done concurrently with analysis, particularly if a developing analysis prompts revisiting the boundaries of a collection and/ or seeking out additional cases that may shed light on puzzles that arise as the analysis progresses. The following questions[14] can thus begin to be applied to *analyzing collections* as soon as even a small handful of cases have been assembled as a collection:

1. What types of MCD(s) or category/ies are implicated? (e.g., Pn-adequate vs. setting-based omni-relevant vs. categories from some other collection; perceptually available vs. unavailable; other possibly relevant distinctions?)
2. What common-sense categorial knowledge (in relation to category-bound activities, category-tied predicates, etc.) do the MCD(s) or category/ies invoke or mobilize?
3. What is the nature of the practice/conduct through which the MCD(s) or category/ies becomes (possibly) relevant?

   a. Does it implicate categorization of Self vs. Co-Present Other vs. Non-Present Third Party?
   b. Does it do so explicitly or tacitly?

4. Where (in a turn, sequence, occasion, etc.) does the candidate categorial phenomenon become (possibly) relevant?
5. What kind of action/activity/course of action is the phenomenon part of?
6. Is there evidence and/or are there regularities in relation to the emergence of the phenomenon from the talk and other conduct that precedes it?
7. What are the compositional features of the phenomenon? (Compositional features include all observable elements of conduct through which a phenomenon is produced, including words, volume, prosody, gestures, and other bodily conduct.)

14 Our composition of this list owes a heavy debt to an unpublished document developed as a teaching aid by Gene Lerner.

8. What does this practice/conduct accomplish interactionally, and/or what contingencies is it observably designed to manage or contend with?
9. Does the phenomenon implicate differential opportunities to participate?

    a. Who (in interactionally and or demonstrably categorially relevant terms) produces it?
    b. Does its production establish or change the prevailing set of explicit or tacit entitlements or obligations?

10. What are its consequences for subsequent actions?

    a. What (if any) expectations does it establish for what should happen next, and/or who should act next?
    b. How is it responded to/taken up by other participants? (Is it aligned with/treated as routine/taken for granted or does it occasion interactional troubles/resistance/challenges/disputes?)
    c. Is there other evidence available subsequent to the target conduct for participants' treatment of its categorial import?

11. Are there alternative realizations of the phenomenon (boundary cases and/or deviant cases) that reveal its otherwise ordinary organization?

By addressing these questions both to each individual case in the collection and to the collection of cases as a whole, the analysis should move towards an account that reflects both the 'core' features that are recurrent across all cases and thus constitutive of the phenomenon, and the potential range of distinctive features that are observable in only some or even just one of the cases. The analysis should thereby seek to document how participants can recognize and use the conduct at hand in ways that include analytic attention to features of both recurrence and distinctiveness, and that thereby provide for both durable features of the social category/ies concerned, and for their flexible adaptation to the case-by-case particularities of their realization.

3.6   Summary and conclusions

There is surely much more that could be said about the methodological principles, practices, and challenges we have discussed in this chapter – and about the longstanding debates associated with them. While explicit engagement with these matters is an important basis for conducting careful and rigorous research, we are also mindful of the following note of caution offered by Schegloff (1999a, p. 580; emphasis in original):

> The danger in exchanges like this is that the contributors and readers get drawn further and further into secondary discussions about the work, and further and further away from *doing* the work – whatever the work they

choose to do is. Indeed, the ultimate danger is that this *becomes* the work they choose to do. . . . Readers need to decide what they find most cogent and compelling to do, and then go do it, or prepare themselves further for doing it, if that is the life stage they are at. . . . Whatever it is, *do* it – or try – before *talking* about doing it.

Consistent with this sentiment, rather than seeking to reopen well-rehearsed debates – much less presume that what we write about them could bring about their definitive resolution – our concern in this chapter has been to describe an empirically grounded and principled approach for *doing* the work. As such, this chapter serves as a bridge between the foundations laid in the preceding chapters and the framework for studying categorial phenomena in social interaction we offer in the remainder of the book. In the chapters that follow, we apply these methodological principles and practices in specifying a set of places in which categorial phenomena can be found, and demonstrating a range of ways of looking for and at them. Those chapters thereby include instances of a wide range of 'collectables,' with many of the analyses we offer in those chapters being based on at most a handful of empirical cases, while providing ripe potential for more detailed exploration of the phenomena concerned based on more extensive and varied collections than we have been able to provide within the scope of a book. In following this approach, we sketch out some of the systematic intersections between categorial phenomena and generic organizations of practice for interaction that could guide additional research employing the approach we have described in this chapter to further flesh out these categorial systematics.

4

FORMING AND MAKING SENSE OF ACTIONS

4.0   Introduction

In January 2021, officers from the Rochester, New York Police Department, who were responding to a report of "family trouble" (Ly & Levenson, 2021) encountered and detained a nine-year-old girl, who had apparently attempted to flee from them upon their arrival. During the course of detaining her, the officers first handcuffed and later pepper-sprayed the girl, sparking widespread outrage that led to the suspension of three of the nine officers present at the scene (Sanchez & Alsharif, 2021). In a distressing exchange (captured by police body camera footage) while the officers' struggled to force the handcuffed child into a police vehicle, and in the moments preceding the pepper-spraying, categorial matters came to be explicitly topicalized by the participants: as Jones (2021, p. 527) notes, "an officer yelled at the girl with obvious frustration, 'You're acting like a child!'" and the girl quickly retorted, "I AM a child!" In taking up this exchange, Jones (2021, p. 527) describes how the girl's retort "interjected a truth into the struggle that had been all but ignored by the armed adults on the scene" and thereby exposed "the lies of law enforcement," and links this truth to "a call for a system, a world, that would treat a Black girl as if she were a child."

Later in this chapter, we build on Jones's (2021) analysis by offering some further observations on this exchange. In order to establish the foundations for doing so, we further develop a key claim we made in Chapter 1: An Introduction to Categories in Social Interaction, where we proposed that *all actions can be inspected for how they are designed by reference to particular categories of actor and/or recipients, and/or how features of their design can be taken up as such by recipients.* Specifically, we examine some of the myriad

DOI: 10.4324/9781003120599-5

observable ways in which, across different actions, the ways participants design and take up one another's actions can be inspected for how they index or take into account participants' categorizations of themselves and one another.[1] We thereby build on conversation analytic findings on the resources participants in interactions use for forming up recognizable actions and for recognition (or "ascription" – see Levinson, 2013, p. 104) of the actions produced by others (also see, e.g., Heritage, 2013; Schegloff, 2007b).

Research on action formation and ascription begins with a key and basic insight underpinning CA as an approach to studying talk-in-interaction: that "talk is constructed and is attended by its recipients for the action or actions it may be doing" (Schegloff, 1995, p. 187). This includes actions that "can be referred to with common vernacular terms" – such as announcing, complaining, (dis)agreeing, noticing, offering, promising, requesting, teasing, telling, and so forth (Schegloff, 2007a, p. 7) – as well as "previously undescribed" (Schegloff, 1996, p. 162) actions that do not correspond to vernacular terms of this sort, but which participants nonetheless recurrently produce and make sense of in empirically describable ways (also see Schegloff, 2007a). What makes the mutual intelligibility of actions possible is their production using practices composed through a wide range of interactional resources, with participants' common-sense cultural knowledge of the ordinary meanings of these practices enabling convergence between their deployment by speakers and their interpretation by recipients (Schegloff, 1996; cf. Garfinkel, 1967).[2]

These interactional resources include those grounded in talk, including the words selected for forming up an action (also see Chapter 5: Referring to and Addressing People); the grammatical format in which it is produced (see, e.g., Couper-Kuhlen, 2014; Ochs et al., 1996; Raymond, 2003); and its phonetic and prosodic features, including pitch, intonation, and emphasis (see, e.g., Couper-Kuhlen & Ford, 2004; Schegloff, 1998b; Selting et al., 2010). Actions can also be composed through other interactionally organized embodied conduct produced either with or independently of accompanying talk, including gestures, manual actions, and features of body position (see, e.g, Goodwin, 2000; Lerner & Raymond, 2021; Mondada, 2016; Sacks & Schegloff, 2002; Schegloff, 1998a; Streeck et al., 2011). In addition to

---

1 In focusing on features of how particular actions are formed and taken up by their recipients over a series of turns, we include attention to *sequential* aspects of the interactions at hand. This contrasts, however, with our examination of *sequence-organizational* matters, which relate to the resources that enable participants to build coherent *courses* of action – and which we take up in Chapter 7: Organizing Sequences of Action.

2 Of course, mutual intelligibility is nonetheless not guaranteed by the use of such practices, and troubles in accomplishing intersubjective understandings are a systematic contingency that may be managed by practices of repair, which we discuss in relation to categories in Chapter 8: Managing Troubles in Speaking, Hearing and Understanding.

these features of the *composition* of actions, a further crucial feature is their *position*. This concerns, most proximately, where they are positioned in ongoing turns and sequences of action (also see Chapter 6: Taking Turns at Talking and Selecting Next Speakers and Chapter 7: Organizing Sequences of Action, respectively), and/or within the overall structural organization of the occasion of interaction. However, it can also include more 'distal' senses of position to which participants may be oriented, including within the course of their relationships with one another, within the unfolding of particular socio-historical events or epochs, and so on (cf. Schegloff, 1998c). Moreover – and of key importance for the present purpose – participants may use background knowledge presumed to be known in common (also see Chapter 9: Managing Knowledge, Experience, and Entitlement), together with their assumptions about who they relevantly are in terms of membership in particular categories, as bases for action and inference.

In order to specify in this chapter some basic features of categorial systematics in relation to action formation and ascription, we begin in Section 4.1 by considering some cases in which participants use categories in forming up actions designed to solve distributional problems they encounter during the course of their interactions. We then build on our observations of the range of explicit and tacit categorial practices they use in doing so by examining, in Sections 4.2 and 4.3, respectively, how participants use explicit mentions of categories and/or category-resonant terms to form and make sense of actions, and how they tacitly treat categories as bases for designing and evaluating actions. After returning in Section 4.4 to the Rochester, NY, encounter we introduced previously to examine some implications of the phenomena developed in the preceding sections for this case, we conclude the chapter in Section 4.5.

4.1 Using categories to solve organizational problems

One way the relevance of categories can come to be observably implicated in the production of actions and activities is where they come to be used to solve organizational problems. By organizational problems, we mean questions as to how responsibilities, entitlements, objects, or other resources – whether positively or negatively valued (cf. Sacks et al., 1974) – are distributed, allocated, or configured. Participants may adopt category-based solutions in anticipation of occasions where they will be needed. For example, categories can be used in formally legislated or policy-based solutions regarding the allocation of benefits (e.g., entitlements accorded to members of categories such as 'veteran,' 'child,' 'citizen,' 'senior citizen'). By virtue of the way categories are organized into collections (MCDs), in every case where a category is used to allocate a resource, it simultaneously serves as the basis for withholding that resource from members of other categories from that MCD – and can thereby constitute a basis for category-based inequalities and troubles. For example, Weinberg (2005) observes that social problems arose from government programs that provided assistance respectively for incumbents of the category 'mentally ill,' and '[drug or alcohol] addict,' but not for those who were 'dually diagnosed' as concurrently members of both these categories – since treatments for mental illness depended on the prescription of drugs, while treatments for addiction focused on total abstinence from drugs. As this example demonstrates, while categories can provide a set of bases for resolving problems, their use can also be a source of related or entirely different or unanticipated problems.

In addition to categories being formally adopted by institutions as pre-planned solutions to distributional problems, participants in interactions may arrive at category-based solutions to problems that arise 'in the moment.' On such occasions, the design and uptake of actions provides a window into both that and how categories come to be treated as locally relevant. Consistent with our discussion of this in Chapter 1: An Introduction to Categories in Social Interaction, and as the cases we examine in this section demonstrate, categories from *Pn*-adequate collections are pervasively available and recurrently deployed in such cases, especially when the prevailing setting-based categories do not offer a 'ready-made' solution to a distributional problem. An initial illustration of this is shown in Extract 4.1, which also demonstrates some of the ways participants can resist such uses of these categories. The relevant setting-based category for this interaction is 'student,' with the participants tasked with carrying out a collaborative writing activity in which, as a group, they must produce descriptions of people in a series of photographs. However, the student participants (S1–S4) use a gender category as a basis for solving an organizational problem relating to the distribution of responsibility for different required elements of this task (also see Extract 8.10 in Chapter 8: Managing Trouble in Speaking, Hearing and Understanding, in which a similar organizational problem is solved in similar ways, 30 years later in a different setting).

```
Extract 4.1: University small group work
01   S1:  D'you reckon she's an instructor then.
02            (0.2)
03   S1:  Of some sort,
04   S2:  Is somebody scribing. who's writin' it.=
05   S1:  =Oh yhe:ah.
06            (0.8)
07   S3:  Well you can't [   r e a d   m y   ]=
08   S1:                 [She wants to do it.]
09   S3:  =writin' once I've [wri:tten it.]
10   S4:                     [ .hehhhh ]
11   S1:  We:ll secretary an' female.
```

```
12              (0.3)
13  S4:  .Hh heh heh heh
14              (0.4)
15  S3:  It's uh::,
16  S4:  Yeah: I'm wearing glasses I must be the secretary.=
17  S2:  =I think- (.) we're all agreed she's physical.
18              (0.2)
 .  .  .
27  S3:  Make a good start.
28  S4:  Heh heh heh .hhh (.) .hhh Okay what's her name.
29              (0.5)
 .  .  .
104 S4:  Am I wri:ting (then.)
105 S1:  Yes: go on.
 .  .  .
123             (0.3)
124 S3:  <Are you getting all this down.=Come on.
125             (1.6)
126 S1:  You've gotta learn this shorthand before you get into
127      the- (0.4) the job market.
```

FIGURE 4.1   S1 points at S4 at line 08

The extract begins with S1 offering an initial contribution to the task, as he speculates as to the occupation of the woman in the photograph they are looking at: "an instructor" (lines 01–03). This observation, however, occasions a registering that to meet the task demands one member of the group must write down their ideas, as S2's query, "is somebody scribing," immediately followed by a further query, "who's writin' it" (line 04), initiates a new sequence prompting a search for the party who will undertake this responsibility. The use of the reference form "somebody" proposes that any of them could be selected (cf. Whitehead & Lerner, 2020), and thereby become the incumbent of a setting-based 'scribe' category. In its sequential placement and design, the resulting search is positioned as ancillary to the main activity – indeed, it is produced as an 'afterthought' (also see Raymond & Lerner, 2014), and aligned with as such by S1's response (line 05). As we shall see, this positions the person who takes on the 'scribe' duties as assisting the other participants, and thus as being potentially accountable to them, rather than engaging on an equal footing in the main activity.

Following S2's initiation of this activity, participants seek to manage their possible selection into the role of scribe: S3 offers a skills-based account for why he cannot do so (lines 07–09), and S1 nominates S4 using a pointing gesture (Figure 4.1; also see Goodwin, 2003) and the pronoun "she" to select S4, as the only woman in the group, for this task – in a context where the setting-based 'student' category does not differentiate between them since all are co-members of this category. S1 thereby exploits a person reference practice (also see Chapter 5: Referring to and Addressing People) as a tacit method for using gender as a basis for selecting S4 without going 'on record' as having used gender to resolve the problem at hand. Moreover, S1 claims to report S4's desire to take up the task – "she wants to do it" (line 08) – thereby obscuring his move to impose the responsibility on S4 despite her having offered no indication she is willing to take it on. Taken together, these resources used by S1 in forming his nomination of S4 for this aspect of the task render the apparent underlying gendered basis for his action readily available and yet unspoken. As a consequence, S4 may have limited options for resisting or rejecting S1's use of gender without being vulnerable to the charge of having introduced a gender-based interpretation of an ostensibly non-gendered action (cf. Whitehead, 2009).

S4's laughing response to S1's claim attempts to treat it as a non-serious transgression rather than an accurate reflection of her willingness to serve as scribe – and thereby tacitly resists S1's proposal while leaving its apparently gendered basis tacit. S1 evidently registers this resistance on S4's part, as he offers a "well"-prefaced justification of his nomination of S4 (line 11). In doing so, he offers the category "secretary" as a replacement for 'scribe' and thereby positions it, and S4 as its proposed incumbent, outside of – and subordinate to – the setting-based 'student' category. Moreover, S1 explicates an ostensibly shared logic whereby this occupational category is bound to the gender category "female," but casts this connection as something he has just noticed in the moment, as opposed to his selection of S4 being motivated from the outset by an effort to target her as a woman. S1 therefore mobilizes common-sense knowledge bound to the "secretary" and "female" categories to exclude him and the other men in the group from possible incumbency in either of these categories.

While S4 concedes to her nomination by picking up her paper and pen, thereby aligning herself with the role and carrying out its preliminary activities, she nevertheless continues to resist S1's use of gender in nominating her. For example, she finds a different basis for distinguishing her from the other group members as the "secretary," tying this category to wearing glasses (line 16). However, once serving as scribe has been treated as an afterthought and tied to gender, this provides an ongoing resource for the other members to continue to treat her as an appropriate recipient of a series of directives, admonitions, and advice (lines 27, 105, 124, and 126–127) that, although apparently designed as teasing or non-serious, unequivocally position her as a subordinate (also see Stokoe, 2008a).

A second case where participants use setting-based and P*n*-adequate categories as alternative bases for solving an organizational problem and making sense of actions produced in relation to this solution is shown in Extract 4.2. This exchange is part of a dinner involving four friends: Vivian and Shane, who are a couple and are hosting the dinner, and Nancy and Michael, a couple who are their guests. Following compliments of the chicken by Nancy and Michael (not transcribed), Vivian announces that there is "one more:- piece" (lines 01–02) thereby raising the problem of how to distribute it – particularly in light of the normative prohibition against being the party who takes a last item. She thereby potentially invites a category-based solution that is most readily provided by the setting-based 'guest' category, given the entitlements associated with membership in this category. However, insofar as both Nancy and Michael are members of this category, this does not resolve the prohibition against taking the last piece, as indicated by the lengthy silence (line 03) that develops following Vivian's announcement. Shane then intervenes, initiating a set of ostensibly joking exchanges grounded first in the 'host'/'guest' pair of categories before a shift to an alternative use of gender and relationship categories.

```
Extract 4.2: Chicken Dinner (5-6)
01  VIV: Thez anothuh pie:ce: (.) one (0.2) one more:- piece a'
02       chicken lef'.
03               (2.9)
04  SH?: °uhh::::°
05               (0.2)
06  SHA: W(h)e a(h)ll we know'ooz getting'tha[:t.] [he-he-ha:::]=
07  MIC:                                      [En ]h[a a h a:ha:]=
08  SHA: =ha[a hu-]  [.hnn-n-i]h
09  VIV:    [Bt th]at['s ↑i:t.]
10  SHA: [(Yes ih)-
```

```
11   MIC:  [It's ↑my hou::[se
12   SHA:          [.ihh huh huh[huh[huh-uh
13   NAN:                      [°mm[-hm-hm-hm-hm°
14   MIC:                  [En ah'm: ea[tin' it.=
15   VIV:                              [heh
16   NAN:  =Ah[think wir g'n[noo- a(h)a(h)ll b]e[fight'n[over it.=
17   SHA:     [.hhhhh       [e h heh heh  heh ] [.hhhh [hhh
18   MIC:  =(Ari'[wait)
19   SHA:        [We gudduh- .i[h .ih
20   MIC:                      [B'd ah'm th'↓gues[:t.
21   SHA:                                       [.huh ha ha hah=
22   MIC:  =B'd ah['m the]↓gues:t.
23   NAN:       [mmm:::]hm-hm-hm-hmgh.=
24   SHA:  =.ih .ih .↑ih .i[h
25   VIV:                  [I gave Michael the bigges' ↑piece- too:.
26           (0.9)
27   SHA:  What?
28           (0.7)
29   ???    °( [ )°
30   NAN:     [Yeh I sa[w tha:]t.
31   SHA:             [Wha:t?]
32   MIC:  We know'oo[rates he:re]:.=
33   VIV:            [Of chicken,]
34   SHA:  =Is this true?
35   MIC:  .t .hh- .hh (0.2) She gaym'the biggis'b'↓ta:y/(potato)
36        the biggis' ↓chicken=
37   SHA:  =nah ↑ha:h ↑O-kay (ul en w') talk about that later.
```

Shane's initial intervention jokingly claims that there is an obvious alternative category-based solution to the dilemma that has emerged, but one that – in keeping with his claim that "we all know" (line 06) – he declines to state directly. We can appreciate the basis for this joke in two ways: first, it invokes a category ('man of the house' – also see Michael's displayed ascription of this in line 11) of which Shane is the sole incumbent; and, second, his use of this category implements a form of humour based on blatant violation of normative expectations (see, e.g., Cheeks & Whitehead, 2024; Stokoe, 2008b) – in this case that guests are entitled to privileged access to food. Michael then takes up Shane's subversion of this expectation by jokingly challenging Shane's proposed solution on the grounds that he is 'the guest' (lines 20 and 22). Thus, once gender privilege is explicitly invoked by Shane's introduction of the 'man of the house' category, Michael explicitly claims (as shown by his use of the definite article 'the') singular membership in the 'guest' category – which also serves to exclude Nancy as a possible recipient of the chicken. This shift transforms the initial dilemma, which of Michael or Nancy would get the chicken, into a dispute over which man will get it, thereby demonstrating how the pervasive availability of gender – as a Pn-adequate category – 'lies in wait' for use by one or more participants at moments when something accountable is happening (also see our discussion of this phenomenon in Chapter 1: An Introduction to Categories in Social Interaction).

Vivian then intervenes in the humorously produced dispute, remarking in line 25, "I gave Michael the biggest piece too." In this way, she aligns with Michael's claim to special entitlements based on his membership in the 'guest' category by reporting how she had previously acted on the basis of these same entitlements. Vivian thereby reflexively (although tacitly) claims membership in the 'host' and 'cook' categories and, as the sole incumbent of this combination of categories, positions herself as the person responsible for distributing the food. Vivian's unhesitating intervention on Michael's behalf, however, is treated by Shane as a betrayal, shown by his claim of shock in his response, "What?" (line 27). Since it cannot be a surprise to him that Vivian, as a co-host, has aligned with Michael's claim of privileges associated with his membership in the 'guest' category, Shane's claimed surprise – and the challenge it implements[3] (Schegloff, 1997a) – requires inferring the relevance of an alternative set of categories in order to make sense as an action. This challenge by Shane thus evidently invokes Shane and Vivian's co-membership in the 'hetero-romantic partner' category, in contrast to Michael's exclusion from this category in relation to Vivian.

In posing this challenge, Shane asserts an entitlement to evaluate Vivian's actions by reference to their co-membership in a different category than the one by reference to which she had evidently produced her action. In this way, Shane's invocation of this alternative set of category relations casts Vivian's preferential treatment of Michael as evidence of a violation of the obligations and prohibitions associated with her respective relationships with each of them. In this respect, we can observe the strong relationship between entitlements and obligations: Where any action is accountable (i.e., witness-ably done for some cause), it may be understood to assert a category-based entitlement or obligation for having been done. And as a consequence, what is done by reference to the *entitlements* associated with one category can be treated as problematic by reference to the *obligations* associated with another category, or vice versa.

In taking up Shane's challenge, Vivian works to re-establish her actions as having been produced under the auspices of the 'host' and 'cook' categories, and by reference to Michael as a guest. That is, by specifying "Of chicken" (line 33), Vivian attends to Shane having 'jokingly' treated her announcement as an admission of a possible sexual betrayal, and reasserts the 'host' category as the basis for her action. Even after this clarification, however, Shane continues to take up her conduct as a betrayal (line 34) – still doing so designedly jokingly but possibly with a more serious treatment being conveyed by his pursuit of this action (also see our discussion of pursuits in Chapter 7:

---

3 Also see our discussion of the use of practices of repair as methods for challenging a prior action in Chapter 8: Managing Troubles in Speaking, Hearing and Understanding.

Organizing Sequences of Action). Michael then intervenes in support of Vivian's claim to have acted on the basis of her and Michael's respective membership in the 'host' and 'guest' pair of categories, reporting that she gave him the biggest potato and the biggest piece of chicken (lines 35–36) – thereby claiming Vivian's actions in this regard to have been fully public and legitimate by reference to these categories. Shane, however, remains undeterred by this, responding by maintaining his non-serious claims of infidelity, as he treats this as an ongoing conflict between himself and Vivian by suggesting that they will "talk about that later" (line 37). Even as Vivian attempts to resolve one type of gender-based trouble, she finds herself subject to an accusation regarding another.

Across this extract, we can appreciate how the participants, through their conduct, maintain the relevance of gender as a tacit feature of their actions and relations. In the process, they reproduce familiar gender-based asymmetries and associated accountability in relation to the division of household labour (see, e.g., Hochschild & Machung, 2012): Vivian has taken responsibility for preparing and distributing the food, thereby becoming vulnerable to complaints about how she has done both; Nancy comes to be excluded as a plausible recipient of a last available food item; Michael and Shane assert their respective entitlements to food; and Shane complains[4] about how Vivian manages the competing relevancies of the 'host' versus 'romantic partner' categories. In this respect, we can note parallels with the participants' use of gender to ground a category-based solution to the distribution of labour in the prior extract. While in Extract 4.1, gender is invoked explicitly to justify S4's selection as "secretary," in Extract 4.2 the parties' reliance on gender remains unspoken – which may make it more difficult for Vivian to resist in the way S4 did in Extract 4.1.

In both Extracts 4.1 and 4.2, we can observe the participants managing activities tied to their membership in setting-based categories ('student,' 'host,' 'cook,' 'guest,' 'romantic partner,' etc.) while also mobilizing categories from Pn-adequate collections (particularly, in these cases, gender) that offer a basis for resolving organizational problems. Their uses of, and resistance to, these categories arise in activities initiated and conducted through a series of actions formed through the use of person reference and other word selection person practices (also see Chapter 5: Referring to and Addressing People), other formulations, and visible embodied conduct. They also include

---

4 In Chapter 6: Taking Turns at Talking and Selecting Next Speakers, Extract 6.5, we examine a segment of this interaction that began around 90 seconds before the stretch shown in Extract 4.2, in which Shane produces a series of complaints about the potatoes, the uptake of which reveal the participants' tacit orientations to the contrasting relevance of gender and relationship categories as bases for alliances in the resulting dispute. Moreover, around 15 seconds prior to the start of Extract 4.2, Shane produces a further complaint about the potatoes following a positive assessment of the chicken by Nancy.

the deployment of both explicit mentions of categories in the formation of actions and tacit orientations to categories as bases for action and inference. In the following sections we turn to more detailed considerations of each of these, while further examining how setting-based and Pn-adequate categories can intersect and/or serve as alternative sets of resources in producing and interpreting actions.

4.2 Explicitly mentioning categories in forming and making sense of actions

As we have already seen in the data we have examined in previous chapters, and will continue to see in the chapters that follow, direct mentions of categories and other explicitly category-resonant words are recurrently used as resources for forming actions – and thereby serve as resources for recipients in making sense of those actions. In this section, we further develop these observations by focusing on some variations in how categories can be introduced in forming up particular actions, and how these variations reflect speakers' orientations to the valence (positive versus negative) of the actions they are producing and the ways they are using categories in doing so. There are three main elements to this analysis: first, we consider how particular, and especially Pn-adequate, categories can be explicitly used in forming up actions. Here we are concerned primarily with how the specific category and its collection contribute to the action being composed, including (where relevant) how its use entails a departure from the prevailing setting-based categories otherwise relevant for the encounter. Second, we examine how speakers select (from a range of available category terms) how to formulate the categories they mention,[5] and how these choices may reflect the speaker's relationship to the mentioned category (see also the discussion of description in action by Schegloff, 1988a). Third, we consider what other categories may be tacitly invoked by these explicit mentions of categories.

As we show in these analyses, explicit uses of Pn-adequate categories may be inspected for the 'special' interactional work they may be used and/or seen to do – which can include managing matters relating to various "-isms" (also see Whitehead & Stokoe, 2015). This can be most directly appreciated in cases where categories are introduced in indirect or euphemistic ways (also see our analysis of Extract 2.7 in Chapter 2: Approaching Membership

---

5 Also see our analysis in Chapter 8: Managing Troubles in Speaking, Hearing, and Understanding of speakers' uses of repair practices to shift from one available category term to another, thereby treating such selections as consequential for the in-progress action, the occasion to which it contributes, and/or the relations between participants and the categories mentioned.

Categorization), and conversely in how direct and unvarnished uses of categories can serve as resources for upgrading the force of negatively valenced actions.

A first case, shown in Extract 4.3, is taken from the opening moments of a call to a holiday company (also see Flinkfeldt et al., 2022) – which we previously examined in Chapter 1: An Introduction to Categories in Social Interaction – in which the caller (C) comes to explicitly categorize herself using gender and age categories, as "a lady of a certain age" (lines 03–05), while requesting assistance from the salesperson (S).

Extract 4.3: Holiday sales

```
01   S:   G'd evenin' Rindley Leisure Hotels, you're speaking to
02        Diane.=↓How c'n I help.
03   C:   Uh- good evenin' Diane. .hh I'm trying to- um. (0.3) I'm
04        a lady of a certain age and going online's giving me a
05        headache.
06   S:   Mhm he heh, [heh,
07   C:               [h I don't know what I've pressed now.
08   S:   Uh heh heh [heh
09   C:              [(I'm trying) t'do a booking, could you check
10        the availability for me ((continues))
```

Extending our previous analysis of this case, we can observe that, in categorizing herself in this way, the caller foreshadows the introduction of some trouble will turn out to have been the basis for the request for help she has called to make, while treating this trouble as linked to her membership in an age category – although without directly stating this category (a matter we return to in the following analysis). She thereby uses this age self-categorization as a resource for providing the background against which action of requesting is being formed up – specifically, in accounting for having called to seek assistance from an institutional representative rather than "going online" (line 04) to do it herself. It is notable that in an institutional occasion designed precisely for requests from customers just like her, the caller nevertheless introduces category-based relevancies to manage her entitlement to make the specific type of request she has called to produce – which she thereby treats as possibly beneath the threshold likely to be expected by a salesperson in this setting. Thus, where a participant treats her actions as falling outside the ordinary scope of the prevailing setting-based categories (here, 'customer' and 'salesperson'), P*n*-adequate categories (here, age and gender) can be introduced as resources for warranting such a departure.

Having identified the basis on which the caller's invocation of age comes to be introduced in relation to making a request, we can now appreciate how the specific formulation she uses – "lady of a certain age" – manages a range of complexities associated with the action she is producing. That is, while it is evident that age is the basis for justifying her request – the caller is accounting for her need for assistance by reference to her age, rather than proposing herself to be a 'helpless woman' – she nevertheless uses a category formulation that takes into account gender-based prohibitions on explicitly using the category 'old.' Said baldly, 'I'm an old lady and . . .' risks being treated as self-deprecation, and thereby as making relevant a disagreeing response (e.g., 'you don't sound old to me'; see Pomerantz, 1984; Speer, 2019). The caller's use of this formulation thus manages self-justification without veering into self-deprecation. By responding with the receipt "Mhm" (line 06) and laughter, the salesperson registers the caller's use of these categories and treats them as designed to feature in her project of seeking assistance, rather than (for example) being done in pursuit of a compliment.

Thus, in a place where the action of requesting could be pursued without a justification for it being expected, Pn-adequate categories can nevertheless be mobilized to manage possible discrepancies between expectations and actions. Moreover, in a place where an unvarnished method of categorization can be used, a speaker instead uses an idiomatic and euphemistic formulation to manage exigencies associated with its more direct alternatives. The following cases provide further illustrations of these routine features of actions involving explicit uses of categories, including uses of Pn-adequate categories as alternatives to setting-based categories and specific practices for formulating those categories as compositional features of the actions being produced.

In Extract 4.4, a radio host (IR) is interviewing a pharmacist (P) about a scheme to sell Viagra directly to customers in high street chemists. While there may be a common-sense association between the use of this drug and particular age ('old[er]') and gender ('men') categories (by virtue of its development as a treatment for erectile dysfunction), the interviewer's question in lines 01–02 invites – or at least enables – the pharmacist to introduce alternative categories that may run counter to these associations. Our interest is in how the pharmacist's response resists the terms of this question and in her use of multiple alternative formulations of the gender category her answer foregrounds.

Extract 4.4: BBC Radio 4, *Case Notes*, 09–07

```
01   IR:  What sort'v people (.) have been co:ming
02        t'you.
03              (0.2)
04   P:   .hh We've had a: wi:de variety of ↓gentlemen
05        coming to see us:. to access the Viagra
06        thro:ugh our programme .hh a lot of men when
07        we ta:lk to them have said I've been meaning
```

```
08        to do something about this for a:ges an' I've
09        just never got round to it, (0.2) ↑typical
10        guy response.=re(h)ally y'know.=.hh an'
11        eventually they think w'll I really do need
12        to do something about it now.=
```

Beyond the common-sense knowledge it may index, the framing of the interviewer's question – through the singular "sort'v people" (as opposed to a plural "sorts'v") – seems to invite the pharmacist's identification of a specific category of person as the primary customer for Viagra. Following a brief delay after the interviewer's question (line 03) that may already indicate trouble (also see Chapter 7: Organizing Sequences of Action), the pharmacist's framing of her response repeats and reformulates the question (lines 04–05), thereby resisting its terms to introduce multiple other categories ("a wide variety") that intersect with the category she treats as primary relevant for this medication ("gentlemen") – which may have been anticipated by the question and is now made explicit in this response. By using gender alone in a context where age may also, as noted previously, have been expected to be relevant, the pharmacist avoids the age stereotyping that the interviewer's question may seem to invite. The pharmacist can thereby also be seen as acting by reference to her occupational category by virtue of encouraging a wider range of potential customers to make use of this medication. Although the pharmacist's turn is composed of various elements, which we discuss in detail later, its beginning, end, and overarching trajectory can thus be understood overall as primarily a sales-related project.

In explicitly using a gender category, however, the pharmacist is confronted with a choice of which category term to use in referring to this category (e.g., 'males,' 'men,' 'guys,' 'dudes,' etc.), thereby making the choice she arrives at is inspectable for how it contributes to the action she is forming up. We can note in this respect that "gentlemen" is the most formal category term available, and her selection of it thus serves to convey the respectable status of her customers – and thereby works against the possible stigma or embarrassment associated with public disclosures of sexuality and especially sexual dysfunction. As she continues her response, the pharmacist uses two further alternative category terms that are selected by reference to the features of the actions accomplished in respective parts of the turn in which she uses them. First, as she begins to report on the delay between her customers' intention to purchase the medication and their actual visit to the pharmacy, the pharmacist uses the generic (and thus less positive) category term "men" (line 06). The pharmacist then produces a negatively valanced characterization of their habits as presumptively known-in-common characteristics for members of this category, using a third category term, "guy" (line 10). As the least formal of the three, this category term most easily permits derisive uses, while also limiting the forcefulness of the derisive use to which the pharmacist puts it in this context. This informality is consistent with the laugh token the pharmacist produces in the word "really" just after the assessment, which, together with the "y'know" that follows (line 10), invites recognition and appreciation of this activity as category-bound.

Our observations thus far have primarily focused on selection and use of category terms in the formation of the pharmacist's response. We can note, however, that these elements participate in the overall organization of that action in different ways: The first two category terms contribute to the pharmacist's response to the interviewer's question, while the third is included in a parenthetical assessment that briefly interrupts the progressivity of this response.[6] In this regard, the parenthetical assessment stands out from the rest of her turn in at least three ways. First, in producing the assessment, the pharmacist shifts from reporting what men say to her to offering her own view on the reported conduct. Second, although negative, this assessment is designedly non-serious, in contrast to the seriousness of the elements of the turn that precede and follow it. And third, the pharmacist uses the assessment, including the aforementioned appended "really y'know" and interpellated laughter, to invite a moment of personal connection with the interviewer, apparently (although tacitly) on the basis of their co-membership in a category from a Pn-adequate collection (gender). In these ways, the pharmacist's parenthetical insertion briefly departs from the relevancies associated with the setting-based categories ('radio host' and 'pharmacist') to invoke their shared (as women) experience of "typical guy" habits, before resuming her treatment of the setting-based categories as relevant by returning to and completing her response (lines 10–12).

In both of the cases we have examined thus far in this section, we have observed how speakers use explicit mentions of Pn-adequate categories in forming actions, and thereby temporarily depart from setting-based categories to accomplish actions that depart from the relevancies of those categories. In Extract 4.5, we see a similar explicit use of Pn-adequate categories as a departure from setting-based categories and their relevancies, but in this case the departure brings about an abandonment of the occasion and its associated categories altogether, on the grounds of a participant's violation of expectations associated with multiple Pn-adequate categories. This case is from a televised interview conducted with tennis player Venus Williams (VW) prior to the first competitive match of her professional playing career at the age of 14 while her father, Richard Williams (RW) sat nearby. In the course of the interviewer's (IR's) questions, Richard Williams intervenes to

---

6 This parenthetical introduction of a Pn-adequate category as an alternative to a setting-based one can be similarly observed in other cases, including Extract 4.3. We take this up in our further analysis of that case in Chapter 7: Organizing Sequences of Action.

forestall the interviewer's questioning, and possibly to end the interview as a whole (see line 16), and to sanction the interviewer (lines 19, 21–23, and 25). In further examining this case in Chapter 6: Taking Turns at Talking and Selecting Next Speakers and Chapter 7: Organizing Sequences of Action, we take up how Richard Williams comes to intervene and how the interviewer objects to Richard Williams's intervention, treating it as interruptive. Here, we focus on how Richard Williams explicates and justifies his intervention on the basis of Venus Williams's membership in a range of categories with intersecting relevance for his conduct, including explicit mentions of age, gender, and race, and a tacit orientation to his membership in the categories 'parent' and 'coach'.

```
Extract 4.5: Venus Williams ABC Interview, 1995
01  IR:  You think you could beat her?
02            (.)
03  VW:  I know I can beat her.
04            (1.2)
05  IR:  You know it?
06            (2.2) ((VW nods, smiles))
07  IR:  Very confident?
08            (1.0)
09  VW:  I'm very confident.
10            (0.8)
11  IR:  You say it so easily.
12            (2.5)
13  IR:  Why?
14            (1.5)
15  VW:  Cuz I bel[ieve it.
16  RW:           [(All right, end that there) if you don't
17       mi:nd.
18            (.)
19  RW:  And let me tell you why:.
20            (1.0)
21  RW:  What she has sa:id, (0.5) she said it with so much
22       confidence the first time, (0.7) but you keep going on
23       and on:.
24  IR:  You-
25  RW:  (Listen to [her.)
26  IR:             [can't keep i- interrupting, I mean i- if you
27       want [(her-)
28  RW:       [You've got tuh understand that you('re) dealing
29       with a image of a fourteen year old chi:ld.
30            (0.3)
31  RW:  And this child gonna be out there playing when your old
32       ass and me gonna be in the gra:ve. When she say
33       something, we done told you what's happen(ed). (.hh)
34       You're dealing with a little Black ki:d, (.) and let her
35       be a kid. <She done answered it with a lot of confidence,
36       LEAVE THAT ALONE!
```

Having intervened in the interview, Richard Williams retrospectively accounts for having done so by formulating an accusation claiming that by "going on and on" (lines 22–23), the interviewer has failed to "understand" who he is "dealing with" (line 28) – that is, "a fourteen year old child" (line 29). By explicitly invoking Venus Williams's age and stage of life categories in this way, Richard Williams escalates the gravity of his accusation: His formulation, "fourteen-year-old child" explicitly positions Venus Williams as a member of the category "child," despite the fact that her age may qualify her as a teenager – a stage of life category that may not be entitled to the same degree of protection. When this accusation is met with silence rather than contrition on the interviewer's part (line 30), Richard Williams continues his accusation, further enhancing it by contrasting the interviewer's (and his own) membership in an age/stage of life category ('old ass') to warrant his protection of her (lines 31–32) and underscore the interviewer's failure to meet this category-bound obligation.

In the talk that follows, Richard Williams invokes Venus Williams's membership in a set of intersecting categories – that is, her status as a "little Black kid" (line 34) – that establish additional distinct axes of variation with the interviewer, who he thereby tacitly categorizes as a 'white adult.' Richard Williams's continuing accusation thus asserts Venus Williams and the interviewer's respective memberships in these contrasting categories as a basis for highlighting her vulnerability to his actions, and thereby treats these categories as superseding the relevance of the setting-based 'tennis prodigy' category that was the main basis for her participation in the interview. Moreover, Richard Williams's use of multiple categories for Venus Williams (and thus the interviewer) departs from Sacks's economy rule, which underscores the interviewer's manifold failures to fulfil the obligations associated with his membership in categories from the collections Richard Williams has used to categorize Venus Williams. Thus, while the interviewer evidently produced actions associated with his setting-based 'interviewer' category, Richard Williams seeks to establish that he has transgressed obligations (e.g., for care and concern) bound to his and Venus Williams's membership in an alternative set of Pn-adequate categories.

As we detail in our further analysis of this case in Chapter 6: Taking Turns at Talking and Selecting Next Speakers, Richard Williams initiates and composes his action by reference to his rights and obligations as Venus Williams's parent and coach, intervening to shield her from potentially damaging questioning by the interviewer. He thereby tacitly acts by reference to these categories, in contrast to his explicit use of multiple Pn-adequate categories as we have just noted. As suggested by our analyses of this extract and the preceding one, even where explicit category formulations feature in the formation of actions, they may also serve to tacitly treat other categories as relevant for the conduct at hand. More generally, circumstances in which one or more participants explicitly categorize themselves or others may also involve tacit categorization, sometimes in relation to the explicit mentions of categories and sometimes independently of them. In the following section, we build on this by considering actions that are not formed using explicit mentions of categories, but for which the design features and type of action nonetheless tacitly index the relevance of one or more categories.

4.3 Tacitly using categories as bases for designing and evaluating actions

As we noted in Chapter 3: Methodological Principles, Practices, and Challenges, although tacit uses of categories have commonly been treated as a significant methodological challenge, in many cases (including those we have examined in the preceding sections of this chapter) they are rendered plainly observable by features of participants' conduct. While the range of ways in which this may become evident in particular cases is indefinite, and therefore a potentially rich site for future research, in this section we offer some considerations based on two main types of cases. In Section 4.3.1 we examine multiple instances of the same action (requesting) as a strategy for revealing how this action is unavoidably composed and/or understood by reference to the speaker and recipient(s)' memberships in one or more categories, and the entitlements and obligations associated with those categories (also see our discussion of these matters in Chapter 2: Approaching Membership Categorization). Then, in Section 4.3.2, we introduce some ways in which participants' orientations to categories and categorial matters can be observed in the features of other types of embodied conduct.

4.3.1 Similar actions formed up in different ways, making tacit uses of categories observable

Requests, offers, and other forms of "recruitment" have been the subject of substantial CA research (e.g., Clayman & Heritage, 2014; Curl, 2006; Curl & Drew, 2008; Drew & Couper-Kuhlen, 2014; Floyd et al., 2020; Kendrick & Drew, 2016). This research has demonstrated how the design features of requests or offers are sensitive to the occasions in which the action is initiated, the speaker's orientation to their entitlement to initiate the action, the recipient's ability to complete the initiated course of action, and the amount of effort on the part of speaker and/or recipient this will entail. Although this work has typically not centrally examined categorial features of requests (but see, e.g., Flinkfeldt et al., 2022; Rossi & Stivers, 2020), how participants can be categorized is a key way in which such entitlements and obligations are managed, patrolled, and defended (cf. Rossi & Stivers, 2020). We illustrate this by examining the array of requests from dinnertime conversations in the extracts that follow. In each case, the design of the request is evidently oriented to different entitlements in relation to the respective category incumbencies of the speaker and recipient.

The first of these, shown in Extract 4.6 (also analysed in Raymond & Lerner, 2014), shows how a recipient of a request may object to the request's design features and thereby expose how it has been inappositely designed in light of the speaker and recipient's respective category memberships. The requester in this case is Rick, who has been invited by his friend Jim to participate in a dinner that is being recorded by Jim's sister as part of a class assignment. The request recipient is Jim's mother, Ms. Tolivey, who objects to the casual form that Rick's request takes.

```
Extract 4.6: Family dinner (GB07 Peppermill)
01  Rick:  Can I have some of dat pasta ther:e.
02            (2.0)
03   MsT:  I have a na:me.
04            (3.0)
05  Rick:  Ms. Tolivey can I °have some pasta°=
06   MsT:  =↑Absolu:tely it would be my pleasur:e (.) to pass
07          the pasta
```

After a lengthy silence (line 02) following Rick's initial request (which foreshadows trouble in relation to the granting of the request – see Chapter 7: Organizing Sequences of Action) during which Ms. Tolivey suspends her current embodied involvements (Raymond & Lerner, 2014), she defers the fulfilment of the request with an objection to (line 03). She thereby treats objecting to the design of the request, and specifically Rick's failure to address her by name, as having a higher priority than granting the request. Rick's subsequent reformulation of the request reveals his analysis of the substance of Ms. Tolivey's objection: in contrast to his prior use of a tacit form of addressing (Lerner, 2003), he begins the reformulated request by addressing her formally, using her title and last name (also see our discussion of address terms in Chapter 5: Referring to and Addressing People). He then adopts a more formal diction in forming up its remaining elements, changing the colloquial noun phrase "some of dat pasta there" to the more standard form, "some pasta," and in the process dropping the non-standard pronunciation, "dat" from the request (line 05). In addition, his quiet delivery of the latter part of the reformulated request registers both the admonishment he has been subjected to and the resulting recalibration of his understanding of the degree of formality relevant for the occasion in which he is participating.

The resulting upgraded formality of the form of Rick's request form indexes a shift from his initial request to its reformulation in what he treats as the relevant setting-based categories. That is, it reveals how the initial request was designed for a co-member of a 'friend' category (or other similar equal-status categorial relationship), while Ms. Tolivey's objection and the subsequent iteration of the request index the unequal status associated with their different age and/or stage of life categories without these categories ever being explicitly mentioned (cf. Raymond's, 2016 analysis of how the T/V distinction in Spanish somewhat more explicitly indexes relative formality and hence categorial relationships of speaker and recipient).

Although Ms. Tolivey's objection only tacitly indexed the categorial source of her objection, her uptake of Rick's reformulation, an emphatic and elaborated granting (lines 06–07), treats its more formal design as having thoroughly corrected its prior shortcomings. Specifically, the granting, "Absolutely," underscores that Rick's entitlement to make the request is unquestionable, and her subsequent elaboration of what is entailed by this granting minimizes the degree of contingency involved in fulfilling the request, claiming it to be a "pleasure" as opposed to a possible imposition. While the exaggerated form of this granting proposes to dispense with the category-bound asymmetry invoked by her preceding objection and acquiesced to in Rick's subsequent reformulation, it also serves as a patronizing positive assessment that 'rewards' the corrective action he has taken and thereby retains this asymmetry.

The objection to the request by its recipient in Extract 4.6 can be contrasted with the trouble-free fulfilment of a similar request to pass a food item (in this case butter) in Extract 4.7. Here, Shane produces a request addressed to Michael, as a continuation of a turn for which Michael was also the primary recipient (line 01), and Michael begins fulfilling the request during its ongoing production and during the silence that follows at line 03 (also see the more detailed analysis of this exchange by Schegloff, 1997c, pp. 180–182).

```
Extract 4.7: Chicken Dinner
01  SHA:  .hhhh Most wishful thinkin' hey hand me some a' dat
02        fuckin budder will you?
03            (0.8) ((MIC hands butter to SHA))
04  SHA:  °°Oh::yeah°°
05            (1.1)
06  NAN:  C'n I have some t[oo
07  MIC:              [mm-hm[hm:
08  NAN:                  [hm-hm-↑h[m    [↑he-ha-]ha  .hehh ]
09  VIV:                            [Ye[h[I wa]nt] some too.]
10  SHA:                              [N[o:. ] [( )-
11  SHA:  No.
12            (0.2)
13  SHA:  Ladie[s la:st.
14  NAN:      [No-
```

The request in this case is produced in a similarly informal register to the initial request in Extract 4.6, as Shane marks its beginning and his shift from his preceding assessment with the informal use of "hey" as a method of addressing that establishes a place for the request that follows. This beginning is further consistent with Shane's use of a high-entitlement and low-contingency grammatical format through the demand form "hand me" and tag question "will you?" (lines 01–02). The informality of the request is also underscored by the pronunciation of "dat" (line 01) similar to what we saw in Extract 4.6, and the use of profanity prior to his naming of the requested item (line 02). While no category is mentioned as a basis for the request, it appears to be designed for a recipient who is a co-member of the category 'friend,' and possibly more specifically 'male friend.' Michael's immediate, unelaborated compliance tacitly aligns him as a co-member of this category by treating the request form as unremarkable, in contrast to the rejection of the request and its associated categorial incumbencies seen in Extract 4.6.

These observations are underscored by further requests for the butter produced in the ensuing moments. The first of these, produced by Nancy at line 06, resembles the second iteration of Rick's request in Extract 4.6, but without the formality of the address term insisted on by Ms. Tolivey and acquiesced to by Rick. The grammatical format of Nancy's request is also lower-entitlement and higher-contingency than Shane's preceding request to Michael, formed up as a request rather than a demand. Together, these features seem to tacitly index Nancy's treatment of Shane as a co-member of the 'friend' category while also departing from the gender-specific friendship category apparently implicated by Shane's request to Michael – and sensitive to her membership in the 'guest' (rather than 'host') category. The second of these further requests, produced by Vivian at line 09, is in turn higher-entitlement and lower-contingency than Nancy's, grammatically formatted as a statement of Vivian's desire for the butter rather than in the question format used by Nancy, while still falling short of the demand format of Shane's request. It thereby appears to be fitted to Vivian's co-membership with Shane in the 'romantic partner' category.

Another key moment follows, in the form of Shane's "ironic or mock rejection" (Schegloff, 1997c, p. 181) of Nancy and Vivian's requests (lines 10 and 11, respectively), and his explicit use of a gender category to account for doing so (line 13). By subverting a 'ladies first' rule and thereby tacitly asserting an alternative 'first come, first served' rule in this way, Shane deploys an ironic use of gender as a means of solving an organizational problem (cf. Section 4.1) posed by Nancy and Vivian's requests potentially competing both with each other and with his own efforts to secure the butter (Schegloff, 1997c). In doing so, he also makes explicit a set of gendered relationships that, as we have proposed in the preceding analysis, may have already been tacitly indexed by the respective design features of the requests produced during the preceding moments.

The requests we have considered thus far can be juxtaposed with a non-serious request in Extract 4.8 by Michael for Nancy to cut his chicken, along with Nancy's blunt rejection in response. This takes place in the aftermath of a tease associated with the fulfilment of a prior request that has been taken up as a humour source (not transcribed), which contributes to providing a context in which Michael can be heard as joking rather than actually requesting.

Extract 4.8: Chicken Dinner

```
01           (2.3)
02  MIC:  ↑Nance kin you- kin you ↓cut my chic↓ken.
03           (0.4)
04  NAN:  Do yer own cut(h)'n(h)n(h)n!
```

Michael's selection of Nancy as the recipient of this joking request is by reference to their co-membership in the 'romantic partner' category, but the substance of the action serves to (jokingly) mis-categorize her as his parent. More specifically, by asking Nancy to perform a task any competent adult could perform for themselves, Michael casts himself as a child and positions Nancy as his mother. He thereby uses a recurrent gender-based complaint about the Oedipal fantasies underpinning men's heterosexual romantic relationships with women (see Freud, 1905/2017) as a basis for joking. Michael's marked pitch shifts in his production of the request further invite its hearing as "doing 'doing being a child'" (cf. Schegloff, 2005b, p. 469), and thus underscore its design as a non-serious action (also see Schegloff, 1987b).

Nancy's response (line 04) shows her orientation to Michael's complete lack of category-based entitlement to produce a request of this nature, together with the lack of any category-based obligation for her to fulfil it, as she bluntly rejects the joke-request. This contrasts with the rejection we saw in Extract 4.6, where Ms. Tolivey's objection to Rick's initial request was to *how the request was formed up* by reference to Rick's and her respective category memberships, which thereby invited Rick to re-issue his request with these design features in mind. Nancy's rejection here indexes her category membership relative to Michael, with her instruction to him to "Do yer own cut'n" implicating an objection to *the request being done at all.* In addition, however, Nancy's subsequent laughter displays her understanding of Michael's action as a joke on the basis of these same category-based (non-)entitlements and (non-)obligations.

Taken together, the cases we have examined in this section demonstrate how categories tacitly provide for the moral valence of how an action is formed up, and for what action(s) a speaker can be understood to have produced. In selecting a ubiquitous and ordinary form of action to examine, our analysis shows that there is virtually unavoidably a reflexive relationship between the compositional practices used to formulate actions, the substantive character of the action, and the relevance of participants' respective memberships in particular categories – a state of affairs that can be further appreciated by reference to many of the cases we examine in the chapters that follow.

4.3.2 Embodied features of action that expose tacit uses of categories

As we noted in Chapter 2: Approaching Membership Categorization, for many categories, membership is presumed to be immediately available based on visual appearances, and/or (following Sacks's viewer's maxim) on the basis of actions or activities – including their visually available embodied features. For participants, this is often entirely tacit and taken for granted, thereby presenting challenges (as we described in Chapter 3: Methodological Principles, Practices, and Challenges) for analysts who seek to empirically ground claims about participants' orientations to particular categories in relation to embodied features of their conduct (also see, e.g., Mondada, 2021; Reynolds, 2017). As we noted in our prior discussion, however, such categorial orientations may be readily available even while remaining completely tacit. This can be appreciated in relation to embodied practices by reference to some classic observations by Sacks (1992, p. 81), which he offered during a segment of a lecture in which he addressed questions from students who had been given an assignment to observe people exchanging glances:

> I was walking down the hall the other day, to give an exam to one girl. She was standing, leaning up against the wall. In between us walked another girl. She passed this girl first, and then me. And the girl who was standing against the wall looked at me and gave a shrug of her shoulders with a big smile, which I returned. And I don't think it was a big puzzle over what was going on. The girl who walked by was smoking a pipe.
>
> Now, the two of us knew what we were noticing. But that can be problematic. For example, on the Berkeley campus or in places in Berkeley, you often find interracial couples wandering around. . . . And people who look like tourists, visitors to the campus, etc. – that is, strangers – will stop and look at these couples and then check with others around. . . . And when they do that, people will not infrequently look back at them and give them a negative stare. As if to say, "Who the hell are *you*" (emphasis in original).

Although he does not use membership categorization terms to describe these phenomena, Sacks's observations are evidently designed to demonstrate how an embodied practice – exchanging glances, along with accompanying gestures (e.g., shrugs) and facial expressions (e.g., smiles) – is recurrently used by participants as a tacit method for registering a departure from category-based expectations. That is, in the instances he describes, observers use glances as a way of sharing their recognition that an activity is being performed by a member of a category (from a Pn-adequate collection) to which it is not bound, and treating it as remarkable by virtue of this. In the first example the glance is reciprocated and the associated categorial orientation and assessment are thereby ratified as mutually shared. In contrast, in the second example it is rejected through the use of a different embodied practice of looking – a "stare" rather than a "glance" – with the parties thereby exposed as diverging in their understandings of what can properly be treated as a departure, and one party sanctioning the other for their evident racism on this basis. Moreover, across these examples, participants' membership in a range of categories is treated as immediately visually available and as a mutually intelligible – albeit in some cases contestable – basis for evaluating their actions.

We can also note in relation to Sacks's observations how eye gaze – and what observers characterize as 'glances,' 'stares,' and other types of looks – are treated by those members as 'for cause' actions. That is, features of eye gaze, including its direction (particularly when directed at another party) and duration, are produced and recognized by members as implementing particular actions and thereby inviting responsive (and especially aligning) actions by other parties. These reciprocally organized forms of embodied conduct thereby share features in common with sequence organization (see Chapter 7: Organizing Sequences of Action), albeit without the supporting infrastructure of a turn-taking system that in part organizes the meaning of talk and/or its absence (see Chapter 6: Taking Turns at Talking and Selecting Next Speakers).

In building on these observations, we consider a further ethnographic fieldnote shared by a colleague, and presented in Extract 4.9. While sharing the feature of a category-related exchange of glances that parallels those described by Sacks, this case demonstrates how this practice can index the sudden consequentiality of the co-membership of the glancing parties themselves in a Pn-adequate category, in relation to the membership of others in the scene in a contrasting category from the same collection.

Extract 4.9: Train (fieldnote, personal communication)

```
01   A British colleague is riding a train, sitting on her own in a
02   car with just a few passengers, quietly working. At the next
03   station, a large group of rowdy football fans – all apparently
04   male – enter the carriage. As the group shows themselves to be
05   staying in the carriage, continuing to drink and shout as they do
06   so, our colleague makes and briefly sustains eye contact with
07   another woman on the train.
```

Although the occasion for their gathering was evidently a football game, the group arriving on the train was composed of persons who could also, based on their immediate visual appearance, be categorized (including by our colleague) as 'men' rather than (only) as 'football fans.' This heightened the potential relevance of our colleague's contrasting membership not only in a 'non-football fan' category but in the gender category 'woman' – as suggested by her orientation to the heightened relevance of her *connection* to the other person visibly categorizable as a woman in the same carriage. That the import of these connections and contrasts are recognizable by and to members can be appreciated in the fact that each of the two women looked to the other at the same moment, with their maintenance of their eye contact suggesting each was oriented to their co-membership in a readily visible category beyond the setting-based 'train passenger' category that now consequentially connected them. That is, although no words were exchanged, making and then sustaining eye contact (e.g., rather than looking away to indicate that the look was incidental or accidental), suggests that for each of them, this contact had a 'for cause' basis tied to the most obvious category co-membership that connected them. While the occasion and data do not allow a definitive analysis of this 'for cause' basis of their exchange of glances, it appears to be a method of mutually registering their shared understanding of their changed circumstances (and thus shared need to be 'on guard') – or perhaps something more, such as a tacit agreement to look out for one another.

Even without definitively settling the shared meaning of this sustained eye-contact, we can recognize its status for the participants as a purposeful, and thus meaningful, action that reflects the relevance of categories and categorization for their conduct and their evaluation of the change in their prevailing circumstances: The two passengers, sitting apart from one another, had no apparent basis for seeing a connection with one another as they pulled into the station; once at the station, however, they found their circumstances altered by the group boarding the train. This changed situation in turn shifted the categorial landscape from their routine and unremarkable co-membership in the 'passenger' category to their consequential co-membership in the 'woman' category. The newly constituted occasion thereby enabled mutual eye contact to be constitutive of one specific action – registering mutual concern – in contrast to alternative potential bases for sustained looks between strangers in other circumstances, such as displaying romantic or other interest in another (cf. Sacks, 1992, p. 50).

Such encounters highlight the systematic (potential) relevance of contrasting category memberships from the same collection as well as co-membership in the same category. Given the ways these connections and contrasts can be used by members to understand their circumstances and compose or inflect actions, observations regarding such occasions open a window onto one methodical basis for the potentially ubiquitous relevance of categories from Pn-adequate collections, and thus one way in which the relevance of such collections of categories can be seen to 'lie in wait.'

Extending the preceding analyses, we can move beyond a specific type of embodied conduct (eye gaze) to consider how a range of bodily behaviours can be inspected for the understandings they display of an encounter and the person's participation and place therein – including by reference to category memberships. This is illustrated by Extract 4.10, which was examined by Lerner and Raymond (2021) as a case of "body trouble." As Lerner and Raymond (2021, p. 281) note, in this encounter, "one member of a dining party (Larry) who is paying for their meal manages the transaction with the cashier, while the other member (Ann), arriving at the counter after him, stands to his side (nearer the door)." Our interest here is in how the closing of the encounter (also see Schegloff & Sacks, 1973) is conducted, and the range of categories the participants treat as relevant and consequential in forming up their participation therein through their talk and especially the accompanying embodied conduct, key features of which are shown in the array of four screenshots (a, b, c, d) from the video recording that follow the extract in Figure 4.2.

```
Extract 4.10: Restaurant payment
01              (0.6)
02   Ton:  We- good to see you folks.
03   Lar:  Ye:a, good to seE you.
04   Ton:  Thank you, an:: (.) >again give my regards to the girls
05         when you talk to 'em.<=
06   Lar:  =Yeah.
07   Ton:  An:: (0.4) >look forward (t')seein' you real ↑soon.<
```

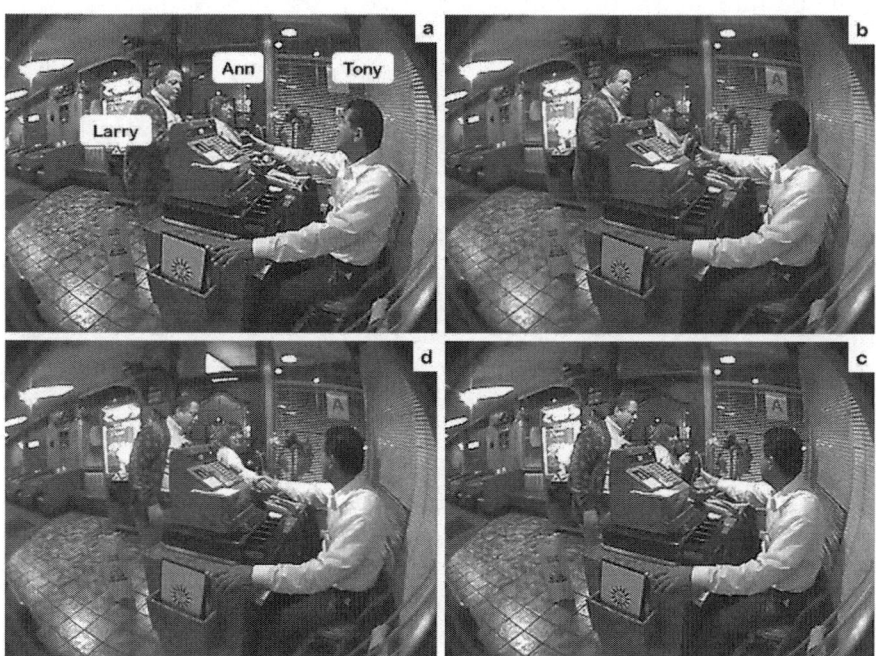

FIGURE 4.2 Restaurant payment

Just after Larry and the restaurant owner, Tony, complete the transaction, Tony initiates closing with an assessment (line 02), which treats Larry and Ann (who are evidently a married couple) as members of the 'customer' category but also a more familiar relational category (e.g., 'acquaintance' or 'friend') associated with repeated encounters and the shared biographical details associated with a personal investment in seeing one another (as conveyed in lines 04–05). Following Larry's reciprocal assessment, which serves to ratify the associated categorial implications of Tony's assessment, Tony thanks Larry and then produces a further action (lines 04–05) that maintains his orientation to a familiar relational category by extending regards to "the girls" (referring to Larry and Ann's daughters). Just as he begins to do this, he initiates a handshake with Larry by beginning to extend his right hand towards him (see Figure 4.2a). On seeing this move, Larry begins a reciprocal move to extend his hand, with the resulting arrival of his hand at just the place and moment projected by Tony's arriving hand, allowing the parties to complete the handshake as Larry affirms Tony's good wishes (line 06).

Throughout the encounter up to this point, Ann's participation (not transcribed) has been attenuated, with her contributions largely following and repeating Larry's. In this respect, the participants have conducted encounter with Larry representing the couple as one party in the situated 'payer'/'payee' pair of categories. We can also see an orientation to this division of labour reflected in the position Ann has taken up near the door and the relaxed body posture and facial expression she has adopted while leaning against it. This division of labour also coincides with their partitioning in terms of gender categories, with the two men participating in the transaction while the woman awaits its completion – a possible reflection of the gender-bound expectations commonly associated with completion of payments for meals among heterosexual couples. This becomes a source of trouble as Tony, after completing his handshake with Larry, turns his gaze and his extended arm towards Ann (Figure 4.2b), initiating a handshake with her. He thereby shifts from an orientation to the 'payer'/'payee' (and intersecting gender) categories to a related but broader 'restaurant owner'/'customer' and/ or 'acquaintance'/'acquaintance' categories as he moves towards closing the encounter. As Lerner and Raymond (2021) note, however, the reduced projectability of this handshake initiation by Tony results in a delay in Ann's extension of her hand, while she moves an object from her right hand to her left (Figure 4.2c) before she extends it for the handshake (Figure 4.2d). As Lerner and Raymond (2021, p. 283) observe,

Beyond (and in addition to) the reduced projectability of Tony's hand proffer, Ann, the other member of the dining party, 'did not see it coming' in another sense: Here, remediation exposes Ann's orientation to the social organization of the occasion, and to her category-bound place within it. Although Ann watches the handshake between the cashier and the bill payer, she makes no move to prepare for a second handshake. She does not free up her right hand (which is holding an object) or otherwise put herself 'on-deck' for a possibly forthcoming next handshake. That is, in sustaining the manner in which the parties conducted the encounter up to this point, she treats the initial handshake as an only handshake – or more precisely, she treats the handshake with her husband as adequate for the party and not as the first-in-a-series of handshakes. Her relaxed body posture and the hand she has left occupied convey that she is not treating the handshake as an *initial* handshake that puts her in line as next-up for a handshake. She then acts surprised when, with little warning . . . the cashier moves his right hand laterally toward her.

We can further note that after Ann's facial expression initially registers surprise, she accelerates the movement of her hand to remediate its delayed arrival and shifts to a smile. Tony accommodates this effort by halting the progressivity of a further utterance he began as he completed his handshake with Larry (see the stretching on "and" and the mid-turn silence in his turn at line 07), thereby treating this utterance and associated categorial implications as addressed to Ann.

As this case and the others we have examined in this section show, tacit orientations to the relevance of categories can be observed in features of participants' embodied conduct, along with (in some, but not all, cases) accompanying talk-based actions. While this includes both setting-based and Pn-adequate categories, embodied orientations to the latter recurrently come to be exposed in particularly visible ways in moments where evident trouble arises in relation to them.

4.4   Using categories in the Rochester police encounter

In returning to the encounter we introduced at the outset of the chapter in light of our discussions on categorial bases for action formation and ascription in the preceding sections, we offer here some further observations on the segment of the encounter on which Jones's (2021) analysis focused, which is shown in Extract 4.11. Prior to this extract, and as noted previously, the police officers have forcefully restrained the girl, Cassie (CAS), handcuffing her before attempting to force her into a squad car. Cassie has strongly resisted the officers' actions, both physically and by repeatedly demanding that they release her and allow her to see her father (also see lines 01 and 03).

```
Extract 4.11: Rochester, NY Police Encounter
01   CAS:  I WANT MY DA:D, ST↑O:P!
02    P1:  (Nothing wrong.)
03   CAS:  .HH HH ST↑O:P!
04    P1:  SIT UP!
05   CAS:  N↑O::=HHH[HO:
06    P1:          [YOU'RE ACTING LIKE A CH[I:LD, STOP!
07   CAS:                                [I DON'T WANNA
08         S- I ↑AM A CHILD, FU:CK! .HH HHH .HHH ↑A:H::
09         MY [(FOOT) UH!
10    P2:     [(Let's get) this one ba:ck to the house.
```

While this transcript covers only a small portion of the encounter, it begins with an *n*th version of Cassie's pleading exclamation (line 01). Virtually every design feature of her plea, "I WANT MY DA:D," (line 01) reflects its category-bound connection to her status as a child: her use of the category 'dad' invokes the relevance of her reciprocal categorization as a 'child' – as *his* child – and is consistent with, and reinforced by, her use of the reference form "*MY* DA:D," and her packaging of this request as an expression of desire ("I WANT") addressed to other co-present adults who can presumably act on it. Thus, beyond the straightforward request for a parent she conveys more immediately, Cassie also tacitly pleads with the officers to be recognized as a child, and thereby reveals her understanding that they have so far failed to see or understand her in these terms. Indeed, it is precisely her tearful rejection of P1's command (line 04) – which, in its realization as a breathy and stretched "N↑O::" that is produced "in a whine-delivery" that "is part of its realization as 'doing complaining'" (Schegloff, 2005a, p. 468), further instantiating the relevance of membership in the 'child' category – that seems to attract the officer's frustration.

P1's use of the admonishing "YOU'RE ACTING LIKE A CH[I:LD" (line 06) serves to escalate his preceding directive (line 04) by employing a shift from the preceding tacit treatment of Cassie as a member of a setting-based 'subject of police authority' category to explicit use of a P*n*-adequate category, 'child,' as a resource for complaining about her non-compliance. As we noted in Chapter 2: Approaching Membership Categorization, Sacks (1972b, p. 336) observes how "positioned" categories can be used to formulate complaints of exactly the form P1 uses here: by claiming that a recipient is "acting like" a member of a 'lower' category in a stage-of-life hierarchy, a speaker can sanction their failure to conduct themselves in accordance with the expectations of a 'higher' category of which they are recognizably a member (also see Sacks's, 1992, vol. 1, p. 544 observations on "intentional mis-identifications"). Precisely because Cassie is a child, however, P1's mis-categorization of her licenses his escalating efforts to compel her compliance instead of shifting to the sort of accommodation and patience that would otherwise be relevant if he acknowledged her membership in the 'child' category, including her tacit self-categorization as such. Thus, this format for the formation of an action in explicitly categorial terms exposes (and confirms for Cassie) how, in treating her as a 'subject of police authority,' P1 (and the other officers in the scene), have also been tacitly treating her as an 'adult,' and have not afforded her the assumption of innocence and need for protection that is bound to the 'child' category (also see Rafaely & Whitehead, 2020). The officers' conduct in this encounter underscores how such deliberate mis-categorization establishes a procedural basis for injustice: mis-categorization can be used to warrant conduct that would not otherwise be relevant or acceptable by reference to the person's recognizable and/or self-identified category membership.

This in turn provides evidence for the officers' tacit orientation to Cassie as a member of the race category 'Black,' by reference to the well-documented phenomenon of Black children being especially vulnerable to being seen and treated, especially by police, as older than they are and/or being mis-categorized as adults (see, e.g., Epstein et al., 2017; Goff et al., 2014). Race thus serves as an available, although entirely tacit and thus defeasible, account for the officers' inapposite categorization of Cassie (also see our discussion of defeasibility in Chapter 3: Methodological Principles, Practices, and Challenges).

In affirming her membership in the 'child' category in her retort to P1, Cassie defends herself against his complaint by counter-complaining about how he and the other officers have failed to *allow* her to be the child that she is (also see our discussion of counters in Chapter 7: Organizing Sequences of Action) – including how they have done so despite her repeated tacit claims of membership in this category through her pleas for access to her father and her other conduct. She thereby casts her preceding resistance to the officers' actions as including resistance to their (possibly racist) mis-categorization of her as an adult.

We can thus observe how, across this encounter, the actions of the participants, and the trouble they give rise to and/or seek to manage, are produced and interpreted by reference to how speaker and recipient are (mis-)categorized. This includes, as we have seen in the preceding sections, both explicit and tacit uses of categories, and their implications for both the moral valence of the particular formats in which actions are produced and the bases for producing them at all.

4.5   Summary and conclusions

In this chapter, we have focused on the distinctive ways that membership categories feature in the formation and ascription of actions, and how these interact with and shape other resources participants use in acting and interpreting others' actions. We have thereby begun to specify some of the details of how categories – and especially those from Pn-adequate collections – 'lie in wait' as 'quiet centres of power and persuasion,' as we discussed in Chapter 1: An Introduction to Categories in Social Interaction. In particular, it is not rigid adherence to or enforcement of category-bound entitlements and obligations that provides for this but rather the flexible, contingent, and often creative ways participants deploy, manage, and/or resist them in particular cases. Thus, by specifying some features of the categorial systematics of actions formed up in particular turns at talk, this chapter lays key foundations for the remainder of the book, which the chapters that follow develop by reference to how categories feature in other generic organizations of practice for interaction. We turn next, in Chapter 5: Referring to and Addressing People, to examine a particularly category-rich sub-domain of word selection and (extending our analyses here) an important set of resources for forming up actions in which persons are explicitly referred to or addressed. We then consider the turn-taking system, which organizes who gets to act, and when (Chapter 6: Taking Turns at Talk and Selecting Next Speakers); what participants should do if and when they are afforded opportunities to act, and how they manage the production of sequences of successive actions (Chapter 7: Organizing Sequences of Action); how participants use the practices of repair to manage various forms of trouble during the course of their own and/or others' actions (Chapter 8: Managing Troubles in Speaking, Hearing, and Understanding); and how participants manage epistemic and related matters during the course of (sequences of) actions (Chapter 9: Managing Knowledge, Experience, and Entitlement) – all with a focus on how categorial systematics and these generic organizations of practice mutually constitute each other.

5

REFERRING TO AND ADDRESSING PEOPLE

5.0   Introduction

On the morning of the United States Memorial Day holiday in May 2020, Amy Cooper became the latest in a series of infamous cases of white women who attempted to direct police authority against Black people with whom they were having disputes. In this case, the target was Christian Cooper,[1] who had asked Amy Cooper to leash her dog, as required by the rules of the part of New York City's Central Park known as "The Ramble" where the dispute took place. When she refused, Christian Cooper began filming her on his smartphone and, as the dispute unfolded, she threatened to call the police and "tell them there's an African American man threatening my life" – a threat she subsequently carried out as he continued filming her. The profile of this incident was launched to even greater heights when, later the same day, a white police officer, Derek Chauvin, murdered a Black man, George Floyd, in Minneapolis, after a store clerk had called emergency services to report a suspicion that Floyd had made a purchase with a counterfeit $20.

News reports and commentary on the Central Park incident (e.g., Armus, 2020; Brett, 2020; Harriot, 2020; Maslin Nir, 2020a, 2020b) centred on Amy Cooper's weaponization of commonplace racist tropes associating Black men with violence and white women with vulnerability to such violence, documenting in broad terms the initiation and unfolding of the dispute. In addition, these discussions related the incident to some of the socio-historical formations reflected and reproduced therein, as well as exploring the personal

---

1 While the two antagonists in this dispute had the same last name, they are not related.

DOI: 10.4324/9781003120599-6

histories and experiences of the protagonists in relation to their actions during the dispute. However, the details of Amy Cooper's conduct, when reported or quoted at all, were generally treated as needing no further explanation – as constituting a self-evident basis for the undisputed consensus regarding the racism embodied in the incident. While it may be suggested that this treatment of her conduct simply reflects how self-evident it in fact was, the consensus in this regard can also be treated as an accomplishment grounded in the details of her actions, and her actions can thus be examined in terms of exactly how they came off in just the way they did. In particular, her references to Christian Cooper (especially as "an African American man," as noted previously), as well as to herself, both during her exchange with him and while speaking to the emergency call-taker, can be examined for precisely how they render as plainly recognizable the deliberate racism of her actions – while also offering insights into how other incidents that share some (but not all) features in common with this one may be viewed as more opaque or controversial with regard to their status as (possible) instances of racism (cf. Durrheim et al., 2015; Stokoe, 2015; Whitehead, 2015).

We will return to an extended analysis of the person references in this case towards the end of this chapter. First, however, in order to lay a foundation for a close examination of these references, we provide in what follows an overview of the intersections between membership categories and practices for referring to and addressing people in interaction. In Section 5.1, we introduce the practices of person reference, including a key distinction between systematic resources for referring to persons and the further interactional work to which person references may contribute. In doing so, we examine 'third-person' reference forms (Section 5.1.1), 'first-person' (self) reference forms (Section 5.1.2), and 'second-person' (recipient) reference forms (Section 5.1.3), before returning in Section 5.2 to apply these discussions to the Central Park case and then summarizing and concluding the chapter in Section 5.3.

5.1 Categories and person reference: systematic resources and their interactional deployments

In his foundational "Partial sketch of a systematics" of practices for person reference in talk-in-interaction, Schegloff (1996, pp. 438–439) poses the following questions, which together constitute an "analytic theme" that has remained central to much of the subsequent conversation analytic research in this area:

> How do speakers do reference to persons so as to accomplish, on the one hand, that nothing but referring is being done, and/or on the other hand that something else in addition to referring is being done by the talk practice

which has been employed? Relatedly, how is talk analyzed by recipients so as to find that 'simple' reference to someone has been done, or that referring has carried with it other practices and outcomes as well?

These questions establish a crucial distinction between "referring *simpliciter*" (Schegloff, 1996, p. 440) and what Haviland (2007, p. 232) later called "referring *dupliciter*" (also see Schegloff, 2009, p. 364). The former of these terms is used in relation to any reference form that is "default or unmarked" in the sense that it "does, and is understood by recipients to be doing, nothing but simply referring to the person it identifies" (Schegloff, 2009, p. 364) – that is, reference forms that are "specified via the *systematics* of person reference" (Schegloff, 1996, p. 467; emphasis in original). In contrast, the latter term is used as a designation for person references that observably depart from these default or unmarked forms and can therefore be inspected for the 'special' interactional work, beyond or in addition to mere reference, they are designed to accomplish – that is, reference forms whose use can be accounted for "by reference to the ensemble of *interactional* exigencies (Schegloff, 1996, p. 467; emphasis in original). As we will see, a key subset of these interactional exigencies involves category-related matters, with person references being a vehicle through which a speaker can introduce the relevance of new categories and/or shift from one set to another – and thus through which speakers can mobilize common-sense knowledge associated with categories in the service of interactional agendas or projects. (Also see our discussions of category maintenance and category change in Chapter 1: An Introduction to Categories in Social Interaction and action formation in Chapter 4: Forming and Making Sense of Actions).

In the following sections, we review some ways in which this distinction between 'system-relevance' and 'interaction-relevance' (cf. Klein, 2011) in a speaker's selection of a form of person reference can be observed in relation to the categories directly used or otherwise made available across three main types of person reference form, namely 'first-person' (or 'self-reference'), 'second-person' (or 'recipient reference'), and 'third-person reference.'[2] We thereby establish a set of systematic analytic resources that can be brought to bear on uses of categories in referring to and addressing people, before returning to the Central Park case as a way of demonstrating their application. We

---

2 While we restrict our discussion to these intersections between person reference and categories, other conversation analytic research (e.g., Button, 1987; Enfield, 2013; Raymond & White, 2017; Schegloff, 1972; Whitehead & Lerner, 2009) has extended some of these considerations to other domains of reference including place, object, time, and event references. Moreover, we focus in particular on practices for referring to specific, identifiable individuals or collectivities, as opposed to references to hypothetical persons or entire categories of people whose referents are indeterminate (cf. Whitehead & Lerner, 2020, pp. 47–48).

begin with third-person reference, since it is the domain for which categories of person are most systematically a central resource, before proceeding to consideration of how categories may figure in first- and second-person reference forms, for which they do not ordinarily serve as system-relevant resources.

5.1.1 Third-person reference forms

References to third persons – that is, persons other than the speaker and their immediate recipient(s) – are systematically grounded in participants' orientations to recipient design considerations, reflecting the speaker's sense of whether the referred-to person (or referent) is known to the speaker and/or recipients (Sacks & Schegloff, 1979; Schegloff, 1996). This provides for two main forms of third-party reference, namely 'recognitional' forms, which treat the referent as known to both the speaker and recipients, and 'non-recognitional' forms, which convey that the referent is not known to the recipients (Sacks & Schegloff, 1979; Schegloff, 1996).

As Sacks and Schegloff (1979) demonstrated in their pioneering study of person reference, the use of recognitional forms is structurally 'preferred' – meaning that participants systematically orient to a preference for using recognitional forms whenever possible – and names are a basic and massively used resource for doing so.[3] Moreover, Schegloff (1996) demonstrates that names are preferred over other recognitional reference forms, such as descriptions that identify a specific person who is proposed to be known-in-common without naming them (but see, e.g., Blythe, 2013; Enfield & Stivers, 2007; Levinson, 2005 for descriptions of cross-language variations).[4] Given that names are an alternative to categories, designedly

---

3 In addition to a preference for using recognitional forms, Sacks and Schegloff (1979) demonstrate a preference for 'minimization' – or the use of a single reference form – and they suggest that "names are prototypical and ideal recognitionals in part because they are minimized reference forms as well" (Sacks & Schegloff, 1979, p. 18). The preference for recognitional reference forms also parallels a preference for place formulations described by Schegloff (1972). Schegloff (1972, p. 97) points out that, in answering questions about, say, an address, people can respond by formulating places, which he calls "G for geographical," including "such formulations as street address (2903 Main Street) and latitude-longitude specifications." Alternatively, formulations that Schegloff (1972, p. 97) calls "Rm for 'relation to members'" may be used – for example, "John's place." Based on his examination of uses of these different ways of formulating places by speakers, Schegloff (1972, p. 100) notes that "the preference rule appears to be: use an Rm formulation if you can." This in turn constitutes a preference for using formulations that "turn on the outcome of a membership analysis, requiring an analysis of who knows whom, who are strangers, whether persons are members of such pair-relationships as would allow use of an Rm term" (Schegloff, 1972, p. 100). That is, using Rm formulations requires the use of categories and category-based relationships.
4 Schegloff (1996, p. 459) calls these "recognitional descriptions" and "recognitional descriptors." As we discuss later, categories are a systematic resource for the production of these descriptions.

referring to a person as an individual rather than as a member of a category of persons, categories are not the systematically preferred or 'default' resource for recognitional references. It is nonetheless possible that one or more categories could be inferable based on the specific name used, as in Extract 5.1, where Hyla's use of the normatively female name "Grace" (line 01) possibly makes inferences about the referent's gender category available.

```
Extract 5.1: Hyla and Nancy (13)
01      Hyl:   .hhh ↑Oh, >you know what< I was talking tuh Gra:ce.
02                   (0.2)
03      Nan:   °Gra[:ce,°
04      Hyl:       ['Member Gra:ce¿ My friend Gra[:ce,
05      Nan:                                      [Ye::ah.=
06      Hyl:   =.hhh Ay:::u::n, .hhhh she has, these best friends.
```

More generally, both first and last names may – for particular speakers and recipients, and depending on other contextual features to which they may be normatively tied – reveal the referent's possible membership in categories from a range of MCDs, including gender, race, ethnicity, class, nationality, and age (cf. Sacks, 1992; Schegloff, 1972). However, the *availability* of inferences of this sort based on a name does not necessarily imply – at least in the absence of additional evidence to this effect – that a speaker's use of the name was *designed* to mobilize such categories for some interaction-relevant end.

In cases in which a name by which both the speaker and recipients know the referent is not available, or where (as in Extract 5.1) recognition is not accomplished through the use of a name alone, speakers may use recognitional descriptions – for which categories serve as a recurrent resource. In this case, when Nancy initially shows she is having difficulty recognizing who Grace is (line 03), Hyla uses the categorial description "My friend" along with a further repetition of her name (line 04), which yields a display of recognition by Nancy (line 05). While this provides for Hyla's explicit mention of the category "friend," and we can note (following Sacks, 1972a, 1972b, 1992) that this category is necessarily chosen from a number of alternative ways in which Grace could 'accurately' be described (also see our discussions of this matter in Chapter 1: An Introduction to Categories in Social Interaction, and Chapter 2: Approaching Membership Categorization), it appears that the basis for choosing this category is securing Nancy's recognition of who Grace is, rather than doing any additional interactional work.

Extract 5.1 also demonstrates a further systematic way in which membership in a category – specifically, in this case, a gender category – can come to be explicitly revealed in relation to a person initially referred to by name. This can be seen in line 06, where Hyla uses the gender-specific pronoun "she" in a subsequent reference to Grace. Schegloff (1996, p. 450) uses the term "locally subsequent" to refer to pronominal reference forms of this sort (e.g., he/him, she/her, they/their), which index a person referred to in a prior ("locally initial") reference – for example, through use of a name, as in this case. Although in as many as two-thirds of the world's languages, these pronominal forms are non-gendered (Siewierska, 2005), and their use is thus not a systematic basis for making a referent's gender category available, in English they are gender-specific.[5] As such, while we return later to a consideration of how special category-related interactional work can be done by locally initial versus locally subsequent reference forms, for now we can register that Hyla's use of this locally subsequent form – and, more generally, similar uses by speakers in other cases – is recognizably system-relevant rather than designedly contributing in other ways to the action formed up in this turn (also see Klein, 2011; Raymond et al., 2021).

In cases where the use of a name as an initial reference form is not available despite the referent being known to both speaker and recipients – either because the speaker does not know or cannot recall it, or because the recipient is assumed not to know the referent by name – a range of categorial forms can be used while nonetheless being treated as unmarked, doing nothing more than referring. These include gender categories (e.g., 'that guy,' 'that woman'), kinship category terms used in recognitional references to a family member of the speaker or recipient (e.g., 'my mom,' 'your brother'), and other categories deployed as part of recognitional descriptions (e.g., 'the guy who was sitting next to you,' 'the tall woman in our class') (Schegloff, 1996; Stivers, 2007). However, in some cases where such a form (most especially a name, given the preference for their use when possible) is evidently available to both a speaker and recipient, a speaker nonetheless selects a different form. These reference forms, which Stivers (2007) calls "alternative recognitionals," expose the additional interactional work, beyond simply referring, the speaker is doing – and categories can figure prominently in this work. This is illustrated by Extract 5.2, showing a call to a South African radio show, during which the host, Eric, has been interviewing a South African-born former athlete, Zola Pieterse (née Budd), who controversially represented Britain in the Olympic Games during the apartheid period, when South Africa was banned from competing in international sporting events. During the course of expressing appreciation for the show, a caller, Rose, uses the alternative recognitional "a fellow South African" (line 08) to refer to Pieterse.

---

5 As Klein (2011) demonstrates, they/their pronouns can be used in cases where the gender category of a referent is not known, but their use as preferred pronouns by people who identify as gender non-binary has become commonplace more recently, and they can thus also be recognized as (at least potentially) indicative of the referent's gender category.

Extract 5.2: Radio call-in (215, SAfm, 7.5.08)
```
01  Rose:   You know what I love, about this programme?
02              (.)
03  Eric:   Mm
04  Rose:   >And I-< an:d I'm loving it tonight, h [is how many::
05  Eric:                                          [Hm
06  Rose:   .h people across the board, (.) phone in, (0.3) .hh
07  Rose:   and ↑just (.) express their delight and gratitu:de, (0.8)
08          for a fellow South ↑Afri↓can.
09  Eric:   Mm:[:.
10  Rose:      [.hh Not worrying about colour, or race, or anything
11          ↑else. <It's just absolutely: marvellous, I love this
12          programme for that. .hh[hh i- it's just (.) lovely to=
13  Eric:                          [°Ya, (   )°
14  Rose:   =hear South Africans of every race, colour and creed
15          phoning in to:: .hh congratulate Zola Budd, a:n::d (.)
16          and ↑thank her, and just tell them how pr↑oud- (0.4)
17          they are of her.
18  Eric:   Yes.
```

Rose's subsequent use of Pieterse's (maiden) name[6] in line 15 makes it clear that her prior use of the category "fellow South African" was selected to contribute to the action she was producing rather than on the basis of not knowing or not recalling the name. In addition to underscoring Pieterse's membership in this citizenship category as a marked alternative to using her name, Rose goes on to convey that she has deployed it as an alternative to using race or religion categories (see lines 10 and 14) as a basis for engaging with Pieterse. She thereby acknowledges and resists potentially racialized understandings of the controversy associated with Pieterse's athletic career, which was widely cast as a betrayal of Black South Africans by a white athlete who placed her Olympic aspirations above their aspirations for an end to apartheid. Rose's use of the category "South African" thus proposes that support for Pieterse on the basis of shared citizenship should take precedence over potential criticism of her on the basis of racial justice, as she praises prior callers to the show whose contributions she claims have embodied this principle.

Extract 5.3 demonstrates that even in cases in which a categorial recognitional reference does not appear to have been designed as interaction-relevant by its speaker, the category used in the reference can nonetheless be subsequently exploited as resource for additional interactional work, with its use in the reference thereby being retrospectively exposed or topicalized (also see Hopper & LeBaron, 1998). In this case, Jennifer's use of a gender category in a reference designed as recognitional for its recipient (Teresa) is seized upon

6 This is the name under which Pieterse competed for the majority of her athletic career, and thus the one by which many people in South Africa know her and continue to refer to her.

by another participant in the scene (Betty, to whom the referent is evidently not known) as the basis for a sexualized joke.

```
Extract 5.3: JBT Housemates (24/17:35-16:00)
01  Bet:   I ↑think we should all like get al[l sassied up one night?
02  Jen:                                     [( )
03  Bet:   (I'm just thinkin') a little (bit of) sa:s[s.
04  Jen:                                             [UH::::
05             (0.8)
06  Jen:   We should.
07             (1.0)
08  Jen:   .hh >We need< tuh hire that girl. ((turns to T on "girl"))
09             (.)
10  Jen:   That girl, Annie.
11             (0.2)
12  Ter:   ↑What girl?
13  Jen:   =Do[n and Jane's friend.
14  Bet:      [We need tuh £hire a girl?£
15  Jen:   There's th[is girl, uh hh=[A(h)nn(h)ie.
16  Bet:             [hhh ((laugh))  [huh huh hah hah hah hah .HHH
17  Jen:   [Um, .hh >I wanna hire- ((making "telephone" gesture))
18  Ter:   [Ha huh [huh huh huh huh huh [huh huh
19  Bet:           [huh huh huh huh huh [huh huh .HHH
20  Jen:                                [hire a girl for som:e (0.3)
21  Ter:   .hhh
22  Jen:   ser↑vices?
23  Ter:   hih [hih uh:: [uh:::
24  Bet:       [hih HA:: [.HHHH
25  Jen:                 [hih hih .hhh
```

After aligning (line 06) with Betty's suggestion to "get all sassied up one night" (line 01), Jennifer proposes hiring someone (who she implies could help them prepare for the proposed night out), referring to her using the recognitional categorial form "that girl" (see Auer, 1984; Sacks, 1992 on "that X" as a recognitional form) and turning towards Teresa as she does so. She thereby treats Teresa as knowing (about) the specific person she is referring to, but as the exchange unfolds Teresa repeatedly fails to show such recognition (lines 09, 11, and 12), and Jennifer pursues her recognition through successive elaborations of the reference (also see Sacks & Schegloff, 1979), including a mention of her name[7] (line 10) and her categorial relationship ("friend") to two other named persons (line 13). Just after Jennifer begins the second of these pursuits, Betty speaks in overlap with her to question her proposal to "hire a girl" (line 14). Betty's use of the indefinite article "a" in this reference,

---

7 This use of a name following a failure to achieve recognition using a categorial form is evidence for Jennifer's orientation to the preference for names in recognitional reference described by Schegloff (1996), as noted earlier.

in contrast to the recognitional "that" used by Jennifer, converts Jennifer's reference to a specific person into a reference to potentially any member of a broader category of people. That is, she treats the category of person Jennifer used rather than the specific individual she used it to refer to as the relevant upshot of the reference.[8] Taken together with the smile she produces as she does this, Betty's question appears to be designed as a sexual inuendo, with "a girl" as an allusive reference to a member of the category '(female) sex worker' (also see our analysis of Extract 2.11 in Chapter 2: Approaching Membership Categorization).

Jennifer initially responds to Betty by beginning to explain who Annie is (line 15), shifting her reference to the non-recognitional categorial form "this girl" and repeating her name. However, after Betty begins to laugh in overlap with her (line 16), Jennifer breaks into laughter just as she begins to repeat the name (line 15), and Teresa joins in shortly thereafter (line 18). Just as Teresa begins to laugh, Jennifer abandons her account and begins to further build on the joke by miming a telephone call during which she makes the sexual innuendo introduced by Betty more explicit, repeating the "hire a girl" formulation (line 20) before pointedly pausing (line 20), and then emphasizing, the word "services" (line 22) – which prompts a further round of laughter from all three participants (lines 23–25). Thus, while the 'sex worker' category is never explicitly mentioned, Jennifer and Teresa both display recognition of Betty's joking exploitation of Jennifer's designedly unmarked initial reference, with Jennifer actively collaborating in the continuing production of the joke.

In contrast to the preference for the use of names in recognitional references, Schegloff (1996, p. 459) notes that "prototypical simple non-recognitional reference forms are expressions such as 'someone,' 'this guy,' 'this woman,' etc.," and suggests that these forms "appear designed to do virtually nothing else but convey non-recognition-ality; they do just 'referring-as-non-recognizable.'" It is noteworthy that included among the examples Schegloff provides here are both reference forms that include a gender category ('this guy,' 'this woman') and those that convey nothing about the referent other than that they are a person ('someone') – which Whitehead and Lerner (2020) call "generic" forms. One basis for gender categories being treated as purely system-relevant in this way in languages with gender-specific pronouns is the systematic potential for subsequent references by recipients of an initial reference who would face the problem of selecting a gender-appropriate pronoun for the referent if gender had not already been built into the initial reference (Klein, 2011).

---

8 In doing this, Betty may be treating Jennifer's initial reference as an alternative recognitional – and thus as having done more than simply referring – by virtue of her initial use of the categorial form "that girl" before subsequently revealing through her use of the name "Annie" that this preferred form was available.

Other studies of gender categories in non-recognitional reference forms (e.g., Kitzinger, 2007b; Klein, 2011; Stockill & Kitzinger, 2007) have demonstrated that they *may* in some cases, as Schegloff suggests, do "nothing else but convey non-recognition-ality."[9] However, in other cases they evidently contribute to gender-related interactional work, and even when they are apparently designed as purely system-relevant they may nonetheless be taken up by recipients for other interaction-relevant uses (Hopper & LeBaron, 1998; Kitzinger, 2007b; Klein, 2011; Stockill & Kitzinger, 2007; also cf. Extract 5.3). These findings thus demonstrate that the use of a gender category in a non-recognitional reference is neither a sufficient nor necessary condition for claiming that gender is relevantly in play for the participants of the interaction. Moreover, when it comes to generic forms, although the reference form itself does not include any category, in many cases the referent's membership in a category can be inferred from the contextual particulars surrounding the use of the reference, "with the tacitly available membership category accounting for the actions being produced or reported" (Whitehead & Lerner, 2020, p. 49). In addition, as Whitehead and Lerner (2020) further demonstrate, generic forms themselves can contribute to delicate interactional work, including muting or even directly suppressing the potential relevance of a category.

A number of these possibilities in relation to both gender categorial and generic non-recognitional reference forms are neatly illustrated by Extract 5.4, taken from a breakfast-time conversation.[10] In this case, Tricia, in providing an account for why she was ejected from a nightclub the previous night, produces two successive versions of a designedly system-relevant non-recognitional reference (lines 03 and 07).

```
Extract 5.4: Sorority breakfast (2, 35-36)
01  Tar:   =Why did you get kicked out?
02            (0.2)
03  Tri:   >C'z I had some guy buy me a drink.<
04            (0.6)
05  Tar:   You did what?
06               (1.0)
07  Tri:   (I) had someone buy me a dr↑ink.
08  Tar:   Mm:.
09               (1.2)
10  Tar:   He kicked you out?
```

9 One possible system-relevant basis for their regular use in this way is that, as noted previously, the pronominal reference forms used for subsequent references in English and many other languages are gender-specific, and thus making the referent's gender available to recipients in the initial reference can avert the possible trouble a recipient may otherwise have in selecting the appropriate pronominal form for subsequent references to the same person (Klein, 2011).
10 Our analysis of this case partially overlaps with that of Whitehead and Lerner (2020, pp. 52–53).

```
11                (0.8)
12   Tri:   I'm >not twenty one an'< I have no form of
13          identification.
14   Tar:   ↑Oh hhm hm
```

While the first reference form Tricia deploys includes a gender category, the referent's gender does not contribute to the account Tricia is producing, and is evidently designed to do nothing more than non-recognitional reference – which is further underscored by her use of the word "some" in the reference. However, the contextual particulars of the telling provide for an inference of an age category that does contribute to the account, namely that, unlike Tricia, the referent was old enough to purchase an alcoholic drink, and having him do this for her was what occasioned her ejection from the nightclub. Although her recipient, Tara, initially fails to register this aspect of the account (see lines 05 and 10), Tricia subsequently specifies her age and lack of identification as the basis for her ejection (lines 12–13), thereby tacitly confirming the relevance of the referent's age category, in contrast to hers, for the events she has reported (also see our analysis of this instance of other-initiated, next-turn repair in Chapter 8: Managing Trouble in Speaking, Hearing, and Understanding).

While the gender category of the person Tricia refers to here plays no relevant role in her telling of this story – and similarly an earlier telling of the same story for a different set of recipients[11] – her orientation to it being (mis)heard as interaction-relevant is evident in the generic form ("someone") she uses in her second reference to him (line 07). That is, by removing the gender category from this second iteration of the reference, she both treats it as "dispensable" (Schegloff, 2004) and exposes her orientation to the possibility that retaining it might occasion a diversion from the main point of her story – for example, as a result of a recipient inferring that the action of drink-buying combined with the gender category of the drink-buyer might imply a potential romantic advance on his part. As such, and somewhat paradoxically, this case demonstrates the use of a generic reference form to do category-related work – muting the otherwise-plausible relevance of a category. Moreover, while the recipients in this case align with Tricia's treatment of her initial use of a gender category as being in the service of nothing more than referring, the system-relevance of this category can be seen in Tara's subsequent use of the male pronoun "he" (line 10) in her (mistaken) registering of the referent's role in Tricia's ejection from the nightclub.

The central implication of the foregoing discussion and analysis is that even the non-recognitional reference forms that are most recurrently entirely system-relevant may on some occasions contribute to interaction-relevant

---

11 The transcript of this earlier telling is not included here but is examined by Whitehead and Lerner (2020, p. 52).

(including category-related) work, and/or may be vulnerable to being taken up as interaction-relevant by recipients even when not designed as such by their speakers. This highlights the importance of case-by-case analyses of whether and how these possibilities may be evident, rather than assuming that these reference forms always do nothing else but convey non-recognition-ality.

The interaction-relevance of categories other than gender used in non-recognitional reference forms should similarly not be assumed without careful analysis. However, once again, following Sacks's (1972a) foundational observation in this regard (as discussed in Chapter 2: Approaching Membership Categorization and Chapter 3: Methodological Principles, Practices, and Challenges), the systematic availability of multiple different categories for referring to any person provides for the inspection of a speaker's selection of a particular category in terms of its interactional relevance rather than its accuracy or (as in the case of gender categories) system-relevance alone. Moreover, in contrast with recognitional references, the selection of a non-recognitional reference form is not a matter of accomplishing recognition of a specific referent. Instead, categories are recurrently used in non-recognitional forms to tacitly mobilize common-sense categorial knowledge that contributes to the action of the utterance in which the reference is used. Thus, while in Extract 5.4 the age category tacitly contributed to the account being produced by the speaker without ever being mentioned directly, categories that are explicitly included in non-recognitional reference forms can contribute to accounting for an action being produced by a speaker without the account ever needing to be directly spelled out. This can be seen in Extract 5.5, in which a caller (C) to an emergency medical service line in South Africa[12] repeatedly uses the category 'child[ren]' to refer to a party for whom he is requesting an ambulance (see lines 02, 04, and 10).

Extract 5.5: Emergency call (WC EMS 10469)
```
01  C:   Hi, >this Mister ↑Fox from Daventry Secondary School,
02       man.< [.h There was a fight between two ↑child↓ren, h
03  CT:        [ (Mm hm?)
04  C:   .hh the one chi:ld i:s um is uh l- >un↑conscious at the
05       moment, h .hh u::m: an' I'm just a bit con↑cerned man.
06  CT:  >Okay, so the ambulance is only< for one patient now?
07  C:   Ya, for one, ya. h (.hh)
08            (.)
09  C:   Can:: ya (o-) coz I'm >j'st a bit< concerned about-
10       you know:, summing >could happen to the child man,<
```

12 We thank Jennifer Watermeyer and the Health Communication Research Unit at the University of the Witwatersrand, Johannesburg, for permitting us to use this data extract.

Given that the caller has just indicated his membership in the category 'teacher' from the setting-based 'school' MCD in identifying himself, the consistency rule provides for the expectation that he would refer to the parties involved in the fight he is reporting as 'students' or 'pupils.' Moreover, other unmarked options available to him include, as described previously, non-categorial forms (e.g., 'people,' 'person') and gender categories. His use of the category "child" is thus observable as a marked choice selected from a range of unmarked alternatives, with this choice evidently being made by reference to potential doubts about whether the matter at hand is sufficiently serious to warrant treatment as an emergency (also see Raymond & Zimmerman, 2016) – perhaps particularly in light of the government-operated service he is calling being over-burdened and under-resourced (Tam et al., 2024). That is, his use of this category tacitly mobilizes common-sense knowledge about the special vulnerability and need for protection of its incumbents (also see Rafaely & Whitehead, 2020), as a basis for warranting his request for the dispatch of a scarce resource. Further evidence for this can be seen in his repeated expressions of concern (lines 05 and 09–10), which underscore his treatment of the need for an ambulance as potentially questionable. (Also see our further analysis of this call, including of some subsequent troubles arising from the caller's choice of categorial reference, in Chapter 8: Managing Trouble in Speaking, Hearing, and Understanding.)

The selection of a category in a non-recognitional reference can similarly supply an account for an action being retrospectively reported by the speaker, as illustrated by Extract 5.6. In this case, Mary's use of the category "friend" (line 03) as a non-recognitional reference tacitly accounts for her reported action of spending the day helping the referent.

```
Extract 5.6: Family call (Munoz 1.8, 1)
01  Cin:  Are you guys at home already?=h
02  Mar:  No, we've been- I got my tooth fixed and we've been in:
03        Ventura, .hhh helping my friend at her new sto:re, .hh
04        all: day. <She:'s opening an↑tique store, .h=pt and
05        since I: (.) >you know< (.) am: so knowledgeable from:
06        when my mother and ↑dad were in the business, all=
07  Cin:  =Right.=
08  Mar:  =their lives, [.hhh
09  Cin:                [>uh huh<
10  Mar:  =I'm: been helping her, <so I'm helping her <price
11        stuff.>
```

It is noteworthy here that just after reporting that she has helped her friend, Mary specifies how she came to have the type of expertise that would make her a good candidate to provide help – an account to which the kinship categories "mother" and "dad" (line 06) contribute. However, an account for why she would give up a full day of her time (also note the emphasis she places on the word "all" in line 04) to provide assistance in this task is provided entirely by the "friend" category – it is tacitly taken-for-granted that she did this because it is the sort of thing friends do for each other. Had she instead used a reference form like 'somebody' or 'this woman,' her recipient would have been left to infer what possible categorial relationship Mary had with the referent that would account for her taking on this task, with the type of trouble shown by the recipient in Extract 5.4 in making such an inference being a possible outcome.

A number of analyses of categorial non-recognitional references (e.g., Kitzinger, 2005a, 2005b; Sacks, 1972a, 1972b, 1992; Whitehead & Lerner, 2009) have demonstrated that, as in Extracts 5.4–5.6, their use as a tacit interactional resource is entirely mundane and taken-for-granted, contributing seamlessly to the production of a range of actions in ways that are, for the participants, completely unproblematic. However, the availability of these resources may vary both with respect to the categories used in the production of person references and the ability of particular categories of speakers to unproblematically deploy them in these ways. For example, Kitzinger's (2005a) study of after-hours medical calls demonstrates how callers from normative heterosexual nuclear families could routinely use kinship categories in referring to a family member in need of medical assistance in ways that accounted for the caller's act of seeking help for the patient, while calls made by non-familial callers were characterized by a range of interactional troubles and in some cases included explicit accounts by callers as to why they (as opposed to a family member) were making the call. A related analysis by Land and Kitzinger (2005) shows a range of interactional difficulties encountered during calls to institutional lines by callers who were in same-gender relationships whose non-gender-specific references to their partners were taken by the call-taker to index an opposite-gender person. This demonstrates how subsequent references using gender-specific pronouns produced by recipients of a non-gender-specific categorial reference can reveal their assumptions about the likely (or normative) gender of the referent – and this similarly serves as a mechanism for exposing participants' orientations to the normatively gendered nature of a range of other categories (see, e.g., Klein, 2011; Stokoe & Smithson, 2001; Stringer & Hopper, 1998).

The historical uses of some MCDs – including race, gender, sexuality, age, (dis)ability, and other Pn-adequate categories – as bases for unequal and oppressive social arrangements, and the political mobilizations that have arisen in opposition to such social arrangements, have made uses of these categories in non-recognitional references a particularly morally fraught matter. That is, such references are recurrently treated by participants as doing more than simply referring – as contributing to either maintaining or resisting the continued marginalization of members of these categories, and as thereby reflexively making available the category membership and/or associated social positioning of the speaker of the reference (also see, e.g., Robles, 2015; Stokoe, 2015; Whitehead, 2009, 2015).

A classic illustration of this can be found in Sacks's (1984b, 1986) analyses[13] of a racial category used in a non-recognitional reference ("colored lady") by a speaker, Ellen, recounting an incident she witnessed outside a department store. As Sacks notes, through the use of this reference, along with a claim that she "wanted to go in the main entrance there where the silver is and all the gifts and things," Ellen "works to put in information relevant to seeing what was happening" (Sacks, 1986, p. 134), implying that the referent was attempting to rob the store. While Sacks (1984b, p. 422) observes that "This lady is not designing a right-wing report. All she is doing is reporting what she saw," he also proposes that Ellen's "massive comfort in her innocence, and in the legitimate audience status that she has" are so taken-for-granted for her that "she can have no sense of an empathy with, for example, a kid in the ghetto" (Sacks, 1984b, p. 422; 1986, p. 137). Sacks therefore notes that despite the ostensibly 'innocent' design of this reference, Ellen's use of it in her report exposes the racism of her actions and makes available inferences about her own category-bound social status. Moreover, although Sacks makes no mention of this in his analyses, it is significant that the reference made by Ellen includes categories from two MCDs, race and gender – where, following the economy rule, a single category would be sufficient for accomplishing adequate reference, and the inclusion of a second category can thus be inspected for the additional interactional work it accomplishes.

As we foreshadowed earlier, a further way in which additional category-related interactional work done by third-person references – both recognitional and non-recognitional – can be exposed relates to the intersection between the position and the form of the reference. Ordinarily, initial references to a person are produced using locally initial reference forms (e.g., names or categories), while subsequent references are produced using locally subsequent forms (e.g., a pronoun). As such, " 'mis-matches' between sequential position and reference form invite immediate attention, both from participants (though not necessarily consciously, of course) and from professional analysts, and may be understood to achieve distinctive outcomes" (Schegloff, 1996, pp. 450–451; also see Raymond et al., 2021) – including category-related outcomes. For example, using a pronoun as an initial reference can be a way of mobilizing a category without directly mentioning it (Wilkinson & Kitzinger, 2003), or of muting the relevance of a category (Kitzinger et al., 2012). Conversely, as Extract 5.7 demonstrates, using a category as a subsequent reference for which a pronoun could have been used can be a way of criticizing or complaining

---

13 Further discussion of these analyses is provided by Whitehead (2021).

about the referent's actions (also see Jackson, 2013) by treating them as recognizably category-bound. This exchange is from a radio show on which the guest, Reshma, is an artist who has created a controversial 12-metre-long walk-in sculpture of a vagina that a caller, Wayne, to the show has characterized as "absurd." In the course of inviting Reshma to respond to Wayne's characterization, the host (Aubrey) refers to him by name (line 01), and as she begins to respond Reshma uses the locally subsequent pronoun "he" (line 05) to refer to him. However, Reshma then abandons what she had started to say in order to formulate it in a different way, in the process using the locally initial categorial form "a <u>white</u> male" (line 06), rather than the further locally subsequent form "him" that she could have used.

Extract 5.7: Radio call-in (691, 702 19.8.13)

```
01   Aub:  So what do y[ou think Wa:yne is ref]erring towhen he
02   Res:              [(and that's the purpose-)]
03   Aub:  speaks of the absurdity of the situation? .hhh
04            (0.2)
05   Res:  .hh Ah- I mean, I- I think he's just- (.) hhh ((chuckle))
06         .hhh £I think it's also easy£ fo:r a:: .hh £a white male,
07         sorry to say that,£ to sit in judgment of it without (.)
08         understanding the: .hh the experiences, or the:
09         perspectives of: u::h .hh b- u::h (.) women in this
10         country or: within patriarchal systems, .hh I think maybe
11         he is a bit (0.5) u::m: disempowered by it.
```

This reference form underscores Reshma's criticism of Wayne's response to her art as being grounded in his own race- and gender-based understandings and experiences (cf. line 08), effectively casting his claim as revealing a racist and sexist social position as opposed to constituting a warranted critique of the art itself. This case thereby demonstrates how categorial reference forms can serve as resources not just for actions that contribute to or reproduce systems of oppression, as noted previously, but also for actions designed to resist or challenge them (cf. Rawls et al., 2020; Sacks, 1992; Whitehead & Lerner, 2009). (Also see further analyses of this interaction in Chapter 7: Organizing Sequences of Action and Chapter 8: Managing Troubles in Speaking, Hearing and Understanding, and in Whitehead & Lerner, 2022.)

These features of initial versus subsequent reference forms also provide for further appreciation of how the caller in Extract 5.5 repeatedly mobilized the category "child" to warrant his request for an ambulance. That is, his reference to "the <u>one</u> chi:ld" (line 04) comes shortly after his report of "a fight between two ↑child↓ren" (line 02), which provides for the possibility of an elided (e.g., "the one") or pronominal (e.g., "one of them") subsequent disaggregation (cf. Lerner & Kitzinger, 2007) of the unconscious party. Moreover, a pronoun could have been used for the caller's subsequent reference to "the child" in line 10. His continued use of the initial (categorial) form of the reference thus serves to underscore the ongoing relevance of the category for the service request he is producing.

5.1.2 First-person (self) reference forms

In contrast to the systematic place of categories in third-person references, individual self-reference in English is largely accomplished through

> the dedicated term 'I' (and its grammatical variants – me, my, mine, etc.). This term is opaque with respect to all the usual key categorical dimensions – age, gender, status and the like, and is also insensitive to the history of prior reference – whether for the first or the nth occasion in some conversation or across multiple conversations, self is referred to as 'I' (Schegloff, 2007a, p. 123; also see Land & Kitzinger, 2007; cf. cross-language variations described by, e.g., Enfield, 2007; Hacohen & Schegloff, 2006; Oh, 2007).

Uses of these forms of "simple self-reference" (Whitehead & Lerner, 2022) leave it to recipients to figure out whether and how a speaker is relevantly speaking as a member of a particular category or categories when referring to self. This can give rise to troubles in relation to either the relevance of a particular category *being* inferred when the speaker has not designed their talk to be heard as such, or to the relevance of a category *not* being recognized when the speaker has assumed it will be readily evident to recipients (Whitehead & Lerner, 2022). As Whitehead and Lerner (2022) demonstrate, speakers may manage the former of these possibilities by explicitly claiming to be speaking "personally" or "as an individual" – although using this practice involves doing more than what is needed to produce a simple or minimal self-reference, and thereby exposes the speaker's orientation to the possibility of otherwise being heard as a member of a category or other collectivity. Similarly, speakers can manage the latter of these possibilities, while at the same time exposing the additional interactional work they are producing in doing so, by explicitly claiming to be speaking as a member of one or more categories (also see Jackson, 2011; West & Fenstermaker, 2002; Whitehead & Lerner, 2022). As Extracts 5.8–5.10 show, this self-categorization practice can be deployed prior to, during the course of, or following the utterance in which a simple self-reference is produced.

Extract 5.8 shows an exchange from the American political news show *Meet the Press* in which the host, Chuck Todd, has introduced the guest, Kellyanne Conway as "counsellor to President Trump" (not transcribed), thereby establishing this as her setting-based category incumbency for the interview. However, when Todd presses Conway on the "morality" of the Trump Administration's reviled policy of separating young migrant children from their parents or guardians upon their entry into the country at the southern border, Conway claims membership in two categories – "mother" and "Catholic" (line 06) – before producing a further self-description (lines 07–09) and then formulating a disavowal of the policy (lines 09–10).

Extract 5.8: *Meet the Press*, NBC (17.6.18, Kellyanne Conway)

```
01  CT:   But as you know, this is- this is a question of morality.
02        This is a question of Am[erican MORALITY.
03  KC:                          [You've heard me- You've heard me
04        weigh in on that.
05  CT:   I did, this is a question of Am[erican morality.
06  KC:                                  [As a mother, as a
07        Catholic, as somebody who:: h's got a conscience, and
08        wouldn't say (.) ((pointing)) the junk that somebody
09        said, (.) uh a- apparently=allegedly, I will tell you
10        that nobody likes this policy.
```

By prefacing this disavowal – which includes the simple self-reference "I" (line 09) – with these claims of category incumbency, Conway orients to the possibility that in the absence of this prefatory work she would be heard as producing a self-serving defence of the administration she represents, rather than a genuine moral sentiment of the sort that she treats as tied to these categories.

In Extract 5.9, from an inquiry call to a mediation service (M) that provides assistance with neighbour disputes, the caller (C, who has complained about noise made late at night by her neighbour's child) temporarily halts the forward progressivity of an utterance in order to insert a parenthetical claim of membership in the compound category "single mother" (line 10) before restarting the utterance she had suspended (cf. Mazeland, 2007; Whitehead, 2020). (Also see our discussion of 'parenthetical sequences' in Chapter 7: Organizing Sequences of Action.)

Extract 5.9: Neighbour mediation initial inquiry

```
01  Cal:   Because I- I: have a little girl who's the s- exactly
02         the same age actually.
03  Med:   Oh ri:ght.
04  Cal:   Um: (0.3) an'- an:, (.) an' I usually get her into bed
05         for half past eight.
06                    (0.2)
07  Cal:   An,=
```

```
08   Med:   =Yeah.
09                  (0.3)
10   Cal:   By that ti- a- cos I'm a single mother, (0.3)
11   Med:   M:mm.=
12   Cal:   =By that time, (0.3) I'm ti:red;
13                  (0.2)
14   Cal:   .hhh
15   Med:   Yeah.=
16   Cal:   An' I don't have many resources left for co:ping with
17          things.
```

Since the caller has already revealed her membership in the 'mother' category (line 01), this inserted self-categorization primarily serves to establish the relevance of this more specific category of mother for the simple self-references ("I'm" and "I") she goes on to produce in her claim of tiredness and her elaboration thereof (lines 12 and 16–17, respectively). Her use of this category thereby provides an account for her tiredness beyond what other parents might experience and thus serves to upgrade her noise complaint (also see Stokoe, 2003, 2009a).

In Extract 5.10 (which partially replicates and extends Extract 5.7), Aubrey responds to Reshma's use of race and gender categories by laughingly confessing to the experience of disempowerment that Reshma has attributed to Wayne (lines 10–11). After beginning with a preface ("I can tell you") that includes a simple self-reference and establishes that the utterance he is producing will offer his perspective on what she has said (lines 12–13), Aubrey goes on to propose that Reshma's use of the racial category "white" in characterizing this experience was overly restrictive (line 15). He then proposes that Reshma's claim also applies to "Black males" (line 17), thereby retrospectively revealing that his earlier preface was designed to index his membership in these categories.

```
Extract 5.10: Radio call-in (691, 702 19.8.13)
06   Res:   .hhh £I think it's also easy£ fo:r a:: .hh £a white male,
07          sorry to say that,£ to sit in judgment of it without (.)
08          understanding the: .hh the experiences, or the:
09          perspectives of: u::h .hh b- u::h (.) women in this
10          country or: within patriarchal systems, .hh I think maybe
11          he is a bit (0.5) u::m: disempowered by it [so he:
12   Aub:                                              [£I can tell
13          you-£ I c(h)an t(h)ell you [R(h)esh, .hh £that it's not
14   Res:                             [(hh) ((chuckle))
15   Aub:   just white males th[at have this£=huh .h
16   Res:                      [hhhh
17   Aub:   [£it's Black males too,£
18   Res:   [hih hih hih
```

These cases thus demonstrate how the elaboration or modification of a simple self-reference using a category exposes the interactional work the speaker is doing in addition to mere referring. It is important to emphasize, however, that although in some cases (as in Extract 5.10) the category or categories the speaker explicitly mentions are those that are evidently relevant for the interactional work being done, in other cases the mentioned categories are designed to replace or override a different (as in Extract 5.8) or less specific (as in Extract 5.9) category that might otherwise be taken to be relevant – with the speaker's orientation to the relevance of the unmentioned category thus (somewhat paradoxically) being revealed by their use of the mentioned categories. This again highlights (as discussed in Chapter 3: Methodological Principles, Practices, and Challenges) the importance of case-by-case analysis, as opposed to assuming that categories that are made explicit are always the (only) relevant ones in play.

Category-related interactional outcomes can also be accomplished through the use of self-reference forms other than the ordinarily used 'I,' 'me,' etc. For example, Schegloff (1996) observes that speakers can use either names or categorial third-person reference forms in self-references, with the former being a way of emphasizing their status as a public figure, and the latter serving to claim the relevance of their membership in the used category for their ongoing talk. A related analysis by Land and Kitzinger (2007) shows how speakers can use third-person reference forms that include categories as self-references, as a way of representing the views of someone else in relation to the speaker's membership in a particular category.

Although collective self-references in English are (like individual self-references) largely accomplished through a set of dedicated terms ('we,' 'us,' 'our,' etc.) that are opaque with respect to categorial dimensions, they also index the speaker's membership in a collectivity – whether a category or a non-categorial group. In some instances, speakers may explicitly tie categories to collective self-references, including through similar practices to those seen in Extracts 5.8–5.10, which directly specify what category or categories a collective self-reference is designed to refer to, or by using collective pronouns to claim co-membership in a category that has just been mentioned (see, e.g., Sacks, 1992; Whitehead, 2012b, 2021). In other cases, speakers may use the collective reference form 'we' as a way of displaying that they are speaking on behalf of an organization, thus tacitly displaying their membership in an organizational category (also see Whalen & Zimmerman, 1990). In still other cases the category or collectivity indexed by a collective self-reference may remain entirely tacit, leaving it to recipients (and thus analysts) to infer from the contextual particulars surrounding the reference (see, e.g., Bull & Fetzer, 2006; Lerner & Kitzinger, 2007; Sacks, 1992; Whitehead, 2020).

Despite ordinarily being used to refer to the speaker as an individual rather than a member of any category of other collectivity, simple individual self-references can also tacitly self-categorize the speaker. Jackson (2011) shows that simple self-references can index the speaker's membership in a gender category when produced in environments in which a different gender category is explicitly mentioned (also see Stokoe, 2010a). Moreover, Whitehead and Lerner (2022) describe a prosodic practice through which speakers can produce simple self-references that tacitly categorize them as a member of a particular category, even in contexts in which no category from the applicable MCD has been mentioned. This practice, "contrastive entanglement" (Whitehead & Lerner, 2022, p. 416), involves the use of contrastive stress (emphasis) on a simple self-reference, which serves to both contrast the speaker with, and juxtapose them to, another person or persons in relation to membership in different categories from the same MCD. An instance of contrastive entanglement produced in a joke told by Michael Che on the television comedy show *Saturday Night Live* is shown in Extract 5.11. Here, Che uses a contrastively stressed self-reference in remarking on then-President Trump's Covid-19 infection being treated with a drug derived from foetal stem cells.

Extract 5.11: *Saturday Night Live* (S46, E2, 10.10.20)

```
01   MC:   It's ↑kinda ↓funny that these old Republicans are so
02         a:nti: abortion, .hh when it comes to everybody else,
03         but then they do a complete one eighty as soon as stem
04         cells can save their lives or when I get their
05         daughter pregnant.
```

While Che explicitly mentions age ("old") and political party ("Republicans") categories in line 01, it is evident that the contrastively stressed "I" he produces in line 04 tacitly implements categorization in terms of a different MCD altogether. That is, in trading on the referents' hypothetical newfound support for abortion in the face of him impregnating "their daughter" (lines 04–05), Che's joke invokes common-sense knowledge about white (and racist) fears of miscegenation. His stressed self-reference thereby serves to tacitly categorize himself as 'Black' and the previously mentioned "old Republicans" as 'white.'

5.1.3 Second-person (recipient) reference forms

Our observations on second-person references will be relatively brief, as they largely mirror the preceding discussion of self-references. This is because addressing a co-present recipient is, in English, largely accomplished using dedicated pronouns ('you,' 'your,' 'yours,' etc.) that "mask the [categorial] relevance of the referent and the reference at that point in the talk" (Schegloff, 1996, p. 447; also see Lerner, 1996c; cf. cross-language variations described by, e.g., Enfield, 2007; Oh, 2007, 2010; Raymond, 2016; Sidnell & Shohet, 2013). Other unmarked forms include names and kinship terms (e.g., 'Mom,' 'Granddad,' etc.), as well as formal address terms or institutional forms of address that may index gender or other institutional categories (e.g., 'Mister Chairman,' 'Madam Speaker'), while nonetheless not being designedly interaction-relevant in their contexts of use (also see, e.g., Clayman, 2013; Enfield, 2007; Levinson, 2007; Schegloff, 1996).

Alternative forms that expose the speaker's use of categories to perform additional interactional work similarly mirror some of the referring practices described in the previous sections, including uses of third-person reference forms instead of a second-person pronoun (Schegloff, 1996), and elaborations of reference forms to specify which category or categories a second-person pronoun is designed to refer to, as illustrated by Extract 5.12 (also cf. Eglin, 2013; Ervin-Tripp, 1972). In this case, from an interview on the comedy news television show *The Daily Show*, host Trevor Noah specifies the category "sociologist" (line 03) in relation to the second-person pronoun "you" (line 04) in asking his guest, Tressie McMillan Cottom, to account for the phenomenon of Black men voting for Donald Trump in larger numbers than Black women (lines 01–07).

```
Extract 5.12: The Daily Show (11.3.20)
01    TN:  One of those things has been (.) r- Black men, (0.2)
02         voting in larger numbers for Donald Trump, (.) Black
03         women staying consistent. (0.2) As a sociologist,do
04         you have any i(h)de(h)a of why this is, w- wh- like
05         what could it possibly be about Donald Trump, that more
06         Black men than usual go like "yeah, I'm gonna go with
07         him."
08              (0.8)
09    TMC: Ma:n:, cocaine is a helluva dru:g. [I:: (.h) Ithink
10    TN:                                     [ih heh hih hih
11    TMC: [the=hah hah his .hh I th(h)in(k) there is forall=
12    TN:  [hih hih hih
13    TMC: =that we talk about rac:e, in this country, and it is
14         significant, and it matters, an:d for all that we talk
15         about class, it is significant, .hh and it matters, (.)
16         what we have learned is that gender (.) also matters.
```

Noah's use of the category "sociologist" in this case exposes his orientation to the possibility that the subsequent "you" might otherwise be heard as tacitly invoking McMillan Cottom's membership in the compound category 'Black woman' (also note his mention of "Black women" in lines 02–03) rather than her expertise as a sociologist, as a basis for asking her this question (also cf. Extracts 5.8 and 5.9). Moreover, evidence for McMillan Cottom's orientation to her membership in this racial category can be seen in her initial response to the question, as she jokingly quotes an iconic line produced by Black singer Rick James in Dave Chapelle's Black-identified sketch comedy series *Chapelle's Show* (line 09), before reverting to enacting the professional category Noah has mentioned by providing a recognizably sociological account for the trend described in his question (lines 11–16).

Similarly again to self-reference practices, the category-relevance of a recipient reference can also be made tacitly available through the use of contrastive stress on a second-person pronoun (Whitehead & Lerner, 2022), or through other features of the content and context of the talk that make the relevance of categories evident without including them as part of the reference itself. In particular, in multi-party interactions, where a turn at talk may be addressed either to all the other participants or to a specific party, the turn in which the recipient reference is included may tacitly categorize the addressed party by virtue of their category membership(s) being what distinguishes them from anyone else in the scene to whom the talk might otherwise have been heard as being addressed. For example, asking "Did you cook this all the way through?" disambiguates who the "you" is addressing (the party who cooked the food) while tacitly categorizing that party in that particular moment as "cook" and possibly also "host" (Lerner, 1993, 1996c, 2003).

5.2   Person references in the Central Park case

Armed with the analytic resources introduced in the foregoing sections, we can now return to the case of the dispute in Central Park (shown in Extract 5.13) with which we began the chapter, in order to conduct a closer examination of how Amy Cooper's uses of all three of the main types of person references we have discussed contribute to what were widely regarded as clearly racist actions. As a further preface to this analysis, and recalling our discussions of intersections and/ or distinctions between setting-based and Pn-adequate categories in preceding chapters, we note that the dispute that was already underway at the onset of the recording was evidently occasioned by reference to the setting-based collection, 'park user,' and the specific categories, 'dog walker' and 'bird watcher.' That is, Amy Cooper has evidently, as a 'dog walker,' complainably failed to fulfil the category-bound obligation of leashing her dog, thereby infringing on the category-bound rights of Christian Cooper as a 'bird watcher' to engage in the eponymous category-bound activity without having the birds scared away by an unleashed dog. As the dispute escalates, Amy Cooper deploys person references that shift to available Pn-adequate (race and gender) categories, using them as resources first for threatening Christian Cooper and then for carrying out this threat, in an attempt to 'win' the dispute.

Of central importance in this regard – as noted previously – is her reference to Christian Cooper as "an A:frican American man" (line 10). While this reference was frequently quoted in news reports of the incident, a crucial and typically unexamined feature thereof is that it is produced while Amy Cooper was speaking directly to Christian Cooper, and thus constitutes a marked departure from the default use of the second-person pronoun 'you' in such references. That is, by using race and gender categories in this recipient reference, Amy Cooper exposes her use of them as a resource for threatening him. Specifically, she mobilizes common-sense knowledge about Christian Cooper's membership in these categories as a basis for his particular vulnerability to being subjected to police violence (also see, e.g., Jones, 2018; Smith Lee & Robinson, 2019) – and does so in the service of securing his compliance with her request that he stop filming her (line 01), which a prior (less specific) threat to call the police (line 04) has failed to accomplish.

Extract 5.13: Central Park (video from Twitter via The Telegraph)

```
01   AC:   Please take your ↑phone off.= ((AC pointing at CC))
02   CC:   =↑Please ↓don't >come close< to me.= ((AC withdraws
03         point))
04   AC:   =(>Then I'm taking picture and calling the cops.<)
05         ((AC holding phone; begins to dial))
06   CC:   Please- Please call the cops. hh
07               (1.0) ((AC engaging with phone/dialling))
08   CC:   Please call the cops.=h
09               (0.2)
10   AC:   .hh I'm gonna tell them there's an A:frican American man
11         threatening my ↑life.
12   CC:   .h Please tell them whatever you ↑like. hhh
13               (2.0) ((AC continuing to dial; stepping away))
14   AC:   Excuse me. ((still dialling; stepping away))
15               (11.7)
16   AC:   I'm sorry, ↑I'm in the Ramble, (.h) and there is a man,
17         African American, he has a biker helmet, .hh he is
18         recording me, and threatening me and my do:g.
19               (2.2)
20   AC:   There is an African American man, .h I am in Central
21         Park, .hh he is recording me, and threatening myself and
22         my dog.
23               (1.8)
24   AC:   And my (d-)
25               (1.8)
```

```
26   AC:   I'm sorry, I can't hear y(h)ou either, .HH ↑I'M being
27         THREATENED BY A MAN IN THE RAMBLE, .H PLEASE SEND THE
28         COPS IMMEDIATELY!
```

The self-reference ("I'm" – line 10) Amy Cooper produces in making this threat is also significant, both in its own right and in relation to the categorial second-person reference that follows. In light of the contrastive stress on this reference, it appears to be an instance of contrastive entanglement, serving to contrast Amy Cooper with Christian Cooper in relation to their respective memberships in categories from the same MCD(s). The race and gender categories she then uses in referring to him – and in particular the contrastive stress she places on both words of the race category – then make explicit that these are the MCDs made relevant by her stressed self-reference. As such, there is evidence not only that this threat is directed at him specifically as a Black man but also that she is oriented to producing it particularly as a white woman, thus providing specific empirical grounding for observations of her exploitation of the trope of white women's vulnerability to Black men's violence (cf. Brett, 2020; Harriot, 2020).

The person references Amy Cooper produces in this threat also constitute a crucial context for the series of person references she subsequently produces during the emergency call. The first of these is another contrastively stressed self-reference ("I'm") followed by a contrastively stressed reference to Christian Cooper as "a man" (line 17), the latter of which is then elaborated into a list including a racial category ('African American'), and a further description of Christian Cooper's appearance, "he has a biker helmet" (line 16). Taken at face value, this list appears to be designed to provide the type of visual identifiers that are routinely either solicited by call-takers or provided by callers without being solicited, as a basis for supplying police officers who may be dispatched to the scene with information that will assist them in identifying the person whose actions have prompted the call (Hill, forthcoming). However, Amy Cooper's use in this list of the exact racial category term she deployed in the threat she produced just seconds earlier, and that she is now carrying out, leave no doubt as to the designed use of this category to do something more than simply providing institution-relevant information – and the contrastively entangled self-reference she has produced just prior to the list serves as further evidence of her orientation in this regard.

Following what appears to have been difficulty on the part of the call-taker in hearing her complaint (presumably indicated to her during the silence shown at line 19), Amy Cooper produces a second version of the complaint, this time starting with a reference to Christian Cooper that includes the racial category in the reference form itself rather than as part of a post-reference list of visual descriptors (line 20). This shift foregrounds relevance of the racial category, while

Amy Cooper's exclusion of the "biker helmet" description from this version of the complaint treats it as a "dispensable" (Schegloff, 2004) element of the original complaint. This further exposes her use of race not just as an institution-relevant description of the target of the complaint but also for highlighting her vulnerability to the violence she claims to have been threatened with.

When the call-taker's apparent trouble in hearing Amy Cooper evidently continues (lines 24–26), she produces a third version of the complaint in which her reference to Christian Cooper is simply an emphasized gender category (line 27). While this serves to treat the previously used racial category as dispensable in the context of an attempt to have a simplest form of the complaint heard and acted-upon, it also retrospectively underscores the work she has done to include this category in the prior versions of the complaint. (In Chapter 7: Organizing Sequences of Action we extend our analysis of this interaction, examining aspects of its unfolding prior to and including the stretch on which we have focused here.)

5.3   Summary and conclusions

The cases we have presented in this chapter build on the discussion of action formation and ascription we presented in the preceding chapter, and further illustrate how categories can feature in a particular domain of word selection, namely in the context of practices for referring to and addressing people. They thereby offer further demonstrations of the mutually constitutive relationship between categories and the generic organizations of practice for interaction we introduced in Chapter 1: An Introduction to Categories in Social Interaction and further developed in Chapter 4: Forming and Making Sense of Actions. Specifically, on the one hand, the structures and practices of person reference provide a systematic set of places for the use (and thus reproduction) of categories in interactions, while on the other hand, categories serve as a central set of resources for referring to and addressing people. While this is so both in cases where the speaker is designing a person reference to do nothing more than referring (reference *simpliciter*) and when the specific reference form is evidently chosen so as to also contribute in some way to the action of the turn in which the reference is produced (referring *dupliciter*), the conversation analytic research we have reviewed in this chapter offers a powerful set of resources for distinguishing cases of the former from cases of the latter – and thus for empirically grounding claims of whether and how speakers are observably oriented to the relevance of particular categories for what they are doing interactionally at particular moments.

As we have pointed out, however, these resources do not provide a recipe for the fool-proof production of iron-clad analyses in the absence of careful consideration of the features evident in any particular case of interest (recall our discussion of distinctiveness and recurrence – practices deployed "for another first time" – in Chapter 3: Methodological Principles, Practices, and Challenges). If person references can be produced in ways that convey nothing 'special' is being done beyond simply referring, then speakers may reflexively use such practices to *claim* 'innocent' or 'unmotivated' use of categories while nonetheless making categorical inferences available to recipients (cf. Whitehead & Lerner, 2020, p. 50). As such – and as illustrated by the Central Park case we examined in the previous section – it is crucial to examine the form of person reference used in relation to all other available features of the 'thick particulars' of the talk and other conduct surrounding it, in order to arrive at characterizations of whether and how it is contributing to the interactional work at hand. In the chapters that follow, we continue to introduce further resources for examining the wide range of interactional details that may be attended to in doing so – and we thereby continue to develop our specifications of the aforementioned mutually constitutive relationship between categories and the generic organizations of practice for interaction.

6

TAKING TURNS AT TALKING AND SELECTING NEXT SPEAKERS

6.0   Introduction

In November 2019, during the House Intelligence Committee hearings in the U.S. Congress's first impeachment of then President Trump, a dispute emerged regarding the refusal of the Committee Chair, Democratic Party Representative Adam Schiff, to allow Republican Party Representative Elise Stefanik to question a witness (former U.S. Ambassador to Ukraine, Marie Yovanovitch). At issue was the basis on which Schiff "gaveled over" Stefanik's successive efforts to speak after Representative Devin Nunes, the top-ranked Republican on the committee, invited her to question Yovanovitch. The very way in which the dramatic set of events unfolded virtually guaranteed – and were perhaps designed to guarantee – coverage that dissected the propriety of Schiff's intervention. Was this (yet another) case of a man interrupting a woman, as asserted by Stefanik and Nunes? Or had Schiff simply held Stefanik to the rules that bound all participants in the hearings, and that had been voted upon prior to the onset of the hearings? These became matters of debate, with Republican supporters charging Democrats as hypocrites for failing to call out the sort of gender-based conduct they had criticized others for engaging in, and Democratic supporters insisting that Schiff was simply fulfilling his responsibilities as Committee Chair. The events were recounted in a column by Hesse (2019):

> Early in the afternoon, Rep. Devin Nunes (R-Calif.), the Republican ranking member of the intelligence committee, attempted to yield some of his time to Stefanik. This attempt, however, violated a House resolution: Only ranking members and their staff counsel were allowed to speak at that moment. So when Stefanik began a question, Schiff gaveled over her.

DOI: 10.4324/9781003120599-7

"What is the interruption for *this* time?" Stefanik asked witheringly. Schiff explained, and then, when Stefanik again spoke, he again cut her off.

Nunes got involved: "You're gagging the young lady from New York?" he fumed, in an interesting turn of phrase. Stefanik is 35 – hardly elderly, but well beyond the age to which "young lady" is reasonably applied.

But "gagging the young lady" makes good television. It's an outrage-inducing sentiment, much more so than if Nunes had accused Schiff of "declining to recognize the congresswoman." It seemed designed to make Stefanik looked wronged and Schiff look misogynistic.

Is that what happened? Did the chair of the intelligence committee mistreat his junior colleague because she's a woman?

For many amateur detectives, the answer was apparently yes.

The conflict in the hearing, and the ensuing public deliberations in the many pieces published about it, point to the visceral reactions people have to being interrupted (and otherwise excluded) and to the ways categorial identities have been understood to feature in who is, and is not, allowed to participate in specific encounters and public life more generally. To understand what is at stake, and how we might improve on the approach taken by the "amateur detectives" derided by Hesse (2019), we review the foundational research on the turn-taking system for conversation and other encounters, how it has been taken up by researchers, and how the notion of "interruption" has shaped the ways that category membership has been connected to it. We thereby specify a set of structures and practices relating to turn-taking, and systematically deployed and oriented to by participants in interactions, that will enable us to return later in this chapter to a more detailed examination of the categorial features of this dispute.

We begin, in Section 6.1, by considering how features of turns at talk and the turn-taking system provide for expectations that, when departed from, can occasion categorial accounts, and how social scientific studies of "interruption" have sought to formalize such accounts. In Section 6.2, we describe the basic elements of the turn-taking system, which include 'turn construction' and 'turn allocation' components, before considering how categories may feature in the allocation of opportunities to speak, and how departures from routine turn-taking practices can be a basis for instantiating the relevance and consequentiality of categories. We then return in Section 6.3 to the Schiff-Nunes-Stefanik exchange, examining how a range of categories figured in the unfolding of the dispute and the turn-taking-related conduct of the antagonists, before concluding the chapter in Section 6.4.

6.1 Turn-taking and categories

Turn-taking is a ubiquitous feature of a wide range of activities, and a crucial mechanism for the collaborative production of actions produced in talk-in-interaction. Early conversation analytic research (Sacks et al., 1974) demonstrated that participants systematically use and orient to a system for conversational turn-taking based on the construction of turns in the form of units of talk with projectable and recognizable completion points ('turn constructional units' or TCUs) and a set of practices and associated rules for allocating turns to a next speaker at or near places where a TCU may be complete ('transition relevance places' or TRPs). This system provides for the possibility of overlapping or simultaneous talk, while ensuring that it is largely localized around TRPs and is recurrently resolved quickly through one or both of the overlapping speakers dropping out in accordance with a 'one speaker at a time' rule (see, e.g., Jefferson, 1986; Sacks et al., 1974; Schegloff, 2000a). In contrast, departures from the routine accomplishment of conversational turn-taking – such as extended periods of overlapping or simultaneous talk (i.e., enduring departures from the 'one speaker at a time' rule) or one party taking a turn at talk despite a different party having been selected to speak next by the prior speaker – may be treated as morally problematic occurrences (e.g., 'interruption,' 'speaking out of turn'), occasioning a search for an account for the behaviour of the offender(s) (see, e.g., Schegloff, 2000a, 2001). The rich set of interpretive resources that categories provide (as described earlier) may thus be mobilized by participants engaging in such explanatory work, with accounts for departures from the ordinary system for turn-taking recurrently invoking the membership of the involved parties in one or more categories (Schegloff, 2001) – and thus the common-sense knowledge associated with the invoked categories being reproduced as a result. More generally, to investigate how practices for taking and distributing opportunities to speak intersects with members' orientations to and uses of membership categorization is to make visible one of the most basic and ubiquitous sites of and occasions for struggles over social inclusion and exclusion.

The use of category membership to account for departures from ordinary turn-taking can be observed in social scientific research that takes the approach of coding participants in interactions as members of particular categories and then statistically compares rates of turn-taking departures across categories. One prominent set of examples in this regard is evident in widely cited studies (e.g., Smith-Lovin & Brody, 1989; West, 1979; West & Zimmerman, 1983; Zimmerman & West, 1975) claiming to show that men interrupt women more often than women interrupt men, and proposing on this basis that these turn-taking violations reflect the operation of gendered power relations at the level of everyday interactions. Indeed, so strong are socio-cultural beliefs in difference[1] – along gender and other categorial lines – that so-called facts

---

1 Critiques of difference-based research do not, of course, halt its progress, especially outside CA, or in research that draws somewhat upon but is not principally based on CA (e.g., Tabassum & Hafeez, 2023). Certainly, research shows that people believe in gender and other

about gender and language have long since passed beyond the realm of academic research and into urban myth (e.g., Gray, 1992; Tannen, 1990). Jefferson (2004b, p. 117) writes about how difference research may have its origins in such beliefs as well as how conversation analysis might be a corrective to such research:

> Working with interactional data, one sometimes observes that a type of behavior seems to be produced a great deal by one category of persons and not all that much by another category. But when put to the test of a straightforward count, the observation does not hold up: Category X does not after all do this thing significantly more often than Category Y does. It may then be that the apparent skewing of the behavior's distribution across categories is the result of selective observation; noticing with greater frequency those cases which conformed to some biased notion held by the observer of how these categories behave. But there seems to be another possibility. It may be that the observation has located, but only roughly and partially described, a complex of behaviors which the observation can then be seen to reflect, refer to, or constitute a 'gloss' for.

Following more than two decades of studies of gender difference in interactional style, including turn-taking, Schegloff (2001, p. 289) observed,

> this line of inquiry and its results engendered . . . a range of contrary stances and findings. . . . The upshot of many of these reports, largely in the context of preoccupations with gender relations, whether from a feminist point of view or other can be put most roughly as 'No they don't' and/or 'That's not the way to look at it, study it, interpret it, etc.'
>
> At the same time, other investigators extended the effort to relate interruption to aspects of social structure and social organization in other directions. For example, taking interruption as an indicator and instrument of hierarchy and dominance relationships, they deployed it in small groups of various sorts to explore such topics as whether dominance relationships were fundamentally grounded in gender categories, or whether gender was itself simply (or not so simply) an index or proxy for status and power relationships (e.g., Kollock et al., 1985, Smith-Loven & Brody, inter alia). The upshot taken from this work can be put most roughly as, 'It depends.'

---

category-based difference or interpret situations using categories. For example, Briggs et al. (2023, p. 1325) found that women *interpreted* men interrupting them as gender bias: "[W]hen faced with condescending explanation, voice nonrecognition, or interruption, women reacted more negatively and were more likely to see the behavior as indicative of gender bias when the communicator was a man" (also see our discussion of "mansplaining" in Chapter 9: Managing Knowledge, Experience, and Entitlement).

The upshot of a review of this entire domain of literature and its variants in the mid-1990s (James & Clarke, 1993) roughly can be characterized as "indeterminate," that is, that few conclusions can be said to be supported other than that men do not interrupt more and that not all interruptions are disruptive or dominating.

While this research has been subject to considerable elaboration and critique, researchers have identified a range of accounts for the profoundly indeterminate findings it produced. These begin with the complexities of associating vernacular conceptions of conduct (i.e., "interruption") with a specific category, in some independence of how participants produce, orient to, and understand a stretch of conduct (also see Weatherall & Edmonds, 2018). However, as anticipated in Schegloff's characterization of this literature, critiques of these studies mostly focus on a range of matters associated with identifying what counts as "interruption," and thus how instances of it are coded and counted. These issues include:

- *Overlap vs. Interruption*: When does overlapping or simultaneous talk constitute an interruption? Overlapping talk is ubiquitous, brief, and most of the time, resolved via the very turn-taking resources that led to its emergence in the first place. Thus, without attending to the timing of the onset of overlapping talk, we cannot determine whether ostensibly interruptive talk is an ordinary by-product of the turn-taking system (and perhaps reflective of *affiliation* rather than domination), or if it is a designed disruption to an in-progress action (Jefferson, 1986; Schegloff, 1997c; Stokoe, 2018; Wilkinson & Kitzinger, 2014). Moreover, in some circumstances, one participant can accuse another of "interruption" even in the absence of overlapping talk. In what follows, we will attend to *overlapping* talk and other interventions that may occasion a search for the (categorial) basis on which two or people come vie for the opportunity to talk.
- *Outcome*: Interruption describes the *outcome* of a potential disruption. It is an intervention designed to stop another person's in-progress, and as yet incomplete, course of action. For the subset of occasions where overlapping talk is initiated outside of or some distance away from the possible completion of a TCU, there is the further question of whether that overlapping talk "succeeds" in promoting the first speaker to abandon an in-progress turn. A claim of "successful interruption" may be complicated because speakers recurrently resume talk that is suspended by reference to overlap in the moments following its resolution (see, e.g., Lerner, 1989). Indeed, some cases of so-called interruption can be the by-product of overlapping talk that emerges from one party resuming a previously suspended in-progress action, raising the question of "who is interrupting whom?" (also see Wilkinson & Kitzinger, 2014).

- *Complainability*: Given the possibility of using overlapping, even disruptively positioned, talk to produce affiliative actions – for example, as in the case of collaborative completions (Lerner, 2004), choral co-production of talk (Lerner, 2002; also see Wilkinson & Kitzinger, 2014), and the like – researchers concerned with using "interruption" to examine power and dominance may be especially concerned with the subset of cases in which participants treat some stretch of overlapping talk as a "complainable" (Schegloff, 2005a) matter. Put simply: do the participants treat the overlapping (or other) talk as problematic? Here a further set of challenges emerge: participants lodging such claims typically do so in, and as part of, a dispute. Consequently, an accused party may resist or reject such claims. Moreover, such complaints or accusations may also reflect and arise out of participants' orientations to, and claims about, whatever differences in status and rights obtain in the encounter. That is, rather than a tacit indicator of power or authority, accusations of interruption may entail an exercise of these very axes of asymmetry.

A full review of these matters exceeds the scope of these introductory remarks. Schegloff (2001) offers a virtuosic, comprehensive overview and discussion of the literature on "interruption" and power, and the issues it raises for social scientific accounts of conduct (also see Wilkinson & Kitzinger, 2008, 2014). Beyond the specific issues Schegloff identifies, we note that approaches assuming straightforward linkage between "interruption" and category membership invites a mechanistic view of interaction in which categories and status differences "drive" both conduct and interactional outcomes.[2] By contrast, we show there is much more to see and understand about how categories matter for interaction if we treat "interruption" (and claims about it) as one among a range of turn-taking phenomena through which parties orient to and instantiate the relevance of who they are for one another in the course of working out who should speak and for how long.

An initial case involving a claim of interruption, shown in Extract 6.1, may help us to see the limitations of these more familiar approaches to turn-taking phenomena and the probative value of the alternative perspective we are proposing (also see the analysis of this case by Stokoe, 2018). In this encounter, a police officer (P) begins interviewing a teenage girl (the suspect, S) who has been arrested on suspicion of criminal damage. The encounter up to this point has entailed a dispute characterized by what might be called

---

2 More recently, Taylor (2016) used experimental studies of gender-based exclusion (including interruptions) in workplaces to challenge essentialist assumptions about the ways men and women respond to stress. Notably, in her experimental design, interruptions (of both men and women) were composed so as to index the category relevant for the form of exclusion being tested.

"mutual misunderstanding," insofar as the parties' claims and conduct reflect contrasting perspectives on the circumstances being discussed. In the immediately preceding talk, the police officer evinces surprise that the suspect claims not to be concerned about the possible consequences of her conduct (up to and including a criminal record and prison), while the suspect appears mystified that the police officer cannot appreciate that her actions were justified by the need to maintain her and her family's dignity and safety in the face of hostile conduct by others.[3] In lines 01–03, the police officer begins formulating what appears to be a further accusation ("do you think that your behaviour . . ."), which the suspect rejects (line 05). Our interest begins with the observation that, although there are actually *no* moments of overlapping talk in this exchange, the police officer claims the suspect has interrupted her (line 08). The suspect, in turn, claims she thought she had allowed the officer to finish speaking before she responded (line 09). How are we to understand this dispute? And how can an analysis of the turn-taking phenomena in the encounter help us to understand what is at stake for the participants?

```
Extract 6.1: Police interview
01  P:  Do you think that- (0.7) your behaviour,
02      (.) coupled with the other: twelve or so that
03      came out,
04             (0.4)
05  S:  No, because everyone coming on the road so they
06      can- y'know-
07             (0.2)
08  P:  Are y'gonna let me finish what I'm sayin'.
09             (0.5)
10  S:  °°I thought you had.°°
```

In asking whether the suspect will "let [her] finish" (line 08), the police officer topicalizes the timing of suspect's denial, which begins before the officer has brought her turn (lines 01–03) to a possible completion. That is, although the suspect's turn (line 05) begins almost half a second after the police officer has stopped speaking, the turn she had been producing was yet to reach a point of grammatical or intonational possible completion (the comma following "out," registers slightly rising, or continuing, intonation), that would make transition to a next speaker (unequivocally) relevant. If the

---

3 The participants' asymmetrical assertions of claims regarding the other's "understanding" are also apparent. In the face of the suspect's justifications for her conduct (not transcribed), the officer complains, "you're not listening to what I'm saying" as a means of claiming that suspect *should* "understand" (and presumably accept or adopt) her perspective. Although the suspect could make the same claim (the officer hasn't understood *her*), she never asserts a reciprocal claim on the officer's attention or understanding. These contrasting orientations point to the ready observability of participants' orientations to hierarchy and dominance relationships in interaction.

police officer has clearly not finished, however, in what way could the suspect claim that she "thought" she had?

As conversation analytic studies of turn-taking (e.g., Jefferson, 1973, 1986; Lerner, 1989, 1996b; Lerner & Takagi, 1999) have noted, next speakers can sometimes start by reference to dimensions other than the possible completion of an in-progress turn. For example, given the context established in the police officer's turn-so-far, both the type of action she is producing – an accusation making relevant an admission – and the grounds for it are readily apparent to the suspect. In addition, together with the multiple delays and disfluencies that emerge throughout the officer's turn (shown by the silences following "that-" and "behaviour" and the stretching on "other" on lines 01–02), the nearly half-second delay following "out" (line 4), may raise questions about whether the officer has abandoned the turn, and so whether she will complete it (also see Lerner, 1996b; Lerner & Takagi, 1999; Schegloff, 1996c). From the suspect's perspective, an accusation has been projected but not completed, leaving the matter of just when she can address its implications up in the air.

This state of affairs may be especially problematic in investigatory interviews, since silences and delays in responding to an accusation are associated with admissions and indicia of guilt. Given this context, a suspect awaiting the chance to defend herself and already selected as next speaker may be under pressure to begin responding lest the growing silence be associated with her hesitancy or failure to speak rather than the police officer's unfinished turn. As these observations suggest, analysing this exchange as an instance of 'interruption' (or even 'possible interruption') would leave us with a disputable set of claims, *precisely because the participants are in the midst of a dispute.* Indeed, as we shall see, the police officer's claim to have been interrupted *pursues* an in-progress dispute, and appears to be a consequential intervention in it.

Even the brief, cursory analysis we have developed should lead us to be sceptical of analytic frameworks that presume a simple or straightforward connection between 'interruption' and social structure (including categories). An analysis of this exchange that takes the police officer's assertion at face value would seem to run counter to the findings reported by researchers concerned with the interruption-power nexus. Along virtually every dimension, this case confounds expectations: whether we consider Pn-adequate categories (e.g., gender, race, age), or setting-based ones (e.g., 'police'/'suspect' – a category pair characterized by profound power inequities), or analyses that take into account how these categories may intersect to produce an aggregate or compound bases for inequality, in this case *the less powerful party has purportedly interrupted the more powerful one.* This might be viewed as an anomaly, or perhaps the exception that proves the rule, but is this so?

Another possibility is suggested if we use our analysis to examine how these participants *use* practices of turn-taking as a set of resources for *locally managing and distributing entitlements and obligations to participate* in an encounter (see Lerner, 2002). In such an analysis we can examine how turn-taking phenomena have a direct bearing on the participants' respective projects of establishing the suspect's guilt or innocence, and thus how their conduct instantiates orientations to their category-bound participation in the encounter, including whatever asymmetries may be associated with those categories or their intersections with others.[4] In a place where the police officer has produced a recognizable, though unfinished, accusation, and the suspect has produced a coherent, responsive turn fitted to it, the officer faces a choice: she can take up the suspect's response (e.g., by challenging or accepting it), or she can treat the timing of its production as problematic, using it as the basis for a further accusation. In choosing the latter option, the officer uses this second accusation to enhance the suspect's vulnerability, thereby underscoring the implication of her prior accusation – namely, that the suspect's *current* conduct has been found wanting, with associated negative implications about her capacity for 'self-control,' lack of concern for others, and the like, ready-to-hand. We can also note, however, that the officer's claim to have been interrupted departs from the mundane or routine turn-taking practices to enforce a *heightened entitlement to speak*. This second accusation, and the assertion of control the officer uses it to establish, results in a marked shift in the suspect's participation. The suspect's defence of herself (line 10) suggests a new appreciation of her diminished access to claims of innocence or justification: As compared with her initial, staunch, full-volume rejection of the officer's perspective, the suspect's whispered back-down, "I thought you had," draws on a practice for establishing the "non-consequential character" of her talk that Schegloff (1988c, p. 117, 2007b, p. 143) calls an "out loud." In this way, the officer's claim to have been interrupted appears to succeed in a way that her initial accusation and earlier prodding had failed. The suspect thereafter abandons her efforts to directly challenge or rebut the officer's claims, highlighting her revised understanding of the precarity of her access to any supportable claims of innocence.

In approaching this exchange by examining how participants *use* turn-taking practices to instantiate the relevance of categories, we find a basis for understanding connections between the phenomena of 'interruption' and 'power' grounded in the participants' orientations to and uses of both. Indeed, in situ claims of, and complaints about, 'interruption' seem to be associated with *heightened entitlements to speak*, precisely because they are made by participants who can pursue and defend such claims, or who are at least willing to risk the attempt to do so. Viewed in this way, the emergence of claims of interruption

---

4 Without a video, we cannot see what prompts the suspect to abandon her in-progress defence, but the cut-offs in line 06 suggest that the police officer's talk in line 08 may have been foreshadowed by the police officer's facial expression or other conduct, raising questions about who is interrupting whom.

by, or on behalf of, members of historically disadvantaged categories may reflect an orientation to a context of incipient or in-progress change. That is, they suggest occasions in which members of advantaged categories remain oblivious to change or cling to rapidly fading status relations, and members of (previously) disadvantaged categories seek to establish a new, more equal set of relations.[5] Moreover, in seeking to understand the participants' orientations to their category-bound participation in the exchange and the forms of inequality with which they are associated, we also gain insight into previously unexplored ways that participants may (seek to) exploit the turn-taking system. Thus, rather than using categories as analysts' resources to account for apparent turn-taking violations, in the remainder of the chapter we proceed by examining how participants themselves observably orient to and mobilize categories to understand their own and others' uses of, and departures from, the use of the turn-taking system to manage who speaks when and for how long. We thereby specify one significant set of interactional mechanisms through which categories can be seen to 'lie in wait' for use as interpretive resources in the way we described in Chapter 1: An Introduction to Categories in Interaction. Our efforts in doing so will be enhanced if we begin by briefly elaborating on our previous introduction to the basic elements of the turn-taking system.

6.2 Turn-taking: basic elements and categorial dimensions

As we noted earlier, the turn-taking system for conversation is comprised of two parts: a turn construction component and a turn allocation component. The turn construction component, as its name implies, describes the resources speakers use to compose turns at talk once they have the opportunity to produce them. Sacks et al. (1974) note that speakers compose turns using turn constructional units (TCUs), which can vary in length from a single word to a phrase or clause, to a full sentence. Crucially, once they are started, TCUs have a sequentially sensitive projectable course and duration that enable both speaker and hearer to track (and adjust) the progressive realization of an in-progress TCU as it moves towards its possible completion. Once a speaker has the right to a turn, they are entitled to speak one such unit 'in the clear' (without any other participant speaking concurrently), with transition to a next speaker becoming relevant at its (projectable) possible completion, or transition relevance place (TRP) (Schegloff, 1996c). Such a system provides a locally organized basis for shaping how turns come to be produced over their course and localizes to the boundaries of TCUs the majority of struggles that might emerge as speakers seek or avoid turns. At such boundaries, the turn allocation component of the system comes into play.

---

5 In this respect, perhaps it is not surprising that research on power and interruption emerged in the aftermath of the civil rights movement and the rise of second-wave feminism.

The turn allocation component is comprised of a set of resources by which next speakers come to be selected: A next speaker can (a) be selected by the current speaker, (b) self-select, or (c) current speaker can continue (Lerner, 2003; Sacks et al., 1974). Participants systematically orient to a set of rules that order the use of these options (a–c) so that if a current speaker selects next, the selected speaker should begin speaking at the next possible opportunity – that is, at the first possible completion of the in-progress TCU. If a turn reaches a possible completion and no speaker has been selected, then a next speaker can self-select (in multi-party conversation, first speaker claims rights to talk), and if no speaker self-selects, current can continue (Sacks et al., 1974). We can note that the ordering of these options (a–c) places pressure to use one before the next option becomes available: If current speakers wish to select a next speaker, they must do so before their current turn reaches a possible completion, lest a next speaker self-select; if no speaker has been selected as next, then a next must self-select at the earliest possible place, lest another participant do so, or current speaker continues. These elements thus furnish a set of resources designed to produce one party speaking at a time, no more and no less, and a basis for all participants involved in a conversation to carefully track what others are doing, in case they are selected to speaker next, or have some basis for self-selecting (Sacks et al., 1974).

The basic elements of this turn-taking system provide a 'context-free form of social organization' that is nevertheless capable of exquisitely 'context-sensitive' operation (Lerner, 2003; Sacks et al., 1974; Schegloff, 2000a, 2001). The range of contexts to which members can adapt (aspects of) the use of the turn-taking system varies considerably and includes common sense conceptions of 'context' such as work settings (e.g., a doctor's office, news interview, university lecture); the persons who may be involved in an encounter; how they may be categorized, and thus the relational and status systems their participation makes relevant (e.g., Drew & Heritage, 1992b; Schegloff, 2001); politico-historical contexts (e.g., Raymond et al., 2019; Whitehead, 2020); and more abstract characterizations related to numbers of parties, activities, and variable deployments of the system itself (e.g., Schegloff, 1979a, 1996c, 2000a, 2001; Schegloff et al., 1977).

Because the turn-taking system provides the basis for members' sequentially organized participation in an encounter, with one turn following a next, it also supplies the basic infrastructure through which members contribute to and maintain a common grasp of their joint circumstances (also see our discussion of sequence organization in Chapter 7: Organizing Sequences of Action). In this way, the turn-by-turn organization of talk-in-interaction also provides a radically different understanding of the relationship between action and context than those conventionally assumed in social scientific analyses of action. That is, in contrast to an approach in which 'distal' (or so-called 'macro') notions of context are understood to circumscribe and impinge on members' conduct, the inexorably local focus demanded by the turn-by-turn organization of interaction disciplines when, where, and how contexts – aspects of the social world beyond the immediate occasion, including social categories – come to be instantiated in some bit of conduct, and thus made relevant for others to contend with as well (also see, e.g., Goodwin & Heritage, 1990; Schegloff, 1987a, 1991, 1997c; Whitehead, 2020).

Given the flexibility of this form of social organization, the range of ways that the practices of turn-taking can be used to display an orientation to the relevance of categories is virtually limitless. In fact, virtually any use of the turn-taking system can be a basis for participants to materially instantiate their category-bound place within an encounter, or for invoking categories to justify their actions or retrospectively account for what has just transpired. Rather than seeking to provide an exhaustive account of the ways that turn-taking phenomena can be associated with relevance and procedural consequentiality (Schegloff, 1987a, 1991, 1992c) of categories in talk-in-interaction, we seek in the remainder of this section to explicate some of the more basic ways the various components of the turn-taking system can be used to ground such claims. Specifically, we primarily examine the ways that participants' use of the turn-taking system (and institution-specific modifications of it) can be shown to reflect their orientation to the relevance of specific categories, emphasizing the practices through which those orientations come to be instantiated in talk, and the ways that these may reflect how the turn-taking system provides a locally organized basis for managing participation and exclusion. As we shall see, such orientations to categories and categorization can be reflected in ordinary uses of the turn-taking system, as well as in departures from it.

6.2.1 Categories and turn allocation: current speaker selects next

To illustrate how the turn-taking system can be used as a basis for locally managing category-based entitlements and obligations to speak, we begin with a simple pair of cases exemplifying the two most common ways participants come to talk – current speaker selects next and next speaker self-selects. The first case is taken from a news interview analysed in Roth (1998, p. 89–90). As conversation analytic research (e.g., Clayman & Heritage, 2002; Heritage & Clayman, 2010) has noted, news interviews are, in part, constituted through a specialized turn-taking system that pre-allocates turns and the activities done in them: interviewers pose questions to interviewees who produce answers. In such encounters, participants' orientations to these setting-based institutional categories can be grounded on a turn-by-turn basis. Moreover, as Roth (1998) observes, interviewers routinely use other categories and categorization to introduce guests in the opening of an interview as a way of accounting for their inclusion as "newsworthy" persons. In doing so, interviewers may cast the interviewees as either "legitimate, marginal, or beyond the pale'" (Roth,

1998, p. 80; cf. Hall, 1973, p. 88) by reference to some moral or political framework. These observations can be extended by noting that, *by virtue of the way turn-taking practices and categorization co-operate in news interviews, interviewers can use practices of questioning to enact, maintain, or move, a society's bureaucratic and ideological boundaries.*

This is illustrated by Extract 6.2, from a television news interview focused on an armed stand-off between federal agents and members of an anti-government militia known as the Freemen. The interview involves two interviewees introduced as members of categories from different collections: one, Kenneth Stern (KS), is introduced as a professor who is "an expert on hate groups," while the other, Norman Olson (NO) is introduced as a member of the "Northern Michigan Militia." Evidently, the interviewees have been invited to provide alternative vantages on the unfolding news events, with contrasting epistemic bases for their claims (also see Chapter 9: Managing Knowledge, Experience, and Entitlement). At one point, following a brief struggle for the floor (lines 02–06; also see Schegloff, 2000a), the interviewer, Phil Jones (PJ) selects Stern as next speaker based on his status as an expert on, rather than membership in, the militia movement (lines 07–08).

```
Extract 6.2: Face the Nation, 31.03.96
01  KS:  . . . that just exacerbates thuh
02        situa[tion and le[ads to a confrontation.
03  NO:        [Well lemme-[
04  PJ:                    [Mister Stern.
05        Mis[ter Stern. M- Let me ask Mister Stern plea:se.=
06  NO:      [Lemme explain.
07  PJ:  =Ah you-you have looked at these militia groups,
08        What do you know about thuh Freemen. [Who are they?
09  KS:                                        [.hhh They're a
10        white supremacist group, their basic belief is
11        something called Christian identity ((continues))
```

Following a longer turn by Stern (concluded in lines 01–02) that criticizes a position previously articulated by Olson, both Olson and Jones pursue alternative projects, producing a struggle for the floor. Olson self-selects, indexing his identity as a militia member by seeking to address Stern's claims and claiming the right and ability to "explain" (lines 03 and 06), while Jones makes multiple efforts to select Stern as next speaker (lines 04 and 05). Once in the clear, Jones warrants his selection of Stern using a characterization of him ("you have looked at these militia groups," line 07) that links back to his introduction of Stern as an "expert" on such groups. Jones's stress on "looked" in his description of Stern builds a contrast (see, e.g., Bolinger, 1961; Schegloff, 1998b; Whitehead & Lerner, 2022) with Olson, indexing his participation in the interview as based on his membership in the militia movement rather than research-based expertise on it. As Roth (1998, p. 90; emphasis in original) notes, "by describing an interviewee *as* an expert on the matter at hand, an interviewer *builds an account* for posing this particular question to this particular interviewee *into the question itself*." In doing so, Jones also maintains Olson's position as outside the mainstream of American political discourse. In the face of Olson's persistent efforts to produce a turn explaining the position Stern has just critiqued – which would thereby constitute his position as one (legitimate) side of a political debate – Jones warrants selecting Stern as next speaker by indexing his prior categorization of him as an expert. Moreover, with Olson dropping out and Stern proceeding to answer the query posed to him, both interviewees ratify, or at least accept, Jones's selection of Stern as next speaker.

In this case, Jones's introduction of the interviewees as militia expert and member establishes the relevance of the participants' category-based identities in a way that casts them as omni-relevant for this encounter. And yet the necessity for *locally* managing entitlements and obligations to participate (or not) in the encounter nevertheless emerges as basis for establishing the procedural consequentiality of their orientations to their respective category-bound places within it. That is, competition over who will speak next makes relevant various adjustments to Jones's in-progress turn, including his account for selecting one party to speak next (over the other). Absent Olson's self-selection, Jones could simply select Stern to speak next by using the address term 'Mr. Stern' to direct a next question to him, as he begins to do in line 04. Once the floor fight emerges from Olson's bid to speak, however, Jones adjusts the practices he uses to select Stern as next speaker: he restarts his turn, obliquely addressing Olson when the latter persists in his bid for the floor (see lines 04–05), and then goes on to give an account that uses contrastive stress to highlight Stern's category membership (as compared to Olson's) as a basis for doing so. It is worth underscoring the potentially generic import of this observation: the relevancies introduced by one person acting on the basis of category membership (as happens when Olson begins speaking in lines 03 and 06) prompts adjustments that "expose" a second party's (Jones's) orientation to a further party's (Stern's) membership in a category from a different MCD. As we saw in Chapter 4: Forming and Making Sense of Actions, where participants must manage the potential relevance of more than one category – which, as we have noted previously, is a systematic possibility – disambiguating which category will be treated as the relevant one can be a basis for the design of actions produced in turns at talk. Thus, while Roth (1998) observes how people are frequently invited to appear on news interviews because of their category-based expertise about, and experiences in and with, newsworthy phenomena, in this case a description of an interviewee as an expert in the course of directing a question to them during an ongoing interview mobilizes such a category to justify that party's selection as next speaker over a differently categorized other party.

6.2.2 *Categories and turn allocation: (next) speaker self-selects*

In the turn-taking system, current selects next is the first method for allocating turns at talk. However, if no speaker has been selected, a next speaker can self-select at the next TRP within in an encounter, or as a way of opening an encounter. While a self-selecting speaker can simply begin speaking, the practices used to claim a turn can also reveal the speaker's orientation to their category-bound participation within the encounter. To examine how practices of speaker self-selection may expose participants' orientations to one or more categories, we return to a case, shown in Extract 6.3, which we previously examined in Chapter 3: Methodological Principles, Practices, and Challenges (Extract 3.2). As we noted previously, this extract shows an encounter with the police regarding a disturbance in a convenience store in which a civilian present in the store upon the arrival of the police seeks to establish his membership in the setting-based 'witness' (and later 'peacekeeper') category before the police ever say a word – and in doing so shows his orientation to his vulnerability, as a member of one or more of the categories 'young,' 'Black,' and 'man,' to being categorized by the police officers as a 'suspect.' This case thereby demonstrates that, once a party has set the turn-taking system in motion in the way this participant does (i.e., addressing his turn to the officers), all of the participants are placed in a situation of choice: they can either respond to the first speaker's turn or leave its claims unaddressed if they pursue some other course of action.

Extract 6.3: Police encounter (SPD7455@20090331021633)

```
((As two officers walk in))
01  C1:  >Hey.=Honestly sir.< (.) I have no issues=
02  P1:  =Let's go out[side.
03  C2:               [These guys are cool.
04  C1:  This guy- I- hon[estly- honestly=
05  C3:                  [He's cool. He's,
06  C1:  =I'm the- I'm [the one that's keeping th[uh peace sir.
07  C2:               [those dudes out there, [
08  C3:                                        [He's- he's
09  C1:  I'm fine.
10  P1:  First of all you're coming outside too
11  C1:  Okay. [No(   ). fine sir
12  C3:        [Hey he's cool though. Please believe me man.
```

The timing and composition of C1's opening turn (line 01) address two elements of the encounter's opening: his understanding that the arriving police officers are entitled to speak first and that they will likely assume his involvement in the dispute unless he does something to avert this. For example, despite being the first to self-select, the opening components of his turn are louder than the surrounding talk and produced at an accelerated pace – two practices speakers use to preempt or subvert potentially competitive turns (Schegloff, 2000a). Moreover, in using this rushed turn-beginning to address the officers, C1 treats recruiting their recipiency as a prerequisite for further action. These elements of C1's turn-beginning reflect an orientation to his diminished entitlement to speak – as compared, for example, with P1's turn in line 02. Once he can see that he has won his bid to take a turn in the clear, C1 slows the pace of his talk to disclaim his involvement in the dispute (line 01). Then, when one of the officers tells him to "go outside" (line 02) instead of taking up his claims, C1 further characterizes his role in trying to resolve the dispute, as a means of establishing how he should be treated. That is, in asserting that he is "the one that's keeping thuh peace" (line 06), and thereby claiming membership in a setting-based 'peacekeeper' category, C1 specifies an alternative basis for his presence at a scene of trouble that the police have been called to resolve – one that claims alignment with their project, rather than acquiescing to their apparent positioning of him as part of those troubles.

It is thus through these speaker self-selection practices that C1 claims membership in the setting-based 'witness' and 'peacekeeper' categories before the officers can act on (any presumed) categorial biases (as described in our analysis of Extract 3.2) that might lead to his categorization as a 'suspect.' We can thereby see how the intersection of turn-taking and membership categorization places C1 in a situation of choice: he can either act to preemptively establish his membership in the 'witness' category or attempt to challenge or dispute the officers' treatment of him as one of the involved parties if they go first and categorize him in this way.

Once a party sets the turn-taking system in motion by talking, it becomes an ongoing basis for locally managed obligations and entitlements that ensnares other co-present parties (even more powerful ones, like the police), until they collectively manage to turn it off by ending the encounter (see, e.g., Raymond & Zimmerman, 2007; Schegloff & Sacks, 1973). In this case, having produced a turn addressed to the arriving officers (and thereby selected them as possible next speakers), whoever speaks next cannot avoid taking a position regarding the competing relevancies set in motion by C1's turn – namely, the officers institutionally grounded rights to 'take control' of the scene and C1's preemptive claims of innocence. Although P1's first turn (line 02) follows C1's, by producing it 'as if' he was the first to speak he nevertheless takes a position on the status of C1's claims by asserting his right to speak first. The directive he produces, in turn, further heightens the situation of choice established by C1's talk: the other co-present civilians can either respond to the officer's directive or address C1's claims. We can note, then, that C2 and C3 take up C1's project by addressing the officers with supportive assessments (lines 03, 05, and 12). Moreover, in doing so, their talk reveals that they share C1's understanding of the officers' likely racial biases and thus the precarity of his situation. Indeed, in speaking on behalf of C1 – and doing so without any apparent concern that they might be viewed as suspects or that their protestations might be treated as 'resistance' warranting the use of force (cf. Sacks, 1984b) – they appear to be acting on the privileges (e.g., the presumption of innocence and credibility) associated with their visible membership in the racial category 'white.' Moreover, their assumptions in this regard prove to be well-founded: after an officer uses pain compliance techniques to forcefully escort C1 outside (not transcribed), C3 casually walks out with another officer, and a third points to C2 (whose conduct prompted the call and who has trailed behind them, unescorted) to ask, "is she involved too?", thereby displaying an openness to the possibility of her innocence that has not at any time been extended to C1.

In the cases we have examined so far, next speakers begin their talk by reference to the ways the turn-taking system routinely organizes opportunities for participation. These are highly robust patterns that reflect the ways that the turn-taking system localizes the relevance of transition to next speakers by reference to the *possible* completion of TCUs (Jefferson, 1986; Sacks et al., 1974) and other opportunities to talk (e.g., in the openings of encounters, as in Extract 6.3). As we noted in Section 6.1, however, participants may depart from the routine accomplishment of conversational turn-taking in ways that occasion a search for an account for their having done so. As we demonstrate in the following section, in these cases participants may mobilize the set of interpretive resources provided by category membership to engage in such explanatory work.

6.2.3 Categories and departures from routine turn-taking practices

In the preceding sections we examined how ordinary uses of the turn-taking system can be a basis on which orientations to the relevance and consequentiality of specific categories come to be instantiated on particular occasions. Our claims have been developed along two intersecting lines of analysis: First, the turn-taking system provides participants a set of practices for locally managing category-based entitlements and obligations to talk (or not). Second, in developing this account we have emphasized that participants' orientations to category membership often become observable in circumstances where conduct produced by reference to alternative or contrasting category memberships becomes salient or possible. Insofar as a specialized turn-taking system can be the basis for instantiating the relevance of specific categories on a turn-by-turn basis (cf. Drew & Heritage, 1992a; Heritage & Clayman, 2010), we might expect that the relevance and procedural consequentiality of specific categories would become most prominent, apparent, or recognizable, where one or more participants depart from or override the presumed local distribution of entitlements and obligations to act or not. In this section, we examine how participants observably orient to and mobilize categories in accounting for their own and others' departures from ordinary turn-taking practices. This can be seen even where departures from ordinary turn-taking practices do not appear to be special or remarkable, as in Extract 6.4, an exchange in a day-care centre analysed by Lerner (2019).

```
Extract 6.4: Day-care center
01    Dad:   BYE BYE An:(.)tonio.
02              (.)
03  a→CG1:  BYE:: Mitch
04              (.)
05    Dad:   [(Bye bye)
06  b→CG1:  [Say bye to your dad?
```

As Lerner (2019, p. 393; emphasis in original) notes, people caring for very young children who are just learning to speak may monitor occasions for circumstances in which a person directs an initiating action to the child, and thereby makes a responsive action by them relevant:

> On each occasion in which a very young child is selected as next speaker, the possibilities of pursuit by the selecting party or intervening action by another party or both may not result from demonstrated inability on that occasion alone but can be oriented to by coparticipants as an omnirelevant possibility. That is, very young children can be treated as not yet competent to respond on their own behalf – an orientation that is not without a basis in fact or experience. Moreover, [as Extract 6.4 demonstrates] . . . such moments of *heightened normativity* can be taken up as teachable moments – as opportunities for both modeling (as at arrow a) and instructing (as at arrow b).

> Here CG1 (at arrow a) seems to be demonstrating a return good-bye for Antonio's benefit. It is just these moments that require something specific of fully fledged participants – and as fully fledged participants, the coparticipants of very young children know just what will count as adequate for the practical sequence-organized matter at hand. One might say that parents and other caregivers are omnirelevant consociates for very young children in these matters. They are, in effect, category-bound consociates.

Thus, in such cases, a party may talk or act in support of, or on behalf of, another who has been selected to do so. It is precisely because one party has been selected to talk that another party who talks in that place can be said to intervene on their behalf. For example, a person can also be found to be "not yet competent to respond on their own behalf" on the grounds that they are not yet competent speakers of one language even though they are competent speakers of another: a married couple visiting a country in which one party is a native speaker of the language while the other only knows a few words or phrases may find that the native speaking member routinely responds to queries directed to the other party. And, as illustrated by Extract 6.5, one speaker intervening on behalf of another can be seen to have done so on the basis of other categories (also see the brief analysis of this case by Lerner, 2019, p. 391). The exchange shown here is initiated by a complaint by Shane (line 01; also see lines 08 and 11), which implicates fault on the part of Vivian, his partner, and the party who prepared the meal that Shane and Vivian are hosting with their friends Nancy and Michael (who are also a couple). After Nancy recruits Michael in her efforts to defend Vivian (line 13), thereby selecting him as the next speaker, Shane intervenes on behalf of Michael by speaking when he has not been selected, using a non-serious query (line 14) that appears designed to redirect the interaction away from the difficult choice with which Michael was faced.

```
Extract 6.5: Chicken Dinner
01  SHA:  Ah can't- Ah can't [get this thing ↓mashed.
02  VIV:                      [Aa-ow.
03              (1.2)
04  NAN:  You[do that too:? Tih yer pota]toes,
05  SHA:     [This one's hard ezza rock.]
06  SHA: ↑Ye[ah.
07  VIV:     [It i:[s?
08  SHA:           [B't this thing- is ↑ha:rd.
09              (0.3)
10  VIV:  It's not do:ne? th'potato?
11  SHA:  Ah don't think so,
12              (2.2)
13  NAN:  Seems done t'me how 'bout you Mi[chael,]
14  SHA:                              [Alri' ]who cooked
15        this mea:l.
16  MIC:  .hh Little ↓bit'v e-it e-ih-ih of it isn'done.
17  SHA:  Th'ts ri:ght.
18              (1.2)
19  MIC:  [°('T's alright)°
20  SHA:  [No it's a(h)lr(h)i(h)ght['t's (h)air(h)i(h)ght]
21  NAN:                       [Theh: F u c k t h e]m it's
22        goo:d o[kay?
22  SHA:         [he-he
```

Having initially attempted to divert attention away from Shane's complaint by observing its implications for their shared potato-mashing practices (line 04), Nancy's turn at line 13 more directly refutes the complaint before explicitly recruiting Michael to align with her in doing so. Nancy thereby displays a sustained orientation to defending Vivian from Shane's repeated complaints, thereby evidently acting by reference to their co-membership in a gendered friendship category and/or as a member of the 'guest' category showing appreciation for and defending the work Vivian has done as a 'host.' Nancy's recruitment of Michael places him in a category-laden position of choosing between taking the side of his partner and concurrently meeting the expectations of being (like Nancy) an appreciative guest versus aligning with his male friend Shane's complaint and thereby rescuing him from the prospect of being left isolated and potentially appearing to be a dispositional 'moaner' or 'whinger' (see Edwards, 2005). Before Nancy is able to finish saying Michael's name in her recruitment of him, however, Shane incurs on her turn by producing a designedly non-serious query, "who cooked this meal" (lines 14–15). In addition to attempting to re-cast his earlier complaints as a joke,[6] this intervening action by Shane forestalls a response by Michael to Nancy's recruitment in which he would have to contend with the fraught categorial choices this would involve – albeit only temporarily so, as Michael responds shortly thereafter (line 16), orienting in the process to the no-win situation in which he has been placed by fumbling his way through a 'middle-ground' position. Shane thus, similarly to what we saw in Chapter 3: Methodological Principles, Practices, and Challenges, Extract 3.1, produces an intervening action on behalf of a co-member of a category (in this case 'male friend') facing a difficult situation, with the departure from ordinary turn-taking involved thereby revealing his orientation to this category.

In Extract 6.4, we saw caregivers intervene to support and encourage action by a party developing the competence to do so on their own. In the day-care setting, the 'parent' and 'child' categories are treated by participants as omni-relevant for, and constitutive of the activities that comprise it. In this regard, turn-taking conduct that is oriented to their relevance can accountably be seen as a routine matter: participants' orientations to the parent-child standardized relational pair are simply part of how the institutional work of that setting is conducted, particularly at the beginning and end of the day where parents drop off and pick up their children. In other settings, where participants' turn-taking conduct is systematically produced by reference to a different set of setting-based categories, one party making relevant such categories – and others as well – can be understood as part of a different, more critically oriented, project that may depart from the categories otherwise treated as omni-relevant for the setting. This can be seen in Extract 6.6, which we previously examined in Chapter 4: Forming and Making Sense of Actions (Extract 4.5). As we noted

6 While Shane formulates this turn as a further complaint rather than a genuine query (given that he knows very well that it was Vivian who cooked the meal), the exaggerated fashion in which he does this serves as a way of backing down from what had previously been apparently serious complaints – which he then underscores with his laugh-interpellated backdown at line 20. Shane thereby works, in the face of his potential isolation as the sole complainer, to provide himself with an 'escape hatch' from the negative inferences that might arise from his complaint being unanimously treated as unfounded or even mean-spirited (cf. Edwards, 2005).

in our previous analysis, this encounter is from a televised interview conducted with tennis player Venus Williams (VW) in which her father, Richard Williams (RW), intervened to forestall the interviewer's (IR's) questioning, occasioning a dispute between them. Here, we take up the interviewer's objection to this intervention, as he treats Richard Williams's talk as an interruption on the basis that he is not an incumbent of the category 'interview participant' (lines 24 and 26–27), after which Richard Williams uses explicit mentions of a range of categories to sanction the interviewer.

Extract 6.6: Venus Williams ABC Interview, 1995

```
01  IR:  You think you could beat her?
02             (.)
03  VW:  I know I can beat her.
04             (1.2)
05  IR:  You know it?
06             (2.2) ((VW nods, smiles))
07  IR:  Very confident?
08             (1.0)
09  VW:  I'm very confident.
10             (0.8)
11  IR:  You say it so easily.
12             (2.5)
13  IR:  Why?
14             (1.5)
15  VW:  Cuz I bel[ieve it.
16  RW:           [(All right, end that there) if you don't
17       mi:nd.
18             (.)
19  RW:  And let me tell you why:.
20             (1.0)
21  RW:  What she has sa:id, (0.5) she said it with so much
22       confidence the first time, (0.7) but you keep going on
23       and on:.
24  IR:  You-
25  RW:  (Listen to [her.)
26  IR:             [can't keep i- interrupting, I mean i- if you
27       want [(her-)
28  RW:        [You've got tuh understand that you('re) dealing
29       with a image of a fourteen year old chi:ld.
30             (0.3)
31  RW:  And this child gonna be out there playing when your old
32       ass and me gonna be in the gra:ve. When she say
33       something, we done told you what's happen(ed). (.hh)
34       You're dealing with a little Black ki:d, (.) and let her
35       be a kid. <She done answered it with a lot of confidence,
36       LEAVE THAT ALONE!
```

In Chapter 7: Organizing Sequences of Action, we return to this case to consider the features of the interactional sequence that occasions Richard Williams's intervention (lines 01–15). Here we will note that Richard Williams intervenes on Venus Williams's behalf (line 16) just after she has begun to respond (line 15) to the strongest in a series of challenging questions the interviewer has produced during this exchange (line 13; also see lines 05, 07, and 11). This intervention entails a departure from both the local relevancies established by the interviewer's prior turn (which selected Venus Williams as next speaker), and the encounter itself insofar as Richard Williams is not a ratified co-participant in the interview, and thus would not ordinarily be selected as a speaker at any point. Although the account Richard Williams initially provides for his interruption (lines 19 and 21–23) takes up the interviewer's questioning of Venus Williams's displays of confidence without explicitly introducing the category-relevance of his own or the interviewer's actions, his intervention on behalf of Venus Williams shows his orientation to his rights and obligations as her parent and coach, serving to shield her from the scepticism conveyed in the interviewer's aggressive questioning – and thus from the potential damage to her confidence he implies such questioning may inflict (see especially lines 21–22 and 35–36).

Then (as we noted in our analysis of this extract in Chapter 4: Forming and Making Sense of Actions), after the interviewer objects to his interruption (lines 24 and 26–27), Richard Williams explicitly invokes Venus Williams's age and stage of life categories (lines 28–29 and 34), in contrast with those of the interviewer and himself (lines 31–32) to warrant his protection of her. Moreover, in his subsequent sanctioning of the interviewer's actions (lines 32–36), Richard Williams invokes Venus Williams's race and (again) stage of life categories, thereby mobilizing these categories as further warranting his interruption of the interview. As in Extract 6.4, in this case a parent intervenes to act on behalf of their child. In this case, however, the intervention constitutes a departure from the currently relevant institutional (interview) turn-taking system and associated categories, and (in further contrast to Extract 6.4) the categorial relevancies that have occasioned the intervention are considerably more complex, involving matters of race, age, respect, confidence and the very different orientations to such matters that may be oriented to by a parent/coach versus a journalist. Moreover, this case demonstrates how the invocation of Pn-adequate categories as alternatives to setting-based ones can be a basis on which institutional turn-taking constraints come to be relaxed or abandoned, with participants moving instead to the most basic ordinary conversational system.

The turn-taking system provides a localized organization for distributing opportunities to speak, yet how any person comes to take a turn – especially a turn not already allocated to them – can be inspected for the category-based projects it might be understood to pursue. While this is a general feature of how departures from ordinary turn-taking may be interpreted, the ways in which Richard

Williams explicitly treats P*n*-adequate categories as superseding the prevailing setting-based ('interviewer'/'interviewee') categories to warrant his intervention exposes their systematic availability as bases for taking a turn at a particular moment. Thus, it is when the interviewer treats Richard Williams's intervention as an illegitimate interruption that Richard Williams invokes Venus Williams's race, gender, and categories as bases for her vulnerability to the type of questioning the interviewer has been pursuing, and hence for the legitimacy of Richard Williams's protective intervention. As we shall see in the following section, this potentially superseding import of P*n*-adequate categories can be more cynically deployed as a resource in pursuit of occasion-based political ends.

6.3 Turn-taking and categories in the Schiff-Nunes-Stefanik dispute

Having specified some of the key intersections between the turn-taking system and participants' orientations to and uses of various (types of) categories, we return to the dispute with which we began this chapter to examine the purported case of interruption it involves, and the contrasting categorical bases invoked to assess and account for it. As noted previously, at issue in the dispute is the basis Adam Schiff (AS) has for 'gaveling' Elise Stefanik's (ES's) contribution out of order following Devin Nunes's (DN's) invitation for her to question Ambassador Yovanovitch. As alluded to by our prior discussion of the dispute, the occasion is organized by reference to categories from a setting-based 'congressional hearing' MCD that throughout the majority of the occasion the participants systematically treat as omni-relevant, constituted by categories that serve as the basis for distributing opportunities to speak. These include 'committee chair' and 'ranking member' (of which Schiff and Nunes respectively are the incumbents), along with 'committee member' (of which Stefanik is an incumbent) and 'witness' (the sole incumbent of which for this specific hearing is Yovanovitch). Also attached to these categories (and again as alluded to previously) is the participants' respective political affiliations with the opposing Democratic (Schiff) and Republican (Nunes and Stefanik) political parties, the former of which was in the majority in the House of Representatives at the time, thereby affording Schiff and Nunes their respective 'committee chair' and 'ranking member' positions.

By virtue of the rules voted in during the process of establishing the impeachment inquiry of which the hearing was a part, the portion of the hearing during which the dispute took place had been pre-allocated to Nunes as ranking member, and/or to his Minority Counsel, a hired attorney who Nunes was permitted to delegate as his agent in questioning Yovanovitch. The dispute, shown in Extract 6.7, emerged shortly after Schiff had yielded the floor to Nunes, who produced some commentary on the hearing before (without asking Yovanovitch any questions nor prompting his counsel to do so) announcing his yielding of the floor to Stefanik (lines 01–02 and 04). Soon after Stefanik begins to speak (lines 05–07), Schiff strikes his gavel (line 08) and directs her "to suspend" (line 10) – that is, to cease talking. This occasions a brief floor struggle (lines 07–10), followed by a series of claims and counter-claims regarding whether Stefanik is allowed to speak, and taking up the categorial bases on which Schiff has interceded to prevent this from happening.

```
Extract 6.7: U.S. House Intelligence Committee, 15.11.19
01   DN:  Uh: I know Miss Stefanik you had a f:: a few quick
02        questions: (.) for the ambassador.
03              (0.5)
04   DN:  I'll- (.) yield to you, Miss Stefa[nik.]
05   ES:                                     [tch ] .hh (.) Thank
06        you, Mister Nunes:.
07        .hh [Ambassador Yovanovitch, [ tha:nk  you ]
08   AS:      [((strikes gavel))       [The gentlewom-]
09   ES:  for b[eing     here         toda:y,]
10   AS:       [The gentlewoman will suspend.]
11              (.)
12   AS:  The gentlewoman wi' suspend.
13   ES:  What is the interruption for this time? It is our time.
14   AS:  Th- >the gentlewoman will suspend,< you're not
15        recognized. Mister Nunes, you or Min[ority Counsel]
16   DN:                                       [  I: jus-   ]
17        I jus: recogn[ized Miss Stefanik. ]
18   AS:               [(Bu)=under the House] >Resolu'n< six sixty
19        you're not allowed to yield time except to Minority
20        Coun[sel.]
21   ES:      [The ] Ranking Member [ yield]ed [time to ano]ther
22   AS:                            [(Yib-)]   [(Gen'lwm-) ]
23   ES:  Mem[ber of Con]gres[s.]
24   AS:     [(Gen'lwm-)]    [ N]o.
25              (0.2) ((AS bangs gavel))
26   AS:  That is not accurate.
27   DN:  You're gagg(h)ing the: [young lady from New] York?
28   ES:                         [ That is accurate. ]
29   AS:  .hhhh [(Remember-)]
30   ES:        [Ambassador ] Yovanovitch, I wanna thank you for
31        [  being  here   today,  ]
32   AS:  [Gentlewoman will suspend.] ((AS strikes gavel on
33        "suspend"))
34              (0.4)
35   AS:  You're not recognized.
36              (1.0)
37        ((exchange continues))
```

Congressional hearings, like other formal settings involving witness testimony (see, e.g., Atkinson, 1992; Atkinson & Drew, 1979), entail specialized rules regarding when speakers can speak, and how they come to have the floor. We can note, then, that Stefanik does not begin speaking following the first possible completion of the turn in which Nunes initially refers to her (line 02), although this turn would have sufficed in selecting her as next speaker in an ordinary conversation. Instead, Stefanik only begins speaking after Nunes explicitly 'yields the floor' to her (line 04), suggesting her recognition that her contributions will be treated as legitimate only if she adheres to the set of specialized turn-taking rules in play. We can also note that Schiff similarly orients to the requirements of his role as chair. For example, he does not immediately gavel Nunes out of order when he proposes that Stefanik may speak next. Rather he intervenes only after Stefanik begins talking, producing his gavel strike and associated directive (lines 08 and 10) just after she has thanked Nunes (line 06) and is beginning to address Yovanovitch (line 07).[7] Nevertheless, the timing of Schiff's intervention is clearly designed to be interruptive – Schiff bangs his gavel and begins speaking *after* Stefanik has recognizably begun a turn-at-talk (that Nunes selected her to produce), and well *before* she reaches a first possible completion. Moreover, in repeating his command (line 12) in the face of Stefanik's efforts to persist to completion (line 09), Schiff demonstrates a commitment to preventing her from speaking, at least at this time. And, of course, as we noted previously, both Nunes and Stefanik register complaints about Schiff's intervention. For example, Stefanik's initial complaint references her party membership as the basis for the complaint by using the collective pronoun "our" (line 13; also see our discussion of collective self-reference in Chapter 5: Referring to and Addressing People), thereby indexing the relevance of this setting-based MCD for organizing turn-taking during the hearing.

Notably, however, following a dispute between Schiff and Stefanik over the latter's right (or lack thereof) to speak (lines 13–26), Nunes escalates matters with his expression of disbelief (in line 27), claiming the relevance of age and gender in accounting for Schiff's conduct. He thereby attempts to cast this as an occasion in which an (old[er]) man (Schiff) has interrupted a "young lady" (Stefanik). The interactional implications of these choices are underscored if we recall how Sacks's economy rule observes that one category can be used to do adequate reference, and thus when more than one is used, participants can

---

7 The video of this exchange does not show all of the participants continuously; instead, coverage moves to include Schiff as he is picking up his gavel. As a consequence, it is not clear whether Schiff has delayed his intervention until the moment Stefanik addresses Yovanovitch, or if the time it took for him to retrieve and use his gavel slightly delayed his intervention.

inspect what is being done by the additional category or categories used (see Chapter 2: Approaching Membership Categorization). In this respect, Nunes evidently draws on common-sense knowledge in relation to the categories he invokes without explicitly spelling out the ways that he is treating 'interruption' as category-bound to 'man.' That is, Nunes evidently mobilizes the intersection of age and gender to underscore Stefanik's vulnerability and need for protection relative to Schiff (also note the parallels with Richard Williams's use of categories to underscore Venus Williams's vulnerability in Extract 6.6). Moreover, Nunes's claims in this regard are emphasized by his use of the word "gagging," which invokes a more hostile or aggressive practice for 'silencing' than that implied by the setting-specific formulations Schiff has used, including "suspend" (lines 10, 12, 14) and "not recognized" (lines 14–15). Indeed, by the lights of Nunes's and Stefanik's claims, we would seem to have (following Schegloff, 2001) a 'textbook' case of a man interrupting a (young) woman: Schiff intervenes in the midst of Stefanik's in-progress TCU, resulting in overlapping talk designed to stop its in-course production (and thus the project or action it conveys), in a way that the participants' treat as complainable.

In contrast, viewed from Schiff's (and his defenders' perspective) we can make several observations that run counter to the claims registered by Nunes, Stefanik, and others who joined calls to condemn the ostensible hypocrisy of Democratic party members who champion gender equity while excusing Schiff's supposed transgression. These observations pertain to Schiff's conduct within the encounter itself, and to the larger point we have been pursuing about attending to the relationship between setting-based and Pn-adequate collections of categories. According to rules cited by Schiff (lines 18–20), only the minority leader (Nunes) and his counsel were permitted to question the witness in this portion of the hearing. (The other committee members from both parties, including Stefanik, would have the opportunity to question Yovanovitch during a later period allocated for this purpose). Beyond the timing of Schiff's intervention (which we noted was designed to halt the turn-taking violation entailed by Stefanik's attempt to question Yovanovitch), we can note other aspects of his conduct seem designed to reflect the limits of his role as chair – and in so doing, establish his incumbency of that category as the basis for his intervention, as opposed to some other category that might be invoked to account for it. For example, although Schiff does respond directly to the complaint Stefanik produces (in line 13), he also does not gavel this turn out of order, or seek to prevent its production. Instead, by stating that Stefanik is not permitted to speak (lines 14–15), noting who can speak (line 15), and then specifying the basis for these assertions (lines 18–20), he first tacitly and then explicitly accounts for his interruptive conduct as arising from the formal rules for the occasion, and his responsibility as chair to insist on committee members' compliance with them (also see Raymond et al., 2022 on 'invoking rules'). In this way, Schiff's interventions allow for (limited) complaints and discussion by members of the committee on how the occasion will be conducted, while preventing departures that would constitute explicit violations of the rules that have been established through a formal vote held prior to the hearing through which the resolution invoked by Schiff in line 18 was adopted. Moreover, in the ensuing discussion, Schiff refuses to engage in a debate about what has happened or can happen, and continues to limit his contributions to alternately directing Stefanik to "suspend" when she addresses Yovanovitch (with accompanying use of gavel strikes) and responding to Nunes's claims and complaints by (re) asserting the rules regarding who can participate. By limiting his conduct in this way, Schiff establishes that he is acting by reference to the 'committee chair' category (and speaking to both Nunes and Stefanik in their capacity as members of the 'ranking member' and 'committee member' categories from the same MCD), and thereby undercuts any claims that his conduct could be accounted for by reference to his or Stefanik's membership in other (especially P*n*-adequate) categories.

We can further note that the conduct of this encounter stands in contrast with Extract 6.6 with respect to ways that setting-based and P*n*-adequate MCDs are treated as relevant or invoked. In Extract 6.6, Richard Williams succeeded in suspending the interview because he could claim that the interviewer should hold Venus to a *different* set of rules by virtue of her being a "little Black kid." That is, he invoked a set of P*n*-adequate categories as a basis for claiming their superseding relevance for the occasion over the setting-based categories by reference to which the interviewer was evidently primarily acting. In Extract 6.7, however, the assertion that Stefanik should be held to a different standard than either Nunes or Schiff would seem to run counter to critiques claiming support for gender equity. Insofar as it appears that Schiff would have prevented any person other than Nunes or his counsel from speaking, his gaveling of Stefanik was in support of the rules and gender equity rather than a contravention of either. As Hesse (2019) noted in her column on the dispute, "sexism isn't about punishing a woman because she's *wrong*. It's about punishing a woman because she's a *woman*" (also see our further analysis of the Schiff-Nunes-Stefanik dispute in Chapter 7: Organizing Sequences of Action, Extract 7.10).

6.4 Summary and conclusions

In this chapter, we have described the turn-taking system as a locally organized basis for managing entitlements and obligations to speak, and thus for including some and excluding others. Both routine uses of, and departures from, the turn-taking system can thereby serve as a basis for establishing the relevance of categorial identities. In each case, the local distribution of entitlements and obligations provides a set of expectations for acting that others can adhere to or violate. In adhering to them, participants will be seen to orient to the relevance of the category or categories that ordinarily serve as bases for the allocation of turns at talk in the interactional environment or setting at hand. In such cases, these categorial orientations tend to remain 'submerged,' with participants using them routinely but entirely tacitly – as we described in Chapter 1: An Introduction to Categories in Social Interaction – as a " 'seen but unnoticed' background of common understandings" (Garfinkel, 1967, p. 44) in relation to when they can or should act. Conversely, in departing from them, participants can be seen to be timing their actions by reference to superseding categorial entitlements and obligations, including supporting and/or admonishing (co-)members of particular categories, pursuing cat- egorial agendas, engaging in category-related disputes, and the like – with the categories involved recurrently surfacing explicitly in the process. Thus, in keeping with the examinations of the mutually constitutive relationship between categories and generic organizations of practice for interaction we began developing in previous chapters, we can appreciate how turn-taking constitutes a systematic site at which categorial matters are reproduced and contested on a moment-by-moment basis, and categorial matters reciprocally serve as bases for acting and/or making inferences about others' actions in relation to turn-taking at particular moments.

7

ORGANIZING SEQUENCES OF ACTION

7.0   Introduction

In July 2015, in Prairie View, Texas, a woman named Sandra Bland was pulled over in an ostensibly routine – but ultimately fateful – traffic stop by a State Trooper, Brian Encinia, who cited her failure to signal a lane change as the basis for the stop. The ensuing encounter became the site of a physical confrontation that ended with Bland being arrested and charged with assaulting a public servant, and three days later she was found dead in her jail cell, with her death being classified as a suicide by hanging (Montgomery, 2015; Ohlheiser & Phillip, 2015). In addition to raising questions about the suspicious nature of Bland's death, public responses to the encounter – which was captured on dashboard camera footage from Encinia's vehicle – included widespread claims that the stop was part of a pattern of racial profiling of Black motorists by police (cf. Meehan & Ponder, 2002), while also interrogating Encinia's conduct in the escalation of the encounter (Barned-Smith & Binkovitz, 2015; Dart, 2015; Montgomery, 2015; Rogers, 2015).[1]

This attention to the interactional unfolding of the encounter has been further developed in subsequent detailed examinations of the recording, which have sought to identify the key moments and mechanisms for its escalation into a violent conflict. For example, Lowrey-Kinberg and Sullivan Buker's (2017) analysis focuses on the moments following a request/command by Encinia for Bland to extinguish a cigarette she had lit during the course of

---

1 Bland's family accepted a $1.9 million settlement after filing a wrongful death lawsuit against Encinia, employees of the jail where Bland died, Waller County, and the Texas Department of Public Safety (Hauser, 2016; Silver, 2016).

DOI: 10.4324/9781003120599-8

the encounter, identifying Encinia's action here as a crucial point of onset for the subsequent rapid escalation of the encounter. However, although they note the significance of an evident pattern of Bland challenging Encinia's institutional authority throughout the encounter, Lowrey-Kinberg and Sullivan Buker (2017) do not engage in a detailed examination of its unfolding prior to this pivotal moment. They thereby focus on the escalation of trouble *after* it has already arisen, rather than considering its initial manifestations earlier in the encounter.

Similarly, Gladwell (2019, p. 280) identifies Encinia's request for Bland to extinguish her cigarette, and Bland's resistant response, as crucial escalatory moments:

> She's right, of course. A police officer has no authority to tell someone not to smoke. He should have said, "Yes. You're right. But do you mind waiting until after we've finished here? I'm not a fan of cigarette smoke." Or he could have dropped the issue entirely. It's only a cigarette. But he doesn't. Something about the tone of her voice gets Encinia's back up. His authority has been challenged. He snaps.

While Gladwell (2019) does note that trouble is evident at earlier points during the interaction, he treats it (similarly to the account in the passage quoted here) as arising from "mistake[s]" (p. 279) on Encinia's part, whereby he "missed opportunit[ies]" (p. 280) to manage Bland's evident emotional responses during the unfolding encounter. Moreover, the transcript Gladwell (2019) provides of these opening exchanges has a number of omissions and thereby does not facilitate a detailed, moment-by-moment account of just how trouble arose in these early parts of the encounter.

In returning to this case later in this chapter, we consider how a close examination of the early moments of its unfolding exhibits evidence of interactional trouble virtually from the outset, with Encinia's actions during these exchanges serving to escalate the encounter in a more active way, rather than doing so merely through errors and missed opportunities. This in turn provides for seeing the rapid escalation concerning the cigarette as the culmination of a trajectory set in motion earlier in the encounter – and one in which categorial matters are of crucial significance. To establish some key resources for this analysis, we sketch out in the sections that follow some of the foundational conversation analytic findings on the sequential organization of courses of action in interaction, while also building on the categorial focus we have been developing in the preceding chapters. We start, in Section 7.1, by exploring how categories figure in a central structure and resource for organizing sequences of action: the 'adjacency pair,' including the notion of 'conditional relevance' and the way that one action in an interaction makes a next one relevant, accountable, missing, 'preferred,' or 'dispreferred.' In

Section 7.2, we develop this focus on adjacency pairs by examining how these basic sequences can be expanded – through actions that come before, between, and after the first and second pair parts of an adjacency pair – while exploring how categories become relevant to such expansions. In Section 7.3, we describe category-related 'parenthetical' sequences. Before concluding the chapter in Section 7.5, we return in Section 7.4 to the Sandra Bland case, focusing in detail on how the sequential unfolding of trouble, evidently grounded in categorial matters, escalates rapidly into physical conflict. We thereby demonstrate how categories function in and as extra-sequential sources of sequence organization.

7.1 Categories in adjacency pair sequences

Since the earliest published work in the field (see especially Schegloff, 1968), a primary focus of conversation analytic research has been on the social organization of sequences of action – that is, on addressing the question of how successive turns at talk are "formed up to be 'coherent' with the prior turn (or *some* prior turn)," and on the nature of that coherence (Schegloff, 2007b, p. xiv; emphasis in original). A central finding is that what Schegloff and Sacks (1973, p. 295) call "adjacency pairs" pervasively serve as a basic resource for participants in building and organizing mutually intelligible courses of action in interaction. Adjacency pairs are (as the term implies) two-part action sequences designed to be placed adjacent to one other, with the production of a 'first pair part' providing a place for another speaker's production of a pair-type related responsive 'second pair part' (Schegloff, 1968, 2007b; Schegloff & Sacks, 1973).[2] The opening moments of the telephone call shown in Extract 7.1 demonstrate the unfolding of a range of different types of adjacency pair sequences.

```
Extract 7.1: Hyla & Nancy
01          ((ring))
02   Nan:   H'llo:?
03   Hyl:   Hi:,
04   Nan:   ↑HI::.
05   Hyl:   Howaryuhh=
06   Nan:   =Fi:ne how're you,
07   Hyl:   Oka:[y,
08   Nan:       [↓Goo:d,
09          (0.4)
```

2 This does not mean, however, that their adjacent placement is empirically realized in all cases; that is, that second pair parts are always produced immediately after first pair parts – a matter we shall return to in the sections that follow.

```
10  Hyl:  .mkhhh[hhh
11  Nan:        [What's doin',
12              (.)
13  Hyl:  aAh:, nothi:n:,
```

As Schegloff (1968, 1986) observes, the ringing of a telephone that occurs when one party calls another (as shown in line 01) constitutes the first pair part (FPP) of a 'summons-answer' sequence, with the called party's response to the ringing (in this case, Nancy's "H'llo:?" in line 02) serving as the second pair part (SPP) made relevant by the FPP. Having heard Nancy's response to the summons – and thereby having established her availability to engage in an interaction – Hyla produces the FPP of a greeting sequence (line 03), with Nancy quickly producing a matching SPP in response (line 04). These initial adjacency pair sequences are followed by an exchange of '"howareyou" sequences' (see Jefferson, 1980; Pillet-Shore, 2018; Sacks, 1975; Schegloff, 1986), each of which is similarly composed of FPPs (Hyla's "Howaryuhh" in line 05 and Nancy's "how're you" in line 06), followed respectively by the SPPs they make relevant (Nancy's "Fi:ne" in line 06 and Hyla's "Oka:y" in line 07). Finally, we have a question-answer sequence (lines 11 and 13), which marks a transition from the "core opening sequences" that are routinely produced at the beginnings of calls like this one (Schegloff, 1986, p. 117) to the remainder of the conversation that is projected to follow.

Despite the seemingly unremarkable "sense of routineness and perfunctoriness" (Schegloff, 1986, p. 114) in sequences like the ones we see here, adjacency pairs serve as crucial "building-blocks" (Schegloff, 2007b, p. 12) by reference to which a great deal of what participants do across a wide range of different types of interactions is produced.[3] In addition, however, the adjacency pairs produced in Extract 7.1 also provide an organizing structure through which the participants collaboratively – but entirely tacitly – achieve co-alignment in the 'friend'/'friend' pair of categories as omni-relevant for this encounter (also see Pomerantz & Mandelbaum, 2005), in and through these routine features of the opening. This can be observed in a number of ways, which we consider in the paragraphs that follow.

As Schegloff (1986) demonstrates, in calls between familiars, participants may recognize each other based only on the small voice samples produced in the opening turns of a call. In such cases, how the parties are known to one another (e.g., as friends, family members, work colleagues) may be the basis for their treatment of the associated collection of categories as omni-relevant once mutual recognition

---

3 Indeed, apart from the ambiguous utterance/out-breath produced by Hyla at line 10, the only talk in Extract 7.1 that does not contribute to either the FPP or SPP of an adjacency pair is the "sequence-closing third" or "minimal post-expansion" (Schegloff, 2007b, p. 118) constituted by Nancy's "↓Goo:d" at line 08 – a matter to which we return later.

has been accomplished in and as part of the sequential unfolding of encounter's opening (also see Psathas, 1999; Whitehead et al., 2024). In this case, it is evident in their reciprocal production (at lines 03 and 04) of "recognitional greetings" (Drew, 2002, p. 486) that the participants have accomplished this mutual recognition. Specifically, the stretched, emphasized, and unelaborated production of both of these greetings and the increased volume of Nancy's return greeting, together display both parties' recognition of who the other is, and who they are to one another (Drew, 2002; Psathas, 1999; Schegloff, 1972, 1986) – and thus their co-alignment in the 'friend'/'friend' pair of categories.

This orientation to the 'friend' category is then underscored by the question-answer sequence at lines 11 and 13, which is produced in the sequential position at which the initiator of the interaction (in this case the caller, Hyla) ordinarily "gets to initiate first topic" or introduce the "reason for the call" (Psathas, 1999, p. 149; Schegloff, 1986, p. 186). After not initially taking up the opportunity to do this during a silence (line 08), and following Nancy's prompting (line 10), Hyla directly declines to introduce a first topic or say why she is calling. As such, Hyla effectively proposes that the reason for the call is 'no reason in particular,' which treats it as an ordinary conversation between co-members of the 'friend' category, as opposed to an interaction with some more specific 'task oriented' or 'institutional' character. This point also underscores how attention to social positions such as 'caller,' 'called,' 'questioner,' and 'answerer' offers resources (for participants, and therefore analysts) for establishing the categorial bases of interactions (also see Chapter 1: An Introduction to Categories in Social Interaction).

While the categorial orientations produced through adjacency pair sequences are in many cases – as in Extract 7.1 – an entirely tacit feature of the unfolding of interactions, a substantial body of research (e.g., Hansen, 2005; Kitzinger, 2005a, 2005b; Shrikant, 2021; Stokoe, 2009a, 2009b, 2010a, 2012a; Stokoe et al., 2017; Whitehead, 2012b, 2013a, 2018, 2020; Whitehead et al., 2024; Wilkinson & Kitzinger, 2003) has demonstrated how a wide range of categories can be deployed more explicitly in particular sequential positions to accomplish or contribute to particular actions. This is illustrated in the following two cases, both of which include uses of categories in a similar sequence type (a complaint sequence), being deployed respectively in the course of producing a first pair part (a complaint) and a second pair part (a complaint response). The first of these, shown in Extract 7.2 (also examined in Chapter 2: Approaching Membership Categorization, Extract 2.8), is from a telephone call to a mediation centre in which a council worker (C) is calling on behalf of a local resident whose house backs onto cricket club grounds. The resident has complained to the council that balls from the club are damaging her roof and make it unsafe to sit in her garden. In the course of formulating a FPP in which she narrates the resident's complaint, and thereby simultaneously requests that the mediation centre mediate between her and the club, the council worker deploys a formulation of the resident's age: "she's eighty three" (line 06).

Extract 7.2: Neighbour mediation initial inquiry

```
01   C:   She can't go in 'er ga:rden an' it's dam- she's paid
02        for: (.) tiles bein' fixed on 'er roof:. Without even
03        contactin' them,=she's says- she knows they're re- (0.2)
04        they kno:w they're responsible [ hh ] but she
05   M:                                  [.pt Yeh.]
06   C:   doesn't want to confront them: she's [eighty three]
07   M:                                        [.hhh ↑↑No: I]'d be
08        uh ↑ye:[ah. ]=it's not *i-* uh y'know: *i-* b- *i-*
09   C:          [(Um)]
10              (0.5)
11   M:   Obviously age: (.) c- *i- i-* (.) could [be an i:ssue]
12   C:                                           [  Ye:ah:   ]
13   M:   with'er but- .hh [↑y'know] it's ↑not something that=
14   C:                    [(Yeah) ]
15   M:   =(0.3) a lo:t of people: um: do: easily.
```

While the council worker formulates the resident's age in years rather than explicitly categorizing her as, for example, 'old,' this formulation invokes common-sense knowledge in relation to age that accounts for her reluctance to confront the club on her own behalf. As we noted in our analysis of this case in Chapter 2: Approaching Membership Categorization, although the council worker does not specify precisely what characteristics of a person this age would provide for this reluctance, she appears to be alluding to age as a marker of frailty, vulnerability to being intimidated, and the like. The council worker thereby uses age as a resource for the moral work involved in formulating the complaint (also see Drew, 1998). That is, the cricket club is proposed not just to be causing damage but to be insensitive to the category memberships of people affected by their actions who are not equally competent, fit, healthy, and so on. Thus, consistent with Schegloff's (2005a, p. 453) observations in this regard, the council worker forges "a link between the complainability of the conduct and the category membership of those implicated in it," and in doing so amplifies its complainability.

The council worker's use of the age category also pre-empts a potential response that would question the validity of the associated request for mediation by proposing that the resident should resolve the issue directly with the club. In her response, the mediator does not fully endorse this use of the age category by the council worker, proposing that "a lo:t of people:" (line 15) do not find confrontation easy, and in doing so perhaps resisting the category as something she ascribes to the client, and/or resisting an ageist implication that older people are unable to do some things for themselves. However, her response does acknowledge that "age . . . could be an i:ssue" (line 11), thereby showing her recognition of the common-sense categorial knowledge the council worker has deployed.

In Extract 7.3 (previously examined in Chapter 5: Referring to and Addressing People, Extracts 5.7 and 5.10), an artist who is guest on a radio show (Reshma) responds to a caller to the show (Wayne) who has complained that the 12-metre-long walk-in sculpture of a vagina Reshma created is "absurd." While Reshma's turn in lines 05–11 is, most immediately, a response to Aubrey's invitation at lines 01 and 03, this invitation recalls Wayne's earlier complaint, making Reshma's turn here also a response to that action.

```
Extract 7.3: Radio call-in (691, 702 19.8.13)
01  Aub: So what do y[ou  think  Wa:yne  is ref]erring to when he
02  Res:             [(and that's the purpose-)]
03  Aub: speaks of the absurdity of the situation? .hhh
04          (0.2)
05  Res: .hh Ah- I mean, I- I think he's just- (.) hhh ((chuckle))
06       .hhh £I think it's also easy£ fo:r a:: .hh £a white male,
07       sorry to say that,£ to sit in judgment of it without (.)
08       understanding the: .hh the experiences, or the:
09       perspectives of: u::h .hh b- u::h (.) women in this
10       country or: within patriarchal systems, .hh I think maybe
11       he is a bit (0.5) u::m: disempowered by it.
```

As noted in our previous analysis of this case, in producing this response, Reshma selects gender and race categories to refer to Wayne, thereby turning his complaint back on him. That is, by deploying common-sense knowledge about the bases of his complaint in his gender- and race-based experiences as a resource for discounting its validity, Reshma uses these categories to produce a counter-complaint against Wayne in response to his complaint against her.

7.1.1 Conditional relevance

Although, as we have seen in the cases we have examined thus far, second pair parts of adjacency pairs recurrently follow first pair parts, the significance of these basic sequential structures as crucial building blocks for the social organization of courses of action does not arise from the empirical or even statistical regularity of their adjacent production (Heritage, 1984b). Instead, their significance lies in the systematic treatment by participants of adjacency pairs as "a *normative* framework for actions which is *accountably* implemented" (Heritage, 1984b, p. 247; emphasis in original). This means that the production of an FPP by one speaker sets in motion an *expectation* that another speaker will produce a matching SPP, such that it will be "noticeably, officially, consequentially, absent" (Schegloff, 2007b, p. 20) if not produced. This feature of adjacency pair organization, which Schegloff (2007b, p. 20) calls "conditional relevance," is most clearly evident in cases where this expectation is *not* met, and participants orient to the relevance of an SPP's absence in a range of ways, including pursuing it, accounting for its non-production, and making associated moral inferences.

As Extract 7.4[4] demonstrates, categories can feature prominently in these cases as resources both for pursuing a 'missing' SPP and for arriving at accounts for and/or moral judgments in relation to its absence. In this case, a caller (Joe) to a radio show complains about the (South African) African National Congress (ANC) government's actions (lines 05–06) in the context of a reported "skills shortage" (line 02). He thereby targets the government as the party responsible for the problem he reports the Deputy President as having recently spoken about (lines 01–02). This complaint constitutes an FPP that makes relevant a responsive SPP – for example, an expression of sympathy, agreement or disagreement, etc. – by its recipient, the host of the show (Clinton). Moreover, Joe's production of the tag question "hey?" at the end of his complaining turn (line 06) serves to explicitly prompt a response from Clinton (cf. Hepburn & Potter, 2010; Heritage, 2002; Sacks et al., 1974).

```
Extract 7.4: Radio call-in (573, 702 23.4.08)
01  Joe:   .hh Uh look, uh: thē: deputy: president uh:: (0.5)
02         was talking about the skills shortage.
03              (1.0)
04  Cli:   Mm [hm?
05  Joe:      [>↑The thing is=is< the ay en cee⁵ government has
06         made a <helluva mess> hey?
07              (0.4)
08  Joe:   And there's no doubt about it.
09              (0.8)
10  Joe:   I'm not a white person, I'm a  Black person.
11              (.)
12  Joe:   .hhhh Number one, they decided to close down=hh most (.)
13         of the nursing colleges. ((continues))
```

When Clinton fails to produce the response that has been made conditionally relevant during a 0.4-second silence at line 07, Joe produces an upgraded reaffirmation of his complaint (line 08) that serves to pursue a responsive SPP from Clinton. He thereby treats an SPP as relevantly absent and renews its relevance by providing another place where Clinton could produce it. Then, when Clinton continues to withhold a response during an even longer (0.8-second) pause at line 09, Joe disclaims his membership in the category "white person" before self-categorizing as a "Black person"

---

4 Also see the analysis of this case in Whitehead (2021); cf. similar cases of pursuits involving categorial mentions and/or inferences examined by Stokoe (2015), Whitehead (2012, 2015), and Whitehead and Lerner (2022).

5 "ANC"

(line 10), thus displaying his use of race as a resource in accounting for Clinton's non-responses. That is, although he does not explicitly spell out the reasoning behind this race-based account, Joe is evidently oriented to his complaint about the government as an action that is bound to the category "white," and thus vulnerable to being discounted as racially motivated rather than principled if produced by a speaker heard as a member of this category (also see Whitehead, 2020; Whitehead & Lerner, 2022). In this way, Joe treats Clinton's non-responses as implicating a negative moral stance towards his complaint and works to manage this implication (also see our discussion of categorial bases for formation and ascription of actions in Chapter 4: Forming and Making Sense of Actions).

Extract 7.5 shows a further case in which, as in Extract 7.4, (mis)-categorization-related trouble is exposed by the absence of FPPs in places where their production is conditionally relevant.[6] This case, from an initial inquiry call from a neighbour to a mediation service, also (like Extract 7.4) demonstrates the potential troubles that may arise from the constrained range of "perceptually available" categories (Jayyusi, 1984) in telephonic interactions (also see our discussion of this feature of some categories in Chapter 2: Approaching Membership Categorization). That is, the participants' lack of visual access to each other in these interactions may give rise to trouble in relation to assumptions about memberships in categories from Pn-adequate collections, together with associated intentions, motivations, and prejudices. We join the extract as the caller (C) describes the basis for the call to the mediator (M): his neighbour has apparently been socializing with people who have been "using her house" (line 02) for noisy parties.

```
Extract 7.5: Neighbour mediation initial inquiry
01  C:  The people she was mixing with .hhh obviously I felt
02      that they were using her house as one of these um (0.2)
03      .hh blues parties.=you know that goes on, .hhhh
04  M:  Oh ri:[ght.
05  C:        [And she's West Indian so she'll have reggae
06      parties an' stuff like that an'
07              (1.3)
08  C:  >But u::m< (0.2) I mean she hasn't had one for some
09      ti:me now.
10              (1.2)
11  C:  But (that was) [when she first initially .hh]hh when she=
12  M:                 [   O::kay not recently.    ]
```

---

6 Also see the analyses of this case by Stokoe and Edwards (2007) and Stokoe (2015), and further convergent analyses of cases of pursuits involving categorial mentions and/or inferences examined by Stokoe (2015), Whitehead (2012, 2015), and Whitehead and Lerner (2022).

```
13       = first got in, .hhhhh but we did 'ave racial abuse in
14       Jan- in December.
15              (0.3)
16   C:  .hhh (0.2) an' a coupla times: since then. .pt. .hhh
17   M:  Ye- racial abuse.
18   C:  Yep.
19   M:  °H:mm.°
20              (1.1)
21   C:  Uh: >I- I-< I'm Asian:: my Wes- my [wi:fe is]
22   M:                                     [ Right. ]
23   C:  West Indian.
24   M:  ↑Oh: o- [okay. (Mm.)]
25   C:          [.hhhh um:: ]
26              (0.9)
27   C:  Um: uh such as (.) Paki family: etcetera hhh
28   M:  O:::h.=right.
```

The caller's characterization of the problem includes a category-resonant description of "blues parties,"[7] produced as a particular and recognizable type of event of which the mediator will share knowledge ("you know that goes on,"; line 03). (Also see our discussion of such descriptions in Chapter 2: Approaching Membership Categorization.) In response, the mediator registers as news this basis for the caller's complaint with the change of stake token "Oh" while claiming prior knowledge of the type of event the caller has described using the word "ri:ght" (line 04). The caller then explicitly specifies the category made relevant by his prior description of the event (line 05), before tying it using the word "so" (Raymond, 2004) to further characterizations of both particular ("reggae parties") and more generalized complainable conduct, "an' stuff like that" (line 06; also see Schegloff, 2005a). These features of the caller's complaint make it vulnerable to being heard as racist by virtue of invoking stereotypical links between the neighbour's ostensibly negative behaviour and her membership in a racial/ethnic category (also see Whitehead, 2018). And indeed, there is evidence that the mediator has heard it in this way, as he withholds a response during the relatively lengthy silence at line 07. Moreover, the caller evidently registers this incipient trouble as he changes his stance following this silence (also see Tadic, 2024; Whitehead, 2015), downgrading his complaint about the neighbour's reported parties by conceding that "she hasn't had one for some ti:me now" (lines 08–09), and thereby providing the mediator with a further opportunity to respond. After a further silence (line 10) marking the mediator's withholding of a conditionally relevant response,

---

7 Blues parties, in British Caribbean communities, "[u]sually hosted in someone's basement, . . . sprung up in the 1970s as safe refuges from Britain's racist clubbing scene" (Frazer-Carroll, 2020).

the caller again pursues a response by reasserting the complaint (line 11), partially in overlap with the mediator's delayed registering of the caller's preceding downgrade (line 12). The caller then reports that "racial abuse" had occurred (lines 13–14), tacitly implicating the complained-about neighbour as the perpetrator, and the mediator initially again withholds a response (line 15), before producing a repeat-receipt only (line 17) after the caller pursues and upgrades this complaint (line 16). The caller's confirmation (line 18) following this receipt by the mediator is hearably 'irritated,' yet the mediator maintains his non-empathic stance towards the complaint with a minimal receipt (line 19), which is followed by another lengthy silence (line 20) that further underscores the trouble at play.

The trouble is then rapidly resolved after the caller provides a category-based account for his accusation – "I'm Asian:: my Wes- my wi:fe is West Indian" (lines 21 and 23) – thereby establishing bases for he and his wife's legitimate membership in the category 'victim of racial abuse.' The caller thereby (like in Extract 7.4) treats the foregoing withheld responses to his complaints as arising from the mediator having tacitly mis-categorized him as 'white' – and thus a 'perpetrator' rather than a 'victim' of racism. The mediator's subsequent responses provide strong evidence of this, as he immediately and emphatically treats the caller's announcement of he and his wife's respective racial/ethnic category memberships as news (line 24). Then, after the caller (following another silence at line 26) follows up with a report of the specific form of the racial abuse (line 27), the mediator produces a further news receipt (line 28) with very different intonation to his prior news receipt at line 24, thereby marking his shift into empathic responses that serve to align him with the caller's complaints.

Categories can also serve as resources for warranting the non-production of a response by the participant whose response has been made conditionally relevant. This can be seen in Extract 7.6, which shows the beginning of the exchange we considered in Extract 7.3, including the production of the complaint by a caller, Wayne, to which Reshma eventually responded, as shown in Extract 7.3. Here, Aubrey uses the practice of contrastive entanglement to invoke his membership in the category 'host,' in contrast to Wayne's membership in the 'caller' category, as a basis for declining to respond to Wayne's complaint (Whitehead & Lerner, 2022). (Also see our discussion of contrastive entanglement in Chapter 5: Referring to and Addressing People.)

```
Extract 7.6: Radio call-in (691, 702 19.8.13)
01  Aub:   ↑Hi, Wayne?
02              (0.5)
03  Way:   Aubrey?
04  Aub:   Yu[h?
05  Way:     [Um, (.) this (.) this is- i- is compl- com-
```

```
06          completely and (.) an- an' to my mind, (.) um: from a:
07          a testosterone um:: filled person, (0.7) u:m: it's a-
08          i- i- im: (.) uh: coming from a mu- a mother, (.) and
09          a father, (0.8) um I ↑find it a <little bit (.) abs↓urd.>
10                (0.4)
11    Way:   Don't ↑you?
12                (0.8)
13    Aub:   (Y)I:: £mean it do(h)esn't m(h)atter what I think, Wayne
14          I wanna know what you th(h)ink.£ .hh
15    Way:   Okay. ((continues, and produces further complaint))
```

In addition to establishing their mutual alignment as host and caller in the opening moments of the call (lines 01–03; cf. Extract 7.1), Wayne's addressing of Aubrey by name and with rising intonation (line 03) prompts Aubrey's confirmation of his availability to hear what is to follow (line 04) and establishes him as its primary recipient (cf. Schegloff, 1986; also see our discussion of pre-expansions in Section 7.3.1). Wayne then formulates his complaint (lines 05–09), with its possible completion with the negative assessment "a <little bit (.) abs↓urd.>" (line 09) making relevant a response by Aubrey. Following a 0.4-second silence during which Aubrey declines to respond, Wayne pursues a response from him (cf. Extract 7.4) by more directly soliciting his alignment with the negatively polarized yes/no question, "Don't ↑you?" (also see Raymond, 2003). Notably, Wayne has invoked his membership in the category 'male' by identifying himself as a "a testosterone um:: filled person" (line 07) as part of the convoluted self-description that he parenthetically inserted into his complaint-in-progress (lines 06–09; also see Whitehead, 2020). His recruitment of Aubrey's alignment with his complaint is therefore evidently by reference to Aubrey's co-membership in this Pn-adequate category. The contrastively stressed self-reference ("I") and other-reference ("you") that Aubrey produces in responding to this pursuit (lines 13–14) serve to tacitly invoke his and Wayne's alternative respective membership in the setting-based 'host' and 'caller' categories in the service of accounting for neither aligning nor disaligning with Wayne's complaint (Whitehead & Lerner, 2022). That is, Aubrey invokes "the category-bound activities and expectations that hosts should facilitate the expression of opinions on the topic at hand, whereas callers should express their opinions" (Whitehead & Lerner, 2022, p. 16) as resources for staking out a "neutral" position on the matter (cf. Clayman, 1988, 1992).

In addition to accounting for his own non-response to Wayne's complaint, this move by Aubrey also serves as what Schegloff (2007b, pp. 16–17) calls a "counter" – an action that serves to reverse the direction of the constraint set in motion by a prior FPP, redirecting the relevance of responding back to the speaker who produced it. Thus, by producing this counter – and using categories as resources for doing so – Aubrey deflects Wayne's attempt to re-cruit his alignment in complaining about Reshma's sculpture. Moreover, by registering his acceptance of Aubrey's counter with an "Okay" (line 15), be-fore producing a further complaint, Wayne aligns with the reversal of the di-rection of conditional relevance that Aubrey has proposed.

With these observations on conditional relevance, pursuits, and counters in mind, we can now return to the case of the dispute in Central Park, which we initially examined in Chapter 5: Referring to and Addressing People (Extract 5.11) in order to provide further analysis of the sequential environment from which her use of race and gender categories in referring to him arose. Specifically, the opening moments of the recording of the in-cident, shown in Extract 7.7, feature a series of pursuits and counters that produce a "sequential standoff" (Raymond et al., 2023; also see Whitehead et al., 2025) that constitutes the immediate context for Amy Cooper's threats to call the police.

Extract 7.7: Central Park (video from Twitter via *The Telegraph*)

```
01   AC:  Would you please stop.
02             (0.8)
03   AC:  Sir, I asking you to stop. ((approaching CC))
04             (.)
05   CC:  hh .hh ↑Please don't come close to me. ((AC continues to
06        approach CC))
07             (0.5) ((AC continues toward CC; CC steps back))
08   AC:  Sir, I'm asking you to stop re↑cording me
09        [with your ↑phone. ((AC begins to step toward CC and
10        reach out with her right hand))
11   CC:  [↑Please ↓don't come close to me. ((AC continues
12        stepping/reaching toward CC))
13   AC:  Please take your ↑phone off.= ((AC pointing at CC))
14   CC:  =↑Please ↓don't >come close< to me.= ((AC withdraws
15        point))
16   AC:  =(>Then I'm taking picture and calling the cops.<)
17        ((AC holding phone; begins to dial))
18   CC:  Please- Please call the cops. hh
19             (1.0) ((AC engaging with phone/dialling))
20   CC:  Please call the cops.=h
21             (0.2)
22   AC:  .hh I'm gonna tell them there's an A:frican American man
23        threatening my ↑life.
24   CC:  .h Please tell them whatever you ↑like. hhh
```

Just after the recording begins, Amy Cooper asks Christian Cooper to stop filming (line 01) – a request that he disattends during a 0.8-second interval (line 2) and that Amy Cooper then pursues (line 03), moving closer to him as she does so.[8] While Christian Cooper continues to withhold a response to Amy Cooper's pursued request during a further brief silence at line 04, he does respond to her movement towards him with a request of his own (line 05) that serves as a counter to her request. Amy Cooper similarly disattends this request, continuing her movement towards Christian Cooper during and just after its production, while Christian Cooper takes a step backwards and continues recording (lines 05–07). Amy Cooper then produces a second, elaborated pursuit of her request – now including a specification of precisely what she is asking him to stop doing ("recording me with your phone") – and thus a further counter (lines 08–09). While she briefly stops moving towards him as she does this, standing a few feet away from him and facing him (and the camera), during the final words of this turn she begins to again step towards him and reach out with her right hand, possibly in an attempt to block the camera's view of her. She thereby displays a continuing unwillingness to comply with Christian Cooper's request, which by this time he is pursuing in overlap with the end of her turn (line 11), thereby implementing a further counter to her request to stop recording and displaying his continuing unwillingness to comply with this request.

Following one further, similar round of pursuits/counters by both Amy Cooper and Christian Cooper (lines 13 and 14), Amy Cooper issues the category-based threats (lines 16 and especially 22–23) discussed in our prior analysis of this exchange. By supplementing that prior analysis with our consideration here of the sequential unfolding of the exchange, we can register the sequential trouble that occasions Amy Cooper's deployment of these threats, and thereby more fully appreciate how her deployment of race and gender categories in line 22 is designed to escalate the dispute by forcing Christian Cooper to back down and thereby bring about a favourable (for her) end to the stand-off that has emerged. We can also note the significance (including categorial) of Christian Cooper's responses to these threats: rather than producing the backdown that they projected as next actions on his part, his encouragement for her to carry them out (lines 18, 20, and 24) serves to tacitly categorize Amy Cooper as a 'law-breaker,' thereby proposing that – despite the spectre of police violence against Black men that she has invoked – summoning the police to the scene would result in further trouble for her rather than for him.

---

8 A further noteworthy feature of the design of this pursuit is the way Amy Cooper begins her turn with an emphasized formal address term "Sir," which appears to be designed to manage the disaffiliative nature of the action she is about to produce (cf. Butler et al., 2011; Clayman, 2013), while registering her orientation to him as a man – and possibly (but tacitly) more specifically as a Black man. Also note the similar use of this address term at the beginning of her similar next turn (line 08).

7.1.2 The organization of (dis)preference in sequences of action

In addition to demonstrating participants' orientations to the conditional relevance of an SPP upon production of an FPP, and some ways that categories may come into play when this expectation is not met, the features of a number of the cases from the foregoing sections also illustrate how categories may figure in what conversation analysts call 'preference organization.' While some FPPs (e.g., greetings) make relevant only one specific SPP (e.g., return greetings), for many others there are alternative possible responses. For example, invitations can either be accepted or declined, requests can either be granted or denied, commands can either be complied with or resisted. In such cases, the possible alternatives are systematically treated by participants as asymmetrical, with SPPs that align with the project of the FPP treated as 'preferred' and those that depart from it treated as 'dispreferred' (for overviews, see Heritage, 1984b; Schegloff, 2007b).

Importantly, rather than concerning the psychological desires of the participants, these terms refer to a *structural* relationship between the first and second parts of adjacency pairs – and the socially constituted expectations embodied therein – which participants reveal they are oriented to through the differential practices they use in producing aligning versus dis-aligning actions. That is, aligning actions are produced as structurally preferred through participants systematically delivering them immediately and in simple or unelaborated forms, while dis-aligning actions are systematically delayed, mitigated, and elaborated by accounts, and thereby produced by participants as structurally dispreferred (Heritage, 1984b; Schegloff, 2007b). In particular, delays in producing an SPP at places prepared for an aligning or dis-aligning response – such as those at lines 07 and 09 of Extract 7.4; lines 07, 10, 15, and 20 of Extract 7.5; and lines 10 and 12 of Extract 7.6 – may be recognized by the FPP speaker as foreshadowing a dis-aligning (dispreferred) response. They may thus provide opportunities for the FPP speaker to do further work in pursuit of alignment, and/or to forestall or mitigate the potential disalignment. Indeed, as noted earlier, this is precisely what the speakers do in Extracts 7.4–7.6: in Extract 7.4, Joe first upgrades his complaint in pursuit of an aligning response (line 08) and then uses racial self-categorization to manage its uptake in terms of its moral status (line 10); in Extract 7.5, the caller downgrades his complaint in line 08, reasserts it in line 11, upgrades it in line 16, and racially categorizes himself and his wife to manage its uptake in line 21; and in Extract 7.6, Wayne explicitly prompts Aubrey to produce an aligning response (line 11).

A further feature of preference organization concerns the potential in some sequential contexts for multiple preferences to be concurrently associated with the range of possible ways a speaker could respond to a first pair

part. In such cases, the constraints associated with these multiple preferences may be 'congruent,' such that "the same response which is preferred
in one is preferred in the other" (Schegloff, 2007b, p. 76). This makes it
possible to satisfy all the prevailing preferences simultaneously with one response type, thus making the production of a second pair part "uncomplicated" (Schegloff, 2007b, p. 76). For example, in Extract 7.2, the council
worker produces a complaint that also serves as a request. In this case, the
multiple preferences associated with these actions are congruent, since it is
possible for the recipient, the mediator, to both align with the complaint
(by registering its validity and displaying sympathy) and grant the request
for mediation. In both of these respects, the mediator's response is in keeping with the expectations of the 'mediator' category, and thereby reaffirm
her orientation to this category.

Alternatively, however, multiple preferences may be "cross-cutting," meaning that "the response which is the preferred second pair part for one aspect
of the first pair part turn is dispreferred for the other" (Schegloff, 2007b,
pp. 76–77). This is demonstrated in Pomerantz's (1978) classic analysis of
responses to compliments, which considers how participants treat compliments as a type of assessment, with agreement being a preferred response,
as well as orienting to a constraint against self-praise that renders agreement
with a compliment a dispreferred response. Since these competing constraints
cannot be simultaneously satisfied by either agreement or disagreement, participants routinely struggle to respond to compliments, thereby displaying
their orientations to the cross-cutting preferences at play (Pomerantz, 1978;
also see Raymond, 2003; Schegloff, 2007b). Extending these foundational
findings, a number of studies have shown that cross-cutting preferences may
also arise from what could be called category-based preferences – that is, the
moral proscriptions associated with actions that could be deemed to constitute
category-based '-isms,' including racism, sexism, and heterosexism (see, e.g.,
Robles, 2015; Stokoe, 2015; Tadic, 2024; Whitehead, 2015; Whitehead &
Stokoe, 2015). A similar set of phenomena may be at play in Extracts 7.4–7.6,
with the recipients in these cases risking being heard as endorsing a racist
(in the case of Extracts 7.4 and 7.5) or sexist (in Extract 7.6) action should
they align with the callers' complaints. If so, the recipients' withholding of
responses in these cases may reflect their orientations to their membership in
the racial category 'white' (in Extracts 7.4 and 7.5) and the gender category
'male' (in Extract 7.6), respectively, as heightening their vulnerability to being
heard in these ways. Moreover, in both of these cases alignment by the recipients may also be oriented to a preference for institutional actors such as radio
hosts and mediators to maintain neutrality with respect to controversial matters, with this category-based expectation being explicitly exposed in Extracts
7.5 and 7.6, as described in our analyses.

As these observations reveal, categories constitute not only a wide-ranging set of resources for the production and interpretation of actions in particular sequential positions but also complex bases for the matters of (dis-)alignment they may implicate and resources for managing participants' positioning in relation to them. Analytic attention to the expectations associated with this range of sequence organizational phenomena, and their intersections with categorial matters, can thus offer revealing insights into both sequential bases for the social organization of categories and categorial bases for the realization of sequences of action-in-interaction.

7.2 Categories in sequence expansions

In the previous section we considered adjacency pairs as basic "building blocks" for sequences of action, the preferences that participants treat as shaping the relationship between actions that initiate courses of action and those that respond to such initiations, and the import of categories across these sequential positions. In this section we extend these foundations by examining how basic adjacency pair sequences can be expanded in a range of ways – before a first pair part, between first and second pair parts, following a second pair part, or through actions inserted 'parenthetically' into actions-in-progress in any these positions (Schegloff, 2007b) – while considering how categories may figure in the realization of all of these types of expansions. As Schegloff (1990, 2007b) notes, and as we shall see in the cases we examine later, expansions of adjacency pair sequences themselves recurrently take the form of further adjacency pair sequences that therefore share the features (including potential categorial features) of adjacency pairs described in the preceding sections.

7.2.1 Pre-expansion

Pre-expansions take the form of sequences that participants treat as "preliminary to something else" (Schegloff, 2007b, p. 28). That is, they project that a speaker will imminently produce the first pair part of a "base sequence" (Schegloff, 2007b, p. 29), while working to establish and/ or shape the terms on which the base sequence will occur – or indeed whether it will occur at all (also see Sacks, 1992; Schegloff, 1980, 2007b). Extract 7.8 shows a case in which a doctor uses multiple pre-sequences (cf. Schegloff, 1980, 2007b, pp. 53–56) to check on the possible membership of a patient's father in categories that would serve as bases for relative expertise regarding the information-giving and decision-making process that is projected to follow (also see Chapter 9: Managing Knowledge, Experience, and Entitlement.)

```
Extract 7.8: Doctor Consultation (1b: 3.15-9.00)⁹
01  Doc:   The next discussion we need to ha:ve is about whether
02         he also needs the next up the ladder, which is: °epipens.
03  Dad:   °Mhm¿°
04  Doc:   .Hhh Just in terms of: helping wi'that discussion.=.hh
05         Are you medical. °in terms o'your background.°=
06  Dad:   =I'm a lawyer.
07  Doc:   You're a lawyer. Oka:y¿ .Hh Uhm: (0.3) And in terms of
08         s:cie::nce and stuff.=What've you- (0.2) How far did
09         you go [£in terms of education'n£
10  Dad:   Science. (.) [ Er:] ((scratching head)) Maths ā level,
11  Doc:                [°(Yeh)°]
12  Dad:   an:d gee cee es ee¹⁰ in chemis[try° 'n°° °physics°°°]
13  Doc:                                 [#Right. Okay  then ok]ay.
14         So you've got< (    ). ((gaze to notes)) .hh (I mean
15         they), (0.7) ↑One of (0.2) the cha:llenges: <we've got in
16         deciding> (0.6) who:: ((gaze to Dad)) needs epi↓pens is
17         we do know: .hh that you get >mild allergic reactions,
18         and severe allergic reactions.< [.hhh] a:n:d >I mean< (.)
19  Dad:                                   [Mhm¿]
20  Doc:   nobody really likes ↑thinking about it¿ but at the
21         severest end you can have< (.) °↑fatal (reac[tions.°)]
22  Dad:                                               [ Yeah.  ]
```

By projecting the nature of the "discussion" that is to follow (lines 01–02), and receiving a "go-ahead" (Schegloff, 2007b, p. 30) from the patient's father (line 03), the doctor secures the father's alignment with a move to begin this piece of business. However, rather than immediately launching the projected discussion following this go-ahead, the doctor produces an FPP enquiring as to the father's possible membership in a medical category (lines 04–05). After the father's responsive SPP, in the form of a self-categorization in a non-medical – but nonetheless highly educated – occupational category (line 06), the doctor asks a further question (lines 07–09) designed to ascertain the degree to which the father's educational background provides for his knowledge of "s:cie::nce and stuff" (line 08). After registering (lines 13–14) the father's response (lines 10 and 12), the doctor then launches the projected discussion of the possible suitability of EpiPens for the patient by informing the father about the medical considerations involved in such decisions (lines 15–18, 20–21). The doctor thus evidently uses the preceding question sequences to gather information regarding the father's medical expertise as a basis for calibrating whether and how to provide him with appropriately

---

9 We are grateful to Laura Jenkins for permitting us to use this data extract.
10 'GCSE': examinations taken by students at age 16 in the UK.

recipient-designed information in the service of his collaboration in these treatment decisions.

7.2.2 Insert expansion

Insert expansions take the form of sequences initiated by a recipient of a base FPP who, rather than immediately producing a corresponding SPP to complete the base sequence, produces an FPP of another sequence. This inserted FPP, and the responsive SPP it makes relevant, are treated as having "been launched to address matters which need to be dealt with in order to enable the doing of the base second pair part" (Schegloff, 2007b, p. 99). That is, unlike counters, which (as discussed previously) reverse the conditional relevance of a (base) SPP, insert sequences are designed to clear the way for its production once the insert sequence has been completed (Schegloff, 2007b).

Extract 7.9 illustrates instances of both of the two main types of insert expansions Schegloff (2007b, pp. 100–109) describes, namely "post-first" and "pre-second" insert expansions, which respectively "look backward" to address troubles in relation to an FPP that require resolution before the relevant SPP can be produced, and "look forward" to establish the conditions on which the SPP will be based. In this case, the FPP of the base sequence is the request for an appointment (lines 04–05) produced by a caller to the reception of a doctor's surgery. (Note how the exchange of greetings in lines 01–02 serves as a pre-sequence that establishes the call-taker and caller's co-alignment in the institutional categories associated with the call, and thereby clears the way for the caller's production of the request – cf. Extracts 7.1 and 7.5.) The receptionist's initial response to the request, "Yea:h" (line 7) displays her willingness to grant it, but instead of moving directly to produce such an SPP (e.g., by indicating a specific candidate time for the appointment, as she eventually does at lines 26–27), she asks a question regarding the type of appointment the caller is requesting (lines 07–08). This question is the FPP a post-first or "backward-looking" insert expansion by virtue of seeking clarification of the nature of the request, and thereby of the specific category of patient for whom the caller has made the request. The caller's response corrects the presupposition of the receptionist's question that the request was most likely for a "routi:ne appointment" (line 07) – and thus 'routine' category of patient (cf. Raymond & Heritage, 2021; Raymond, 2003) – instead describing symptoms that place the patient in the category 'acutely ill' (lines 09–11).

```
Extract 7.9: GP reception call
01   R:   Good morning surger:y J[ a n e ] speakin:g,
02   C:                         #[>Hello.<]#
03             (0.6)
04   C:   (Uh/H'llo) >c'n I make< an appoi:ntment for
```

```
05        Edward Potter please.
06             (0.4)
07   R:   Yea:h is it a r- (.) routi:ne appointment you're
08        requiring,
09   C:   U- no he's been up all night wi'a pain in his ear-
10        <well from yesterday he's got a pain in his ear
11        an' it's going down into his ne:ck.
12             (0.2)
13   R:   >Okay< (.) uh:m how old is Edward.
14             (1.2)
15   C:   He's sixty-one.
16             (0.4)
17   R:   (Oh/All) ri(h)hg(h)t.=.hh
18   C:   Huh huh H[UH huh huh huh]
19   R:            [ah HAH HAH HAH] ah huh-huh huh heh .hh
20   R:   UH what's h[i-
21   C:              [£You didn't expect that did you.£=
22   R:   =N(h)o I di(h)dn't mhuh huh .hh Wha- huh hah hah
23        what's uh:m (.) .ptk (.) what's the address there
24        plea:se.
25   C:   It's eighty Wordsworth R[oa:d.
26   R:                           [hh=hih O(h)k(h)ay £I can£
27   ──── book him in at twenty past ni:ne this morning,
28   C:   Th(h)at's l(h)ovel(h)y.
29   R:   All right, twenty past nine this morning.
30   C:   £Lovely, thanks a lot.£
31   R:   Thank you:.
32             (.)
33   R:   B[ye bye.]
34   C:    [ Bye:. ]
35   R:   > Bye bye. <
```

Having clarified the nature of the request through this post-first expansion, the receptionist then, as is commonly the case in service encounters (Schegloff, 2007b), initiates two pre-second or "forward-looking" insert expansions in the form of questions designed to gather additional routine information needed in order grant the request (lines 13 and 23). The first of these in particular is category-related, implicating the patient's membership in an age or stage of life category. It is notable that this question by the receptionist may tacitly reveal her assumption that the patient is a child, especially given receptionists in other calls from this corpus regularly ask for the patient's "date of birth" in the service of correctly identifying them in the computerized record systems, checking eligibility, and so on (see, e.g., Sikveland & Stokoe, 2017). Moreover, although the caller in this case never specifies her relationship to the patient, aspects of her conduct may allow for (or even encourage) the receptionist to make assumptions about the standardized relational pair that she and the patient occupy in relation to one another – namely, that she calling to make an appointment for her child (cf. Kitzinger, 2005a). That is, consistent with the viewer's maxim, the caller's request for an appointment on another's behalf, and reporting of symptoms of an ear infection (which are common in infants and young children), converge in enabling the receptionist's presumptive categorization of the caller as the patient's parent or guardian. The caller's response, "He's sixty-one" (line 15), then reveals that the patient is in fact an adult rather than a child. Moreover, the 1.2-second silence between the question and this response (line 14) may – consistent with our previous discussion of delays in relation to preference organization – be evidence of the caller's treatment of the question as inapposite for this patient. The subsequent unfolding of the interaction provides retrospective evidence for this analysis, while also taking the form of a further type of sequence expansion, namely post-expansion.

7.2.3 Post-expansion

While sequences can be recognizably complete (for participants) following the production of an SPP, they may instead be expanded through the production after the SPP of further actions that continue the 'business' of the preceding adjacency pair (Schegloff, 2007b). Post-expansions can take the "minimal" form of one further turn – a "sequence-closing third" – following the SPP of a sequence (Schegloff, 2007b, p. 118). Alternatively, they can be "non-minimal" (Schegloff, 2007b, p. 148), taking the form of further full adjacency pair sequences, which (as noted previously) can themselves be further expanded by pre-sequences, insert expansions, or yet more post-expansions.

Both of these main possibilities, along with attendant illustrations of how post-expansions can expose and/or be used to manage categorial matters, are evident in lines 17–22 of Extract 7.9. First, after a brief silence (line 16) following the caller's answer to the receptionist's question about the patient's age (as discussed in the previous section), the receptionist produces a laughing sequence-closing third that assesses the unexpected or surprising nature of the answer (line 17; cf. Wilkinson & Kitzinger, 2006).[11] She thus effectively confirms that she had been tacitly (mis-)categorizing the patient as a child, albeit without directly acknowledging this.

While the sequence *could* have ended after this post-expansion[12] by the receptionist – for example, by the receptionist moving directly to the FPP

---

11 See Schegloff (2007b, pp. 118–148) for further discussion of the range of specific forms that sequence-closing thirds recurrently take, and the types of interactional work they can perform.

12 This illustrates again how the statuses of objects such as "sequence-closing thirds" are interactional accomplishments rather than fixed 'essences' – while such practices do recurrently bring sequences to a close, and have earned their technical analytic labels accordingly, whether they do so in any specific case is thoroughly contingent on what the participants in the scene choose to do next.

of the next sequence, which she eventually produces in the form of the question at lines 23–24 – it is instead further expanded by an additional full adjacency pair. That is, after producing reciprocal laughter (lines 18–19), the caller explicitly registers the receptionist's surprise with the question, "£You didn't expect that did you.£" (line 21), which the receptionist answers affirmatively (line 22). This non-minimal post-expansion serves to manage the evident category trouble, in the form of the receptionist's mis-categorization of the patient, that has arisen, thereby more explicitly exposing this trouble. It is noteworthy, however, that this trouble is resolved – in the sense of the participants evidently mutually understanding and sharing a joke over what has just happened – even though who the patient is to the caller is never confirmed. While Kitzinger (2005a) demonstrates that participants systematically treat kinship categories as providing a warrant for calling for medical assistance on behalf of another, which provides for the availability to the receptionist of an inference that the patient was the caller's spouse or another member of her family, this is ultimately never explicitly stated. As such, if the receptionist has indeed made such an inference, then she has done so as a further instance of the type of tacit 'background' categorization through which she previously mis-categorized the patient.

While the trouble that has arisen in Extract 7.9 is resolved through a single post-expansion adjacency pair (along with the accompanying affiliation produced through shared laughter), post-expansions can extend over multiple sequences. In general, as Schegloff (2007b, p. 117) notes, "preferred responses tend to lead to closing the sequence, while dispreferred responses regularly lead to expansion of the sequence." As such, disputes or conflicts are a recurrent basis for extended post-expansions – and in such cases, categories can serve as key resources for parties seeking to escalate, resolve, or account for a dispute (also see Whitehead et al., 2018).

An instance of this can be seen in Extract 7.10 (a longer version of which we previously examined in Chapter 6: Taking Turns at Talking and Selecting Next Speakers, Extract 6.7), showing the dispute between Representatives Adam Schiff, Devin Nunes, and Elise Stefanik during the first impeachment of Donald Trump. As we noted in our previous analyses, the culmination of the dispute in this exchange is Nunes's use of age and gender categories in referring to Stefanik as a "young lady" (line 27) in accusing Schiff of "gagging" Stefanik. We can now build on our prior analysis by noting how the escalation of this dispute is part of a non-minimal post-expansion following an adjacency pair comprised of Schiff's directive for Stefanik to "suspend" (line 12) and Stefanik's complaining – and thus disaligning, resistant – response (line 13).

Extract 7.10: U.S. House Intelligence Committee, 15.11.19

```
12  AS:  The gentlewoman wi' suspend.
13  ES:  What is the interruption for this time? It is our time.
14  AS:  Th- >the gentlewoman will suspend,< you're not
15       recognized. Mister Nunes, you or Min[ority Counsel]
16  DN:                                     [   I: jus-   ]
17       I jus: recogn[ized Miss Stefanik. ]
18  AS:              [(Bu)=under the House] >Resolu'n< six sixty
19       you're not allowed to yield time except to Minority
20       Coun[sel.]
21  ES:      [The ] Ranking Member [ yield]ed [time to ano]ther
22  AS:                            [(Yib-)]   [(Gen'lwm-) ]
23  ES:  Mem[ber of Con]gres[s.]
24  AS:     [(Gen'lwm-)]    [ N]o.
25       (0.2) ((AS bangs gavel))
26  AS:  That is not accurate.
27  DN:  You're gagg(h)ing the: [young lady from New] York?
28  ES:                        [ That is accurate. ]
```

Following Stefanik's response, Schiff pursues his directive, thus reissuing the FPP with which Stefanik's response resisted complying, along with an account for the directive invoking the rules of the hearing (lines 14–15). Schiff thus seeks in this post-expansion to bring the prior sequence to a close, but Nunes and Stefanik's continued disputing of the legitimacy of his directive (lines 16–24) serves to further extend the sequence. Schiff's "No" in line 24 in particular marks the impasse that the dispute has reached by this point: consistent with Schegloff's (2007b, p. 151) observation that a recurrent way in which conflict is managed is "by trying to treat it as a problem of misunderstanding," Schiff has, in his two prior turns (lines 14–15 and 18–20), provided accounts for his directives that invoke the rules for the hearing, thereby treating the dispute as possibly arising from Nunes and Stefanik not adequately understanding or being aware of the rules. In contrast, his simple refutation of their claims in line 24 treats them as knowingly pursuing a course of action that violates the rules, and unequivocally rejects their attempt to do so. We can thus observe how Nunes produces his category-laden accusation at line 27 in the face of this sequential impasse, as he attempts to tilt the outcome of dispute in his and Stefanik's favour, and/or (as we noted in our prior analysis) to discredit Schiff should he stand firm in asserting his power as the committee chair to enforce the rules of the hearing. It is thus reminiscent of Amy Cooper's use of race and gender categories in the face of a similar impasse in Extract 7.7 – although in a different sequential environment.

We now return to another case examined in Chapter 4: Forming and Making Sense of Actions (Extract 4.5) and Chapter 6: Taking Turns at Talking and Selecting Next Speakers (Extract 6.6) – in the form of the exchange from the Venus Williams interview reproduced here as Extract 7.11. This case provides further illustrations of how the management of troubles in non-minimal post-expansions can provide for categorial inferences and/or mobilization of categorial resources in efforts to escalate or resolve them. Specifically, we can now consider how Richard Williams's intervention is occasioned by the interviewer's repeated post-expansions of the question sequence initiated at line 01, as he questions of Venus Williams's assertions of confidence in her ability to beat her forthcoming opponent (lines 05–15).

```
Extract 7.11: Venus Williams ABC Interview, 1995
01  IR:  You think you could beat her?
02           (.)
03  VW:  I know I can beat her.
04           (1.2)
05  IR:  You know it?
06           (2.2) ((VW nods, smiles))
07  IR:  Very confident?
08           (1.0)
09  VW:  I'm very confident.
10           (0.8)
11  IR:  You say it so easily.
12           (2.5)
13  IR:  Why?
14           (1.5)
15  VW:  Cuz I bel[ieve it.
16  RW:           [(All right, end that there) if youdon't
17       mi:nd.
18           (.)
19  RW:  And let me tell you why:.
20           (1.0)
21  RW:  What she has sa:id, (0.5) she said it with so much
22       confidence the first time, (0.7) but you keepgoing on
23       and on:.
24  IR:  You-
25  RW:  (Listen to [her.)
26  IR:             [can't keep i- interrupting, I mean i- if you
27       want [(her-)
28  RW:       [You've got tuh understand that you('re) dealing
29       with a image of a fourteen year old chi:ld.
30           (0.3)
31  RW:  And this child gonna be out there playing when your old
32       ass and me gonna be in the gra:ve. When she say
33       something, we done told you what's happen(ed). (.hh)
34       You're dealing with a little Black ki:d, (.) and let her
35       be a kid. <She done answered it with a lot of confidence,
36       LEAVE THAT ALONE!
```

The interviewer's further questioning in this post-expansion emerges from the contrast between the design of his initial question, which treats Venus Williams's ability to win as squarely in question, and Venus Williams's response (line 03), which treats as inapposite the presumption entailed in the query. This trouble can be seen in Venus Williams's nonconforming response in answering a yes/no-type question with something other than a "yes" or "no" (Raymond, 2003), and in her use of contrastive stress on "<u>know</u>," which upgrades the "th<u>i</u>nk" in the interviewer's question. The interviewer's successive pursuits following Venus Williams's strongly affirmative responses (lines 05–13) challenge her displays of confidence, casting her responses as inadequate or problematic (cf. Drew, 2003), and thereby possibly revealing the interviewer's orientation to her category memberships as a 'teenager' and/or 'novice tennis professional' as undermining her grounds for such confidence.[13] As our analysis of this exchange in Chapter 6: Taking Turns at Talking and Selecting Next Speakers noted, Richard Williams's intervention comes just as Venus Williams has begun responding to the most challenging query by the interviewer thus far (lines 13 and 15), and he subsequently deploys a range of categories from Pn-adequate MCDs as resources in pursuing his dispute with the interviewer (lines 28–36). Richard Williams thus designs his intervention as responsive to persistent aggressive questioning by the interviewer, which may be a routine feature of news interviews conducted with adults (and especially newsworthy ones, such as politicians, sports figures) but is treated as sanctionable by reference to Venus Williams and the interviewer's contrasting respective membership in categories from these Pn-adequate devices.

7.3 Categories in parenthetical sequences

In the preceding sections we have sought to describe some of the basic sequential structures that serve to organize extended stretches of interaction, and the categorial matters produced and managed in and through them. In this section we consider a final sequence type that occurs "at the interface of two levels of the organization of talk: turn taking and sequence organization" (Mazeland, 2007, p. 1818) – which Schegloff (2007b, p. 241) calls "parenthetical sequences." These sequences are characterized by a first speaker's temporary suspension of the progressivity of an ongoing *turn* in order to produce the first pair part of a distinct *sequence*, making relevant a response by a second speaker, following which the first speaker resumes the temporarily suspended

---

13 It is noteworthy that Venus Williams won this match, defeating the vastly more experienced Shaun Stafford in straight sets, and thereby demonstrating that the confidence she displayed in this interview was entirely warranted.

turn (Mazeland, 2007; Schegloff, 2007b).[14] Parenthetical sequences thereby serve as a means of "initiating a subsidiary activity" that is "supportive of and subordinate to the action that is underway in the TCU it is inserted into" (Mazeland, 2007, pp. 1818–1819) – and, as Whitehead (2020) demonstrates, these subsidiary activities can include the deployment of categories and/or management of categorial matters in relation to the action into which the parenthetical sequence is inserted.

While Whitehead's (2020) analysis focused on speakers' use of parentheticals to manage the implications of their membership in the race category 'white' during the course of complaints, their use can also be seen in relation to other action types and categories, as illustrated by Extract 7.12 (which we also examined in Chapter 1: An Introduction to Categories in Social Interaction, Extract 1.1, and Chapter 4: Forming and Making Sense of Actions, Extract 4.3). In this case, showing the opening exchanges of a call to a holiday sales booking company, the caller uses a parenthetical sequence to deploy an age-based account for calling to request assistance.

```
Extract 7.12: Holiday sales
01  R:  G'd evenin' Rindley Leisure Hotels, you're speaking to
02      Diane.=↓How c'n I help.
03  C:  Uh-·good evenin' Diane. .hh I'm trying to- um. (0.3) I'm
04      a lady of a certain age and going online's giving me a
05      headache.
06  R:  Mhm he heh, [heh,
07  C:              [h I don't know what I've pressed now.
08  R:  Uh heh heh [heh
09  C:             [(I'm trying) t'do a booking, could you check
10      the availability for me ((continues))
```

Following the exchange of greetings at the outset of the call through which the call-taker and caller accomplish alignment as members of the 'customer' and 'customer service representative' categories respectively (lines 01–03; cf. Extracts 7.1, 7.6, and 7.9), the caller begins to produce a request – projected by "I'm trying to" (line 03). However, she then suspends the progressivity of this action in order to parenthetically insert an age-based account for having made the call in the first place, and thus for the request she has begun to produce. Specifically, she produces a euphemistic but nonetheless explicitly

---

14 Parenthetical sequences can thus be inserted into turns-in-progress (and the actions they are in the progress of implementing) produced at any of the sequential positions described in the foregoing sections – that is, they can be produced during the course of first or second pair parts of adjacency pairs, before a base FPP, between a base FPP and SPP, following a base SPP, and so on.

category-rich self-description (cf. Schegloff, 2007a) – "I'm a lady of a certain age" (lines 03–04) – to claim membership in the age category 'old,' which serves as account for calling to ask for the agent's help with a project that she might otherwise have completed herself using the company's website (Flink-feldt et al., 2022). That is, by invoking a mismatch between her age category and the relatively recent emergence of what has nonetheless become a wide-spread technology for accomplishing the task she has called to request help completing, the caller treats a category-based less knowledgeable or "[K–]" epistemic status (Heritage, 2012b, p. 4) as warranting a more expansive enti-tlement to help than might be afforded to other customers (also see Chapter 9: Managing Knowledge, Experience, and Entitlement). The agent's responsive laughter (lines 06 and 08) tacitly accepts the caller's account as well as appreci-ates the humour embedded in its delivery, thereby completing the parentheti-cal sequence, after which the caller resumes her previously projected request (lines 09–10).

7.4 The sequential unfolding of trouble in the Sandra Bland case

In returning to the Sandra Bland case, we consider how – in light of our preceding discussion – sequential trouble can be seen in the two segments of the interaction that precede and set the scene for its subsequently rapid escalation into a physical conflict. The first of these, shown in Extract 7.13a[15], shows the opening phase of the encounter, beginning immediately after Bland (SB) and Encina (BE) have pulled over, and Encinia has walked from his car to the passenger side of Bland's. As prior analyses of the openings of police encounters (e.g., Kidwell, 2018; White-head et al., 2024) have demonstrated, a primary project of the sequences of which they are typically comprised is to accomplish the participants' alignment with re-spect to their membership in the setting-based institutional categories that are systematically treated as omni-relevant for the subsequent unfolding of the en-counter. As such, the multiple instances of sequential trouble that are evident in this opening phase together indicate the participants' categorial misalignment. That is, while Encinia treats this as a routine stop structured by their respective memberships in the 'state trooper' and 'driver accused of a traffic violation' cat-egories, Bland evidently tacitly resists being positioned in latter category, and thus resists the legitimacy of the occasion as a whole.

```
Extract 7.13a: Sandra Bland arrest
01  BE:   Hello ma'am.
02              (.)
03  SB:   Hi↓::.
```

15 We are grateful to Albert J. Meehan for drawing our attention to this part of the encounter and providing us with the video and a draft transcript of the segment shown here.

```
04   BE:   ( Now, ) >we're the Tex' Highway Patrol, the reason for
05         your< sto:p is you didn't fai::l- you failed to signal
06         (.) your lane change. >You got yer driver's lic'=an'
07         insurance with ya?<
08               (2.5) ((possible paper rustling sounds))
09   BE:   tch=What's wrong?
10               (1.5)
11   SB:   Nothin's wrong.
12               (16.0) ((SB reaching into glove compartment; handing
13         BE documents))
14   BE:   ( Thank=you. )
15               (0.5)
```

From as early as Bland's return greeting (line 03), there is evidence of trouble, in the form of a slight delay (line 02) in responding to Encinia's greeting (line 01), along with the informal register she adopts in her selection of a greeting format (a simple "Hi," in contrast to Enicnia's "Hello" + [formal address term] format), as well as the pitch change and stretching on her production of the greeting. These features of this SPP may register her orientation to the stop as unwarranted or questionable by tacitly disaligning with the FPP with which he has started this opening phase of the traffic stop (see Kidwell, 2018).

Then, following Enicnia's production of a highly routinized and quickly spoken account for the stop and request for her license and registration in lines 04–07 (cf. Kidwell, 2018), further trouble emerges. While Bland may be in the process of beginning to comply with Encinia's preceding request during the 2.5-second silence at line 08 – the video footage does not provide a clear view of her embodied conduct during this time, but the audio suggests possible movement and/or rustling of papers on her part, and she does ultimately hand something to Encinia during the silence at line 12 – she does not provide any spoken acknowledgement or acceptance of his account of the reason for the stop, nor any spoken indication of her willingness to fulfil the request. She may thus be actively resisting the course of action Encinia has initiated through the dual FPPs (account and request) he has produced by withholding responsive SPPs – and, indeed, Encinia then explicitly registers this silence as evidence of trouble, as he initiates an expansion of this request sequence by asking Bland what is wrong (line 09). This question by Encinia may be a sincere inquiry as to the nature of the possible trouble he has inferred but may alternatively be designed to show her that he has noticed her incipient resistance, and to warn her of the potential consequences of more direct resistance and prompt her to 'get with the program' (cf. Raymond et al., 2022; Van Maanen, 1978). While Bland's responsive denial (line 11) does not conclusively indicate whether she has taken Encinia's inquiry at face value or as a veiled warning, the further substantial silence that precedes it (line 10) marks the denial as reluctantly produced, and thus constitutes further evidence of trouble in relation to this sequence in particular, and thus the unfolding encounter more generally.

Insofar as Bland's evident resistance indicates her disalignment from the 'driver accused of a traffic violation' category, it also serves as evidence of her treatment of the stop as motivated by something other than her ostensibly unlawful conduct as a driver. In other words, it poses, for her, a potential puzzle as to why Encinia may have pulled her over, if not on a legitimate legal basis. Bland does not explicitly offer a possible solution to this puzzle, either in this opening phase of the encounter or at any other time prior to the subsequent emergence of a physical confrontation – a matter to which we return later. However, as the cases we presented in the preceding sections demonstrate, categories constitute a systematic set of resources for 'solving' such puzzles (also see Whitehead, 2009). The trouble we see here, and its further escalation in the segment that follows, may thus be tacit evidence for Bland's orientation to Encinia's decision to pull her over as being motivated by visibly available categories – for example, race and/or gender – other than those that provide institutionally relevant (i.e., legal) bases for such encounters.

The second segment we examine, shown in Extract 7.13b, begins around five-and-a-half minutes after the end of the prior segment. During this time, Encinia has asked Bland some additional 'routine' questions (including about how long she has been in Texas and where she is now heading), before walking to the front of the car and looking in the direction of the front license plate, then walking back along the passenger side and returning to his car for approximately four minutes, and then walking to Bland's driver-side window to resume his interaction with her. This segment includes the request/command[16] by Encinia for Bland to extinguish her cigarette identified by Lowrey-Kinberg and Sullivan Buker (2017) and Gladwell (2019) as a key point in the escalation of the encounter (lines 40–41), and ends with the first moments of the physical conflict that followed. Before considering those exchanges, however, we examine the trouble in the sequences that lead up to these moments, in light of what we have already seen in the previous extract.

Extract 7.13b: Sandra Bland arrest

```
16  BE:   Okay, ma'am,
17              (4.5) ((BE takes out pen and prepares to write))
18  BE:   You ok↑a:y?
19              (0.8)
20  SB:   ↑I'm waiting on you:, you:::- (.) This is your jo::b. I'm
21        waitin' on you, whenever you want [(me tuh go.)
22  BE:                                     [>I dunno,< you seem
```

---

16 While this action is grammatically formulated as a question, thus ostensibly constituting a request, it nonetheless claims a right to direct Bland's actions, and is hearable as a command by reference to Encinia's institutional category and associated authority (Lowrey-Kinberg & Sullivan Buker, 2017) – which it thereby also possibly invokes.

```
23          very irritated.=
24   SB:   =I am. I- I really am, I feel like what's cra:p is
25         what I'm gettin' a ticket for. <I was getting: out of
26         your way, you were speedin' up, (.h) tailing me, (.h) so
27         I move over and you stop me. So, yeah, I am a little
28         irritated bu:t (.)that doesn't stop you from giving me a
29         ticket, so
30               (0.8)
31   SB:   ( where's the ticket? )
32               (2.0)
33   BE:   Are you done?
34               (1.0)
35   SB:   You asked me what w's wro:ng and I told you.
36   BE:   Okay.
37   SB:   So now, I'm do:ne, yeah.
38   BE:   Okay.
39               (3.0) ((BE clicks pen and moves to start writing))
40   BE:   You mind puttin' out your cigarette, pleas:e.
41         >If y' don'< mind?
42               (2.5)
43   SB:   I'm in my ca:r, why'd I have to put out my cigarette.
44   BE:   Well you can step on out now.
45               (0.8)
46   SB:   ↑I don't have to step out of my [car ( )
47   BE:                                    [Step out of the car.
48               (3.0) ((BE places clipboard on car hood and moves
49         to open driver's door))
50   SB:   Why'm I a-
51         (0.5) ((BE opening driver's door))
52   BE:   S[tep ou:t of thuh car.
53   SB:    [No::, you don't hav- No, you don't have the right-
54   BE:   =[STE:P OUT OF THE CAR. ((hyper articulation))
55   SB:   =[YOU DO NO:T ha-
56   SB:   You do not have the right to do that.
57   BE:   I do have the right, now ste[p out or I will remove you.
58   SB:                                [I refuse to say-
59   SB:   I refuse to talk to you:, other than to identify myself,
60         [(and )
61   BE:   [STEP OUT, OR [I WILL REMOVE YOU.
62   SB:                 [(I am no-)
63   SB:   I am getting removed for:: a [failure to ↑signal?
64   BE:                                [S:TEP OUT,
65               (.)
66   BE:   or I will remove you. <I'm givin' you a lawful order.
67               (1.2)
68   BE:   Get outta thuh car now.
69               (.)
70   BE:   Or I'm [gonna remove you.
71   SB:          [(Talk to) my lawyer. And I'm calling my
72         [lawyer.
73   BE:   [I'm gonna yank you outta here [(now). ((reaching
```

```
74         inside car))
75   SB:                                  [Okay, you gonna yank me
76         outta my ↑car:?
77   BE:   Get ou:[t (of there.) ((grabbing/pulling SB))
78   SB:        [↑Oka:y.
79             (0.2)
80   SB:   ↑All right.
81             (0.8)
82   BE:   Twenny five [forty seven, (come in.)
83   SB:               [Let's- let's do this.
84             (.)
85   BE:   Yeah. We're going to[:. ((grabbing/pulling SB))
86   SB:                        [Yeah.
87             (.)
88   SB:   Let's- don't touch me!
```

In resuming his interaction with Bland upon his return to her car, Encinia projects that he is moving to the next phase of the traffic stop, which could include issuing a ticket or a warning. This is evident in his utterance at line 16, and his apparent move towards writing something on the paper he is holding, having taken a pen out of his pocket during the silence at line 17. However, he then suspends his progress towards this projected course of action to initiate a parenthetical sequence with a question that registers and takes up her emotional state (line 18), and that echoes the question at line 09 we discussed previously. Like that prior question, this may be designed as either a sincere inquiry about Bland's wellbeing but may alternatively be a warning designed to register signs of frustration or resistance on her part and prompt her to back down from displaying them. In contrast to her denial (and thus possible backdown) in response to his prior question, on this occasion Bland (following a silence at line 19 that foreshadows the trouble that follows) treats the question as an accountable delay in the proceedings, directing a complaint in this regard at Encinia (lines 20–21). She thus sequentially counters his attentiveness to – or warning about – her own conduct by initiating a competing course of action that targets his conduct, and prompts him to abandon the parenthetical sequence he has initiated with his question and instead return to the primary institutional 'business' of the encounter in the service of bringing it to a close and allowing her to leave. Moreover, she ties her complaint to his institutional category by asserting, "This is your job" (line 20), and by proposing that he is in control of when she can leave (line 21), thereby treating him as failing to fulfil the obligations associated with membership in this category.

Rather than produce one of the range of responses made conditionally relevant by Bland's complaint – for example, a preferred response in the form of an apology or offer of a remedy, or a dispreferred response in the form of a rejection of the validity of Bland's complaint (Schegloff, 1995, 2005a) – Encinia pursues the course of action to which Bland's complaint was a counter. That is, by remarking more directly on her emotional state (lines 22–23), he pursues and upgrades the FPP of the parenthetical sequence he produced at line 18, countering her counter by attending again to her conduct rather than his. He thereby issues a third potential warning – again in a format that could instead be taken at face value as a sincere query about her wellbeing – providing another place where she is prompted to choose how to respond in light of these possibilities. This pursuit by Encinia may also serve to imply that any continued progress towards closure of the encounter is contingent on addressing the emotional matter he has observed. On this occasion, Bland responds by treating Encinia's question at face value, acknowledging and accounting for her irritation (lines 24–27), before registering her expectation that he will nonetheless issue her a ticket (lines 27–29 and 31). Thus, while she implements a further complaint against Encinia, she ends her turn by conveying her lack of expectation of a remedy for her complaint and prompts Encinia again to resume movement towards closure of the encounter. Moreover, it more directly renews the puzzle as to why Encinia pulled Bland over, thus providing further evidence for her possible tacit treatment of his actions as motivated by categories such as race and gender, and her resistance of the relevance of categories relating to her conduct as a driver as a basis for the stop.

Rather than aligning with the course of action Bland has proposed, Encinia launches a post-expansion of this sequence that retrospectively confirms that his prior action (and perhaps, by extension, the two prior iterations of this action) was a warning rather than a sincere inquiry. Rather than working to repair her face-value uptake of his action, however, he treats Bland as having deliberately escalated the trouble that has already emerged. Specifically, by asking "Are you done?" (line 33) following a substantial silence after she had ended her turn (line 32), he complains that she has talked beyond a point at which she *should* have stopped, and thus tacitly proposes that she has knowingly resisted his warning. This complaint thereby exposes his orientation to the category-based authority that he treats her as having deliberately violated. In addition to working retrospectively in this way, this action by Encinia also serves as a further warning and prompt for Bland to back down by affirming that she is indeed "done," and thereby comply with the category-based authority he has tacitly asserted. Following another silence (line 34), which again marks the trouble at hand, Bland responds by resisting Encinia's complaint about her prior action, accounting for it as having been prompted by him (line 35), before proposing closure of this expanded sequence by affirming that she is done (line 37).

Although the responses Encinia produces at lines 36 and 38 serve as sequence-closing thirds, claiming acceptance of what she has said and thus proposing an end to this expanded sequence, it is noteworthy that Encinia thereby withholds any possible remedial action or other response in light of Bland's complaints about the circumstances under which he initiated the traffic stop. He then projects his resumption of the ticket-issuing phase of the encounter by clicking his pen and beginning to write again (line 39), and thereby belatedly aligns with her prompt for him to return to this activity, while leaving unresolved her objections to the actions that began the encounter in the first place.

It is evidently during this interlude that Bland has lit a cigarette, occasioning Encinia's request/command for her to extinguish it (lines 40–41). We can now observe that this action is an nth sequence expansion deferring progress towards closure of the encounter, occurring just moments after she has directly complained about such delays. Its status as an escalatory action by Encinia is more than just a matter of Bland's legal right to smoke in her car but also arises from its particular sequential placement. In addition, its status as a command oriented to Encinia's category-based authority takes on heightened significance in the context of the puzzle Bland has directly raised regarding the categorial bases for Encinia's actions. That is, it may be designed as a means of (re-)establishing his institutional authority specifically in the face of Bland having just resisted it. The rapid escalation that ensues when Bland – after another long silence (line 42) that again foreshadows the trouble that is to follow – counters this action by asserting her right to smoke in her car (line 43) is thus thrown into sharper relief by reference to the sequential environment in which it is produced.

Similarly, the further expansion of this sequence through Encinia's directive for Bland to leave her car (line 44), and the confrontation and standoff that then emerges (lines 45–72) and escalates into a physical confrontation (lines 73–88), constitute a continuing escalation of the categorial misalignment that has been increasingly explicitly evident throughout the encounter, rather than arising 'out of the blue.' Specifically, Encinia repeatedly invokes his legal authority through his commands (lines 47, 52, 54, 57, 61, 64, 68, and 77); threats (lines 57, 61, 66, 70, and 73); by more directly asserting it (lines 57 and 66); and by calling for backup (line 82). In contrast, Bland repeatedly disputes the legal basis of his directives (lines 46, 53, 55–56, 58–59, and 71–72) and asks questions that invoke other possible (e.g., categorial) motivations for his actions (lines 50 and 63). While Bland never explicitly mentions which specific categories she may have inferred as being relevant, thereby rendering claims in this regard unavoidably equivocal (cf. our discussion of ambiguity in Chapter 3: Methodological Principles, Practices, and Challenges), this may be further evidence of her having inferred such biases on his part: the more she sees his actions as reflecting such biases, the more dangerous she may recognize it to be for her to directly name them.

7.5   Summary and conclusions

In keeping with the examination of the mutually constitutive relationship between categories and generic organizations of the practice of interaction we have been developing in the preceding chapters, the cases we have presented here show both how the structures and expectations of sequences provide places for the use and/or management of categories; and how categories serve as extra-sequential sources of the sequential organization of interactional occasions, providing resources for the ongoing mutual intelligibility of each next action and sequence of actions. This is particularly evident in cases where interactional trouble can be observed, with categorial trouble being exposed in and through sequential trouble, while sequential trouble may arise in the first place from categorial trouble – and with categories also serving as participants' resources both for recognizing the nature of some trouble that has arisen and for managing and/or escalating associated conflicts or disputes.

This shows the value of examining interactions – and interactional troubles – through both sequential and categorial lenses: by identifying the sequential position and type of sequence embodied by each successive action in an unfolding exchange (basic adjacency pairs, pre- insert- and post-expansions, and parenthetical sequences), and the choices and contingencies with which participants are contending in light of this, we can examine whether and how the categories in play are shifting (or not) from one action to the next, and how participants are using and managing categories in light of the prevailing sequential exigencies. In doing so, we can begin to specify mechanisms through which categorial matters shape interactional sequences as well as sequential matters providing for the reproduction of categories.

8

MANAGING TROUBLES IN SPEAKING, HEARING, AND UNDERSTANDING

8.0   Introduction

In June 2020, British *Sky News* journalist Sophy Ridge conducted a live televised interview with the UK government's then Health Secretary, Matt Hancock. This interview took place in the weeks following the murder of George Floyd (also see Chapter 5: Referring to and Addressing People) and was contextualized as such by Ridge in her remarks prior to introducing Hancock, as she reported on a Black Lives Matter protest held in London that day in response to Floyd's death and other issues of systemic anti-Black racism. The interview was the subject of substantial media attention, focusing especially on an exchange that began around four minutes in, when Ridge asked Hancock how many Black cabinet members there were in the government – thereby alluding to the complete lack of Black cabinet members at that time as emblematic of the type of structural racism against which the Black Lives Matter movement was protesting. This question became an even more exposed occasion for category trouble when Hancock eventually responded by referring to a broader composite category commonly used in the UK to encompass multiple categories of people of colour, "Black and minority ethnic," before naming two cabinet members from Asian background. When pressed by Ridge to address the question about "Black people specifically" in the cabinet, Hancock claimed that the two cabinets he had served in under then Prime Minister Boris Johnson were "the two most diverse cabinets I have ever sat in."

In addition to being challenged by Ridge in the interview itself for "lump-[ing] everyone from non-white backgrounds together," Hancock was widely criticized for his responses to Ridge's questions, including being accused of

DOI: 10.4324/9781003120599-9

either not knowing or not being willing to acknowledge that there were no Black cabinet members (see, e.g., Duffy, 2020; Martin, 2020; Singh, 2020). While the commentary on Hancock's conduct in this interview thus took up some key substantive issues in relation to the category trouble that characterized it, it was invariably based "cleaned up" (also see Bucholtz, 2000; Potter & Hepburn, 2005) renderings of both Hancock and Ridge's talk. This resulted in the omission of several fine-grained details of the unfolding trouble that – in keeping with the approach we have developed throughout the preceding chapters – we contend are important to attend to.

Before returning later in the chapter to an extended examination of the Ridge-Hancock interview, we introduce a set of resources for the analysis of practices speakers can use to repair interactional trouble in general and category trouble in particular. As Schegloff (1987a, p. 210) notes, interactional trouble

> includes such occurrences as misarticulations, malapropisms, use of a 'wrong' word, unavailability of a word when needed, failure to hear or to be heard, trouble on the part of the recipient in understanding, incorrect understandings by recipients, and various others.

Such troubles are a pervasive feature of social interaction: as Hayashi et al. (2013, p. 1) observe, "[a]ny serious effort to contend with the real time production and understanding of human actions in everyday interaction can scarcely avoid noting that they are characterized by the routine occurrence of troubles, 'hitches,' misunderstandings, 'errors,' and other infelicities" (also see Bolden et al., 2022).

In focusing in this chapter on the management of category trouble as a particular sub-class of these types of interactional trouble, we examine how participants can use practices of 'repair' to manage trouble that can occur when producing, partially producing, correcting or altering, hearing, and understanding categorial phenomena in social interaction. In Section 8.1, we describe the main types of repair identified by conversation analysts, focusing particularly on how they may be used to address category-related troubles in speaking, hearing, and understanding. As we will see, practices and occasions of repair constitute a rich and systematic set of places in which the relevance (for participants) of a particular category or set of categories for an in-progress course of action can become observable because of the work participants do to manage, and thereby expose, these troubles. In examining these types of repair, we show when and how particular categories become sources of trouble and introduce a range of practices – including those for which categories serve as resources – that can be used to manage it. We then return in Section 8.2 to the Ridge-Hancock interview, considering how the details of the focal exchange can be illuminated by examining the numerous instances, and multiple types, of category-related repair that occurred in its unfolding. We conclude in Section 8.3 by reflecting on what category trouble, and the practices used to repair it, reveal about broader sociological and psychological matters as they play out in unfolding interactions, and thereby how it provides a kind of litmus test for where we are as a society. These reflections are thus connected to the issues discussed in Chapter 1: An Introduction to Categories in Social Interaction, about the power of conversation analytic research focused on categories to shed light on the workings of oppression, inequalities, and social change.

8.1 Categories and repair

Conversation analysts use the term 'repair' to refer to the recurrent practices through which potential or actual troubles in speaking, hearing, and understanding can be managed – and thereby become observable because of an in-progress turn or sequence being temporarily suspended in order to address them (see, e.g., Jefferson, 2018; Schegloff et al., 1977). The practices through which a trouble is 'fixed' can ensure "that the interaction does not freeze in its place when trouble arises, that intersubjectivity is maintained or restored, and that the turn and sequence and activity can progress to possible completion" (Schegloff, 2007b, p. 14).

As Kitzinger (2013, pp. 241–242) notes,

> Sometimes a repair is just a repair; that is, it is doing no more than it purports to do, which is to fix a possible problem in speaking, hearing or understanding the talk. . . . However, repair can also be used in the service of the action the speaker means to be doing with the talk.

That is, speakers may deploy repair practices for managing how an action is formed up and how it is or has been taken up by its recipients (also see Chapter 4: Forming and Making Sense of Actions), and thus in relation to both matters of recipient design and a range of "self-presentation" (Goffman, 1959; cf. Whitehead & Lerner, 2022) or "subject side" (Edwards, 2005) considerations. As we demonstrate in this section, the full range of these bases for using repair practices can involve categorial matters.

Foundational conversation analytic research on repair (e.g., Drew, 1997; Jefferson, 2018; Schegloff, 1979b, 1992d, 1997a, 1997b, 2000b, 2013; Schegloff et al., 1977) has examined its structurally systematic features, identifying a main set of places, relative to a 'trouble source' or 'repairable,' at which repair can be initiated and the practices recurrently used to complete it (also see the review by Kitzinger, 2013). These intersect with a fundamental distinction between *initiation* of repair by the same speaker who produced the trouble source ("self-initiated repair") and repair initiated by another party ("other-initiated repair"), along with a related distinction between self- versus other-*completion* of the repair (Schegloff et al., 1977). In the sections that follow, we sketch out the core features of the resulting main types of repair – namely, self-initiated same-turn (Section 8.1.1) and transition space (Section 8.1.2) repair; other-initiated, next-turn repair (Section 8.1.3); and repair after next turn (Section 8.1.4) – focusing on some ways in which all of these types of repair can be addressed to various sorts of categorial matters.

8.1.1   Self-initiated, same-turn repair

This type of repair is produced by the speaker of a trouble source within the same turn – and often, but not exclusively, within the same turn-constructional unit or TCU (see Chapter 6: Taking Turns at Talking and Selecting Next Speakers) – as the trouble source (Schegloff, 2013). That is, the repair is initiated by a speaker who both produces a trouble and notices and works to repair it before bringing the turn in which it occurs to completion, and thus prior to any other participant taking a subsequent turn at talk. These repairs can involve the use of one or more "operations" that a speaker can use "to deal with some putative trouble-source in an ongoing turn-at-talk in conversation or to alter it in some interactionally consequential way" (Schegloff, 2013, p. 43). Schegloff (2013) describes ten such operations, namely *replacing, inserting, deleting, searching, parenthesizing, aborting, sequence-jumping, recycling, reformatting*, and *reordering*.[1]

The initiation of "repair segments" (Schegloff, 2013, p. 41) typically, although not invariantly, becomes visible in and through features of the "broken surface" (Jefferson, 2018) of talk – that is, when "the speaker breaks the progressivity of the turn at talk, thereby exposing a bit of talk . . . as having been in some way inadequate or erroneous" (Bolden et al., 2022, p. 203; also see Schegloff, 2000b, 2013). Their onset is thus recurrently marked by various forms of disfluency, including cut-offs, repetitions, restarts, silences and other forms of delay (Kitzinger, 2013). The key component of the repair segment is the "repair *outcome* – whether solution or abandonment of the problem" (Schegloff, 2000b, p. 207; emphasis in original). In cases in which there *is* a solution, a comparison of where the turn was projectably headed prior to the initiation of repair with where it ends up following the repair solution can reveal just what the speaker took the trouble source to be, and thus what they have accomplished – including in relation to categorial matters – by completing the repair.

Other components that may also be present in repair segments include prefaces such as "actually," "I mean," "no," "or," and "well," which can contribute in various

---

1 The cases we present in this section include instances of the majority of these operations. We refer readers to Schegloff (2013) for detailed descriptions and empirical illustrations of the full range of them.

ways to the action of the turn in which the repair is produced (see, e.g., Clift, 2001; Kitzinger, 2013; Lerner & Kitzinger, 2015, 2019); apologetic terms such as 'sorry' and 'pardon me' through which the speaker can acknowledge their responsibility and/or express regret for the error or indiscretion being repaired (see, e.g., Bolden et al., 2022; Heritage & Raymond, 2016; Kitzinger, 2013; Robinson, 2004); and other commentary or self-talk that further contributes to managing or assessing the trouble at hand (see, e.g., Bolden et al., 2022; Kitzinger, 2013).

In the remainder of this section, we examine a range of extracts that illustrate many (although not all) of these operations and components of self-initiated, same-turn repair segments. We have selected these cases of repair to demonstrate some (but again not all) of the ways that speakers, in producing same-turn, self-initiated repair, can manage – and thereby expose their orientations to – various categorial contingencies. (We also provide a summary of these cases in Table 8.1.)

We begin with a group of repairs that are addressed to correcting errors – or what the speaker treats as such in producing the repair. They thereby relate to a set of phenomena, variously referred to as "speech errors, (Freudian) slips, slips of the tongue, gaffes, etc." (Bolden et al., 2022, p. 203), and regularly reported on in news and popular media when produced by politicians, celebrities, and other public figures. For example, in 2010, a radio presenter accidentally introduced the UK's then Culture Secretary, Jeremy Hunt, as "Jeremy Cunt" live on air. As Cookney (2014) reports, "[h]e later apologised, saying he "got into an awful tangle" and explained he mixed up the words "Hunt" and "culture" (for a transcript and analysis, see Bolden et al., 2022). These sorts of cases illustrate immediately the interest that anyone might have in such errors, which are often (following Freud, 1901) interpreted as making the speaker's unconscious thoughts visible, exposing what people 'really' mean, think, intend, and so on. In contrast to this deep-psychological account, conversation analysts have considered the social and interactional contingencies that may give rise to such phenomena, and the observable surface-level practices through which they may be addressed and/or managed (also see, e.g., Bolden et al., 2022; Burford-Rice & Augoustinos, 2018; Jefferson, 1996).

A first recurrent type of category-related error that occasions repair is what Jefferson (1996, p. 9; also see Jefferson, 1974) calls 'category-formed errors,' observing that they appear to arise from

> objects that very strongly belong together; sometimes as contrasts, sometimes as co-members, very often as pairs. Up-down, right-left, young-old, husband-wife. What seems to happen is that a gross selection-mechanism delivers up a category, but not the specific *member* of that category, and it's sort of a matter of pot luck whether the correct one gets said. It's like the whole package gets dropped down, and it's up to . . . who knows what? your taste buds? to decide which word is going to come out (emphasis in original).

Jefferson thus shows that some repairs result from categorial errors in which speakers select the 'wrong' category from a collection, with those 'wrong' categories thereby being strongly associated with the 'correct' category that the speaker was presumably heading for, as in Extract 8.1.

```
Extract 8.1 [GH:FN] (Jefferson, 1996, p. 10)
01  Lar:  Hi. I'm Carol's sister- uh brother.
```

Consistent with their aforementioned potential treatment as 'Freudian slips,' and as Jefferson (1996, p. 9) similarly notes, cases such as this may be taken "as having deep psychological import" – for example, in this case, that Larry has unintentionally revealed something about his gender identity. Independently of such psychological matters, however, we can observe the interactional organization of these 'slips': in this case, Larry produces the entire word "sister" before initiating repair by cutting off at the end of this word; further delays the continued production of his turn with "uh"; and then produces the repair solution in the form of the alternative category, "brother," thereby implementing the repair through the operation of *replacing* the 'incorrect' category with the 'correct' one. Although the trouble source ("sister") is exposed by being fully produced before the initiation of repair, Larry otherwise treats it as a simple error that can be straightforwardly corrected. While it is possible that this reflects an active effort on his part to 'cover up' any psychological inferences this error may give rise to, the key point here is how Larry *interactionally* produces it as relatively unremarkable in and through his use of these repair practices.

In contrast, category-related 'errors' may be more explicitly and elaborately managed, and thereby exposed, as interactionally and morally fraught matters through speakers' production of additional practices in the repair segment (see Bolden et al., 2022), or – as in Extract 8.2 – at some point after the repair has been completed. This case is from the reality television show *Love Island*, a dating game show that aired originally in the UK but now has multiple international versions around the world. The format involves equal numbers of previously unacquainted heterosexual male and female contestants, called 'Islanders,' living in a large villa ('The Villa') in Mallorca, Spain. The Islanders 'couple up' with each other to see if a romantic connection forms, and regularly 're-couple' to form new relationships. The producers set up numerous obstacles to 'test' the romantic connection between the contestants and the public votes for its favourite Islanders as the weeks go by. The winning couple wins a cash prize at the end. In the scene shown in Extract 8.2a, one of the Islanders, Gemma (G), is currently 'coupled up' with Luca (L). However, Gemma's real-life ex-boyfriend, Jacques (J), has recently entered The Villa as a contestant. Here, all three are located around a table. Gemma is sitting on a bar stool with Luca standing behind her, while Jacques stands perpendicular to them. Luca is physically teasing Gemma by pulling at her shoulders to move her back and forth against his chest. In the course of protesting against this action, she begins to call him "Jacques," before initiating repair midway through saying this incorrect name and addressing him instead using his correct name (also see Chapter 5: Referring to and Addressing People).

Extract 8.2a: *Love Island* (8th British series, June 2022)
01 G: Uwgh- ↑N:o.=Jac- (0.4) um (0.5) Luca ↓don'.

At the start of line 01, Gemma produces a non-lexical vocalization (also see, e.g., Keevallik & Ogden, 2020) in the form of a 'vomit' sound that serves to negatively assess Luca's pulling her into his chest. She then articulates her resistance lexically, telling him, "↑N:o" before immediately latching what is likely to be the beginning of a negative imperative, before cutting off just after beginning to address him as "Jac-." Following some further hesitation in the form of two silences separated by an "um," she completes the repair by *replacing* the incorrect partially produced "Jacques" with the correct "Luca" before completing the production of her imperative with "↓don'[t]."

What makes this repair such a fraught matter is that it is not just about correcting an address term but also concerns the category-relevant trouble exposed by the initial error: Gemma has referred to her current boyfriend (or, in *Love Island* language, the person she is 'coupled up' with) with her ex-boyfriend's name, while both are co-present. These relationship categories, and their arrangement in standardized pairs ('boyfriend'/'girlfriend') are associated with obligations and rights – for example, that one should know and use one's partner's name, and can expect one's partner to know and use one's name – such that an error of this sort may occasion inferences about whether Gemma sees Jacques rather than Luca as her actual or preferred partner. Indeed, much of the rest of this episode of *Love Island* is dedicated to the fallout from Gemma's repair, focusing on her feelings of guilt and Luca's resulting insecurity about their relationship. For example, Extract 8.2b shows a short segment in which Gemma reports what happened to some other Islanders.

Extract 8.2b: *Love Island* (8th British series, June 2022)
01 G: I said "o:hh £stop it Jha::hchques.£"
02   (0.8)
03 G: An' it was Lu::ca.h
04   (0.3)
05 G: An' Jacques was stood like <u>right</u> next t'me.

By comparing the transcripts, we can see that when Gemma reports her error to others later, she presents as direct reported speech something that is nevertheless an 'upgraded' reformulation of what she actually uttered in the moment. In the moment, the "degree of error" (Jefferson, 1974, p. 185) and degree of exposure of the trouble is relatively small, since "Jac-" is cut-off mid-production. However, when telling the story later, Gemma changes the prosodic features (emphatic but low-pitched in the moment versus breathy, smiley, and with accompanying laugh tokens in the report); the words uttered ("don't" in the original versus "oh stop it" in the report); and the completeness to which she uttered the trouble source ("Jac-" in the moment versus "Jha::hchques" in the report). Thus, although the report is delivered in an entirely separate conversation, to different recipients, it has a quality of what Bolden et al. (2022, p. 210) call "over-exposed" correction, noting that such cases may implicate "a failure to keep up with one's relational or epistemic obligations."

In contrast to the cases we have considered thus far, a great number of repairs are addressed to trouble sources that do not seem to technically constitute errors but that speakers nonetheless treat as inadequate or problematic in some way, including in relation to categorial matters. As Extract 8.3 demonstrates, these repairs can also be over-exposed through the production of additional practices that serve as sources of evidence of the contingency being managed by the speaker through the repair. This case is from a police interview with a suspect (S) arrested on suspicion of criminal damage to his neighbour's door. In the course of asking the suspect about his alleged confession to the neighbour, the police officer (P) refers to the neighbour as "this girl" before repairing to the alternative category term "woman" (lines 02–03).

Extract 8.3: Police interview (PN-19)
```
01  P:  [Right- YE:ah.=so] that comment's: wrong then:.
02      that you didn't- (0.2) y'didn't admit. To this
03      girl then. (.) °that-° this woman >sorry< that uh::
04      you punched 'er door.
```

The police officer initiates this repair after having fully produced the category term "girl" and projected his continuation of his turn with the word "that," before cutting off on the end of this word to *replace* "girl" with "woman" (line 03). The trouble source is a category term commonly used as an alternative to the repair solution (also see Extract 8.4), with both referring to members of the same category from the same MCD. The basis for the repair is thus not an error of the sort seen in Extracts 8.1 and 8.2, but instead relates to what the police officer treats as a difference in moral valences between these alternative category terms (also see our discussion of this matter in Chapter 4: Forming and Making Sense of Actions). That is, in addition to *recycling*[2] both the pre-frame ("this") and the post-frame ("that"), the police officer over-exposes the repair by producing the explicit apology, "sorry" just after the repair solution. He thereby treats "woman" as the default or unmarked category term and "girl" as a potentially offensive alternative, such that using it warrants an apology (also see our discussions of gender categories as unmarked reference forms in Chapter 5: Referring to and Addressing People). In doing so, he displays his orientation to feminist critiques of "girl" as a sexist reference form that conveys status-downgraded inferences relative to "woman," and to the associated importance of being 'gender aware' – that is, to the trouble that may arise from using sexist language (also see Extracts 8.11 and 8.12, and the extended analysis and discussion of this phenomenon by Stokoe, 2011a).

The repair in this case echoes an early discussion by Jefferson (1974, p. 192) of defendants in a traffic court who replaced the word "cop" with "officer," thereby conveying

> not merely that someone happened to be on the verge of saying 'cop' and replaced it with 'officer', but that this is the sort of person who habitually uses the term 'cop' and replaced it with 'officer' out of deference to the courtroom surround; someone who is to be recognized as operating in unfamiliar territory, e.g., a regular guy talking to a Judge in a courtroom.

The moral transgression to which the police officer's apology in this case is oriented may thus involve not just having used the term "girl" on this occasion but to the potential inference that this is a form he habitually uses in his interactions outside of workplace settings such as this one. It may thereby may also constitute evidence for his orientation to the omni-relevance of his membership in the setting-based 'police officer' category in this interaction, and to his transgression of the professional obligations associated with this category.

Extract 8.4, similarly to Extract 8.3, involves trouble with the selection of a gender category term, but with the speaker evidently managing a quite different contingency than that seen in Extract 8.3. This case, also analysed in Stokoe (2011a) is from a 'speed-date,' organized by a dating company, in which pairs of heterosexual men and women spend approximately five minutes talking to each other before the man moves on to a next participant. Here, the woman (W) has just agreed for her five-minute conversation to be recorded and is talking to her current interlocutor (M) about the researcher who has set up the recording equipment.

---

2 As Schegloff (2013, p. 59) observes, "recycling can be a repair operation in its own right" in some cases, while in others – as in this one – "the recycled element(s) *figure* in the repair segment but *not* as the repair *itself*" (emphasis in original).

Extract 8.4: Speed dating (SD-28)
```
01  W:   Just igno:re- this (.) lād- this gi:rl who's doing
02       um:: (0.4)
03  M:   I know, don' worry.
04             (0.3)
05  W:   Sociology degr*ee:,*
```

This extract also shows an apparent instance of "successive repairs" (Schegloff, 1979a, p. 277), "two-stage repair" (Lerner & Kitzinger, 2007, p. 536), or "cascading troubles" (Lerner & Kitzinger, 2009), "where an initial repair solution is subsequently treated as a trouble source" (Lerner & Kitzinger, 2012, p. 112).[3] The first of the successive repairs is marked by the cut off at the end of "igno:re" and the subsequent micropause following "this" (line 01), which indicate a brief instance of *searching*, reflecting that the woman has had some difficulty in selecting an appropriate way of referring to the researcher while telling the man to ignore her. The initial solution to this trouble is the gender category term 'lady,' which the woman can be heard to be headed towards from the way the 'a' in the cut-off "lād-" following the micropause (line 01) is produced as 'ay' (rather than 'a' as in 'lad').[4] By cutting off her production of this word, the woman treats it as a further trouble source before completing a second repair, in this case *replacing* it with an alternative gender category term, "gi:rl" (line 01). This second repair is also marked by the woman's recycling of the word "this" from prior to the micropause as a pre-frame for the repair solution.

This raises a potential puzzle as to what the basis for this repair might be, given that "this lady who's doing um Sociology degree," could do the job of referring quite adequately, and that the repair solution "girl" constitutes a shift to just the alternative category term that in Extract 8.3 was treated as potentially offensive. In contrast to the police officer's orientation to gender politics in Extract 8.3, it appears that the category trouble the woman is oriented to in this case concerns age, with the repair solution "girl" implicating someone younger than a "lady," and the woman thus evidently treating "lady" as a reference form that is 'too old' to be apposite for the researcher – who is a postgraduate student, and around 10–15 years younger than the woman. Furthermore, in the context of reassuring the man about having their interaction recorded, the woman's replacement of

---

3 These cases underscore the potential for literally any utterance or part thereof becoming a repairable, as even talk designed to repair (potential) trouble can itself become a source of trouble and in turn be repaired.
4 This eliminates any possibility that the further repair that follows may have arisen from a category-formed error of the type seen in Extract 8.1.

"lady" with "girl" may implicate the category by reference to which the researcher is doing the recording, positioning her as a 'harmless student.' Even more speculatively, this repair may serve to formulate the researcher as too young to be a participant as opposed to an observer in the current speed-dating setting, and thus to rule her out as a potential alternative partner for the man!

Extract 8.5 shows another case of successive repairs in which the outcome of a *searching* operation is cut off and subjected to a further repair operation – in this case, *deleting*. In previously examining this exchange in Chapter 5: Referring to and Addressing People (Extracts 5.7 and 5.10) and Chapter 7: Organizing Sequences of Action (Extract 7.3), we considered how Reshma, an artist being interviewed on a radio show, used gender and racial categories to respond to a complaint from a caller, Wayne, about her art. In continuing her response to Wayne, Reshma initially projects that she is headed towards a reference to "Black women" before cutting off after producing the "b-" sound and (following further delays indicating another instance of *searching*[5]), to omit the projected race category.

```
Extract 8.5: Radio call-in (691, 702 19.8.13)
01   Res:    .hhh £I think it's also easy£ fo:r a:: .hh £a white male,
02            sorry to say that,£ to sit in judgment of it without (.)
03            understanding the: .hh the experiences, or the:
04            perspectives of: u::h .hh b- u::h (.) women in this
05            country or: within patriarchal systems, .hh I think maybe
06            he is a bit (0.5) u::m: disempowered by it.
```

Having just referred to Wayne using race and gender categories (line 01), the consistency rule provides for Reshma's use of categories from these MCDs in the contrastive collective reference that she has projected – through the formulation "the experiences, or the: perspectives of:" (lines 03–04) – is to follow. This also provides for hearing the cut-off "b-" in line 04 as clearly headed towards "Black" (as a contrast to "white"), and thus the subsequent repair solution "women" as having been arrived at by deleting "Black" from the initially projected "Black women." The repair thus contributes to Reshma's discounting of Wayne's criticism by expanding the constituency she claims as likely supportive audiences for her work.

A further repair quickly follows, as Reshma initially circumscribes the category "women" by appending "in this country" (thereby constructing a 'gender +

---

5 The searching here can be seen as a practice used in the course of implementing the deletion, rather than as itself a distinct instance of repair (cf. the related discussion of recycling in Schegloff, 2013, p. 59). That is, the trouble source and repair solution for the searching operation here are one and the same as the repair solution for the deleting operation, with deleting thereby being the primary project completed by the speaker in this segment.

country of residence' compound category) before using or-initiated repair to *replace* the latter part of this compound category with a vastly more inclusive alternative, "within patriarchal systems" (lines 04–05). This repair is in keeping with the preceding one, serving to expand the collectivity encompassed by the resulting compound category in such a way that still includes those referred to in the initial version (see Lerner & Kitzinger's 2015 account of or-prefacing as a practice for substituting one formulation for another without altogether discarding the initial one).

The converse of deleting is *inserting*, a case of which is shown in another exchange from a radio call-in show, Extract 8.6, which parallels Extract 8.5 in the gender and race categories present in the repair segment. During the course of producing an assessment, a caller, Gugu, begins to produce the category-specific collective self-reference "us: women" (also see our discussion of self-reference in Chapter 5: Referring to and Addressing People) before cutting off midway through the category term "women" and inserting the race category "Black" into the self-reference.

```
Extract 8.6: Radio call-in (57, Kaya, 5.6.08)
01  Gugu:   John, I think, as somebody who has suffered double
02          prejudice, this week has turned out to be one, .hh
03          that is quite momentous in our ↑history?
04  John:   Mm hm?
05  Gugu:   Firstly we've got a Black man being recognized in
06          the United ↑States, in thee: form of Barack Obama,
07  John:   Mm hm?
08  Gugu:   and now we've got a ↑woman taking: .h u:m (0.6) a
09          >position of ↑leadership< within our- our- our
10          customs. <This is a very good win for us: wom-
11          Black women.
```

In prefacing her reason for calling into the show, Gugu claims membership in two unnamed categories subjected to prejudice (lines 01–02), before tying this to the news of Barack Obama's victory in the Democratic Party presidential primaries (lines 05–06), thereby revealing one of these categories as "Black." She then specifies the second category, "woman" (line 08), describing a judgment made in the South African Constitutional Court the previous day that a woman would succeed her father as the Chief of the Valoyi traditional community, having previously been disqualified on the basis of gender from taking up this position (lines 08–10). In doing so, she also alludes to her membership in, and the relevance for the court ruling of, a racial/ethnic category with the formulation "our customs" (lines 09–10). This provides for assessment of the implications of the ruling either for women more broadly, or more specifically for women of the racial/ethnic category associated with the Valoyi community, with

Gugu's initial assessment focusing on the former possibility and the repair to insert the race category "Black" opting for the latter – and thereby linking the assessment to both categories made relevant by her mention of "double prejudice" in her earlier preface.

Extract 8.7 shows a further case produced in a radio call-in show, and involving categories that overlap with those seen in Extracts 8.5 and 8.6. This case illustrates a caller's use of *parenthesizing*[6] to laminate a set of categories onto a simple self-reference (again, see our discussion of self-reference in Chapter 5: Referring to and Addressing People).

```
Extract 8.7: Radio call-in (368, 702 8.5.07)
01  Jen: What do you think about: about the DA now?
02           (0.2)
03  Abi: You know, I- (b-) I've- I've always been of the opinion
04       that we are- o- myself, a:nd I'm a Black female, twenny
05       eight, .hhh nowhere near ready to have a white president,
06       Or a white potential president,=h (.) but this woman she
07       just comes across as just being so genuinely interested
08       in this country and this continent.
```

In response to a question by the host, Jenny, regarding the caller's opinion of the DA[7] (line 01), the caller, Abigail, initially employs a simple self-reference (line 03), repeating it twice, before beginning to offer her opinion in answer to Jenny's question (lines 03–04). Abigail then suspends the progressivity of her turn just as she is about to formulate her opinion in order to instead produce another self-reference ("myself," line 04) that explicitly separates her from the collectivity ("we") she has just mentioned (cf. Lerner & Kitzinger, 2007, pp. 540–546). She then parenthetically (also see Mazeland, 2007; Whitehead, 2020) categorizes herself in race, sex, and age categories (lines 04–05) that she thereby treats as relevant for the opinion she subsequently offers (lines 06–08). By situating her opinion categorially, Abigail casts her positive assessment of the DA's new (white) leader as incongruent with her intersecting memberships in these categories – and as a departure from the more category-congruent opinion she reports having "always" (line 03) previously held. By doing this, she upgrades the proposed significance of the exception (marked by "but" in line 06) she has now adopted, thereby sharpening her positive assessment (or even possible endorsement) of this leader.

---

6 As Schegloff (2013, p. 51, emphasis in original) observes, this operation functions in a related way to *inserting* by adding something to the turn that was initially not projected, but "*unlike* insertings, they are ordinarily composed of clausal TCUs, and are implemented by different practices – by a different 'technology' – than is found with insertings."

7 This acronym refers to the Democratic Alliance, the official opposition to the ruling African National Congress (ANC) in South Africa.

A case showing the combined use of *aborting* and *reformatting* can be seen in Extract 8.8, from an interview on *The Late Show* involving the show's host, Stephen Colbert (SC) and actor Jason Segel (JC). In responding to Colbert's optimistic assessment of his age (line 07) following an exchange regarding his recent birthday (lines 01–06), Segel begins to formulate a more pessimistic upshot in a way that would implicate Colbert's membership in a different age or stage of life category than himself, before abandoning this formulation in favour of one that positions himself and Colbert as co-members of a category from this MCD.

```
Extract 8.8: The Late Show, Jason Segel, 19.1.21
01  SC:  ↑Oh and: uh speaking of uh >this year next year<
02        ha:ppy b↑irthday_was yesterday, ↑right?
03             (.)
04  SC:  How many years: (.) have we been on the pla:net?
05             (0.8)
06  JS:  I've been on the planet for forty one years:.
07  SC:  Oh, that's [nothin' man. That's nothin'.
08  JS:            [Yeah.
09           (1.0)
10  JS:  That's what I keep hearing. That's nice, but I hear it
11       hih hih_fr(h)om p(h)eop(h)le wh(h)o are- .HHH (0.2)
12       I don't hear it_from kids. hih hih huh [huh .hhh
13  SC:                                          [No.
14  JS:  No- no young kids say f(h)ort(h)y £one is nothin'.£
```

After initially aligning with and appreciating Colbert's assessment of his age (line 10), Segel projects, with the word "but" (line 10), a contrasting upshot. As he continues, he marks the delicate nature of the formulation-in-progress by laughing as he speaks (also see Jefferson, 1985; Lerner, 2013), before cutting off on the word "are" – just at the point where the projected next word that would bring the formulation to completion is "old(er)," or some variation thereof. Continuing the formulation to this completion would clearly implicate Colbert as the party who has just produced the type of assessment Segel is reflecting on and, given that he is in fact more than 15 years older than Segel, as a member of the category Segel is headed towards uttering. It would also serve to contrast Segel's age with Colbert's, positioning him as a member of an older or later age or stage of life category than Segel. After *aborting* this formulation, Segel produces a *reformatted* version of it that adjusts its potentially troublesome categorial implications. That is, rather than reporting who he *doesn't* hear this type of assessment from, he shifts to a report of who he *does* hear it from: "kids" (line 12) – a category that thereby contrasts with that of both Colbert and himself, tacitly positioning them as co-members of a 'not kids' category. By producing this repair, Segel averts what he treats as a potentially offensive or insulting categorization of Colbert (and others of similar or older ages) as "old," orienting in doing so to old(er) age as a stigmatized stage of life.

While we have now presented cases illustrating a range of repair operations, the types of trouble sources we have considered have been relatively uniform, taking the form of explicit mentions of categories and/or references to persons. This is both useful for the purpose of cross-case comparisons and is a reflection of the highly recurrent nature of these as trouble sources and thus their plentiful availability in our data. However, it is important to note that self-initiated, same-turn repairs of innumerable other types of turn components can also be done on the basis of, and/or reveal speakers' orientations to, categorial matters. To provide just two illustrations of this in rounding off this section, we consider two repairs, shown in Extract 8.9, on lexical items produced in relatively close proximity to one another. The first of these reveals the speaker's orientation to his own previous membership in the category 'person experiencing a mental health crisis,' and the second exposes a different speaker's orientation to his recipient's membership in that same category. This extract is from an interview on the radio show and podcast *This American Life* in which the interviewee, Zach, is recounting his experience of a psychotic break characterized by what is known as a "Truman Show delusion," in which the sufferer believes their entire life is – like Jim Carrey's character on the film, *The Truman Show* – a staged production being filmed for a broadcast audience (also see Gold & Gold, 2012).

```
Extract 8.9: This American Life (677)

01  Zach:   I r- I sprinted acro:ss:. (.) the intersection of (0.4)
02          I think it was Houston and First Avenue.
03              (0.3)
04  Zach:   Uh:[:
05  Sean:      [While cars were ↑moving?
06  Zach:   Oh, yea:h:.
07              (.)
08  Sean: That's in- (0.5) ↑credibly dangerous:.
09              (.)
10  Zach:   Not if it's professional drivers on a closed course.
```

In recounting his conduct during the course of one part of this episode, Zach reports crossing a busy intersection in Manhattan (lines 01–02). In doing so, he cuts off what appears to be headed towards the word "ran" on the "r" sound, *replacing* this with the more extreme "sprinted" (line 01). This repair to use an extreme case formulation (Edwards, 2000; Pomerantz, 1986) serves to underscore the extremity of his conduct arising from the psychotic break, with this shift in word selection thereby revealing his ongoing orientation to the omni-relevance of the category 'person experiencing a mental health crisis' in relation to the events he is recounting.

After seeking and receiving confirmation that Zach did this "While cars were ↑moving" (lines 05–06; also see our discussion of next-turn, other-initiated repair in Section 8.1.3), the interviewer, Sean, assesses this part of Zach's report, producing an extraordinarily artful instance of *replacing* as he does so. This repair becomes visible as Sean cuts off on the "in" sound of what seems to be headed towards the assessment, "That's insane" (line 08). While this is a widely used idiomatic formulation indicating that something is extreme, incredible, unbelievable, etc.,[8] its literal meaning may be deemed prejudicial or at least insensitive, especially in the context of assessing the reported conduct of a party whose membership in the 'person experiencing a mental health crisis' category has been established as the relevant setting-based one for the events he is recounting. Following a relatively lengthy silence during which Sean evidently searches for an alternative but still contextually fitted way of completing the assessment, he then does so by appending "↑credibly dangerous" to the suspended assessment-in-progress. He thereby repurposes the cut-off "in-" as the first syllable of the repair solution "incredibly dangerous," producing it as if it were merely a hitch in the progressivity of an assessment that was designed all along to be formed up in just this way (cf. Lerner & Raymond's, 2017 analysis of the "practical re-intentionalization" of embodied actions).

It is, of course, possible that this was merely a hitch in Sean's production of what was always designed to be the word "incredibly" rather than being the repair we have proposed, as his cut-off on "in-" is produced just in time to make the inference that he was about to say "insane" at least somewhat equivocal. However, the very presence of a mid-word silence of this sort potentially raises, for participants, the question of what the basis for such a hitch might be, thereby providing for inferences along the lines of the account we have offered. This case thus also underscores how some degree of speculation may be needed to analyse cases of same-turn repair in which the trouble source is not fully produced prior to the initiation of repair, while also demonstrating that and how such speculation can nonetheless be grounded in the empirical details at (also see our discussion of these matters in Chapter 3: Methodological Principles, Practices, and Challenges).

Other research on same-turn, self-initiated repair further demonstrates how it exposes participants' orientations to categorial matters and/or provides resources for managing them. In a recent study, Svensson (2024) shows how self-repair during the pronunciation of other people's names can be a category-bound activity. She examines the way chairpersons introduce

---

8 See, for example, www.italki.com/en/post/question-473040; www.reddit.com/r/ThatsInsane/.

TABLE 8.1 Selected category-related self-initiated, same-turn repairs

Extract	Trouble source	Repair solution	Repair operation
8.1	"sister"	"brother"	Replacing
8.2	"Jacques"	"Luca"	Replacing
8.3	"girl"	"woman"	Replacing
8.4	(Projected reference to co-present researcher)	"lady"	Searching
8.4	"lady"	"girl"	Replacing
8.5	(Projected reference to collectivity)	"Black women"	Searching
8.5	"Black women"	"women"	Deleting
8.5	"in this country"	"within patriarchal systems"	Replacing
8.6	"women"	"Black women"	Inserting
8.7	"I"/"myself"	"I'm a Black female, twenny eight"	Parenthesizing
8.8	"I hear it from (old/er people)"	"I don't hear it from kids"	Aborting, Reformatting
8.9	"ran"	"sprinted"	Replacing
8.9	"insane"	"incredibly dangerous"	Replacing

next speakers by name at a political party conference and how, though "problems with pronouncing the names . . . manifested through hitches, pauses, self-repair, and stretched sounds" (p. 17), such practices are accountable "as (politically) immoral" or "normatively deviant" (p. 26). Specifically, Svensson demonstrates how names can be prosodically realized in unmarked ways as 'ordinary' or as 'strange' and 'non-normative' and thus "related to membership categories and the situated construction of social identities" (p. 1). Thus, somewhat like Edwards's (2005) notion of the way people build actions to deal with both 'object-' and 'subject-side' concerns, Svensson argues that "the marked pronunciation is heard as attributing categorial features to its bearer and this, in turn, prompts the participant to attribute categorial features of ignorance to the chairperson(s)" (p. 26).

Related research has examined pronunciation, use, and self-repair of categories and category-implicative words and phrases in relation to second language acquisition (SLA) interactions (see, e.g., Firth & Wagner, 1997) or those in which participants do not all speak the same 'native' language. For example, Maheux-Pelletier and Golato (2008) show, in their analysis of conversations among French speakers from different speech communities, how repairs of lexical items can "be used to negotiate linguistic membership . . . [and] establish, confirm, or insist on speakers' belonging to one particular speech community over another" (p. 689). Similarly, Bolden (2014) examines "intercultural moments" in which a speaker displays "an assumption that the addressee does not understand a lexical item or a cultural reference and repairs it" (p. 212), observing how such repairs "convey a presumption of asymmetrical expertise and, thereby, (re)produce the lack of co-membership in the relevant cultural domain" (p. 220). (Also see our discussion of category-related expertise in Chapter 9: Managing Knowledge, Experience, and Entitlement.)

8.1.2 Transition space repair

The distinctive feature of transition space repairs is that they are initiated after the turn in which a trouble source is spoken has been brought to possible completion, but before any other speaker takes a turn at talk (Schegloff et al., 1977) – and thus, in the space at which transition from one speaker to a next is relevant (also see our discussion of turn transition in Chapter 6: Taking Turns at Talk and Selecting Next Speakers). These repairs are otherwise similar to same-TCU repairs, being initiated and completed by the speaker who produced the trouble source, using a similar set of operations (Kitzinger, 2013). In light of this, and since there is little systematic research on this type of repair (Kitzinger, 2013), we restrict our examination of them in this section to three cases that illustrate the structural position at which they are produced while offering interesting variations on naturally occurring talk-based data by virtue of including cases from a scripted television interaction and a textual interaction (also see our discussion of data sources in Chapter 1: An Introduction to Social Categories in Interaction).

The first of these cases can be seen in Extract 8.10, which comes from British reality television show, *The Underdog: Josh Must Win*. The set-up involves four hosts (who are all well-known in the UK, including for being ex-reality TV stars), Nick Grimshaw (NG), Vicky Pattison (VP), Amber Gill (AG), and Pete Wicks (PW). The hosts' job is to watch and manipulate, from behind one-way mirrors and cameras, contestants who believe they are in a reality TV show called *The Favourite*. Among the cast is a contestant called Josh, who is visibly out of place in the world of reality TV. In the exchange shown, the four hosts are viewing a round of voting between the contestants. Our interest is how the organizational task of recording participants' votes becomes, like Extract 4.1 in Chapter 4: Forming and Making Sense of Actions, resolved by leveraging categories, and how Pete Wicks produces a transition space repair in the course of objecting being nominated to serve as the scribe.

```
Extract 8.10: The Underdog: Josh Must Win, March 2024
Channel 4
01  NG:   D'y'think we need t'be taking notes.=
02  f?:   =Yeh.
03              (0.3)
04  PW?:  (I thi[nk)
05  NG:         [Pe:te.=d'you wanna be scri:be.
```

```
06                     (.)
07   PW:  Am I the se:cretary now.=The [bu:tler.
08   AG:                                [↓Yeh.
09   NG:  Ye:[ah.
10   VP?:    [Yeh.
11   NG:  Oh- Yea[:h.
12   AG?:        [(↑Yeah.) >go'on,<
13                     (0.2)
14   f?:  [.uhh ↑HAH ↑HAH ↑hah ↑hah hah
15   m?:  [( )- Huh huh
16                     (0.8) ((PW gets up to collect paper and pen))
```

   In Extract 4.1, we saw how one of the students involved in a collaborative writing task becomes incumbent in the setting-based category "scribe" via another participant categorizing her in the occupational category "secretary" and tying that to the gender category "female" ("well, secretary, female"). In noting the striking parallels between that case and Extract 8.10 (which took place 30 years after Extract 4.1), our particular (repair-related) interest is Wicks's production of a transition space repair of a category term at line 07. Like Extract 4.1, the sequence starts with one party (Nick Grimshaw) noticing that the task of note-taking should occur (line 01). At lines 02 and 04, one of the women hosts confirms that this task is needed, and Wicks begins a turn which he may be – but is probably not, given what comes next – beginning to volunteer to take notes, before Grimshaw nominates Wicks to be "scribe" (line 05). After a brief silence (line 06), and rather than a yes or no, which would be a grammatically fitted response to the design of Grimshaw's preceding question (Raymond, 2003), Wicks accepts the nomination but with a somewhat ironic, faux-outrage confirmation-seeking expansion: "Am I the secretary now" (line 07). Then, immediately after reaching the possible completion of this complaint, Wicks uses a transition space repair to replace the category "secretary" with the alternative "butler" (line 07). In doing so – and in contrast to the explicit binding of "secretary" to "female" we saw in Extract 4.1 – Wicks manages the ostensible basis for his faux-outrage at being nominated as "scribe," claiming it to be grounded in an objection to class-based subservience, rather than on a sexist view that "scribes" are 'female.' By replacing "secretary" with "butler," however, he also exposes his treatment of the former as stereotypically 'female' (and thus inapposite for him) and the latter as stereotypically 'male' (and thus more fitting, even if nonetheless objectionable).[9]

---

9 Also noteworthy is Wicks's display of surprise at his nomination as scribe, in contrast to the also-resistant but apparently unsurprised response by the female participant nominated for this category in Extract 4.1, which exposes the degree to which the association of this category with the gender category 'female' is taken-for-granted by participants in both cases.

Extract 8.11 shows a scripted case from an episode of the US television comedy *Friends*. Two of the characters, Ross and Phoebe, are discussing recent events in which Ross, already twice married and divorced, married another character, Rachel, while they were both drunk while visiting Las Vegas. Rachel wants to get the marriage annulled, and Ross has told her that he has done so. However, he admits to Phoebe that he has not gone through with the annulment and is telling her why. In responding sceptically to Ross's reasoning, Phoebe produces a transition space repair that is strikingly similar to the case of same-turn repair shown in Extract 8.3 (and to other cases examined by Stokoe, 2011a).

```
Extract 8.11: Friends: 'The one where Ross hugs Rachel'
01  Ross:  ↑All I know is: I- I ↑can't have another (.) failed
02         ma:rriage.
03  Phoe:  ↑So: okay what.=you're gonna be ↑ma:rried ↑to a
04         ↑girl who ↑doesn' even know: ↑about ↑it?
05              (0.2)
06  Phoe:  ↓O:h. WO:man. SO:rry.
```

While in Extract 8.3, the speaker-initiated repair by cutting off a TCU in progress, in this case the TCU in which the trouble source (the category term 'girl,' line 04) is produced is brought to possible completion without repair being initiated. This is shown by the grammatical completeness and rising intonation at the end of Phoebe's challenging question to Ross (line 04), and the brief silence that follows (line 05), during which Ross could be expected to produce a response (also see our discussion of adjacency pair sequences and conditional relevance in Chapter 7: Organizing Sequences of Action). However, like the one in Extract 8.3, this repair is produced as a replacement, with the repair solution taking the form of the alternative category term "woman" (line 06), and being followed by an explicit apology (line 06). Thus, like the one in Extract 8.3, Phoebe's apology is oriented to her category selection and is designed (in this case by the scriptwriters) by reference to the same 'subject-side' concerns about claiming a 'gender-aware' identity. That is, Phoebe's character is probably the most 'feminist' in the show (see Desai & Kim, 2020), so this bit of scripting gets its humour from her uncharacteristic use of a 'sexist' formulation. Also noteworthy is Phoebe's embodied production of the repair, an exaggerated parody of an eye-roll that accompanied a speaker's similar repair from "girls" to "women" in another similar case analysed by Stokoe (2011a, pp. 96–98). In addition, Phoebe's pained facial expression and accompanying arm movements, along with the prosodically marked change of state token "↓O:h" (line 06), work in aggregate to emphasize her display of 'noticing' that there was trouble in her preceding talk. Moreover, the increases in volume in her production of the repair solution and the apology, which she also produces with a lengthy grimace, further underscore the parodied portrayal of a common sexist *faux pas*, and repair thereof (cf. Cheeks & Whitehead, 2024).

Writing about the "absence of repair from the sentences with which linguists (especially syntacticians?) concern themselves," Schegloff (1979b, p. 263) argues that "much of the available analysis is for written sentences or for 'might-as-well-be-written' sentences." However, Extract 8.12 demonstrates that in some cases the types of repair we more commonly see in spoken discourse can also be produced in written texts (also see the further instances of self-initiated repair in written data sources presented by Stokoe, 2011a). In this case, from an internet blog, the author completes a sentence with a categorization of a referent as "a girl," before effecting a written transition space repair that is otherwise much like the cases in Extracts 8.3 and 8.11, beginning a new sentence with the alternative category term "Woman" followed by an apology (line 04).

```
Extract 8.12: www.anothermonkey.blogspot.com
01  There's definitely a girlish quality about it, in the
02  way that the Lifetime channel or a Lisa Loeb video have
03  a girlish feel to them. Which is not surprising, given
04  that Jen is, in fact, a girl. Woman. Sorry. Woman.
```

What is particularly interesting about this repair is the fact *that* it is written. Why purposefully mark a repair when the associated *faux pas* could be deleted, such that only the 'corrected' version is revealed publicly (see Meredith & Stokoe, 2014)? Unlike the use of this practice to display 'gender awareness' in Extract 8.3, it appears that the author in this case is *doing* 'doing repair' by reference to potential objections to the use of the category term "girl" as a way of parodying or ironicizing this common practice – and thus, similarly to Extract 8.11, using categorial repair as a resource for producing humour.

8.1.3 Other-initiated, next-turn repair

Other-initiated repair occurs when a subsequent speaker initiates repair to address a trouble that the preceding speaker has not treated as such in any of the ways described in the foregoing sections – with such repairs being overwhelmingly produced in the turn immediately following the trouble source turn, hence "next-turn" (Schegloff et al., 1977).[10] As Kitzinger (2013, p. 231) notes, "the party who initiates repair is usually not the party who

---

10 Although Schegloff (1992, 2000) considers cases in which other-initiated repair is produced in later turns, the categorial bases and features of such cases are similar to those of next-turn repair, so we focus on these more common cases in our discussion here.

produces the repair solution. Instead, the initiation serves as an invitation or request to the trouble-source speaker to provide the repair solution him/herself, such that one party initiates repair and the other effects it" (also see Schegloff et al., 1977). Practices used for these repair initiations range from those that display a 'weak(er)' grasp of the trouble source turn to those that display a 'strong(er)' grasp (Kitzinger, 2013; Schegloff et al., 1977) – and this range of practices has been shown to be universal across spoken languages around the world (Dingemanse et al., 2015). For example, what Drew (1997) calls "open class" initiators (e.g., 'what?,' 'sorry?,' or 'huh?') indicate only that something in a prior turn has been a trouble source without specifying what or where it was. In contrast, interrogatives such as 'who?,' 'where?,' and 'when?' indicate that the trouble source was a person, place, or time; repeating part or all of the trouble source serves as a claim that it has been heard but not understood (Robinson & Kevoe-Feldman, 2010); and candidate understandings (e.g., 'you mean . . . ?') claim to have heard and possibly understood the trouble source, while nonetheless seeking to confirm that they have adequately done so (e.g., Benjamin, 2012; Helmer & Zinken, 2019; Schegloff et al., 1977).

Other initiation of repair systematically provides for potential inferences about the (in)competence of the participants involved: the speaker of a trouble source may be seen as incompetent by virtue of having failed to register it and initiate repair in the same turn or the transition space, while a party who initiates repair in a next turn may be seen as incompetent on the basis of having failed to hear or understand the prior turn (see, e.g., Bolden, 2024; Jefferson, 1987; Lerner, 1996a; Robinson, 2006) – and these possibilities systematically intersect with the use of categories as accounts for these inferred lapses in competence. For example, extending our discussion in Section 8.1.1 of the literature on SLA and 'intercultural' interactions, other-initiated repairs in these interactions "may be treated as indicative of the recipient's linguistic or cultural novicehood" (Bolden, 2014, p. 233). Similarly, Egbert's (2004, p. 1470) analysis of interactions involving " 'non-native [sic] speakers of German" showed that, "in other-initiated repair, interactants may orient to regional origin, place of residence, and linguistic variety" as bases for trouble in hearing or understanding (also see, e.g., Bae & Oh, 2013; Bolden, 2024; Hoey & Raymond, 2024; Hosoda, 2000; Huensch, 2017; Park, 2007).

In another recent paper, Raymond (2019a) describes how other-initiated repair is a recurrent site for what he calls "category accounts," which "make use of normative assumptions about identities and membership categories in order to explain away moments of what the participants view as category deviance" (p. 585). The following extract from Raymond's (2019a) collection demonstrates the recurrent sequential structure of category accounts and their relationship to other-initiated repair. This case is from an advertisement for the US-based store Big Lots, in which "a young boy of about ten years old asks Lottie —designated on our version of the transcript as "Lot"— (the Big Lots mascot, a personified orange exclamation point) about the availability of various toys on sale" (Raymond, 2019a, p. 591).

```
Extract 8.13: Raymond (2019a, p. 591), "Big Lots 'Barbies'"
01  Lot:  Hello:: sir:?=a:nd (.) w:elcome to Big Lots.=
02  Boy:  Are you Lottie?
03  Lot:  Yes I am.
04  Boy:  Do you like being orange?
05  Lot:  Ah:::=I: guess so?
06  Boy:  Have any Hot Wheels?
07  Lot:  >Yes.<
08  Boy:  Nerf sets?
09  Lot:  >Yes.<
10  Boy:  Barbies_
11  Lot:  Ye-< Bar:bie:s,? ((furrows brow))
12  Boy:  It's for my li'l sister.
13  Lot:  Nice choice. ((smirk and wink))
14        ((scene change))
15        ((narrator begins announcing this week's sales))
```

Raymond's (2019a, p. 292) analysis focuses on lines 10–14: the boy's question (line 10) about "Barbies" (a type of female doll) is treated as accountable by Lottie's other-initiated repair (line 11), which indicates a trouble in understanding. This occasions a category account by the boy (line 12), with this account treating the trouble targeted by the repair initiator as involving the question of why someone like him would be asking about a toy of this nature. The account also tacitly affirms Lottie's treatment of a boy being interested in Barbies as normatively unexpected by claiming his interest to have been on behalf of someone whose gender category is fitted to an interest in this type of toy. Lottie's aligning response (line 13) then treats the account as adequately resolving what was previously a source of confusion, thereby affirming both the boy's inference about the categorial basis for Lottie's initiation of repair and his claim of his sister as a suitable candidate recipient of such a toy.

We can add to Raymond's (2019a) analysis that Lottie's initiation of repair in this case reveals an orientation not just to the boy's gender category but also to his age/stage of life category: while a question about Barbies by a male-presenting adult may be taken up as being asked on behalf of another for whom the questioner could be inferred to be buying a gift, Lottie's apparent assumption that the boy could only have been asking on his own behalf treats him as an incumbent of the 'child' category. The other-initiation of repair in this case does not, however, implicate the category membership(s) of Lottie – the party who initiated the repair – in any evident way. This contrasts with Extract 8.14, in which an other-initiated repair has potential category-related reputational implications for both the party who initiates the repair and the speaker of the trouble source, with the latter using a category account to manage these implications. This case is from another episode of *The Late Show* in which host Stephen Colbert (SC) interviewed actor, writer, and producer Issa Rae (IR). In this segment of the interview, a trouble in understanding gives rise to successive other-initiated repairs, with Colbert also exploiting the trouble as a resource for producing humour before retrospectively accounting for it by reference to his membership in an ethnic/cultural category – which serves as an alternative to potential inferences in relation to other available categories that audience members could use in making sense of it.

Extract 8.14: *The Late Show*, Issa Rae, 20.10.21

```
01   SC:   D'you sing? Do you enjoy singing?
02   IR:   No, I'm a terrible singer. [But I enjoy singing terribly.
03   SC:                             [(↑What?)
04              (0.8)
05   SC:   See? .h Tha- you'd fit right in with my fa:mily
06         [because we're not that good, but .hh Katie bar the doo:r:
07   IR:   [hih hih hih
08   SC:   uh: (.) near the end of a wedding.
09                                                                 (.)
10   IR:   Wh::[o- w(h)a(h)i(h)t=hh hh w:::hy::?
11   AUD:      [((laughter))
12   SC:   What? ((audience laughter continuing))
13   IR:   She barred the door:: near the [(end-)
14   SC:                                 [Katie bar the door, you
15         ever heard that te[rm?
16   IR:                     [No, I've never heard tha:t.
17   SC:   That means there's gonna be a Donnybrook for- there is gonna
18           be a fisticuffs in this room, there's [gonna be a ba:ttle
19   IR:                                           [>That is< so many
20         words that I don't know, oka[y, now I know.
21   SC:                               [Oka:y::
22   AUD:                              [((laughter, continues through
23         line 29))
24   SC:   There's gonna be a battle, a Donnybrook, a Don[nybrook,
25   IR:                                                 [Okay, a
26   SC:   [you kno:w:: (>get a bit<) of the old Jack Johnson, .hhh
27   IR:   [Donnybrook ((audience laughter continuing))
28   SC:   a:n:d: that means- Katie bar the door means .h honey, lock
29         the door, I'm gonn[a kick everybody's ass [>in this room,<
30   IR:                     [OH::                    [Katie: uhhih
31   SC:   Katie bar the door, (.) we're gonna [fight,
32   IR:                                       [((slaps table and
33         begins silently laughing))
34                                                      [((laughter, cheers,
35           applause, continues through line 42))
36   SC:   that's what that means.
```

```
37                   (1.5) ((IR continues silently laughing))
38   SC:   Does that make sense to you: [now?
39   IR:                                 [YES!
40                   (0.8) ((IR continues silently laughing))
41   SC:   [It's a grea- it's an Irish (.) it's an ol[d Irish express-
42   IR:   [I GOT IT! (Y- eh)                         [OH::: you ( )
43   SC:   [I'm Irish. I'm Irish, >yeah yeah yeah.<
44   IR:   [(                     I got you)
```

The trouble source that occasions this exchange is the idiomatic formulation Colbert produces (lines 06 and 08) in the course of affiliating with Rae's response (line 02) to his prior question (line 01). In initiating repair on this formulation, Rae initially begins producing a repair initiator ("Wh::o . . .") that would target as the trouble source the name ("Katie"), indicating a trouble either in hearing this name or in recognizing the person it refers to (also see our discussion of recognitional reference forms in Chapter 5: Referring to and Addressing People). However, Rae self-initiates repair on her repair-initiator-in-progress, shifting to one ("W:::hy::?") that indicates a trouble in understanding what Colbert has just said, while also treating this trouble as a source of humour through her interpellated laughter (line 10), with laughter from the studio audience (line 11) similarly appreciating it as such. This in turn occasions further trouble, as Colbert produces an open-class interrogative (line 12) and Rae then produces a further attempt at repair of the original trouble source by partially repeating it (line 13). After Colbert registers and seeks confirmation of the nature of the trouble (lines 14–15) and Rae confirms her lack of understanding of the idiom he has used (line 16), Colbert seizes on the opportunity to offer an explanation (lines 17–18) evidently designed to produce further trouble sources that will also continue the humour produced by the preceding ones – and it is taken up as such by Rae's self-effacing joke that serves as another text-turn repair initiator (lines 19–20) and by the audience's further laughter (line 22). After Rae eventually registers her understanding of the idiom (line 20), and Colbert elicits further laughter from Rae and the audience with an extended elaboration of his explanation (lines 24–40), Colbert produces a category account, describing the idiom by reference to the category 'Irish' (line 41) before self-categorizing as a member of this category (line 43). He thereby attributes both his use of the idiom and Rae's difficulty in understanding it to their respective (non-)membership in this category, and Rae responds by accepting and aligning with the account (lines 42 and 44).

Colbert's use of an ethnic category in this way is a recognizable alternative to other available inferences that would implicate potential relational and reputational risks for both Colbert and Rae. That is, having designed his turn in lines 05–06 and 08 to affiliatively cast his family (including himself) and Rae as co-members of a locally constituted 'enjoyer of singing terribly' category, using an idiom that Rae does not understand potentially undermines this relational work. Even more potentially fraught is the puzzle of how Colbert could evidently assume Rae would unproblematically understand the idiom only for her to not do so, which implicates issues of competence that participants could account for by reference to categories such as age, race, and gender. For example, this could be seen as an out-of-touch old(er) white man using a formulation with which a young(er) Black woman could/should not be expected to be familiar, or even as a deliberate attempt by Colbert to show Rae up as ignorant by reference to her membership in these categories. Thus, by using an ethnic category in his account, Colbert manages these potential risks, and in the process treats the ethnic category as a less risky basis for the asymmetries in knowledge exposed by the repair (also see our discussion of category-related epistemic matters in Chapter 9: Managing Knowledge, Experience, and Entitlement).

While the cases we have examined thus far in this section demonstrate some ways in which other-initiated repair can be produced and/or accounted for directly by reference to categorial matters, it can also serve as a site for the surfacing of categorial orientations even when the category in play evidently does not directly feature in the trouble source or repair initiation. We can appreciate this by reference to a case, shown as Extract 8.15, that we previously examined in Chapter 5: Referring to and Addressing People, Extract 5.4. As we noted in our previous analysis, in describing how she was ejected from a night club for underage drinking, Tricia successively refers to the person who bought her the drink as "some guy" (line 03) and then "someone" (line 07), thereby omitting what she treats as an irrelevant gender category from the second iteration of the reference. We can now register more explicitly that Tricia's production of two versions of this person reference arose from Tara's other-initiation of repair (line 05) on the turn in which the first of the references appeared.

```
Extract 8.15: Sorority Breakfast 2 (35-36)
01  Tar:    =Why did you get kicked out?
02                (0.2)
03  Tri:    >C'z I had some guy buy me a drink.<
04                (0.6)
05  Tar:    You did what?
06                (1.0)
07  Tri:    (I) had someone buy me a dr↑ink.
```

The basis for Tara's initiation of repair in this case appears to be a trouble in hearing, as she claims with "You did what?" an understanding that Tricia has formulated the conduct for which she was ejected while indicating trouble in hearing precisely what Tricia has described. While Tricia's near-verbatim repeat of her prior turn displays her orientation to the trouble as one of hearing (Schegloff, 2004), the one amendment to the second version of the turn – the change in the reference form – exposes her orientation to the inferences that might otherwise arise from the gender category in the initial reference form. Tara's initiation of repair thus occasions Tricia's shift from a categorial to non-categorial reference form, and the tacit-but-observable orientation to inferences about gender and sexuality it is designed to tamp down, that may have remained entirely hidden had Tara adequately heard Tricia's account at the first attempt. That is, while the repair in this case is not *about* the gender category and associated common-sense knowledge, it provides a place where its procedural consequentiality for the interaction *becomes visible*.

8.1.4 Repair after next turn

In cases where what turns out to have been a trouble source has not been recognized as such and repaired by the speaker of the turn in which it was spoken, nor by any speaker who responded to that turn, there is one remaining and related pair of places where repair may systematically occur. Schegloff (1992d) calls these "third position" (p. 1299) and "fourth position" (p. 1323) repair respectively, and refers to them together as "repair after next turn" (p. 1295). By far the more common of these (Schegloff, 1992d) – and thus the one we will primarily focus on in this section – is third position repair, which Schegloff (1997d, p. 31) describes as occurring when

> some party to the conversation has produced an utterance, the response to which (ordinarily in the following turn) reveals a problematic understanding. The 'misunderstood' speaker may then undertake to set the matter straight, and does so in the turn following the one which displayed the problematic understanding.[11]

Fourth position repair, in the rare cases in which it occurs, is initiated by a recipient of the trouble source turn ('position 1') who, having initially has not registered the trouble in their initial response ('position 2'), but then comes to do so on the basis of some aspect of a further turn spoken by the trouble source speaker ('position 3'), and then takes action to address the trouble (Schegloff, 1992d, 1997b). Third and fourth positions constitute the last local sequential opportunities for averting the continuation in the ongoing interaction (or beyond it) of an unaddressed misunderstanding, and on this basis,

---

11 Schegloff (1997d) distinguishes third *position* repairs from third *turn* repairs: The former "show themselves to be prompted by the response (position 2) to some earlier utterance (position 1)" (pp. 31–32), while the latter involve a speaker registering and repairing a trouble source in a prior TCU, but only after an intervening turn has been produced by another speaker. This intervening turn is thus "incidental" to the repair rather than being (as with third-position repairs) the basis for its initiation, making third turn repairs much like transition space repairs in all respects other than the presence of the intervening turn (also see Kitzinger, 2013; Schegloff, 1992d).

Schegloff (1992d, p. 1325) refers to them as "the last structurally provided defence of intersubjectivity."[12]

A relatively straightforward case of a category-related third position repair is shown in Extract 8.16, which comes from an exchange on Twitter between a British supermarket account (S) and "Jennifer" (J)[13] that occurred during the first summer of the Covid-19 pandemic. The trouble source in this case is the inclusion of "Karen" at the end of the initial tweet from the supermarket account (line 03).

```
Extract 8.16: Twitter exchange, July 2020
01  S:  We won't be challenging customers without a mask
02      when they enter or when they are in store since
03      they may have a reason not to wear a mask. Karen
04  J:  Highly offensive putting the Karen at the
05      end..stick it
06  S:  Hi Jennifer, sorry for the confusion. Karen is the
07      name of the colleague who responded to the query.
08      Barry
```

The trouble source in this case is the "Karen" (line 03) included at the end of the initial tweet from the supermarket account – which thus constitutes the 'position 1' turn for the instance of third position repair that follows. In the 'position 2' response to this turn, Jennifer treats this "Karen" as a category, complaining about the supermarket account's "Highly offensive" inclusion of it (lines 04–05). That is, Jennifer evidently reads the position 1 turn as targeting people of the category 'Karen,' which Blitvich (2022) describes as a category attributed to middle-aged white women who act in rude and entitled ways, target service workers, and were associated with anti-mask positions during the pandemic. The third position response from the supermarket account then corrects Jennifer's (mis)understanding of the "Karen" in the initial tweet, thereby defusing Jennifer's complaint about its inclusion. Moreover, by signing off as "Barry"[14] (line 08) the person who wrote this tweet treats the format in which "Karen" was included in the initial tweet as a conventional one used by employees who staff the account, thereby further discounting any potential inference that the "Karen" was used in this way to target a particular category while providing for deniability in the process. In

---

12 It is, of course, possible for prior unaddressed troubles to be detected after – and even long after – fourth position. As Schegloff (1992d, p. 1325) notes, however, "after these positions there is no systematic provision for catching divergent understandings. In general, after third position, such repair as gets initiated can at best be characterized as being initiated when the trouble source is 'next relevant.' Of course, it may never again be relevant."

13 Since this user subsequently deleted her tweet, we have replaced her name with a pseudonym.

14 The third position repair in this case is thus evidently produced by a different person than the turn in which the trouble source appeared but is nonetheless produced by a representative of the same *party* – the supermarket account staff (also see Bolden, 2013).

addition, Jennifer's subsequent deletion of her tweet indicates her acceptance of the correction and her acknowledgement that her complaint arose from a misunderstanding.

While Extract 8.16 provides a case in which the three turns relevant for a third position repair are produced consecutively, they may also be separated by intervening turns and sequences while still exhibiting the canonical features of this type of repair (Schegloff, 1992d). This is illustrated by returning to a case we partially examined in Chapter 5: Referring to and Addressing People, Extract 5.5, an extended segment of which is shown in Extract 8.17. As we noted in our previous analysis, the repeated use of the person reference form "child[ren]" by a caller to an emergency medical services line in this case (see lines 02, 04, and 10) appears to be designed to warrant his request for emergency assistance on the basis of common-sense knowledge about the vulnerability and need for protection of members of this category. In examining the subsequent unfolding of the call, we can see how this choice of reference form emerges as a trouble source several turns later.

```
Extract 8.17: Emergency call (WC EMS 10469)
01  C:    Hi, >this Mister ↑Fox from Daventry Secondary School,
02        man.< [.h There was a fight between two ↑child↓ren, h
03  CT:        [(Mm hm?)
04  C:    .hh the one chi:ld i:s um is uh l- >un↑conscious at the
05        moment, h .hh u::m: an' I'm just a bit con↑cerned man.
06  CT:   >Okay, so the ambulance is only< for one patient now?
07  C:    Ya, for one, ya. h (.hh)
08              (.)
09  C:    Can:: ya (o-) coz I'm >j'st a bit< concerned about-
10        you know:, summing >could happen to the chi[ld man,<
11  CT:                                              [Is it- is it
12        a high ↑school, o:r:
13  C:    Sorry?
14  CT:   Is it a- it a high school, Davism- m-
15        [(Dav- is a) high school.
16  C:    [Daventry, yes.
17  CT:   Is it a high school sir?
18  C:    Yes.
19              (0.8)
20  CT:   Okay, um:: approximately how old is the guy- >u- (dis=is)
21        the< thuh (.) bo:y.
22              (.)
23  C:    Sorry? It's a [girl. 't['sa girl.
24  CT:                 [Uh      [(        you said) girls?
25  C:    Ya.
26  CT:   So- (.) u- g- two girls fight?
27              (0.2)
28  C:    Ya.
```

```
29  CT:  Okay, how ↑old is (s)he?
30  C:   .h I think she's about ↑thir↓teen.=hh
```

The 'position 2' response that exposes the trouble source in this case is not produced in the immediate next turn due to a series of intervening insert sequences (lines 06–16) that follow the caller's report of the incident in relation to which he is requesting assistance (also see our discussion of insert sequences in Chapter 7: Organizing Sequences of Action). These include sequences initiated by requests for clarification by the call-taker of the number of patients involved (line 06) and nature of the place to which the ambulance is to be dispatched (lines 11–12), the latter of which occasions trouble resulting in two other-initiated repair sequences (lines 13–15 and 17–18). Following the resolution of these troubles, the call-taker produces a question about the patient that is responsive to the turns in which the caller used the category 'child,' while instead referring to the patient as "the guy" (line 20) before repairing to replace this with "thuh (.) boy" (line 21). This self-initiated repair is interesting in its own right, indicating the care the call-taker is exercising in selecting a reference form that matches the age category invoked by the caller's use of "child" by shifting from a hearably 'adult' form to an alternative 'child' form, and thereby anticipating the potential trouble that could arise from being heard as treating the patient as an adult. What the call-taker evidently does not anticipate, however, is that using a gender-specific reference form, in contrast to gender-neutral form used by the caller, exposes what turns out to be an erroneous assumption about the patient's gender category – with this assumption apparently grounded in common-sense knowledge of the reported activity (fighting) being bound to this gender category.

In response to this question, after initially producing another next-turn repair initiator ("Sorry?"), the caller evidently registers and moves to correct the call-taker's assumption about the patient's gender using a third position repair that categorizes her as "a girl," while underscoring the correction by repeating it and placing emphasis on the category term in both iterations (line 23). This occasions further trouble as the call-taker initiates next-turn repair to confirm her hearing of the correction (line 23) and then, even after the caller has confirmed this hearing (line 24), producing a further understanding check (line 26) before finally moving to a new question about the patient's age (line 29) after the caller's further affirmative response (line 28).

This extract thus provides a rich case demonstrating how a mis-categorization grounded in a participant's orientation to an activity as category-bound can be exposed in and through third-position repair (also see the scripted category-related third-position repairs examined by Okazawa, 2024). In addition, it demonstrates both how category-related troubles of this nature can delay time-sensitive institutional activities (in this case providing emergency assistance) and how the practices of repair serve as crucial resources for getting interactions back on track in such cases.

8.3 Using repair to avert and pursue category trouble in the Ridge-Hancock interview

Armed with the analytic – and participants' – resources introduced in the foregoing sections, we can now return to a more detailed examination of the Sophy Ridge-Matt Hancock interview with which we opened the chapter. In doing so, we can observe that the focal segment of the interview, shown in Extract 8.18, includes category-related instances of all the main types of repair described in the foregoing sections.[15] In the analysis that follows we consider how these repairs serve as resources for both Ridge and Hancock during the course of the exchange, and how they thereby figure in the category troubles observed by commentators following the interview.

The stretch of the interview shown in Extract 8.18 is initiated by Ridge's question (lines 01–03), which serves as a challenge to Hancock, given that a factual answer would be "zero" or "none," and straightforwardly giving such an answer would implicate the government of which Hancock is a part in having failed to undertake the type of "doing more" Ridge has mentioned in the preface to her question (also see, e.g., Clayman & Heritage, 2002).

```
Extract 8.18: Ridge/Hancock 7.6.2020
01   SR:  We've been talking about thē: >you know<
02        imp̲o̲rtance of: (.) doing more, um:: (0.2) ↑how m'ny
03        Black people are in cabinet?
04             (2.0)
05   MH:  .hh I'm s̲o̲ sorry, I didn' (.) c̲a̲tch that question,
06        Sophy.
07             (0.2)
08   SR:  h=H̲ow m'ny:: (.) Bl̲a̲ck people are:: (.) in
09        the current #↓cabinet?#
10             (2.0)
11   MH:  .hh U::m: (0.2) thē:: ↑W'll, (0.2) ↓#Uh-
12        th- we've go- there's a- wh̲o̲le ↑s̲e̲ries of
13        people from a:=h (0.3) Bl̲a̲ck an' mah- min̲o̲rity
14        ethnic background? .h Uh:: the Chancellor >(a' thē)<
15        Exch̲e̲quer, .h the H̲o̲me S̲e̲cret'ry, .hh um: is:: to
16        n(h)am(h)e b(h)ut £two.£ .hh Uh
17        so[:: the- it's uh >you know,< there actually (is a )
```

---

15 A caveat to this is that transition space repair does not feature in the exchange – but, as we noted in Section 8.1.2, transition space repair shares most of the features of self-initiated, same-turn repair.

```
18   SR:    [I'm j'st talking about Black s::- sorry (I-)
19               (.)
20   SR:    I'm talking about Black people specific'ly, b'cause
21          I do think it's quite important not to:: .hhh lump
22          everyone from non-white backgrou:nds together,
23          because obviously: .hhh Asian people for example:
24          face prejudice too, but it ↑might be a different
25          prejudice to that .hh faced by Black people:, um
26          sixty two percent for example, .hhh of GCSE pupils
27          from Indian backgrounds got a strong pass in English
28          and maths, .hh twenty seven percent of Black
29          Caribbean, .hh you're three times as likely to be
30          stopped and searched if you're Black than if you're
31          Asian, so th↑at's why I was specifically asking about
32          .hh how many Black people there are .h (.) in the
33          current cabinet?
34               (1.5)
35   MH:    .hh Uh- well, uh- the cabinets that I've- the two
36          cabinets I've sat i:n:: .h uh with:: uh:: Boris
37          Johnson as Prime Ministe:r: are the two most diverse
38          cabinets I've ever sat in. .h Um: an::d uh- you know,
39          right at the top of: (.) government, i- including in
40          the great offices of state people from Black and
41          minority ethnic backgrounds, Kwasi Kwarteng: .h was:
42          sitting around the cabinet table, (.) uh: with me:,
43          (0.2) um- i- i- so[:: a- ↑actually I think tha:t:
44   SR:                       [>£He's not anymore though.£< hhh
45          ((chuckle))
45   MH:    Bori- (u::) well I think that Boris Johnson's got a
46          very good record on this.
```

The first instance of repair on which we focus is initiated by Hancock's next-turn repair initiator, prefaced by an apology (lines 05–06), following a lengthy silence (line 04) after Ridge's question. While we cannot know whether Hancock genuinely failed to hear Ridge's question as he claims, or whether he was using an initiation of repair as a resource for deferring an answer to the question-as-posed, it is worth entertaining the latter possibility, given the difficult position in which the question places him. Either way, Hancock's initiation of repair provides for at least an outside chance of Ridge's completion of the repair leaving him with a more manageable version of the question to answer. Ridge does not oblige, however, repeating the question verbatim with the exception of the addition of the words "the current" before "cabinet" (line 09), thereby narrowing the constraints the question puts on Hancock by explicitly excluding as a legitimate answer anything pertaining to previous cabinets – the import of which we return to shortly.

Hancock's response to the question (lines 11–17) – which he begins after another lengthy silence (line 10) and following further delays and silences after he begins to speak (line 11) – is littered with self-initiated, same-turn repair. His first apparent attempt to address the question appears with the word "thē::" (line 11), but he quickly produces a first instance of same turn repair by aborting (and then abandoning) this TCU. He then restarts with what appears to be the beginning of a well-prefaced repair, uttering only the preface "↑W'll" (line 11) before again aborting this TCU and then aborting two further apparent attempts to begin answering, as shown by his cut off "th-" and "we've go-" (line 12). Also noteworthy is the further self-initiated, same-turn repair on line 13, as Hancock apparently begins to articulate the word "majority," before initiating repair by cutting off its production to replace it with "minority." He appears to be disaggregating the acronym 'BME' as 'Black and Minority Ethnic,' in which the word 'majority' would be an inaccurate disaggregation. This repair is thus an error correction, but one that – together with the preceding series of repairs – underscores the evident difficulty Hancock is having in addressing a challenge regarding the absence of Black cabinet members of the Cabinet, and is potentially hearable as reflecting a lack of comfort or familiarity on his part with diversity-related terminology such as this – and, by extension, the government's shortcomings in dealing with the diversity-related issues implicated by Ridge's question.

Hancock's substantive response (lines 12–14) orients to the way the "how m'ny" in Ridge's question calls on him to supply a number but also departs from the constraints of the question by adding the further compound category 'minority ethnic background' to the category 'Black' specified by Ridge in the question. Hancock thereby seeks to evade the challenge posed by the question by expanding to a broader set of categories than the single one specified by Ridge. This enables him to offer a non-zero number as a response to the question, which he elaborates by naming two British Indian members of the cabinet (lines 14–15) before claiming there are others he could also name (lines 15–16). This occasions a third position repair by Ridge, as she asserts that her question was "about Black people specific'ly" (line 20). Rather than simply completing the repair, Ridge offers an account for her rejection of the expanded set of categories Hancock has sought to introduce, exhorting him not to "lump everyone from non-white backgrou:nds together" (lines 21–22) by reference to examples of the differential types and degrees of "prejudice" faced by Black people in particular (lines 23–31). This repair and accompanying account thereby provide an occasion for sanctioning Hancock and providing further context for her question before reasserting the question (lines 32–33) as a verbatim repeat of the prior iteration from lines 08–09 – and it is in responding to this reassertion of the question regarding *current* cabinet members that Hancock mentions *former* cabinet member Kwasi Kwarteng. The version of the question Ridge initially produced following Hancock's next-turn repair initiator in lines 05–06 thus serves to heighten the discrediting nature of his mention of Kwarteng – and Ridge herself treats it as such with her dismissive, and even somewhat mocking (as shown by her smiling delivery and subsequent chuckle), interjected response in line 44.

In sum, the various types of repair we have considered in this chapter were central to the circumstances under which Hancock produced the remarks that were taken up by commentators in the wake of this interview. While the condemnation arising from the interview is understandable without attending to the litany of repairs involved, we can further appreciate the category troubles at play by examining how these repairs figured as contexts for, and integral features of, their unfolding.

8.4   Summary and conclusions

The practices of repair we have examined in this chapter provide a set of methods that participants can deploy in managing a wide range of troubles relating to categorial matters, including by implementing or proposing the addition or removal of categories as bases for action and inference in relation to some ongoing action or project, by shifting from one operative category or set of categories to another, and by addressing categorial mis-hearings or misunderstandings. These practices exhibit highly systematic features that intersect with the main positions relative to a trouble source at which they can be deployed – in the same turn, next turn, or after the next turn. Repair in general, and specific types and sub-types of repair in particular, are not necessarily present in any and every stretch of interaction in the way some of the other 'generic orders of organization' for talk-in-interaction unavoidably are (e.g., action formation and ascription, word selection, turn-taking, and sequence organization). However, repair is ubiquitous enough to serve as a plentiful and readily identifiable source of 'collectables' that are visible at the "rich" (Edwards, 2006), "broken" (Jefferson, 2018) surface of social interaction. Examining what sorts of things participants treat as potential troubles (especially in self-initiated repair) and/or encounter as fully realized troubles (in all forms of repair), along with the ways participants contend with categorial matters ranging from the mundane and unproblematic to the morally fraught, thereby provides unique windows into participants' orientations to normative – including category-related – social arrangements. As such, we can appreciate that and how repair – like the other generic orders – stands in a mutually constitutive relationship with categories: repair provides places and practices for managing categorial matters, and category-related troubles serve as recurrent bases for using practices of repair.

9

MANAGING KNOWLEDGE, EXPERIENCE, AND ENTITLEMENT

9.0   Introduction

In a segment on the American news-comedy show *The Daily Show with Trevor Noah*, one of the show's correspondents Roy Wood Jr. visits Boston to ask residents, "Is Boston racist?" In a discussion of the segment for a *Beyond the Scenes from the Daily Show* podcast (published August 2, 2022), Wood Jr. talks with the segment's producer, CJ Hunt, about making it. The broadcast segment included parts of Wood Jr.'s interviews with two groups of people: representatives from anti-racist organizations familiar with the city's history of racial exclusion and oppression and 'person-on-the-street' interviews with white residents. In the podcast, Wood Jr. and Hunt highlight and replay a series of responses from white interviewees responding to the Wood Jr.'s focal query, "Is Boston racist?" While all the interviewees included in the series claim that Boston is not racist, the third interviewee's response conveys the strongest or most emphatic assertion in this regard: "I don't think of Boston as a racist city at all." This response sets up the sequence that becomes the main target of Wood Jr. and Hunt's subsequent ire and commentary: Wood Jr. asks, "How do you know?" and the interviewee responds, "I don't feel it."

The comedic impact of the sequence emerges from the discrepancy between the relevance of race raised by Wood JR.'s queries and the interviewees' responses. Thus, in asking this question, Wood Jr. and Hunt challenge the interviewee, and the overhearing listeners, to consider: how did white interviewees come to make such readily challengeable assertions? Is there more to say about this interview than highlighting the evident racial privilege in these interviewees' responses? An introduction and overview to the sub-field

DOI: 10.4324/9781003120599-10

of CA known as 'epistemics' offers the basis for a better understanding of how such blindness can come to be produced in interaction.

Epistemics has a special connection to the ways that persons embody or orient to the relevance of categories and categorization of self and other. CA researches have established that, across settings and occasions, "participants in interaction display sensitivity to what they have rights to know and say relative to their co-participants" (Raymond & Heritage, 2006, p. 680; also see Drew, 1991; Goodwin & Goodwin, 1987; Kamio, 1997; Stivers, 2005). As a consequence, the resources through which participants patrol and defend their differential access to territories of knowledge are woven into the very fabric of social interaction. Indeed, two of the most basic grammatical forms used to compose utterances – declaratives and interrogatives – are primarily distinguished by the distinct ways that they index the relative epistemic rights of speaker and recipient, and speakers are accountable for using them in ways that are sensitive to the sequential positioning of the actions conveyed by them (Heritage, 2012b; Heritage & Raymond, 2012; Raymond, 2010). As a consequence, across a wide range of actions, persons cannot avoid taking a position regarding what they know relative to their co-participants by virtue of the identities and experiences associated with specific domains of knowledge (Heritage, 2012b; Raymond & Heritage, 2006). The ubiquity with which participants manage their relative epistemic rights in composing and conducting courses of action, then, provides analysts with a set of methods for grounding how participants' orientations to categories and category membership come to be consequential for the ways that they conduct encounters. Rather than beginning with identities and sifting through 'haystacks' (cf. van Dijk, 1987, p. 119), one can instead identify "various practices of speaking through which participants can make relative access to knowledge and information relevant, and then demonstrate how those practices can be used to evoke the relevance of a specific identity" (Raymond & Heritage, 2006, p. 680).

In this respect, the organization of epistemics opens a window onto what Schegloff (1991, p. 48) called "the interaction social structure nexus" by identifying the elementary linguistic and sequential practices through which persons manage their differential rights to knowledge in composing actions (also see our discussion of action formation in Chapter 4: Forming and Making Sense of Actions). For example, as Raymond and Heritage (2006, p. 700) observe,

By looking at how persons manage the rights and responsibilities of identities – the territories of ownership and accountability that are partly constitutive of how identities are sustained *as identities* – we are witnessing a set of resources through which identities get made relevant and consequential in particular episodes of interaction. In this respect, [such analyses explicate] how an identity gets formed up as a personal characteristic of a speaker, how it comes to have interactional significance and is made real in a situated encounter, and how, ultimately, through repetition and reproduction, it comes to be sustained as an enduring feature of a person.

These observations suggest that participants' use of and reliance on the practices that comprise the organization of epistemics provide a set of locally organized methods for composing sequentially organized actions that reveal participants' orientations to how they can be categorized in the encounter. In short, examining participants' management of epistemic issues provides analysts with a set of resources for uncovering how participants orient to categorial matters at the level of action sequencing (also see Chapter 7: Organizing Sequences of Action).

This chapter builds on these observations by reviewing the field of epistemics and its relation to categorial phenomena. We begin in Section 9.1 by introducing the domain of epistemics, using an analysis of an extended series of assessment sequences to examine how participants orient to their relative rights to evaluate a state of affairs as emerging from the categories they treat as relevant and consequential for this domain. In Section 9.2, we track how analyses of epistemics developed to encompass the much broader range of sequence types initiated by interrogatives and declaratives, using these advances to introduce other basic resources participants, and thus analysts, can draw upon in conducting action sequences, including epistemic status and stance and their interaction. Specifically, in Sections 9.2.1–9.2.3 we develop observations regarding the distinctive relevancies associated with using declaratives versus interrogatives to initiate sequences, using these analyses to develop the notion of category-bound domains of knowledge. Finally, in Section 9.3, we revisit the segment from *The Daily Show with Trevor Noah* introduced earlier, before concluding the chapter in Section 9.4.

9.1 Action types, epistemics, and categories

The relevance of epistemics for talk-in-interaction, and for participants' orientations to linkages between membership categorization and the conduct of sequences of action specifically, can be most directly observed in assessment sequences – that is, on occasions where the participants jointly evaluate some known-in-common state of affairs, and thus establish whether they agree with one another about them. As Heritage and Raymond (2005) observe, even within sequences of action designed to achieve agreement (which is preferred – see Chapter 7: Organizing Sequences of Action) participants can become involved in complex negotiations concerning the management of their relative rights to knowledge and information. These negotiations emerge because (i) persons treat their relative access to the state of affairs being evaluated as relevant for the matter of 'who is agreeing with whom?' (also see Schegloff,

1996), and (ii) offering a first assessment carries an implied claim that the speaker has primary rights to evaluate the matter assessed.

The fundamental association between the sequential position of an assessment and the epistemic claims implied by that positioning are reflected in "the distribution of practices in first and second position, the frequency of their deployment in each of these positions, and the putative rights of the speakers who deploy them in these positions" (Raymond & Heritage, 2006, p. 685). Specifically, as illustrated in Table 9.1,

> (i) The distribution of practices described in Heritage and Raymond (2005) suggests a recurrent social need to compensate for the primary claims of first position and the secondary claims of second position. . . . Practices for downgrading claimed rights to assess cluster in first position, while practices for upgrading claims cluster in second position. (ii) The deployment of these practices reflects speakers' recurrent need to manage the same contingency: First position assessments are rarely upgraded in the several hundred ordinary conversations examined, but they are quite commonly downgraded; similarly, second position assessments are rarely downgraded, but they are quite commonly upgraded (Raymond & Heritage, 2006, pp. 684–685).

Given the strong linkages between epistemics and category membership noted previously, it may be tempting to think that, for participants, establishing the categories relevant for a course of action and the state of affairs evaluated over its course would provide ready-made solutions regarding how to design and sequentially position their actions. As it happens, however, the type of action being conducted and the relative epistemic rights that may be associated with category membership give rise to countervailing contingencies that must be managed over the action's course. For example, in sequences of action preoccupied with agreement, participants with lesser socio-epistemic rights cannot simply defer to persons with greater socio-epistemic rights without risking the appearance that they are merely going along with the other

TABLE 9.1 Resources for marking epistemic authority/subordination in assessment sequences

	First position	*Second position*
Unmarked	[Declaratives]	[Declaratives]
Downgraded	Evidentials	
	[Assessment]+ [Tag Question]	
	Downgraded-"firstness"	
Upgraded	Negative Interrogatives	[Confirmation] + [Agreement]
		[Oh] + [Assessment]
		[Assessment]+ [Tag Question]
		Negative Interrogatives

speakers' claims rather than genuinely agreeing with them. We illustrate this basic observation by tracking how two friends discuss a known-in-common state of affairs, how they manage their relative rights to know about that state of affairs across a range of sequences of action, and how they manage the associated troubles that arise over the course of the exchange.

9.1.2   Agreement and category bound rights to knowledge: the case of 'owning' grandchildren

The stretch of talk shown in Extract 9.1 was recorded in Britain in the 1980s as part of a larger corpus of phone calls. The conversation was initiated (and recorded) by Jenny, who is returning the call of her friend, Vera, who had called Jenny earlier in the day. As Raymond and Heritage (2006, p. 681) note,

> The conversation directly follows, and largely focuses on, a visit by Vera's married son, daughter-in-law, and grandchildren. When the family arrived at Vera's house after a long car drive, the intervention of a neighbor recruited by Vera directed them to Jenny's house, where they had a cup of tea and waited for Vera to return.

Much of the initial conversation between Vera and Jenny focuses on appreciating Vera's grandchildren, which is initiated by her apology to Jenny (line 05) for the obligations associated with hosting her family. Jenny rejects the need for an apology, and occasions the ensuing discussion of Vera's family, and their joint evaluations of Vera's two grandsons, by casting Vera's family's visit as "luvly" and a "nice surpri:ze" (line 07). Evidently, by virtue of her status as the grandmother of the two children, Vera has primary epistemic rights to evaluate the children, despite Jenny's direct observation of the children in her own home prior to Vera's arrival. For the purposes of this chapter, we are particularly interested in how,

> [a]cross this extended stretch of talk, the participants' management of their different epistemic rights complicates the consensus that both parties are otherwise striving for. In the very process of trying to agree with each other, while managing the conflicting exigencies of establishing the independent basis for their assessments and simultaneously respecting their different rights to assess Vera's family, Jenny and Vera become entangled in a struggle regarding Vera's primary epistemic rights to assess her own grandchildren. (Raymond & Heritage, 2006, p. 699–700)

An analysis of the entire exchange between Jenny and Vera can be found in Raymond and Heritage (2006). In this chapter, we will focus on Jenny's assessment of one of Vera's grandchildren as a "bri:ght little boy:" in line 22.

Extract 9.1 Two friends [Rahmen 14, pg. 2]

```
01   VER:    =[Yes,
02   JEN:    =[eeYe:s::[Mm hm,
03   VER:     [Yes.
04   JEN:    Oh[: ( ).
05   VER:     [I'm sorry yih hahd th'm all o[n you[J e n n y]like that]
06   JEN:                                     [.hhh[↑Oh don't]b e sill]y=
07   JEN:    =No: thaht wz luvly it wz a nice surpri[:ze
08   VER:                                          [Yeh[s ( )
09   JEN:                                              [Ahn' they look
10           so well.the chilreh theh go:hrg[iss ahrn't they]
11   VER:                                   [D'you know theh-]
12   VER:    He wz- they w'rr ez good ez go:ld,
13                (.)
14   JEN:    Yes:[:
15   VER:        [Yihknow ah'v hehrd such bad repo:hrts.about them.
16   JEN:    Oh:: they w'sm[ashi:ng.]
17   VER:                  [ Ah::::n]d eh- they w'good heah they
18           pla:yed yihkno:w,
19   JEN:    Ah::[:?
20   VER:        [ehr: they readjer comics:'n evrythink yihkn[o:w
21   JEN:                                                    [Yeh: w'l
22           I think he's a bri:ght little boy: u[h:m
23   VER:                                        [I: do=
24   JEN:    =l[ittle Ja]:[:m e s,]uh [Pau:l.  yes.]
25   VER:      [ Pau:l, ] [ mm-  m]mm [P a u : : l,]
26   JEN:    Mm:.[Yes.
27   VER:        [Yes.
28                (0.3)
29   VER:    [Yes (            )]
30   JEN:    [Yeh James's a little] divil ihhh ↑heh heh
31   VER:    [That-
32   JEN:    [.huh .hh[h He:-
33   VER:    [James is a little buugger[isn'e.
34   JEN:                              [Yeh- Yeah
35   JEN:    =[(     ) evrythi]ng
36   VER:    =[Mindju eez good]Jenny, 'e wz mischievous but w-'e wz good.
37   JEN:    Oo 'e wz beautiful heahr[wuuz↑n't'ee.=
38   VER:                            [↓Yes
39   JEN:    ='E[wz verry well be[he:ved.
40   VER:       [@Yes.           ['E wz well behaved he:uh[too:.
41   JEN:                                                 [Ye:s they're
42           lovely little boy:s.
43   VER:    Ye::[s,
44   JEN:        [Mm[I: bet they proud o:f the fahm'ly.=
45   VER:           [Ye:s.
46   JEN:    =They're[a luvly fahmily now ah'n't[they.
47   VER:           [ Mm:._              [They ahr: ye[s.
48   JEN:                                               [eeYe[s::,
49   VER:                                                    [Yes,
50   JEN:    'N: all they need now is a little guhrl tih complete i:t.
```

As Raymond and Heritage (2006, pp. 698–699) observe,

Despite these efforts to agree with Vera, however, Jenny's assessment occasions some troubles of its own. In her effort to join with Vera in rebutting the *bad reports* of the children, Jenny's assessment eventuates in a contamination of their agreement by grounding the rebuttal in her own experiences of their behavior. We can notice that in line [17], Vera abandons an *and*-projected continuation of her talk at line [15] in favor of mobilizing a 'counter-agreement' – *they were good here* – that explicitly asserts (with *here*) her own home as the epistemic basis for her claims. Vera's conduct strongly suggests that, in the face of Jenny's *oh*-prefaced assessment, the task of asserting her epistemic rights in the matter of assessing the grandchildren's conduct has assumed real priority.

Subsequently in this sequence, following the flurry of negative evaluations of the children begun by Jenny (discussed above), the issue of managing epistemically aligned, full-bodied agreement explicitly reemerges at line [36]. Vera says, *mind you he was good Jenny, he was mischievous, but he was good*. By prefacing her assessment with *mind you* Vera initiates a reversal of the terms in which James is to be assessed from the general and negative evaluations (e.g., as in *little devil* and *little bugger* in lines [30 and 33]) to a particularized and positive evaluation based in her immediate experience of his behavior. Indeed, two features of Vera's turn at line [36] – the *mind you* preface and the address term *Jenny* – position this assessment as markedly contrastive with the vision of James that Jenny has so far collaborated in constructing. This environment poses special challenges for Jenny on two grounds. First, she must now find a way of credibly reversing her evaluation of James, a child she has just referred to as a *little devil*. Second, she must accomplish this in second position while avoiding the appearance of a merely "reactive" agreement, given her relatively diminished rights to assess the boy. In effect, Jenny must find a way of reversing the position she has just taken without appearing to be simply going along with Vera.

Jenny formats her new assessment in line 37 to address just these issues: *Oo he was beautiful here wasn't he*. Three features of her turn are critical. First, by *oh*-prefacing her assessment Jenny asserts independent access to the child's behavior – a stance that is further indexed by her use of the word *here*, which markedly invokes her personal access to the children's behavior at her own home, as the basis for her revised position. Second, through the tag question Jenny positions what is, in real time, an agreeing responsive assessment as a 'first position' assessment to be itself agreed with by Vera. While these features of Jenny's turn manage to avoid the appearance of mere 'reactivity,' her subsequent assessment of the child's conduct – *He wz very well beha:ved* – backs off from the raw assertiveness of that position. Nonetheless, after acknowledging Jenny's assessments with *Yes* (lines [40 and 43]), Vera renews her earlier assessment with a further agreement (*'E wz well behaved he:re too:*) that reasserts her own experience of the children as a further and final basis for the conclusion they are converging upon. In this sequence, then, while the parties are working to achieve full agreement about the behavior of the children, they are also discomforted by how that agreement is to be managed, and which account will have epistemic priority as the basis for the conclusions they are jointly reaching. Jenny is attempting to establish the independent basis for her assessments so as to achieve full agreement, and thereby to avoid the appearance of mere reactivity. Vera, on the other hand, is careful to police the boundaries of her knowledge rights by asserting her epistemic priority as the children's grandparent.

As this exchange underscores, simply knowing which party has primary epistemic rights regarding a state of affairs does not resolve the matter of how they will come to agreement about it. Across the exchange, the manner in which both parties deploy resources for managing epistemic primacy and subordination reflects what appears to be a basic dilemma of self-other relations. As Raymond and Heritage (2006, p. 701) note,

> In managing her discussion with Vera, Jenny must both manage her independent access to the matters being assessed and avoid intervening too far into the "territorial preserves" (Goffman, 2017 [1971]; Heritage & Raymond, 2005) – territories of feelings, knowledge, and ownership – that Vera evidently defends as her own.
>
> This dilemma appears to be a direct product of the participants' management of their intersubjective grasp of the world, the relationship they build with each other based on that intersubjective grasp, and their simultaneous insistence on the independence of their access to the events under discussion. In this respect, the struggles evident in Vera and Jenny's interaction are an instance of what we might term the "distance-involvement" dilemma involved in constructing intimate self-other relations generally. In acts of affiliation, persons must manage the twin risks of appearing disengaged from the affairs of the other, or appearing over-involved with and even appropriating them. Given the fundamental character of this dilemma, it should not be surprising that we can identify a range of linguistic and sequential resources for managing epistemic priority and subordination. It is notable, however, that such resources, which are highly general, can nevertheless be used as materials in the fabrication of identities of exquisite specificity and particularity.

As the single case analysis in Extract 9.1 demonstrates, when persons evaluate states of affairs, they cannot avoid having to contend with the fundamental connection between the sequential positioning of their utterances, the assertions of epistemic rights associated with this positioning, and the grammatical and other linguistic resources used to compose their assessments. By virtue of these fundamental connections, persons cannot avoid having to manage their relative epistemic rights in composing their contributions. But of course, the very fact that knowledge is socially distributed – that some persons know things that other persons don't know – can be basis for initiating sequences of actions via practices associated with asking and telling. As Raymond (2018, p. 63) notes, "the systematic relevance of epistemics for interaction" can be appreciated

> if we consider that the contrasting methods that declaratives (which in their default usage convey information) and interrogatives (which in their default usage request it) provide for composing utterances occur in every language subject to systematic investigation thus far (Dryer, 2013). In this regard, these forms must be among the most basic – and ubiquitous – procedural building blocks of (sequence-initiating) actions available to speakers (see Heritage, 2012a, 2018; Raymond & Heritage, 2013; Schegloff, 2007b, among others).

In Section 9.2 we turn to consider how the use of declaratives and interrogatives to compose and conduct sequences of actions can also therefore be analysed to reveal participants' orientations to categories and category membership (also see our discussion of category-based entitlements and obligations in Chapter 2: Approaching Membership Categorization).

9.2   Epistemic status and stance: initiating sequences via telling versus asking

The ubiquity of participants' orientations to the relevance and consequentiality of epistemics, and its association with categorial phenomena, can be appreciated if we consider how it is associated with the most common bases for initiating courses of action: asking and telling. As a backdrop to considering such matters, however, we first need to review how issues of action formation and ascription (also see Chapter 4: Forming and Making Sense of Actions) are linked to participants' relative rights to knowledge regarding the state of affairs being discussed. As Heritage (2012a, 2012b, 2013) shows, and Raymond (2018, p. 64, emphasis in original) summarizes, in composing and making sense of actions participants attend to:

- *Epistemic status*: Speakers producing FPPs for recipients must take into account their relative access to, and/or rights to know about, the states of affairs relevant for the matters formulated in it. As Heritage (2012b, p. 6) observes, persons, by virtue of their social relationships, experiences and the like, 'occupy different positions on an epistemic gradient (more knowledgeable [K+] or less knowledgeable [K–]), which itself may vary in slope from shallow to deep.'

- *Epistemic stance*: Speakers composing a wide range of FPPs select one of the two basic alternative grammatical forms that adopt contrasting *epistemic stances*: declaratives, which in their default usage *assert* information, and interrogatives, which in their default usage *request* information. In addition, speakers can draw on a range of lexical and grammatical resources (including tag questions) to vary the *epistemic gradient* enacted by these forms (see Heritage, 2012b; Heritage & Raymond, 2012).

- *Epistemic status and stance interact* in shaping the relevancies set in motion by an FPP composed using a declarative or interrogative. There is a preference for a congruent relationship between epistemic status and stance: in most cases, speakers with a K– status pose interrogatives (which request information) and persons with a K+ status use declaratives (which convey information); however, it is possible for speakers to deploy forms that are incongruent with their epistemic status. Where there is a mismatch between epistemic status and stance, the speaker's status 'trumps' the default orientation of the grammatical form, so that declaratives produced by K– speakers will be heard to request information, and interrogatives produced by K+ speakers will be heard to either assert information (when speakers use negative syntax) or to pose 'exam' questions when speakers use positive syntax) (Heritage, 2012b, 2013).

The elements of this framework suggest a number of features of the larger forms of social organization – particularly action sequencing (also see Chapter 7: Organizing Sequences of Action) – of which they are a part. As Raymond (2018, pp. 65–66, emphasis in original) notes:

- First, because the forms speakers use have a *default directional orientation* (i.e., as requesting or asserting information) that can be reversed, their use unavoidably indexes their speaker's epistemic status. Or, put differently, because the default directional valence of declaratives and interrogatives can be reversed by an FPP speaker's epistemic status, *FPP speakers must take into account their relative epistemic status in composing actions* and *responding speakers must track their relative epistemic status as a basis for 'solving' the possible alternative sequential import of those FPPs*. In addition, speakers can use the ways that epistemic status and stance interact to invoke specific contexts for the sequences they initiate (e.g., as in the case of 'exam questions') or alter or inflect the relevancies their FPPs set in motion (e.g., as in the case of K+ speakers using interrogatives to assert information).

- Second, the basic features of these resources for composing FPP actions also point to an underlying basis for *initiating* sequences of action: discrepancies between the participants' relative knowledge can be a basis for producing FPPs/initiating sequences of actions (Heritage, 2012a).
- Third, given the import of the participants' relative epistemic status at the inception of such sequences – as a basis for initiating a sequence and for selecting the relevant practice for implementing the FPP that will do so – it should not be a surprise that epistemics also features in the overall structural organization of these courses of action. As Heritage (2012a) observes, a base sequence (Schegloff, 2007b) can be subject to pre-expansion (e.g., to establish what a recipient knows; Terasaki, 1976/2004) and post-expansion via the introduction of additional increments of information. Furthermore, exhausting or resolving (in various ways) the discrepancy between what a K– and K+ speaker knows can be a basis for bringing a sequence to a possible completion.

Given the generic or ubiquitous character of these components and features we can appreciate how they have a systematic import across a range of sequence types, activities, and institutional settings. Indeed, the basic resources participants use to compose and make sense of utterances as actions in this framework provide a recurrent method by which they also make relevant or orient to the various possible ways that they can be categorized. Although participants use such generic resources to manage recurrent interactional contingencies, in any specific case they "can nevertheless be used as materials in the fabrication of identities of exquisite specificity and particularity" (Raymond & Heritage, 2006, p. 701).

Having focused on categorial features of the matter of establishing agreement regarding a known-in-common state of affairs in Extract 9.1, in the following sections we explicate connections between knowledge, categories, and actions across two other basic activities types: sequences initiated via K+ speakers (using declaratives) and K– speakers (using interrogatives), focusing on variations in the sequential trajectories that emerge from participants' orientations to the categories made relevant by sequence initiating actions. In doing so, we show how participants' orientations to categories can be explicated via examination of their routine uses of epistemic resources, as well as how these basic practices can be systematically modified to reveal or expose specialized inferential frameworks, or the use of stereotypes associated with "-isms." In this way, we show how analysts can examine participants' uses of epistemic practices to uncover members' orientations to aspects of social structure across a range of contexts, and how these are made visible in context-specific adaptations of this context-free form of the organization of interaction. As Drew (2018, p. 183) notes, epistemics is most evident in the recipient design of turns at talk; again, a speaker's orientation to the other and to the other's identity includes their relative epistemic statuses, and is manifest in the speaker's epistemic stance towards the other.

As we will show in the following sections, participants orient to systematic connections between categories and bodies or domains of knowledge – a phenomenon we will call '*category-bound knowledge*' to capture the ways in which demonstrable or claimed familiarity with a body of knowledge can be associated with category membership, and vice-versa. Given this connection, we can observe that just how participants use epistemic status and stance to compose and make sense of actions regarding some state of affairs provides analysts with systematic ways of observing their otherwise tacit orientations to the ways they and their recipients can be categorized.

9.2.1   K+ initiated actions

Sacks's (1992) discussion of storytelling included what may seem like an obvious rule, "Don't tell others what you figure they already know" (see Schegloff, 1992b, p. xv), as a basis for raising and discussing the recurrent need for category-based exemptions to it. As Sacks (1992) notes, given category-based obligations and entitlements that prioritize sharing news with spouses before sharing it with others, without such an exemption, any occasion in which friends and their spouses gather would pose challenges to the sharing of any stories at all. One way that K+ speakers can manage this when delivering news to others is by directing their tellings to co-present recipients who are uninformed (or have a K– status). Given the connections between turn-design, action formation, and categorization discussed in Chapter 4: Forming and Making Sense of Actions, analysts can inspect both who a speaker selects as a K– recipient of their news, and how the news they convey is formed as relevant for that recipient in particular, as a method for establishing how the speaker is tacitly categorizing the recipient. To explore these connections between membership categorization and news tellings, we revisit an extract and analysis drawn from a classic paper that was crucial to the emergence of conversation analysis as a field: Charles Goodwin's (1979, p. 97) analysis of the "interactive construction of a sentence." As readers familiar with this paper may recall, Goodwin analyses an utterance, "I gave up smoking cigarettes one week ago today actually" (p. 98), produced by a speaker in the midst of a dinner table conversation among family and friends. As Goodwin (1979) shows, the sentence – as an utterance – is produced incrementally, with the speaker producing and adding specific segments to serially address a range of potential recipients. The focus of Goodwin's (1979) analysis was primarily devoted to establishing how speakers' use of the turn-taking system can be shown to shape the internal composition of a sentential TCU by attending to how it is composed for specific recipients who stand in different relations to the matters conveyed in it. Goodwin (1979) emphasizes how the utterance-in-progress is designed for these varied recipients by attending to what they can be presumed to know about the matter being announced. For the present purpose, we invert this focus, using an analysis of the practices and organization of epistemics to uncover how the speaker's in-progress adjustments reveal his orientation to relevancies associated with the different ways his possible recipients can be categorized.

The participants in this encounter are John and Beth, a married couple who are hosting the meal for their friends Don and Ann, who are also married. Early in the dinner, at a possible sequence boundary, John initiates a new sequence, telling his friend Don about a recent life change he made, "I gave up smoking cigarettes" (line 03).

```
Extract 9.2: Chinese Dinner (from Goodwin, 1979)
01   JER: °(          ),
02   DON: ((clears throa[t ))     ]
03   JOH:               [I gave,] I gave up smoking cigarettes::.=
04   DON: =Yea:h,
05   JOH: 1-uh: one-one week[ago t'da:y. acshlly,
06   DO?:                   [°(Y-ehhh)
07   ANN: Rilly? en y'quit fer good?
08   JOH: Yu[p hh
09   BET:   [Mhm?
10             (0.5)
11   ANN: Wuhduz it[feel like.
12   JOH:          [Fer all times.
13             (0.3)
14   ANN: hh hih-hih-huh-hnh=
```

Beginning in line 02, John turns (his head and eyes) towards Don, and, following a restart (line 03) that solicits Don's reciprocal gaze (Goodwin, 1979), conveys the news that he has quit smoking. John evidently selects Don as a recipient by virtue of his co-membership with Jon in the category, 'friend,' which here attends to two relevancies associated with the latter's categorization in these terms: this is the first occasion on which John has seen Don since quitting, thereby positioning Don as having a K– epistemic status relative to John and distinguishing Don from others at the table (especially Beth, John's wife) who already know John's news. Don is more than merely uninformed, however. The change John reports is specifically relevant for Don as a friend, both as an achievement to be acknowledged, encouraged, or even possibly celebrated, but also because the latter might otherwise engage in actions (e.g., offering a cigarette or an occasion for one) premised on the understanding that he still smokes, and thereby complicate or undermine John's ongoing effort to quit. In this regard, by conveying this news to Don on a first possible occasion for doing so, John's formation of the utterance as announcement reflects how it has been designed by reference to Don's categorization as John's friend, and not for his wife, Beth. Goodwin (1979, pp. 115–116) grounds his claims in this regard by drawing on Sacks's observations that linking sharing news (or "tellables") with membership categories for which they have a distinct relevance:

> Sacks (10–19–71) notes that tellables and news of various types are organized so that one should tell particular others about some piece of news at the first opportunity. . . . For spouses the class of events that one member of the couple should tell the other is extremely large, and in fact if a spouse tells others some piece of news that he could have told his partner but didn't, this can constitute grounds for complaint. . . . Sack's analysis makes explicit some of the structures enabling all participants in the present data to legitimately see that Beth should know that John has given up smoking cigarettes. This analysis also provides a systematic basis for the co-presence of knowing and unknowing recipients.

Despite John having directed this news to a friend[1] in this way, Don's uptake is rather tepid (line 04). While John could have left matters there, he instead

---

1 As suggested in Sacks's work on tellables (quoted by Goodwin), category membership can entail obligations that make relevant sharing tellables. Tellings that invoke the relevance of those obligations can be differentiated from locally occasioned mentions of a matter that turn out to be news. For example, a person can mention to their friend that they quit smoking as a way of explaining their mood. While this may be news to the recipient who is also a friend, its telling has not been formed up as an announcement that conveys news for a friend, with consequences for how it comes to be appreciated. In the following extract, Emma has called Barbara for help after her husband, Bud, has left her – a state of affairs that dominates the call, having an evident overarching significance for virtually every sequence in it. In accounting for Bud's departure, Emma notes that she "gets on his nerves," and mentions that she quit smoking, apparently as an account for why this might be so (lines 01–02).

```
NBIV.7 (from Drew, 2003)
01  Emm:  I: GET ON HIS NER:VES I gi-
02        I:'ve quit s:mokin ↓yihknow en evryth*ing hh
03              (0.7)
04  Bar:  Well wenjih stop tha*:t.
05  Emm:  THE DAY YOU LE:FT.h
06              (0.6)
07  Bar:  Left whe:re.
08  Emm:  From here in September=
09  Bar:  =e-How m'ny cigarettes yih had.
10              (0.5)
11  Emm:  ↑↑NOGH:NE.
12  Bar:  Oh rea↑lly?
13  Emm:  NO:.
```

pursues a more robust appreciation of his news from a different recipient: in line 05, John turns to Beth (his wife) and refashions his in-progress utterance to register the current occasion as an anniversary of his effort ("one week ago today"). Although Goodwin (1979) does not use the terminology of membership categorization, his analysis establishes that John's invocation of an anniversary reflects the relevance and procedural consequentiality of Beth's status as John's wife or partner. As Goodwin (1979, p. 101) notes,

> An anniversary is constructed via the lamination of events at two separate moments in time, an original event which becomes the object of celebration, and the anniversary itself. The two are related by the occurrence of some regular period of time between them. . . . An anniversary is an appropriate object to call to the attention of someone who shared experience of the event celebrated by it with the speaker. More precisely, interest in the anniversary is contingent upon interest in the event being celebrated by it.

By virtue of her status as John's partner or wife, Beth will have a "shared experience of the event celebrated" by the anniversary and thus may also have an interest in celebrating the achievement conveyed by the completion of this unit of time. Moreover, while Beth may know that John has quit smoking, she may not have registered that this is the one-week anniversary of the event. In this way, John's revised utterance is now designed for Beth as a possible K– recipient of the telling – or at least as a person who could join him in celebrating 'as if' this were news, as a method for instructing others how they might also respond (also see our discussion later of Goffman's observations on 'shills'). Indeed, such minor personal 'anniversaries' may have little relevance for persons other than those occupying categories that virtually oblige them to align as possible celebrants of the teller's news, such as parents and partners. As it happens, as John produces and completes this increment, he finds that

```
14                    (.)
15  Bar:  ↑Very ↑goo↓*:d.
16  Emm:  VERY good.=
17  Emm:  =.hhh ↑WILL YOU ↓AH'LL k- uhAh'll CALL [YIH D U H]MORROW 't=
```

The 'bad news' sequential context in which this possibly good news has been conveyed (also see Maynard, 2003) poses challenges for how Barbara can take it up, as suggested by the silence in line 03. We can note, then, that Barbara uses a series of questions about Emma's quitting (lines 04, 07, 09, and 12) to establish a context in which Emma's achievement can be appreciated and celebrated (lines 15–16) before Emma immediately redirects their talk to her request for Barbara's help (line 17). Here, although Barbara ultimately responds as a friend to Emma's news that she quit smoking (e.g., by celebrating it, line 15), Emma's initial mention of this fact was not conveyed as an announcement to a friend but instead as a locally occasioned justification for her marital troubles and specifically Bud's frustration with her.

Beth has not returned his eye gaze and instead remains engaged in the task of eating, suggesting that she is unavailable as a possible responding recipient.

Finding Beth thus preoccupied, John redirects the utterance to Ann, the one adult at the table who remains a possible K– recipient of his news. In adding, "actually" John again reshapes the emerging meaning of his utterance for a third time, *precisely because the anniversary is not relevant for her*. As Goodwin (1979, p. 111) notes,

> Rather than being asked to recognize the anniversary the recipient is told that in fact the event being marked by it did occur a week ago. The addition of "acshilly" thus again reconstructs the emerging meaning of John's sentence so that once more it becomes appropriate to its recipient of the moment.

Although Goodwin's classic analysis focuses on how a turn comes to be interactively constructed over its course, the epistemic phenomena he analyses in doing so nevertheless reveal how membership categorization constitutes a key resource for understanding how participants manage pervasive matters of recipient design. Across the incremental production of this news, John refashions his utterance on the fly, shaping it to index the epistemic status associated with how each person he selects (via eye gaze) as a possible recipient can be categorized and the attendant forms of appreciation his news makes relevant for them. We can further note, then, that although actions such as informings may be composed to index category-bound entitlements and obligations that make a party an appropriate recipient of the telling, and thus the response it makes relevant, such actions can also be refashioned to take into account the relevancies associated with a recipient who is a member of a different category. In this respect, we can appreciate how the epistemic resources available for managing recipient design nevertheless offer speakers considerable latitude in shaping how they will be resolved in any specific circumstance. Conversely, because speakers must recurrently attend to matters of recipient design in forming their actions, the organization of epistemics provides analysts with resources for uncovering how participants orient to and use specific categories to compose and make sense of actions (also see our discussion of these matters in Chapter 4: Forming and Making Sense of Actions).

In Extract 9.2, we saw how participants' use of epistemic resources to compose and respond to actions relevant for the setting-based categories associated with the occasion. In Extract 9.3, we consider a more complicated encounter in which a non-serious or joking dispute emerges regarding what a recipient can be expected to know that is conducted, in part, by attending to how she might relevantly be categorized. This is an extract we previously examined in Chapter 3: Methodological Principles, Practices, and Challenges, as Extract 3.1. As we noted previously, this encounter is from a radio comedy quiz show featuring Olympic bobsledder Elana Meyers Taylor (EMT), hosts Peter Sagal (PS) and Bill Kurtis (BK), and guest participants Alzo Slade (AS), Negin

Farsad (NF), and Paula Poundstone (PP). The extract begins as Sagal transitions from interviewing Meyers Taylor to introducing the game she will be playing (lines 07–09), its rules, and the listener she will be playing on behalf of (lines 11–16), which entails collaborating commentary by Kurtis (lines 01–09 and 11–16). In elaborating the basis for the game, Sagal recalls Meyers Taylor's personal experience as an Olympic medalist (line 07) as the basis for proposing a quiz in which she will be asked questions about the musical genre, heavy metal. Meyers Taylor's laughing exclamation (line 10) regarding the proposed quiz conveys a lack of confidence in her prospects of success. Perhaps registering Meyer's Taylor trepidation, Slade produces an intervening action (see Lerner, 2019) to challenge the fairness of the game (line 18), briefly delaying its start. Our analysis tracks how the ensuing non-serious or joking dispute about the fairness of the game unfolds, focusing specifically on the participant's treatment of knowledge about heavy metal as category-bound knowledge.

```
Extract 9.3 [NPR, Wait Wait. . . Don't Tell Me, March 12,
2022]
01   PS: Well, Ela:na, we are de↑lighted to talk to you, we
02       have more questions but we have business to do, we
03       have a competition of our own, (.) Bill, (0.2) what
04       is the na:me of the ga:me?
05   BK: pt=.hh "You've Medalled all Right in:: (0.2) Death
06       Metal:."
07   PS: So, (.) we were ↑think↓ing, (.) Olympic medals, as
08       you well know, are famously quite heavy, so we
09       thought we'd ask you about (0.5) heavy metal.
10   EMT: O(h)h(h) boy! heh [heh!
11   PS:                    [>Answer two out of three questions
12       about< heavy metal bands and you'll win >our prize
13       for one of our listeners, the voice of anyone they
14       might choose for their voicemail.< .hh Bill who:: is
15       Elana Meyers playing for?
16   BK: Jason Ha:ll of Austin Texas.
17   PS: All::: righty then.
18   AS: I feel like this ain't right, Peter.
19   PS: Why- why is it not ri[ght?
20   AS:                      [This ain't right. ih- ((chuckle))
21       d'y- I mean, .hh £it's enough that the: Black woman is
22       already in[: bobsledding, now you gonna ask her£
23   EMT:          [°hhh huh huh huh°
24   AS: t[uh- tuh b(h)e- £tuh be knowledgeable about death=
25   EMT: [huh huh huh .hh
26   AS: =metal?£ [ hih   hih   hih   hih   hih   hih
27   PP:          ['Ts- I- I think it's- she's a shill.
28   AS: [hih hih hih hih .hhh
29   PP: [I think it's gonna turn out=
30       =[she knows a:ll:: abo[ut death metal.
```

```
31   NF:   [Yea:h:                    [(she doe[s) ↑that is her thing ( ).
32   EMT:                             [ uh      [ huh huh huh .hhh
33   PS:                                         [A(h)l(h)l r(h)ig(h)ht.
34   PS:   [.hh All right. We- we're gonna find out.
35   EMT:  [I don't know ab- bout that. (But) let's go.
36         (0.2)
37   PS:   He:re (.) is your first question.
```

As a preface to our analysis of the extract, it is worth recalling that the use of questions as part of a quiz differs from interviews insofar as it entails the use of so-called known information questions (Mehan, 1979) that position the speaker posing the query as having a K+ status (i.e., Sagal knows the answers to the questions he poses), which is then used to evaluate the response provided by the recipient, Meyers Taylor, as correct or incorrect. In this respect, even in the context of a light-hearted comedic show, the proposed quiz entails something different than asking Meyers Taylor interview questions about heavy metal, because Sagal's queries will establish a sequential environment in which the adequacy of her knowledge will be evaluated – and possibly used as a basis for further joking about her. We can note, then, that Slade composes his intervening action at line 18 using a turn-final address term that selects Sagal as its recipient, thereby positioning him as the relevant (K–) recipient for this news. Sagal, by inviting Slade to elaborate his objection (line 19), aligns as a K– recipient and, given the comedic underpinning of the show (which entails privileging possible-jokes over maintaining progressivity of the show's 'official' activities), positions himself as the butt of a possible joke by Slade, thus allowing Slade to elaborate his challenge in the clear.

Slade's ensuing turn is composed of two parts: a reduced repeat of the objection produced in overlap with the completion of Sagal's invitation (line 20) and an elaboration of the basis for the challenge (lines 21–22, 24, and 26), that is delayed by three separate restarts of the TCU. Notably, the first restart allows Slade to introduce a brief chuckle (line 20), thereby inviting others to treat what follows as joking or non-serious (Jefferson et al., 1987), a status that he thereby treats as requiring emphasis, perhaps to undercut the potentially serious-sounding repetition of his initial objection, "This ain't right." Moreover, the multiple restarts that follow (line 21) reveal Slade to be treating the projected joke/accusation as, in some way, delicate (also see Lerner, 2013). Through these design features, Slade treats the informing he goes on to produce as something his recipient may find problematic or objectionable, despite its evident design as a joke. He then underscores *his* treatment of it as non-serious by prefacing the punchline of the joking challenge with talk that is thoroughly interpolated with laughter (line 24), giving the appearance that he is almost struggling to produce the talk.

So, what is the joke? As we noted in our prior analysis of this extract, Slade uses common-sense knowledge about the incongruity between knowledge of heavy metal and Meyers Taylor's race, gender, and stage of life categories as resources for proposing the unfairness of the task she is facing. Moreover, Slade also evidently treats his co-membership in the racial category 'Black' as a basis for producing this joking challenge. However non-serious this challenge may be, it effectively turns the tables on the game Sagal has set up. While Sagal and the show's writers may have anticipated that the incongruity of asking a "Black woman" about heavy metal would provide opportunities for humour, Slade's challenge treats the game as entailing a kind of racial blindness that risks publicly humiliating Meyers Taylor. We note, for example, that although Sagal has aligned himself as a recipient of this informing, and Slade has prefaced the objection with chuckles and produced its punchline to invite laughter, Sagal is not hearable as one of the parties laughing at its possible completion, as only Meyers Taylor and Slade do so.

In overlap with Slade's and Meyers Taylor's laughter, Poundstone intervenes to offer a possible defence of Sagal – that is, a basis on which the game may not be unfair in the way that Slade has jokingly alleged it is (line 27). Poundstone accomplishes this by producing a further K+ initiated informing (similarly positioning Sagal, Slade, and others as K– recipients) that proposes a possible resolution of the apparent discrepancy between Sagal's assumption that is fair to ask Meyers Taylor questions about heavy metal music and Slade's assertions that it is not. Competing in overlap with the laughter (also see Schegloff, 2000a), Poundstone produces an utterance that starts as an apparent assertion (with a version of "it's" in line 27), which she later brings to completion as an assertion that Meyers Taylor "knows all about death metal" (line 30). Poundstone initiates same-turn repair (also see Chapter 8: Managing Troubles in Speaking, Hearing and Understanding), to initially produce a more mitigated form of disagreement (line 27, "I think it's"), which she also abandons in favour of an altogether different sort of assertion: "she's a shill" (line 27). Poundstone then unpacks the basis for her assertion: "I think it's gonna turn out she knows a:ll:: about death metal" (lines 29–30), thus completing the utterance she abandoned in line 27.

While there is much to say about Poundstone's intervention, we make two main observations here. First, Poundstone begins, and then abandons, an assertion about what she "thinks" (and thus what she could reasonably claim to believe or know) about Meyers Taylor in favour of making an alternative joking assertion, "she's a shill." As a consequence of these multiple repairs, Poundstone's subsequent claims that Meyers Taylor "knows all about death metal" emerges from, and is framed by, her invocation of an entirely different (setting-based) category, "shill," thereby also invoking the relevance of her own setting-based category on the show. In this way, Poundstone avoids directly challenging Slade's claims about what Meyers Taylor might know on the basis of their shared membership in the racial category 'Black,' suggesting Poundstone's orientation to troubles that might arise from any action that highlighted the relevance of her own membership in the contrasting racial category, 'white.'

Second, we note that "shill" is an activity-specific category that provides an entirely different basis for judging the encounter as 'unfair.' In this regard, Poundstone's joking claim of Meyers Taylor's membership in this category exploits a discrepancy between what the party *claims* to know about some state of affairs (and thus what others may also take for granted about them) and their *actual* epistemic status. As Goffman (1959, p. 146) observes, "A shill is someone who acts as though he [sic] were an ordinary member of the audience but is in fact in league with the performers." In casting Meyers Taylor as a "shill," then, Poundstone is proposing she is more informed than Slade has presumed, and thus instead of claiming Meyers Taylor *shouldn't be expected to know* about heavy metal (as Slade does), Poundstone claims Sagal has already established that she *does know* about it. Thus, instead of Sagal posing questions that Meyers Taylor can't possibly answer (as claimed by Slade) – which thereby casts the quiz as a vehicle for her public humiliation – Poundstone proposes that Sagal will be posing questions that he *knows* Meyers Taylor can answer, raising questions about whether this is a quiz at all.

Poundstone's subsequent elaboration of this claim attempts to underscore that she is not accusing Meyers Taylor of engaging in fraud. Instead, her claim that Meyers Taylor knows "all about death metal" points to the ubiquitous and routine character of such epistemic performances in everyday life. As Goffman (1959, pp. 146–147; emphasis added) observes,

> We must not take the view that shills are found only in non-respectable performances. . . . For example, at informal conversational gatherings, it is common for a wife to look interested when her husband tells an anecdote and to feed him appropriate leads and cues, *although in fact she has heard the anecdote many times and knows that the show her husband is making of telling something for the first time is only a show.* A shill, then, is someone who appears to be just another unsophisticated member of the audience and who uses his [sic] unapparent sophistication in the interests of the performing team.

Although Goffman did draw on what we now know about links between the organization of epistemics and action formation to describe how shills perform in everyday life, we can nevertheless note that 'shill,' as a category (and by extension other categories in the collection it is from, e.g., a 'mark'), evidently exploits participants' reliance on the inferred or presumed epistemic status of others in producing and conducting action sequences with others that may not know, or only partly know (i.e., just about everyone). In the context of the quiz, working successfully as a shill entails a person claiming to have an as-yet-unknown epistemic status regarding the matters formulated in the quiz's questions (with their actual epistemic status to be revealed in their responses and the quiz organizer's evaluations of their adequacy), when they in fact have a K+ epistemic status regarding those affairs. We can further note, then, that Poundstone's claims do not disregard the relevance of Meyer's Taylor's categorization as Black woman and the treatment of knowledge about heavy metal as category-bound to a contrasting set of race, gender, and stage of life categories. Rather, in Poundstone's version of events, Meyers Taylor's racial categorization as a Black woman apparently simply aids her performance as a shill. We can also note that Poundstone's claim pre-emptively casts doubt on any subsequent claims by Meyers Taylor, despite her K+ status regarding the musical genres she is likely to be familiar with. Although she disavows knowing about heavy metal, her rejection is mitigated, particularly in light of her K+ status in the matter ("I don't know about that," line 35) and only addresses Poundstone's subsequent elaboration in lines 29–30. Once she has been called a shill, any rejection of that assertion can be heard as consistent with the claim that she *is* one.

Across this exchange, then, the participants' treatment of knowledge of heavy metal as category bound to race, gender, and stage of life categories can be appreciated in at least two ways. In a most basic sense, the connection between such knowledge and these categories constitutes part of the general stock of knowledge that participants and audience members can be counted on to know, such that it can be not just a basis for action, but for jokes. Moreover, whether the parties contend that Meyers Taylor has a K– or K+ status regarding heavy metal, neither treats that status as consistent with her categorization as a Black woman: she either doesn't know about heavy metal *because* she is a Black woman, or she knows about it *despite* being one. Thus, across the exchange, the parties manage what anyone knows about a specific stock of knowledge as a category-bound phenomenon that is independent of what the participants in a particular encounter might know about it.

As we shall see, this connection between categories and specific domains of knowledge can be observed in other settings and situations. In the next section we examine how disputes about what participants can or should be presumed to know can occasion category-bound complaints about the epistemic presumptions entailed by another's conduct, specifically by characterizing it as "mansplaining."

9.2.2 Categories and epistemics: The case of "mansplaining"

Our examination of participants' pervasive orientations to connections between the epistemic status and stance claimed or established in talk, and how these reflect orientations to how they or others might be relevantly categorized, has thus far focused on encounters in which participants' claims about their relative epistemic status has mostly been confirmed in subsequent talk, or at least has gone unchallenged. As Raymond (2018, p. 74) notes, however, participants' orientations to the import of epistemic status as a feature of action formation can be "most vividly exposed where [participants] encounter some sort of problem with the epistemic status they claim." In this section, we take up connections between such troubles and categorial phenomena by considering instances of the phenomenon of "mansplaining." As Joyce et al. (2021, p. 4) observe,

> The term "mansplaining" entered the English vocabulary over 10 years ago. It originated from a short autobiographical essay by feminist writer Rebecca Solnit (2014), entitled "Men explain things to me (Facts didn't get in their way)." In the essay, Solnit recounts an interaction she and her friend had with a man who kept telling her about an important book he discovered but had not actually read. Meanwhile, her friend tried to intervene to inform him that Solnit was the author of that book. This scenario, in which a man seems to assume that he knows more about a topic than the woman with whom he is interacting when, in fact, it is the other way around, resonated with countless women who had had similar experiences.

As both the term and its brief history suggest, "mansplaining" links persons' management of epistemics, action formation, and categories: claiming that a man is engaged in "mansplaining" entails a category-based explanation for a norm violation. As Joyce et al. (2021, p. 5) observe,

> a charge of "mansplaining" works as a membership categorization device (Sacks, 1989), making not only the interlocutor's categorial identity (man) relevant, but at the same time placing the accuser in the paired membership category "woman." This results in highlighting a patriarchal organization of gender, with women presumed to be inferior – here having less knowledge/expertise – than men.

Charges of mansplaining thus parallel claims about men interrupting women, although in this case grounded in the organization of epistemics rather than turn-taking. As we noted in discussing "interruption" (see Chapter 6: Taking Turns at Talk and Selecting Next Speakers), despite a lively sense that many have about these claims, establishing that men do in fact interrupt women more than women interrupt men proved challenging to establish empirically due to complications associated with defining "interruption," identifying instances in which gender (as opposed to some other category) was relevant, or where the interrupted party treated the overlapping talk as a complainable matter. Charges of "mansplaining" are different. Because matters of epistemic status and stance are managed at the surface level of action formation and sequencing and therefore cannot be avoided (e.g., in producing a next action one cannot avoid taking a position on whether one has been informed by a prior speaker's telling), complaints of mansplaining may surface more recurrently than complaints about "interruption." That is, complaints about interruption may well go unremarked upon precisely because raising them would entail a "counter" interruption, in which the interrupted speaker must interrupt the other party to register the claim that they have been interrupted. In contrast, charges of mansplaining can be produced as next actions, and so can be used to move sequences towards possible completion, in part because they are so regularly produced in the course of conflicts. In highlighting these claims, Joyce et al. (2021) differentiate instances of mansplaining from the occasional, typically unremarkable matter of one speaker presuming to be K+ when they are in fact K– (see Raymond, 2018 for examples). When a person levels the charge of mansplaining, "Not only are [the accused parties] guilty of wrongly claiming more/better knowledge, but they are also evidently sexist in presuming to be more knowledgeable than their women interlocutors and therefore treating them as clueless or ignorant" (Joyce et al., 2021).

Joyce et al. (2021) also observe that accusations of "mansplaining" are routinely produced as counter-complaints (see our discussion of "counters" in Chapter 7: Organizing Sequences of Action) – that is, as a complaint about a prior action that entails a complaint or reports "complainables" (Schegloff, 2005a, p. 452).[2] In what follows, we examine two cases from Joyce et al. (2021), drawing on their analysis, which explicates aspects of

---

2 Indeed, such "epistemic errors" (i.e., assumptions that recipients have one epistemic status rather than another) appear to be one recurrent basis speakers have for producing a counter: speaker A presumptively adopts an epistemic status in producing an initiating action and selecting a recipient (B); speaker B's response, however, "turns-the tables" to assert that that they do not in fact have the epistemic status presumed by speaker A. For example, in the following case (analysed by Schegloff, 2007) Marsha has called her ex-husband Tony to find out if their son Joey has arrived home after visiting her in a different city.

```
MDE:MTRAC:60-1:2 -- STOLEN
01  Marsha:    Hello:?
02  Tony:      Hi: Marsha?
03  Marsha:    Ye:ah.
04  Tony:      How are you.
05  Marsha:    Fi::ne.
06                    (0.2)
07  Marsha:    Did Joey get home yet?
08  Tony:      Well I wz wondering when 'e left.
09                    (0.2)
10  Marsha:    'hhh Uh:(d) did Oh: .h Yer not in on what ha:ppen'.
11  Tony:      No(h)o=
```

the environments where these occur and the features of the offending turn that render them objectionable. In developing these observations, we also attend to what these epistemic disputes can reveal about how other categories relevant when the conflict emerges can be understood or oriented to as having been relevantly (if tacitly) gendered – and how the parties either seek to maintain or reject this tacit gendering via charges of (and defences to) mansplaining.

Joyce et al. (2021, pp. 7–8) begin with an especially clear exemplar of the phenomenon,

> taken from an episode of an internet sports show called "Barstool run-down", which is based in the United States. The episode features three hosts – Dave (DP), Kevin (KC), and Dan (DK) – and five guests – Liz (LG), Frankie (FB), Jared (JD), Eric (EH), and Tommy (TS) . . . . The participants are reviewing a recent baseball game between the Red Sox and Yankees, won by the former. Before line 01, the participants have been disapprovingly discussing Liz's reaction to the loss, specifically a clip she recorded after the game, in which she reaffirms her devotion to the Yankees by stating she would rather be a loser than become a Red Sox fan.

Extract 9.4: (Joyce et al., 2021, p. 8)

```
01  FB:  <I mean like [no one's sayin' we- like.
02   C:              [((laughter))
03  FB:  =whe- when your [ team ] loses you don't be like.
04  EH:                  [ nope ]
05  FB:  ↓I wanna become a Red >Sox fan<. We're just saying
06       like THEY're in a better spot than us Do you get that?
07           (0.6)
```

As the call and her query in line 07 suggest, Marsha presumes that Joey has possibly arrived, or at least communicated with Tony about when he will do so. Tony's counter (line 08) – which turns the tables and redirects the matter back to Marsha – reveals this assumption to be problematic: Joey hasn't arrived and Tony doesn't even know when he left. This, in turn, prompts Marsha's reported realization (line 10) regarding Tony's epistemic status, and the focus of the call is recalibrated from an occasion in which Marsha asks Tony about Joey into one in which she tells Tony about him. One recurrent basis for producing a counter, then, appears to be resolving circumstances in which the presumption about a recipient's epistemic status, incorporated into the design of a speaker's FPP, turns out to be incorrect. In the cases of mansplaining analysed in Joyce et al. (2021), one party uses a telling to accuse or admonish a recipient of having failed to take into account relevant background knowledge that they could or should have known about (see Raymond & Sidnell, 2019). In response, the recipient of this "informing" turns the tables by casting the prior action as an instance of "mansplaining," thereby asserting both that they did not need to be informed and offering a category-based complaint regarding the basis for the other party's mistaken assumptions regarding what they know or need to know. Also see Raymond's (2018, pp. 73–75) examination of epistemic troubles of a different sort.

```
08  LG:  ↑Oh i- .Hh (0.2) Do I get [↑that?]
09   ?:                              [Uh   ]  [↓o:h
10  FB:                                       [>like<.
11   C:  O:h no: [:   :   : , .aw:   :   :   :  :].
12  LG:          [Are you mansplaining that we just]=
13   C:  [((very [loud voices))
14  LG:  [(      [ )
15  FB:          [THAT'S NOT MANSPLAINING. NO.
16       [THAT'S NOT 'SPLAINING..
17  KC:  [Uhr:: : : : ((shakes fists in the air))
```

Frankie's turn (spanning lines 01, 03, and 05–06) entails a complaint that Liz has mischaracterized a prior contribution by him ("Nobody is saying that . . .) as a preface to offering a restatement of his earlier claim, now produced as a correction. Insofar as Frankie is explicating an understanding of his own talk, he can claim a K+ status (relative to Liz) regarding its proposed meaning or import. Nevertheless, since this re-assertion is itself produced in response to a critique of Liz's prior talk, she can treat it as misguided or ineffective by treating it as uninformative, thereby challenging the epistemic underpinning of its status as an informing (e.g., by saying "I know" – see Mikesell et al., 2017). Perhaps to pre-empt that possibility, Frankie appends a post-positioned query, "do you get that?" that, in effect, insists on its status as an informing by asserting a steep epistemic gradient relative to Liz. However, this adjustment profoundly changes the action his turn accomplishes: while Frankie's earlier correction treated Liz as uninformed about basic dimensions of fandom (e.g., the meaning or import of post loss commentary), the appended query treats her capacity to understand the logic or import of the disputed action as 'in question.' It is this escalation that apparently opens Frankie to the charge of "mansplaining." Frankie's query shifts the response options for Liz to a choice between accepting that her competence needed to be established or defended (by responding to his query) or calling out the prior action as a complainable. In this respect Liz's, "Are you mansplaining . . ." turns the tables both by making a response from Frankie relevant next, and by using a query that invites Frankie's admission that his prior conduct was premised on category-bound assumptions about what women know about a specialized domain of knowledge – here, being a 'sports fan' (Joyce et al., 2021).[3]

---

3 In their analysis of a further case, Joyce et al. (2021) observe that in a discussion of a Supreme Court nominee's judicial philosophy related to abortion, one of the more left-leaning panellists interjects with "don't do that. You're heading right toward mansplaining" when her conservative colleague begins his contribution with, "I'm trying to explain to you what a conservative philosophy is . . ." Evidently, in formulating his in-progress action as "trying to explain" he casts his efforts-so-far as having failed (with "trying"), thereby casting his recipient's competence as in question. Conversely, by seeking to disrupt his effort in this regard with the warning that he is

In the exchange shown in Extract 9.4, Liz's charge of mansplaining treats Frankie's utterance as having positioned her as incompetent in a domain historically – if problematically, given the number of athletes and fans who are women – patrolled and defended as bound to the gender category 'man.' In this regard, Liz's accusation of mansplaining turns the tables in a further way: it unmasks (or treats) Frankie's effort to cast Liz's participation as illegitimate or unworthy as having been done on the basis of an incompetency associated with *his* (relatively privileged) status as male, and thus as part of an unwarranted effort to cast her as an outsider. The charge, in this sense, works against an intersectional basis for inequality by challenging presumed or taken-for-granted linkages between 'sports fan' and gender (as a *Pn*-adequate collection of categories).[4] *In this regard, we can begin to see how more specialized categories (such as 'sports fan') that may be category-bound to Pn-adequate categories provide a systematic basis for using one such category to do something by the reference to the other.*[5]

"headed toward mansplaining," his recipient positions any continuation of his efforts as entailing category-bound assumptions by him regarding her status as a woman. In both cases, women raising the possibility that the other party has engaged in mansplaining, or is about to, and thereby treat the accusation as defeasible, providing the accused with a way out of the charge – if he stops now or backs down.

4 We note that our account of "mansplaining" in this and other extracts departs from the one developed by Joyce et al. (2021), who contend that such charges invoke gender as a *replacement* of other categories that had been treated by the participants as relevant. For example, in summarizing their argument, they note that

> Across all cases, gender categories were made salient *and replaced other identity categories* such as Yankee fan . . . or political opponent. . . . As a membership categorization device "mansplaining" instantiates the "viewers' maxim" (Sacks, 1992) by tying participants' gender categories to their situated conduct: the men who assume more knowledge than their women interlocutors do that as men rather than as Republicans, TV hosts, or politicians, which renders their conduct into a sexist act (Joyce et al., 2021, p. 21; emphasis added).

While we do not dispute that charges of mansplaining invoke the relevance of the participants' gender status via Sacks' viewer's maxim, it is not clear that such charges *replace* the relevance of the other categories. We suggest instead that they point to the speaker's effort to challenge or dispute the targeted speaker's presumption about, and treatment of, the domains of knowledge as themselves bound to a specific gender category.

5 This suggests a possible corollary to Sacks' viewers maxim: *Where a category is itself category-bound to a Pn-adequate category, then view any challenges to the competence or ability of a member of category as a reflection on their membership in the associated Pn-adequate category.* For example, a purportedly incompetent comment about sports by a fan categorized as a man can be a basis for calling the speaker's masculinity into question; conversely a person categorized as woman who makes a similarly discrediting comment can have her apparent incompetence as a sports fan attributed to or 'explained by' her gender. In this respect, these cases resemble the treatment of knowledge of heavy metal music as associated with members of a racial category we saw in Extract 9.3.

A further case of "mansplaining which exposes patronising conduct" can be observed in the following extract, which Joyce et al. (2021, pp. 10–11) introduce as being

> from Tucker Carlson Tonight, a TV show in the United States. Here the conservative political commentator, Tucker Carlson (TC), and his guest, Monica Klein (MK), a political strategist, disagree about Susan Collins's character – a Republican senator who supported Brett Kavanaugh's nomination to the US Supreme Court of the United States, despite sexual assault allegations against him.

```
Extract 9.5: (Joyce et al., 2021, p. 11)
01  MK:  [An' I think she will be vo:ted out]
02  TC:  [I think th't your world view is  s]cary,=
03  MK:  =because women are extremely frustrated with
04       Susan ↑Collins right now because she's
05       [supported a SEXUAL predator. ]
06  TC:  [Well not every woman feels th]at way,=And
07       [you don't speak for all women j]ust so you know.
08  MK:  [↑OKAY but there is a   thirty ]
09            (.)
10       ↓Oka[y thank ] you for [ mansp]laining that t(h)o me.
11  TC:      [°Mo↓nica°]         [°okay°]
12            (0.6)
13  TC:  £hhum£ I'm not mansplaining, (0.4) I'm saying something
14       that's obviously true.
15  MK:  [There  is  a  thirty  per    ]cent gap
16  TC:  [I appreciate you coming on. Thanks.]
```

In the course of Klein's comments about the reaction of women to Susan Collin's support for Brett Kavanaugh despite the allegations about him (lines 01, 03–05), Carlson produces an other-correction that focuses on Klein's use of "women." While Klein evidently uses her reference to "women" to formulate how a *plurality* of women feel (see line 15), Carlson's objection, that "not every woman feels that way" and "you don't speak for women" (lines 06–07), treats Klein as having made assertions bound to the *category* "women" and so made on behalf of *all* members of the category as a kind of constituency. While such a deliberate mis-hearing of Klein's remarks might be objectionable on its own, Carlson's ratchets up his complaint by adding the tag, "just so you know." As in the prior case, the appended comment appears designed to enhance the epistemic gradient that might otherwise be asserted by Carlson's rebuttal, and thus to insist that his utterance is informative *for Klein's understanding of her own conduct.*[6] In this respect, Carlson's formulation "just so you know" (and his post-positioned address term, "Monica") challenge Klein's competence by specifically asserting that she has overlooked an 'obvious truth,' and therefore *needs* to know what he has conveyed based on what she has just said. In just the way Carlson renders his objection to Klein's claims as if were helpful, he also escalates the degree to which it is explicitly patronizing, reflecting a sense of superiority on his part. We can note, then, that Klein's objection to Carlson's claims register precisely these features of it: her use of a gratuity token, "thank you" (line 10), produced with a "mocking tone" (Joyce et al., 2021, p. 12) positions her as the 'beneficiary' of Carlson's objectionable conduct (see Raymond & Zimmerman, 2016), a practice that can be used for blaming another person for the unwelcome consequences associated with the 'help' ostensibly offered by them.

As Joyce et al. (2021, p. 12) note in summarizing the import of this case,

> The accusation of mansplaining exposes [Carlson]'s conduct as patronising. That is, [Klein] calls out [Carlson] for treating her as though she does not understand that she does not speak for all women; moreover, it neatly addresses the irony that [Carlson] has claimed authority to speak on behalf of women. [Carlson] denies the accusation of mansplaining by resisting the nominated action as a gendered category-bound activity, thus orienting to mansplaining as a stigmatised action label. He produces a competing formulation of his conduct as "saying something that's obviously true", by which he substitutes the accused mansplaining as something known-in-common (Wowk, 1984).

Moreover, in summarizing their findings, Joyce et al. (2021, p. 22) contend that

> spontaneous accusations of mansplaining index an epistemic injustice and hold the accused responsible for that imbalance. Moreover, by building gender into these accusations as the ostensible motive behind the transgression, the culpability of the conduct is compounded by sexism. Mansplaining, unlike accusations of being patronising or condescending, package a sanctionable action with an ostensible motive and thus make visible sexism as deliberate conduct.

---

6 Here, the "just so you know" accomplishes 'insistence' by addressing questions of relevance that might otherwise provide the basis for rejecting his comment. As noted earlier, K+ informings not only propose that K– recipients are uninformed about the matters they convey, *but that the matter is specifically relevant for the K– recipient* (see Heritage & Raymond, 2012; Raymond, 2018; Raymond & Heritage, 2013).

Beyond the clarity of these observations about interaction as a site of struggles for social justice, here we are particularly interested in the ways their observations link the patrol and management of rights to knowledge with conceptions of 'injustice.' In this regard, their paper fulfils a possibility anticipated in early work on epistemics:

> By examining how such rights to knowledge and action are shared by speakers, or how they are distributed between them, how they are respected or how they might be violated, and how they are used to establish agreement or how they might be used to foster conflict, we can begin to explicate how identities are produced and reproduced in specific episodes of interaction. In turn, this provides a window into how the complexity of social structure is produced and reproduced through actual conduct (Raymond & Heritage, 2006, p. 701).

The phenomenon described as mansplaining is plainly not new, despite its relatively recent naming by Solnit. The fact that women now raise it as a charge may be evidence of a realignment or reconfiguration between these gender categories as their members patrol and defend epistemic boundaries that were once transgressed with impunity, which may give rise to adjustments to the entitlements and obligations with which they are associated. While the long, slow process of such incremental change may not be visible in individual extracts of talk, it may be hard to accomplish at all without the forms of conduct analysed by Joyce et al. (2021).

In this section we have focused on actions initiated by speakers with (presumed) K+ status on behalf of recipients who are presumed to have a K– status. The actions we have examined, such as tellings or informings, stand in contrast to those initiated by K– speakers' use of queries, which we turn to in our next section. Our discussion of such K+ initiated actions began with a discussion of the rule that Sacks's formulated in his lectures "Don't tell others what you figure they already know." As we have seen, violations of this rule can be treated as a kind of moral failing, precisely because of what is entailed by presuming that someone doesn't know what they should or need to know. While there doesn't seem to be a similar rule for K– initiated actions, precisely because there are such strong connections between membership categories and domains or types of knowledge, the set of practices associated with K– initiated actions – including the design and posing of interrogatives or other queries – provide participants with systematic resources for establishing and disputing the relevance of categorial phenomena.

9.2.3 K– initiated actions

In the preceding cases we have examined how members patrol and defend rights to knowledge in their conduct, and how the management of such epistemic phenomena provides systematic bases for establishing the partici-pants' orientations to the relevance of specific categories. As we anticipated in our analysis of the Extract 9.1, persons can use such connections between knowledge, experiences and category membership as a basis for action and inference. In some cases, however, persons may disavow such knowledge, per-haps as a way of disavowing their membership in the category to which it is bound.

To explore these matters, we examine an encounter in which a police officer enforces the Civil Sidewalk Ordinance or CSO. The CSO prohibits persons from sitting or lying on the sidewalk between 7 a.m. and 11 p.m., and was adopted by voters in "Golden City," California, two years before the encounter shown in Extract 9.6 took place. Like other so-called "quality of life laws," the CSO bans specific behaviours in specific places, creating a network of laws that effectively criminalize "life-sustaining behaviours" of the chronically homeless (Coalition on Homelessness, 2015). Although communities ostensibly adopt such 'quality of life' laws to provide law enforcement officials with the legal means to manage forms of conduct that can lead to disputes and other forms of disorder, sociologists have argued that they are perhaps better understood as emerging out of "society's perception of a continuing need to control some of its 'suspicious' or 'undesirable' members" (Chambliss, 1964, p. 75). Raymond et al. (2022) provide an analysis of how police enforce this ordinance using a database of several hundred hours of video and interviews collected in ride-alongs with the Golden City Police Department.

In taking up these matters here, we consider aspects of Raymond et al.'s (2022) analysis to explicate how police officers orient to subjects poten-tially categorizable in two intersecting categories, 'homeless' and 'local resident,' in making inferences about who should be aware of the law, and thereby who can be reasonably and legally held accountable to its provi-sions.[7] Although the CSO applies to every person in the city, police officers and members of the public treat the ordinance as applying specifically to (chronically[8]) homeless persons. For example, Raymond et al. (2022) show that patterns of enforcement adopted by the GCPD are specifically sensitive

---

7 For both police and the homeless subjects that they encounter, the latter's status as a 'local' (or not) routinely emerges as a basis for establishing what they can be expected to know. For exam-ple, one person whittling a stick (and so possessing a small knife) announces "I'm not a native bird" to pre-emptively account for his uncertainty about whether that activity is the grounds for the officer's approach.

8 We add "chronically" as a modifier of "homeless" because persons who are only temporarily homeless may live in cars, move between the houses of friends and relatives, or stay briefly in shelters, and thus may not live for sustained periods on the street in the way that chronically homeless residents do (e.g., with their sleeping bags and other belongings). Thus, when mem-bers of the public refer to the "homeless," they are typically referring to chronically homeless persons.

to the daily routines of homeless residents, thereby tailoring its enforcement to them. Conversely, persons claiming that they should not be subject
to its provisions typically do so by claiming that they are not homeless. For
example, a news article on the law quotes the experience of one resident of
the city, who reports, "I was sitting down talking to a kid, I was having my
coffee . . . It was literally breakfast – 7:30, 8 a.m. – just kneeled down to
talk to a kid. A cop just happened to roll up, just assumes that I'm homeless and whatnot'" (KALW, 2012). As this quote suggests, members of the
public treat being subject to enforcement of the CSO as category-bound to
a person's status as homeless.

By virtue of being the primary targets of the law, and thereby subject to
its routine enforcement, homeless residents are presumed to know about the
CSO (which is a condition of the law as a *mala prohibita* offense). In this
respect, an officer's enforcement of the CSO is sensitive to their understanding
of "what socially defined types of persons are legitimately entitled to have what
kinds of trouble" (Garfinkel, 1967, p. 156). For example, they treat homeless
residents as responsible for showing that they know about the law by either
moving to pre-empt its enforcement when they see officers see them, or for
apologizing when their current state (e.g., sleeping) has left them vulnerable to
being 'caught' (see Raymond et al., 2022, pp. 168–173). Given this pattern,
officers mostly enforce the CSO by maintaining a focused presence in areas
and times where it is strictly enforced. In this respect, officers enforcing the
CSO routinely categorize the subjects they encounter sitting or lying on a
sidewalk or in a park as both homeless (on the basis of their appearance and
conduct) and local residents of the city, by virtue of their presence. From the
officers' perspective, persons who are seen as members of these two categories
are presumed to be aware of the CSO, and thus can be expected to conduct
themselves on the basis of this awareness.

By contrast, officers approaching subjects whose appearance and conduct
does not fit this profile (e.g., they may not be obviously recognizable as
homeless, or they remain sitting or lying on the sidewalk after seeing that
officers have seen them) may entertain a range of possible accounts for
the subject's apparent inaction. For example, in Extract 9.6, when a police
officer's sustained gaze and greeting fail to prompt a sitting subject (S) to
move, the police officer (P) explores the possibility that he may not be a
local resident instead of simply treating him as uncooperative. Notably, in
this encounter the young man's clothing, as well as the place and position
in which he is sitting (on a milk crate in front of a drugstore at midday),
suggest that he may be homeless. At the same time, his apparently groomed
appearance and the absence of a bedroll suggest that he has a location to
sleep, shower, and store his belongings. Complicating matters still further,
he does not move or otherwise acknowledge the officer as soon as she

appears, conduct that suggests either a wilful violation of the CSO or possible ignorance of it.

In examining Extract 9.6, we unpack how the underlying epistemic framework of the sequences initiated by the police officer's investigative queries (beginning in line 13) reflect an orientation to the subject's status as a homeless resident who, by virtue of his membership in both of these categories, cannot reasonably claim to be unaware of the CSO. As Raymond et al. (2022, p. 176) note, however, the police officer's initial approach and contact with the sitting subject establishes some basis for uncertainty in this regard:

> As the officer takes note of [the subject] sitting in a shopping area subject to police scrutiny, she uses a step-wise approach to establishing contact that provides the subject several opportunities (lines 1–5) to preempt or avoid a full-blown encounter with her (e.g., by standing or moving). She initially stops a short distance from him and announces her presence with a summons (line 1) when the subject does make eye contact with her. . . . Only after the subject fails to begin moving in the midst of a substantially delayed exchange of greetings (lines 3 and 4) does the officer step closer and initiate the more sustained encounter that follows with a request for identification (lines 6). In these ways, over the course of this extended opening, the subject passes on the multiple opportunities the officer provides for anticipating the basis for her contact.

Extract 9.6 GCPD_SitandLieArrest_MI_08052013

```
01  P:  Hello:,
02              (1.3)
03  S:  Hi.
04  P:  Hi,
05              (.)
06      Got your ID on you?
07              (0.3)
08  S:  U::mm (0.3) °no.°
10  P:  No, yih don't,<you from the city?
11              (.)
12  S:  Yeah.
13  P:  You're aware of the civil sidewalk ordinance?
14              (1.5)
15  S:  No:.
16  P:  They call it sit lie. You heard've it,
17              (2.0)
18  S:  U:mm
19  P:  How long've you been in thuh city:
20              (1.4)
21  S:  Several years.
22  P:  Okay:uh 'cause they uh approved that in uh two
```

```
23       thousand ten.
((four lines omitted regarding reason for recording))
28  S:   uh:[mm
29  P:      [°Okay.° So do you have your ID or not.
30  S:   No: I don't have no ID on me.
31              (0.3)
32  P:   You've never been wa:r:ned or::
33  S:   °Nope.°
34  P:   Told anything about thuh: >civil sidewalk<
35       ordinance.
36  S:   No.
37  P:   'n what's yer name?
((50 seconds omitted; P gathers information from subject, including
his address, and radios to verify he has been contacted re: CSO))
38  S:   Can you explain this sit lie law?
39  P:   Yeah there's uh rule th't sitting or lying on thuh
40       sidewalk. . .
((4 lines omitted re: ordinance))
45       I'll give you a flyer about it. So you're more
46       informed [about it
47  S:            [yeah, uh: do ya have one?
48  P:   Yeah. As soon as I confirm that there isn't
49       documentation that you've already been warned
50       about it.
```

Instead of moving directly to enforcing the CSO (e.g., by requesting or demanding that the subject get up and move, as routinely happens when police officers encounter homeless residents whom they recognize or know), the police officer seeks to establish whether he is a local (lines 10–12) and, based on his claimed status as a local (line 12), begins to pursue what he knows about the CSO. We can note that once the police officer establishes that the subject is a local (lines 10–12), the declarative query she uses to initially probe his familiarity with the CSO (in lines 13) establishes an epistemic gradient that strongly presumes (Heritage & Raymond, 2012) he already knows about the ordinance (lines 10–12). In this way, the design of her action also tacitly categorizes him as homeless. This orientation can also be further appreciated in the ways that she takes up his response, despite her K– status relative to him regarding what he knows. After the subject flatly disclaims any knowledge of the CSO (line 15), the police officer's follow-up queries (in lines 16, 19, and 22–23) convey her scepticism regarding this claim, given how long the ordinance has been enforced (see especially lines 19, 22–23). Raymond et al. (2022, pp. 177–178) observe that

Following a series of negatively framed declarative questions that convey the officer's continuing skepticism regarding the resident's claims (lines 32, 34–35), the civilian attempts to embody his lack of awareness of the CSO by positioning himself as a willing recipient of the officer's "expla[nation of] the law" (line 38). In doing so, this resident displays at least an openness to hearing about the ordinance, thereby avoiding the possible implication that his current violation of it is willful or flagrant as it would be if he knew of the law and remained sitting despite the presence of the officer. . . . Such a claim would be undercut if the resident has already been warned, however, and this officer remains unmoved. While she explains the law and mentions a flyer she can give him (lines 45–46), she suspends the realization of this offer until after she confirms the he hasn't been informed of the CSO (lines 48–49).

Thus, although just what the subject knows about the CSO comes to be contested across this exchange, the police officer's use of queries designed to convey to her the suspicion that he is aware of the CSO because has already been officially warned about it (which she makes explicit in lines 48–50) reflects her implicit, if tentative, categorization of him as homeless. As Raymond et al. (2022, p. 178) observe,

> [h]ad the officer categorized the subject as a chronically homeless person from the outset [as officers had done in other cases examined in the analysis], she would likely have presumed he knew about the ordinance and adopted a different method of enforcement. . . . Similarly, had the subject simply admitted that he knew of the CSO and walked away, he very likely would have avoided arrest.[9]

We further note that the subject's persistent claims to have no knowledge or awareness of the CSO reflects a relatively underdeveloped aspect of epistemics. On the whole, the field of epistemics has developed by examining how participants orient to the relevance of one party's epistemic authority in composing actions and conducting sequences of action where access to the body of knowledge or state of affairs indexed by an action is positively valued by those participants. Less attention has been paid to the complexities introduced by circumstances in which epistemic access may be treated by participants as a basis for negative inferences, accusations, stigma, or other trouble, as in Extract 9.6. We can see further implications for how participants' orientation to the experiential basis of a domain of knowledge, as well as their orientation to qualities associated with its status as a 'social problem,' can be appreciated in the ways that participants patrol and defend who has rights to

---

9 The subject was arrested following a search for his name in the CSO database, which revealed that he had an outstanding warrant on an unrelated matter.

that knowledge by returning, in the following section, to matters we raised at the beginning of the chapter.

9.3 Revisiting K– initiated actions: queries and alternative possible categories

Having introduced and discussed the basic elements of the field of epistemics, we can now return to more closely examine the encounter we introduced at the beginning of this chapter. As noted previously, the encounter of interest emerged on a podcast discussing a segment that appeared in *The Daily Show with Trevor Noah* in which white residents of Boston were asked, "Is Boston racist?" In discussing the segment, with producer CJ Hunt (CJH), as shown in Extract 9.7, Wood Jr. (RWJ) recalls the interviewees' (IE1, IE2, IE3, and IE4) claims that Boston is not racist, commenting on the logic of this and other responses to their queries in ways that intersect with the epistemic and categorial matters we have discussed in this chapter.

```
Extract 9.7 Beyond the Scenes: The Daily Show with Trevor
Noah
01   RJW:   . . . I- I distinctly remember us asking one person you know is
02          there racism.=she goes £well ↑I've never seen it,£
03          ((transition sound effect to broadcast))
04   IE1:   I don't see that racism.=myself, honestly.
05   IE2:   ↑No I don't think Boston's a racist city
06   IE3:   I don't think've Boston as a racist cit[y: at all
07   IE4:                                         [ I don't think it's
08          true
09   RWJ:   So how do you know?
10              (0.8)
11   IE3:   I don't fee:l it.
12          ((sound effect marking transition on podcast))
13   RWJ:   As if that's the only way it can be confirmed.
14              (.)
15   RWJ:   Is: you must see it and exp- you mus' witness a Black person
16          getting: kicked out of a store or thuh cops beatin' his ass
17          .hhh to believe that it's real, and I- I though that- that
18          was kinda disheartening in a way . . .
```

We begin with some simple observations. First, although Wood Jr. and Hunt (who are both Black) have arranged to pose the segment's focal query to interviewees who appear white, they report being "disheartened" (as Wood Jr. later says) that the interviewees make strong claims to know about racism, and thus to confidently report that Boston is free of it. For example, the series of responses from the broadcast (from lines 04 to 06) resist, in different ways, the query's preference for a "yes" or confirming response, ranging from subjectivizing confessions – "I don't see that racism myself, honestly" (line 04) – to bald assertions that Boston is not racist "at all" (line 06).

The main target of Wood Jr. and Hunt's commentary is produced in the sequence initiated by Wood Jr.'s follow-up query to the third and strongest of these assertions (line 08), "How do you know?" (line 09). Evidently, this utterance can be heard in at least two ways: first, it can be heard as a challenge of the interviewee's strong assertions by tacitly indexing a possible basis for *not* knowing – if racism is directed at Black residents, how can a white resident be sure that there is none "at all"? Or, alternatively, it can be heard as a simple question that invites the interviewee to elaborate the basis for the claim – something like, 'tell us how you know.' After a gap (line 10) – suggesting some consideration of his response – IE3 reports a personal, subjective basis for his claim, "I don't feel it" (line 11), thereby treating Wood Jr.'s follow-up as a simple query inviting elaboration. It thus does not seem to have occurred to IE3 that Wood Jr. may have been challenging his claims by indexing a possible basis for *not* knowing: if racism is directed to Black residents, how can a white resident be sure that there is none "at all"? Having reviewed research on epistemics, we can now see that this difference in making sense of Wood Jr.'s query turns on the different epistemic status the participants presume is relevant for making sense of *both* of the queries he poses: as a simple question, the query positions the recipient at a K+ respondent across each sequence; as a challenge, it positions the recipient as having a K– status across both sequences, thereby revealing problems with each response.

Before unpacking how the interviewee heard the query, we first consider Wood Jr.'s subsequent commentary. The comedic impact of the sequence emerges from the discrepancy between the relevance of race raised by Wood Jr.'s queries and IE3's responses, which evidently disattend the possibility that he may not be aware of or have "felt" racism *precisely because of his race* – because he is white. Wood Jr.'s comments to Hunt (lines 13–18) successively explicate this logic. His initial comment (line 13) points to the absurdity of IE3's claim but leaves the basis for its absurdity unspoken. Following a brief silence, however, his appended elaboration (line 15–17) problematizes these responses in a way that highlights the relevance of IE3's racial category. In the formulation "witness a Black person" (e.g., as opposed to "another Black person"), Wood Jr. tacitly categorizes IE3 as white (also see Whitehead, 2009) and proceeds to locate him as lacking knowledge of *experiences* of racism and therefore as, at best, a possible "witness" to its most extreme or obvious forms.

The special relevance of experience to Wood Jr.'s claims and elaboration is underscored by his same turn repair (line 15; also see Chapter 8: Managing Troubles in Speaking, Hearing and Understanding), which replaces his projected use of "experience" (in "see it and exp-") with "witness." This formulation also incorporates seeing, while highlighting the tragic and/or special character of the observed events – that is, one "sees" ordinary events, and "witnesses" tragic or momentous ones. This apparently minor shift reveals how, by design or happenstance, interviews such as this one exploit what persons can be counted on to know (or not know) based on experiences associated with their membership in specific categories. Insofar as persons categorized as white cannot *experience* racism (except, perhaps, as perpetrators of it), the basis for any such person claiming that Boston is *not* racist can be challenged precisely on the grounds that, as 'witnesses,' they have only second-hand – and therefore infrequent or incidental – access to its possible occurrences. As we noted previously, the question here is, *how would they know?*

These observations return us to the question we raised in the opening paragraphs of the chapter: how did white interviewees come to make such readily challengeable assertions? Is this merely an expression of racial blindness and privilege, or can we learn something about how such blindness and privilege come to be produced as an interactional phenomenon by attending to categorial features of epistemics? We can note that the segment's focal query invokes the possible relevance of two alternative collections of categories. The first of these, the 'local'/'outsider' pair of categories (also see Schegloff, 1972), is tied to the setting-based 'interviewer'/'interviewee' pair, since the basis for being selected to be interviewed is being a Boston resident ('local') by an 'outsider' interviewer in Wood Jr.. The second and alternative pair of categories is the (P*n*-adequate) race collection. Each of these alternative category pairs is associated with different epistemic entitlements grounded in the participants' contrasting membership therein. As a visitor to the city, Wood Jr. asks locals about its character, invoking the relevance of a category that positions the interviewees as having a K+ status, associated with greater entitlement and access to local knowledge relative to Wood Jr.'s K– status as an 'outsider.' In this hearing (which the interviewees reveal in their responses), Wood Jr.'s follow-up query about Boston is also conveyed to a person with K+ status, and thereby invites the recipient to elaborate his prior claims by reference to this status. At the same time, Wood Jr.'s query about *racism* in Boston can be understood to probe a state of affairs to which *he* can claim K+ access, by virtue of his status as a Black person who has experienced and knows about racism, relative to white interviewees who have, at best, second-hand knowledge of such matters. If the query is heard as posed by a K+ speaker to a K– speaker, it invites treatment of the follow-up questions as a challenge to the interviewees' prior claims, and thus invites a backdown from those (e.g., "you're right, how would I know?"). In light of this, we can observe that IE3's response (like the preceding responses by IE1 and IE2) is produced by reference to the setting-based 'local' category as opposed to the alternative P*n*-adequate category 'white,' and thereby treats Wood Jr. as an 'outsider' with K– status. Moreover, IE3 (and the other interviewees) thereby formulate what they treat as a 'best case' scenario in response to Wood Jr.'s query (see Heritage & Raymond, 2021). That is, the interviewees appear to have presumed that reporting the absence of racism would be reassuring to a Black recipient rather than a "disheartening" denial of its reality. We can thereby appreciate how IE3's failure to entertain the possibility that Wood Jr.'s follow-up was a challenge arises from and reflects his orientation to by reference to the prevailing setting-based categories as the default and 'obvious' ones of relevance – but, in doing so, produced a response that was vulnerable to Wood Jr. and Hunt's critiques by reference to alternative Pn-adequate categories.

In putting a segment like this together, Wood Jr. and Hunt cannot leave to chance the possibility that person-on-the-street interviews will generate material that is both funny and illuminating about the topic of the segment – here, race-related phenomena in a city with a longstanding reputation for anti-Black racism. As our analysis suggests, Wood Jr. and Hunt appear to have used their tacit understanding of linkages between category membership, experience, and rights to knowledge in formulating and posing queries to white residents. Moreover, these queries succeed in eliciting what we might call *category-bound errors*: these are problematic forms of conduct associated with category membership in a privileged category. In effect, in these cases Wood Jr. succeeds in getting the interviewees to respond on the basis of their membership in a setting-based category in ways that are treated as demonstrating racial incompetence that appears to be invisible to them (cf. Cheeks & Whitehead, 2024; Rawls & Duck, 2020).

9.4   Summary and conclusions

In this chapter, we have briefly canvassed connections between the subfield of epistemics and categorial phenomena, which include a growing body of research that establishes how participants' conduct reflects their monitoring, patrol, and defence of rights to knowledge associated with experience and identities – and especially identities grounded in category memberships. The connections between epistemics and categories are deep, pervasive, and more complicated than might be expected at first glance. Because social actions are conducted by reference to the ways participants may be categorized, category membership structures and contributes to members' experiences, and what they know others will know or presume about them. In reviewing the basic or elementary practices and inferential frameworks established by research on epistemics thus far, as well as developing analyses associated with "-isms," we have shown how the domain of practices associated with epistemics can also be used to reveal participants' orientations to differences between the bodies of knowledge and experience that feature in both ordinary and morally problematized practices. As we have demonstrated, analysts have only begun to scratch the surface of what might be discovered through analyses of the use of these practices and inferential frameworks (but see Harms et al., 2021;

Heritage, 2011). Rounding out the set of ways we have specified features of the mutually constitutive relationships between generic organizations of practice for interaction and categorial matters, we can now note how participants' memberships in categories provide bases for managing epistemic matters, and their practices for managing of epistemic matters can reflect their orientations to particular categories. We see exciting possibilities for future research on categorial systematics across these domains of interaction, and it is to the future that we turn to next, in our final chapter.

10

WHAT NOW AND WHAT NEXT? DOMAIN-SPECIFIC APPLICATIONS OF CATEGORIZATION PRACTICES

10.0 Introduction

In August 2013, a British social media campaign with the hashtag #HelloMy-NameIs went viral. The campaign was created by a doctor, Kate Granger, who was also terminally ill with cancer. She made the following observation during one of her stays in hospital:

> [M]any staff looking after me did not introduce themselves before delivering my care. It felt incredibly wrong that such a basic step in communication was missing. . . . Introductions are about making a human connection between one human being who is suffering and vulnerable, and another human being who wishes to help. They begin therapeutic relationships and can instantly build trust in difficult circumstances.

The campaign was a huge success and, since 2013, has underpinned the communication practices of many in healthcare and medicine, and, in turn, has been much researched and evaluated (e.g., Ban et al., 2021).

The two interactional components of the campaign – a greeting ("hello") and self-identification ("my name is . . .") – are actions which can be done in different ways, following the principles of person reference (also see Chapter 5: Referring to and Addressing People), recipient design, and epistemic matters (also see Chapter 9: Managing Knowledge, Experience, and Entitlement). For example, the self-identification part in the campaign is done via one form of self-reference ('names') rather than another (e.g., 'occupation'). There are many alternatives to "my name is Kim," such as "my name is Dr Roberts"; "my name is Kim Roberts"; "my name is Dr Kim"; "I'm Kim"; "I'm Dr Kim"; "I'm

DOI: 10.4324/9781003120599-11

Dr Kim Roberts"; "I'm Dr Roberts"; "I'm the consultant"; and "I'm your consultant." Each of these is doing the same basic action, self-introduction, but with different affordances and connotations.

There is extensive research across conversation analysis on the way greetings, introductions, and identifications are done, showing not just their systematicity in terms of say, turn design and sequential location but also their variation, according to the principles noted earlier (e.g., Fitzgerald & Housley, 2002; Pillet-Shore, 2011, 2012, 2018; Psathas, 1999; Schegloff, 1979a, 1986, 2007a; Whitehead et al., 2024). So, while the #HelloMyNameIs campaign underlined the importance of introductions and self-identifications as fundamental features of human sociality, by using an invariant and static method for doing so it accounted neither for recipient design nor for evidence about how introductions are actually done by medics, and others, in interaction. In other words, the intervention, while powerful, was not based on evidence about what participants treat as the most effective ways to do self-identification in particular settings, for particular recipients.

We will return to the #HelloMyNameIs campaign in the section that follows. In the remainder of this final chapter, we aim to draw out some of the applications of the approach developed in the preceding chapters for domains outside academia. Conversation analysis has demonstrated its applied benefits for many years, with an increasingly strong track record in delivering practical and policy intervention in institutional settings, including education, law, healthcare, defence, policing, medicine, politics, and media (e.g., Antaki, 2011; Haddington & Stokoe, 2023; Lester & O'Reilly, 2018; Richards & Seedhouse, 2005). In terms of "what happens to the results of our research" (Bygate, 2004, p. 18), there are numerous examples of the ways in which research in in sister disciplines such as discursive psychology (e.g., Lamerichs & te Molder, 2011; Lester, 2014; Stokoe, 2020) and applied linguistics (e.g., Avineri & Martinez, 2021; Grujicic-Alatriste, 2015; McIntyre & Price, 2018) has addressed the most pressing issues of our time – including social justice, sustainability, access to services, identities and inequalities, and public health in the time of Covid-19.

Of course, given that conversation analysis as a field began with Sacks's (1966) analysis of interaction in an institutional setting (the Los Angeles Suicide Prevention Center), the potential for creating applications, interventions, and impacts from the analysis of actual practitioners doing real things was built into conversation analysis from the start. Similarly, there are several decades of research in applied ethnomethodology (e.g., Heap, 1990) in the domains of work-related technology, design, "situated action" (Suchman, 1987), "technomethodology" (Dourish & Button, 1998), and other approaches to human-computer interaction, including research conducted directly in and for technology companies such as Xerox (see Blackwell et al., 2017) and, more recently, IBM and Microsoft (e.g., Moore et al., 2018; Rintel, 2013). Indeed, some of this research includes membership categorization as a key focus in studies of online social media and video-mediated interactions (e.g., Housley et al., 2018; McLay, 2019; Mlynář et al., 2018; Rintel, 2015) and human-robot and human-assistant interaction in conversational AI (e.g., Albert et al., 2019; Krummheuer, 2016; Pitsch & Koch, 2010).

While many of the category-rich interactions we have analysed in the book seek to understand categories in 'applied' interactional contexts – that is, in institutional or organizational settings – in this chapter we describe cases where a further step has been taken: co-producing research with external non-academic partners and using findings to inform and benefit professional or industry practice. In Section 10.1, we reconsider the #HelloMyNameIs campaign in the context of research on how institutional parties introduce themselves and what would count as an evidence base on which to build such a campaign. In doing so, we show how an evidence-based approach to designing an action as apparently uncomplicated as self-introduction can change how practitioners interact in real settings where the stakes are high: the case of suicide crisis communication. Next, in Section 10.2, we map a course from category-based interaction research to conversation design and the world of chatbots and conversational AI, including the relevance and use of category-based analyses within conversational technologies including virtual assistants like *Siri* and *Alexa*. We also consider the way assistants, chatbots, and other software interfaces are designed for particular categories of 'users' who are referred to, in these industries, as 'personas,' while considering how these technologies are complicated by interactional considerations relating to recipient design, as well as being shot through with problematic assumptions and biases. This takes us into Section 10.3, in which we describe how EMCA research on '-isms' has underpinned communication training for different groups of practitioners.

Thus, the main aim of this chapter is to focus specifically on applications of category-focused research. However, as it is the final chapter, a further aim is, of course, to revisit the themes that the book as a whole has addressed, in a future-oriented conclusion (Section 10.4), in which we outline five areas for future research for which we propose the systematic investigation of categorial matters will be crucial.

10.1 "Hello, my name is . . ."

We begin with an instance of category-related trouble from the start of a suicide crisis negotiation (also see Sikveland et al., 2020; Whitehead et al., 2024). The extract comes from a collection of crisis communication encounters that were audio-recorded and provided by a British police hostage and crisis negotiation unit as part of routine practice – that is, they were not produced for research in the first instance, and no video-recordings were made. The project was initiated and funded by the Hostage and Crisis Unit of the Metropolitan

Police with the purpose of producing research-based communication training for negotiators as part of the project. One of us (Stokoe) had previously met two senior officers from the unit while delivering a "Conversation Analytic Role-Play Method" (CARM) training workshop (see Stokoe, 2011b, 2014) for non-academic stakeholders – on this occasion, for mediators and conflict resolution practitioners.

With Derek Edwards, Stokoe had conducted extensive analyses of initial inquiry (or 'intake') calls into community mediation (and related) services focusing on how identity matters – cashed out in categorial terms – impacted the trajectory of the dispute between parties (e.g., Stokoe & Edwards, 2009). Towards the end of the project, Stokoe began to focus particularly on whether callers became clients of community mediation organizations by the end of their encounter with a mediator. Such intake calls are treated as separate from and outside of an actual mediation and had, before Edwards and Stokoe's study, received no attention from either researchers or the mediation industry. But because services secure funding partly based on recognized need – on the size of their client base – it is crucial that mediators successfully convert callers to the service into clients of their service, into clients of mediation 'proper' (Charkoudian, 2010). Analysis of intake calls revealed potential clients' doubt about the usefulness of mediation compared to other services such as going to the police, a lawyer, or court – in other words, institutions that are more explicitly on the client's side, can intervene in a conflict, and sanction the behaviour of the other party. Given that the outcome of intake calls is a bottom-line issue for mediation services, the project's findings were to be of direct relevance to mediation organizations.

Starting with such findings about mediation, then, Stokoe began to develop an approach to communication training underpinned by selected aspects of the research. Her approach was in stark contrast to traditional forms of training based on simulation or role-play, since it took research findings about effective practice as the basis. The basis of the method, which she termed 'CARM' (the Conversation Analytic Role-play Method), involved identifying examples of effective and less effective practices; for example, for describing and offering mediation to sceptical callers. She anonymized audio and video extracts from recordings and played them and synchronously with transcripts, to enable participants to 'live through' real encounters without knowing what would happen next. Workshop attendees discuss what they might do next to handle the situation. For example, if Party A makes a particular sort of comment, how might Party B respond most appropriately? Finally, Party B's actual response is revealed and discussed, and the workshop moves on. Stokoe's (2011b, 2014) work developing CARM has been used to train thousands of professionals across hundreds of organizations in the UK, USA, and Australia, starting with mediators but evolving into work with police officers, police crisis negotiators, sales people, medics and healthcare providers, and teachers (as part of the Conversation Analytic Innovation for Teaching Education [CAiTE] project; see Skovholt et al., 2021).

It was at a mediation CARM workshop, then, where Stokoe met the two Metropolitan Police crisis negotiators, because they were also volunteering at their local mediation centre. Seeing the potential of the CARM approach for crisis negotiation, the head of UK national negotiation training "took the rare step of releasing negotiation tapes" (Rupasinha, p.c.) in order to co-produce research-based communication training. The training was delivered to the Metropolitan Police and Police Scotland between 2017 and 2019 (for an overview of the underpinning research, see Sikveland et al., 2022).

One area for empirical research was the opening phase of the negotiation, in which the negotiator attempts to engage the person in crisis and get the interaction moving towards the activities of negotiation and/or providing assistance. In Extract 10.1, a police negotiator (N) is working to open a conversation with a person in crisis (PiC). The negotiator struggles to accomplish alignment with the person in crisis vis-à-vis these setting-based categories, treating his incumbency in 'police' and/or 'negotiator' categories as a potential source of trouble, and identifying himself using his name as an alternative to using these categories. With the foregoing discussion of the "my name is" format in mind, we now offer further consideration of the negotiator's use of this format (line 01). While crisis negotiation is not the same as the medical interactions in which the #HelloMyNameIs campaign was developed, we want to show that and how taking an evidence-based approach *before* building a social media campaign may have benefits and other unforeseen consequences.

Extract 10.1: Police crisis negotiation (HN5 2:33)

```
01   N:    Hi darling. <My n- my name is David.
02              (0.6)
03   N:    Uh[m  ]
04  PiC:     [Who] are you,
05              (0.2)
06   N:    I'm just here to try and help.
07              (0.7)
08  PiC:  Yeah. Who are you.=You know from where.
09              (0.3)
10   N:    Oh- I- I'm from the police.
```

The negotiator's use of only his first and not surname is consistent with the goal articulated in the #HelloMyNameIs campaign: to make "a human connection" to another "human being who is suffering and vulnerable" and to "instantly build trust in difficult circumstances" (www.hellomynameis. org.uk, 2021). However, the interactional trouble that arises from this formulation – with the person in crisis resisting aligning with the course of action and associated categories it pursues, and the negotiator ultimately using a categorial self-identification (line 10) – raises questions as to whether this is an effective way to do such an action to, and build trust with, a stranger in stressful circumstances. Ironically, the person in crisis does not resist movement into the negotiation phase of the interaction on the basis that the negotiator is, in fact, a police officer, but instead on the basis of not being able to ascertain which category the negotiator is acting as a member of in the first place. Moreover, this case is not an isolated or idiosyncratic instance of this type of trouble: as Sikveland et al. (2022) show, the "my name is" format is routinely resisted and responded to by persons in crisis with pursuit of an occupational self-identification. Extract 10.2 provides a further case of this.

```
Extract 10.2: Police crisis negotiation (HN34)
01  PiC:   Hello.
02    N:   Mosi my n- my name is Riley.
03                (0.8)
04    N:   Can we talk,
05                (1.5)
06  PiC:  Who's that.
07                (0.5)
08    N:    (mm)
09                (0.3)
10    N:   My- my name is Riley=I just want to talk to you.
11                (0.9)
12  PiC:  Who are you.
```

From their collaboration with experienced negotiators, Stokoe knew that the negotiators were concerned about being immediately categorizable as 'police officers' and assumed that persons in crisis would respond better to someone more easily categorizable as 'neutral parties.' This concern evidently underpinned the use of the "my name is" self-identification practices observed in Extracts 10.1 and 10.2. Yet, Sikveland et al. (2022) found no evidence for this concern in the actual crisis negotiations analysed. Indeed, persons in crisis not only sometimes requested to talk to a police officer (e.g., in cases where a uniformed officer first encountered the person in crisis before professional negotiators arrived at the scene), but also displayed resistance to self-identification as "a negotiator," as Extract 10.3 shows.

```
Extract 10.3: Police crisis negotiation (HN1_1)
01  N:  Hi Oliver?
02              (0.8)
03  N:  My name is Chris.
04              (1.0)
```

```
05    N:    One of the negotiators?
06              (1.9)
07    N:    Just seeing if we can .hhh help you come
08          down safely, (0.6) and we can sort this out.
09              (0.3)
10    PiC:  (Then) why is there a negotiator.
11              (1.0)
12    PiC:  There's nothing to negotiate.
13              (2.2)
14    PiC:  I'm not robbing a bank, Why is there a nego- negotiator here.
```

Note the gap following the negotiator's greeting (line 02) and
self-identification using the "my name is" format (line 04), in which the person in crisis does not respond. At line 05, the negotiator adds incrementally
to his self-identification, stating his membership in the category 'negotiator.'
A longer gap ensues at line 06, marking the person in crisis's withholding
of a response and thus resistance of the course of action implied by the negotiator's self-identification (also see our discussion of sequential trouble in
Chapter 7: Organizing Sequences of Action). The negotiator then pursues
a response by taking another turn in which he formulates an account for his
presence at the scene – to help the person in crisis come down safely (lines
07–08) – thereby addressing the person in crisis's evident resistance to the
'who' of the negotiator's presence by explaining the 'why.' The person in
crisis's response then shows that it is, in fact, the 'who' that is problematic,
as he asks, "(Then) why is there a negotiator" (line 10), thereby challenging
(Koshik, 2003) the basis for the negotiator's presence at the scene. Following
this question, the negotiator remains silent (line 11), thereby orienting to any
possible response as a likely source of further trouble – that is, treating it as
an "unanswerable" question (Koshik, 2003, p. 55). The person in crisis then
continues, formulating his account for why a "negotiator" is not relevant to
his situation (line 12), which occasions the longest silence yet (line 13), as
the negotiator continues to treat the person in crisis's challenges as unanswerable. The person in crisis then issues a further challenge, explicitly formulating the lack of fit between the activity in which he is (not) engaged and
the participation of a negotiator in the encounter (line 14). Thus, in this case,
neither the use of first name terms nor that of a categorial self-identification
facilitated movement into a negotiation phase of the negotiation.

As well as generating resistance, then, rather than 'human connection' – at
least in the crisis setting – the practice of self-identification via "my name
is" as an institutional norm and 'script' is one that evidently does not actually accomplish what it is designed to do. To be clear, we are not arguing
that doing the actions of greeting and self-identification or introduction are
themselves problematic but that doing them based on normative understandings simply creates an invariant occasion for the ensuing interaction. That is,

scripting the starts of interactions creates a 'static' first pair part rather than a recipient-designed approach.

Further evidence for the problems with assuming an invariant format ("my name is") for constructing an action (self-identification) comes from other research on police and medical training encounters in which officers and doctors are assessed on their communication competences. For example, Stokoe (2013) compared the way police officers introduced themselves in the openings of real and simulated interviews with actual suspects and with actors playing the parts of suspects in training sessions. What happens in openings is heavily prescribed by law – the Police and Criminal Evidence Act (PACE, 1984). This means that, in both cases, the police interviewers' first job is to turn the written law into spoken turns at talk with the suspect, which includes the following: *The interviewer shall give their name and rank and that of any other interviewer present.* Extract 10.4 shows how the two police officers, P1 and P2, present in turn this item of the law into spoken talk, recorded on tape as part of standard legal process.

```
Extract 10.4 Police interview
01   P1:   Um: (0.3) my name is pee cee Hargreaves, as we've >already
02         discussed< please call me Linda?
03   P2:   .pt my name's uh- pee cee two three seven: .hh Tim Jensen:
04         but-  feel free to call me Tim,
```

Both police officers use an announcement to identify themselves, and both follow a format that starts with "my name is." P1 completes the announcement with her police rank and surname: "pee cee Hargreaves" (line 01), thus combining a name-based identification with a categorial one. P2 then produces an amended version of the announcement, including his rank ("pee cee"), 'badge number' ("two three seven:"), and full name ("Tim Jensen:"). While the PACE guidelines state that "the interviewer" should supply the "name and rank and that of any other interviewer present" – implying one officer can introduce all officers present – in fact the two officers do this in tandem. Moreover, although the guidelines do not specify that officers should provide their badge numbers, P2 in this case does so. Also noteworthy is that both officers invite the suspect to use their first names (lines 02, and 04), with P1 also reminding the suspect that they have "already discussed" this (lines 01–02). This seems to have a similar purpose to the "my name is" campaign – to build personal affiliation and lessen the formality of institutional identifications – while at the same time meeting the legal requirements of formal identifications 'for the benefit of the tape' (also see Stokoe, 2009b).

A further instance of the same PACE item being turned into spoken interaction is shown in Extract 10.5:

```
Extract 10.5 Police interview
01  P1:  .hh ↑I'm pee cee ↓treble six eight Smith attached to
02       Boroughtown p'lice station,
03              (0.4)
04  P1:  Also present is my collea:gue,
05              (0.2)
06  P2:  .pt Pee cee four two four Torball: also attached to:
07       Boroughtown police   station.
```

In this case, P1 (like P2 in Extract 10.4) announces his rank, badge number, and surname, before also (unlike the officers in Extract 10.4) specifying his station affiliation (lines 01–02) – a further detail not specified by PACE. P1 then projects the introduction of P2, thereby evidently heading towards following the guidelines by introducing "all officers present," before suspending his turn mid-course (note the silence at line 05) to allow P2 to collaboratively complete the introduction (also see Lerner, 1991) – which, like P1's self-introduction, includes a rank, station affiliation. In this case, unlike in Extract 10.4, neither officer supplies their first name, and nor do they issue an invitation to the suspect regarding how to refer to them.

Extract 10.5 comes from a real police interview, with a real suspect, while 10.4 comes from a role-play, in which the police officers are interacting with an actor playing the part of a suspect. Their task is to pass the interview training they are participating in. In comparing these two settings, Stokoe (2013) found that introductions were accomplished differently in each, with 'I'm PC X' and collaborative completions in real interviews versus 'My name is' self-introductions done by each officer separately in role-plays. That is, under evaluation and assessment, the officers each took their own full turns to introduce themselves, while in real interviews, the officers, ironically, work more visibly as a team rather than as individuals.

Why do officers use the 'my name is X' format in role-plays but use a 'I'm PC X' format when they know they are being evaluated? Notably, Atkins et al. (2016; also see Atkins, 2019) found a similar pattern in the use of alternative formats for doing introductions in doctor-patient interactions compared to simulations thereof: in real encounters, general practitioners introduce themselves by saying, 'I'm Dr X,' but when being assessed on their consulting skills in simulations, they were more likely to say, 'My name is Dr X.' In doing so, they worked to ensure that the 'assessable' communication practices were clearly present, to be ticked off by the observing assessor, and thus to pass their "Objective Structured Clinical Examination" (OSCE). Furthermore, if a candidate used the 'I'm Dr X' format in the simulation, they were likely to be marked negatively for doing so. As Atkins et al. (2016, p. 1) point out, "the linguistic problems and differences that arise from interacting in artificial settings are of considerable importance in assessment, where we must be sure that the exam construct adequately embodies the skills expected for real-life practice."

It appears, then, that different occupations are trained to make introductions in the same way, by saying 'My name is X.' Doctors and police officers use this format when being assessed. But they use 'I'm X' in real encounters – with no evidence that this is less effective for the comprehensibility of the action or for any other function. It is therefore difficult to discern what underpins the solidification into guidance and evaluation of one practice over another. This is underscored by other examples of introductions in designedly standardized interactions, such as in Maynard et al. (2011) series of studies of survey design and verbal questionnaires, in which they found that "My name is" was part of the script provided for interviewers by the survey company. Training, guidance, and scripts for, and assessment of, communicative encounters are often apparently built from people's attempts to make explicit their tacit knowledge and build that into guidance and recommendations. This may, however, lead to failures in identifying the right 'trainables' or 'assessables,' because people's memories of their communicative encounters are shaped by many factors, from sheer processing capacity to matters of stake and interest (Edwards & Potter, 1992), and their tacit knowledge of how particular practices in such encounters should be carried out may thus differ from how they are done in naturally occurring instances.

To reiterate, our point is not that stating "my name is" rather than a categorial or other way of referring is intrinsically flawed, or not found endogenously in real occasions. Rather, we argue that prescribing ways of talking falls foul of not just the principle of recipient design but also the evidence of how people actually talk in any given situation, where effective practice may be identified more robustly. The examples given earlier, in addition to several other key practices identified in the crisis negotiation data, were used to train the entire 'cadre' of Metropolitan Police negotiators at their UK National Hostage course, as well as visiting attendees from regional police forces, international guests from the FBI, and from other areas of policing. Following the training, testimonials from negotiations attested to better outcomes "as a direct result of the language used" and noted that the training "had a specific impact on our negotiations from the opening gambit and throughout the dialogue . . . and help[ed] bring incidents to a swift conclusion." Subsequently, the Head of Border Policing Command at the Organised Crime and Counter Terrorism Unit invited Stokoe and colleagues to roll out the training across Police Scotland. Following the training in 2019, the heads of training and operations reported that "the research is fully embedded within negotiator training courses and materials" (see Stokoe & Sikveland, 2021). The reach of the training was extended beyond negotiators to every new Police Scotland officer via the hostage and crisis unit's input into tactical communication.

In the next section, we consider more examples of the way categories are used to compose actions that have implications for both communication training and evaluation, and for the development of Large Language Models (LLMs), conversational AI, and 'conversation design' as a field – particularly in light of the rapid ascent of robots, virtual assistants, ChatGPT, and related software-as-a-service (SaaS) technologies.

10.2 Categories and design

> Sacks' insight can help us make sense of the abiding interest that those committed to the reproduction of an established institutional order might have in replacing the contested moral grounds of organizational commitment and accountability with a scheme of standardized, universalistic categories, *administered through technologies implemented on the desktop* (Suchman, 1994, p. 188; emphasis added).

Another area in which research on categories in social interaction has had impact started in an unlikely place: the veterinarian practice. Stokoe et al. (2020) analysed incoming inquiry calls from pet owners as part of another co-produced CARM project. The goal of the project was to identify effective practices to underpin training for a large veterinary customer experience organization (often abbreviated in industry as 'CX' or 'UX') whose purpose is to "inspire change and create customer-centred practice so that pets, horses and livestock receive the best care."

The organization provided recordings of real calls from pet owners to different practices, as well as 'mystery shopper' calls. Mystery shopping is "a form of participant observation," in which mystery shoppers "act as customers or potential customers to monitor the quality of processes and procedures used in the delivery of a service" (Wilson, 1998, p. 414). Incumbency in the category 'mystery shopper' involves 'passing' (cf. Garfinkel, 1967, p. 116): the practices through which members produce authentic and accountable social activity associated with the 'shopper' category. The mystery shopper approach is seen as superior to post-hoc CX surveys because it can evaluate the process of service as it happens. For example, in a study of the selling of 'restricted medicines,' Norris (2002) found that mystery shoppers struggled to distinguish between 'pharmacists' (who were qualified to sell restricted drugs) and pharmacy staff (who were not), and that the former were only involved in transactions in 46% of visits.

However, a fundamental – and untested – assumption of the mystery shopping methodology is that mystery shoppers produce requests and other actions in the same way as customers who actually use the services. If mystery shoppers are unable to reproduce a genuine service encounter, then their reports back to the organization are, at best, reduced in validity and, at worst, potentially damaging for the employees who have interacted with them. Stokoe et al. (2020) found a series of differences between the two types of calls to veterinary practices, including in call length (real calls were significantly longer), reason for call (real callers phoned to make appointments; mystery shoppers to ask about the cost of services), and call outcome (real calls typically ended with a service being progressed; mystery shopper calls ended with no further actions on the part of the caller or vet practice). They found no evidence, however, that receptionists knew if and when the caller was a mystery shopper since, across the tens and hundreds of calls they deal with, they may encounter small numbers of instances, or none at all, during the course of their work. It is only by comparing large datasets of both types of call, then, that any differences become readily visible.

Another key difference was in the ways in which callers referred to their pets in their reason for calling. Compare Extracts 10.6, from a real caller, and 10.7, from a mystery shopper. The receptionist is unaware that the caller is a mystery shopper.

```
Extract 10.6: RC Other 1
01  C:  .h Hello::.=I:t's Joanna Clarke here.=I'm ringing regarding
02      um my lab Brownie, .hh he:'s (0.2) off his food,
```

```
Extract 10.7: MS 2
01  C:  Hi.=I [(got) a new d- uh: puppy the other day.
02  V:        [((coughs))
03  C:  .hh s'wonderin' how much it'd cost t'get the jabs done.
04      please.
```

Note the difference between "my lab Brownie" and "a new d- uh puppy" as ways of referring to pets. Stokoe et al. (2020) found that real callers were more likely to use a possessive pronoun ("my"); the category of animal in terms of breed (e.g., "lab"), and their pet's name (e.g., "Brownie") in their reason for call, than were mystery shoppers. Mystery shoppers never volunteered the name or breed of the subject of their hypothetical inquiry. Instead, mystery shoppers were more likely to refer to their pet in categorial terms using the indefinite article, such as in Extract 10.7 ("a new d- uh puppy"; note the repair from "dog" to "puppy," the latter being a more age-appropriate category for a vaccination inquiry). Mystery shoppers were also more likely than real callers to initiate repair on, delay, or otherwise 'stumble' in responding to queries about the pet breed and weight. These differences made relevant or closed subsequent trajectories in talk. For instance, given that mystery shoppers did not volunteer the name of their pet, receptionists sometimes asked.

Much like the earlier examples from crisis negotiation and police and medical interviews, one implication of the research is that mystery shopper callers did not reproduce the social actions that comprise real customer telephone calls to veterinary practices. Instead, they produced a limited set of interactional 'scenarios' for the receptionists to progress, which were generally atypical of real callers. The research also shows that and how a person's stake in encounters matters (also see Edwards & Potter, 1992). For mystery shoppers, who do not have a pet – or at least do not have the hypothetical pet about which they are calling – their stake arises from their membership in the category 'assessor of interaction.' For real callers, their stake, as members of the 'pet owner' (or, for some, 'pet parent') category, is in showing care for their pet – for example, by referring to them by name rather than just by category, making timely requests for medical interventions that do not start with their cost, and the like. Stokoe took findings back to the organization to enable the redesign of the 'scripts' for mystery shoppers, including the recommendation to, for example, make appointments for pets (and then later cancel them – something real pet owners also do!), as well as how to formulate their 'reason for the call.'

Stokoe et al. (2020) draw out some implications of their mystery shopper research for the development of conversational AI systems such as Apple's *Siri*, Amazon's *Alexa*, and Google's *Duplex* (Leviathan & Matias, 2018) that attempt to emulate naturalistic spoken interaction. There is a rapidly growing body of conversation analytic research that shows how constrained the 'conversations' are in such interactions (e.g., Albert et al., 2019; Fischer et al., 2019; Porcheron et al., 2018; Reeves, 2017; Reeves et al., 2018). Stokoe et al.'s (2020) findings suggest that, worse still, even humans who are simulating other humans do not produce social actions (e.g., requests) in the same way when the stakes – including categorial stakes – are different. If humans attempting to simulate other humans do not – at least from the evidence in this study – convincingly simulate social actions, the developers of artificial agents face an even tougher challenge. Before even approaching any engineering problems, they must first solve the long-standing empirical question of how social actions are formed and recognized in interaction (see our discussion of this matter in Chapter 4: Forming and Making Sense of Actions). In other words, how and what sorts of conversational turns are coded for speech analytics systems used to assess employees' performance in call-centres? How are chatbot turns at interaction designed for (categories of) recipients, progressivity, and sequence, and (how) can they be programmed to adequately use and handle practices of repair? What kind of training data underpins the algorithms for conversational agents? One route into these empirical questions is via research in conversation analysis, including consideration of the range of intersections between categories and the generic orders of practice for interaction we have considered in the preceding chapters.

An article co-authored by Stokoe and colleagues, including Google's User Experience Lead, Cathy Pearl (Stokoe et al., 2021), discusses the ubiquity in academia and industry of conversation design as a concept and practice in the world of chatbots, virtual assistants, and 'conversational user interfaces' (CUIs). For some designers, the aim is to enable CUIs to respond to and progress requests from users (e.g., turn devices off and on; make purchases, initiate video or telephone calls; and so on) – within minimal misunderstanding and friction. For others, the aim is farther-reaching, to enable CUIs "to mimic human, turn-based conversation and to use natural language in written or spoken form" (Vitali & Arquilla, 2019, p. 60). Yet, despite huge investment, massive technical progress, and the proliferation of CUIs across domestic, transport, and workplace spaces, a review recently stated that "no system is able to lead a half-decent coherent conversation" (Kopp & Krämer, 2021, p. 1). That said, during the time we have written this book, large language models, or LLMs, have become available for mass market users, and we are witnessing the rapid escalation of conversational technologies and their capabilities – alongside concerns about their veracity, integrity, and ethics (e.g., Bender et al., 2021; Liesenfeld & Dingemanse, 2022; Zhang, 2021). While it seems obvious that EMCA research should have a close and productive relationship with conversational products of all kinds, there has until recently been relatively little interaction between the two domains (although with some notable exceptions; e.g., Moore et al., 2018; Stokoe et al., 2024). As we finish writing the book, we can only mark a moment in time regarding research on how categories and their interaction analysis will come to figure in this space.

A key feature of conversation design practice is to produce conversation flows for recipients, or 'users' – including particular categories of users – suggesting a tangible point of connection between EMCA (including the foregoing chapters in this book) and industry. For example, Baker et al. (2005, p. 40; emphasis added) note, in relation to a study of a technical helpline, that call-takers may attend "to much more than the technical competence of the caller – it includes hearing and responding to '*identity* matters'"; while Schegloff (2007b, p. 89; emphasis added) notes that, alongside recipient design considerations for person references and other lexical choices, these also feature in topic selection "either individually *or categorically*." As McHoul (2007, p. 460) remarks, "[t]his is not 'stereotyping' or anything of the sort" but a logical consequence of the generic organization of word selection – the way that language provides an indefinite number of ways to describe, reference, and categorize something or someone. Moreover, Nguyen (2011, p. 200, emphasis in original) contends that most work to date on recipient design focuses on "aspects of talk that are designed for the participant(s) in *one* particular conversation" and shows that and how recipient design may be achieved longitudinally, as revealed in an analysis of a pharmacy intern's interactions with patients over time. That is, "some aspects of recipient design can be carried over to a next interaction," and thus the "recipient" in "recipient design" "may be understood as *members of the same category* and not just one particular co-participant in a given conversation" (Nguyen, 2011, p. 200, emphasis in original).

This notion is embedded in conversation design through the construction of data-driven user-based target market personas such as "Nerdy Nina" (McCready, 2021) or "Facilities Manager Fred" (Wells, 2021). Personas are designed to help focus language choices for a likely recipient. However, personas, once created, are static. Indeed, the very consistency of tone of voice used to create brand distinction can, at the same time, backfire by becoming monotonous or stereotypical (Fuat Firat & Shultz, 1997). Furthermore, critics argue that segmentation reproduces the preferences of dominant cultural groups (e.g., Bedi, 2019), and stereotypes and bias can easily backfire on marketers and advertisers. It is easy to imagine how following a persona-based script when interacting with an actual client could go wrong (Flinkfeldt et al., 2022). For instance, if the persona is designed as an older person, it may lead to assumptions that produce what has been termed 'elderspeak,' which includes speaking more loudly, slowly, or simply, among other adjustments to voice quality (see, e.g., Kemper, 1994; Shaw et al., 2020). This might not create friction if such adjustments are warranted, but can be experienced as "the baldest form of ageism" if not (Friend, 2017).

However, while questioning the possibility or value of targeting predefined categories of people, such critiques fail to consider that conversational encounters are *already* shaped for recipients and that this, in turn, may have less to do with 'segmentation' as marketers define it, and more to do with the way interaction fundamentally works. As Flinkfeldt et al. (2022) argue, examining real interaction enables us to see that and how people design communication *moment-to-moment* for a client or customer who is responding synchronously. In contrast to the inevitably static and stereotypical categories onto which marketers build strategies, interlocutors may adapt to each other in real time, and this may be underpinned by the category memberships they are presumed to occupy *in that moment*. This is demonstrated by Flinkfeldt et al.'s (2022) comparative analysis (cf. Sidnell, 2009) of telephone calls to a holiday sales call-centre for 'seniors' and a university admissions call-centre for 'young' students. While topically different, call-takers in both datasets requested callers' email addresses in order to progress service. Flinkfeldt et al. (2022) examined how these requests were designed, where and how age was made relevant, and how subsequent service provision was handled in a way that matched callers' presumed age categories. One key finding of Flinkfeldt et al.'s (2022) study was that explicit categorizations about (older) age were produced only by callers themselves, not by call-takers. For example, in Extract 10.8 (previously examined as Extracts 1.1, 4.3, and 7.12), a caller (C) to the holiday sales company (S) begins her request with a parenthetical account, which includes an explicit self-categorization as "a lady of a certain age" (line 04) along with categorial inferences that older people are less technologically competent (lines 04–05).

Extract 10.8: Holiday_sales
```
01  S:  G'd evenin' Rindley Leisure Hotels, you're speaking to
02      Diane.=↓how c'n I help.
03  C:  Uh- good evenin' Diane. .hh I'm trying to- ↓um. (0.3) I'm
04      a lady of a certain age and going online's giving me a
05      headache.
```

In contrast, in the 'young' dataset, call-takers explicitly categorized callers as such. For example, Extract 10.9 shows how the university call-taker (U) addresses the student caller (S) using an age-based category (also see Chapter 4: Referring to and Addressing People).

Extract 10.9: University admissions call centre
```
07  U:  ↓Hi.=are ↑you um: the student enquiring about Human Biology.
08           (0.4)
09  S:  I am.=yes[:.
10  U:           [.pt Okay,=what's your name.=↓young la:dy,
```

In both extracts, the gender category "lady" is also used, in combination with age. Across the datasets, it was routinely treated as acceptable to categorize someone else as 'young' but refer only to oneself as 'old.'

While Extracts 10.8 and 10.9 involved cases of explicit uses of categories, Flinkfeldt et al.'s (2022) study also showed that similar recipient design considerations can be seen at work in cases where no category is mentioned, but where the practices used by participants in producing particular actions reveal their orientations to their recipients as being members of particular age categories. This can be seen by comparing Extracts 10.10 and 10.11, which illustrate how call-takers in the two data sets both used routinized practices for requesting a caller's email address and designed these requests for recipients thereby treated as either 'old' or 'young.'

Extract 10.10: University admissions call centre
```
01  U:  .hhh And what's your email address,
02              (0.5)
03  S:  .tch uh::m, .h s:uze:? anderson,
```

Extract 10.11: Holiday sales
```
01  S:  Lovely. (.) Thank you: and uh do you have an email
02      address #at all:#.
03  C:  No.
```

In Extract 10.11, the university call-taker's request is 'and-prefaced,' lending the question a routine character (Heritage & Sorjonen, 1994). The request also presupposes that the student caller has an email address, and (albeit after a brief delay; lines 02–03) the student aligns with this presupposition by producing an email address (line 03; also see Heritage & Clayman, 2010; Heritage & Raymond, 2021). By contrast, in Extract 10.12, although the salesperson's question is also and-prefaced, the request it carries does not presuppose that the caller has an email address and will supply it with no problem. The "do you have" construction serves as a pre-sequence that projects a forthcoming solicitation of the caller's email address while orienting to the relevance of first establishing whether such a request is apposite for the (category of) recipient at hand (also see our discussion of pre-expansion in Chapter 7: Organizing Sequences of Action). In addition, the negative polarity item "#at all:#." (line 02) projects that the caller is likely to produce a negative response and thereby block the caller's production of the projected request (Heritage & Clayman, 2010; Heritage & Raymond, 2021; Raymond & Heritage, 2021) – and indeed this is precisely what the caller does at line 03. By showing that email requests varied systematically across the two datasets, Flinkfeldt et al. (2022) revealed how, without ever directly mentioning or categorizing callers in terms of age, call-takers design otherwise-routinized actions for recipients of particular age categories (also see Wilkinson's [2011b] analysis of practices that reveal call-takers' orientations to the hearable gender of callers). That is, call-takers evidently use what is commonsensically known about the probability of 'young' versus 'old' recipients being email users as a basis for requesting email addresses in more versus less 'optimistic' ways (also see Heritage & Raymond, 2021; Raymond & Heritage, 2021).

Eliciting an email address is a mundane component of almost any customer or user experience in the digital era. The action of requesting it is also mundane, yet we can see the work involved in constructing requests in different ways for different recipients, including using self- and/or other-categorizations, extending requests with pre-sequences, and fitting the presuppositions and polarity of questions to what is presumed about the category of recipient at hand. Thus, in contrast to static notions of 'segments' and 'personas,' these findings show how recipient design is bound up with categorial considerations while being responsive to the live unfolding of actual interaction. These are therefore the sorts of findings that could underpin better conversation design, while pointing to the recipient design-related challenges for the development of CUIs that are capable of interacting like humans rather than acting in static or invariant ways – independently of in-the-moment inferences participants may make about the (categories of) recipients they are addressing.

But let us take this one step further: are conversational agents, chatbots, etc. – and the designers who write scripts and computer scientists who generate training data for algorithms – able to take the evidence discerned from how people respond to preceding actions as a basis for deciding whether a course of action or an interaction as a whole can be brought to a close, or whether further expansions are in order? (Also see our discussion of sequence expansions in Chapter 7: Organizing Sequences of Action.) Consider Extract 10.12, which shows how even in cases where an email address is on file, call-takers do not presume it will be the preferred way to receive a booking confirmation.

```
Extract 10.12 Holiday sales
01  S:  .h Tha::t's it. >So what I'll do now for you, I'll
02      get your confirmation sent straight through. .hh
03      Now I have got your email address here, but would
04      you like it sent via the post instead? What would
05      be your preference?
06  C:  Um- (0.3) will you: will you send it through the
07      post [actually,] [ because  I ] will give
08  S:       [  .hh.   ] [>↑Of course<]
09  C:  Pauline her own¿
10  S:  Oh of cou::rse.
```

In lines 01–02 the salesperson projects the closing of the encounter by informing the caller that the confirmation of the booking will be "sent straight through." However, in line 03, the salesperson then expands the sequence in order to register that she has the caller's email address but nonetheless offer to send the confirmation "via the post instead" (line 04). The salesperson thereby treats the caller as a member of a category that may have a "preference" (line 05) for this alternative despite being an email user. In response, the caller indeed selects "send it through the post," while orienting to this as non-default (and possibly extra work for the salesperson) by adding "actually" in line 07 and supplying an account (that she will give a copy to her travel companion) in lines 07 and 09.

In response to Stokoe's (2021) presentation of these findings at an industry event, the Conversation Design Institute Festival, the host of the event offered a pessimistic assessment of the possibility of CUIs ever being capable of dealing with these questions, saying, "Well, we can all pack up and go to the pub now, since AI is never going to be able to do stuff like this." Her presentation at the same organization's 2024 event, focused on how the action of requesting is often accomplished through non-request actions (e.g., descriptions, positioned as pre-sequences), was deemed "terrifying" by the next speaker. While this outlook may be well-founded, given that current CUIs lack the capacity to manage such recipient design considerations in anything approaching how human participants demonstrably do (see Stokoe et al.'s [2024] comparison of LLM versus human turn-taking), conversation analytic research has (as noted at the beginning of this chapter) been making in-roads into the technology industry for some time. There is a strong and growing presence of EMCA researchers at CUI and HCI (human-computer interaction) events, and many rapidly evolving research collaborations (see Stokoe et al., 2024, forthcoming). In terms of the direct shaping of 'Software as a Service' (SaaS) products, Stokoe has translated her own and much other conversation analytic work on questioning, progressivity, and recipient design into the SaaS industries, via industry fellowships at *Typeform* (www. typeform.com) and *Deployed* (www.deployed.co) – two companies that produce 'conversational' templates for online data collection. The benefits of these collaborations have been articulated by both companies:

> The immediate beneficiary is *Typeform* itself, but the end user is the real beneficiary – our customers who are actually now creating typeforms with different templates and different guidance. Their forms are a critical part of their business process, we want to maximize their changes for as good a completion rate as possible, so that they can convert a potential new lead into a customer and then into revenue (Typeform; quoted in Stokoe & Sikveland, 2021, p. 5).

> [The conversation analytic] insights and guidance set the path to our strategic decision to build a solution where users interact with conversational Q&A that follow the principles of question science (Kayleigh Kuptz, co-founder, Deployed, LinkedIn post, June 2023).

Being 'conversational' is not the only challenge for the conversation design industry, however. Big Tech, start-ups, and SaaS industries and their employees have, since their inception, become categories themselves. Employees are the types of "smart, socially awkward engineers" (Goldhaber-Gordon & Goldhaber-Gordon, 2006, p. 723) represented on the television series *Silicon Valley*. They are also stereotypically, and actually, largely white men, who populate 'Brotopia' (Chang, 2019). Even the CUIs themselves, as technological products, are categorized in terms of gender, age, and race (e.g., Schlamb, 2019), via their names (e.g., "Alexa," "Siri"). Indeed, researchers have shown that such devices "suffer constant verbal aggression by the users" (Santos & Polivanov, 2021, p. 1). For example, in data collected by Lauren Hall and Saul Albert, we see a user, Ann, become increasingly frustrated with Amazon CUI Alexa's inability to play a particular song that Ann has requested to hear. Note line 36, where, following an extended set of sequence expansions in which this trouble continues, Ann sanctions the CUI using an assessment formulated with a gender category.

Extract 10.13 Hall/Albert (slightly modified from original transcript)

```
01  Ann: A̲lexa̲.
02            (1.0)
03  Ann: Cn you play Garth Hewitts (.) I shall be made thy music.
04            (2.0)
05  CUI: I can't find the song I shall be made by Garth Hewitt on
06       Spotify.
07            (7.5)
((13 lines omitted in which Ann repeated pursues request))
20  Ann: Alexa, (1.3) play (.) I shall be made thy music (.) by Garth
21       Hewitt.
22  CUI: Playing specific songs is only available with Amazon Music
23       Un[limted (            ) ]
24  Ann:    [Oh for g̲oodness sa::ke,]
25  CUI: Studio add tape nineteen seventy one by Bob Dylan this
26       service may contain interest based ads.
27  Ann: [It's the n̲ame of an a̲:lbum. ]
28  CUI: [(To learn more (.) including)] how to set your preferences
29       go to Amazon dot co do uk slash interest (.) based (.) ads.
30  CUI: [(              (Plays music))              ]
31  Ann: [You're u̲seless. (3.2) utterly u̲seless. ]
32  CUI: [((Continues to play music))]
33  Ann: [       >Alexa STOP.<        ]
34  CUI: ((music fades))
35            (2.7)
36  Ann: St↑upid st↑upid woman. hh
37            (9.3)
38  Ann: °Let's try a different way°
```

Although Ann has formulated several turns that convey frustration and annoyance with the CUI (e.g., lines 24, 31, 33) – and this is a shortened version of the full sequence – at line 36, Ann produces a negative assessment of the CUI composed with the extreme case formulation "St↑upid st↑upid" followed by the gender category "woman." Not only does this echo larger scale studies about how users gender Alexa (e.g., Fortunati et al., 2022), it provides evidence of how such gendering occurs in real interaction, embedded in an action that accomplishes an extreme negative assessment in a context of interactional trouble. This case also draws together some of the major themes of the book, such as how participants recurrently use categories in the face of trouble.

Despite many initiatives, "inequality remains a pernicious problem" in tech industries (Wynn, 2020, p. 107). The structural inequalities that are evident in Silicon Valley employees are also reproduced in AI and tech products. For example, Buolamwini and Gebru (2018, p. 77) found that, in facial recognition software, training "datasets are overwhelmingly composed of lighter-skinned subjects." These inequalities were further documented in the 2020 film *Coded Bias*, which explores the work of Joy Buolamwini, founder of the Algorithmic

Justice League. One of the conclusions drawn in the film is that, if it is mostly white men who do the mathematics and coding required to build algorithms, it is not surprising that "computers are worse at recognising women and people of colour than white men" (Venkatraman, 2020, p. 30). Similar sorts of 'coded bias' can be found in voice recognition software, which is less able to understand accents, genders, and ages – when it comes to the accuracy of automatic speech recognition in voice assistants as well as the word accuracy and speaker identity diarization in speech-to-text translation (see Parslow et al., 2021). With the rapid escalation in 2023 of LLMs, such as ChatGPT, new biases are being discovered daily (e.g., Appignani & Sanchez, 2024; Liang et al., 2023).

This brings us to a final illustration of the way EMCA research on categories, in particular, may benefit stakeholders outside the academy: how interactional participants identify instances of possible '-isms' (Stokoe, 2015; Whitehead & Stokoe, 2015) and how they decide what to say in response.

10.3 "How to say when it's not okay"

Many of the data extracts used in this book include cases of possible '-isms' – including racism, sexism, heterosexism, ageism, and ableism – and, as discussed in the introduction, one of the goals of category-based work in social interaction has often been to address topics of power, inequality and inclusion at the heart of what started as a crucially sociological and social psychological endeavour (Stokoe, 2012b). As we have seen in the preceding chapters, matters of category (mis)attribution, ascription, resistance, transformation, deletion, and entitlement are fundamental features of social organization and are entirely imbricated in the turn-by-turn machinery of social interaction.

Thus, as noted in Chapter 1: An Introduction to Social Categories in Interaction, there is a long trajectory of work across EMCA and discursive psychology the categorial basis of prejudice, discrimination, and inequalities. To cite just a handful of examples from the wealth of literature in this regard, recent studies have examined how Asian American immigrants to the USA orient to and resist essentialize notions of race (Shrikant, 2018); how managers categorize different generational cohorts in their workplaces (Baker Rosa & Hastings, 2016); how carers support and disempower patients with intellectual disabilities (Chinn & Antaki, 2021); how normative gender categorization practices challenge an organization's attempts to create gender neutral accessible bathrooms (Kiguwa, 2018); how pronouns in particular languages enable interlocutors to avoid indexing gender as relevant to both the topic and the participants to interaction (Miltersen, 2020); how occasioned categories in medical encounters in Latinx communities along the "borderland transnational" context of the US-Mexico border marginalize patients (Vickers,

2020), and how stratified social structures and social class categories can be respecified as members' orientations (Lee, 2018).

In an analysis of a large dataset of telephone calls from clients to landlords and real estate agencies across different city districts in Germany, Du Bois (2019) found that Turkish-named callers were more likely to secure property viewing appointments if they spoke with a standard German accent than a Turkish accent. This study also showed a relationship between social class and linguistic discrimination, since Turkish-accented speakers were more likely to secure a viewing of properties in poorer neighbourhoods than expensive ones. Du Bois (2019) also reports her experience of taking findings back to estate agents themselves, who were "very receptive" to the findings but denied such discrimination at their organizations. She further notes that, while German law prevents discrimination in theory, language-based discrimination "occurs on subtle and implicit levels" and "cannot always be proven" (Du Bois, 2019, p. 107; also see Wright, 2023).

Du Bois's personal website reports other applications of her research on telephone gatekeeping and discrimination, in a series of intercultural and diversity training workshops. Elsewhere, researchers have also taken their category-based findings about 'isms' to other stakeholders in their research. This includes using membership categorization approaches to interrogate the inclusiveness of research itself and make recommendations about how to discuss roles and responsibilities across research teams comprising researchers with and without intellectual disabilities (Frankena et al., 2018). Furthermore, Paulsen (2018, p. 144) explains how he used membership categorization for evaluation and programme planning in the context of "how individuals define the micro-processes of their work, fidelity of implementation, or outcome evaluations of interventions designed to change one's worldview."

One of the most popular training sessions that used the CARM approach introduced earlier started out as a response to a request from community mediators. As part of her funding for 'knowledge transfer,'[1] Stokoe offered two CARM workshops to mediation services across the UK and USA: a general session bringing together different findings that showed how mediators could most effectively convert initial inquiries from callers into clients of their services, and a second 'bespoke' session that would be designed to meet whatever need the mediation centres had. One organization asked for a session on 'hate speech.' To best meet this need – and to move away from traditional role-play or experience- or scenario-based training – Stokoe developed a workshop

---

1   Economic and Social Research Council RES-189-25-0202 project entitled, "Mediating and policing community disputes: Developing new methods for role-play communication skills training."

based on different strands of research in which categories such as age, gender, race, and ethnicity, as well as accusations of racism, sexism, and other forms of prejudice, became live issues in the inquiry calls (see, e.g., Stokoe, 2009a, 2015; Stokoe & Edwards, 2007). For example, Extract 10.14 comes from a mediation session encountered in Chapter 2: Approaching Membership Categorization (Extract 2.7) in which three parties in a dispute are co-present (C1, C2, C3), with two mediators (M1, M2). This extract is over halfway through a 90-minute session, and the ostensible cause of the dispute is a shared garden space which has been, according to C2 and C3, 'colonized' by C1's plants. Here, C1 is explaining what she sees as the ostensible root of the problem.

```
Extract 10.14: Neighbour mediation multi-party meeting
01  C1:   I remember (0.3) uh having a word with Gary about something
02        he accused me of being uh- (0.5) like a Barbra Streisand.
03        Which meant I must be aggressive (0.5) Jewish, (0.3) which I
04        am neither,
```

As we have noted previously, this case is interesting not least because of the way C1 turns "Barbra Streisand" into a category (note the indefinite article "a," at line 02) and unpacks what she takes to be the category-bound predicates that turn the categorization into a possible instance of anti-Semitism. In the CARM workshop, the audio recording and transcript stop here. Participants discuss questions about what kind of accusation this is (and their evidence for it) and what – if they were the mediator – they may say in response. Most workshop participants say that their response would topicalize the categorization and explore it further, including asking C2 for his account. This is what actually happens next:

```
Extract 10.15: Barbra Streisand
05              (0.4)
06  C1:  Um::
07              (0.4)
08  M2:  I- I think- [I'm not- I'm not sure that this is helpful
09  M1:              [Is this helpful?
```

Following a number of delays, hitches, and mitigations (lines 05–08) that foreshadow their disalignment from the preceding action (also see our discussion of preference organization in Chapter 7: Organizing Sequences of Action), the mediators simultaneously question whether the course of action C1 has initiated is "helpful" (lines 08 and 09). In doing so, they decline to address her accusation, instead closing off the sequence in favour of returning to a discussion of the garden and what might happen to the plants.

The participants in the CARM workshop use this case as the basis for further discussion, including about the nature and purpose of mediation itself. Indeed, similar to findings from a survey of mediators reported by Rendon (2007), some mediators "believed that prejudice and discrimination issues are irrelevant distractions from mediation's goal of case resolution, and therefore should be ignored or put aside," while others argued that "the mediator should meet the issues 'head on' by bringing them to the table." What CARM sessions offer in contrast to abstracted and individualized survey responses, however, is that mediators – sometimes from the same organization – are able to discuss actual cases, and see actual mediator responses, and discover that not everyone shares an understanding of what counts as an 'ism' or even whether the organization shares an ethos about the purpose of mediation.

The '-isms' workshop was delivered to numerous mediation centres in both the UK and USA between 2011 and 2013. Since then, it has evolved further, most recently into a co-produced resource by Loughborough University's Discourse and Rhetoric Group and its 'Maia' women's network, led by Stokoe. The one-page guidance, '*How to say when it's not okay: Tackling prejudicial -isms in workplace conversation*,'[2] is designed to stand alone as well as accompany the continually refreshed CARM workshop. There are three key aspects to the guidance: first, it is based on research in EMCA and discursive psychology and what people actually do and say (e.g., Pino, 2017; Robles, 2015; Stokoe & Edwards, 2007; Whitehead, 2015, 2018); second, it foregrounds the issue that what people say they would do to 'call out' an '-ism,' or be an ally, differs from what typically happens in real interaction, and third, it describes eight possible responses to an 'ism' based on research. These include – in non-technical language – how to leverage the preference for self-correction ("Pause, with an expectant look"); how to generate self-repair via other-initiation of repair ("Huh?"); indirect, embedded, and mitigated challenges; and direct challenges. It also discusses how to intervene as a third party (also see Joyce & Sterphone, 2022). The resource has been downloaded many times and Stokoe continues to present CARM workshops to organizations across the UK.

Writing about CARM in 2011, Stokoe suggested that, perhaps because EMCA is the study of members' practices, the conversational materials presented in workshops are immediately of interest and accessible to members whether or not they are trained in conversation analysis, ethnomethodology, or membership categorization. As we noted in Chapter 1: An Introduction to Categories in Social Interaction, people "do not have to consult a textbook" to talk to each other or analyse the social world – "*They just do it*" (Silverman, 1998, p. 86; emphasis added). The data presented in CARM workshops, and the discussions that are scaffolded on the basis of them, are grounded

---

2 Available online: www.lboro.ac.uk/media/media/campaigns/iwd/how-to-say-when-its-not-okay.pdf.

uncompromisingly in empirical findings about those data. There is no pressure to either 'dumb down' or 'theorize up': material is presented in much the same way as it might be in any conversation analytic "data session" (also see, e.g., Antaki et al., 2008; Stevanovic & Weiste, 2017). Using it for communication training, however, allows the users of research to engage authentically, without simulation, with their everyday professional practice. CARM's effectiveness as a method for changing communication practice has been evaluated and demonstrated across multiple sectors (e.g., Church & Bateman, 2019; White et al., 2021), including in a feasibility randomized controlled trial in teacher education (Sikveland et al., 2023), thus demonstrating some of the range, scope, and impact of applying findings from studies of categories in social interaction across the academy and beyond.

The application domains described earlier, as well as in the previous two sections, serve to demonstrate the power of research on categories in social interaction and the value of using both naturally occurring materials and conversation analytic methods. The application cases also serve, more broadly, to show the bringing together of the book's core themes as set out in Chapter 1: An Introduction to Categories in Social Interaction. That is, they enable us to further see (1) how categorial phenomena relate to foundational conversation analytic findings on the basic structures and practices that constitute conversational and institutional occasions of talk-in-interaction; (2) how the full range of different types or 'categories of categories' are mobilized by participants through which they design their interactional conduct and/or interpret the conduct of others; and (3) how the practices through which the 'operative' category/ies may be maintained or changed a moment-by-moment during the course of an unfolding interaction.

By returning to these themes, we are coming full circle. In the final section, we revisit the book's aims and set out our views about the future of research on categories in social interaction.

10.4   Categories in social interaction: returning to our aims, predicting the future

Leveraging the methods and findings of research in social interaction to develop 'conversational products' – such as communication guidance and training, or other technologies and tools – is where we bring this chapter, and the book overall, to a close. A key contribution of the book – as with all other research in conversation analysis and membership categorization – is to provide numerous instances of people's interactions 'in the wild,' as they actually are, as they unfold, as they happen – rather than simulate, experimentally produce, report or reflect upon them. Conversation analysts can identify, describe, and share what constitutes authentic and (in)effective practices – including categorial practices – that can be used to underpin how we evaluate, train, or build tools, products, and processes that rely on knowledge of social interaction.

We turn now to some final reflections on the primary aim of the book: to assemble a systematic framework for exposing that and how categories and categorial phenomena are (re)produced in naturally occurring social interaction and texts of all kinds. In part, we wanted to address Schegloff's (2007d, p. 477) proposal that work on membership categorization should embrace "the rest of the field of which it is presumptively a part and what has been learned in it – I mean, conversation analysis." Thus, as discussed in Chapter 1: An Introduction to Categories in Social Interaction, we wrote this book in part to develop a specifically *conversation analytic* framework for the analysis of categorial phenomena. In doing so, we also embrace Watson's (2021, p. 17) call for an "inclusive approach" by working towards converging and unifying the different areas of focus that originated in Sacks's work.

Thus, our aim has been to provide as comprehensive an account as possible in a book-length treatment of the areas where categories and social interaction come together. We chose to build, first and foremost, on the several decades of research that is inspired by and develops Sacks's original work on membership categorization, as they intersect with the "generic orders of organization in talk-in-interaction" identified by Schegloff (2007b, p. 13) – all of which, of course, also owe a heavy debt to Sacks's work. We have thereby sought to specify some of the ways that categories necessarily or contingently feature and function within person reference (and other aspects of word selection), turn-taking, action formation, sequence organization, repair, and epistemics. In keeping with Schegloff's (2007b, p. 264) description of how these domains of interaction individually and together comprise "the stuff of social life," our accounts across Chapters 4–9 of some of the ways categories intersect with each of them can be read both individually, as accounts of the distinct features of each domain, and together, as comprising a larger account of "categorial systematics" (Stokoe, 2012a). But, of course, there are many gaps to fill in and as-yet-unknown expansions and transformations to occur – as we also noted in Chapter 1, we have really only provided "a sketch" or even "a sketch of a sketch" (Schegloff, 1996, p. 471) of a systematics. There is, therefore – as we have noted previously – much potential for future research to flesh out any number of details of our sketch that are missing, incomplete, or even incorrect.

This future work may reflect and/or be aligned to whatever personal, local, regional, national, or international agendas, concerns, or landscapes are pertinent to the participants in the interactions used as data – and thus potentially those of the researchers who selected or created the data. We nevertheless suggest five areas where the systematic investigation of categorial matters will be crucial – and, across each of these, where an excavation of the practices of (in)justice, inclusion, equity, and diversity, across the widest and most inclusive understanding of categorizations, may be conducted:

1. *Fundamental research*: Since we have located our work on categories within the field of (ethnomethodological) conversation analysis, we argue that wherever any and all developments in EMCA go, within and beyond the generic organizations of practice for interaction, categories can and should be a key consideration in pursuing empirical analyses and theoretical understandings of the basic machinery of social interaction.

2. *Application, benefit, and impact*: As outlined in this chapter, the application, benefit, and impact of EMCA research has grown enormously in recent years and the ability and importance of researchers to work with non-academic partners, including governments, industry, third, public, private, commercial, and charity sectors, is clear and vital.

3. *Technology as a research resource*: The study of categories in social interaction began, as with the rest of EMCA, with analysis of telephone interactions, though quickly came to include attention to physically co-present interaction and embodied conduct. Since the early development of EMCA, researchers have fully embraced and even pioneered the use of each emerging technology (e.g., audio recording, video recording, screen capturing, virtual reality) in order to capture and study features of social interaction as it unfolds across all the senses and modalities (e.g., gesture, prosody, gaze, embodied conduct, speech, writing, signing). As technologies continue to develop, they will no doubt be mobilized as tools to enable EMCA to reach interactions in the social world that have not yet been studied.

4. *Technology as a research topic*: Of course, technologies do not just provide tools with which to record social interaction but (as we have discussed in this chapter) are studyable in and of themselves as part of human-technology interaction, human-computer interaction, and, proliferating at a rapid rate, interactions with conversational technologies such as robots, voice assistants, and chatbots – many of which are developed using machine learning and artificial intelligence. Both the basic workings of these technologies and the designed-in 'isms' they may exhibit are directly relevant to and studyable by EMCA researchers, including those focused on categories.

5. *Universality, comparative work and language 'cultures'*: While foundational conversation analytic work has sought to document "candidate universals in human interaction," it has also always attended to "cultural variability" (Schegloff, 2006, p. 83). Indeed, it is only by reference to, and with an adequate grasp of, what is universal about interaction that we can appreciate variations arising from specific features of cultures, languages, geographical regions, etc. We are therefore excited by the trajectories of EMCA research that are providing for both comparative analyses and cross-language,

multi-language universals in terms of the interactional practices that constitute the foundations of human sociality. There is much to explore about where categorial practices feature within these emerging research trajectories.

We opened this book with the observation "To categorize is human." We hope that, across its chapters, we have inspired and energized colleagues – those already working with categories in social interaction within EMCA; those who have typically worked or self-identified as 'conversation analysts' or 'ethnomethodologists' or 'membership categorization analysts,' or 'discursive psychologists'; as well as those working in other fields and even in industry (who may discover this book by accident!) – to take our 'sketch of a sketch' and extend the categorial systematics we have begun to build.

REFERENCES

Ablitt, J. (2020). Walking in on people in parks: Demonstrating the orderliness of interactional discomfort in urban territorial negotiations. *Emotion, Space and Society*, *34*, 100648.

Ainsworth-Vaughn, N. (1992). Topic transitions in physician-patient interviews: Power, gender, and discourse change. *Language in Society*, *21*(3), 409–426.

Albert, S., Housley, W., & Stokoe, E. (2019). In case of emergency, order pizza: An urgent case of action formation and recognition. In *Proceedings of the 1st International Conference on Conversational User Interfaces*, 1–2.

Alcoff, L. M., & Mendieta, E. (Eds.) (2003). *Identities: Race, class, gender, and nationality*. Blackwell.

Alejandro, A. (2021). How to problematise categories: Building the methodological toolbox for linguistic reflexivity. *International Journal of Qualitative Methods*, *20*, 1–12.

Anderson, D. C. (1978). Some organizational features in the local production of a plausible text. *Philosophy of the Social Sciences*, *8*(2), 113–135.

Anderson, E. (2015). The white space. *Sociology of Race and Ethnicity*, *1*(1), 10–21.

Anderson, E. (2022). *Black in white space: The enduring impact of color in everyday life*. University of Chicago Press.

Anderson, R. J., & Sharrock, W. (2017). *Has ethnomethodology run its course?* www.sharrockandanderson.co.uk/wpcontent/uploads/2019/10/Run-its-Course-VII.pdf

Antaki, C. (2011). *Applied conversation analysis: Intervention and change in institutional talk*. Palgrave Macmillan.

Antaki, C., & Horowitz, A. (2000). Using identity ascription to disqualify a rival version of events as "interested". *Research on Language and Social Interaction*, *33*(2), 155–177.

Antaki, C., & Widdicombe, S. (Eds.). (1998a). *Identities in talk*. Sage.

Antaki, C., & Widdicombe, S. (1998b). Identity as an achievement and as a tool. In C. Antaki & S. Widdicombe (Eds.), *Identites in talk* (pp. 1–14). Sage.

Antaki, C., Biazzi, M., Nissen, A., & Wagner, J. (2008). Accounting for moral judgments in academic talk: The case of a conversation analysis data session. *Text & Talk*, *28*(1), 1–30.

Antaki, C., Billig, M., Edwards, D., & Potter, J. (2003). Discourse analysis means doing analysis: A critique of six analytic shortcomings. *Discourse Analysis Online*, *1*(1). https://extra.shu.ac.uk/daol/articles/open/2002/002/antaki2002002-paper.html

AP. (2020). Explaining AP style on Black and white. *AP News.* https://apnews.com/article/archive-race-and-ethnicity-9105661462

Appiah, K. A. (2020, June 18). The case for capitalizing the *B*in Black. *The Atlantic.* www.theatlantic.com/ideas/archive/2020/06/time-to-capitalize-blackand-white/613159/

Appignani, T., & Sanchez, J. (2024). AI and racism: Tone policing by the Bing AI chatbot. *Discourse Studies.* https://doi.org/10.1177/14614456241235075

Armus, T. (2020, May 27). White woman "terminated" from job after calling police on Black birdwatcher who asked her to leash her dog, company says. *The Washington Post.*

Ashmore, M., & Reed, D. (2005). Innocence and nostalgia in conversation analysis: The dynamic relations of tape and transcript. *Historical Social Research/Historische Sozialforschung, 30*(1), 73–94.

Ásta, Á. (2018). *Categories we live by: The construction of sex, gender, race, and other social categories.* Oxford University Press.

Atkins, S. (2019). Assessing health professionals' communication through role-play: An interactional analysis of simulated versus actual general practice consultations. *Discourse Studies, 21*(2), 109–134.

Atkins, S., Roberts, C., Hawthorne, K., & Greenhalgh, T. (2016). Simulated consultations: A sociolinguistic perspective. *BMC Medical Education, 16,* Article 16.

Atkinson, J. M. (1992). Displaying neutrality: Formal aspects of informal court proceedings. In P. Drew & J. Heritage (Eds.), *Talk at work: Interaction in institutional settings* (pp. 199–211). Cambridge University Press.

Atkinson, J. M., & Drew, P. (1979). *Order in court.* Macmillan.

Atkinson, P. (1988). Ethnomethodology: A critical review. *Annual Review of Sociology, 14*(1), 441–465.

Auer, P. (1984). Referential problems in conversation. *Journal of Pragmatics, 8*(5–6), 627–648.

Avineri, N., & Martinez, D. C. (2021). Applied linguists cultivating relationships for justice: An aspirational call to action. *Applied Linguistics, 42*(6), 1043–1054.

Bae, E. Y., & Oh, S.-Y. (2013). Native speaker and nonnative speaker identities in repair practices of English conversation. *Australian Review of Applied Linguistics, 36*(1), 20–51.

Baker, C. (1984). The "search for adultness": Membership work in adolescent-adult talk. *Human Studies, 7*(1), 301–323.

Baker, C. (1997). Membership categorization and interview accounts. In D. Silverman (Ed.), *Qualitative research: Theory, method and practice* (pp. 130–143). Sage.

Baker, C. (2000). Locating culture in action: Membership categorization in texts and talk. In A. Lee & C. Poynton (Eds.), *Culture and text: Discourse and methodology in social research and cultural studies* (pp. 99–113). Routledge.

Baker, C. (2004). Membership categorization and interview accounts. In D. Silverman (Ed.), *Qualitative research: Theory, method and practice* (pp. 162–176). Sage.

Baker, C., Emmison, M., & Firth, A. (2005). Calibrating for competence in calls to technical support. In C. Baker, M. Emmison, & A. Firth (Eds.), *Calling for help: Language and social interaction in telephone helplines* (pp. 39–62). John Benjamins.

Baker Rosa, N. M., & Hastings, S. O. (2016). Managers making sense of millennials: Perceptions of a generational cohort. *Qualitative Research Reports in Communication, 17*(1), 52–59.

Bakshi, P. (2024). Language, religion, and workplace discrimination: Intersectional microaggressions in India. *Asian Ethnicity, 25*(2), 185–214.

Ban, S., Baker, K., Bradley, G., Derbyshire, J., Elliott, C., Haskin, M., MacKnight, J., & Rosengarten, L. (2021). "Hello, my name is . . .": An exploratory case study of inter-professional student experiences in practice. *British Journal of Nursing*, *30*(13), 802–810.

Barned-Smith, S. J., & Binkovitz, L. (2015, July 21). Dash cam in Bland case shows escalating confrontation. *Houston Chronicle*.

Bedi, S. (2019). Marketing's ethical blind spot: Catering to consumer preferences. *Kelley School of Business Research Paper*, 19–50.

Bender, E. M., Gebru, T., McMillan-Major, A., & Shmitchell, S. (2021). On the dangers of stochastic parrots: Can language models be too big? In *Proceedings of the 2021 ACM Conference on Fairness, Accountability, and Transparency*.

Benjamin, T. (2012). When problems pass us by: Using "you mean" to help locate the source of trouble. *Research on Language & Social Interaction*, *45*(1), 82–109.

Benson, D., & Drew, P. (1978). "Was there firing in Sandy Row that night?": Some features of the organisation of disputes about recorded facts. *Sociological Inquiry*, *48*(2), 89–100.

Benwell, B., & Stokoe, E. (2006). *Discourse and identity*. Edinburgh University Press.

Billig, M. (1995). *Banal nationalism*. Sage.

Billig, M. (1999a). Conversation analysis and the claims of naivety. *Discourse & Society*, *10*(4), 572–576.

Billig, M. (1999b). Whose terms? Whose ordinariness? Rhetoric and ideology in conversation analysis. *Discourse & Society*, *10*(4), 543–558.

Bilmes, J. (2009). Kinship categories in a Northern Thai narrative. In H. Nguyen & G. Kasper (Eds.), *Talk-in-interaction: Multilingual perspectives* (pp. 29–56). University of Hawai'i, National Foreign Language Resource Center.

Bishop, D. (2018). *A woman of a certain age!* https://womanofacertainageinparis.com/blog/2018/08/07/a-woman-of-a-certain-age/

Blackwell, A. F., Blythe, M., & Kaye, J. (2017). Undisciplined disciples: Everything you always wanted to know about ethnomethodology but were afraid to ask Yoda. *Personal and Ubiquitous Computing*, *21*, 571–592.

Blain, H., & Diskin-Holdaway, C. (2023). Destabilizing racial discourses in casual talk-in-interaction. *Applied Linguistics*, *44*(4), 631–657.

Blitvich, P. G.-C. (2022). Karen: Stigmatized social identity and face-threat in the on/offline nexus. *Journal of Pragmatics*, *188*, 14–30.

Blommaert, J. (2001). Context is/as critique. *Critique of Anthropology*, *21*(1), 13–32.

Blommaert, J. (2005). *Discourse: A critical introduction*. Cambridge University Press.

Blythe, J. (2013). Preference organization driving structuration: Evidence from Australian aboriginal interaction for pragmatically motivated grammaticalization. *Language*, *89*(4), 883–919.

Bogen, D. (1999). *Order without rules: Critical theory and the logic of conversation*. SUNY Press.

Bolden, G. B. (2013). Unpacking "self" repair and epistemics in conversation. *Social Psychology Quarterly*, *76*(4), 314–342.

Bolden, G. B. (2014). Negotiating understanding in "intercultural moments" in immigrant family interactions. *Communication Monographs*, *81*(2), 208–238.

Bolden, G. B. (2024). Correcting others in other-initiated other-repair sequences. *Research on Language and Social Interaction*, *57*(2), 193–214.

Bolden, G. B., Hepburn, A., Potter, J., Zhan, K., Wei, W., Park, S. H., Shirokov, A., Chun, H. C., Kurlenkova, A., & Licciardello, D. (2022). Over-exposed self-correction: Practices for managing competence and morality. *Research on Language and Social Interaction*, *55*(3), 203–221.

Bolinger, D. L. (1961). Contrastive accent and contrastive stress. *Language*, *37*, 83–96.

Bologh, R. W. (1992). The promise and failure of ethnomethodology from a feminist perspective: Comment on Rogers. *Gender & Society*, *6*(2), 199–206.

Bowker, G. C., & Star, S. L. (1999). *Sorting things out: Classification and its consequences.* MIT Press.

Bredal, A., Stefansen, K., & Bjørnholt, M. (2024). Why do people participate in research interviews? Participant orientations and ethical contracts in interviews with victims of interpersonal violence. *Qualitative Research, 24*(2), 287–304.

Brett, M. (2020, May 28). Amy Cooper played the damsel in distress. That trope has a troubling history. *The Washington Post.*

Briggs, C. Q., Gardner, D. M., & Ryan, A. M. (2023). Competence-questioning communication and gender: Exploring mansplaining, ignoring, and interruption behaviors. *Journal of Business and Psychology, 38*(6), 1325–1353.

Bucholtz, M. (2000). The politics of transcription. *Journal of Pragmatics, 32*(10), 1439–1465.

Bucholtz, M. (2003). Theories of discourse as theories of gender: Discourse analysis in language and gender studies. In J. Holmes & M. Meyerhoff (Eds.), *The handbook of language and gender* (pp. 43–68). Blackwell.

Bull, P., & Fetzer, A. (2006). Who are we and who are you? The strategic use of forms of address in political interviews. *Text & Talk, 26*(1), 3–37.

Buolamwini, J., & Gebru, T. (2018). Gender shades: Intersectional accuracy disparities in commercial gender classification. In *Proceedings of the 1st Conference on Fairness, Accountability and Transparency.*

Burford-Rice, R., & Augoustinos, M. (2018). 'I didn't mean that: It was just a slip of the tongue': Racial slips and gaffes in the public arena. *British Journal of Social Psychology, 57*(1), 21–42.

Burger, M., & Fitzgerald, R. (2019). Good professional reasons for bad journalism practice: Inventing audience contributions in a live TV debate. *Journalism Practice, 13*(10), 1185–1199.

Butler, C. W., Danby, S., & Emmison, M. (2011). Address terms in turn beginnings: Managing disalignment and disaffiliation in telephone counseling. *Research on Language & Social Interaction, 44*(4), 338–358.

Butler, C. W., & Fitzgerald, R. (2010). Membership-in-action: Operative identities in a family meal. *Journal of Pragmatics, 42*(9), 2462–2474.

Butler, J. (1990). *Gender trouble: Feminism and the subversion of identity.* Routledge.

Buttny, R. (1993). *Social accountability in communication.* Sage.

Button, G. (1987). On member's time. In B. Conein, M. De Fornel, & L. Quéré (Eds.), *Les Formes de la Conversation* (pp. 161–182). CNET.

Button, G. (1991). *Ethnomethodology and the human sciences.* Cambridge University Press.

Button, G., Lynch, M., & Sharrock, W. (2022). *Ethnomethodology, conversation analysis and constructive analysis: On formal structures of practical action.* Routledge.

Button, G., & Sharrock, W. W. (1993). A disagreement over agreement and consensus in constructionist sociology. *Journal for the Theory of Social Behaviour, 23*(1), 1–25.

Bygate, M. (2004). Some current trends in applied linguistics: Towards a generic view. *AILA Review, 17*(1), 6–22.

Byun, S. (2024). Interactional practices of inviting minoritized students to whole-class mathematics discussions. *Educational Studies in Mathematics, 115*, 321–350.

Cahill, S. E. (1983). Reexamining the acquisition of sex roles: A social interactionist approach. *Sex Roles, 9*, 1–15.

Caldas-Coulthard, C. R. (2010). "Women of a certain age": Life styles, the female body and ageism. In *Femininity, Feminism and Gendered Discourse: A Selected and Edited Collection of Papers from the Fifth International Language and Gender Association Conference (IGALA5)*, Newcastle upon Tyne.

Cameron, D. (1997). Demythologizing sociolinguistics. In N. Coupland & A. Jaworski (Eds.), *Sociolinguistics: A reader and course book* (pp. 55–67). Macmillan.

Cameron, D. (2008). Talk from the top down. *Language & Communication, 28*(2), 143–155.

Carlin, A. (2003). Observation and membership categorization: Recognizing 'normal appearances' in public space. *Journal of Mundane Behavior, 4*(1), 77–91.

Carlin, A., Marques, J. B., & Moutinho, R. (2021). Seeing by proxy: Specifying "professional vision". *Learning, Culture and Social Interaction, 30,* 100532.

Chambliss, W. J. (1964). A sociological analysis of the law of vagrancy. *Social Problems, 12*(1), 67–77.

Chang, E. (2019). *Brotopia: Breaking up the boys' club of Silicon Valley.* Portfolio/Penguin.

Charkoudian, L. (2010). Giving police and courts a break: The effect of community mediation on decreasing the use of police and court resources. *Conflict Resolution Quarterly, 28*(2), 141–155.

Cheeks, L., & Whitehead, K. A. (2024). Using racial incompetence as a comedic device and tacit method of anti-racist education. In H. Z. Waring & N. Tadic (Eds.), *Critical conversation analysis: Inequality and injustice in talk-in-interaction* (pp. 174–194). Multilingual Matters.

Chepinchikj, N. (2022). *Interactional approach to cinematic discourse: How do Woody Allen's characters talk?* Palgrave Macmillan.

Chinn, D., & Antaki, C. (2021). Answering the clinicians' questions: Do carers support or disempower patients with intellectual disabilities? *Journal of Applied Research in Intellectual Disabilities, 34*(5), 1233–1234.

Cho, S., Crenshaw, K. W., & McCall, L. (2013). Toward a field of intersectionality studies: Theory, applications, and praxis. *Signs: Journal of Women in Culture and Society, 38*(4), 785–810.

Church, A., & Bateman, A. (2019). Methodology and professional development: Conversation Analytic Role-play Method (CARM) for early childhood education. *Journal of Pragmatics, 143,* 242–254.

Clayman, S., & Heritage, J. (2002). *The news interview: Journalists and public figures on the air.* Cambridge University Press.

Clayman, S., & Heritage, J. (2014). Benefactors and beneficiaries: Benefactive status and stance in the management of offers and requests. In P. Drew & E. Couper-Kuhlen (Eds.), *Requesting in social interaction* (pp. 55–86). Benjamins.

Clayman, S. E. (1988). Displaying neutrality in television news interviews. *Social Problems, 35*(4), 474–492.

Clayman, S. E. (1992). Footing in the achievement of neutrality: The case of news interview discourse. In P. Drew & J. Heritage (Eds.), *Talk at work: Interaction in institutional settings* (pp. 163–198). Cambridge University Press.

Clayman, S. E. (2013). Agency in response: The role of prefatory address terms. *Journal of Pragmatics, 57,* 290–302.

Clayman, S. E., & Whalen, J. (1988). When the medium become the message: The case of the rather-bush encounter. *Research on Language and Social Interaction, 22*(1–4), 241–272.

Clift, R. (2001). Meaning in interaction: The case of actually. *Language, 77*(2), 245–291.

Clift, R., & Raymond, C. W. (2018). Actions in practice: On details in collections. *Discourse Studies, 20*(1), 90–119.

Coalition on Homelessness. (2015). https://hsh.sfgov.org/wp-content/uploads/201 6/06/2015-San-Francisco-Homeless-Count-Report_0-1.pdf

Collins, H. M. (1983). The sociology of scientific knowledge: Studies of contemporary science. *Annual Review of Sociology, 9*(1), 265–285.

Collins, P. H. (1995). Symposium: On West and Fenstermaker's "doing difference". *Gender & Society, 9*(4), 491–494.

Collins, P. H., & Bilge, S. (2020). *Intersectionality.* Polity.

Colman, N. (2020). Why we're capitalizing Black. *New York Times.* www.nytimes.com/2020/07/05/insider/capitalized-black.html

Cookney, F. (2014, March 4). George Bush, Prince William, Kanye West and more: The best Freudian slips and linguistic gaffes ever. *Daily Mirror*. www.mirror.co.uk/news/world-news/best-freudian-slips-linguistic-gaffes-3206919

Coser, L. A. (1975). Presidential address: Two methods in search of a substance. *American Sociological Review, 40*(6), 691–700.

Couper-Kuhlen, E. (2014). What does grammar tell us about action? *Pragmatics Quarterly Publication of the International Pragmatics Association (IPrA), 24*(3), 623–647.

Couper-Kuhlen, E., & Ford, C. E. (Eds.). (2004). *Sound patterns in interaction: Cross-linguistic studies from conversation*. John Benjamins.

Crabtree, A. (2000). Remarks on the social organisation of space and place. *Journal of Mundane Behaviour, 1*(1), 25–44.

Crawley, S. L. (2022). Queering doing gender: The curious absence of ethnomethodology in gender studies and in sociology. *Sociological Theory, 40*(4), 366–392.

Crawley, S. L., Whitlock, M., & Earles, J. (2021). Smithing queer empiricism: Engaging ethnomethodology for a queer social science. *Sociological Theory, 39*(3), 127–152.

Creider, S. C. (2024). I'm just saying: Being explicit in a mixed-race conversation about racism. In H. Z. Waring & N. Tadic (Eds.), *Critical conversation analysis: Inequality and injustice in talk-in-interaction* (pp. 155–173). Multilingual Matters.

Crenshaw, K. W. (1989). Demarginalizing the intersection of race and sex: A Black feminist critique of antidiscrimination doctrine, feminist theory, and antiracist politics. *University of Chicago Legal Forum, 14*, 538–554.

Cuff, E. C. (1994). *Problems of versions in everyday situations: Studies in ethnomethodology and conversation analysis*. University Press of America.

Curl, T. S. (2006). Offers of assistance: Constraints on syntactic design. *Journal of Pragmatics, 38*(8), 1257–1280.

Curl, T. S., & Drew, P. (2008). Contingency and action: A comparison of two forms of requesting. *Research on Language and Social Interaction, 41*(2), 129–153.

Dart, T. (2015, July 17). 'What happened to Sandy?' Protesters tie Sandra Bland case to US race tensions. *The Guardian*.

Davis, K. (1988). Paternalism under the microscope. In A. Dundas Todd & S. Fisher (Eds.), *Gender and discourse: The power of talk*. Ablex.

DeFrancisco, V. L. (1991). The sounds of silence: How men silence women in marital relations. *Discourse & Society, 2*(4), 413–423.

DeLand, M. F. (2021). Men and their moments: Character-driven ethnography and interaction analysis in a park basketball rule dispute. *Social Psychology Quarterly, 84*(2), 155–176.

Deppermann, A. (2011). Notionalization: The transformation of descriptions into categorizations. *Human Studies, 34*, 155–181.

de Rijk, L., Breukelman, M., Dalmaijer, E., & Stommel, W. (2024). 'This uh. . . young lady young gentleman': Gender attribution in the context of a gender-ambiguous robot. *Discourse & Communication*. https://doi.org/10.1177/17504813241267 1

Desai, J., & Kim, T. (2020). The one with post feminism and hegemonic masculinity in friends. *RTF Gender and Media Culture*. https://rtfgenderandmediaculture.wordpress.com/2020/11/18/the-one-with-post-feminism-and-hegemonic-masculinity-in-friends/

Dickerson, P. (2000). 'But I'm different to them': Constructing contrasts between self and others in talk-in-interaction. *British Journal of Social Psychology, 39*(3), 381–398.

Dingemanse, M., Liesenfeld, A., Rasenberg, M., Albert, S., Ameka, F. K., Birhane, A., Bolis, D., Cassell, J., Clift, R., & Cuffari, E. (2023). Beyond single-mindedness: A figure-ground reversal for the cognitive sciences. *Cognitive Science, 47*(1), e13230.

Dingemanse, M., Roberts, S. G., Baranova, J., Blythe, J., Drew, P., Floyd, S., Gisladottir, R. S., Kendrick, K. H., Levinson, S. C., & Manrique, E. (2015). Universal principles in the repair of communication problems. *PLoS One, 10*(9), e0136100.

Dominguez-Whitehead, Y., & Whitehead, K. A. (2014). Food talk: A window into inequality among university students. *Text & Talk, 34*(1), 49–68.

Dourish, P., & Button, G. (1998). On "technomethodology": Foundational relationships between ethnomethodology and system design. *Human-Computer Interaction, 13*(4), 395–432.

Drew, C. (2021). 8 examples of social identity (race, class and gender). *Helpful Professor.* https://helpfulprofessor.com/social-identity-examples/

Drew, P. (1978). Accusations: The occasioned use of members' knowledge of 'religious geography' in describing events. *Sociology, 12*(1), 1–22.

Drew, P. (1991). Asymmetries of knowledge in conversational interactions. In I. Markova & K. Foppa (Eds.), *Asymmetries in dialogue* (pp. 29–48). Harvester/Wheatsheaf.

Drew, P. (1992). Contested evidence in courtroom cross-examination: The case of a trial for rape. In P. Drew & J. Heritage (Eds.), *Talk at work: Interaction in institutional settings* (pp. 470–520). Cambridge University Press.

Drew, P. (1997). 'Open' class repair initiators in response to sequential sources of troubles in conversation. *Journal of Pragmatics, 28*(1), 69–101.

Drew, P. (1998). Complaints about transgressions and misconduct. *Research on Language and Social Interaction, 31*(3&4), 295–325.

Drew, P. (2002). Out of context: An intersection between domestic life and the workplace, as contexts for (business) talk. *Language & Communication, 22*(4), 477–494.

Drew, P. (2003). Precision and exaggeration in interaction. *American Sociological Review, 68*, 917–938.

Drew, P. (2005). Conversation analysis. In K. L. Fitch & R. E. Sanders (Eds.), *Handbook of language and social interaction* (pp. 71–102). Lawrence Erlbaum.

Drew, P. (2018). Epistemics in social interaction. *Discourse Studies, 20*(1), 163–187.

Drew, P., & Couper-Kuhlen, E. (Eds.). (2014). *Requesting in social interaction.* Benjamins.

Drew, P., & Heritage, J. (1992a). Analyzing talk at work: An introduction. In P. Drew & J. Heritage (Eds.), *Talk at work: Interaction in institutional settings* (pp. 3–65). Cambridge University Press.

Drew, P., & Heritage, J. (1992b). *Talk at work: Interaction in institutional settings.* Cambridge University Press.

Drew, P., & Penn, C. (2016). On failure to understand what the other is saying: Accountability, incongruity, and miscommunication. In J. D. Robinson (Ed.), *Accountability in social interaction* (pp. 47–72). Oxford University Press.

Drury, J., & Stokoe, E. (2022). The interactional production and breach of new norms in the time of COVID-19: Achieving physical distancing in public spaces. *British Journal of Social Psychology, 61*(3), 971–990.

Dryer, M. S. (2013). Polar questions. In M. S. Dryer & M. Haspelmath (Eds.), *WALS online (v2020.3)* [Data set]. Zenodo. http://wals.info/chapter/116

Du Bois, I. (2019). Linguistic discrimination across neighbourhoods: Turkish, US-American and German names and accents in urban apartment search. *Journal of Language and Discrimination, 3*(2), 92–119.

Due, B. L. (2024). Ocularcentric participation frameworks: Dealing with a blind member's perspective. In P. Haddington, T. Eilittä, A. Kamunen, L. Kohonen-Aho, T. Oittinen, I. Rautiainen, & A. Vatanen (Eds.), *Ethnomethodological conversation analysis in motion* (pp. 63–82). Routledge.

Duffy, N. (2020). Matt Hancock proclaims Boris Johnson's cabinet, which includes no Black or openly LGBT+ people, the "most diverse in history". *PinkNews.* www.thepinknews.com/2020/06/08/matt-hancock-black-lgbt-sophy-ridge-diverse-cabinet-boris-johnson-priti-patel-backlash/

Duneier, M., & Molotch, H. (1999). Talking city trouble: Interactional vandalism, social inequality, and the 'urban interaction problem'. *American Journal of Sociology, 104*(5), 1263–1295.

Durrheim, K., Greener, R., & Whitehead, K. A. (2015). Race trouble: Attending to race and racism in online interaction. *British Journal of Social Psychology*, *54*(1), 84–99.

Edmonds, D. M., & Pino, M. (2023). Designedly intentional misgendering in social interaction: A conversation analytic account. *Feminism & Psychology*, *33*(4), 668–691.

Edwards, D. (1991). Categories are for talking: On the cognitive and discursive bases of categorization. *Theory & Psychology*, *1*(4), 515–542.

Edwards, D. (1995). Sacks and psychology. *Theory & Psychology*, *5*(4), 579–596.

Edwards, D. (1997). *Discourse and cognition*. Sage.

Edwards, D. (1998). The relevant thing about her: Social identity categories in use. In C. Antaki & S. Widdicombe (Eds.), *Identities in talk* (pp. 15–33). Sage.

Edwards, D. (2000). Extreme case formulations: Softeners, investment, and doing nonliteral. *Research on Language and Social Interaction*, *33*(4), 347–373.

Edwards, D. (2005). Moaning, whinging and laughing: The subjective side of complaints. *Discourse Studies*, *7*(1), 5–29.

Edwards, D. (2006). Discourse, cognition and social practices: The rich surface of language and social interaction. *Discourse Studies*, *8*(1), 41–49.

Edwards, D., & Potter, J. (1992). *Discursive psychology*. Sage.

Edwards, D., & Potter, J. (2020). A word is worth a thousand pictures: Language, interaction, and embodiment. In S. Wiggins & K. Osvaldsson Cromdal (Eds.), *Discursive psychology and embodiment* (pp. 275–301). Palgrave.

Edwards, D., & Stokoe, E. H. (2004). Discursive psychology, focus group interviews and participants' categories. *British Journal of Developmental Psychology*, *22*(4), 499–508.

Egbert, M. (2004). Other-initiated repair and membership categorization – some conversational events that trigger linguistic and regional membership categorization. *Journal of Pragmatics*, *36*(8), 1467–1498.

Eglin, P. (1979). Resolving reality disjunctures on Telegraph Avenue: A study of practical reasoning. *Canadian Journal of Sociology/Cahiers Canadiens de Sociologie*, *4*(4), 359–377.

Eglin, P. (2013). Ethnomethodology and conversation analysis. In D. L. Brunsma, K. E. Iyall Smith, & B. K. Gran (Eds.), *The handbook of sociology and human rights*. Paradigm.

Eglin, P., & Francis, D. (2016). Editors' introduction. In S. Hester, P. Eglin, & D. Francis (Eds.), *Descriptions of deviance: A study in membership categorization analysis*. University of Southern Denmark.

Eglin, P., & Hester, S. (1992). Category, predicate and task: The pragmatics of practical action. *Semiotica*, *88*(3/4), 243–268.

Eglin, P., & Hester, S. (2003). *The Montreal massacre: A story of membership categorization*. Wilfred Laurier University Press.

Eglin, P., & Wideman, D. (1986). Inequality in professional service encounters: Verbal strategies of control versus task performance in calls to the police. *Zeitschrift Für Soziologie*, *15*(5), 341–362.

Ehrlich, S. (2002). Legal institutions, nonspeaking recipiency and participants' orientations. *Discourse & Society*, *13*(6), 731–747.

Elliott, A. (2019). The rise of identity studies: An outline of some theoretical accounts. In A. Elliott (Ed.), *Routledge handbook of identity studies* (pp. 3–17). Routledge.

Enfield, N. J. (2007). Meanings of the unmarked: How 'default' person reference does more than just refer. In N. J. Enfield & T. Stivers (Eds.), *Person reference in interaction: Linguistic, cultural, and social perspectives* (pp. 97–120). Cambridge University Press.

Enfield, N. J. (2013). Reference in conversation. In J. Sidnell & T. Stivers (Eds.), *The handbook of conversation analysis* (pp. 433–454). Wiley-Blackwell.

Enfield, N. J., & Levinson, S. C. (Eds.). (2006). *Roots of human sociality: Culture, cognition and interaction*. Berg.

Enfield, N. J., & Stivers, T. (2007). *Person reference in interaction: Linguistic, cultural and social perspectives.* Cambridge University Press.

Epstein, R., Blake, J., & González, T. (2017). *Girlhood interrupted: The erasure of Black girls' childhood.* Georgetown Law, Center on Poverty and Inequality.

Ervin-Tripp, S. M. (1972). On sociolinguistic rules: Alternation and co-occurrence. In J. J. Gumperz & D. Hymes (Eds.), *Directions in sociolinguistics: The ethnography of communication* (pp. 213–250). Holt, Rinehart and Winston.

Fenstermaker, S., & West, C. (2002). *Doing gender, doing difference: Inequality, power, and institutional change.* Routledge.

Figgou, L., Bozatzis, N., & Kadianaki, I. (2023). 'Guilty as charged': Intersectionality and accountability in lay talk on discrimination and violence. *British Journal of Social Psychology, 62*(3), 1215–1229.

Firth, A., & Wagner, J. (1997). On discourse, communication, and (some) fundamental concepts in SLA research. *The Modern Language Journal, 81*(3), 285–300.

Fischer, J. E., Reeves, S., Porcheron, M., & Sikveland, R. O. (2019). Progressivity for voice interface design. In *Proceedings of the 1st International Conference on Conversational User Interfaces*, Dublin.

Fisher, S. (1984). Doctor-patient communication: A social and micro-political performance. *Sociology of Health & Illness, 6*(1), 1–29.

Fishman, P. M. (1978). Interaction: The work women do. *Social Problems, 25*(4), 397–406.

Fitzgerald, R. (2019). The data and methodology of Harvey Sacks: Lessons from the archive. *Journal of Pragmatics, 143*, 205–214.

Fitzgerald, R. (2021). Sacks: Omni-relevance and the layered texture of interaction. In R. J. Smith, R. Fitzgerald, & W. Housley (Eds.), *On Sacks: Methodology, materials and inspirations* (pp. 88–100). Routledge.

Fitzgerald, R., & Evans, B. (2019). Entering the liminal zone: Generating news with occasioned objects in live TV news reporting. *Journalism Studies, 20*(8), 1130–1148.

Fitzgerald, R., & Housley, W. (2002). Identity, categorization and sequential organization: The sequential and categorial flow of identity in a radio phone-in. *Discourse and Society, 13*(5), 579–602.

Fitzgerald, R., & Housley, W. (Eds.). (2015). *Advances in membership categorisation analysis.* Sage.

Fitzgerald, R., Housley, W., & Butler, C. W. (2009). Omnirelevance and interactional context. *Australian Journal of Communication, 36*(3), 45–64.

Fitzgerald, R., Housley, W., & Rintel, S. (2017). Membership categorisation analysis: Technologies of social action. *Journal of Pragmatics, 118*, 51–55.

Flinkfeldt, M., Parslow, S., & Stokoe, E. (2022). How categorization impacts the design of requests: Asking for email addresses in call-centre interactions. *Language in Society, 51*, 693–716.

Floyd, S., Rossi, G., & Enfield, N. J. (2020). *Getting others to do things: A pragmatic typology of recruitments.* Language Science Press.

Fortunati, L., Edwards, A., Edwards, C., Manganelli, A. M., & de Luca, F. (2022). Is Alexa female, male, or neutral? A cross-national and cross-gender comparison of perceptions of Alexa's gender and status as a communicator. *Computers in Human Behavior, 137*, 107426.

Fox, S., Ramanath, A., & Swan, E. (2023). You people: Membership categorization and situated interactional othering in BigBank. *Gender, Work & Organization, 30*(2), 574–595.

Francis, D. (1994). The golden dreams of the social constructionist. *Journal of Anthropological Research, 50*(2), 97–108.

Francis, D. W. (1986). Some structures of negotiation talk. *Language in Society, 15*(1), 53–79.

Francis, D., & Hester, S. (2004). *An invitation to ethnomethodology: Language, society and interaction.* Sage.

Francis, D., & Hester, S. (2017). Stephen Hester on the problem of culturalism. *Journal of Pragmatics, 118*, 56–63.

Frankena, T. K., Naaldenberg, J., Bekkema, N., van Schrojenstein Lantman-de Valk, H. J., Cardol, M., & Leusink, G. (2018). An exploration of the participation of people with intellectual disabilities in research – a structured interview survey. *Journal of Applied Research in Intellectual Disabilities, 31*(5), 942–947.

Frankena, T. K., Naaldenberg, J., Tobi, H., van der Cruijsen, A., Jansen, H., van Schrojenstein Lantman-de Valk, H., Leusink, G., & Cardol, M. (2019). A membership categorization analysis of roles, activities and relationships in inclusive research conducted by co-researchers with intellectual disabilities. *Journal of Applied Research in Intellectual Disabilities, 32*(3), 719–729.

Frazer-Carroll, M. (2020). Lovers rock gives life to the joyful black history of blues parties. *The Guardian.* www.theguardian.com/commentisfree/2020/nov/24/lovers-rock-black-history-blues-parties-steve-mcqueen-film

Freud, S. (1901). *The psychopathology of everyday life.* Hogarth.

Freud, S. (2017). *Three essays on the theory of sexuality: The 1905 edition.* Verso. (Original work published 1905).

Friend, T. (2017, November 20). Why ageism never gets old. *The New Yorker.*

Frith, H. (1998). Constructing the 'other' through talk. *Feminism & Psychology, 8*(4), 530–536.

Fuat Firat, A., & Shultz, C. J. (1997). From segmentation to fragmentation: Markets and marketing strategy in the postmodern era. *European Journal of Marketing, 31*(3/4), 183–207.

Fukuda, C. (2024). Interactional and categorial analyses of identity construction in the talk of female-to-male (FtM) transgender individuals in Japan. *Pragmatics, 34*(3), 319–346.

Galanter, M. (1974). Why the haves come out ahead: Speculations on the limits of legal change. *Law & Society Review, 9*(1), 95–160.

Garcia, A. C. (2022). A preliminary investigation of the use of racial/ethnic categories in emergency telephone calls in the United States. *Journal of Applied Communication Research, 50*(4), 345–362.

Garfinkel, H. (1967). *Studies in ethnomethodology.* Prentice-Hall.

Garfinkel, H. (1991). Respecification: Evidence for locally produced, naturally accountable phenomena of order, logic, reason, meaning, method, etc. in and as of the essential haecceity of immortal ordinary society (I) – an announcement of studies. In G. Button (Ed.), *Ethnomethodology and the human sciences* (pp. 10–19). Cambridge University Press.

Garfinkel, H., & Sacks, H. (1970). On formal structures of practical actions. In J. C. McKinney & E. A. Tiryakian (Eds.), *Theoretical sociology: Perspectives and developments.* Appleton-Century-Crofts.

Gashaj, V., Stokoe, E., Formaz, C., & Trninić, D. (forthcoming). When failing generates (mathematics) anxiety instead of learning. In C. Chinn, E. Tan, C. Chan, & Y. Kali (Eds.), *Proceedings of the 16th International Conference of the Learning Sciences – ICLS 2022*, International Society of the Learning Sciences, 1465–1468.

Gibson, S. (2019). *Arguing, obeying and defying: A rhetorical perspective on Stanley Milgram's obedience experiments.* Cambridge University Press.

Giles, D. C. (2016). Observing real-world groups in the virtual field: The analysis of online discussion. *British Journal of Social Psychology, 55*(3), 484–498.

Gladwell, M. (2019). *Talking to strangers: What we should know about the people we don't know.* Little, Brown and Company.

Goff, P. A., Jackson, M. C., Di Leone, B. A. L., Culotta, C. M., & DiTomasso, N. A. (2014). The essence of innocence: Consequences of dehumanizing Black children. *Journal of Personality and Social Psychology, 106*(4), 526.

Goffman, E. (1959). *The presentation of self in everyday life.* Anchor Books.

Goffman, E. (1963). *Behaviour in public places.* Free Press.

Goffman, E. (1976). Gender display. *Studies in the Anthropology of Visual Communication*, *3*, 69–77.

Goffman, E. (2017). *Relations in public: Microstudies of the public order*. Routledge. (Original work published 1971).

Gold, J., & Gold, I. (2012). The "truman show" delusion: Psychosis in the global village. *Cognitive Neuropsychiatry*, *17*(6), 455–472.

Goldhaber-Gordon, I., & Goldhaber-Gordon, D. (2006). Silicon stranger. *Nature Physics*, *2*, 723.

Goodman, S., & Burke, S. (2010). "Oh you don't want asylum seekers, oh you're just racist": A discursive analysis of discussions about whether it's racist to oppose asylum seeking. *Discourse & Society*, *21*(3), 325–340.

Goodman, S., & Speer, S. A. (2007). Category use in the construction of asylum seekers. *Critical Discourse Studies*, *4*(2), 165–185.

Goodwin, C. (1979). The interactive construction of a sentence in natural conversation. In G. Psathas (Ed.), *Everyday language: Studies in ethnomethodology* (pp. 97–121). Irvington.

Goodwin, C. (2000). Action and embodiment within situated human interaction. *Journal of Pragmatics*, *32*(10), 1489–1522.

Goodwin, C. (2003). Pointing as situated practice. In S. Kita (Ed.), *Pointing: Where language, culture and cognition meet* (pp. 217–241). Lawrence Elrbaum.

Goodwin, C., & Goodwin, M. H. (1987). Concurrent operations on talk: Notes on the interactive organization of assessments. *IPrA Papers in Pragmatics*, *1*, 1–55.

Goodwin, C., & Heritage, J. (1990). Conversation analysis. *Annual Review of Anthropology*, *19*(1), 283–307.

Gordon, C. (2013). Beyond the observer's paradox: The audio-recorder as a resource for the display of identity. *Qualitative Research*, *13*(3), 299–317.

Gray, J. (1992). *Men are from Mars, women are from Venus: The classic guide to understanding the opposite sex*. HarperCollins.

Greatbatch, D. (1992). On the management of disagreement between news interviewees. In P. Drew & J. Heritage (Eds.), *Talk at work: Interaction in institutional settings*. Cambridge University Press.

Greenfield, B. (2021). Here's why some LGBTQ youth are now embracing the nonbinary pronoun 'it/its'. *Yahoo News*. https://uk.news.yahoo.com/heres-why-some-lgbtq-youth-are-embracing-non-binary-pronoun-it-its-223331366.html?guccounter=1

Grujicic-Alatriste, L. (2015). *Linking discourse studies to professional practice*. Multilingual Matters.

Hacohen, G., & Schegloff, E. A. (2006). On the preference for minimization in referring to persons: Evidence from Hebrew conversation. *Journal of Pragmatics*, *38*(8), 1305–1312.

Hadden, S. C., & Lester, M. (1978). Talking identity: The production of "self" in interaction. *Human Studies*, *1*(4), 331–356.

Haddington, P., & Stokoe, E. (2023). Social interaction in high stakes crisis communication. *Journal of Pragmatics*, *208*, 91–98.

Halkowski, T. (1990). "Role" as an interactional device. *Social Problems*, *37*(4), 564–577.

Hall, S. (1973). A world at one with itself. In S. Cohen & J. Young (Eds.), *The manufacture of news: Social problems, deviance, and the mass media* (pp. 85–94). Constable.

Hammersley, M. (2001). Obvious, all too obvious? Methodological issues in using sex/gender as a variable in educational research. In B. Francis & C. Skelton (Eds.), *Investigating gender: Contemporary perspectives in education*. Open University Press.

Hammersley, M. (2022). Is 'representation' a folk term? Some thoughts on a theme in science studies. *Philosophy of the Social Sciences*, *52*(3), 132–149.

Hansen, A. D. (2005). A practical task: Ethnicity as a resource in social interaction. *Research on Language and Social Interaction*, *38*(1), 63–104.

Harms, P., Koole, T., Stukker, N., & Tulleken, J. (2021). Expertise as a domain of epistemics in intensive care shift-handovers. *Discourse Studies, 23*(5), 636–651.

Harriot, M. (2020, May 29). Amy Cooper is the kind of white woman Black families warn their children about. *The Washington Post.*

Hart, H. L. A. (1948). The ascription of responsibility and rights. *Proceedings of the Aristotelian Society, 49*(1), 171–194.

Hauser, C. (2016, September 15). Sandra Bland's family settles $1.9 million civil lawsuit, lawyer says. *The New York Times.*

Hauser, E. (2011). Generalization: A practice of situated categorization in talk. *Human Studies, 34,* 183–198.

Haviland, J. B. (2007). Person reference in Tzotzil gossip: Referring dupliciter. In N. J. Enfield & T. Stivers (Eds.), *Person reference in interaction: Linguistic, cultural, and social perspectives* (pp. 226–252). Cambridge University Press.

Hayashi, M., Raymond, G., & Sidnell, J. (2013). *Conversational repair and human understanding.* Cambridge University Press.

Heap, J. L. (1990). Applied ethnomethodology: Looking for the local rationality of reading activities. *Human Studies, 13*(1), 39–72.

Heidinger, L., & Cotter, A. (2020). *Perceptions of personal safety among population groups designated as visible minorities in Canada during the COVID-19 pandemic.* Statistics Canada/Statistique Canada.

Helmer, H., & Zinken, J. (2019). Das Heißt ("that means") for formulations and Du Meinst ("you mean") for repair? Interpretations of prior speakers' turns in German. *Research on Language and Social Interaction, 52*(2), 159–176.

Henderson, E. F. (2022). 'So it's not necessarily about exclusion': Category use in naturally occurring transphobic talk. *Journal of Language and Discrimination, 6*(2), 213–240.

Hepburn, A., & Bolden, G. B. (2017). *Transcribing for social research.* Sage.

Hepburn, A., & Potter, J. (2010). Interrogating tears: Some uses of 'Tag questions' in a child protection helpline. In A. F. Freed & S. Ehrlich (Eds.), *Why do you ask? The function of questions in institutional discourse* (pp. 69–86). Oxford University Press.

Hepburn, A., & Potter, J. (2011). Recipients designed: Tag questions and gender. In S. A. Speer & E. Stokoe (Eds.), *Conversation and gender* (pp. 135–152). Cambridge University Press.

Heritage, J. (1984a). A change of state token and aspects of its sequential placement. In J. M. Atkinson & J. Heritage (Eds.), *Structures of social action* (pp. 299–345). Cambridge University Press.

Heritage, J. (1984b). *Garfinkel and ethnomethodology.* Polity.

Heritage, J. (2002). The limits of questioning: Negative interrogatives and hostile question content. *Journal of Pragmatics, 34,* 1427–1446.

Heritage, J. (2011). Territories of knowledge, territories of experience: Empathic moments in interaction. In T. Stivers, L. Mondada, & J. Steensig (Eds.), *The morality of knowledge in conversation* (pp. 159–183). Cambridge University Press.

Heritage, J. (2012a). The epistemic engine: Sequence organization and territories of knowledge. *Research on Language and Social Interaction, 45*(1), 30–52.

Heritage, J. (2012b). Epistemics in action: Action formation and territories of knowledge. *Research on Language & Social Interaction, 45*(1), 1–29.

Heritage, J. (2013). Action formation and its epistemic (and other) backgrounds. *Discourse Studies, 15*(5), 551–578.

Heritage, J. (2018). The ubiquity of epistemics: A rebuttal to the 'epistemics of epistemics' group. *Discourse Studies, 20*(1), 14–56.

Heritage, J., & Clayman, S. (2010). *Talk in action: Interactions, identities, and institutions.* Wiley-Blackwell.

Heritage, J., & Raymond, C. W. (2016). Are explicit apologies proportional to the offenses they address? *Discourse Processes, 53*(1–2), 5–25.

Heritage, J., & Raymond, C. W. (2021). Preference and polarity: Epistemic stance in question design. *Research on Language and Social Interaction, 54*(1), 39–59.

Heritage, J., & Raymond, G. (2005). The terms of agreement: Indexing epistemic authority and subordination in talk-in-interaction. *Social Psychology Quarterly, 68*(1), 15–38.

Heritage, J., & Raymond, G. (2012). Navigating epistemic landscapes: Acquiescence, agency and resistance in responses to polar questions. In J. P. de Ruiter (Ed.), *Questions: Formal, functional and interactional perspectives* (pp. 179–192). Cambridge University Press.

Heritage, J., & Sorjonen, M. L. (1994). Constituting and maintaining activities across sequences: And-prefacing as a feature of question design. *Language in Society, 23*(1), 1–29.

Hesse, M. (2019, November 18). Sexism is a serious issue, not a cheap shot. *Washington Post.*

Hester, S. (1998). Describing "deviance" in school: Recognizably educational psychological problems. In C. Antaki & S. Widdicombe (Eds.), *Identities in talk.* Sage.

Hester, S., & Eglin, P. (1992). *A sociology of crime.* Routledge.

Hester, S., & Eglin, P. (1997a). *Culture in action: Studies in membership categorization analysis.* University Press of America.

Hester, S., & Eglin, P. (1997b). The reflexive constitution of category, predicate and context in two settings. In S. Hester & P. Eglin (Eds.), *Culture in action: Studies in membership categorization analysis* (pp. 25–48). University Press of America.

Hester, S., Eglin, P., & Francis, D. (2016). *Descriptions of deviance: A study in membership categorization analysis.* EMCA Legacy.

Hester, S., & Francis, D. (1994). Doing data: The local organization of a sociological interview. *British Journal of Sociology, 45*(4), 675–695.

Hester, S., & Francis, D. (2000). Ethnomethodology, conversation analysis, and 'institutional talk'. *Text & Talk, 20*(3), 391–413.

Hester, S., & Francis, D. (2003). Analysing visually available mundane order: A walk to the supermarket. *Visual Studies, 18*(1), 36–46.

Hester, S., & Hester, S. (2012). Categorial occasionality and transformation: Analyzing culture in action. *Human Studies, 35*, 563–581.

Hester, S., & Housley, W. (2002). *Language, interaction and national identity.* Ashgate.

Hill, M. J. (forthcoming). *Doing racial projects in requests for police service.*

Hochschild, A., & Machung, A. (2012). *The second shift: Working families and the revolution at home.* Penguin.

Hoey, E. M., & Raymond, C. W. (2024). Racist renditions: Mock language in interaction. In H. Z. Waring & N. Tadic (Eds.), *Critical conversation analysis: Inequality and injustice in talk-in-interaction* (pp. 49–70). Multilingual Matters.

Hollander, M. M., & Turowetz, J. (2023). *Morality in the making of sense and self: Stanley Milgram's obedience experiments and the new science of morality.* Oxford University Press.

Holmes, E. J. B. (2019). *Interaction, identity and social class.* University of York.

Honeyman, V. (2023). The Johnson factor: British national identity and Boris Johnson. *British Politics, 18*(1), 40–59.

Hopper, R., & LeBaron, C. (1998). How gender creeps into talk. *Research on Language and Social Interaction, 31*, 59–74.

Hosoda, Y. (2000). Other-repair in Japanese conversations between nonnative and native speakers. *Issues in Applied Linguistics, 11*(1), 39–65.

Housley, W., & Dahl, P. (2024). Membership categorisation, sociological description and role prompt engineering with ChatGPT. *Discourse and Communication, 18*(6), 848–858.

Housley, W., & Fitzgerald, R. (2002). The reconsidered model of membership categorization analysis. *Qualitative Research, 2*(1), 59–83.

Housley, W., & Fitzgerald, R. (2009). Membership categorization, culture and norms in action. *Discourse & Society, 20*(3), 345–362.

Housley, W., & Fitzgerald, R. (2015). Introduction to membership categorisation analysis. In W. Housley & R. Fitzgerald (Eds.), *Advances in membership categorisation analysis* (pp. 1–21). Sage.

Housley, W., Webb, H., Edwards, A., Procter, R., & Jirotka, M. (2017a). Digitizing sacks? Approaching social media as data. *Qualitative Research, 17*(6), 627–644.

Housley, W., Webb, H., Edwards, A., Procter, R., & Jirotka, M. (2017b). Membership categorisation and antagonistic Twitter formulations. *Discourse & Communication, 11*(6), 567–590.

Housley, W., Webb, H., Williams, M., Procter, R., Edwards, A., Jirotka, M., Burnap, P., Stahl, B. C., Rana, O., & Williams, M. (2018). Interaction and transformation on social media: The case of Twitter campaigns. *Social Media + Society, 4*(1), 1–12.

Huensch, A. (2017). How the initiation and resolution of repair sequences act as a device for the co-construction of membership and identity. *Pragmatics and Society, 8*(3), 355–376.

Humă, B., & Stokoe, E. (2020). The anatomy of first-time and subsequent business-to-business "cold" calls. *Research on Language and Social Interaction, 53*(2), 271–294.

Hummelstedt, I., Holm, G., Sahlström, F., & Zilliacus, H. (2021). 'Refugees here and Finns there' – categorisations of race, nationality, and gender in a Finnish classroom. *Intercultural Education, 32*(2), 145–159.

Ilomäki, S., & Ruusuvuori, J. (2020). From appearings to disengagements: Openings and closings in video-mediated tele-homecare encounters. *Social Interaction: Video-Based Studies of Human Sociality, 3*(3).

Ivanov, A., Nikonova, Z., Frolova, N., & Muratbayeva, I. (2023). Linguistic potential of COVID-19 neologisms in the metaphoric language of socio-political discourse. *Communication and the Public, 8*(3), 237–253.

Jackson, C. (2011). The gendered 'I'. In S. A. Speer & E. Stokoe (Eds.), *Conversation and gender* (pp. 31–47). Cambridge University Press.

Jackson, C. (2013). 'Why do these people's opinions matter?' Positioning known referents as unnameable others. *Discourse Studies, 15*(3), 299–317.

James, D., & Clarke, S. (1993). Women, men, and interruptions: A critical review. In D. Tannen (Ed.), *Gender and conversational interaction* (pp. 231–280). Oxford University Press.

James, D., & Drakich, J. (1993). Understanding gender differences in amount of talk: A critical review of research. In D. Tannen (Ed.), *Gender and conversational interaction* (pp. 281–312). Oxford University Press.

Järviluoma, H., Moisala, P., & Vilkko, A. (2003). *Gender and qualitative methods.* Sage.

Jayyusi, L. (1984). *Categorization and the moral order.* Routledge & Kegan Paul.

Jefferson, G. (1973). A case of precision timing in ordinary conversation: Overlapped tag-positioned address terms in closing sequences. *Semiotica, 9*(1), 49–96.

Jefferson, G. (1974). Error correction as an interactional resource. *Language in Society, 2*, 181–199.

Jefferson, G. (1980). On troubles-premonitory response to inquiry. *Sociological Inquiry, 50*(3), 153–185.

Jefferson, G. (1985). An exercise in the transcription and analysis of laughter. In T. van Dijk (Ed.), *Handbook of discourse analysis* (pp. 25–34). Academic Press.

Jefferson, G. (1986). Notes on 'latency' in overlap onset. *Human Studies, 9*(2), 153–183.

Jefferson, G. (1987). On exposed and embedded correction in conversation. In G. Button & J. R. E. Lee (Eds.), *Talk and social organisation* (pp. 86–100). Multilingual Matters.

Jefferson, G. (1990). List construction as a task and resource. In G. Psathas (Ed.), *Interaction competence* (pp. 63–92). University Press of America.

Jefferson, G. (1996). On the poetics of ordinary talk. *Text and Performance Quarterly, 16*(1), 1–61.

Jefferson, G. (2004a). Glossary of transcript symbols with an introduction. In G. H. Lerner (Ed.), *Conversation analysis: Studies from the first generation* (pp. 13–23). John Benjamins.

Jefferson, G. (2004b). A note on laughter in 'male-female' interaction. *Discourse Studies, 6*(1), 117–133.

Jefferson, G. (2018). *Repairing the broken surface of talk: Managing problems in speaking, hearing, and understanding in conversation.* Oxford University Press.

Jefferson, G., Sacks, H., & Schegloff, E. A. (1987). Notes on laughter in the pursuit of intimacy. In G. Button & J. R. E. Lee (Eds.), *Talk and social organisation* (pp. 152–205). Multilingual Matters.

Jerolmack, C., & Khan, S. (2014). Talk is cheap: Ethnography and the attitudinal fallacy. *Sociological Methods & Research, 43*(2), 178–209.

Jimerson, J. B., & Oware, M. K. (2006). Telling the code of the street: An ethnomethodological ethnography. *Journal of Contemporary Ethnography, 35*(1), 24–50.

Jones, N. (2018). *The chosen ones: Black men and the politics of redemption.* University of California Press.

Jones, N. (2021). "I am a child!": A girl-child's truth and the lies of law enforcement. *Gender & Society, 35*(4), 527–537.

Jones, N., Brown, K., Bautista Duran, E., Heitz, K., Kelekay, J., Rothschild Elyassi, G., & Raymond, G. (2023). "Other than the projects, you stay professional": "Colorblind" cops and the enactment of spatial racism in routine policing. *City & Community, 22*(1), 3–21.

Jones, N., & Raymond, G. (2012). "The camera rolls": Using third-party video in field research. *The Annals of the American Academy of Political and Social Science, 642,* 109–123.

Joyce, J. B., Humă, B., Ristimäki, H.-L., Almeida, F. F. D., & Doehring, A. (2021). Speaking out against everyday sexism: Gender and epistemics in accusations of "mansplaining". *Feminism & Psychology, 31*(4), 502–529.

Joyce, J. B., & Sterphone, J. (2022). Challenging racism in public spaces: Practices for interventions into disputes. *Journal of Pragmatics, 201,* 43–59.

KALW. (2012). *How effective are sit/lie laws?* www.kalw.org/cops-courts/2012-10-25/how-effective-are-sit-lie-laws

Kamio, A. (1997). *Territory of information.* John Benjamins.

Keevallik, L., & Ogden, R. (2020). Sounds on the margins of language at the heart of interaction. *Research on Language and Social Interaction, 53*(1), 1–18.

Kemper, S. (1994). Elderspeak: Speech accommodations to older adults. *Aging, Neuropsychology and Cognition, 1*(1), 17–28.

Kendrick, K. H., Brown, P., Dingemanse, M., Floyd, S., Gipper, S., Hayano, K., Hoey, E., Hoymann, G., Manrique, E., & Rossi, G. (2020). Sequence organization: A universal infrastructure for social action. *Journal of Pragmatics, 168,* 119–138.

Kendrick, K. H., & Drew, P. (2016). Recruitment: Offers, requests, and the organization of assistance in interaction. *Research on Language and Social Interaction, 49*(1), 1–19.

Kerby, J., & Rae, J. (1998). Moral identity in action: Young offenders' reports of encounters with the police. *British Journal of Social Psychology, 37*(4), 439–456.

Kessler, S. J., & McKenna, W. (1978). *Gender: An ethnomethodological approach.* University of Chicago Press.

Kidwell, M. (2018). Early alignment in police traffic stops. *Research on Language and Social Interaction, 51*(3), 292–312.

Kiguwa, P. (2018). Talking about gender neutral bathrooms: Reproducing gender in online interaction. *Annual Review of Critical Psychology*, *15*, 115–135.

Kitzinger, C. (1998). Feminist psychology in an interdisciplinary context. *Journal of Gender Studies*, *7*(2), 199–209.

Kitzinger, C. (2000). Doing feminist conversation analysis. *Feminism & Psychology*, *10*(2), 163–193.

Kitzinger, C. (2005a). Heteronormativity in action: Reproducing the heterosexual nuclear family in after-hours medical calls. *Social Problems*, *52*(4), 477–498.

Kitzinger, C. (2005b). 'Speaking as a heterosexual': (How) does sexuality matter for talk-in-interaction? *Research on Language and Social Interaction*, *38*(3), 221–265.

Kitzinger, C. (2007a). Feminist conversation analysis: Research by students at the University of York, UK. *Feminism & Psychology*, *17*(2), 133–148.

Kitzinger, C. (2007b). Is 'woman' always relevantly gendered? *Gender and Language*, *1*(1), 39–49.

Kitzinger, C. (2008). Developing feminist conversation analysis: A response to Wowk. *Human Studies*, *31*(2), 179–208.

Kitzinger, C. (2009). Doing gender: A conversation analytic perspective. *Gender & Society*, *23*(1), 94–98.

Kitzinger, C. (2013). Repair. In J. Sidnell & T. Stivers (Eds.), *The handbook of conversation analysis* (pp. 229–256). Wiley-Blackwell.

Kitzinger, C., & Mandelbaum, J. (2013). Word selection and social identities in talk-in-interaction. *Communication Monographs*, *80*(2), 176–198.

Kitzinger, C., Shaw, R., & Toerien, M. (2012). Referring to persons without using a full-form reference: Locally initial indexicals in action. *Research on Language & Social Interaction*, *45*(2), 116–136.

Kitzinger, C., & Wilkinson, S. (2017). Referring to persons: Linguistic gender and gender in action – (when) are husbands men? In G. Raymond, G. H. Lerner, & J. Heritage (Eds.), *Enabling human conduct: Studies of talk-in-interaction in honor of Emanuel A. Schegloff* (pp. 189–204). John Benjamins.

Klein, N. L. (2011). Doing gender categorization: Non-recognitional person reference and the omnirelevance of gender. In S. A. Speer & E. Stokoe (Eds.), *Conversation and gender* (pp. 64–82). Cambridge University Press.

Kollock, P., Blumstein, P., & Schwartz, P. (1985). Sex and power in interaction: Conversational privileges and duties. *American Sociological Review*, *50*(1), 34–46.

Kopp, S., & Krämer, N. (2021). Revisiting human-agent communication: The importance of joint co-construction and understanding mental states. *Frontiers in Psychology*, *12*, Article 580955.

Korobov, N. (2001). Reconciling theory with method: From conversation analysis and critical discourse analysis to positioning analysis. *Forum Qualitative Sozialforschung/ Forum: Qualitative Social Research*, *2*(3).

Koshik, I. (2003). Wh-questions used as challenges. *Discourse Studies*, *5*(1), 51–77.

Krummheuer, A. L. (2016). Who am I? What are you? Identity construction in encounters between a teleoperated robot and people with acquired brain injury. In *Social Robotics: 8th International Conference*, Kansas City, MO.

Labov, W. (1972). Some principles of linguistic methodology. *Language in Society*, *1*, 97–120.

Lamerichs, J., & te Molder, H. (2011). *Reflecting on your own talk: The discursive action method at work*. Palgrave Macmillan.

Land, V., & Kitzinger, C. (2005). Speaking as a lesbian: Correcting the heterosexist presumption. *Research on Language and Social Interaction*, *38*(4), 371–416.

Land, V., & Kitzinger, C. (2007). Some uses of third-person reference forms in speaker self-reference. *Discourse Studies*, *9*(4), 493–525.

Laurier, E. (2014). The graphic transcript: Poaching comic book grammar for inscribing the visual, spatial and temporal aspects of action. *Geography Compass*, *8*(4), 235–248.

Leary, M. R., & Tangney, J. P. (Eds.). (2012). *Handbook of self and identity.* Guilford Press.

Lee, J. (1984). *Innocent victims and evil-doers.* Women's Studies International Forum.

Lee, J. (2018). Methodological applications of membership categorization analysis for social class research. *Applied Linguistics, 39*(4), 532–554.

Lepper, G. (2000). *Categories in text and talk: A practical introduction to categorization analysis.* Sage.

Lerner, G. H. (1989). Notes on overlap management in conversation: The case of delayed completion. *Western Journal of Speech Communication, 53*(2), 167–177.

Lerner, G. H. (1991). On the syntax of sentences-in-progress. *Language in Society, 20,* 441–458.

Lerner, G. H. (1993). Collectivities in action: Establishing the relevance of conjoined participation in conversation. *Text, 13*(2), 213–246.

Lerner, G. H. (1996a). Finding 'face' in the preference structures of talk-in-interaction. *Social Psychology Quarterly, 59*(4), 303–321.

Lerner, G. H. (1996b). On the 'semi-permeable' character of grammatical units in conversation: Conditional entry into the turn space of another speaker. *Studies in Interactional Sociolinguistics, 13,* 238–276.

Lerner, G. H. (1996c). On the place of linguistic resources in the organization of talk-in-interaction: 'Second person' reference in multi-party conversation. *Pragmatics, 6*(3), 281–294.

Lerner, G. H. (2002). Turn-sharing: The choral co-production of talk in interaction. In C. E. Ford, B. Fox, & S. A. Thompson (Eds.), *The language of turn and sequence.* Oxford University Press.

Lerner, G. H. (2003). Selecting next speaker: The context-sensitive operation of a context-free organization. *Language in Society, 32,* 177–201.

Lerner, G. H. (2004). Collaborative turn sequences. In G. H. Lerner (Ed.), *Conversation analysis: Studies from the first generation* (pp. 225–256). John Benjamins.

Lerner, G. H. (2013). On the place of hesitating in delicate formulations: A turn-constructional infrastructure for collaborative indiscretion. In J. Sidnell, M. Hayashi, & G. Raymond (Eds.), *Conversational repair and human understanding* (pp. 95–134). Cambridge University Press.

Lerner, G. H. (2019). When someone other than the addressed recipient speaks next: Three kinds of intervening action after the selection of next speaker. *Research on Language and Social Interaction, 52*(4), 388–405.

Lerner, G. H., & Kitzinger, C. (2007). Extraction and aggregation in the repair of individual and collective self-reference. *Discourse Studies, 9*(4), 526–557.

Lerner, G. H., & Kitzinger, C. (2009). *Cascading troubles in the organization of repair.* Paper presented at the Convention of the National Communication Association, Chicago, IL.

Lerner, G. H., & Kitzinger, C. (2012). Research at the intersection of reference and repair: Introduction to the special issue. *Research on Language & Social Interaction, 45*(2), 111–115.

Lerner, G. H., & Kitzinger, C. (2015). Or-prefacing in the organization of self-initiated repair. *Research on Language and Social Interaction, 48*(1), 58–78.

Lerner, G. H., & Kitzinger, C. (2019). Well-prefacing in the organization of self-initiated repair. *Research on Language and Social Interaction, 52*(1), 1–19.

Lerner, G. H., & Raymond, G. (2017). On the practical re-intentionalization of body behavior: Action pivots in the progressive realization of embodied conduct. In G. Raymond, G. H. Lerner, & J. Heritage (Eds.), *Enabling human conduct: Studies of talk-in-interaction in honor of Emanuel A. Schegloff* (pp. 299–313). John Benjamins.

Lerner, G. H., & Raymond, G. (2021). Body trouble: Some sources of difficulty in the progressive realization of manual action. *Research on Language and Social Interaction, 54*(3), 277–298.

Lerner, G. H., & Takagi, T. (1999). On the place of linguistic resources in the organization of talk-in-interaction: A co-investigation of English and Japanese grammatical practices. *Journal of Pragmatics, 31*(1), 49–75.

Lester, J. N. (2014). Discursive psychology: Methodology and applications. *Qualitative Psychology, 1*(2), 141–143.

Lester, J. N., & O'Reilly, M. (2018). *Applied conversation analysis: Social interaction in institutional settings.* Sage.

Leviathan, Y., & Matias, Y. (2018). Google duplex: An AI system for accomplishing real-world tasks over the phone. *Google AI Blog.* https://research.google/pubs/pub49194/

Levin, S. (2016). Delta accused of 'blatant discrimination' by Black doctor after incident on flight. *The Guardian.* www.theguardian.com/us-news/2016/oct/13/delta-discrimination-black-doctor-incident

Levinson, S. C. (2005). Living with Manny's dangerous idea. *Discourse Studies, 7*(4–5), 431–453.

Levinson, S. C. (2007). Optimizing person reference-perspectives from usage on Rossel Island. In N. J. Enfield & T. Stivers (Eds.), *Person reference in interaction: Linguistic, cultural, and social perspectives* (pp. 29–72). Cambridge University Press.

Levinson, S. C. (2013). Action formation and ascription. In T. Stivers & J. Sidnell (Eds.), *The handbook of conversation analysis* (pp. 103–130). Wiley-Blackwell.

Liang, W., Yuksekgonul, M., Mao, Y., Wu, E., & Zou, J. (2023). GPT detectors are biased against non-native English writers. *arXiv preprint arXiv:2304.02819.*

Liesenfeld, A., & Dingemanse, M. (2022). Building and curating conversational corpora for diversity-aware language science and technology. In *Proceedings of the Thirteenth Language Resources and Evaluation Conference.*

Linton, R. (1936). *The study of man: An introduction.* Appleton-Century.

Liu, R.-Y. (2024). Co-constructing parenthood in multiparty interaction: Orienting to parents' rights and responsibilities to act on behalf of others. *Discourse Studies, 26*(1), 48–66.

Liu, Z. (2023). An adult daughter's identity construction: Membership categorization analysis of daily Chinese-Australian family talk. *Journal of Pragmatics, 207,* 1–16.

Lorber, J. (2000). Using gender to undo gender: A feminist degendering movement. *Feminist Theory, 1*(1), 79–95.

Lowrey-Kinberg, B. V., & Sullivan Buker, G. (2017). "I'm giving you a lawful order": Dialogic legitimacy in Sandra Bland's traffic stop. *Law & Society Review, 51*(2), 379–412.

Ly, L., & Levenson, E. (2021). Rochester police officers handcuff and pepper-spray a 9-year-old girl after call of 'family trouble'. *CNN.*

Lynch, M. (1993). *Scientific practice and ordinary action: Ethnomethodology and social studies of science.* Cambridge University Press.

Lynch, M. (2022). Comment on Martin Hammersley "is 'representation' a folk term?" *Philosophy of the Social Sciences, 52*(4), 258–267.

Maheux-Pelletier, G., & Golato, A. (2008). Repair in membership categorization in French. *Language in Society, 37*(5), 689–712.

Mair, M., & Sharrock, W. (2021). Action, meaning and understanding: Seeing sociologically with Harvey Sacks. In R. J. Smith, W. Housley, & R. Fitzgerald (Eds.), *On Sacks: Methodology, materials, and inspirations* (pp. 19–31). Routledge.

Maldonado, L. A. (1995). Symposium: On West and Fenstermaker's "doing difference". *Gender & Society, 9*(4), 494–496.

Marques, A. C. (2019). Displaying gender: Transgender people's strategies in everyday life. *Symbolic Interaction, 42*(2), 202–228.

Marques, A. C. (2020). Displaying trans (in)visibilities. In J. M. Ryan (Ed.), *Trans lives in a globalizing world: Rights, identities and politics* (pp. 17–33). Routledge.

Martikainen, J. (2022). Membership categorization analysis as means of studying person perception. *Qualitative Research in Psychology, 19*(3), 703–721.

Martin, G. (2020). Matt Hancock criticised for "not knowing" how many Black people there are in the cabinet. *Yahoo! News.* www.yahoo.com/video/matt-hancock-black-people-cabinet-110154200.html

Maslin Nir, S. (2020a, June 14). How 2 lives collided in Central Park, rattling the nation. *The New York Times.*

Maslin Nir, S. (2020b, May 26). White woman is fired after calling police on Black man in Central Park. *The New York Times.*

Maynard, D. W. (2003). *Bad news, good news: Conversational order in everyday talk and clinical settings.* University of Chicago Press.

Maynard, D. W. (2013). Defensive mechanisms: I-mean-prefaced utterances in complaint and other conversational sequences. In M. Hayashi, G. Raymond, & J. Sidnell (Eds.), *Conversational repair and human understanding* (pp. 198–233). Cambridge University Press.

Maynard, D. W. (2014). News from somewhere, news from nowhere: On the study of interaction in ethnographic inquiry. *Sociological Methods & Research, 43*(2), 210–218.

Maynard, D. W. (2019). Why social psychology needs autism and why autism needs social psychology: Forensic and clinical considerations. *Social Psychology Quarterly, 82*(1), 5–30.

Maynard, D. W., & Clayman, S. E. (2018). Mandarin ethnomethodology or mutual interchange? *Discourse Studies, 20*(1), 120–141.

Maynard, D. W., & Heritage, J. (2022). *The ethnomethodology program: Legacies and prospects.* Oxford University Press.

Maynard, D. W., & Schaeffer, N. C. (2006). Standardization-in-interaction: The survey interview. In P. Drew, G. Raymond, & D. Weinberg (Eds.), *Talk and interaction in social research methods.* Sage.

Maynard, D. W., Schaeffer, N. C., & Freese, J. (2011). Improving response rates in telephone interviews. In C. Antaki (Ed.), *Applied conversation analysis: Intervention and change in institutional talk* (pp. 54–74). Palgrave Macmillan.

Maynard, D. W., & Turowetz, J. (2022). *Autistic intelligence: Interaction, individuality, and the challenges of diagnosis.* University of Chicago Press.

Mazeland, H. (2007). Parenthetical sequences. *Journal of Pragmatics, 39*(10), 1816–1869.

McCready, R. (2021). 20+ user persona examples, templates and tips for targeted decision-making. *Venngage.* https://venngage.com/blog/user-persona-examples/

McHoul, A. (1987). An initial investigation of the usability of fictional conversation for doing conversation analysis. *Semiotica, 67*(1–2), 84–104.

McHoul, A. (2007). 'Killers' and 'friendlies': Names can hurt me. *Social Identities, 13*(4), 459–469.

McHoul, A., & Rapley, M. (2005). Re-presenting culture and the self: (Dis) agreeing in theory and in practice. *Theory & Psychology, 15*(4), 431–447.

McIntyre, D., & Price, H. (2018). *Applying linguistics: Language and the impact agenda.* Routledge.

McKenzie, K. (2016). Invoking the specter of racism: Category membership as speaker topic and resource. *Qualitative Sociology Review, 12*(3), 44–83.

McLay, K. F. (2019). Geeks, gamers, and girls: Revealing diverse digital identities with membership categorisation analysis. *Discourse: Studies in the Cultural Politics of Education, 40*(6), 946–961.

Meehan, A. J. (1989). Assessing the 'police-worthiness' of citizen complaints to the police: Accountability and the negotiation of 'facts'. In D. Helm, W. T. Anderson, A. J. Meehan, & A. Rawls (Eds.), *Interactional order: New directions in the study of social order.* Irvington.

Meehan, A. J., & Ponder, M. C. (2002). Race and place: The ecology of racial profiling African American motorists. *Justice Quarterly, 19*(3), 399–430.

Mehan, H. (1979). 'What time is it, Denise?": Asking known information questions in classroom discourse. *Theory Into Practice, 18*(4), 285–294.

Meier zu Verl, C., & Meyer, C. (2024). Ethnomethodological ethnography: Historical, conceptual, and methodological foundations. *Qualitative Research, 24*(1), 11–31.

Meredith, J. (2020). Conversation analysis, cyberpsychology and online interaction. *Social and Personality Psychology Compass, 14*(5), 285–294.

Meredith, J., & Stokoe, E. (2014). Repair: Comparing Facebook 'chat' with spoken interaction. *Discourse & Communication, 8*(2), 181–207.

Mikesell, L., Bolden, G. B., Mandelbaum, J., Robinson, J. D., Romaniuk, T., Bolaños-Carpio, A., Searles, D., Wei, W., DiDomenico, S. M., & Angell, B. (2017). At the intersection of epistemics and action: Responding with I know. *Research on Language and Social Interaction, 50*(3), 268–285.

Miltersen, E. H. (2020). Singular de and its referential use in talk-in-interaction. *Scandinavian Studies in Language, 11*(2), 22–61.

Mlynář, J., González-Martínez, E., & Lalanne, D. (2018). Situated organization of video-mediated interaction: A review of ethnomethodological and conversation analytic studies. *Interacting with Computers, 30*(2), 73–84.

Moerman, M. (1974). Accomplishing ethnicity. In R. Turner (Ed.), *Ethnomethodology: Selected readings* (pp. 54–68). Penguin.

Moerman, M. (1988). *Talking culture: Ethnography and conversation analysis.* University of Pennsylvania Press.

Mondada, L. (2016). Challenges of multimodality: Language and the body in social interaction. *Journal of Sociolinguistics, 20*(3), 336–366.

Mondada, L. (2021). Membership categorization and the sequential multimodal organization of action: Walking, perceiving, and talking in material-spatial ecologies. In R. J. Smith, W. Housley, & R. Fitzgerald (Eds.), *On sacks: Methodology, materials and inspirations* (pp. 101–117). Routledge.

Montgomery, D. (2015, July 20). New details released in Sandra Bland's death in Texas jail. *The New York Times.*

Moody, S. J. (2023). Social relationships and institutional roles: Categorizing "novice" and "expert" in foreign language housing. In C. Bushnell & S. J. Moody (Eds.), *Navigating friendships in interaction* (pp. 79–100). Routledge.

Moore, R. J., Szymanski, M. H., Arar, R., & Ren, G.-J. (2018). *Studies in conversational UX design.* Springer.

Nguyen, H. T. (2011). Achieving recipient design longitudinally: Evidence from a pharmacy intern in patient consultations. In J. K. Hall, J. Hellermann, & S. P. Doehler (Eds.), *L2 interactional competence and development* (pp. 173–205). Multilingual Matters.

Nguyen, H. T., & Kasper, G. (Eds.). (2009). *Talk-in-interaction: Multilingual perspectives.* National Foreign Languager Resource Center.

Nielsen, M. F. (2024). Gendered subtle bias in Danish TV election debates. *Pragmatics and Society.* https://doi.org/10.1075/ps.22109.nie

Nikander, P. (2000). 'Old' versus 'little girl': A discursive approach to age categorisation and morality. *Journal of Aging Studies, 14*(4), 335–358.

Norris, P. T. (2002). Purchasing restricted medicines in New Zealand pharmacies: Results from a "mystery shopper" study. *Pharmacy World and Science, 24,* 149–153.

Ochs, E. (1992). Indexing gender. In A. Duranti & C. Goodwin (Eds.), *Rethinking context: Language as an interactive phenomenon* (pp. 335–358). Cambridge University Press.

Ochs, E., Thompson, S. A., & Schegloff, E. A. (Eds.). (1996). *Interaction and grammar.* Cambridge University Press.

Oh, S.-Y. (2007). Overt reference to speaker and recipient in Korean. *Discourse Studies, 9*(4), 462–492.

Oh, S.-Y. (2010). Invoking categories through co-present person reference: The case of Korean conversation. *Journal of Pragmatics, 42,* 1219–1242.

Ohlheiser, A., & Phillip, A. (2015, July 22). 'I will light you up!' Texas officer threatened Sandra Bland with Taser during traffic stop. *The Washington Post.*

Okazawa, R. (2021). Resisting categorization in interaction: Membership categorization analysis of sitcom humor. *Journal of Pragmatics, 186,* 33–44.

Okazawa, R. (2022). Membership categorization, humor, and moral order in sitcom interactions. *Discourse, Context & Media, 46,* 1–8.

Okazawa, R. (2024). Fictional characterization through repair, membership categorization, and attribute ascription. *Text & Talk.* https://doi.org/10.1515/text-2023-0033

Oliver, C., Turnbull, J., & Richardson, M. (2024). Claiming veganism and vegan geographies. *The Geographical Journal, 190,* e12546.

Paoletti, I. (2002). Caring for older people: A gendered practice. *Discourse & Society, 13*(6), 805–817.

Paoletti, I. (Ed.). (2024). *Creating new meanings for old age: Plans and projects after eighty.* Palgrave Macmillan.

Paravina, A. (2024). A discussion of gender, ethnicity, and intersectionality, at the Serb Business Association forum. *Frontiers in Sociology, 8,* 1231050.

Park, J.-E. (2007). Co-construction of nonnative speaker identity in cross-cultural interaction. *Applied Linguistics, 28*(3), 339–360.

Parker, I. (2005). *Qualitative psychology: Introducing radical research.* Open University Press.

Parker, I. (2012). Discursive social psychology now. *British Journal of Social Psychology, 51*(3), 471–477.

Parker, I. (2013). Discourse analysis: Dimensions of critique in psychology. *Qualitative Research in Psychology, 10*(3), 223–239.

Parslow, S., Stokoe, E., & Albert, S. (2021). Using conversation analysis to challenge the notion of emotional tone in sentiment analysis. In *17th International Pragmatics Conference,* Winterthur.

Parsons, T. (1937). *The structure of social action.* Free Press.

Parsons, T. (1951). *The social system.* Free Press.

Paulsen, J. (2018). Membership categorization analysis as an important qualitative method in evaluation. *Evaluation and Program Planning, 67,* 138–145.

Paulus, T., Warren, A., & Lester, J. N. (2016). Applying conversation analysis methods to online talk: A literature review. *Discourse, Context & Media, 12,* 1–10.

Pike, K. L. (1954). Emic and etic standpoints for the description of behavior. In K. L. Pike (Ed.), *Language in relation to a unified theory of the structure of human behavior* (pp. 8–28). Summer Institute of Linguistics.

Pillet-Shore, D. (2011). Doing introductions: The work involved in meeting someone new. *Communication Monographs, 78*(1), 73–95.

Pillet-Shore, D. (2012). Greeting: Displaying stance through prosodic recipient design. *Research on Language & Social Interaction, 45*(4), 375–398.

Pillet-Shore, D. (2018). How to begin. *Research on Language and Social Interaction, 51*(3), 213–231.

Pino, M. (2017). I-challenges: Influencing others' perspectives by mentioning personal experiences in therapeutic community group meetings. *Social Psychology Quarterly, 80*(3), 217–242.

Pino, M., & Edmonds, D. M. (2024). Misgendering, cisgenderism and the reproduction of the gender order in social interaction. *Sociology.* https://doi.org/10.1177/00380385241237194

Pitsch, K., & Koch, B. (2010). How infants perceive the toy robot pleo. An exploratory case study on infant-robot-interaction. In *Proceedings of Second International*

Symposium on New Frontiers in Human-Robot Interactions, De Montfort University, Leicester.

Plunkett, R. (2009). Fashioning the feasible: Categorisation and social change. *Australian Journal of Communication, 36*(3), 23–44.

Poggio, B. (2006). Outline of a theory of gender practices. *Gender Work and Organization, 13*(3), 225.

Police and Criminal Evidence Act. (1984). https://www.legislation.gov.uk/ukpga/1984/60/contents

Pollner, M. (1974). Mundane reasoning. *Philosophy of the Social Sciences, 4*(1), 35–54.

Pollner, M. (1975). The very coinage of your brain: The anatomy of reality disjunctures. *Philosophy of the Social Sciences, 5*, 411–430.

Pollner, M., & Emerson, R. M. (2007). Ethnomethodology and ethnography. In P. Atkinson, A. Coffey, S. Delamont, J. Lofland, & L. Lofland (Eds.), *Handbook of ethnography* (pp. 118–135). Sage.

Pomerantz, A. (1978). Compliment responses: Notes on the co-operation of multiple constraints. In J. Schenkein (Ed.), *Studies in the organization of conversational interaction* (pp. 79–112). Academic Press.

Pomerantz, A. (1980). Telling my side: 'Limited access' as a 'fishing' device. *Sociological Inquiry, 50*(3–4), 186–198.

Pomerantz, A. (1984). Agreeing and disagreeing with assessments: Some features of preferred/dispreferred turn shapes. In J. M. Atkinson & J. Heritage (Eds.), *Structures of social action: Studies in conversation analysis* (pp. 57–101). Cambridge University Press.

Pomerantz, A. (1986). Extreme case formulations: A way of legitimizing claims. *Human Studies, 9*, 219–229.

Pomerantz, A., & Mandelbaum, J. (2005). Conversation analytic approaches to the relevance and uses of relationship categories in interaction. In K. L. Fitch & R. E. Sanders (Eds.), *Handbook of language and social interaction* (pp. 149–171). Lawrence Erlbaum.

Porcheron, M., Fischer, J. E., Reeves, S., & Sharples, S. (2018). Voice interfaces in everyday life. In *Proceedings of the 2018 CHI Conference on Human Factors in Computing Systems*, New York.

Potter, J. (1996). *Representing reality: Discourse, rhetoric and social construction.* Sage.

Potter, J. (2002). Two kinds of natural. *Discourse Studies, 4*(4), 539–542.

Potter, J., & Hepburn, A. (2005). Qualitative interviews in psychology: Problems and possibilities. *Qualitative Research in Psychology, 2*, 281–307.

Potter, J., & Wetherell, M. (1987). *Discourse and social psychology: Beyond attitudes and behaviour.* Sage.

Preece, S. (2016). The Routledge handbook of language and identity. Routledge.

Previtali, F., Nikander, P., & Ruusuvuori, J. (2023). Ageism in job interviews: Discreet ways of building co-membership through age categorisation. *Discourse Studies, 25*(1), 25–50.

Psathas, G. (1979). *Everyday language: Studies in ethnomethodology.* Irvington.

Psathas, G. (1999). Studying the organization in action: Membership categorization and interaction analysis. *Human Studies, 22*(2–4), 139–162.

Puchta, C., & Potter, J. (2004). *Focus group practice.* Sage.

Rafaely, D. (2021). 'Cropped out': The collaborative production of an accusation of racism. *Discourse Studies, 23*(3), 324–338.

Rafaely, D. (2024). Self-categorization: A resource for the management of experiential entitlement in talk about child death. *Text & Talk, 44*(2), 249–269.

Rafaely, D., & Whitehead, K. A. (2020). Extraordinary emergencies: Reproducing moral discourses of the child in institutional interaction. *Pragmatics and Society, 11*(1), 45–69.

Rapley, M. (1998). 'Just an ordinary Australian': Self-categorization and the discursive construction of facticity in 'new racist' political rhetoric. *British Journal of Social Psychology*, *37*(3), 325–344.

Rapley, T. J. (2001). The art(fulness) of open-ended interviewing: Some considerations on analysing interviews. *Qualitative Research*, *1*(3), 303–323.

Rawls, A. W., & Duck, W. (2020). *Tacit racism*. University of Chicago Press.

Rawls, A. W., Duck, W., & Turowetz, J. (2018). Problems establishing identity/residency in a city neighborhood during a Black/white police-citizen encounter: Reprising Du Bois' conception of submission as 'submissive civility'. *City & Community*, *17*(4), 1015–1050.

Rawls, A. W., & Lynch, M. (2024). Ethnography in ethnomethodology and conversation analysis: Both, neither, or something else altogether? *Qualitative Research*, *24*(1), 116–144.

Rawls, A. W., Whitehead, K. A., & Duck, W. (2020). Introduction. In A. W. Rawls, K. A. Whitehead, & W. Duck (Eds.), *Black lives matter: Ethnomethodological and conversation analytic studies of race and systemic racism in everyday interaction* (pp. 4–38). Routledge.

Raymond, C. W. (2016). Linguistic reference in the negotiation of identity and action: Revisiting the T/V distinction. *Language*, *92*(3), 636–670.

Raymond, C. W. (2019a). Category accounts: Identity and normativity in sequences of action. *Language in Society*, *49*(4), 585–606.

Raymond, C. W. (2019b). Intersubjectivity, normativity, and grammar. *Social Psychology Quarterly*, *82*(2), 182–204.

Raymond, C. W., Caldwell, M., Mikesell, L., Park, I., & Williams, N. (2019). Turn-taking and the structural legitimization of bias: The case of the Ford-Kavanaugh hearing by the United States Senate Committee on the judiciary. *Language & Communication*, *69*, 97–114.

Raymond, C. W., Clift, R., & Heritage, J. (2021). Reference without anaphora: On agency through grammar. *Linguistics*, *59*(3), 715–755.

Raymond, C. W., & Heritage, J. (2021). Probability and valence: Two preferences in the design of polar questions and their management. *Research on Language and Social Interaction*, *54*(1), 60–79.

Raymond, C. W., & White, A. E. C. (2017). Time reference in the service of social action. *Social Psychology Quarterly*, *80*(2), 109–131.

Raymond, G. (2000). The voice of authority: The local accomplishment of authoritative discourse in live news broadcasts. *Discourse Studies*, *2*(3), 354–379.

Raymond, G. (2003). Grammar and social organization: Yes/no interrogatives and the structure of responding. *American Sociological Review*, *68*(6), 939–967.

Raymond, G. (2004). Prompting action: The stand-alone 'so' in ordinary conversation. *Research on Language and Social Interaction*, *37*, 185–218.

Raymond, G. (2010). Grammar and social relations: Alternative forms of yes/no-type initiating actions in health visitor interactions. In A. Freed & S. Ehrlich (Eds.), *'Why do you ask?': The function of questions in institutional discourse* (pp. 87–107). Oxford University Press.

Raymond, G. (2018). Which epistemics? Whose conversation analysis? *Discourse Studies*, *20*(1), 57–89.

Raymond, G., Chen, J., & Whitehead, K. A. (2023). Sequential stand-offs in police encounters with the public. *Journal of Language and Social Psychology*, *42*(5–6), 653–678.

Raymond, G., & Heritage, J. (2006). The epistemics of social relations: Owning grandchildren. *Language in Society*, *35*(5), 677–705.

Raymond, G., & Heritage, J. (2013). One question after another: Same-turn repair in the formation of yes/no type initiating actions. In M. Hayashi, G. Raymond, &

J. Sidnell (Eds.), *Conversational repair and human understanding* (pp. 135–171). Cambridge University Press.

Raymond, G., Jungleib, L., Zimmerman, D., & Jones, N. (2022). Rules and policeable matters: Enforcing the civil sidewalk ordinance for 'another first time'. In J. Heritage & D. W. Maynard (Eds.), *The ethnomethodology program: Legacies and prospects* (pp. 162–187). Oxford University Press.

Raymond, G., & Lerner, G. H. (2014). A body and its involvements: Adjusting action for dual involvements. In P. Haddington, T. Keisanen, L. Mondada, & M. Nevile (Eds.), *Multiactivity in social interaction: Beyond multitasking* (pp. 227–246). John Benjamins.

Raymond, G., & Sidnell, J. (2019). Interaction at the boundaries of a world known in common: Initiating repair with 'what do you mean?' *Research on Language and Social Interaction, 52*(2), 177–192.

Raymond, G., & Zimmerman, D. H. (2007). Rights and responsibilities in calls for help: The case of the Mountain Glade Fire. *Research on Language and Social Interaction, 40*(1), 33–61.

Raymond, G., & Zimmerman, D. H. (2016). Closing matters: Alignment and misalignment in sequence and call closings in institutional interaction. *Discourse Studies, 18*(6), 716–736.

Reeves, S. (2017). Some conversational challenges of talking with machines. In *Workshop at the 20th ACM Conference on Computer-Supported Cooperative Work and Social Computing*, Portland, OR.

Reeves, S., Porcheron, M., & Fischer, J. (2018). 'This is not what we wanted': Designing for conversation with voice interfaces. *Interactions, 26*(1), 46–51.

Rendon, J. (2007). Facing prejudice in mediation. What should mediators do? *Mediate.com: Mediators & Everything Mediation.* https://mediate.com/facing-prejudice-in-mediation-what-should-the-mediator-do/

Reuters. (2006). https://web.archive.org/web/20080212002833/http://uk.news. launch.yahoo.com/dyna/article.html?a=%2F06122006%2F325%2Fsmith-seeks-cure-writers-block.html&e=l_news_dm

Reynolds, E. (2017). Description of membership and enacting membership: Seeing-a-lift, being a team. *Journal of Pragmatics, 118*, 99–119.

Reynolds, J., & Wetherell, M. (2003). The discursive climate of singleness: The consequences for women's negotiation of a single identity. *Feminism & Psychology, 13*(4), 489–510.

Richards, K., & Seedhouse, P. (2005). *Applying conversation analysis.* Palgrave Macmillan.

Richardson, E., Haworth, K., & Deamer, F. (2022). For the record: Questioning transcription processes in legal contexts. *Applied Linguistics, 43*(4), 677–697.

Rintel, S. (2013). Tech-tied or tongue-tied? Technological versus social trouble in relational video calling. In *46th Hawaii International Conference on System Sciences.*

Rintel, S. (2015). Omnirelevance in technologised interaction: Couples coping with video calling distortions. In R. Fitzgerald & W. Housley (Eds.), *Advances in membership categorisation analysis* (pp. 123–150). Sage.

Robinson, J. D. (2000). Book review: Identities in talk. Charles Antaki & Sue Widdicombe (Eds.). *Journal of Language and Social Psychology, 19*(4), 494–498.

Robinson, J. D. (2004). The sequential organization of "explicit" apologies in naturally occurring English. *Research on Language and Social Interaction, 37*(3), 291–330.

Robinson, J. D. (2006). Managing trouble responsibility and relationships during conversational repair. *Communication Monographs, 73*(2), 137–161.

Robinson, J. D., Clift, R., Kendrick, K., & Raymond, C. W. (Eds.). (2024). *The Cambridge handbook of methods in conversation analysis.* Cambridge University Press.

Robinson, J. D., & Kevoe-Feldman, H. (2010). Using full repeats to initiate repair on others' questions. *Research on Language and Social Interaction, 43*(3), 232–259.

Robles, J. S. (2015). Extreme case (re)formulation as a practice for making hearably-racist talk repairable. *Journal of Language and Social Psychology, 34*(4), 390–409.

Robles, J. S., & Joyce, J. B. (2024). Stereotypes in conducting interactional disputes in civil service contexts. In A. Kurylo & Y. Hu (Eds.), *Communicated stereotypes at work* (pp. 187–206). Lexington Books.

Robles, J. S., & Xie, Y. (2024). Managing blame for racism in broadcast media. *Discourse, Context & Media, 59*, 100785.

Roca-Cuberes, C. (2008). Membership categorization and professional insanity ascription. *Discourse Studies, 10*(4), 543–570.

Rogers, K. (2015, July 16). F.B.I. investigating police accounts of Black woman's death in custody. *The New York Times.*

Rogers, M. F. (1992a). Resisting the enormous either/or: A response to Bologh and Zimmerman. *Gender & Society, 6*(2), 207–214.

Rogers, M. F. (1992b). They all were passing: Agnes, Garfinkel, and Company. *Gender & Society, 6*(2), 169–191.

Rossi, G., & Stivers, T. (2020). Category-sensitive actions in interaction. *Social Psychology Quarterly, 84*(1), 49–74.

Roth, A. L. (1998). Who makes the news? Descriptions of television news interviewees' public personae. *Media, Culture & Society, 20*(1), 79–107.

Roulston, K. (2019). *Interactional studies of qualitative research interviews.* John Benjamins.

Sacks, H. (1966). *The search for help: No one to turn to.* Unpublished Ph.D. Dissertation, University of California, Berkeley.

Sacks, H. (1972a). An initial investigation of the usability of conversational data for doing sociology. In D. N. Sudnow (Ed.), *Studies in social interaction* (pp. 31–74). Free Press.

Sacks, H. (1972b). On the analyzability of stories by children. In J. J. Gumperz & D. Hymes (Eds.), *Directions in sociolinguistics: The ethnography of communication* (pp. 325–345). Holt, Rinehart and Winston.

Sacks, H. (1975). Everyone has to lie. In M. Sanches & B. G. Blount (Eds.), *Sociocultural dimensions of language use* (pp. 57–79). Academic Press.

Sacks, H. (1979). Hotrodder: A revolutionary category. In G. Psathas (Ed.), *Everyday language: Studies in ethnomethodology* (pp. 7–14). Irvington.

Sacks, H. (1984a). Notes on methodology. In J. M. Atkinson & J. Heritage (Eds.), *Structures of social action* (pp. 21–27). Cambridge University Press.

Sacks, H. (1984b). On doing 'being ordinary'. In J. M. Atkinson & J. Heritage (Eds.), *Structures of social action* (pp. 413–429). Cambridge University Press.

Sacks, H. (1986). Some considerations of a story told in everyday conversation. *Poetics, 15*, 127–138.

Sacks, H. (1989). Lecture six: The M. I. R. membership categorization device. *Human Studies, 12*(3/4), 271–281.

Sacks, H. (1992). *Lectures on conversation.* Blackwell.

Sacks, H., & Schegloff, E. A. (1979). Two preferences in the organization of reference to persons in conversation and their interaction. In G. Psathas (Ed.), *Everyday language: Studies in ethnomethodology* (pp. 15–21). Irvington.

Sacks, H., & Schegloff, E. A. (2002). Home position. *Gesture, 2*(2), 133–146.

Sacks, H., Schegloff, E. A., & Jefferson, G. (1974). A simplest systematics for the organization of turn taking in conversation. *Language, 50*, 696–735.

Saft, S. (2024). Talk in local news broadcasts: Reinforcing negative views towards the Hawaiian Language. In H. Z. Waring & N. Tadic (Eds.), *Critical conversation analysis: Inequality and injustice in talk-in-interaction* (pp. 71–90). Multilingual Matters.

Salter, J. (2023). I confronted Suella Braverman because as a Holocaust survivor I know what words of hate can do. *The Guardian.* www.theguardian.com/commentisfree/2023/jan/17/confronted-suella-braverman-holocaust-survivor-refugees-home-secretary

Sambaraju, R. (2024). "My mother did not have civil rights under the law": Family derived race categories in negotiating positions on critical race theory. *Journal of Social Issues, 80*(1), 1–24.

Sanchez, R., & Alsharif, M. (2021). Three Rochester police officers are removed from patrol after a 9-year-old girl is handcuffed and pepper-sprayed. *CNN.*

Santos, L. C. D., & Polivanov, B. (2021). What do Alexa, Siri, Lu and Bia have in common? Digital assistants, sexism and ruptures of gender performances. *Galáxia, 46,* 1–24.

Sarangi, S. (2017). En'gaze'ment with text and talk. *Text & Talk, 37*(1), 1–23.

Scarpetta, F., & Spagnolli, A. (2009). The interactional context of humor in stand-up comedy. *Research on Language and Social Interaction, 42*(3), 210–230.

Schaller, M., & Neuberg, S. L. (2012). Chapter one – danger, disease, and the nature of prejudice(s). *Advances in Experimental Social Psychology, 46,* 1–54.

Schegloff, E. A. (1968). Sequencing in conversational openings. *American Anthropologist, 70,* 1075–1095.

Schegloff, E. A. (1972). Notes on a conversational practice: Formulating place. In D. N. Sudnow (Ed.), *Studies in social interaction* (pp. 75–119). Free Press.

Schegloff, E. A. (1979a). Identification and recognition in telephone conversation openings. In G. Psathas (Ed.), *Everyday language: Studies in ethnomethodology* (pp. 23–78). Irvington.

Schegloff, E. A. (1979b). The relevance of repair to syntax-for-conversation. In T. Givon (Ed.), *Syntax and semantics, volume 12: Discourse and syntax* (pp. 261–286). Academic Press.

Schegloff, E. A. (1980). Preliminaries to preliminaries: "Can I ask you a question?" *Sociological Inquiry, 50*(3–4), 104–152.

Schegloff, E. A. (1986). The routine as achievement. *Human Studies, 9*(2–3), 111–151.

Schegloff, E. A. (1987a). Between micro and macro: Contexts and other connections. In J. Alexander (Ed.), *The micro-macro link* (pp. 207–234). University of California Press.

Schegloff, E. A. (1987b). Some sources of misunderstanding in talk-in-interaction. *Linguistics, 25*(1), 201–218.

Schegloff, E. A. (1988a). Description in the social sciences I: Talk-in-interaction. *IPrA Papers in Pragmatics, 2*(1–2), 1–24.

Schegloff, E. A. (1988b). From interview to confrontation: Observations of the bush/rather encounter. *Research on Language and Social Interaction, 22,* 215–240.

Schegloff, E. A. (1988c). Goffman and the analysis of conversation. In P. Drew & A. Wootton (Eds.), *Erving Goffman: Exploring the interaction order* (pp. 89–135). Polity.

Schegloff, E. A. (1990). On the organization of sequences as a source of "coherence" in talk-in-interaction. In B. Dorval (Ed.), *Conversational organization and its development* (pp. 51–77). Ablex.

Schegloff, E. A. (1991). Reflections on talk and social structure. In D. Boden & D. H. Zimmerman (Eds.), *Talk and social structure: Studies in ethnomethodology and conversation analysis* (pp. 44–70). Polity Press.

Schegloff, E. A. (1992a). In another context. In A. Duranti & C. Goodwin (Eds.), *Rethinking context: Language as an interactive phenomenon* (pp. 191–228). Cambridge University Press.

Schegloff, E. A. (1992b). Introduction. In G. Jefferson (Ed.), *Lectures on conversation* (pp. ix–lii). Blackwell.

Schegloff, E. A. (1992c). On talk and its institutional occasions. In P. Drew & J. Heritage (Eds.), *Talk at work: Interaction in institutional settings* (pp. 101–134). Cambridge University Press.

Schegloff, E. A. (1992d). Repair after next turn: The last structurally provided defense of intersubjectivity in conversation. *American Journal of Sociology, 97*(5), 1295–1345.

Schegloff, E. A. (1995). Discourse as an interactional achievement III: The omnirelevance of action. *Research on Language and Social Interaction, 28*(3), 185–211.

Schegloff, E. A. (1996). Confirming allusions: Toward an empirical account of action. *American Journal of Sociology, 102*(1), 161–216.

Schegloff, E. A. (1996a). Issues of relevance for discourse analysis: Contingency in action, interaction and co-participant context. In E. H. Hovy & D. R. Scott (Eds.), *Computational and conversational discourse: Burning issues – an interdisciplinary account* (pp. 3–38). Springer-Verlag.

Schegloff, E. A. (1996b). Some practices for referring to persons in talk-in-interaction: A partial sketch of a systematics. In B. Fox (Ed.), *Studies in anaphora* (pp. 437–485). John Benjamins.

Schegloff, E. A. (1996c). Turn organization: One intersection of grammar and interaction. In E. Ochs, S. A. Thompson, & E. A. Schegloff (Eds.), *Interaction and grammar* (pp. 52–133). Cambridge University Press.

Schegloff, E. A. (1997a). 'Narrative analysis' thirty years later. *Journal of Narrative and Life History, 7*(1–4), 97–106.

Schegloff, E. A. (1997b). Practices and actions: Boundary cases of other-initiated repair. *Discourse Processes, 23*(3), 499–545.

Schegloff, E. A. (1997c). Whose text? Whose context? *Discourse & Society, 8*(2), 165–187.

Schegloff, E. A. (1997d). Third turn repair. In G. R. Guy, C. Feagin, D. Schiffrin, & J. Baugh (Eds.), *Towards a social science of language: Papers in honor of William Labov. Volume 2: Social interaction and discourse structures* (pp. 31–40). John Benjamins.

Schegloff, E. A. (1998a). Body torque. *Social Research, 65*(3), 535–596.

Schegloff, E. A. (1998b). Reflections on studying prosody in talk-in-interaction. *Language and Speech, 41*(3/4), 235–263.

Schegloff, E. A. (1998c). Reply to wetherell. *Discourse & Society, 9*(3), 413–416.

Schegloff, E. A. (1999a). Naivete vs sophistication or discipline vs self-indulgence: A rejoinder to Billig. *Discourse & Society, 10*(4), 577–582.

Schegloff, E. A. (1999b). 'Schegloff's texts' as 'Billig's data': A critical reply. *Discourse & Society, 10*(4), 558–572.

Schegloff, E. A. (2000a). Overlapping talk and the organization of turn-taking for conversation. *Language in Society, 29*(1), 1–63.

Schegloff, E. A. (2000b). When "others" initiate repair. *Applied Linguistics, 21*(2), 205–243.

Schegloff, E. A. (2001). Accounts of conduct in interaction: Interruption, overlap and turn-taking. In J. H. Turner (Ed.), *Handbook of sociological theory* (pp. 287–321). Springer.

Schegloff, E. A. (2003). On ESP puns. In P. Glenn, C. LeBaron, & J. Mandelbaum (Eds.), *Studies in language and social interaction: In honor of Robert Hopper* (pp. 531–540). Lawrence Erlbaum.

Schegloff, E. A. (2004). On dispensability. *Research on Language and Social Interaction, 37*(2), 95–149.

Schegloff, E. A. (2005a). On complainability. *Social Problems, 52*(4), 449–476.

Schegloff, E. A. (2005b). On integrity in inquiry . . . of the investigated, not the investigator. *Discourse Studies, 7*(4–5), 455–480.

Schegloff, E. A. (2005c). Whistling in the dark: Notes from the other side of liminality. In *Texas Linguistic Forum 48: Proceedings of the 12th Annual Symposium about Language and Society*, Austin (SALSA), 17–30.

Schegloff, E. A. (2006a). Interaction: The infrastructure for social institutions, the natural ecological niche for language, and the arena in which culture is enacted. In N. J. Enfield & S. C. Levinson (Eds.), *Roots of human sociality: Culture, cognition and interaction* (pp. 70–95). Berg.

Schegloff, E. A. (2006b). On possibles. *Discourse Studies, 8*(1), 141–157.

Schegloff, E. A. (2007a). Conveying who you are: The presentation of self, strictly speaking. In N. J. Enfield & T. Stivers (Eds.), *Person reference in interaction: Linguistic, cultural, and social perspectives* (pp. 123–148). Cambridge University Press.

Schegloff, E. A. (2007b). *Sequence organization in interaction: A primer in conversation analysis.* Cambridge University Press.

Schegloff, E. A. (2007c). Categories in action: Person-reference and membership categorization. *Discourse Studies, 9*(4), 433–461.

Schegloff, E. A. (2007d). A tutorial on membership categorization. *Journal of Pragmatics, 39*(3), 462–482.

Schegloff, E. A. (2009). One perspective on conversation analysis: Comparative perspectives. In J. Sidnell (Ed.), *Conversation analysis: Comparative perspectives* (pp. 357–406). Cambridge University Press.

Schegloff, E. A. (2013). Ten operations in self-initiated, same-turn repair. In M. Hayashi, G. Raymond, & J. Sidnell (Eds.), *Conversational repair and human understanding* (pp. 41–70). Cambridge University Press.

Schegloff, E. A., & Sacks, H. (1973). Opening up closings. *Semiotica, 8,* 289–327.

Schegloff, E. A., Jefferson, G., & Sacks, H. (1977). The preference for self-correction in the organization of repair in conversation. *Language, 53*(2), 361–382.

Schilt, K. (2016). The importance of being agnes. *Symbolic Interaction, 39*(2), 287–294.

Schilt, K., & Lagos, D. (2017). The development of transgender studies in sociology. *Annual Review of Sociology, 43,* 425–443.

Schilt, K., & Westbrook, L. (2009). Doing gender, doing heteronormativity: "Gender normals," transgender people, and the social maintenance of heterosexuality. *Gender & Society, 23*(4), 440–464.

Schlamb, M. (2019). Alexa loses her voice: Deconstructing representations of race and gender in Amazon's Alexa loses her voice. *Journal of Student Research at Indiana University East, 1*(2), 6–14.

Schütz, A. (1953). Common-sense and scientific interpretation of human action. *Philosophy and Phenomenological Research, 14,* 1–38.

Schütz, A. (1962). *Collected papers, volume 1.* Martinus Nijhoff.

Schütz, A. (1964). *Collected papers, volume 2.* Martinus Nijhoff.

Sciubba, E., Shrikant, N., & Williamson, F. (2020). *Guest blog: EM/CA for racial justice.* https://rolsi.net/2021/06/02/guest-blog-em-ca-for-racial-justice/

Seale, C. (1998). Qualitative interviewing. In C. Seale (Ed.), *Researching society and culture.* Sage.

Selting, M., Reber, E., & Barth-Weingarten, D. (Eds.). (2010). *Prosody in interaction.* John Benjamins.

Seuren, L. M., Wherton, J., Greenhalgh, T., Cameron, D., A'Court, C., & Shaw, S. E. (2020). Physical examinations via video for patients with heart failure: Qualitative study using conversation analysis. *Journal of Medical Internet Research, 22*(2), e16694.

Shapiro, D. (1994). The limits of ethnography: Combining social sciences for CSCW. In *Proceedings of the 1994 ACM Conference On Computer Supported Cooperative Work,* New York.

Sharrock, W. (1974). On owning knowledge. In R. Turner (Ed.), *Ethnomethodology: Selected readings* (pp. 45–53). Penguin.

Shaw, C., Gordon, J., & Williams, K. (2020). Understanding elderspeak: An evolutionary concept analysis. *Innovation in Aging, 4*(1), 451.

Shrikant, N. (2018). The discursive construction of race as a professional identity category in two Texas chambers of commerce. *International Journal of Business Communication, 55,* 94–117.

Shrikant, N. (2021). Cultural difference as a resource for arguments in institutional interactions. *Communication Monographs, 88*(2), 219–236.

Shrikant, N. (2022). Membership categorization analysis of racism in an online discussion among neighbors. *Language in Society, 51*(2), 237–258.

Shrikant, N., & Sambaraju, R. (2021). 'A police officer shot a Black man': Racial categorization, racism, and mundane culpability in news reports of police shootings of Black people in the United States of America. *British Journal of Social Psychology, 60*(4), 1196–1217.

Sidnell, J. (Ed.). (2009). *Conversation analysis: Comparative perspectives*. Cambridge University Press.

Sidnell, J., & Shohet, M. (2013). The problem of peers in Vietnamese interaction. *Journal of the Royal Anthropological Institute, 19*(3), 618–638.

Siewierska, A. (2005). Gender distinctions in independent personal pronouns. In M. Haspelmath, M. S. Dryer, D. Gil, & B. Comrie (Eds.), *The world atlas of language structures*. Oxford University Press.

Sikveland, R. O., & Stokoe, E. (2017). Enquiry calls to GP surgeries in the United Kingdom: Expressions of incomplete service and dissatisfaction in closing sequences. *Discourse Studies, 19*(4), 441–459.

Sikveland, R. O., Kevoe-Feldman, H., & Stokoe, E. (2020). Overcoming suicidal persons' resistance using productive communicative challenges during police crisis negotiations. *Applied Linguistics, 41*(4), 533–551.

Sikveland, R. O., Kevoe-Feldman, H., & Stokoe, E. (2022). *Crisis talk: Negotiating with individuals in crisis*. Routledge.

Sikveland, R. O., Moser, T., Solem, M. S., & Skovholt, K. (2023). The effectiveness of the Conversation Analytic Role-Play Method (CARM) on interactional awareness: A feasibility randomized controlled trial with student teachers. *Teaching and Teacher Education, 129*, 104136.

Silver, J. (2016, September 15). Sandra Bland's family settles wrongful death lawsuit, lawyer says. *The Texas Tribune*.

Silverman, D. (1998). *Harvey Sacks: Social science and conversation analysis*. Oxford University Press.

Singh, A. (2020). Matt Hancock names two Asians when asked to identify Black cabinet members. *Huffington Post*. www.huffingtonpost.co.uk/entry/black-cabinet-matt-hancock-protests_uk_5edc9ffdc5b6aedebbc6a27a

Skovholt, K., Solem, M. S., Vonen, M. N., Sikveland, R. O., & Stokoe, E. (2021). Asking more than one question in one turn in oral examinations and its impact on examination quality. *Journal of Pragmatics, 181*, 100–119.

Smith, D. (1978). K is mentally ill: The anatomy of a factual account. *Sociology, 12*(1), 23–53.

Smith, R. J., Housley, W., & Fitzgerald, R. (Eds.). (2021). *On Sacks: Methodology, materials and inspirations*. Routledge.

Smith Lee, J. R., & Robinson, M. A. (2019). "That's my number one fear in life. It's the police": Examining young Black men's exposures to trauma and loss resulting from police violence and police killings. *Journal of Black Psychology, 45*(3), 143–184.

Smith-Lovin, L., & Brody, C. (1989). Interruptions in group discussions: The effects of gender and group composition. *American Sociological Review, 54*(3), 424–435.

Solnit, R. (2014). *Men explain things to me*. Haymarket Books.

Speer, S. A. (1999). Feminism and conversation analysis: An oxymoron? *Feminism & Psychology, 9*(4), 471–478.

Speer, S. A. (2002a). "Natural" and "contrived" data: A sustainable distinction? *Discourse Studies, 4*(4), 511–525.

Speer, S. A. (2002b). Sexist talk: Gender categories, participants' orientations and irony. *Journal of Sociolinguistics, 6*(3), 347–377.

Speer, S. A. (2005). *Gender talk: Feminism, discourse and conversation analysis*. Routledge.

Speer, S. A. (2012). Feminist conversation analysis: Who needs it? *Qualitative Research in Psychology, 9*(4), 292–297.

Speer, S. A. (2015). Responding to *-isms*. *Journal of Language and Social Psychology, 34*(4), 464–470.

Speer, S. A. (2017). Flirting: A designedly ambiguous action? *Research on Language and Social Interaction, 50*(2), 128–150.

Speer, S. A. (2019). Reconsidering self-deprecation as a communication practice. *British Journal of Social Psychology, 58*(4), 806–828.

Speer, S. A., & Hutchby, I. (2003). From ethics to analytics: Aspects of participants' orientations to the presence and relevance of recording devices. *Sociology, 37*(2), 315–337.

Speer, S. A., & Parsons, C. (2006). Gatekeeping gender: Some features of the use of hypothetical questions in the psychiatric assessment of transsexual patients. *Discourse & Society, 17*(6), 785–812.

Speer, S. A., & Potter, J. (2000). The management of heterosexist talk: Conversational resources and prejudiced claims. *Discourse and Society, 11*(4), 543–572.

Speer, S. A., & Stokoe, E. (2011a). An introduction to conversation and gender. In S. A. Speer & E. Stokoe (Eds.), *Conversation and gender* (pp. 1–28). Cambridge University Press.

Speer, S. A., & Stokoe, E. (2011b). *Conversation and gender*. Cambridge University Press.

Speer, S. A., & Stokoe, E. (2014). Ethics in action: Consent-gaining interactions and implications for research practice. *British Journal of Social Psychology, 53*(1), 54–73.

Stanley, L., & Wise, S. (1993). *Breaking out again: Feminist ontology and epistemology*. Routledge.

Sterphone, J. (2022). Negotiating the mainstream: Proximate stance-taking and far-right policy proposals in bundestag debates. *Journal of Sociolinguistics, 26*, 335–361.

Stevanovic, M., & Weiste, E. (2017). Conversation-analytic data session as a pedagogical institution. *Learning, Culture and Social Interaction, 15*, 1–17.

Stivers, T. (2005). Modified repeats: One method for asserting primary rights from second position. *Research on Language and Social Interaction, 38*(2), 131–158.

Stivers, T. (2007). Alternative recognitionals in person reference. In N. J. Enfield & T. Stivers (Eds.), *Person reference in interaction: Linguistic, cultural, and social perspectives* (pp. 73–96). Cambridge University Press.

Stivers, T., & Enfield, N. J. (Eds.). (2009). *Person reference in interaction linguistic, cultural and social perspectives*. Cambridge University Press.

Stivers, T., Enfield, N. J., Brown, P., Englert, C., Hayashi, M., Heinemann, T., Hoymann, G., Rossano, F., De Ruiter, J. P., & Yoon, K.-E. (2009). Universals and cultural variation in turn-taking in conversation. *Proceedings of the National Academy of Sciences, 106*(26), 10587–10592.

Stockill, C., & Kitzinger, C. (2007). Gendered 'people': How linguistically non-gendered terms can have gendered interactional relevance. *Feminism & Psychology, 17*(2), 224–236.

Stokoe, E. (2003). Mothers, single women and sluts: Gender, morality and membership categorization in neighbour disputes. *Feminism & Psychology, 13*(3), 317–344.

Stokoe, E. (2008a). Categories and sequences: Formulating gender in talk-in-interaction. In K. Harrington, L. Litosseliti, H. Sauntson, & J. Sunderland (Eds.), *Gender and language research methodologies* (pp. 139–157). Palgrave.

Stokoe, E. (2008b). Dispreferred actions and other interactional breaches as devices for occasioning audience laughter in television 'sitcoms'. *Social Semiotics, 18*(3), 289–307.

Stokoe, E. (2009a). Doing actions with identity categories: Complaints and denials in neighbour disputes. *Text and Talk*, *29*(1), 75–97.

Stokoe, E. (2009b). "For the benefit of the tape": Formulating embodied conduct in designedly uni-modal recorded police – suspect interrogations. *Journal of Pragmatics*, *41*(10), 1887–1904.

Stokoe, E. (2009c). "I've got a girlfriend": Police officers doing "self-disclosure" in their interrogations of suspects. *Narrative Inquiry*, *19*(1), 154–182.

Stokoe, E. (2010a). 'I'm not gonna hit a lady': Conversation analysis, membership categorization and men's denials of violence towards women. *Discourse and Society*, *21*(1), 59–82.

Stokoe, E. (2010b). "Have you been married, or . . . ?": Eliciting and accounting for relationship histories in speed-dating interaction. *Research on Language and Social Interaction*, *43*(3), 260–282.

Stokoe, E. (2011a). 'Girl – woman – sorry!': On the repair and non-repair of consecutive gender categories. In S. A. Speer & E. Stokoe (Eds.), *Conversation and gender* (pp. 85–111). Cambridge University Press.

Stokoe, E. (2011b). Simulated interaction and communication skills training: The "conversation analytic role-play method". In C. Antaki (Ed.), *Applied conversation analysis: Changing institutional practices* (pp. 119–139). Palgrave Macmillan.

Stokoe, E. (2012a). Categorial systematics. *Discourse Studies*, *14*(3), 345–354.

Stokoe, E. (2012b). Moving forward with membership categorization analysis: Methods for systematic analysis. *Discourse Studies*, *14*(3), 277–303.

Stokoe, E. (2013). The (in)authenticity of simulated talk: Comparing role-played and actual interaction and the implications for communication training. *Research on Language & Social Interaction*, *46*(2), 165–185.

Stokoe, E. (2014). The Conversation Analytic Role-play Method (CARM): A method for training communication skills as an alternative to simulated role-play. *Research on Language and Social Interaction*, *47*(3), 255–265.

Stokoe, E. (2015). Identifying and responding to possible-isms in institutional encounters: Alignment, impartiality and the implications for communication training. *Journal of Language and Social Psychology*, *34*(4), 427–445.

Stokoe, E. (2018). *Talk: The science of conversation*. Hachette.

Stokoe, E. (2020). Psychological matters in institutional interaction: Insights and interventions from discursive psychology and conversation analysis. *Qualitative Psychology*, *7*(3), 331.

Stokoe, E. (2021, July). *What does it mean to be conversational? Conversation analysis and conversation design*. Conversation Design Festival, Conversation Design Institute.

Stokoe, E., & Albert, S. (2024). A method in search of a problem: The power of conversation analysis. In H. Z. Waring & N. Tadic (Eds.), *Critical conversation analysis* (pp. 197–223). Multilingual Matters.

Stokoe, E., Albert, S., Buschmeier, H., & Stommel, W. (2024). Conversation analysis and conversational technologies: Finding the common ground between academia and industry. *Discourse and Communication*, *18*(6), 837–847.

Stokoe, E., Albert, S., Parslow, S., & Pearl, C. (2021). Conversation analysis and conversation design: Where the moonshots are. *Medium*. https://elizabeth-stokoe.medium.com/conversation-design-andconversation-analysis-c2a2836cb042

Stokoe, E., Albert, S., & Pearl, C. (forthcoming). *Conversation analysis and conversational technologies*. Routledge.

Stokoe, E., & Attenborough, F. (2015). Prospective and retrospective categorisation category proffers and inferences in social interaction and rolling news media. In R. Fitzgerald & W. Housley (Eds.), *Advances in membership categorization analysis* (pp. 51–70). Sage.

Stokoe, E., & Edwards, D. (2007). 'Black this, Black that': Racial insults and reported speech in neighbour complaints and police interrogations. *Discourse & Society*, *18*(3), 355–390.

Stokoe, E., & Edwards, D. (2009). Accomplishing social action with identity categories: Mediating and policing neighbour disputes. In M. Wetherell (Ed.), *Theorizing identities and social action* (pp. 95–115). Palgrave Macmillan.

Stokoe, E., Hepburn, A., & Antaki, C. (2012). Beware the 'Loughborough School' of Social Psychology? Interaction and the politics of intervention. *British Journal of Social Psychology*, *51*(3), 486–496.

Stokoe, E., & Sikveland, R. O. (2021). *Transforming communication training to improve engagement and experience in public, private, and third sector organizations.* https://results2021.ref.ac.uk/impact/179ac72d-cbac-4325-b9e6-639cebf1ed1c?page=1

Stokoe, E., Sikveland, R. O., Albert, S., Hamann, M., & Housley, W. (2020). Can humans simulate talking like other humans? Comparing simulated clients to real customers in service inquiries. *Discourse Studies*, *22*(1), 87–109.

Stokoe, E., Sikveland, R. O., & Huma, B. (2017). Entering the customer's domestic domain: Categorial systematics and the identification of 'parties to a sale'. *Journal of Pragmatics*, *118*, 64–80.

Stokoe, E., & Smithson, J. (2001). Making gender relevant: Conversation analysis and gender categories in interaction. *Discourse & Society*, *12*(2), 217–244.

Stokoe, E., & Weatherall, A. (2002). Gender, language, conversation analysis and feminism. *Discourse & Society*, *13*(6), 707–713.

Stokoe, E., Whitehead., K., & Raymond, G. (2025). Categories in social interaction: Unlocking the resources of conversation analysis and membership categorization for psychological science. *Annual Review of Psychology*, 76.

Stokoe, E. H. (2005). Analysing gender and language. *Journal of Sociolinguistics*, *9*(1), 118–133.

Stolier, R. M., & Freeman, J. B. (2016). The neuroscience of social vision. In J. R. Absher & J. Cloutier (Eds.), *Neuroimaging personality, social cognition, and character: Traits and mental states in the brain* (pp. 139–157). Elsevier.

Stommel, W., Plug, I., Olde Hartman, T. C., Lucassen, P. L. B. J., Van Dulmen, S., & Das, E. (2022). Gender stereotyping in medical interaction: A membership categorization analysis. *Patient Education and Counseling*, *105*(11), 3242–3248.

Streeck, J., Goodwin, C., & LeBaron, C. D. (2011). *Embodied interaction: Language and body in the material world.* Cambridge University Press.

Stringer, J. L., & Hopper, R. (1998). Generic he in conversation? *Quarterly Journal of Speech*, *84*(2), 209–221.

Strong, P. M., & Dingwall, R. (2018). *The ceremonial order of the clinic: Parents, doctors and medical bureaucracies.* Routledge.

Suchman, L. (1994). Do categories have politics? *Computer-Supported Cooperative Work*, *2*, 177–190.

Suchman, L., Gerst, D., & Krämer, H. (2019). "If you want to understand the big issues, you need to understand the everyday practices that constitute them." Lucy Suchman in conversation with Dominik Gerst & Hannes Krämer. *Forum: Qualitative Social Research*, *20*(2), Article 1.

Suchman, L., & Jordan, B. (1990). Interactional troubles in face-to-face survey interviews. *Journal of the American Statistical Association*, *85*(409), 232–241.

Suchman, L. A. (1987). *Plans and situated actions: The problem of human-machine communication.* Cambridge University Press.

Svensson, H. (2024). Name(ing) norms: Mispronunciations and ethnic categories in political talk. Language in Society, 53(1), 99–128.

Tabassum, A., & Hafeez, M. R. (2023). Turn taking strategies and gender: A conversational analysis of Pakistani politicians in TV shows. *Pakistan Languages and Humanities Review*, *7*(1), 389–398.

Tadic, N. (2024). Preference organization and possible-isms in institutional interaction: The case of adult second language classrooms. *Language in Society, 53*(2), 211–237.

Tadic, N., Waring, H. Z., & Reddington, E. (2024). Investigating raciolinguistic ideologies in interaction. In H. Z. Waring & N. Tadic (Eds.), *Critical conversation analysis: Inequality and injustice in talk-in-interaction* (pp. 27–48). Multilingual Matters.

Tajfel, H., & Turner, J. C. (1986). *The social identity theory of intergroup behaviour.* Nelson-Hall.

Takagi, D. Y. (1995). Symposium: On West and Fenstermaker's "doing difference". *Gender and Society, 9*(4), 496–497.

Tam, C. L., Whitehead, K. A., & Raymond, G. (2024). Inequality in action: Granting emergency service requests in a highly resource-constrained context. In H. Z. Waring & N. Tadic (Eds.), *Critical conversation analysis: Inequality and injustice in talk-in-interaction* (pp. 91–114). Multilingual Matters.

Tannen, D. (1990). *You just don't understand: Women and men in conversation.* William Morrow.

Taylor, C. J. (2016). "Relational by nature"? Men and women do not differ in physiological response to social stressors faced by token women. *American Journal of Sociology, 122*(1), 49–89.

Terasaki A. K. (2004). Pre-announcement sequences in conversation. In G. Lerner (Ed.), *Conversation analysis: Studies from the first generation* (pp. 171–223). John Benjamins. (Original work published 1976).

Thorne, B. (1995). Symposium: On West and Fenstermaker's "doing difference". *Gender & Society, 9*(4), 497–499.

Tietbohl, C. K., & White, A. E. C. (2022). Making conversation analysis accessible: A conceptual guide for health services researchers. *Qualitative Health Research, 32*(8–9), 1246–1258.

Tieu, M. (2023). *Self and identity: An exploration of the development, constitution and breakdown of human selfhood.* Routledge.

Tileagă, C., & Stokoe, E. (2016). *Discursive psychology: Classic and contemporary issues.* Routledge.

Tuncer, S. (2016). The effects of video recording on office workers' conduct, and the validity of video data for the study of naturally-occurring interactions. *Forum Qualitative Sozialforschung/Forum: Qualitative Social Research, 17*(3).

Turner, J. C., Hogg, M. A., Oakes, P. J., Reicher, S. D., & Wetherell, M. S. (1987). *Rediscovering the social group: A self-categorization theory.* Blackwell.

Turner, R. (1970). Words, utterances, and activities. In J. Douglas (Ed.), *Understanding everyday life* (pp. 169–187). Aldine.

Turner, R. (Ed.). (1974). *Ethnomethodology: Selected readings.* Penguin Books Canada.

Turowetz, J., & Maynard, D. W. (2016). Category attribution as a device for diagnosis: Fitting children to the autism spectrum. *Sociology of Health & Illness, 38*(4), 610–626.

van de Weerd, P. (2019). "Those foreigners ruin everything here": Interactional functions of ethnic labelling among pupils in the Netherlands. *Journal of Sociolinguistics, 23*(3), 244–262.

van de Weerd, P. (2020). Categorization in the classroom: A comparison of teachers' and students' use of ethnic categories. *Journal of Multicultural Discourses, 15*(4), 354–369.

van den Berg, H., Wetherell, M., & Houtkoop-Steenstra, H. (Eds.). (2003). *Analyzing race talk: Multidisciplinary approaches to the interview.* Cambridge University Press.

van Dijk, T. A. (1987). *Communicating racism: Ethnic prejudice in thought and talk.* Sage.

Van Maanen, J. (1978). The asshole. In P. K. Manning & J. Van Maanen (Eds.), *Policing: A view from the street* (pp. 221–238). Goodyear.

Velody, I., & Williams, R. (1998). Introduction. In I. Velody & R. Williams (Eds.), *The politics of constructionism* (pp. 1–12). Sage.

Venkatraman, V. (2020). Bias in the machines. *New Scientist, 247*(3295), 30.

Vera-Gray, F. (2018). *The right amount of panic: How women trade freedom for safety.* Policy Press.

Vickers, C. H. (2020). Occasioned membership categorization in a transnational medical consultation: Interaction, marginalization, and health disparities. *Journal of Sociolinguistics, 24*(5), 574–592.

Vitali, I., & Arquilla, V. (2019). Conversational smart products: A research opportunity, first investigation and definition. *DeSForM 2019. Beyond Intelligence, 60*–68.

Vom Lehn, D. (2014). *Harold Garfinkel: The creation and development of ethnomethodology.* Left Coast Press.

Walker, G. (2012). Phonetics and prosody in conversation. In J. Sidnell & T. Stivers (Eds.), *The handbook of conversation analysis* (pp. 455–474). Wiley-Blackwell.

Watson, D. R. (1978). Categorization, authorization and blame-negotiation in conversation. *Sociology, 12*(1), 105–113.

Watson, D. R. (1987). Interdisciplinary considerations in the analysis of pro-terms. In G. Button & J. R. E. Lee (Eds.), *Talk and social organization* (pp. 261–289). Multilingual Matters.

Watson, D. R., & Weinberg, T. S. (1982). Interviews and the interactional construction of accounts of homosexual identity. *Social Analysis: The International Journal of Social and Cultural Practice, 11*, 56–78.

Watson, G. (1994). A comparison of social constructionist and ethnomethodological descriptions of how a judge distinguished between the erotic and the obscene. *Philosophy of the Social Sciences, 24*(4), 405–425.

Watson, R. (1997). Some general reflections on 'categorization' and 'sequence' in the analysis of conversation. In S. Hester & P. Eglin (Eds.), *Culture in action: Studies in membership categorization analysis* (pp. 49–76). University Press of America.

Watson, R. (2005). The visibility arrangements of public space: Conceptual resources and methodological issues in analysing pedestrian movements. *Communication and Cognition, 38*, 201–229.

Watson, R. (2009a). *Analysing practical and professional texts: A naturalistic approach.* Routledge.

Watson, R. (2009b). Constitutive practices and Garfinkel's notion of trust: Revisited. *Journal of Classical Sociology, 9*(4), 475–499.

Watson, R. (2021). Discovering Sacks. In R. J. Smith, W. Housley, & R. Fitzgerald (Eds.), *On Sacks: Methodology, materials and inspirations* (pp. 12–18). Routledge.

Weatherall, A. (2000). Gender relevance in talk-in-interaction and discourse. *Discourse & Society, 11*(2), 286–288.

Weatherall, A., & Edmonds, D. M. (2018). Speakers formulating their talk as interruptive. *Journal of Pragmatics, 123*, 11–23.

Weber, L. (1995). Symposium: On West and Fenstermaker's "doing difference". *Gender & Society, 9*(4), 499–503.

Weinberg, D. (2005). *Of others inside: Insanity, addiction, and belonging in America.* Temple University Press.

Weinberg, D., Raymond, G., & Drew, P. (2006). *Talk and interaction in social research methods.* Sage.

Wells, J. (2021). 5 persona examples that work in any industry. *Brafton.* www.brafton.co.uk/blog/strategy/persona-examples-from-around-the-web-and-why-they-work/

West, C. (1979). Against our will: Male interruptions of females in cross-sex conversation. *Annals of the New York Academy of Sciences, 327*(1), 81–97.

West, C., & Fenstermaker, S. (1993). Ethnomethodology and "idealist determinism": A reply to Wilson. In P. England (Ed.), *Theory on gender: Feminism on theory* (pp. 357–361). Aldine De Gruyter.

West, C., & Fenstermaker, S. (1995a). Doing difference. *Gender & Society*, *9*(1), 8–37.

West, C., & Fenstermaker, S. (1995b). Reply: (Re)doing difference. *Gender & Society*, *9*(4), 506–513.

West, C., & Fenstermaker, S. (2002). Accountability in action: The accomplishment of gender, race and class in a meeting of the University of California Board of Regents. *Discourse & Society*, *13*(4), 537–563.

West, C., & Garcia, A. (1988). Conversational shift work: A study of topical transitions between women and men. *Social Problems*, *35*(5), 551–575.

West, C., & Zimmerman, D. H. (1983). Small insults: A study of interruptions in cross-sex conversations between unacquainted persons. In B. Thorne, C. Kramarae, & N. Henley (Eds.), *Language, gender and society* (pp. 102–117). Newbury House.

West, C., & Zimmerman, D. H. (1987). Doing gender. *Gender & Society*, *1*, 124–151.

Wetherell, M. (1998). Positioning and interpretative repertoires: Conversation analysis and post-structuralism in dialogue. *Discourse & Society*, *9*(3), 387–412.

Wetherell, M., & Edley, N. (1999). Negotiating hegemonic masculinity: Imaginary positions and psycho-discursive practices. *Feminism & Psychology*, *9*(3), 335–356.

Whalen, M. R., & Zimmerman, D. H. (1990). Describing trouble: Practical epistemology in citizen calls to the police. *Language in Society*, *19*(4), 465–492.

Whelan, P. (2012). Oxymoronic and sociologically monstrous? Feminist conversation analysis. *Qualitative Research in Psychology*, *9*(4), 279–291.

White, S. J., Ward, K., & Hibberd, E. (2021). A pilot of modified conversation analytic role-play method for one-to-one clinical communication training. *Patient Education and Counseling*, *104*(11), 2748–2755.

Whitehead, K. A. (2009). 'Categorizing the categorizer': The management of racial common sense in interaction. *Social Psychology Quarterly*, *72*(4), 325–342.

Whitehead, K. A. (2011). Some uses of head nods in 'third position' in talk-in-interaction. *Gesture*, *11*(2), 103–122.

Whitehead, K. A. (2012a). Moving forward by doing analysis. *Discourse Studies*, *14*(3), 337–343.

Whitehead, K. A. (2012b). Racial categories as resources and constraints in everyday interactions: Implications for non-racialism in post-apartheid South Africa. *Ethnic and Racial Studies*, *35*(7), 1248–1265.

Whitehead, K. A. (2013a). Managing self/other relations in complaint sequences: The use of self-deprecating and affiliative racial categorizations. *Research on Language and Social Interaction*, *46*(2), 186–203.

Whitehead, K. A. (2013b). Race-class intersections as interactional resources in post-apartheid South Africa. In C. M. Pascale (Ed.), *Social inequality and the politics of representation: A global landscape* (pp. 49–63). Sage.

Whitehead, K. A. (2015). Everyday antiracism in action: Preference organization in responses to racism. *Journal of Language and Social Psychology*, *34*(4), 374–389.

Whitehead, K. A. (2018). Managing the moral accountability of stereotyping. *Journal of Language and Social Psychology*, *37*(3), 288–309.

Whitehead, K. A. (2020). The problem of context in the analysis of talk-in-interaction: The case of implicit whiteness in post-apartheid South Africa. *Social Psychology Quarterly*, *83*(3), 294–313.

Whitehead, K. A. (2021). On Sacks and the analysis of racial categories-in-action. In R. J. Smith, R. Fitzgerald, & W. Housley (Eds.), *On Sacks: Methodology, materials and inspirations* (pp. 195–207). Routledge.

Whitehead, K. A., & Baldry, K. (2018). Omni-relevant and contingent membership categories in research interview and focus group openings. *Qualitative Research*, *18*(2), 135–152.

Whitehead, K. A., Bowman, B., & Raymond, G. (2018). 'Risk factors' in action: The situated constitution of 'risk' in violent interactions. *Psychology of Violence*, *8*(3), 329–338.

Whitehead, K. A., Hill, M. J., & Sterphone, J. (forthcoming). Race in action: Theorizing the situated (re)production of race.

Whitehead, K. A., & Lerner, G. H. (2009). When are persons 'white'? On some practical asymmetries of racial reference in talk-in-interaction. *Discourse and Society*, *20*(5), 613–641.

Whitehead, K. A., & Lerner, G. H. (2020). Referring to somebody: Generic person reference as an interactional resource. *Journal of Pragmatics*, *161*, 46–56.

Whitehead, K. A., & Lerner, G. H. (2022). When simple self-reference is too simple: Managing the categorical relevance of speaker self-presentation. *Language in Society*, *51*, 403–426.

Whitehead, K. A., Raymond, G., & Bowman, B. (2025). Cross-cutting preferences in interactional trajectories toward violence. *American Journal of Sociology*, *130*(5).

Whitehead, K. A., Raymond, G., & Stokoe, E. (2024). Analyzing categorial phenomena in talk-in-interaction. In J. D. Robinson, R. Clift, K. Kendrick, & C. W. Raymond (Eds.), *The Cambridge handbook of methods in conversation analysis* (pp. 534–569). Cambridge University Press.

Whitehead, K. A., & Stokoe, E. (2015). Producing and responding to -*isms* in interaction. *Journal of Language and Social Psychology*, *34*(4), 368–373.

Wible, P. (2016). Her story went viral. But she is not the only Black doctor ignored in an airplane emergency. *The Washington Post*. www.washingtonpost.com/national/ health-science/tamika-cross-is-not-the-only-black-doctor-ignored-in-an-airplane- emergency/2016/10/20/3f59ac08-9544-11e6-bc79-af1cd3d2984b_story.html

Widdicombe, S. (1998). 'But you don't class yourself': The interactional management of category membership and non-membership. In C. Antaki & S. Widdicombe (Eds.), *Identities in talk*. Sage.

Widdicombe, S. (2015). 'Just like the fact that I'm Syrian like you are Scottish': Ascribing interviewer identities as a resource in cross-cultural interaction. *British Journal of Social Psychology*, *54*(2), 255–272.

Widdicombe, S., & Wooffitt, R. (1995). *The language of youth subcultures: Social identity in action*. Harvester/Wheatsheaf.

Wieder, D. L. (1999). Ethnomethodology, conversation analysis, microanalysis, and the ethnography of speaking (EM-CA-MA-ES): Resonances and basic issues. *Research on Language & Social Interaction*, *32*(1–2), 163–171.

Wieder, D. L., & Pratt, S. (1990). On being a recognizable Indian among Indians. In D. Carbaugh (Ed.), *Cultural communication and intercultural contact* (pp. 45–64). Lawrence Erlbaum.

Wiggins, S., & Osvaldsson Cromdal, K. (Eds.). (2020). *Discursive psychology and embodiment*. Palgrave.

Wilkes, J., & Speer, S. A. (2021). Reporting microaggressions: Kinship carers' complaints about identity slights. *Journal of Language and Social Psychology*, *40*(3), 303–327.

Wilkinson, S. (2011a). Constructing ethnicity statistics in talk-in-interaction: Producing the "White European". *Discourse & Society*, *22*(3), 343–361.

Wilkinson, S. (2011b). Gender, routinization and recipient design. In S. A. Speer & E. Stokoe (Eds.), *Conversation and gender* (pp. 112–134). Cambridge University Press.

Wilkinson, S., & Kitzinger, C. (2003). Constructing identities: A feminist conversation analytic approach to positioning in action. In R. Harre & F. Moghaddam (Eds.), *The self and others: Positioning individuals and groups in personal, political and cultural contexts* (pp. 157–180). Praeger.

Wilkinson, S., & Kitzinger, C. (2006). Surprise as an interactional achievement: Reaction tokens in conversation. *Social Psychology Quarterly*, *69*(2), 150–182.

Wilkinson, S., & Kitzinger, C. (2008). Using conversation analysis in feminist and critical research. *Social and Personality Psychology Compass, 2*(2), 555–573.

Wilkinson, S., & Kitzinger, C. (2014). Conversation analysis in language and gender studies. In S. Ehrlich, M. Meyerhoff, & J. Holmes (Eds.), *The handbook of language, gender, and sexuality* (pp. 141–160). Wiley Blackwell.

Willemsen, A., Cromdal, J., & Broth, M. (2023). Expecting the unpredictable: Categorisation of children and youth during driver training. *Discourse Studies, 25*(6), 823–845.

Williams, R. (2000). *Making identity matter: Identity, society and social interaction.* Sociology Press.

Williamson, F. (2024). Black methodologies as ethnomethods: On qualitative methods-making and analyzing the situated work of doing being hybridly human. *Qualitative Research in Psychology.* https://doi.org/10.1080/14780887.1478202 4.12347590

Wilson, A. M. (1998). The role of mystery shopping in the measurement of service performance. *Managing Service Quality: An International Journal, 8*(6), 414–420.

Winant, H. (1995). Symposium: On West and Fenstermaker's "doing difference". *Gender & Society, 9*(4), 503–506.

Wooffitt, R. (2007). Communication and laboratory performance in parapsychology experiments: Demand characteristics and the social organization of interaction. *British Journal of Social Psychology, 46*(3), 477–498.

Wowk, M. T. (1984). Blame allocation, sex and gender in a murder interrogation. *Women's Studies International Forum, 7*(1), 75–82.

Wowk, M. T. (2007). Kitzinger's feminist conversation analysis: Critical observations. *Human Studies, 30*(2), 131–155.

Wright, K. E. (2023). Housing policy and linguistic profiling: An audit study of three American dialects. *Language, 99*(2), e58–e85.

Wu, X., & Fitzgerald, R. (2021). 'Hidden in plain sight': Expressing political criticism on Chinese social media. *Discourse Studies, 23*(3), 365–385.

Wynn, A. T. (2020). Pathways toward change: Ideologies and gender equality in a Silicon Valley technology company. *Gender & Society, 34*(1), 106–130.

Xie, Y. (2024). Reporting racism in broadcast interview. *European Journal of Social Psychology, 54*(1), 170–182.

Xie, Y., & Durrheim, K. (2024). Handling racism in a radio phone-in programme: Telling it like it is. *Journalism.* https://doi.org/10.1177/14648849241250196

Xie, Y., Kirkwood, S., Laurier, E., & Widdicombe, S. (2021). Racism and misrecognition. *British Journal of Social Psychology, 60*(4), 1177–1195.

Yu, B., & Sterponi, L. (2023). Toward neurodiversity: How conversation analysis can contribute to a new approach to social communication assessment. *Language, Speech, and Hearing Services in Schools, 54*(1), 27–41.

Yu, D. (2024). Delegitimizing the "other" at US congressional town hall meetings. In H. Z. Waring & N. Tadic (Eds.), *Critical conversation analysis: Inequality and injustice in talk-in-interaction* (pp. 115–129). Multilingual Matters.

Zhang, J. (2021). *Towards actionable understandings of conversations: A computational approach.* Cornell University.

Zhang, T. (2022). Accounting for discrimination through categorization work: An examination of the target-of-discrimination group members' practices. *Discourse & Society, 33*(2), 264–286.

Zhang, T. (2023). Contesting reports of racism, contesting the rights to assess. *Social Psychology Quarterly, 86*(2), 130–150.

Zimmerman, D. H. (1978). Ethnomethodology. *The American Sociologist, 13*(1), 6–15.

Zimmerman, D. H. (1992). They were all doing gender, but they weren't all passing: Comment on Rogers. *Gender & Society, 6*(2), 192–198.

Zimmerman, D. H. (1998). Identity, context and interaction. In C. Antaki & S. Widdicombe (Eds.), *Identities in talk*. Sage.

Zimmerman, D. H., & Pollner, M. (1970). The everyday world as a phenomenon. In J. Douglas (Ed.), *Understanding everyday life: Toward the reconstruction of sociological knowledge* (pp. 80–103). Routledge & Kegan Paul.

Zimmerman, D. H., & West, C. (1975). Sex roles, interruptions and sciences in conversations. In B. Thorne & N. Henley (Eds.), *Language and sex: Difference and dominance* (pp. 105–129). Newbury House.

INDEX

Abigail 254
ableism 335
Ablitt, J. 55n2
accomplishment, categorization 71
action(s): ABC interview of Venus
    Williams 136–139; categories for
    solving organizational problems
    124–132; categories in Rochester
    police encounter 150–152; chicken
    dinner(s) 128–132, 141–143,
    143–144; composition and position
    124; embodied features of, exposing
    tacit uses of categories 144–150;
    explicitly mentioning categories
    in forming and making sense of
    132–139; family dinner 140–141;
    formation and ascription of 123,
    123n1, 152; forming and making
    sense of 13, 122–124; holiday sales
    133–134; organizing sequences
    of 14; radio host interviewing a
    pharmacist 134–136; restaurant
    payment 147–150, *148*; similar
    actions formed in different ways
    139–144; tacitly using categories as
    bases for designing and evaluating
    139–150; train (fieldnote, personal
    communication) 145–147; university
    small group work 125–128, *126*;
    see also sequences of action
action-formation problem, interaction
    37–38

adjacency pair sequences 14; categories
    in 210–224; Hyla and Nancy extract
    210–211
African National Congress (ANC), radio
    call-ins 215–216
age: category 70; research of stage of life
    and generational cohort 10
ageism 335
Agnes, 26–28
agoraphobia 73
Ainsworth-Vaughn, N. 28
Albert, J. 234n15
Albert, S. 9, 18, 48, 317, 327, 333, 334
Albert, Saul, discussion on *Alexa* and
    user 333–334
Alcoff, L. M. 16
Alejandro, A. 16, 20
Alexa: discussion by Hall and Albert
    333–334; virtual assistant 317, 327
Algorithmic Justice League 335
Almeida, F. F. D. 9, 297–304
Al-Qaeda, categorial ways 89–90
Alsharif, M. 122
Amazon, *Alexa* 317, 327
Ameka, F. K. 49, 95, 263
analysts' categories 17, 20
analysts' resources 20
Anderson, D. C. 47
Anderson, E. 83, 114
Anderson, R. J. 48
Angell, B. 300
Ann, 147–149, 288, 291, 333–334